Human Communication in Society

6TH EDITION

Jess K. Alberts
Arizona State University

Thomas K. Nakayama
Northeastern University

Judith N. Martin
Arizona State University

Content Development: Marita Sermolins Bley
Content Management: Pamela Chirls
Content Production: Katharine Glynn,
　Colleen McQuaid

Product Management: Amber Mackey
Product Marketing: Rachele Strober
Rights and Permissions: Annette Linder

Please contact https://support.pearson.com/getsupport/s/contactsupport with any queries on this content.

Library of Congress Cataloging-in-Publication Data

Names: Alberts, Jess K., author. | Nakayama, Thomas K., author. |
　Martin, Judith N., author.
Title: Human communication in society / Jess K. Alberts, Arizona State
　University, Thomas K. Nakayama, Northeastern University,
　Judith N. Martin, Arizona State University.
Description: 6th edition. | Hoboken, NJ : Pearson, [2022] | Includes bibliographical references and index. |
　Summary: "Human Communication in Society, Sixth Edition, like previous editions, covers the full range of
　topics addressed in existing textbooks but also introduces some useful innovations. We begin by describing
　the theoretical foundations of the study of communication, including models of communication and the role
　of identity and perception in communication. We present the factors of verbal and nonverbal communication,
　a new chapter on in-person conversation, and a chapter on listening and responding. We then explore
　communication in various contexts such as culture, close relationships, small groups, and organizations.
　Ours is the first book to provide comprehensive coverage of rhetoric (Chapter 12), and we devote full
　chapters to communication and mass media (Chapter 13) and to the continuing important topic of interactive
　(social) media (Chapter 14). Overall, we discuss the full range of paradigmatic approaches in the field, offering
　a balance between theory and practice"-- Provided by publisher.
Identifiers: LCCN 2021002995 | ISBN 9780136863878 (paperback)
Subjects: LCSH: Communication--Social aspects.
Classification: LCC HM1206 .A43 2022 | DDC 302.2--dc23
LC record available at https://lccn.loc.gov/2021002995

1 2021

Rental Edition:
ISBN-10:　　0-13-686387-6
ISBN-13: 978-0-13-686387-8

Print Offer:
ISBN-10:　　0-13-686365-5
ISBN-13: 978-0-13-686365-6

Brief Contents

Contents

14 Communicating through Social and Other Interactive Media   374

As experienced researchers and instructors in the field of communication, we continue to be impressed by the breadth and depth of scholarship in our discipline; we also recognize that this scholarship presents challenges for students and instructors in the introductory survey course. For example, which research traditions should be covered: the traditional functionalist and psychological perspectives, the interpretive-qualitative perspectives, or the critical perspectives? Which subfields should be covered: intercultural communication, communication technologies, nonverbal communication, or rhetorical studies? Should instructors focus primarily on helping students develop communication skills or should they focus primarily on theories and inquiry?

Our struggle to answer these questions led us to write the first edition of this text, which we believe met the goals we established early on: first, to expose beginning students to the breadth and depth of our discipline's scholarship, and second, to provide a balance between theory and application. Finally, our third goal was to present a lively overview of the discipline, to meet students "where they live," and to engage them in exploring the implications of communication in their daily lives.

Our overarching theme for the first edition was the interaction between the individual and society. In subsequent editions, we've enhanced the emphasis on this theme, adding new examples, illustrations, and pedagogical materials that connect the more traditional individual-centered, functionalist approach—that is, "who you are affects how you communicate"—with more contemporary critical approaches, which focus on the impact of societal structures and history on communication outcomes.

By highlighting this tension between individual and societal forces, we encourage students to recognize the value of multiple perspectives in understanding communication. Students need to be encouraged to think more reflexively about their individualism, as well as their and others' social identities. Students often recognize that if they say the same thing as someone else, the message could be interpreted quite differently due to the differences in gender, age, sexuality, race, and other societal forces. It is important for students to understand how to connect their individuality with larger societal forces that shape their communication experiences. The COVID-19 pandemic has again highlighted these issues for all of us. The conflicts over wearing masks highlight the struggle over individual freedom versus our collective bond to other human beings.

Human Communication in Society, Sixth Edition, like previous editions, covers the full range of topics addressed in existing textbooks but also introduces some useful innovations. We begin by describing the theoretical foundations of the study of communication, including models of communication and the role of identity and perception in communication. We present the factors of verbal and nonverbal communication, a new chapter on in-person conversation, and a chapter on listening and responding. We then explore communication in various contexts such as culture, close relationships, small groups, and organizations. Ours is the first book to provide comprehensive coverage of rhetoric (Chapter 12), and we devote full chapters to communication and mass media (Chapter 13) and to the continuing important topic of interactive (social) media (Chapter 14). Overall, we discuss the full range of paradigmatic approaches in the field, offering a balance between theory and practice.

Revel™

Revel is an interactive learning environment that deeply engages students and prepares them for class. Media and assessment integrated directly within the authors' narrative lets students read, explore interactive content, and practice in one continuous learning path. Thanks to the dynamic reading experience in Revel, students come to class prepared to discuss, apply, and learn from instructors and from each other.

Learn more about Revel

www.pearson.com/revel

Rather than simply offering opportunities to read about and study human communication, Revel facilitates deep, engaging interactions with the concepts that matter most. For example, students can complete a self-assessment to gauge their own communication style and explore ways to improve upon their skills. Students can respond to ethical issues in communication and see how their responses compare to others'. Students may interactively explore different theories of and approaches to communication, see how communication shapes identity, review the components of language and stages of listening, assess models for relationship development, and analyze group roles and communication structures in organizations. Students may interactively see how individual factors, cultural influences, and ethnocentric biases shape the way people perceive others and their world. By providing opportunities to read about and practice communication in tandem, Revel engages students directly and immediately, which leads to a better understanding of course material. A wealth of student and instructor resources and interactive materials can be found within Revel. Some of our favorites include:

- **Videos and Video Quizzes** Videos throughout the narrative show the various ways such factors as ethics, culture, language, and listening skills shape the act of communication to boost mastery. Many videos are bundled with correlating self-checks, enabling students to test their knowledge.

Watch:
Why Do Gender Stereotypes Persist Online?

- **Critical Thinking Prompts** These prompts allow students to answer questions that require them to apply their personal experiences to the concepts within the text.

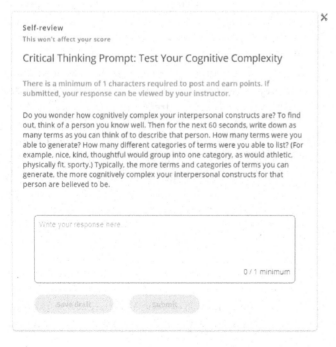

- **Animated Figures** Animated figures help students understand hard-to-grasp concepts through interactive visualizations.

Figure 1.3
The Synergetic Model

The Synergetic Model presents communication as a transactional process in which meaning is influenced by cultural, societal, and individual forces.

- **Audio Narratives** In-text audio narratives bring the "It Happened to Me" stories to life, adding dimension and reinforcing learning in a way that a printed text cannot.

It Happened to Me

Nagesh

Audio
Listen to the Audio

> ▶ Listen to the Audio

- **Integrated Writing Opportunities** To help students connect chapter content with personal meaning, each chapter offers two varieties of writing prompts: the Journal prompt, eliciting free-form topic-specific responses addressing topics at the module level, and the Shared Writing prompt, which encourages students to share and respond to one another's brief response to high-interest topics in the chapter.

Shared Writing: Ethical Dilemmas

There is a minimum of 1 characters required to post and earn points. If submitted, your response can be viewed by your classmates and instructor, and you can participate in the class discussion.

This week, watch three of your favorite television shows (or three episodes of your favorite show) and observe the number of ethical dilemmas related to communication that people and characters confront. Note their response to each dilemma. How many people/characters make choices that you consider ethical? How many do not? What justifications or reasons do people/characters give for their choices? What consequences, if any, are portrayed? What conclusions can you draw about the portrayal of communication ethics on television?

Write a comment

0 / 1 minimum

Save draft   Submit

For more information about all of the tools and resources in Revel and access to your own Revel account for *Human Communication in Society*, Sixth Edition, go to www.pearson.com/revel.

New to This Edition

In addition to the immersive learning experience offered by Revel, we've refined and updated the content in this new edition to create a powerful and contemporary resource for helping speakers connect to their audience. We've added several new features and revised features that both instructors and students have praised.

In this edition, general changes include new examples, theories, and applications, as well as updated photos that reflect the pervasiveness of social and other interactive media. Also, all chapters incorporate examples of studies and applications that include LGBTQIA+ communicators.

New features in the sixth edition of *Human Communication in Society* include:

- A new chapter on in-person conversation, emphasizing the importance of conversational skills needed to complement the constant connectivity of interactive/social media.
- More examples of specific research studies, particularly those that address LGBTQIA+ as well as heterosexual relational communication—in all three major paradigms.
- Updated videos that cover a wide range of new topics, including listening skills in the classroom, code switching, social media's impact on communication, and the value of effective group communication.
- Chapters 13 and 14 ("Mass Media and Communication" and "Communicating Through Social and Other Interactive Media") have been updated and revised to

more clearly differentiate between communication processes that occur in mass media and interactive media, respectively.

- References in each chapter have been updated to reflect the most recent available research on the topics addressed.
- Updated examples that address contemporary events and trends including the communication challenges of the pandemic that help students connect the concepts to their personal experiences and concerns.

Chapter-by-Chapter Descriptions

Part 1

Chapter 1 explains the theme of this book—the interaction between the individual and society—as well as introducing important communication concepts and models. This chapter includes depictions of the linear, transactional, and synergetic models of communication, presented in a simple and clear format to assist student comprehension. Revel includes interactive models of the figures, allowing students to view the components in more depth. It also features an interactive survey that asks students to assess their communication skills and compare the results with their classmates.

Chapter 2 explores the importance of identities in communication. This edition includes updated examples with a focus on contemporary issues, such as Black Lives Matter, the current discussions over whether Middle Eastern people should be counted as "white" in the census, and Islamophobia. This edition also introduces new identity terms such as BIPOC and enby. We also introduce the concept of intersectionality and how it is applied to identities. Revel includes a multimedia gallery that shows how people perform their identities, along with a video and video quiz that delve into how race impacts perception and identity.

Chapter 3 focuses on communication and perception, including a discussion of schemas and the role of primacy and recency on selective attention. New material includes updated examples that address important issues of the day—for example, a new "Did You Know" feature describing the important function of argot in marginalized or stigmatized groups. Revel includes several interactives that test the student's knowledge of the concepts, including a self-quiz on distinguishing between schemas, prototypes, and scripts as well as a matching assessment that requires students to differentiate between physical, cognitive, and interpretive approaches to communicate.

Part 2

Chapter 4 highlights the elements of verbal communication. This edition includes a discussion of argot and how it functions. It is also includes a discussion on the status of English as a world language and whether English speakers need to learn other languages. This chapter also includes a discussion of hate speech in the digital environment and the controversy over Facebook's handling of such language use. Revel includes an interactive fill-in-the-blank exercise on "I" statements along with an image gallery that demonstrates the functions of language.

Chapter 5 addresses issues of nonverbal communication. This edition includes more inclusive examples (disability, transgender) and concepts (microaggressions) as well as a new "Did You Know?" feature describing how the meaning of the "OK" nonverbal sign has changed throughout history and in various communities. Revel includes interactive images with informational pop-ups that delve into the nonverbal messages shown within.

Chapter 6 is an entirely new chapter that focuses on in-person conversational interaction and the underlying skills needed to be a successful conversationalist. It covers perspective taking and conversational awareness and addresses how students can more competently initiate conversations, communicate hurtful messages, communicate sexual consent, and apologize, as well as how to recognize and manage manipulative conversation strategies, among others. The chapter also includes a discussion of how race, gender, and socioeconomic class affect conversational interactions. Revel includes videos related to hurtful messages.

Chapter 7 is devoted to listening and responding. The distinction is made early on between hearing and listening, and new material focuses on the notion of online lurkers as listeners—providing an important audience for online content—as well as an updated listening style framework based on recent research. The chapter also discusses the recent civil unrest, suggesting that those with privilege in society need to listen to others "in a manner that is long-term and systemic." Revel delves into the four stages of listening, requiring students to properly identify the key components of each stage. It also features an interactive video self-assessment that asks students to listen to a problem and then respond appropriately.

Part 3

Chapter 8 includes new material on cultural values reflected in U.S. Americans' response to the pandemic health guidelines in comparison to responses of other cultural groups. The chapter also presents updated statistics on U.S. ethnic and racial demographics, migration patterns, refugee trends, and recent hostility directed at Asians and Asian Americans in intercultural encounters. Revel videos showcase various scenarios that involve intercultural communication. Students review these situations in video quizzes and video self-assessments, both of which require students to identify the communication patterns within.

Chapter 9 discusses communication in close relationships. In this edition, the focus of the chapter has been broadened to include more information on friendships (stage model of friendships, turning point model, maintenance behavior) and family communication. It also addresses new topics, like depression and gaslighting, appeals to broader interests (cosplay), and adds a discussion of passive-aggressive communication. Revel features an interactive model of Knapp's stages of romantic relational development.

Chapter 10 explores small group communication, and this edition includes updated material on communication technologies and small group communication. Given the increased importance of virtual communication in educational and professional contexts, this chapter includes an extended discussion of effective virtual small group work, including the factors affecting virtual teamwork as well as guidelines for handing conflict and the unique role of leadership in virtual small group interaction. There are also new examples and description of symptoms of groupthink. Revel includes interactives that delve into small group task roles, small group relational roles, and small group individual roles, with accompanying student audio.

Chapter 11 explores organizational communication. It has been revised to include a discussion of employee dissent, including potential communication strategies for both employees and supervisors in handling dissent. The chapter also includes new discussion on the potential impacts of the pandemic on organizational leadership, the increasing role of mobile communication technologies in home and work contexts, and their impact on work-life conflict. Revel includes an interactive simulation that asks students to put themselves in the mindset of a manager, presenting them with a series of workplace scenarios that require appropriate and ethical responses. Revel content also features new videos related to using technology at work.

Chapter 12 covers public communication and the use of strategic and persuasive communication. Rhetoric is presented with an emphasis on its historical, theoretical, societal, and ethical aspects. Updates are included in this edition as well as a discussion of the power of visual images of African Americans killed by police and the debates over Confederate monuments. This chapter also introduces how people use Twitter as an activist tool. This edition includes more Revel videos to help students prepare to speak in public.

Chapter 13 discusses communication and mass media. This edition updates the contemporary research on hostile media effects, cultivation theory, and the current trends in online viewing of television. We also look at the close relationship between media content and media ownership, as demonstrated in the case of Disney's purchase of large parts of 20th Century Fox and what happened to the Fantastic Four in the move to a new owner. This edition also introduces the work on frame analysis as another way to understand mass media. Revel interactives delve into the evolution of popular media, explore how media use differs across cultures, and explore how high-power individuals—such as Stephen Colbert—can influence public opinion on current issues.

Chapter 14 covers interactive (social) media and communication. This chapter offers extensive new material, again focusing on the constant communication choices students make in deciding which medium to use to send messages and the consequences of these choices in both personal and professional contexts, as well as how media choices evolve to serve the needs of communicators. The chapter also includes new material on doxing, cancel culture, and problematic social media use (PSMU). There are updated examples, statistics, and research findings reflecting current scholarship and trends in interactive media use as well as guidelines for effective interactive/social media use in the virtual classroom and in interpersonal and professional contexts. Revel includes student testimony videos that explore how they use social media.

Features

Key features retained in this new edition reflect our four goals for this textbook.

Accessible Presentation of Communication Theory

In addition to using a down-to-earth writing style and providing plenty of examples, *Human Communication in Society*, Sixth Edition, offers specific tools throughout the text to help students understand the theory and key concepts:

- **Key terms** are glossed in the margins of the page where the term is first used and defined, listed at the end of each chapter with the page number where the term and definition can be found, and compiled in a convenient Glossary at the end of the text.

KEY TERMS

identity p. 26	self-respect p. 33	enby p. 40
symbolic interactionism p. 28	performance of identity p. 33	gender identity p. 40
reflected appraisals p. 28	self-presentation p. 33	cisgender p. 41
looking-glass self p. 28	enacting identities p. 33	transgender p. 41
particular others p. 29	role expectations p. 35	sexual identity p. 41
generalized other p. 29	mutable p. 35	gender fluid p. 41
reference group p. 30	racial identity p. 37	age identity p. 42
self-fulfilling prophecy p. 30	multiracial identity p. 38	social class identity p. 42
stereotype threat p. 31	national identity p. 38	disability identity p. 44
self-concept p. 32	ethnic identity p. 39	religious identity p. 45
self-esteem p. 32	BIPOC p. 40	intersectionality p. 46

- **Chapter summaries** conclude each chapter.

SUMMARY

2.1 **Identify six reasons identity is important to communication.**

- We bring our identities to each communication interaction.
- Communication interactions create and shape identities.

Emphasis on Ethics in Communication

Each chapter includes one or more detailed sections discussing ethical issues relevant to that chapter's communication topic.

Opportunities to Apply What Was Learned

We advocate a hands-on approach to the study of communication. For this reason, we've included "Apply What You Know" questions to encourage students to work through challenging concepts.

Student Engagement

We like to think that we have translated our commitment to the field and our love of teaching into a text that will engage students. We encourage this involvement with the following pedagogical features:

- **"It Happened to Me"** boxes offer real-life accounts of student experiences that provide a "hook" to important communication concepts.
- **"Alternative View"** boxes offer perspectives that challenge mainstream thinking or offer an interpretation of a chapter-related topic counter to conventional wisdom.
- **"Communication in Society"** boxes serve to reinforce the connection between the individual and society as applied to chapter-related topics.
- **Critical Thinking Prompts**, placed in the margins at strategic intervals, encourage students to reflect on how major concepts connect with their everyday experiences.
- **"Did You Know?"** boxes offer examples of chapter-related material that students may find surprising or unfamiliar.
- **"Journal Prompts"** offer students direction in writing about various issues that arise in the chapters. They give the students some direction in thinking about these issues.

Instructor and Student Resources

Key instructor resources include an Instructor's Manual (ISBN 9780136863984), Instructor's Solutions Manual, (ISBN 9780136863953), and PowerPoint Presentation Package (ISBN 9780136864035). These supplements are available on the catalog page for this text on Pearson.com/us (instructor login required). MyTest online test generating software (ISBN 9780136863724) is available at www.pearsonmytest.com (instructor login required). For a complete list of the instructor and student resources available with the text, please visit the Pearson Communication catalog, at www.pearson.com/communication.

Pearson MediaShare

MediaShare integration makes it easier than ever for students and instructors to share and comment on speeches, as well as other videos, documents, images, and more. Users can upload original content for peer and instructor feedback or embed YouTube content with just a few clicks. Having these share-and-comment tools available directly within Revel™ makes for an even more interactive learning experience.

The best of MediaShare functionality, including student video submissions with grading and video quizzes, is now available to use and assign within Revel, making Revel an even more complete solution for Communication courses. By placing these key components of MediaShare within Revel, students have one all-inclusive space to practice and have their performance assessed while actively learning through interactive course content. Revel with MediaShare is an unparalleled immersive learning experience for the Communication curriculum.

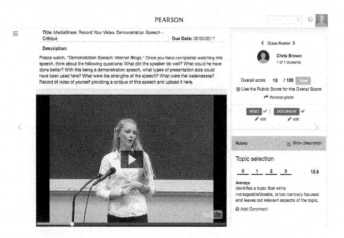

- Use MediaShare to assign or view speeches, video-based assignments, role plays, and more in a variety of formats including video, Word, PowerPoint, and Excel.

- Assess students using customizable, Pearson-provided rubrics or create your own around classroom goals, learning outcomes, or department initiatives.

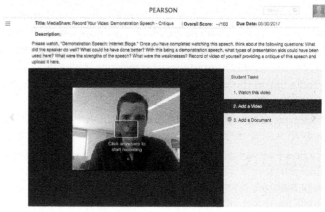

- Set up assignments for students with options for full-class viewing and commenting or private comments between you and the student.

- Record video directly from a tablet, phone, or other webcam.

- Embed video from YouTube via assignments to incorporate current events into the classroom experience.

- Set up quiz questions on video assignments to ensure students master concepts and interact and engage with the media.

- Import grades into most learning management systems.

- Ensure a secure learning environment for instructors and students through robust privacy settings.

A Word about Language

The text's commitment to presenting comprehensive coverage of the complex field of communication carries with it a responsibility to use language thoughtfully. We recognize the fact that, for complex historical and political relations, identity labels carry strong denotative meanings that may vary from person to person and across time. We have made an effort to use inclusive terms to represent the heterogeneity of opinions within various ethnic and racial groups.

For example, the term *Hispanic* was created and used in 1980 by the U.S. government for the census and other purposes of collecting census statistics. However, many individuals of Spanish descent prefer *Latina/o* or *Latinx*. We endeavor to use the latter terms to refer to U.S. Americans of Spanish descent from a specific ancestral nation like Argentina, Mexico, or any country in Latin America or Spain. We also use *Mexican American* when referring to individuals coming more directly from Mexico or *Chicana/o* to designate a more political consciousness among persons of Mexican descent.

Similarly, we use the inclusive term *Asian American* unless the context refers to individuals with a specific national origin (e.g., Japan or the Philippines). We have tried to use the more inclusive term *Black* when it is preferred by those using it (e.g., Black Lives Matter). *Black* is often used as more inclusive, as it includes those from the Caribbean or other parts of the world. We have tried to use *African American* when it is referring more specifically to people who identify in this way. We also use *Native American* and *American Indian* interchangeably, recognizing that individuals are divided in their preferences for each of these terms.

We should also note that we use both *White* (which emphasizes race) and *European American* (which emphasizes ethnicity) to refer to U.S. Americans of European ancestry. At the same time, we recognize that some individuals prefer to emphasize their more specific origins (*Japanese American* rather than *Asian American*, *Yaqui* rather than *Native American*, or *German American* rather than *White*).

We are learning to think more internationally in our use of language. Many of our neighbors in Latin and South America as well as in Canada find it offensive when we use the term *American* to refer to ourselves. (After all, these people are Americans as well.) Therefore, we prefer the term *U.S. American* in recognition of the fact that we are only one society out of many that make up the continents of North and South America.

Finally, in this edition, we also introduced some emerging identity terms, such as enby (NB: non-binary) and BIPOC (Black Indigenous People of Color). Some of these terms may stay relevant or disappear in the coming years, but it is important for students to be aware of the dynamic nature of these terms.

Acknowledgments

We are once again grateful to all the students and instructors who have provided invaluable feedback to us as we wrote the six editions of *Human Communication in Society*. Unfortunately, we are unable to list here all of the students who participated, but we would like to acknowledge the instructors who have helped to shape and define all editions of our book.

Reviewers (First Edition)

Bob Alexander: University of Louisiana–Monroe
Isolde K. Anderson: Hope College
Jay Baglia: San Jose State University
Cheryl L. Bailey: Western Illinois University
John R. Baldwin: Illinois State University
E. Tristan Booth: Arizona State University
Joseph Bridges: Malone College
Lynn S. Cockett: Juniata College
Elisia L. Cohen: Saint Louis University
Lisa Coutu: University of Washington
Peter A. DeCaro: California State University–Stanislaus
Aaron Dimock: University of Nebraska–Kearney
Donald G. Ellis: University of Hartford
Larry A. Erbert: University of Texas at El Paso
Marty Feeney: Central College
Charles Feldman: George Washington University
Sarah L. Bonewits Feldner: Marquette University
Karen A. Foss: University of New Mexico
Kenneth D. Frandsen: University of New Mexico
John Gareis: University of Pittsburgh
Sonja M. Brown Givens: University of Alabama in Huntsville
Carroll Glynn: Ohio State University
Beryl S. Gutekunst: Chestnut Hill College
Thomas Edward Harkins: New York University
Carla Harrell: Old Dominion University
Brian L. Heisterkamp: California State University, San Bernardino
Dr. Patrick J. Hérbert: University of Louisiana–Monroe

Christine Courtade Hirsch: State University of New York–Oswego
John Katsion: Hannibal-LaGrange College
Joann Keyton: University of Kansas
Larry J. King: Stephen F. Austin State University
Thomas J. Knutson: California State University–Sacramento
Peter Lah: Saint Louis University
William A. Lancaster: Northeastern University
Sara McKinnon: Arizona State University
Jennifer Mease: Arizona State University
Diane Millette: University of Miami
Todd Norton: University of Utah
Shirley Oakley: Coastal Georgia Community College
Richard K. Olsen, Jr: University of North Carolina–Wilmington
Karen Otto: Florida Community College at Jacksonville–North Campus
Frank G. Pérez: University of Texas at El Paso
Linda Pledger: University of Arkansas–Little Rock
Steven B. Pratt: University of Central Oklahoma
Leanne Stuart Pupchek: Queens University of Charlotte
John C. Reinard: California State University–Fullerton
Brian Reynolds: State University of New York–Buffalo
Scott J. Robson: Washburn University
Pamela Schultz: Alfred University
David Schulz: California State University–Stanislaus
Kristina Horn Sheeler: Indiana University Purdue University Indianapolis
Deborah Shelley: University of Houston–Downtown
Nancy J. Street: Texas A&M University
Crispin Thurlow: University of Washington
Sarah Tracy: Arizona State University
April Trees: University of Colorado, Boulder
Kathleen J. Turner: Davidson College
Kyle Tusing: University of Arizona
Sam Wallace: University of Dayton
Toni S. Whitfield: James Madison University
Bill Yousman: University of Hartford

Reviewers (Second Edition)

Marcia S. Berry: Azusa Pacific University
Lynn S. Cockett: Juniata College
Larry A. Erbert: University of Colorado–Denver
Emma K. Gray: Portland Community College
Carla J. Harrell: Old Dominion University
Christine Courtade Hirsch: SUNY Oswego
Heather A. Howley: Cazenovia College
Thomas J. Knutson: Sacramento State University
Joanna Kostides: Holyoke Community College
Tema Milstein: University of New Mexico
Cynthia Ridle: Western Illinois University
Renee Beth Stahle: Aquinas College
Jenny Warren: Collin College

Reviewers (Third Edition)

Erin Baird: University of Oklahoma
Anthony Hurst: California State University–San Marcos
Vicki L. Karns: Suffolk University
Dan Lair: University of Denver
Valerie L. Manusov: University of Washington
Tema Milstein: University of New Mexico
Shane Semmler: University of South Dakota
Caitlin Wills-Toker: University of Georgia

Reviewers (Fourth Edition)

Becki Bowman: McPherson College
Kari Duffy: Carthage College
Mary Horner: St. Louis Community College
Gilberto Martinez: Texas A&M International University
Kerry Osborne: College of the Canyons
Leonard Schulze: Carthage College
Carl Thameling: University of Louisiana–Monroe

Reviewers (Fifth Edition)

Jessica Reeher: SUNY Oswego
Daryle Nagano: Los Angeles Harbor College
Sabeen Sheikh: Northern Virginia CC - Annandale
Farah Sanders: Utah Valley University
Emily Holler: Kennesaw State University
Karen Erlandson: Albion College
Carla Stevens: St. Ambrose University
William Price: Georgia Perimeter College

Reviewers (Sixth Edition)

Monika Alston Miller: Columbia College
James Billings: University of Montevallo
Thomas Damp: Central New Mexico Community College
Louis K. Falk: University of Texas at Rio Grande Valley
Kerry Hoey: Carthage College

Additional Acknowledgments

We would also like to thank our colleagues and students for their invaluable assistance and moral support: a special thanks to Professor Pauline Cheong for providing foundational ideas for our chapter on computer-mediated communication, Professor Clark Olson who generously contributed his knowledge on small-group communication, and Professor Pauline Davies for her insightful feedback (and suggestions) regarding content, based on her extensive experience teaching the textbook material. Professor Karen Ashcraft (University of Utah) for her substantial assistance with the organizational communication chapter, and Professor Angela Trethewey for her support and help throughout this project.

And, of course, we need to thank the many, many students, at Arizona State University, Northeastern University, and elsewhere, who have good-naturedly provided invaluable feedback on all previous editions and helped us make the necessary changes in the sixth edition.

Thanks also to our editorial assistants, Ms. Megan Stephenson and Ms. Alison Hawn, Arizona State University, as well as Dr. Elizabeth Glowacki, Northeastern University, who spent hours searching for (and finding) the most recent and relevant research articles, updated examples, and contemporary margin material. We especially appreciate their assistance given that they had their own work to do and the deadlines were extremely tight.

Thanks to the team at Pearson who made it all happen. We could not have managed without their expertise, patience, and practiced hand guiding us through the always complicated publishing process. Thanks also to Marita Sermolins Bley, development editor, for her insightful editing, patience, and hard work. We also want to acknowledge the work of project managers Nicole Suddeth and Sindhuja Vadlamani at SPi Global.

Finally, to our partners—James LeRoy, David Karbonski, and Ronald Chaldu—who continue to tolerate our frequent absences with good grace. We give them our deepest thanks for their support throughout this and many other projects.

About the Authors

Jess Alberts is President's Professor in the Hugh Downs School of Human Communication at Arizona State University. She is an interpretive scholar who focuses on interpersonal communication and specializes in the study of conflict. **Thomas Nakayama** is a professor in the Department of Communication Studies at Northeastern University. He is a critical scholar who focuses on rhetoric and intercultural communication. **Judith Martin** is professor emerita in the Hugh Downs School of Human Communication at Arizona State University. She is a social scientist whose expertise is in intercultural communication.

Jess Alberts   **Thomas Nakayama**   **Judith Martin**

Introduction to Human Communication

LEARNING OBJECTIVES

1.1 Explain why it is important to study human communication.

1.2 Name and describe the seven primary components of communication.

1.3 Explain how the Synergetic Model of Communication differs from previous models.

1.4 Formulate your own communication ethic.

1.5 Articulate what makes a communicator competent.

CHAPTER TOPICS

The Importance of Studying Human Communication

What Is Human Communication?

A Model of Human Communication: The Synergetic Model

Communication Ethics

Putting It All Together: Communicating Competently

> *"If good communication skills were just common sense, then communication would not so often go awry."*

On her way to class, Charee called her dad to let him know what time she would arrive home; she then scrolled through TikTok to see what others were doing while planning her next video. While she waited for class to begin, she checked her Instagram to see how many likes her post had received this morning and looked at one of the community organizations she liked to see what they were organizing today. When the professor arrived, she muted her phone and listened as the class began.

Most people, like Charee, exist in a sea of communication. They text and message their friends and family; spend time on Instagram, TikTok, and Twitter, creating new content and keeping up-to-date with the latest trends; occasionally stream movies; attend class lectures (sometimes online); and are inundated by media images as they are working out, biking to campus, and hanging out with friends. They remember how quickly they adapted their communication during the pandemic, like elbow bumping instead of shaking hands or hugging. Students interacted with professors and classmates more online than in classrooms. People socialized more on video chats, FaceTime, and Zoom than face-to-face; attended virtual graduations, concerts, weddings, and parties; and some stopped interacting with elderly relatives for a period of time or saw them only virtually. Communicating during and after the pandemic highlights the myriad of verbal, nonverbal, and virtual communication options available and how various contexts can necessitate adaptation.

With so many communication options now available and the occasional necessity for quick adaptation to changing contexts, people need a wider range of communication knowledge, skills, and flexibility than ever before. Successful communicators must converse effectively face-to-face and online; determine what messages to send via social media or in person; and absorb the norms and etiquette surrounding the use of social media. Becoming an effective communicator involves a nimbleness and understanding of the components and processes of communication and putting them into practice in every stage of life. As you work in this course to improve your communication knowledge and skills, you may see positive changes in your relationships, your career, your engagement in civic life, and even your identity. How many other courses can claim all that?

The Importance of Studying Human Communication

1.1 Explain why it is important to study human communication.

As you begin this course, several questions may arise. First, you may wonder exactly how the study of human communication differs from other studies of humans, such as psychology. Communication differs from other social science disciplines because it focuses exclusively on the exchange of messages to create meaning. Scholars in communication explore what, when, where, and why humans interact (Emanuel, 2007). They do so to increase our understanding of how people communicate and to help individuals improve their abilities to communicate in a wide variety of contexts. In addition, unlike most social sciences, the study of communication has a long history—reaching back to the classical era of Western civilization when Socrates, Plato, and Aristotle wrote about the important role of communication in politics, the courts, and learning (National Communication Association [NCA], 2003; Rogers & Chafee, 1983). However, the ability to speak effectively and persuasively has been valued since the beginning of recorded history. As early as 3200–2800 BCE, the Precepts of Kagemni and Ptah-Hotep commented on communication (NCA, 2003).

Second, you may question why anyone needs to study communication; after all, most people have probably been doing a reasonably good job of it thus far. And isn't most communication knowledge just common sense? Unfortunately, it is not. If good communication skills were just common sense, then communication would not so often go awry. In fact, most people struggle with how to communicate well: they don't know how to listen so that other people feel heard; they aren't sure how to convince others to see their point of view; and they often aren't able to settle disagreements with people they care about deeply. Because communication is a complex activity, we need to learn skills that allow us to adapt our communication so others will hear, understand, connect with and care for us. Think of times when you felt others failed to communicate effectively with you. Have you ever felt that one of your teachers talked down to you? Have you had a relationship end because you and your partner had a misunderstanding? Or have you failed to get what you wanted—a job, an invitation, your parents' support—because you couldn't figure out how to interact with others in specific contexts? In sum, talking is not equivalent to communicating. We can drown others in words, but if they do not understand, connect with, and care about those words, then we have not communicated with them at all.

Now that we have so many ways to communicate and maintain relationships with others, some scholars have begun to ask if it is possible to have too much communication. Do you think this is possible or likely? To learn how some communication scholars answer this question, see *Alternative View: Co-rumination: When Too Much Talk Is as Bad as Not Enough*.

Finally, you may think of communication as a set of skills but believe that they are easily learned and wonder why there is an entire course (even a major!) that focuses on communication. Although it is true that every day people use communication to accomplish practical goals such as inviting a friend to see a movie, resolving a conflict with a colleague, or persuading the city council to install speed bumps in their neighborhood, communication is more than just a set of skills, like baking, that one can use in a variety of contexts and settings with little alteration. Rather, communication is an intricate process whose effective performance requires an in-depth understanding of how it works and the ability to apply one's critical thinking skills to communication experiences to learn from and improve them.

ALTERNATIVE VIEW
Co-rumination: When Too Much Talk Is as Bad as Not Enough

You have probably heard that to have good relationships, people need to "communicate more." However, sometimes communicating a lot can have negative effects. One type of "over-communication" that can cause harm is co-rumination. Co-rumination occurs when we talk—again—and again—and again—with others about a problem in our lives. It has been linked to negative outcomes such as depression, anxiety, binge eating, binge drinking, and self-harm (Nolen-Hoeksema et al., 2008).

Co-rumination often occurs among friends because that is to whom we turn most often when we encounter problems. In an attempt to console or support each other, such as when a breakup occurs, friends often tolerate or even encourage each other to talk extensively about what happened and how they feel. Individuals are most likely to engage in co-rumination during adolescence and young adulthood.

Why is co-rumination unhealthy? During co-rumination, participants' communication focuses incessantly on the issue and its negative effects rather than on solutions. It can even damage relationships, causing "depression contagion." If the co-ruminating friend repeatedly draws the other into negative conversations, it can make both more depressed and lead the friend to avoid the co-ruminator, as such discussions may make one feel worse and helpless to do anything about it. Consequently, experts suggest that a goal should be to balance "problem talk" with positive activities and that one should revisit their joys and successes with friends just as they would their problems (Schwartz-Mette & Smith, 2018).

Can you think of other occasions when people talk "too much"?

SOURCES: Nolen-Hoeksema S., Wisco, B., & Lyubomirsky, S. (2008). Rethinking rumination. *Perspectives on Psychological Science*, 3, 400–424.

Schwartz-Mette, R. A., & Smith, R. L. (2018). When does co-rumination facilitate depression contagion in adolescent friendships? Investigating intrapersonal and interpersonal factors. *Journal of Clinical Child & Adolescent Psychology*, 47(6), 912–924.

▲ If your romantic partner doesn't answer a text message, it could be because she is studying and set her phone on "do not disturb."

Critical Thinking: A Key to Successful Communication

Critical thinking requires that one become a critic of one's own thoughts and behavior. That is, rather than responding automatically or superficially, critical thinkers reflect on their own and others' communication, behavior, and ideas before responding (Paul & Elder, 2008). Scholars have proposed various definitions of critical thinking; the one we advocate describes it as a process that involves the following steps (Passer & Smith, 2004):

1. Identify the assertion or action.
2. Ask, "what is the evidence for and against the assertion or action?"
3. Ask, "what does the bulk of evidence point to?"
4. Ask, "what other explanations or conclusions are possible?"
5. Continue to keep an open mind for new evidence and new ways of evaluating the assertion.

How might one apply this process to communication interactions? Let's explore this with a simple and common example, showing the steps in the process.

Step 1: Identify the action: Imagine that you send a text message to your romantic partner on a Friday evening but hours later have not heard back. How should you interpret the lack of reply, and consequently, how should you respond? If you were thinking non-critically, you might interpret the behavior negatively (my partner is cheating on me!) even though you have little or no evidence to support this interpretation. You then might respond by dashing off an accusatory message.

Step 2: Evaluate your interpretations and beliefs: Critical thinkers evaluate their interpretations and beliefs before responding by asking themselves, "What evidence do I have for this belief or interpretation?" Thus, if their first impulse was to doubt their partner, they would ask themselves, "What evidence exists that my partner is cheating?" Does failing to return a text necessarily mean the partner is intentionally refusing to respond? Even if the partner is purposely refusing to respond to a text, does that mean the reason for refusing is unfaithfulness?

Step 3: What does the bulk of evidence point to? The critical thinker would then question whether this interpretation is supported by sufficient evidence and experience. A critical thinker would ask: What does the bulk of the evidence point to—for example, has my partner cheated before? Does my partner usually respond quickly to messages? Is my partner normally trustworthy?

Step 4: What other conclusions are possible? Next they would consider what other explanations are possible. For example, my partner's phone battery is dead; my partner fell asleep early and didn't receive my messages; my partner is studying and set her phone on "do not disturb."

Step 5: Keep an open mind and evaluate new information as it is presented: Only after following this process would a critical thinker settle on a likely interpretation and response. Even then, the critical thinker would continue to keep an open mind

Critical Thinking Prompt
Now that you have reviewed the steps involved in critical thinking, would you consider yourself high or low in critical thinking skills? What topics or situations are most likely to cause you to use your critical thinking skills? What can you do to improve these skills?

and evaluate new information as it was presented. Thus, even if you decided that there was no evidence that your partner was cheating, you might reevaluate your conclusion if your partner repeatedly failed to reply to texts on Friday nights.

Advantages of Studying Human Communication

There are many advantages to studying human communication. Individuals use communication to meet people, to develop professional and personal relationships, and to terminate dissatisfying ones. Communication scholar Steve Duck (1994) argues that relationships are primarily communicative. Moreover, the relationships we have with others—including how we think and feel about one another—develop as we communicate. Through communication interactions, relationship partners develop shared meanings for events, explanations for their shared past, and a vision of their future together (Alberts et al., 2005; Dixon & Duck, 1993). So, if you tell your romantic partner, "I have never loved anyone as much as I love you, and I never will," you are simultaneously redefining your past romantic relationships, creating shared meaning for the present relationship, and projecting a vision of your romantic future together. Similarly, through communication with friends, coworkers, and acquaintances, we all define and redefine our relationships.

Perhaps most fundamentally, your communication interactions with others allow you to establish who you are to them (Gergen, 1982; Mead, 1934). As you communicate, you attempt to reveal yourself in a particular light. For example, when you are at work, you may try to establish yourself as someone who is pleasant, hardworking, honest, and competent. With a new roommate, you may want your communication behavior to suggest you are responsible, fun, and easygoing. However, at the same time that your communication creates an image of who you are for others, *their* communication shapes your vision of yourself. For example, if your friends laugh at your jokes, compliment you on your sense of humor, and introduce you to others as a funny person, you probably will see yourself as amusing. In these ways, communication helps create both our self-identities and our identities as others perceive them.

Communication has the potential to transform your life—both for the better and for the worse. (To read how one student's communication created a transformation, see *It Happened to Me: Chelsea*.) As many people have discovered, poor or unethical communication can negatively affect lives. How? Communicating poorly during conflict can end relationships, inadequate interviewing skills can result in unemployment, and negative feedback from conversational partners can lessen one's self-esteem. Sometimes communication can have even more significant effects. In 2019, actor Jussie Smollett went to the Chicago police claiming that he had been attacked by two men who hurled racist and homophobic slurs and tied a rope around his neck. Questions about the incident led to a deal in which the charges were dropped in exchange for community service and losing his bond money. In February 2020, prosecutors charged him with making false police reports (Jussie Smollett, 2020), and in June 2020, a judge ruled that these charges did not constitute double jeopardy (Hendrickson, 2020). At the time of this writing, the judicial proceedings have not concluded, but Smollett is being charged for specific, illegal communication acts (filing false police reports).

It Happened to Me
Chelsea

When the professor asked us to identify a time when communication was transformative, many examples came to mind. Finally, I settled on one involving a negative relationship. In high school there's usually one person you just don't get along with. Boyfriend drama, bad-mouthing, you name it. I remember dreading seeing this one girl, and I'm sure she felt the same about me. Graduation came and went, and I completely forgot about her. A year later, I came across her Facebook page as I was searching for old classmates online. As I thought about how petty our arguments were and how cruel we were to each other, I felt smaller and smaller. So I decided to end it. After friending her, I sent her a private message to apologize for my bad behavior. A couple days later I received a response from her saying she felt the same way and was also sorry for the way she acted. Next week we're going to have a cup of coffee together to really put the past behind us. Maybe to some people that doesn't seem all that life-changing, but after hating this girl for two years, it's an amazing transformation for me.

In contrast, as you can see from Chelsea's story, developing excellent communication skills also can transform your life for the better. The three authors of this book have all had students visit months or years after taking our communication classes to tell us what a difference the classes have made in their lives. A student in a public speaking class reported that, because of her improved presentation skills, she received the raise and promotion she had been pursuing for years; another student in a conflict and negotiation class revealed that her once-troubled marriage became more stable once she learned to express disagreements better. A third student felt more confident after he took a persuasion class that taught him how to influence people.

Studying human communication may also benefit you by opening doors to a new career path. A degree in communication can prepare you for a wide variety of communication careers.

Journal Prompt 1.1: Studying Communication
How does the study of communication differ from other social science disciplines?

What Is Human Communication?

1.2   Name and describe the seven primary components of communication.

Broadly speaking, human communication can be defined as a process in which people generate meaning through the exchange of verbal and nonverbal messages. In this book, however, we emphasize the influence of individual and societal forces and the roles of culture and context more than other definitions do. Because we believe these concepts are essential to understanding the communication process completely, we developed a definition of human communication that included them. Accordingly, we define **human communication** as a transactional process in which people generate meaning through the exchange of verbal and nonverbal messages in specific contexts, influenced by individual and societal forces and embedded in culture. In the following sections, we will illustrate our definition of human communication and explore the meaning of each of these concepts and their relationships.

human communication
A transactional process in which people generate meaning through the exchange of verbal and nonverbal messages in specific contexts, influenced by individual and social forces, and embedded in culture.

Components of Human Communication

Consider the following scenario:

Charee grew up in the United States and knew she needed to talk to her father, Pham, who was reared in Vietnam, about her desire to participate in political rallies in their city. The rallies were protesting police actions in the Black community following George Floyd's death in Minneapolis. She was concerned about how the conversation would go. She knew that, as immigrants, her parents were very patriotic and would not look favorably on activist protests against law enforcement or any other government entity. She hoped to convince her father that it was a good idea for her to participate to make changes to policing as well as show that many Asian Americans support Black Lives Matter. Yet she also wanted to display respect for him as her father and the head of the household. To ensure that things went well, she decided that they should meet at his favorite neighborhood café in the early afternoon so they could talk privately. She rehearsed how she would convey information that he might not be happy to hear and practiced responses to the objections she expected him to raise.

▼ As this picture illustrates, communication is symbolic in that the words we use to communicate an idea such as "I love you" are arbitrary and are not inherently connected to the concept to which they refer.

As this example reveals, communication is a complex process that can require considerable thought and planning. The complexity inherent in communication is a result of the variety of factors that compose and influence it. The seven basic components of communication to consider in planning an interaction are *message creation, meaning creation, setting, participants, channels, noise,* and *feedback.* Each of these features is central to how a communication interaction unfolds. To help you understand this process, we analyze Charee's experiences with her father.

Message Creation **Messages** are the building blocks of communication, and the process of taking ideas and converting them into messages is called **encoding**. (Receiving a message and interpreting its meaning is referred to as **decoding**.) Depending on the importance of a message, people are more or less careful in encoding their messages. In our example, Charee was concerned with how she encoded her messages to her father. She particularly wanted to both persuade him that she should become more politically active and assure him that this would not change their close relationship. To accomplish this, she decided to encode her idea into this message: "I promise that I will make sure to stay in touch while I'm at rallies, I'll do my best to stay safe, and I'll text you."

When we communicate, we encode and exchange two types of messages—verbal and nonverbal—and most of these messages are symbolic. A **symbol** is something that represents something else and conveys meaning (Buck & VanLear, 2002). For example, a Valentine's Day heart symbolizes the physical heart, it represents romantic love, and it conveys feelings of love and romance when given to a relational partner. The verbal system is composed of linguistic symbols (that is, words), whereas the nonverbal message system is composed of nonlinguistic symbols such as smiles, laughter, winks, vocal tones, and hand gestures.

When we say *communication is symbolic,* we are describing the fact that the symbols we use—the words we speak and the gestures we use—are arbitrary, or without any inherent meaning (Dickens, 2003). Rather, their meaning is derived as communicators employ agreed-on definitions. For instance, putting up one's hand palm forward would not mean "stop" unless people in the United States agreed to this meaning, and the word *mother* would not mean a female parent unless speakers of English agreed that it would. Because communicators use symbols to create meaning, different groups often develop distinct words for the same concept. For instance, the common word for a feline house pet is *cat* in English but *neko* in Japanese. Thus, there is no intrinsic connection between most words and their meanings—or many gestures and their meanings.

Because human communication is predominantly symbolic, humans must agree on the meanings of words. Consequently, words can, and do, change over time. For example, the term *gay* typically meant "happy" or "carefree" from the seventeenth century through much of the twentieth century. Although the term was occasionally used to refer to same-sex relationships as early as the 1800s, it has come to be used widely only since the late 1990s, when users agreed to this meaning and usage. Nonetheless, people may have different meanings for specific symbols or words, especially if they come from different ethnic or national cultures. Read about one student's difficulties communicating while on a trip to Europe in *It Happened to Me: Alyssa.*

messages
The building blocks of communication.

encoding
Converting ideas into messages.

decoding
Receiving a message and interpreting its meaning.

symbol
Something that represents something else and conveys meaning.

It Happened to Me
Alyssa

Recently I traveled in Europe; I had no idea how difficult it would be to communicate, even in Scotland. I spent the first few days navigating Edinburgh on my own. It was so hard! People tried to help, but because of the differences in word choice and accents, I couldn't fully understand their directions. After Edinburgh I went to Germany, where I had an even harder time communicating due to the language barrier. So I resorted to using nonverbal gestures, like calling the server in a restaurant by raising a hand/finger. Turns out this gesture is not the way to get the attention of a server, as I read later in my guidebook; it can even be considered rather rude.

As Alyssa's experience reveals, though most people recognize that cultures vary in the words they use for specific ideas and items, they don't always realize that nonverbal gestures can have varied meanings across cultures as well. Creating messages is the most fundamental requirement for communication to occur, but it certainly is not enough. Messages also create shared meanings for everyone involved in the interaction.

Meaning Creation   The goal of exchanging symbols—that is, of communicating—is to create meaning. The messages we send and receive shape meaning beyond the symbols themselves. We also bring to each message a set of experiences, beliefs, and values, often influenced by our culture, that help shape specific meanings. For example, *Top Chef* host Padma Lakshmi, in her Hulu show *Taste the Nation*, describes the way food creates, continues, and preserves culture (especially in immigrant communities). This also means that people can hear the same message but understand it differently. Charee was aware of this as she planned the conversation with her father. She knew they didn't always have precisely the same meanings for every word. For example, the phrase *independent thinker* to describe a son or daughter carried positive meanings for her as a millennial-age college student, but she knew it carried more negative and potentially upsetting meanings for her father. Therefore, when talking to her father, she would never argue that participating in political rallies was good for her because it would help her become more independent.

Meaning is made even more complex because, as the example suggests, each message carries with it two types of meaning—content meaning and relationship meaning. **Content meaning** includes denotative and connotative meaning. Denotative meaning is the concrete meaning of the message, such as the definition you would find in a dictionary. Connotative meaning describes the meanings suggested by or associated with the message and the emotions triggered by it. For example, denotatively the word *mother* refers to one's female parent, whereas connotatively it may include meanings such as warmth, nurturance, and intimacy. **Relationship meaning** describes what the message conveys about the relationship between the parties (Robinson-Smith, 2004; Watzlawick et al., 1967). For example, if a colleague at work told you to "run some copies of this report," you might become irritated, but you probably wouldn't mind if your boss told you to do the same thing. In both cases the relationship message may be understood as "I have the right to tell you what to do," which is appropriate if it comes from your supervisor—but not if it comes from a peer.

Finally, communication helps create the shared meanings that shape families, communities, and societies. Specifically, the meanings we have for important issues including politics, civil behavior, family, and spirituality—as well as for less important concerns such as what food is tasty or what type of home is desirable—are created through people's interactions with one another. For example, if you were asked what your family "motto" is (that is, what is important in your family), what would you say? Some people might say it is "family first," whereas others declare it is "do the right thing." How do families come to have these shared beliefs and meanings? They do so through the countless interactions they have with one another; through these conversations and everyday experiences they create a meaning for what is important to their family. What do you think happens when two people marry, one of whom believes "family first" and another who thinks "do the right thing" is more important than even family? Like the families they grew up within, they will interact, live together, and jointly develop shared meanings for their family beliefs. A similar process occurs when people come together to form groups, organizations, communities, and societies. In sum, our relationships, our understanding of the world, and our beliefs about life and death are created through the interactions we have with others.

Setting   The physical surroundings of a communication event make up its setting. **Setting** includes the location where the communication occurs, environmental conditions, time of day or day of the week, and the proximity of the communicators. Together these factors create the physical setting, which affects communication interaction.

content meaning
The concrete meaning of the message and the meanings suggested by or associated with the message, as well as the emotions triggered by it.

relationship meaning
What a message conveys about the relationship between the parties.

setting
The physical surroundings of a communication event.

Why do you think Charee chose to meet in midafternoon at her father's favorite café as the setting for their conversation? She did so for several reasons. First, her father would be more likely to feel relaxed and in a good mood in a familiar location that he liked. Second, she selected the middle of the afternoon so they would have more privacy and fewer interruptions. Finally, she chose a public setting because she believed her father would remain calmer in public than in a private setting, such as at home. As you can see, Charee carefully selected a comfortable setting that she believed would enhance her chances of being successful.

Participants   During communication, **participants**—two or more people—interact. The number of participants, as well as their characteristics, will influence how the interaction unfolds. Typically, the more characteristics participants share (cultural, values, history), the easier they will find it to communicate because they can rely on their common assumptions about the world.

participants
The people interacting during communication.

As Charee planned her conversation, she recognized that she and her father shared a number of important characteristics—respect for elders in the family, a communal approach to relationships, and a desire for harmony. However, she also realized that they differed in important ways. Although she was close to her family, she desired more independence than her father would want for himself or for her. In addition, she believed it was acceptable for young, single women to make their own decisions about how to think and how to live their lives, a belief she was sure her father didn't share to the same extent.

The type of relationship communicators have and the history they share also affect their communication. Whether communicators are family members, romantic partners, colleagues, friends, or acquaintances affects how they frame, deliver, and interpret a message.

channel
The means through which a message is transmitted.

noise
Any stimulus that can interfere with or degrade the quality of a message.

Because Charee was talking with her father rather than her boyfriend, she focused on displaying respect for his position as her father and asking (rather than telling) him about wanting to attend a protest rally that week. As we have suggested already, the moods and emotions that communicators bring to and experience during their interaction influence it as well. Because Charee wanted to increase the likelihood that the conversation with her father would go well, she tried to create a situation in which he would be in a calmer and happier frame of mind.

Channels   For a message to be transmitted from one participant to another, it must travel through a channel. A **channel** is the means through which a message is conveyed. Historically, the channels people used to communicate with one another were first face-to-face and then written. Today, thanks to technology, we have many more communication channels—email, texting, social networks such as Facebook, Instagram, and Twitter, to name just a few.

▼ Mobile messaging is one channel of communication. What other channels do you often use?

The channel that a person selects to communicate a message can affect how the message is perceived and its impact on the relationship. For example, if your romantic partner broke up with you in an Instagram post or by changing their Facebook relationship status instead of by talking to you face-to-face, how would you respond? Because Charee was sensitive to the importance of the communication channel she used with her father, she elected to communicate with him face-to-face because it was a channel her father was familiar with and would find appealing.

Noise   **Noise** refers to any stimulus that can interfere with or degrade the quality of a message. Noise includes external signals of all kinds: not only loud music and voices but also

Critical Thinking Prompt
How do you choose which channel to use when you communicate with others? Do you consider who they are, the topic, the importance of the message, or something else? Overall, do you think you pick the best channel most of the time? If not, what do you need to do to select more appropriately?

feedback
The response to a message.

Journal Prompt 1.2: Defining Communication
How do the authors define human communication? What are the seven basic components of the communication process?

distracting clothing or hairstyles, uncomfortably warm or chilly temperatures, perceptions of prejudice or racism, and so on. Noise can also come from internal stimuli, such as hunger or sleepiness. Semantic interference, which occurs when speakers use words you do not know or use a familiar word in an unfamiliar way, is another form of noise. If you have ever tried to have a conversation with someone who used highly technical language in a noisy room while you were sleepy, you have experienced a "perfect storm" of noise.

How did the noise factor affect Charee's choices? She chose to meet at a café in the middle of the afternoon, avoiding the crowded lunch and dinner hours. There would be fewer competing voices and sounds, and the waitstaff would be less likely to interrupt with meal service, so there would be fewer distractions. By choosing a setting that minimized interference, she improved the chances that her message would be clear.

Feedback   Finally, the response to a message is called **feedback**. Feedback lets a sender know if the message was received and how the message was interpreted. For example, if a friend tells you a joke and you laugh heartily, your laughter serves as feedback, indicating that you heard the joke and found it amusing. Similarly, if you fall asleep during a lecture, you provide feedback to your professor that either you are tired or you find a Zoom lecture boring. Thus, your feedback serves as a message to the sender, who then uses the information conveyed to help shape his or her next message.

Although Charee wasn't sure what type of feedback her father would provide or what type she would need to give him, she did spend time anticipating what they each would say. She also knew that she would need to be sensitive to his messages and be prepared to offer feedback that was both supportive and persuasive.

A Model of Human Communication: The Synergetic Model

1.3   Explain how the Synergetic Model of Communication differs from previous models.

To help people understand complex processes, scientists and engineers, among others, create visual models to show how all components of a process work together. Scholars of human communication have done the same. They have developed models to reveal how the seven components described work together to create a communication interaction.

The first such model of human communication depicted communication as a linear process that primarily involved the transfer of information from one person to another (Eisenberg et al., 2010; Laswell, 1948; Shannon & Weaver, 1949). In this model, communication occurred when a sender encoded a message (put ideas into words and symbols) that was sent to a receiver who decoded (interpreted) it. Then the process was believed to reverse: the receiver became the sender, and the sender became the receiver (Laswell, 1948). This model (see Figure 1.1) also included the components of "noise" and "channel." A linear model assumes, for example, that your professor encodes her ideas into a lesson that she communicates to you via a face-to-face or video lecture (the channel) and that you hear her message and decode its meaning unless some noise interferes, such as the video failing to load or a loud noise outside drowning out her words. However, you can see some of the limitations of this model. It assumes that if a message is perfectly crafted its meaning will be clear to the audience, regardless of their own ages, experiences, and interpretations. You can probably think of times where this was not true. Because of these limitations, other, more complex models, such as our Synergetic Model, have been created to show a greater variety of factors that interact with one another to influence the communication process.

Synergetic Model
A transactional model that emphasizes how individual and societal forces, contexts, and culture interact to affect the communication process.

The **Synergetic Model** is a transactional model that, like most previous models, depicts communication as occurring when two or more people create meaning as they respond to each other and their environment. In addition, it is based on a belief in the

Figure 1.1 A Linear Model of Communication

Early models depicted communication as a linear process that primarily involved the transfer of information from one person to another.

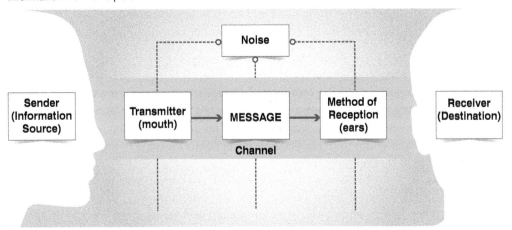

important roles of individual and societal forces, contexts, and culture in the communication process. We call the model synergetic because synergy describes when two or more elements work together to achieve something either one couldn't have achieved on its own. For example, in the ubiquitous volcano science fair project, "lava" is created by adding vinegar to baking soda. Once the two products interact, something new is created. Similarly, when two people work together on a class project, often the outcome is better than either could have created on his own. Thus, our communication model is synergetic in that the different elements of communication work together to create something different, and greater, than just the sum of its parts. We discuss each of these elements, and to help clarify the concepts, we revisit Charee's interaction with her father once again to illustrate how they function during the communication process.

After carefully planning for the interaction with her father about her desire to be more politically active, Charee engaged in the following conversation with him:

CHAREE: I feel it's my civic responsibility to protest what's been going on in our city's police department. *(While talking, Charee notices a quizzical look on her father's face.)*

DAD: *(frowning, speaking uncertainly)* Why you? The police have never done anything to us. Why do you have to put yourself in danger? Couldn't you just write a letter or post some questions to the police department's website?

CHAREE: My friends and I have done this, and the university group I belong to has tried many ways to facilitate change, and it hasn't worked.

DAD: So when and where are you gonna do this?

CHAREE: *(looking away, speaking hesitantly)* Well, there's an organized rally tonight downtown.

DAD: I still don't understand! Why do you think you have to do this?

CHAREE: *(speaking patiently)* Do you and Mom remember what it was like when you were in Vietnam and the government didn't respect people's viewpoints? Do you remember what it was like when I was bullied in school and the teacher denied it was happening? I know it's 10 times worse for my Black friends, in school and on the streets. And I think it's patriotic to make sure *all Americans* are treated fairly. And I know you love this country and feel very patriotic, just as I do.

DAD: *(shaking his head, speaking firmly)* Well, I wish you didn't have to express your patriotism in this way, but I remember hearing about the problems in the police department here. I just worry about you! I want you to be safe.

CHAREE: *(nodding her head, smiling)* I know you worry about me, and I kinda like that. I promise I'll keep in touch and be careful.

Communication Is Transactional

To say that *communication is a transaction* (see Figure 1.2) captures the fact that (1) each participant is a sender and receiver *at the same time*, (2) meaning is created as people communicate together, (3) communication is an ongoing process, and (4) previous communication events and relationships influence its meaning (Warren & Yoder, 1998; Watzlawick et al., 1967). What does this mean?

First, all participants in a communication event both receive and send messages simultaneously, even if those messages are sent only nonverbally. As you may have noted, when Charee explained that she thought it was her civic responsibility, she realized from her father's nonverbal behavior that he was confused. That is, she received his message even as she talked, and he sent a message even as he listened.

Second, a transactional model of communication assumes speakers collaborate through an exchange of messages with the goal of understanding one another. That is, the purpose is not for receivers to perfectly understand the message senders have encoded, but that through working together participants can arrive at agreed-upon meanings. Rather, similar to experiences you have had with your parents, meaning was created as Charee and her dad communicated together; she made a statement, he showed his lack of understanding, and Charee offered more information until they shared similar understandings or meaning.

Third, describing communication as ongoing highlights the fact that it is a process whose specific beginnings and endings can be difficult to discern. All of the interactions one has had with individuals in the past influence one's communication in the present, just as a person's current communication affects his or her expectations for and experiences of future interactions. For example, when you talk with your best friend you often can talk in shorthand, because you can rely on shared communication and events you have had in the past. Similarly, Charee planned her interaction and communicated with her father based on her previous experiences with him. Specifically, she knew he would rather she not participate in political activism, so she was prepared to offer arguments for why participating was best for her. She also knew that while they were both patriotic, she needed her father to understand that they expressed that patriotism in different

Figure 1.2   Communication Is Transactional

Transactional models express the idea that meaning is created as people communicate.

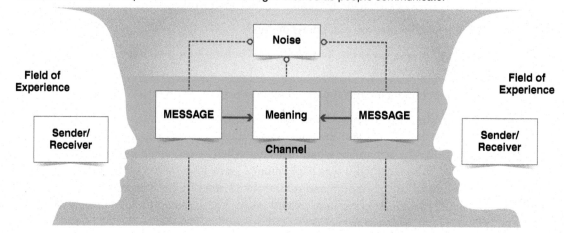

ways. Her experiences with her father, then, affected the messages she crafted for their conversation. In addition, she recognized that their conversation would influence how they communicated with each other in the future. If he became angry, he likely would communicate with her less or more negatively. This, in turn, would influence her future messages to him, and so on.

Finally, because communication is ongoing and interactive, when people communicate, they and their conversational partner(s) reaffirm or alter their identities and relationships. Thus, Charee's conversation with her father is likely to change how they see each other. He might see her as more adult and independent because of her desire to engage in an activity that he didn't really approve of, or he may now perceive her as a less loving child. Similarly, she may view him as less of an authority figure and more of a peer, or she might believe he is more authoritarian and rigid than she previously thought.

Communication Is Influenced by Individual Forces

The individual is a primary focus in communication. Many separate individual forces or characteristics contribute to your identity, and these in turn affect your communication. Individual forces include your demographic characteristics such as age, race, ethnicity, nationality, gender/sex, sexual orientation, regional identity, and socioeconomic class, as well as such factors as personality and cognitive and physical ability. In addition, individual forces include your **field of experience**, such as your education and experiences.

field of experience
The education and experiences that a communicator possesses.

For example, Charee is female, 20, and a college student, whereas her father is a male in his late 40s who operates an automotive repair shop. Each of these individual factors influences the way they communicate as well as the ways others communicate with them and about them. Because of her experiences as a college student, Charee knows what "systemic racism" is and feels strongly that young people must take a stand against inequities and unfair treatment toward all communities of color. By contrast, her father is not as aware of these issues, and based on his culture and his experiences, he believes that loyalty and law-abiding behavior are the most important qualities of a citizen.

The combination of these individual characteristics is unique for every person, so people communicate in distinctive ways. However, every society places limits on the variations that are deemed acceptable. For example, not all men speak assertively, enjoy talking about sports, and engage in "mansplaining" or "manspreading." In mainstream U.S. culture, though, many people consider these behaviors as normal for males. Speaking in a more "female" style, such as speaking quietly or politely talking about fashion, or using nonverbal gestures that could be considered more stereotypically feminine is typically considered inappropriate for men and boys. Those who veer somewhat from the norm may be seen as odd, or they might even be threatened or bullied; those who veer too far from the norm may be labeled as mentally ill. So although we are each individuals, society places constraints on the range of our individualism, a topic we will explore later.

Communication Is Influenced by Societal Forces

As we suggested, individual differences are not value free. They are arranged in a hierarchy in which some individual characteristics are more highly valued than others. For example, being Caucasian is often advantageous in U.S. society, being young has advantages over being old, and being physically able is more advantageous than having a disability. How society evaluates these characteristics affects how we talk to— and about—people who display them. For example, read Nathan's

It Happened to Me
Nathan

I don't look like the stereotypical gay guy. I am fairly athletic, I work out, and I was an athlete in college. Sometimes people say anti-gay things around me, as they assume that I'm not gay. I always have to decide if I need to say something. I am always forced to make communication decisions, depending on my relationship with them. Sometimes I feel that I'm forced to come out to these people. Is it any of their business?

▲ Being gay is both an individual and cultural factor.

experience. While his communication choices are partly due to his relationships with others, the choices are partly due to society's stereotypes of LGBTQIA+ individuals.

The political, historical, economic, and social structures of a society influence this value hierarchy and affect how we view specific individual characteristics. The historical conditions under which many U.S. racial and ethnic groups arrived in the United States, for instance, continue to affect their identities, with many people making assumptions about individuals' occupation and/or social status based on their culture or ethnicity. For example, immigrants who move to the United States often are not fluent in English, so they create businesses of their own—as restaurant owners, shopkeepers, or service professionals. Consequently, many people fail to realize that immigrants also work as technology innovators, lawyers, professors, and physicians. Asian immigrants often flee to America from countries with more authoritarian governments. Happy to be in a country with a representative form of government, their instinct might be to trust a U.S. government and police force that, for the most part, has protected them. The values attributed to individual characteristics such as age, sexual orientation, and sex also come from these larger societal forces—whether communicated to us through the media, by our friends and family, or by organizations such as schools, religious institutions, or clubs. For example, the teachings of religious groups shape many people's views on sexual orientation, and because most societies historically have been patriarchal, they continue to value women in the public realm less than they do men.

In Charee's case, two societal forces were at work in her interaction with her father: how society views women and parent–child interactions. Pham was reared in a culture and time where males held considerably more power than females and parents were assumed to know what was best for their children even when the children were grown. Consequently, he tends to hold the belief that fathers should have considerable decision-making power over their children, especially their unmarried female children. And, in Vietnam, he wasn't part of a minority group. By contrast, Charee grew up in a culture and time where men and women are seen as more equal and parents exert less control over their children's lives as the children grow up.

Social hierarchies wherein men are more valued than women or older people's opinions are considered more worthwhile than younger people's arise from the meanings that societal structures impose on individual characteristics, and communication maintains these hierarchies. For example, cultures that value maleness over femaleness have many more stereotypes and negative terms for women than they do for men. Moreover, these cultures value certain types of communication over others. Thus, men in leadership positions are expected to communicate decisively and avoid appearing "weak" by apologizing or admitting mistakes, whereas the same is not usually true for women. We will explore social hierarchies in more detail in later chapters.

Communication Is Influenced by Culture

Communication also is embedded in culture. **Culture** refers to the learned patterns of perceptions, values, and behaviors shared by a group of people. Culture is dynamic and heterogeneous (Martin & Nakayama, 2018), meaning that it changes over time and that despite commonalities, members of cultural groups do not all think and behave alike. You probably belong to many cultures, including those of your gender, ethnicity, occupation, and religion, and each of these cultures will have its own communication patterns.

When you identify yourself as a member of a culture defined by age, ethnicity, or gender, this culture-group identity also becomes one of your individual characteristics. For example, as people move from their teen years into young adulthood, middle age, and old age, they generally make a transition from one age-related culture to another. Because each cultural group has a unique set of perceptions, values, and behaviors, each also has its own set of communication principles. As you become an adult, then, you probably stop using language you used as a teenager. And even though changing your language is an individual decision, it is influenced by cultural and societal expectations as well.

Culture affects all or almost all communication interactions (Martin & Nakayama, 2018). More specifically, participants bring their beliefs, values, norms, and attitudes to each interaction, and the cultures they belong to shape each of these factors. Cultural beliefs also affect how we expect others to communicate. As we discussed, because he is Vietnamese, Charee's father values family closeness, loyalty, and the role of the father as head of the family. Because she is Vietnamese American, Charee holds many of these same beliefs, but she also values independence and individuality in ways that her father does not. Ethnic background can also influence communication behaviors. Charee felt somewhat torn about where Asian Americans should position their politics in this policing case: while Asian Americans generally do not share the experiences of White Americans or African Americans, she felt that she and other Asian Americans should work toward a society that treats everyone fairly.

In addition to participants' cultural backgrounds, the culture in which a communication event takes place influences how participants communicate. In the United States, politicians routinely mention religion in their public addresses and specifically refer to God; however, in France, because of a stricter separation between church and state, politicians typically do not mention religion or deities in their public communication and would be criticized if they did. Regional culture can also affect participants' expectations for appropriate communication behavior. For instance, Southerners in the United States tend to be more nonverbally demonstrative and thus might hug others more than do Northeasterners (Andersen et al., 1990). Of course, other cultural differences (ethnic background, religious background) might influence these nonverbal behaviors as well.

Communication Is Influenced by Context

Each communication interaction occurs in a specific context. Context includes the setting, or aspects of the physical environment, in which an interaction occurs. It also includes which and how many participants are present, as well as the specific occasion during which the interaction unfolds (for example, a Sunday dinner or a birthday party). Context can exert a strong influence on how people communicate with one another. For example, you could argue with your close friend in private when just the two of you are present, during a social event when you are part of a group, during a staff meeting at work, on a television talk show about feuding friends, or on the sidewalk at campus. Can you imagine how each of these contexts would influence your communication? You might be more open if the two of you are alone and in private; you may try to get others involved if you are with friends; you could be more subdued in public on campus; you

culture
Learned patterns of perceptions, values, and behaviors shared by a group of people.

Figure 1.3   The Synergetic Model

The Synergetic Model presents communication as a transactional process in which meaning is influenced by cultural, societal, and individual forces.

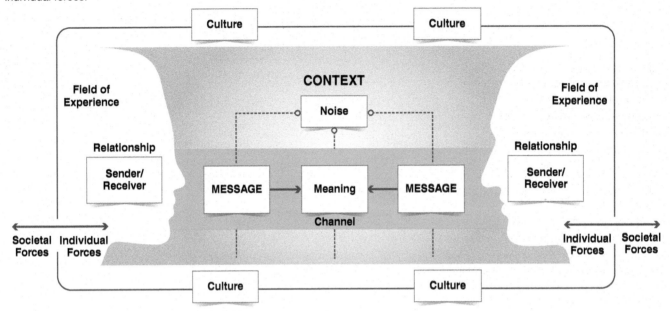

might refrain from mentioning anything too negative on television; or you might be more hostile in an email or text. It is because context strongly affects individuals' interactions that Charee arranged to talk with her father at his favorite café in the afternoon.

The tensions that exist among individual forces, societal forces, cultures, and contexts shape communication and meaning. To help clarify this tension, let's return yet again to Charee's conversation with her father. Their conversation was influenced by the context (a restaurant), multiple individual forces (each person's age, sex, cultural background, and education), multiple societal forces (the importance of racial politics in policing and protesting) as well as their cultures (the meanings of independence, loyalty, and family). Thus, in the conversation between Charee and her father, the context in which the conversation occurred, their individual experiences with racism and the cultural meaning of the parent–child relationship all came together to influence the communication interaction. These components and their relationships to one another are depicted in Figure 1.3.

As we stated at the beginning of the chapter and as is revealed in our model, for us, communication is a transactional process in which people generate meaning through the exchange of verbal and nonverbal messages in specific contexts, influenced by individual and societal forces and embedded in culture. This is the definition and model of communication that will guide you as you explore the remainder of this book. After you complete this course, we recommend that you return to this section to assess how your own understanding of the communication process has changed and deepened.

Our goal in developing this model is to provide a framework for students to organize, read, and understand this complex process we call communication. However, before moving on, we need to discuss one more essential concept that frames and guides all of your communication efforts—ethics.

Journal Prompt 1.3:
The Synergetic Model
According to the Synergetic Model, what are the individual and social factors that influence the communication process?

Communication Ethics

1.4   Formulate your own communication ethic.

A diary study found that college students lied in one out of about every three social interactions, and over the course of a week only 1 percent of students said they told no lies at all (DePaulo, 2011). In a more recent survey of 70,000 undergraduate and graduate students,

95 percent admitted to cheating on a test or homework or committing plagiarism (Danilyuk, 2019). And it isn't only college students who admit to deceiving others. In a recent survey conducted by the National Endowment of Financial Education (2018), 41 percent of respondents confessed to lying to their marital and living partners about money, often with disastrous consequences. "Operation Varsity Blues," in which some wealthy parents paid about $25 million in bribes and misrepresented their children's application materials to get into elite schools, is another example of deception (Reilly, 2020).

Given examples such as these, one may wonder if a communication ethic still exists. We strongly believe that it does. Even if unethical communication is widespread and some people get away with their misbehavior, most people are still held responsible for the messages they create (Anderson & Tompkins, 2015; Fritz, 2019; Lipari, 2009). If you spread gossip about your friends, lie to your employer, or withhold information from your family, justifying your behavior by pointing to the ethical failures of others will not excuse you. Those who know you and are close to you still expect you to meet basic standards for ethical communication.

Why are communication ethics so important? First, they sustain professional success. Yes, unethical people may prosper in the short run, but over time unethical practices catch up with the people who engage in them. To a great extent, your reputation as a person of integrity determines whether others want to hire you, work for you, or conduct business with you. Once that reputation is damaged, it can be difficult if not impossible to regain; consequently, communicating and behaving ethically is just good business.

Communication ethics are vital to personal relationships as well. Maintaining intimate and caring relationships can be difficult, but they become virtually impossible if one communicates unethically by lying, manipulating, or verbally abusing friends and lovers. Intimate relationships are grounded in trust. Without trust, people can't be open and vulnerable with one another, behaviors that are essential to intimacy. When one person abuses that trust by his or her unethical conduct, the other party often is deeply wounded and finds it difficult to ever again be intimate within the relationship. Far too many people have learned the hard way that a lack of ethics destroys relationships.

> **Critical Thinking Prompt**
> What are three specific communication behaviors you believe are unethical? What principles guide your decisions regarding whether a given communication behavior is ethical or unethical?

As a communicator, you will face many ambiguous and difficult choices of both a professional and a personal nature. If you develop your own set of communication ethics, you will be better prepared to face these difficult choices. Therefore, in this section we provide some basic principles of ethical communication for you to consider as you critically review your own ethical standard.

Fundamentally, individuals, groups, and communities develop ethical codes to reflect their beliefs and values. Clearly the guidelines we offer reflect our own communication ethics. We do not expect you to adopt our beliefs wholesale. Rather, we present this information throughout this book so that you can analyze it critically to determine to what extent it reflects your own beliefs and behavior, what evidence supports it, and what other guidelines may be as useful or more useful for you. Thus, we want you to use your critical thinking skills specifically to critique our claims here and to use that analysis to form your own ethical code.

Defining Your Communication Ethic

Communication ethics describes the standards of right and wrong that one applies to messages that are sent and received. When you hear the term *communication ethics*, you might think we are simply referring to whether messages are truthful. Although truthfulness is one of the most fundamental ethical standards, communicating ethically requires much more than simply being truthful. It also involves deciding what information can and should be disclosed or withheld, and assessing the benefit or harm associated with specific messages. Individuals have a responsibility to evaluate the ethics of their own and others' communication efforts. Similarly, corporations ought to weigh the ethics of sharing or withholding information that might affect the value of their

communication ethics
The standards of right and wrong that one applies to messages that are sent and received.

stock shares, and media companies should decide whether it is ethical to report private information about individuals. Let's look at some of the issues you need to reflect on as you develop your code of ethics.

Truthfulness   Truthfulness plays a fundamental role in ethical communication for two reasons: First, others expect messages to be truthful, and second, messages have consequences. Because people inherently expect speakers to be truthful, we actually may make it easier for them to deceive us (Burgoon et al., 1996). If an audience is not suspicious, they probably won't look for cues that the speaker is lying (McCornack & Parks, 1986). However, because of the implicit contract to be honest, discovery of deception can severely damage relationships. The more intimate the relationship, the greater the expectation people have that their partners will be truthful, and the more damaging any deception will be.

As we've implied, people rely on messages to be truthful because they have consequences. One's communication can influence the beliefs, attitudes, and behaviors of others. For example, an individual's communication could persuade a customer to purchase an item, a friend to lend money, or an acquaintance to become romantically involved with him or her. The more consequential the outcome of your message, the more likely you will be held accountable to the truth. You might not be criticized too harshly for exaggerating your salary during a flirtation with a stranger, but an employer will most likely consider it unethical if you lie about your salary on a job application.

Sharing or Withholding Information   A related fundamental principle of ethical communication concerns what information should be divulged and what can be withheld. When is withholding information a matter of legitimate privacy, and when is it a matter of inappropriate secrecy? Thus, you have to determine whether to tell your romantic partner how many sexual partners you have had, media organizations have to decide whether to reveal the identity of confidential news sources, and government officials decide what information to "leak" to the press.

In our view, a message can be considered legitimately private when other parties have no right to expect access to it. Inappropriate secrecy, by contrast, occurs when other parties might legitimately expect access to a message that is withheld. This distinction is important because it is generally ethical to maintain privacy, but it may be unethical to engage in secrecy.

What's the difference between privacy and secrecy? We believe communicators have an ethical responsibility to share information that other people require to make informed decisions. For example, if you have only dated someone once or twice, you may choose to keep private that you have a sexually transmitted disease. However, if the two of you consider becoming sexually intimate, you probably have an ethical obligation to reveal the information. Without this information, your partner cannot make an informed decision about whether to engage in sexual contact. What will happen to your relationship if you withhold the information and your partner contracts your disease—and finds out later that you withheld the information? Similarly, your friends may not need to know why you were fired from your last job, but your new boss may have a legitimate need for access to this information.

By contrast, revealing information can sometimes be unethical. For example, if you have agreed to maintain confidentiality about a topic, it could be considered unethical to reveal what you know. However, if you violate

▼ Is it ethical to gossip or share others' private information?

a confidence because of a higher ethical principle, most people would likely consider your behavior ethical. For example, if you have a duty of confidentiality to your employer, but your company engages in illegal toxic dumping, it likely would be more ethical to break this confidence. Here, the ethic of protecting the public health likely supersedes the ethic of keeping a confidence. These are not easy decisions, but they reflect the type of complex ethical choices that people have to make.

Now that you have read our guideline for differentiating secrecy and privacy, do you find yourself agreeing or disagreeing with it? Can you think of situations in which it would not apply? Can you think of a better principle one could use to make decisions about whether to withhold or reveal information? Again, it is not important that you adopt our guideline but that you think through and develop one that is in line with your own ethical code.

You can begin to think through your position on this issue by exploring a standard practice in job searches—Internet searches by corporations to gather information on potential or current employees as well as the practice of potential or current employees hiding social media information from employers. When individuals create fake Instagram accounts, "finstas," or Facebook spam accounts, do you believe they are engaging in secrecy or privacy attempts? How would you defend your position to someone who disagrees with you? That is, what evidence and examples would you use to argue for your belief? What arguments might someone make who disagrees with you? To what extent does the context of social media communication influence your response?

Benefit and Harm of Messages   To determine the most ethical choice, you also should consider the benefit or harm associated with your messages. A classic example concerns whether it is right to lie to a potential murderer about the whereabouts of the intended victim. A principle of honesty suggests that you should tell the truth. But in this case, once you evaluate the potential harm of sharing versus withholding the information, you might well decide to withhold the information.

More typically, issues of harm and benefit are less clear. For example, if you discover your best friend's romantic partner is being unfaithful, should you share that information? Will it result in more harm or more benefit? If you know that a relative cheated on her taxes, should you report her to the IRS?

Because many communication events are complex and the underlying ethical principles are not definitive, you will need to gradually develop your own philosophy of ethical communication and apply it on a case-by-case basis. This is one requirement of being an effective communicator. However, just as you develop your own ethical standards and decisions, others will do so as well, which means you and others in your life may not always agree.

Absolutism versus Relativism   A fundamental decision in communication ethics concerns how **absolute** or **relative** your ethical standards will be. Will you use the same absolute standards for every communication interaction, or will your ethical choices be relative and depend on each situation? The Greek philosopher Plato and the German philosopher Immanuel Kant conceptualized the absolutist perspective (Kant, 1949), and both believed there is a rationally correct, moral standard that holds for everyone, everywhere, every time. Relativists such as French philosopher Jean-Paul Sartre, by contrast, hold the view that moral behavior varies among individuals, groups, and cultures. They argue that because there is no universal standard of morality, there is no rational way to decide who is correct (Sartre, 1973).

If you hold to the absolutist perspective that lying is always wrong, then in the previous example regarding the potential murderer, you would be obligated not to lie about the whereabouts of the intended victim. But if you adhere to a relativistic position regarding truth and deception, you would decide in the moment what the most ethical choice is based on the specific circumstances. You might tell a lie to save a life.

In reality, few people develop an ethical standard that is completely absolute or relative. Instead, absolutism and relativism are the opposite ends of a continuum, and

absolutism
The belief that there is a single correct moral standard that holds for everyone, everywhere, every time.

relativism
The belief that moral behavior varies among individuals, groups, and cultures and across situations.

▲ Should a salesperson admit that a competitor's product might be as good as the product they are selling?

most people's standards lie somewhere along that continuum.

The issue for you is to decide how absolute or relative your ethical standards will be. If you strongly believe that deception is wrong, you may choose the path of deception only when you believe the truth will cause great harm—a standard that falls toward the absolutist end of the continuum. However, if you favor a more relative view, you will consider a variety of factors, in addition to harm, as you make your decisions.

Communication Ethics in Practice

In this discussion of ethics, we have offered guidelines for creating your own communication ethics. However, in practice, many situations arise that are ambiguous, complex, and multilayered. At times you may not see how you can be ethical and accomplish important goals at the same time. For example, if you know that a friend and classmate has plagiarized a paper, what should you do? Should you keep quiet and maintain your friendship, or should you maintain your personal ethics and tell the instructor? Similarly, if you are a salesperson, how do you respond if a potential client asks whether a competitor's product is as good as yours, and you don't believe it is? Do you tell the truth and thus jeopardize a potential sale? People who tend toward an absolutist view say that you must always tell the truth, so you should only sell a product you truly believe is superior. Others may tell you that no one expects salespeople to be completely truthful in this context; therefore, you are not bound to share your opinion (Diener, 2002; Wokutch & Carson, 1981).

We believe that all communicators need to create an ethical stance based on their own beliefs, values, and moral training. Once *you've* established your ethical stance, you will be prepared to make thoughtful and deliberate communication choices.

Journal Prompt 1.4: Code of Ethics
Why is developing one's own code of communication ethics important?

Putting It All Together: Communicating Competently

1.5 Articulate what makes a communicator competent.

The goal of this book is to help you improve your communication skills so that you can become a more successful, or competent, communicator. A competent communicator is one who is able to use communication to achieve his or her (realistic and appropriate) goals. More specifically, communicators are competent when they use their understanding of themselves, others, the context, and communication principles to adapt their communication to achieve their goals (Friedrich, 1994).

Communication competence is composed of two elements: **appropriateness**, which is defined as following the relevant rules, norms, and expectations for specific relationships and situations; and **effectiveness**, which involves achieving one's goals successfully. Speakers are competent when they understand the expectations regarding their behavior and are able to behave in a way that fulfills those expectations. For example, a best man offering a wedding toast is expected to be amusing, complimentary, and

communication competence
The ability to adapt one's communication to achieve one's goals.

appropriateness
Following the rules, norms and expectations for specific situations or relationships.

effectiveness
Achieving one's goals successfully.

brief (as well as sober!). Failure to fulfill these expectations not only results in a poor toast, but it often also results in audience members negatively evaluating the speaker. If the toast seriously violates these expectations, the consequences may even include terminated relationships.

Effectiveness refers to the ability to achieve one's goals for an interaction without interfering with other, potentially more important goals. Taking the earlier example, a person giving a toast may have a goal of being humorous. However, if the best man makes jokes that are in poor taste, he might meet his goal of making the audience laugh, but he may fail another, more important goal of remaining friends with the bride and groom.

Generally, speakers have three types of goals that are important during an interaction: content, relationship, and identity. *Content* goals describe the concrete outcomes you would like to achieve during an interaction—to receive a job offer, earn a high grade on a speech, or to successfully initiate a new relationship. *Relationship* goals refer to your desire to change or maintain your relationship with another, for example, when you say "I love you" to your romantic partner in hopes of increasing your commitment to one another, or when you apologize so your romantic partner won't leave you. Finally, *identity* goals describe how we would like others to see us or help us see ourselves. When complaining about a grade, for instance, you likely want your grade changed (a content goal) but you probably also want your instructor to see you as deserving the higher grade (an identity goal).

Based on this definition, a communication behavior is judged to be competent only within specific situations or relationships (Cupach et al., 2009). That is, a behavior that might be appropriate or effective for one situation may not be so for another. For example, although "trash talking" may be competent (that is, appropriate and effective) in a sports context, is not likely to be appropriate during a discussion with one's romantic partner, even if it were effective. Communication competence requires that you understand yourself, your relationships and specific situations well enough that you can pull from your repertoire of communication skills exactly the right ones to use at this time, in this place, with this person, on this topic.

If you think all of this sounds like a lot to do, you are beginning to understand why learning to communicate well is so complex. The good news is that we are here to help you develop the skills you need to be competent in a wide range of interactions. As you read through the remaining chapters in the book, reflect on how each concept can help you become a more competent communicator.

**Journal Prompt 1.5:
Competent Communication**
What does it mean to be a competent communicator?

SUMMARY

1.1 Explain why it is important to study human communication.

- Studying human communication can enrich and transform your life professionally and personally.
- *Critical thinking*, which involves reflection and weighing evidence, is a key to successful communication.
- Communication skills are crucial in developing relationships, establishing identity, and opening career doors.

1.2 Name and describe the seven primary components of communication.

- The *process of communication* involves seven basic components: message creation, meaning creation, setting, participants, channels, noise, and feedback.

1.3 Explain how the Synergetic Model of Communication differs from previous models.

- The *Synergetic Model* views communication as a transactional process; it emphasizes that all communication interactions are influenced by the intersection of individual and societal forces, that they are embedded in culture, and that they occur in specific contexts.

1.4 Formulate your own communication ethic.

- Key aspects of communication ethics to consider as you make decisions include truthfulness, decisions regarding sharing or withholding information, and the benefit and harm associated with one's choices.
- Communicators' ethical choices are affected by their position on the continuum of absolutism versus relativism, which in turn influences their language use and how they receive and how they respond to others' communication efforts.

1.5 Articulate what makes a communicator competent.

- Understanding communication processes and the ethics of your own communication choices is the first step toward you becoming a more *competent communicator*.
- Competent communicators strive to be both effective and appropriate in their interactions with others.

KEY TERMS

APPLY WHAT YOU KNOW

1. **Guidelines for Using Communication Technologies**
   Much debate has raged over whether it is appropriate to talk or text on one's cell phone in restaurants, in front of friends, or in the car. The Federal Aviation Administration is considering whether to allow airline passengers to use their cell phones during flights—and many people complain vocally about the possibility. The widespread use of mobile messaging and the ability to access our messages almost anywhere have made the issues surrounding the appropriate use of virtual communication even more complex. To guide your own decisions, develop a list of rules for how, when, and with whom it is appropriate to use or not use communicative media.

2. **Creating a Communication Ethic**
   (a) Interview three people and ask them to describe the underlying ethic(s) that guide their communication choices.

   (b) Then write a brief statement that describes your own communication ethic when using social media, considering the following questions:

   How do you decide what messages to post where? For example, how do you decide *what* you post and how you *present yourself* on different sites? Are you presenting yourself authentically, even if it's unflattering or revealing? Or are you just presenting the best parts of yourself?

   How do you decide *whom* you add on which sites? Do you add or omit certain people (e.g., family members or friends) in order to curate specific audiences and followers?

Communicating Identities

 LEARNING OBJECTIVES

CHAPTER TOPICS

2.1 Identify six reasons identity is important to communication.	The Importance of Identity
2.2 Define *identity*.	What Is Identity?
2.3 Clarify how reflected appraisals, social comparisons, self-fulfilling prophecies, and self-concept contribute to identity development.	The Individual and Identity
2.4 Identify examples of racial, national, ethnic, gender, sexual, age, social class, disability, and religious identities.	The Individual, Identity, and Society
2.5 Discuss three ethical considerations for communicating in a sensitive manner to and about others' identities.	Ethics and Identity
2.6 Explain three ways to communicate more effectively about identities.	Skills for Communicating about Identities

> *"We cannot separate our identities—as individuals or as members of society—from our communication experiences."*

When you think about identity, you may be pondering who you "really" are and how you got to be that way. When Charee thinks about her identity, she thinks about the many identities that make her who she is. Sometimes she thinks about her national identity as a U.S. citizen (e.g., when she applies for jobs and is asked if she is eligible to work in the United States). Other times she thinks about her ethnic identity as an Asian American from an immigrant family. As mentioned in Chapter 1, her father is an immigrant from Vietnam, and she sees herself as a Vietnamese American. Sometimes she thinks about her gender identity in other contexts. Can you choose to be whomever you want, or do your background and social environment determine who you are? In this chapter, we address these identity questions as well as the important role communication plays in them.

As we discussed in Chapter 1, communication is a deeply cultural process. In this chapter, we explore how individual characteristics, such as gender and age and the societal meanings associated with them, interact to create cultural identities—and the important role communication plays in that development. Within cultures, communication patterns, habits, values, and practices develop around specific individual characteristics such as race, gender, sexuality, age, social class, and religion. For example, in the United States, people commonly understand that it is not acceptable to tell racist or sexist jokes, particularly in the workplace, at job interviews, and in other formal settings. This understanding exists because people are aware of the impact of this type of communication on people's identities. We all possess many cultural identities because we identify with genders, races, ethnicities, religions, organizational affiliations, schools, and so on. Some of these identities affect our communication experiences more than others. We know that if you send the same message as someone else, it might be interpreted quite differently because of differences in race, gender, or other identities. We explain which identities are most influential and why. We also examine how societal forces influence identity and discuss ethical issues associated with communication and identities. We conclude by looking at some skills for communicating about identities.

The Importance of Identity

2.1 Identify six reasons identity is important to communication.

Identity has a tremendous impact on the communication process in a number of ways. How we communicate, as well as how our communication is received by others, can be shaped by our identities and the identities of others. Let's look at some of the ways that identity influences communication. First, because individuals bring their self-images or identities to each communicative encounter, every communication interaction is affected by their identities. For example, when elderly people converse with teenagers, both groups may have to accommodate for differences in their experiences and language use.

Second, communication interactions create and shape identities (Carbaugh, 2007). If older adults treat teenagers with respect and admiration during their conversations, these young people may view themselves as more mature and more valuable than they did previously. Conversely, communication can also be used to denigrate other identities and create tension between groups. It is always important to think about the impact of communication on various identity groups.

Third, identity plays an important role in intercultural communication, which is something that has become increasingly common in our global, technology-based world. As more and more businesses have international branches and subsidiaries, workers are increasingly likely to have contact with people from other cultures. The more familiar they are with the values related to identity in these cultures, the better prepared they will be to succeed in today's society.

Fourth, understanding identity is useful because so much of U.S. life is organized around and geared toward specific identities (Allen, 2004). In the United States, we have television stations such as Black Entertainment Television and Telemundo and, as more people get rid of cable subscriptions, *Black Stories* on Hulu, for example, that offer programming for primarily African American audiences. Magazines like *Ebony* and *Out*, among many, are targeted to groups based on their race, age, gender, or sexuality. We also have entertainment venues such as Disneyland and Club Med that are developed specifically for families, romantic couples, and singles. In this identity-based climate, individuals often communicate primarily with others who share their identities. Consequently, learning how to communicate effectively with individuals whose identities vary from yours may require considerable thought and effort.

Fifth, identity is a key site in which individual and societal forces come together to shape communication experiences. Although we each possess identity characteristics such as social class or nationality, the society where our communication takes place defines the meanings of those characteristics. For example, depending on whether you are in the United States or visiting a country where anti-American sentiment is common, what it means to be an "American" can have different nuances. Moreover, we cannot separate our identities—as individuals or as members of society—from our communication experiences.

Finally, identity is an important part of how we send and receive messages. When someone wants to speak for or against a proposed change in restaurant regulations at a city council meeting, they may preface the remarks by noting that they are an owner of a restaurant in the city and then make their arguments. In other situations, people may identify themselves as parents, consumers, fans, and other identities. Sometimes identities are used to mobilize people to act, such as the Black Lives Matter protests held in the wake of the killing of George Floyd in Minneapolis. Not all protestors were African Americans and all African Americans did not participate, but we are a complex set of interconnected identities. We explain this interaction more fully throughout this chapter.

Journal Prompt 2.1: Communication and Society
What are six advantages to understanding the relationship between communication and identity?

What Is Identity?

2.2 Define *identity*.

When you enrolled in college, you were most likely required to provide a piece of identification, such as a birth certificate, passport, or driver's license. Identity is tied closely to identification; it refers to who you are and the specific characteristics that make you different from other individuals. In communication studies, *identity* includes not only who you are but also the social categories you identify yourself with and the categories that others identify with you. Society creates social categories such as *middle aged* or *college student*, but they only become part of one's identity when one identifies with them or others identify you in these categories. For example, you may think of yourself as short, but others may classify you as being of average height. Many young people in their late teens and early twenties identify with the category *college student*, but a growing number of people in their thirties, forties, and even older are also returning to school and identifying with this category. The many social categories that exist can be divided into two types: *primary* and *secondary identities* (Loden & Rosener, 1991; Ting-Toomey, 1999). Primary identities are those that have the most consistent and enduring impact on our lives, such as race, gender, and nationality. Secondary identities, such as college major, occupation, and marital status, are more fluid and more dependent on situation.

To help define the term **identity**, let's examine its essential characteristics. The first characteristic is that identities exist at the individual and the societal levels. Jake Harwood (2006) explains this concept: "At the individual (personal identity) level, we are concerned

identity
Who a person is; composed of individual and social categories a person identifies with as well as the categories that others identify with that person.

with our difference from other individuals, and the things that make us unique as people. At the collective (social identity) level, we are concerned with our group's differences from other groups, and the things that make our group unique" (pp. 84–85). For example, if you are athletic and you are thinking about your athleticism in relation to others who are more or less athletic than you are, you are focusing on one aspect of your individual identity. If you are thinking about the social role of "athletes" in society, then you are focusing on a different aspect of your social identity.

We should note that identities are not necessarily only individual or social; they can be both, depending on the situation. How is this contradiction possible? Let's look at an example. Many of you are U.S. Americans, and your national identity is part of your social identity. Because you are surrounded by others from the United States, you may not be conscious of this as being part of your individual identity. But if you travel abroad, your national identity becomes part of your individual identity because this significant characteristic differentiates you from others.

▲ Our communication with others helps us understand who we are and how others perceive us.

A second important aspect of identity is that it is both fixed and dynamic. Again, this seems like a contradiction. If you think about it, however, you will realize that certain aspects of our identities, although stable to some extent, actually do change over time. For instance, a person may be born male, but as he grows from an infant to a boy to a teenager to a young man to a middle-aged man and then to an old man, the meanings of his male identity change. He is still a male and still identifies as a male, but what it means to be male alters as he ages, and social expectations change regarding what a boy or a man should be (Kimmel, 2005).

A third characteristic of identity is that individual and social identities are created through interaction with others. The relationships, experiences, and communication interactions we share with others shape how we see ourselves. For example, people who travel abroad and then return home may experience stress, but they also experience growth and change—and communication with those they meet as they travel plays a key role in both (Martin & Harrell, 1996).

A fourth consideration is that identities need to be understood in relation to historical, social, and cultural environments. The meaning of any identity is tied to how it has been viewed historically and how people with that identity are situated in a given culture and society (Hecht et al., 2003; Johnson, 2001). For instance, throughout history, we have had varied notions of what it means to be female (Bock, 1989).

For example, Harriet Tubman, who led many slaves to freedom, and Susan B. Anthony, who fought for women's right to vote in the nineteenth century, were significant exceptions to their racial and gender identities. In their times and for much of history, women have been perceived as intellectually inferior, physically delicate, or morally weak when compared to men. African Americans were also seen as unable to be leaders. Because of these beliefs, in many cultures women and African Americans were denied voting and property rights.

Thus, a hierarchy exists across cultures in which some identities are preferentially treated over other identities. You can probably think of other examples in which preferential treatment was given—or denied—based on race, sexuality, religion, social class, or age (Allen, 2004).

Journal Prompt 2.2: Understanding Identity
Describe the four characteristics that are important in understanding identity.

In sum, identity is key to understanding communication, and communication is key to understanding identity. As Abrams et al. (2002, p. 237) have stated, "identity and communication are mutually reinforcing."

The Individual and Identity

2.3 Clarify how reflected appraisals, social comparisons, self-fulfilling prophecies, and self-concept contribute to identity development.

Although it can be tempting to boil a person's identity down to one word—say, *nerd, jock,* or *sorority girl*—in reality, everyone is more complex than that. If you had to pick only one word to describe yourself and you had to use it in every situation—personal and professional—what word would you choose? For most people this task is impossible, for we all see ourselves as multidimensional, complex, and unique. People in the United States, especially, are invested in the notion that they are unique. Twins often go to great lengths to assure people that they are *not* the same. Perhaps the most famous example of this is the Olsen twins, Mary-Kate and Ashley. Mary-Kate dyed her hair dark so she would look less like her sister, and when the sisters received a star on Hollywood's Walk of Fame, they requested that they be given separate stars (a request that was denied). Like almost everyone, they recognize and value their uniqueness—and they would like others to do so as well.

How is it possible that people who are as much alike as twins can still have distinct identities? It is possible because of the ways in which identities are created and how these identities are "performed" in daily life.

Identity Development through Communication

In communication, our understanding of identity development arises out of a theory called **symbolic interactionism** (Blumer, 1969; Mead, 1934). According to this theory, individuals' meanings for the objects, actions, and people around them arise out of social, or symbolic, interaction with others. What you define as beautiful, ethical, and even edible is based on what you have heard and experienced during your interactions with others. You likely learned through observing and communicating with others that eating lobster is a luxury but that eating bugs is disgusting. We develop and reveal identities through communication interactions in much the same way. In this section, we describe three communication processes involved in identity development—*reflected appraisals, social comparison,* and *self-fulfilling prophecies*—and explore how they shape one's sense of self, or self-concept.

Reflected Appraisals A primary influence on identity development is a communication process called **reflected appraisals** (Sullivan, 1953). The term describes the idea that people's self-images arise primarily from the ways that others view them and from the many messages they have received from others about who they are. This concept is also often referred to as the **looking-glass self** (Cooley, 1902; Edwards, 1990), a term that highlights the idea that your self-image results from the images others reflect back to you.

---

symbolic interactionism
A theory that describes how we develop meaning and identities through our communication with others.

reflected appraisals
The idea that people's self-images arise primarily from the ways that others view them and from the many messages they have received from others about who they are.

looking-glass self
The idea that self-image results from the images others reflect back to an individual.

▼ Our self-images arise from how others communicate and interact with us. If others flirt with you, your notion of how others see you may be influenced by that type of communication.

The process of identity development begins at birth. Although newborns do not at first have a sense of self (Manczak, 1999; Rosenblith, 1992), as they interact with others, their identities develop. How others act toward and respond to them influences how infants build their identities. For example, as infants assert their personalities or temperaments, others respond to those characteristics. Parents of a calm and cheerful baby are strongly drawn to hold and play with the infant, and they describe the child to others as a "wonderful" baby. By contrast, parents who have a tense and irritable baby may feel frustrated if they cannot calm their child and might respond more negatively to the infant. They may engage in fewer positive interactions with their baby and describe the child as "difficult." These interactions shape the baby's identity for himself or herself and for the parents, as well as for others who have contact with the family (Papalia et al., 2002).

The reflected appraisal process is repeated with family, friends, teachers, acquaintances, and strangers as the individual grows. If as a child you heard your parents tell their friends that you were gifted, your teachers praised your classroom performance, and acquaintances commented on how verbal you were, you probably came to see yourself those ways. However, if family, friends, and acquaintances commented on how you couldn't "carry a tune in a bucket" and held their ears when you sang, then over time you likely came to view yourself as someone who couldn't sing. Through numerous interactions with other people about your appearance, your abilities, your personality, and your character, you developed your identities as a student, friend, male or female, or singer, among others. To read about one student's experiences with reflected appraisals, see *It Happened to Me: Bianca*.

It Happened to Me
Bianca

I really relate to the concept of reflected appraisals. I was born in Brazil with an Italian mother and a Brazilian father. When I attended an all-girls private school in Cleveland, Ohio, I had a very difficult time blending in. After spending so much time with these other students, however, I gradually began feeling like one of them. I was speaking English all the time, even at home with my parents (whose first language is not English). I felt like I was an American. People communicated to me as an American. In my junior year, I moved back to Brazil. Being Brazilian and speaking Portuguese fluently, their views of me made me feel completely Brazilian and I began to lose my sense of American identity. Even today, at a U.S. college, I feel confused about my selfhood because of the different ways I am reflected off of people depending on which nationality group I am hanging out with.

Interaction with two types of "others" influences this process of identity development. George Herbert Mead (1934) described them as *particular others* and the *generalized other*. **Particular others** are the important people in your life whose opinions and behavior influence the various aspects of your identity. Parents, caregivers, siblings, and close friends are obvious particular others who influence your identity. Some particular others may strongly influence just one of your identities or one aspect of an identity. If you perceive that your soccer coach believes you have no talent, then you may see yourself as a poor soccer player even if friends and family tell you otherwise.

particular others
The important people in an individual's life whose opinions and behavior influence the various aspects of identity.

Your sense of yourself is also influenced, however, by your understanding of the **generalized other**, or the collection of roles, rules, norms, beliefs, and attitudes endorsed by the community in which you live. You come to understand what is valued and important in your community via your interactions with significant others, strangers, acquaintances, various media such as movies, books, and television, and the social institutions that surround you. For example, if you notice that your family, friends, and even strangers comment on people's appearances, that the media focus on people's attractiveness, that certain characteristics consistently are associated with attractiveness, and that people who look a certain way seem to get lighter sentences in criminal proceedings, get more attention at school, and are hired for the best jobs, then you develop an internalized view of what the generalized other values and rewards with regard to appearance. You then will compare yourself to others within your community

generalized other
The collection of roles, rules, norms, beliefs, and attitudes endorsed by the community in which a person lives.

▲ Children's self-images are affected by their teachers' reflected appraisals. The teachers in your life are particular others.

to see if you fulfill the norms for attractiveness, which then affects how this aspect of your identity develops.

Gradually, you begin to see yourself in specific ways, which in turn influences your communication behavior, which further shapes others' views of you, and so on. Thus, individual identities are created and re-created by communication interactions throughout one's life.

However, reflected appraisals aren't the only type of communication interaction that shapes identity. Each of us also engages in a process called *social comparison*, which influences how we see and value our identities.

reference group

Others to whom we compare ourselves to make judgments about our identities.

Social Comparisons   Not only do we see ourselves as possessing specific characteristics, we also evaluate how desirable those characteristics are. As we discussed, the generalized other becomes the basis for our understanding of which characteristics are valued. For example, Amish children learn through their interactions with family, friends, the church, and their community that aggression is a negative trait that one should minimize or eliminate (Kraybill, 1989). In contrast, in gangs, aggression is valued and encouraged, and community members learn this as well (Sanders, 1994).

Once we understand what characteristics are valued (or disdained) in our communities, we assess whether we individually possess more, or less, of them than do others in our communities. We compare ourselves to others to determine how we measure up, and through this social comparison, we evaluate ourselves. In this way, the groups we compare ourselves to—our **reference groups**—play an important role in shaping how we view ourselves.

We compare ourselves to others in our identity group and decide how we rate. A woman might say, "I look good for my age," comparing herself to others in her reference group, which in this case is other women her age. Similarly, classmates often want to know each other's test scores and grades so that they can decide how to view their own performances. For example, how would you feel if you earned a 78 on an exam and your grade was the highest in the class? What if 78 were the lowest grade in the class? Thus, your evaluation of yourself and your abilities is shaped not only by a specific trait but also by how it compares to the traits of others in your reference group. However, your self-evaluation can vary depending on what you use as a reference group. LeBron James, a basketball player for the Los Angeles Lakers, is 6' 9" tall. If his reference group is U.S. American men who average 5' 9" tall, then he may feel very tall. If his reference group is other NBA players, who average 6' 7", he may only feel a little bit taller.

self-fulfilling prophecy

When an individual expects something to occur, the expectation increases the likelihood that it will, as the expectation influences behavior.

Self-Fulfilling Prophecy   Communication interactions can also influence one's identity through a process known as the **self-fulfilling prophecy**, meaning that when an individual expects something to occur, the expectation increases the likelihood that it will because the expectation influences behavior. For example, if you believe you can perform well on an exam, you are likely to study and prepare for the exam, which typically results in your doing well. Others also have expectations for you that can influence your behavior. For example, if your sales manager believes you are a poor salesperson, she may assign you to a territory where you won't have access to big accounts, and she may refuse to send you to sales conferences where your skills could be honed. If you still succeed, she may believe that you just got lucky. However, because you have a poor territory, don't have the opportunity to enhance your sales skills, and receive no rewards for your successes, you probably will not be a very good salesperson.

Thus, the belief in a particular outcome influences people to act and communicate

▲ We compare ourselves with others in our reference group and decide how we measure up.

in ways that will make the outcome more likely; in turn, the outcome influences how we perceive ourselves. For example, parents often unwittingly influence how their children perform in math and how their children perceive themselves as mathematicians. If a child hears her mother complain about her own poor math skills and how unlikely it is that her child will do better, the child is unlikely to succeed in math classes. When the child encounters difficulty with math, the messages she heard from her mother may increase the likelihood that she will give up and say, "Well, I'm just not good at math." By contrast, if a child hears messages that she is good at math, she is more likely to keep trying and work harder when faced with a difficult math problem. This, in turn, will influence her to see herself as a competent mathematician.

Self-fulfilling prophecies can have a powerful effect on an individual's performance, especially when they are grounded in stereotypes of one's identity. For example, stereotypes exist that Asian students excel at math, that African American students are less verbally competent than White students, and that females are worse at math and spatial reasoning than males. Studies have shown that even subtly or implicitly reminding individuals of these stereotypical expectations can impact their performance, a concept called **stereotype threat**.

In one study, African Americans who were simply reminded of their race performed significantly worse on a verbal exam than when the issue of race was not mentioned (Steele & Aronson, 1995); and in another study, Asian American students performed better on a math test when reminded of their race (Shih et al., 1999). In a similar study, females who were cued to think about gender performed worse on math and spatial ability tests than when the issue of gender was not raised (McGlone & Aronson, 2006). Yet another study found that White male engineering students solved significantly fewer problems when told that they were part of a study to examine why Asian Americans perform better in math than when told it was simply a timed test (Smith & White, 2002).

These studies reveal that individuals' performances can be enhanced or hampered when they are reminded, even implicitly, of expectations related to important identities. This is true not only of sex and gender but also has been shown to be true of socioeconomic status (Croizet & Claire, 1998) and age. These findings remind us that we need to be careful about creating self-fulfilling prophecies for others and allowing others' expectations to become self-fulfilling prophecies for us.

stereotype threat
Process in which reminding individuals of stereotypical expectations regarding important identities can impact their performance.

Through repeated communication interactions such as reflected appraisals, social comparisons, and self-fulfilling prophecies, we come to have a sense of who we are. This sense of who we are is referred to as one's *self-concept*.

Self-Concept   As we have suggested, identity generally continues to evolve, as people age and mature, and, at the same time, individuals also have some fairly stable perceptions about themselves. These stable perceptions are referred to as self-concept. **Self-concept** includes your understanding about your unique characteristics as well as your similarities to, and differences from, others. Your self-concept is based on your reflected appraisals and social comparisons. However, reflected appraisals only go so far. When someone describes you in a way that you reject, they have violated your self-concept. For example, if you think of yourself as open and outgoing, but a friend calls you "a very private person," you are likely to think the friend doesn't know you very well. Thus, your self-concept is an internal image you hold of yourself. It affects the external image you project to others, and in turn, your self-concept influences your communication behavior. If you think of yourself as ethical, you may correct others or assert your views when they behave in ways you believe are unethical.

Self-esteem is part of an individual's self-concept. It describes how you evaluate yourself overall. It arises out of how you perceive and interpret reflected appraisals and social comparisons. Like identity, self-esteem can change over time. It functions as a lens through which we interpret reflected appraisals and social comparisons, which may make it hard to change. For example, if you have relatively high self-esteem, you may discount negative reflected appraisals and overgeneralize positive ones. So, if a student with high self-esteem fails an exam, he may attribute the failure to external factors (e.g., the test was unfair) rather than to himself. On the other hand, a person with low self-esteem may see negative reflected appraisals where none exist and may consistently compare herself to unrealistic reference groups. In addition, this person is more likely to attribute a failure to the self (I'm not smart enough) than to external factors.

Because self-esteem is such a powerful lens through which you see the world, your self-concept may not be entirely consistent with how others see you. Several additional factors can create a mismatch between how you see yourself and how others do. First, your self-image and the feedback you receive may be out of sync because others don't want to hurt your feelings or because you respond negatively when faced with information that contradicts your self-image. Few people tell their friends and loved ones that they are not as attractive, talented, smart, or popular as they themselves think they are. Why? They don't want make others feel bad or they don't want to deal with the recipient's feelings of anger or sadness.

Second, if you hold onto an image of yourself that is no longer accurate, you may have a distorted self-image—or one that doesn't match how others see you. For example, if you were chubby in grade school, you may still think of yourself as overweight, even if you are now slim. Similarly, if you were one of the brightest students in your high school, you may continue to see yourself as among the brightest students at your college, even if your GPA slips.

Finally, people may not recognize or accept their positive qualities because of modesty or because they value self-effacement. If your social or cultural group discourages people from viewing themselves as better than others, you may feel uncomfortable

self-concept

The understanding of one's unique characteristics as well as the similarities to and differences from others.

self-esteem

Part of one's self-concept; arises out of how one perceives and interprets reflected appraisals and social comparisons.

▼ Communication plays an important role in how we develop our self-concept.

hearing praise. In such cases, the individual may only compare himself to exceptionally attractive or talented people or may refuse to acknowledge his strengths in public settings. In Japanese culture the appearance of modesty (*kenkyo*) is highly valued (Davies & Ikeno, 2002). A similar trait of "yieldedness to others" (*glassenheit*) leads the Amish to downplay their accomplishments (Kraybill, 1989). As you can see, both culture and identity are deeply embedded in our communication.

Yet another aspect of self-concept is self-respect. Whereas self-esteem generally refers to feeling good about one's self, **self-respect** describes a person who treats others—and expects themselves to be treated—with respect (Rawls, 1995). Self-respect demands that individuals protest the violation of their rights and that they do so within the boundaries of dignity and respect for others. However, people with high self-esteem may not necessarily have self-respect (Roland & Foxx, 2003). For example, some people with high self-esteem may not treat others with respect or respond to violations of the self with dignity. Many atrocities, such as those committed by Syrian President Bashar al-Assad against his people, have been waged by those who, because of their sense of superiority, thought they had the right to dominate and harm others.

> **self-respect**
> Treating others and expecting to be treated with respect and dignity.

Throughout this discussion of identity development, we have focused on four separate constructs: reflected appraisals, social comparison, self-fulfilling prophecy, and self-concept. However, identity development is a circular process in which these constructs are interrelated. For example, reflected appraisals influence your self-concept, which affects your communication behavior, which in turn shapes how others see you and, ultimately, what they reflect back to you. Then the process starts all over again. The issue of identity goes beyond this complex process of development, however. In everyday life, we enact or "perform" these identities. Let's see how this process works.

Performance of Individual Identity

The **performance of identity** refers to the process or means by which we show the world who we think we are and is related to **self-presentation**—the notion that in performing identity we try to influence others' impressions of us, by creating an image that is consistent with our personal identity. For example, many Green Bay Packers fans express their identity by wearing team colors, calling themselves Cheeseheads, and wearing plastic cheese wedges on their heads. In contrast, Pittsburgh Steelers fans often wave "the terrible towel" to cheer on their team. People also perform their identities in more subtle ways every day—with the type of clothing or jewelry (including wedding rings) that they choose to wear or the name they use. Some celebrities have taken stage names that the public is more familiar with than their legal birth names. For example, Charlie Sheen's name is Carlos Estevez. Lady Gaga's real name is Stefani Germanotta. What do these different names communicate to the public? How do these names help these celebrities perform their public identities?

> **performance of identity**
> The process or means by which we show the world who we think we are.
>
> **self-presentation**
> Influencing others' impressions by creating an image that is consistent with one's personal identity.

Communication style is another way people perform, or enact, their identities. For example, do you speak to your mother in the same way that you speak with your friends? If you bring a friend home, do you feel like a different person as he watches you communicate with your family? If so, you're not alone. Most people adapt their communication to the identity they wish to perform in a given context.

In fact, the branch of communication studies called performance studies focuses on the ways people perform, or communicate, their various roles. In other words, people **enact identities** by performing scripts that are proper for those identities. In their analysis of how men use body size as a positive identity, communication scholars Tony Adams and Keith Berry (2013) analyze the performance of a heavy size as a positive identity on FatClub.

> **enacting identities**
> Performing scripts deemed proper for particular identities.

DID YOU KNOW?
Identities in Conflict

Why do different identities come into conflict? What might be triggering these conflicts? How we communicate about identities can reflect very different worldviews and social realities. After the deaths of George Floyd, Breonna Taylor, and Rayshard Brooks in 2020, many Black Lives Matter protests arose across the nation. When you hear "Black Lives Matter," do you hear "Black lives matter more than other lives"? Or "Black lives also matter"? In response, some people invoked the phrase "All Lives Matter." This back-and-forth has been going on since Black Lives Matter emerged in 2013. Vice President Mike Pence, when pressed repeatedly on his refusal to say "Black lives matter," echoed those words on *Face The Nation* when he said, "I really believe all lives matter" (Capatides, 2020). When someone says, "all lives matter," what does it communicate? For some, it's a denial of their lived reality as an African American. For others, it's a provocation, a dismissal of the calls for change in policing. In addressing people who say "all lives matter," writer Troy Smith says that they "must open their eyes or even a history book to understand that if all lives truly mattered to everyone in the first place, America wouldn't be in this mess" (Smith, 2020). Think about how our identities are entwined in history, as well as current, everyday life, and how those experiences shape how we communicate and interpret messages.

SOURCES: Capatides, C. (2020, July 8). Why saying "all lives matter" communicates to Black people that their lives don't. *CBS News*. https://www.cbsnews.com/news/all-lives-matter-black-lives-matter/

Smith, T. L. (2020, June 29). Saying "all lives matter" doesn't make you racist, just extremely ignorant. *Cleveland.com*. https://www.cleveland.com/entertainment/2020/06/saying-all-lives-matter-doesnt-make-you-racist-just-extremely-ignorant.html

com. On the one hand, "members explicitly reframe weight gains and bigger bodies as desirable and erotic," but they also know that "affirming performances and relationships do not proceed without the possibility for criticism" (p. 321). Here the question of identity and what that identity means is answered through communication. The members of this website use communication to recreate different meanings about what a large size body means, but they also recognize that they are open to negative criticism of their body size by others in a culture that generally looks down on large bodies. Their performances reject dominant images of attractiveness and perform different identities as their "orientations toward and uses of bigger bodies are creative, and the community offers a pedagogical space in which to imagine distinct and often-devalued ways of relating"(p. 322). Performing their identities becomes a way to resist the dominant negative view of large bodies.

Nadene Vevea (2008) analyzed how people use tattoos and body piercing to perform their identities. In her interviews, she found that people use body art for many different reasons, to communicate many different feelings. For example, "some of the fraternity brothers who responded to my survey all got matching tattoos to signify their membership but use body art as a positive connection between friends to show loyalty to one another" (p. 22).

Sometimes we enact family roles; other times we enact occupational roles. The enactment of identity is closely tied to one's movements into and out of different cultural communities and one's expectations regarding particular roles. Lawyers, physicians, and teachers also enact particular roles in performing their occupations. If one of these professionals—say, a teacher—steps out of the appropriate role and tries to be the best friend of her students, problems can arise. In June 2020, six women filed civil lawsuits against U.S.A. Swimming "saying the national governing body for the sport failed to protect them from coaches who were sexual predators when they were preteens and teenagers" (Macur, 2020). While swimming is not the only sport dealing with issues of sexual harassment and sexual assault, we expect coaches to perform the identity of "coach" in certain ways. When their communication behavior—verbal and nonverbal—crosses outside the appropriate role of a coach, problems can arise.

▲ We show the world who we think we are through the performance of identity—in this case, these sports fans are enacting their enthusiasm for soccer and performing their Polish identity.

Thus, we perform various roles and communicate with others based on **role expectations**. If you are pulled over for a traffic violation, you expect the police officer to perform in a particular way. In turn, you communicate with the officer based on a prescribed script. If you do not enact the expected role or if the police officer does not enact the prescribed role, then confusion—or worse—can occur. Everyone carries many scripts with them into all kinds of interactions. For example, the authors of this book are all pet owners. When we speak to our pets, we sometimes repeat communication patterns that our parents used with us when we were children. Pets are not children, yet we often communicate to them as if they were because the script is familiar to us.

role expectations
The expectation that one will perform in a particular way because of the social role occupied.

As we noted previously, identities are **mutable**, or subject to change. When people change identities, they also change the way they perform them. For example, as people age, if they perform the "grown-up" role appropriately, they hope others will treat them more like adults. If they don't change the way they behave, then they might be told to "stop acting like a child."

mutable
Subject to change.

Because identities are not fixed, sometimes you see mismatches between the performance of identity and any single identity category. Sometimes the difference between identity performance and identity category can be rather benign. For example, if we say that someone is young at heart, we are saying that we perceive that person's identity performance to resemble that of someone much younger in years. Thus, two people may be the same chronological age, but one may listen to contemporary music, watch current films and television shows, and dress according to the latest fashion trends. The other may listen to oldies radio stations and dress as they did years ago.

Sometimes this disconnect is viewed much more negatively. When people enact a gender identity at odds with the cultural identity category, such as when males perform identity scripts that are typically female, they may be ridiculed, ostracized, or worse. Still, how do particular identity categories, or ways of performing them, acquire meaning? How do you know what a particular category is supposed to "look like" or how it is to be performed? The answer has to do with societal forces, the subject we take up next.

Journal Prompt 2.3: Identity Development
What are the key concepts in identity development? How is identity performed?

The Individual, Identity, and Society

2.4 Identify examples of racial, national, ethnic, gender, sexual, age, social class, disability, and religious identities.

The development of individual identities is influenced by societal forces. Therefore, you cannot understand yourself or others without understanding how society constructs or defines characteristics such as gender, sexuality, race, religion, social class, and nationality. For example, as a child, you were probably told (some of) the differences between boys and girls. Some messages came from your parents, such as how boys' and girls' clothing differs or how girls should behave as compared with boys. Other messages came from your schoolmates, who may have told you that "they" (either boys or girls) had "cooties." You may also have picked up messages about gender differences, or about any of the identity categories mentioned, from television or other media. By combining messages from these various sources, you began to construct images of what is considered normal for each identity category.

Communication scholars are particularly interested in how identities are communicated, and created, through communication. For example, in his work focusing on communication interactions, Donal Carbaugh (2007) is particularly interested in studying intercultural encounters, and he focuses on how communication interaction reveals insights into cultural identities.

When people enact identities that are contrary to social expectations, they may be pressured to change their performance. Thus, boys and girls who do not perform their gender identities in ways prescribed by society might be called "sissies" or "tomboys." There are some Jewish people who eat shrimp and some Latter-Day Saints (Mormons) who drink coffee, but they may not do so when around other people.

Those who do not conform to expected social communication or performance patterns may become victims of threats, name calling, violence, and even murder (Sloop, 2004). These aggressive responses are meant to ensure that everyone behaves in ways that clearly communicate appropriate identity categories. For example, after a lengthy lawsuit, Shannon Faulkner became the first woman to enroll at the Citadel, South Carolina's formerly all-male military college. During the time that she attended the school, she received death threats and had to be accompanied by federal marshals (Bennett-Haigney, 1995). Thus, some groups in society have strong feelings regarding how identities should be performed, and they may act to ensure that identities are performed according to societal expectations.

In this section of the chapter, we will look at a range of primary identity categories. Note that each is a product of both individual and societal forces. Thus, whatever you think your individual identity might be, you have to negotiate that identity within the larger society and the meanings society ascribes to it.

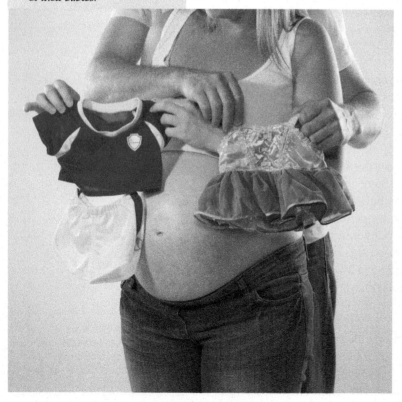

▼ Many parents choose clothes that communicate the gender of their babies.

Racial Identity

Despite its frequent use, the term *race* is difficult to define. Historically, races were distinguished predominantly by physical aspects of appearance that are generally hereditary. A race was defined as a group with gene frequencies differing from those of other groups. However, many physical anthropologists and other scholars now argue that because there is as much genetic variation among the members of any given race as between racial groups, the concept of race has lost its usefulness (Hirschman, 2003).

Despite the difficulty in accurately delineating the various races, race is still a relevant concept in most societies, and individuals still align themselves with specific racial groups, which we discuss next.

Racial identity, the identification with a particular racial group, develops as a result of societal forces—because society defines what a race is and what it is called. This means that racial categories are not necessarily the same from country to country. For example, the 2001 census in the United Kingdom did not include Chinese in the "Asian/Asian British" category, but the 2011 census "re-positioning of the 'Chinese' tick box from 'Any other ethnic group' to Asian/Asian British" shows that these racial categories are fluid (Office for National Statistics, 2012). Their census includes the "Irish Traveller" category that the U.S. census does not.

racial identity
Identification with a particular racial group.

Even within the United States the categorization of racial groups has varied over time. The category *Hispanic* first appeared on the U.S. census form as a racial category in 1980. In the 2000 census, however, Hispanic was categorized as an ethnicity, which one could select in addition to selecting a racial identity. Therefore, one could be both *Asian* (a race) and *Hispanic* (an ethnicity), or one could be both *White* (a race) and *Hispanic* (again, an ethnicity). Similarly, as Susan Koshy (2004) has noted, people from India were once labeled "non-white Caucasians," but today are categorized with Asian Americans on the U.S. census. These categorizations are important because historically they have affected the way people are treated. Although discrimination based on race is no longer legal, we continue to live with its consequences. For example, although slavery ended almost 150 years ago in the United States, many churches, schools, and other social institutions remain racially segregated (Blake, 2020; Hacker, 2003; Meatto, 2019; Nittle, 2019). For a more recent discussion about racial categories on the U.S. census, see *Alternative View: Are Middle Eastern/North African People Also White People?*

What do you think you would do if a total stranger began making racist or other bigoted comments to you? How would you react?

Although people often think of racial categories as scientifically or biologically based, the ways they have changed over time and differ across cultures highlight their cultural rather than their biological basis. How cultures describe and define specific races affects who is considered to belong to a given race and, consequently, how those individuals are treated. As anthropologist Gloria Marshall explains: "Comparative studies of these popular racial typologies show them to vary from place to place; studies of these popular racial classifications also show them to vary from one historical period to another" (1993, p 117). Moreover, communication is a strong factor in furthering,

ALTERNATIVE VIEW
Are Middle Eastern/North African People Also White People?

People who identify their roots in the Middle East or North Africa (MENA) are counted by the U.S. census as "White." Since at least the 1980s, Arab Americans have called for a separate category in the census but were repeatedly denied. However, "in March 2017, the Bureau reversed its own and other executive agencies' position; it recommended that Americans of Arab and North African descent be granted a separate category starting in 2020" (p. 18). Controversy arose over the term *Arab* as well as the problems in counting this group. Ultimately, MENA were not counted separately in the 2020 census, but the debate will continue over creating a separate category in the 2030 census. What do you think? Should MENA identities be counted as "White"?

SOURCE: Hobeika, M. O. N., & Nakayama, T. K. (2020). Check-mate: The MENA/Arab double-bind. In H. Bhabra, F. Z. C. Alaoui, S. Abdi, & B. M. Calafell (Eds.), *Negotiating identity & transnationalism: Middle Eastern and North African communication and critical cultural studies* (pp. 17–30). Peter Lang.

affecting, or altering racial categories and identities to serve different social needs. For example, Guzmán and Valdivia (2004) studied the media images of three Latinas—Salma Hayek, Frida Kahlo, and Jennifer Lopez—to see how gender and Latinidad are reinforced through the media (see Chapter 11). Face-to-face communication also influences peoples' ideas about racial identities. If individuals have little contact with people of a different racial group, it is especially likely that one or two encounters may lead them to draw conclusions about the entire group.

multiracial identity
One who self-identifies as having more than one racial identity.

Beginning with the 2000 census, the U.S. government has allowed people to claim a **multiracial identity** (Jones & Smith, 2001). This category recognizes that some people self-identify as having more than one racial identity. So, how should we categorize Barack Obama? Although "there is much to celebrate in seeing Obama's victory as a victory for African Americans," writer Marie Arana (2008) also thinks that "Obama's ascent to the presidency is more than a triumph for blacks." She feels that "Barack Obama is not our first black president. He is our first biracial, bicultural president." What difference does it make if we see Obama as our first African American president or as our first biracial president? As you think through this issue, you can see the complexities of race and racial politics within a culture.

Multiracial identities have arisen as a result of history as well. The Dutch colonization of Indonesia led to many mixed race children who were known as "Indische Nederlanders," or Dutch Indonesians. The actor Mark-Paul Gosselaar is an example of a Dutch Indonesian, as is CNN reporter Atika Shubert. There is even a Facebook page devoted to the Dutch Indonesian community. What other multiracial identities have resulted from the many ways that people have migrated around the world (e.g., through colonization, slavery, wars, invasions, and so on)?

National Identity

national identity
A person's citizenship.

Racial identity can often be confused and conflated with **national identity**. We often misuse the notion of nationality when we ask someone "What's your nationality?" but what we really want to know is their ancestry or ethnic background. *Nationality* or national identity refers to a person's citizenship. In other words, Lady Gaga's nationality is not Italian but U.S. American because she holds U.S. citizenship. John F. Kennedy's nationality was not Irish; he was a U.S. citizen. Many U.S. Americans did not actively choose their national identity; they simply acquired it by being born in the United States. Although many of us have not actively chosen our national identity, most of us are content with—or even proud of—it.

Like our other identities, the importance placed on national identity can vary, depending on many factors. Sports are one context in which national identities can be important, but they are not equally important across all countries. International competitions, such as the World Cup and the Olympics, tend to emphasize national identities. A recent study found that "[i]n general, countries with low GDPs and low levels of democracy and cultural globalization are clearly more sport nationalistic than other countries" (Seippul, 2017). The importance of national identity can vary from context to context, and it can serve different needs.

Yet, above and beyond these contextual issues, communication in a common language was the bond of national identity: "Of the national identity attributes included in the Pew Research Center survey, language far and away is seen as the most critical to national identity. Majorities in each of the 14 countries polled say it is *very* important to speak the native language to be considered a true member of the nation" (Stokes, 2017). Communication plays a key role in national identity.

Ethnic Identity

Although race and ethnicity are related concepts, the concept of ethnicity is based on the idea of social (rather than genetic) groups. Ethnic groups typically share a national or tribal affiliation, religious beliefs, language, or cultural and traditional origins and background. A person's **ethnic identity** comes from identification with a particular group with which they share some or all of these characteristics. Thus, some U.S. citizens say that they are Irish because they feel a close relationship with Irish heritage and custom, even though they are no longer Irish citizens—or perhaps never were. Likewise, in the United States many U.S. Americans think of themselves as Italian, Greek, German, Japanese, Chinese, or Swedish even though they do not hold passports from those countries. Nonetheless, they feel a strong affinity for these places because of their ancestry. Unlike national identity, ethnic identity does not require that some nation's government recognizes you as a member of its country. It is also unlike racial identity, in that any racial group may contain a number of ethnic identities. For example, people who are categorized racially as White identify with a range of ethnic groups, including Swedish, Polish, Dutch, French, Italian, and Greek.

In other parts of the world, ethnic identities are sometimes called *tribal identities*. For example, "in Kenya, there are 50 tribes, or ethnic groups, with members sharing similar physical traits and cultural traditions, as well as roughly the same language and economic class" (Wax, 2005, p. 18). Tribal identities are important not only across Africa, but also in many nations around the world, including Afghanistan (Lagarde, 2005). In some societies, tribal or ethnic identity can determine who is elected to office, who is hired for particular jobs, and who is likely to marry whom. In Malaysia the three major ethnic groups are Malay, Indian, and Chinese. Because the Malay are in power and make decisions that influence all three groups, being Malay gives one an important advantage. In the United States, however, the ethnic identities of many White Americans are primarily symbolic because they have minimal influence in everyday life (Waters, 1990). Even if ethnic identity does not play an important role in your life, it can carry great significance in other parts of the world.

ethnic identity

Identification with a particular group with which one shares some or all of these characteristics: national or tribal affiliation, religious beliefs, language, and/or cultural and traditional origins and background.

▼ People can perform gender identity in many different ways; there is no right or wrong way to perform gender identity.

Gender Identity

Similar to race, gender is a concept constructed through communication. *Gender* refers to the cultural differences between masculinity and femininity, whereas *sex* refers to the biological differences between males and females. Gender describes the set of expectations cultures develop regarding how men and women are expected to look, behave, communicate, and live. For example, in U.S. culture women (who are biologically female) are expected to perform femininity (a cultural construction) through activities such as nurturing, crossing their legs and not taking up too much room when sitting, speaking with vocal variety and expressivity, and wearing makeup. How do people respond to women who cut their hair in a flattop, sit sprawled across the couch, speak in an aggressive manner, and refuse to wear makeup? Often, they call them names or ridicule them; occasionally they even mistake them for males because these behaviors are so culturally attached to notions of masculinity. Like ethnic identities, gender identities are also dynamic and changing. In order to communicate about identities, new terms are always emerging (See *Alternative View: Emerging Identity Terms*).

gender identity
How and to what extent one identifies with the social construction of masculinity and femininity.

Gender identity refers to how and to what extent one identifies with the social construction of masculinity and femininity. Gender roles and expectations have changed enormously over the centuries, and cultural groups around the world differ in their gender expectations. How do we develop our notions of gender, or what it means to be masculine or feminine? We learn through communication: through the ways that people talk about gender, through the media images we see, and through observing the ways people communicate to males and females. For example, although crying is acceptable for girls, young boys receive many messages that they are not supposed to cry.

BIPOC
Acronym for Black, Indigenous, People of Color.

enby
Someone who does not identify as either male or female, or non-binary.

A leading scholar on gender, Judith Butler (1990, 1993) was one of the first to argue that gender identity is not biological but based on performance. She asserted that people's identities flow from the ways they have seen them performed in the past. In other words, a man's performance of male identity rests on previous performances of masculinity. Because the performances of traditional masculinity have been repeated for so long, individuals come to believe that masculine identity and behaviors are natural. However, some people choose to enact their identity in nontraditional ways, and their performances will be interpreted against the backdrop of what is considered acceptable and appropriate.

ALTERNATIVE VIEW
Emerging Identity Terms

The many categories with which we do or do not identify change frequently to respond to the realities of our complex lived experiences. Throughout our lives, we will encounter new terms for identities, and we have to make communication choices about how we will respond to these changes. Some emerging terms include **BIPOC** (Black, Indigenous, People of Color) and **enby** (non-binary person). There are likely many more terms to come in the future. BIPOC attempts to create a larger political identity that some see as preferable to "people of color" as "[t]he other two letters, for black and Indigenous, were included in the acronym to account for the erasure of black people with darker skin and Native American people" (Garcia, 2020). Enby people do not identify as either male or female. Enby can be a noun (e.g., "They're an enby," "I'm enby") or a modifier (They're an enby person"). The dating website *OkCupid* has put together a guide for non-binary dating that includes a lot of helpful information on communicating with enby people (e.g., never ask their "dead name," but do ask which pronouns to use) (A quick guide, 2020).

Whether you identify with these identities or not, pay attention to these and other identity terms that will emerge in the coming years. Some will endure; others will not. Make ethical and respectful decisions about how you use these terms in your communication.

SOURCES: Garcia, S. E. (2020, June 17). Where did BIPOC come from? *The New York Times*. https://www.nytimes.com/article/what-is-bipoc.html

A quick guide for non-binary dating. (2020, July 9). *OkCupid*. https://help.okcupid.com/article/207-a-quick-guide-for-non-binary-dating

Sometimes people distinguish between cisgender and transgender as ways of thinking about gender identity. **Cisgender** refers to a matching between one's gender identity and their biological body. A cisgender man is someone who identifies as male and was born into a male body. In contrast, **transgender** refers to someone who identifies with a different gender than their biological body. A transgender man is someone who identifies as a man but was born into a female body.

The complexity of how people identify with gender is reflected in Facebook's 2014 change to the gender options. "Facebook offers 56 options. You can use up to 10 of them on your profile" (Weber, 2014). Yet even this array of choices may not capture the diversity of gender identifications possible in people's everyday lives (see *Alternative View: Gender Fluidity*).

cisgender
Someone whose gender identity matches their biological sex.

transgender
Someone whose gender identity does not match their biological sex.

Sexual Identity

Sexual identity refers to which of the various categories of sexuality one identifies with. Because our culture is dynamic, it has no set number of sexual identity categories, but perhaps the most prominent are heterosexual, gay or lesbian, and bisexual. Although most people in our culture recognize these categories today, they have not always been acknowledged or viewed in the same ways. In his *History of Sexuality*, French historian and theorist Michel Foucault (1988) notes that over the course of history, notions of sexuality and sexual identities changed. In certain eras and cultures, when children were born with both male and female sexual organs, a condition referred to as *intersexuality*, they were not necessarily operated on or forced to be either male or female.

Many people think of sexuality or sexual identity as private, but it frequently makes its way into the public arena. In everyday life, we often encounter people who will personally introduce us to their husbands or wives, a gesture that shares a particular aspect of their sexual identity. However, our society often exposes an individual's sexual identity to public scrutiny. For example, we don't know the sexual identities of other people unless they tell us how they identify. Actor Michael C. Hall, who played on *Six Feet Under* and *Dexter*, identifies as primarily heterosexual but says, "I would say I was not all the way heterosexual." He describes his sexual identity as on "a spectrum" (qtd. in Teeman, 2018). In contrast, rapper Lil Nas X self-identifies as gay (Trammell, 2019). He doesn't describe his sexual identity as "fluid." And singer Ariana Grande has made the communication choice not to identify her sexuality. She once tweeted out: "I haven't before and still don't feel the need to now which is okay" (qtd. in Jackson, 2019).

sexual identity
Which of the various categories of sexuality one identifies with.

gender fluid
Someone whose gender identity is not fixed but is dynamic and changes in different contexts at different times.

ALTERNATIVE VIEW
Gender Fluidity

Although many people identify with the categorization of cisgender and transgender, there are other people who identify in more **gender fluid** ways. These people may feel more feminine at some times and more masculine at others. Cisgender and transgender do not capture the dynamic and fluid nature of how they identify with gender. Sometimes the term *genderqueer* is used, but there are other terms that try to capture the complexity of gender.

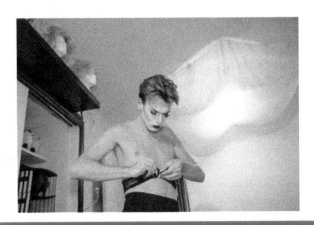

People can identify in different ways and also make communication choices about communicating (or not communicating) those identities to others.

Because identity categories are social constructions, there is not always agreement about what they mean. Clearly, in the public arena, people manipulate these identity categories to help retrieve their reputations when their sexual activities become public.

In daily life, a person's sexual identity plays a role in such mundane matters as selecting which magazines to read and which television shows and movies to watch, as well as choosing places to socialize, people to associate with, and types of products to purchase. Television shows, magazines, books, Internet sites, and other cultural products are targeted toward particular sexual identities, or they assume a certain level of public knowledge about sexual identities and groups. For example, *The Bachelor/ Bachelorette, Millionaire Matchmaker,* and *Real Housewives of Orange County* presume an understanding of U.S. heterosexual culture. In contrast, the Here TV cable channel is specifically geared to LGBTQIA+ viewers. *Modern Family* includes gay characters, whereas *Pose* and *The Politician* center on characters with diverse sexualities. These communication texts can reinforce, confirm, or challenge our notions of various categories of sexual identity.

Age Identity

age identity
A combination of self-perception of age along with what others understand that age to mean.

Age, when thought of strictly as the number of years you've been alive, is an important identity for everyone. But your **age identity** is a combination of how you feel about your age as well as what others understand that age to mean. How old is "old"? How young is "young"? Have you noticed how your own notions of age have changed over the years? When you were in first grade, did high school students seem old to you? Although *age* is a relative term, so are the categories we use for age groups. Today, for example, we use the terms *teenager, senior citizen, adult,* and *minor,* but these terms have meaning only within our social and legal system. For example, the voting age is 18, but people have to wait until they are 21 to buy liquor. Someone who commits a heinous crime can be charged as an adult, even if they are not yet 18. Still, whether a person feels like an adult goes beyond what the law decrees and comes from some set of factors that is far more complex.

Other age-related concepts are culturally determined as well. For example, the notion of "teenager" has come into use only relatively recently in the United States, and it is certainly not a universal category (Palladino, 1996). The notion that people have "midlife" crises is not a universal cultural phenomenon, either. Moreover, these age categories are relatively fluid, meaning that there are no strict guidelines about where they begin and end, even though they do influence how we think about ourselves (Trethewey, 2001). For example, because people today generally live longer, the span of years thought of as middle age comes later in our lives. These changes all illustrate the dynamic nature of age identity and the categories we have for it.

The use of terms for generations tries to group people by age groups, such as the Greatest Generation, Baby Boomers, or Millennials. There are stereotypes that go along with these age groups that influence how we think about them. Negative attitudes and stereotypes about Baby Boomers led to the hashtag #BoomerRemover to trend when COVID-19 first emerged in the United States. What are some stereotypes about your generation?

Social Class Identity

social class identity
An informal ranking of people in a culture based on their income, occupation, education, dwelling, child-rearing habits, and other factors.

Social class identity refers to an informal ranking of people in a culture based on their income, occupation, education, dwelling, child-rearing habits, and other factors (Online Glossary, 2005). Examples of social classes in this country include working class, middle class, upper-middle class, and upper class. Most people in the United States identify themselves as middle class (Baker, 2003). However, only about half of the United States is now middle class: "The share of American adults who live in middle-income households has decreased from 61% in 1971 to 51% in 2019," and those leaving the middle class create greater income inequality in the nation: "From 1971 to 2019, the share of adults in the upper-income tier increased from 14% to 20%. Meanwhile, the share in the lower-income tier increased from 25% to 29%" (Horowitz et al., 2020).

For Ken Eisold, social class "is really more about identity" (qtd. in Horn, 2013). In other words, the amount of money that people earn is only one part of identifying as middle class.

In his work on social class, French sociologist Pierre Bourdieu (1984) found that people of the same social class tended to view the world similarly: They defined art in similar ways, and they enjoyed similar sports and other aspects of everyday life. Moreover, based on his study of social class, Paul Fussell (1992) noted that U.S. Americans communicate their social class in a wide variety of ways, some verbal and some nonverbal. For example, middle-class people tend to say "tuxedo," whereas upper-class people are more apt to say "dinner jacket." In the category of nonverbal elements that express social class identity, he included the clothes we wear, the way we decorate our homes, the magazines we read, the kinds of drinks we imbibe, and the ways we decorate our automobiles. We will discuss more about class and verbal and nonverbal communication in the next two chapters.

Critical Thinking Prompt
How does your own speech reveal your social class background and identity? Can you identify aspects of your family's home, yard, interior decorating, and clothing that reveal social class identity?

Those in occupations such as nursing, teaching, and policing soon may no longer be considered middle class. What other occupations have fallen or might fall from middle-class status? In their study *The Fragile Middle Class*, Teresa Sullivan and her colleagues noted the increasing numbers of bankruptcy filings (2001), especially among those in occupations that we consider securely middle class, such as teachers, dentists, accountants, and computer engineers. In the wake of the COVID-19 pandemic, there has been increasing discussion on how different sectors of the economy have profited while others have suffered. The pandemic has drawn attention to the increasing wealth of some people and the ability of some to work from home, while others have to work in face-to-face situations or have lost their jobs entirely. These discussions may portend a new focus on social class identity.

One reason people in the United States avoid discussing social class is because they tend to believe that their country is based on *meritocracy*, meaning that people succeed or fail based on their own merit. This idea leads to claims such as "anyone can grow up to be president." However, this has not proven to be true. For example, until the election of Barack Obama in 2008, every president in the United States has been White, male, and, in all cases but one, Protestant. Social identity and class have a powerful impact on one's life because they can determine where you go to school (and what quality of education you receive), where you shop (and what quality of resources you have access to), which leisure activities you participate in (on a scale from constructive and enriching to destructive and self-defeating), and who you are most likely to meet and with whom you are mostly likely to socialize. In this way, social class identity tends to

▼ Social class identity is an important influence in the ways that people socialize and engage in leisure activities.

reproduce itself; the social class one is born into is often the same as the social class one dies in. People who are working class tend to live around other working-class people, make friends with working-class people (who influence their expectations and behavior), and attend schools that reinforce working-class values. In an early study that showed how communication was used to perform social class identity in conjunction with gender and race, Gerry Philipsen (1992) noted that men tended to speak much less than women and rarely socialized outside their working-class community, which he called "Teamsterville." More recently, Kristen Lucas (2011) studied how family is an important site for communication messages that "both encourage and discourage social mobility" (p. 95). By examining how families reproduce their working-class identity, we can see how there are contradictory messages sent to the children about social class and moving toward white-collar occupations.

It Happened to Me
Melinda

My parents went through a divorce when I was two, and my mother has worked hard so we could have a comfortable life. Throughout my life, I've gone to private schools and universities with other students whose families had much more money than mine. I've always tried to fit in with the other students. Recently my mother has gone into debt, and I am having trouble adjusting to this change. I haven't told any of my upper-class friends because I am afraid they won't understand my situation. It can be a struggle to be honest with people you don't think will understand your situation, but it is a struggle that I have to overcome. People should accept each other for who they are, not what social class they fit into.

Disability Identity

disability identity
Identification with physical or mental impairments that substantially impact everyday life.

People can identify with or be identified as disabled for many different reasons. **Disability identity** is often defined as having an impairment of some kind. Some people experience differences in hearing, sight, or mobility. Not all disabilities are visible or evident to others. In 1990, the United States passed the Americans with Disabilities Act, which recognized disability as an important identity that needed federal protection from discrimination. This act also defines "disability" in Section 12102:

> The term "disability" means, with respect to an individual:
>
> **(A)** a physical or mental impairment that substantially limits one or more major life activities of such individual;
>
> **(B)** a record of such an impairment; or
>
> **(C)** being regarded as having such an impairment. (Americans with Disabilities Act, 1990, 2008)

Although this legal definition may be helpful to some, it does not tell us what this identity means and how it is performed by those who identify as disabled, nor does it tell us how disability is viewed by others.

It is through communication that "disability" as an identity gains its meaning in our society. As Deanna Fassett and Dana L. Morella explain:

> while someone might have a medical or physical condition that structures her/his experience, it is in her/his interactions with others that that condition takes on meaning and becomes what our collective social environment would consider disability, with all the punishments and privilege that entails. We build this social environment in our own mundane communication, in classrooms and faculty meetings; we learn and reiterate, often unknowingly, as institutional members, what is normal and what is not and what that means. (2008, p. 144)

If we are swimming in a sea of communication, the many meanings that we generate in everyday communication give meaning to disability.

Like other identities, disability is performed; it is "always in the process of becoming, then disability is something we do, rather than something we are" (Henderson and Ostrander, 2008, p. 2). Disability, in this view, is about how it is enacted and lived; it is not about a fixed state of being. For example, in his study on disabled athletes who play wheelchair rugby, Kurt Lindemann found that "performances of disability, especially in a sport context, can subvert the stigma associated with physical disability in surprisingly effective ways" (2008, p. 113). By focusing on athletic activities, disabled people attempt to challenge stereotypical views of those with disabilities. More recently, disabled actors have complained about media productions that feature able-bodied actors portraying disabled characters, such as Kevin McHale's portrayal of Artie Abrams in *Glee*. Some question whether there is a stereotype that disabled actors can't perform and work as well on studio sets as able-bodied actors.

People who are not disabled can become disabled and then develop this new identity as a part of their larger configuration of identities. For example, many people, as they grow older, may experience increasing hearing loss, reduced visual acuity, or other physical or mental impairments that can render them disabled. But disability, of course, is not limited to older people. How we talk about disability, see it in media images, and experience it in everyday life are all part of how we communicate about and construct the meanings of disability as an identity. In her study on autobiographical narratives of those growing up with chronic illness or disability, Linda Wheeler Cardillo found that "communication at all levels has a powerful impact on these persons and their experiences of difference. A deeper understanding of this experience and how it is shaped by communication can lead to more sensitive, respectful, affirming, and empowering communication on the part of health-care providers, parents, teachers, and others" (2010, p. 539).

Religious Identity

In the United States today, **religious identity** is changing rapidly. On the one hand, religious identification continues to decline, as fewer U.S. Americans identify with Christianity, the largest religious identity in the nation. As these people leave the Catholic and Protestant churches, they are generally not affiliating with other religions but identify as "none" (In U.S., decline of Christianity, 2019). On the other hand, as the COVID-19 pandemic has spread across the United States, those who do identify with a religion report that "their religious faith has strengthened as a result of the outbreak," but for most U.S. Americans, "their faith hasn't changed much (47%) or that the question isn't applicable because they were not religious to begin with (26%)" (Gecewicz, 2020).

religious identity
Aspect of identity defined by one's spiritual beliefs.

Religious identity is defined by one's spiritual beliefs. For example, although Greg hasn't been to a Catholic church in decades, he still identifies himself as Catholic because of his upbringing and the impact the religion has had on his outlook. Most researchers and writers agree that "religion is certainly one of the most complex and powerful cultural discourses in contemporary society, and religion continues to be a source of conflict between nations, among communities, within families, and . . . within one's self" (Corey, 2004, p. 189). Although you may believe that your religious identity is part of your private life and irrelevant outside your family, this is not true. For example, in the aftermath of the 2001 September 11 attacks, Muslim identity has been viewed with particular suspicion. A 2004 study done by researchers in the Department of Communication at Cornell University found the following attitudes about Muslim Americans.

Critical Thinking Prompt
How would you describe your religious identity? How do you communicate it to others? Do you ever conceal it? If so, when and why?

About 27 percent of respondents said that all Muslim Americans should be required to register their location with the federal government, and 26 percent said they think that mosques should be closely monitored by U.S. law enforcement agencies. Twenty-nine percent agreed that undercover law enforcement agents should infiltrate Muslim civic and volunteer organizations to keep tabs on their activities and fund-raising. About 22 percent said the federal government should profile citizens as potential threats based on the fact that they are Muslim or have Middle Eastern heritage. In all, about 44 percent said they believe that some curtailment of civil liberties is necessary for Muslim Americans (Cornell University, 2004).

Religious identity also takes on public significance because it correlates with various political views and attitudes (Corey & Nakayama, 2004). For example, the 2004 Cornell study found that Christians who actively attend church were much more likely to support differential treatment of Muslim Americans. In contrast, the nonreligious or those less active in their churches were less likely to support restrictions on civil liberties of Muslim Americans.

However one responds to other people's religious beliefs, most U.S. Americans feel a strong need to embrace and enact personal religious identities (Corey & Nakayama, 2004). In 2000, for example, 46 percent of U.S. Americans belonged to religious groups, and approximately 40 percent of U.S. Americans claimed to attend religious services regularly (Taylor, 2005). Thus, in their article on "religion and performance," Frederick Corey and Thomas Nakayama (2004) write that individuals feel a "tremendous need to embody religious identities and reinforce those identities through spirited, vernacular performances" (p. 211). Religion can serve different needs to people. To understand how one student's religious identity affects his life, read *It Happened to Me: James.*

It Happened to Me
James

When I was growing up, my family went to an African Methodist Episcopal (AME) Church. It was very important to connect with others in the African American community. Today, I feel a strong desire to connect to the community, but not so much to the religious part. When I am home with my family, we go to church and church events, which I find enjoyable. But when I'm away at college, I spend more time with other African American political and social groups. I don't feel that my parents' religious identity is as significant to me, and I would describe my own religious affiliation as "none."

The virtual environment has also been influenced by and influences religious identity. Sometimes people find religious communities online, and some people even use their iPhones for prayer and other religious purposes. Others resist the Internet for fear it would compromise or challenge their religious beliefs. Communication scholar Heidi Campbell notes: "Digital religion as a concept acknowledges not only how the unique character of digital technology and culture shapes religious practice and beliefs, but also how religions seek to culture new media contexts with established ways of being and convictions about the nature of reality and the larger world" (2013, p. 4).

Intersectionality

intersectionality
How different identities combine to shape our communication experiences.

Intersectionality is not an identity itself but refers to the ways that various identities come together in different contexts to shape our communication experiences. The term is most often credited to Kimberlé Crenshaw (1989), who focused on how race and gender shaped justice in the legal system. She emphasized that the experiences of African American women are not the same as "women" as a legal class or "African Americans" as a legal class but lie at the intersection of both identities.

Since her original article more than 30 years ago, the idea has been used in communication studies to explore the ways that multiple identities come together to shape our communication experiences and choices. Intersectionality "describes the way people from different backgrounds encounter the world. The lived experiences—and experiences of discrimination—of a black woman will be different from those of a white woman, or a black man, for example" (Coaston, 2019).

Often, we cannot understand communication through the lens of any single identity. Whether in interpersonal interactions or social media and other communication contexts, we need to consider how many identities work together. In their study of the television series *Downtown Los Angeles (DTLA)*, Shinsuke Eguchi and Myra Washington (2016) examine the ways that racial, sexual, and gender identities function in *DTLA*. While they

ALTERNATIVE VIEW
Islamophobia

What responsibilities do we have to use communication to work against Islamophobia, or the fear of Muslims?

High-profile terrorist attacks in a number of countries have created significant fear of Muslims and prejudicial attitudes against them. A number of hateful acts have been committed against Muslims and mosques in recent years. In January 2017, a lone gunman entered a mosque in Quebec City and opened fire, killing six and injuring 19 people. A number of politicians have spoken out against this type of violence against the Muslim community, including Joël Lightbound, a member of the Canadian Parliament representing this area. In his speech, he explains the role of communication. In part, he said:

Today, I also want to apologize to them. I apologize for having observed stigmatization and ostracization over the past few years, having seen the mistrust, the fear, and the hatred among my peers. And having tried to respond, but not having done enough.

Silence also has consequences. Never again.

SOURCE: Lum, Z. A. (2017, February 2). Joël Lightbound urges no more silence over Islamophobia after Quebec City mosque attack. *Huffington Post Canada*. http://www.huffingtonpost.ca/2017/02/02/joel-lightbound-quebec-shooting_n_14575968.html

ultimately conclude that the representations of intersectionality here only reinforce the status quo rather than challenge it, they see potential in the possibilities of new ways of representing everyday life. Even when it might not seem as if multiple identities are involved, Mack and McCann (2019) demonstrate how intersectionality can lend insight into an event. In the case of Brock Turner, a White Stanford University student who was convicted of sexual assault of a White woman, their analysis focuses on the recall campaign against the judge, Aaron Persky, a White male, for the perceived light sentence given to Turner. Gender was not the only identity at play here, they argue, but White identity as well, and taken together they help us understand why the recall campaign was successful.

You may have encountered or read about "Karens," White women who feel empowered to call the police on people of color doing ordinary, everyday things or refuse to wear masks during the COVID-19 pandemic, among other public behaviors. For some White women, gender and racial identities come together in this way of entitlement and empowerment that can endanger others. It has become common enough that this communication behavior of "the Karen has risen to outstanding levels of notoriety in recent weeks, thanks to a flood of footage that's become increasingly more violent and disturbing" (Lang, 2020).

We've shown throughout this chapter that aspects of our personal identity such as race, nationality, ethnicity, gender, age, social class, and religion develop through the tension between individual and societal forces. We also looked at intersectionality as a way to consider how various identities come together to shape our experiences. Although we may assert a particular identity or view of ourselves, these views must be negotiated within the larger society and the meanings that the larger society communicates about that identity. See *Alternative View: Islamophobia* for an example of how communication can be used to deal with religious differences and the dangerous role of silence. In the next section, we discuss the role of ethics in communication about identity.

**Journal Prompt 2.4:
Identify Categories**
What are the primary identity categories? Define each and give an example of how identity might be performed for each primary identity category.

Ethics and Identity

2.5 Discuss three ethical considerations for communicating in a sensitive manner to and about others' identities.

As you are probably aware, a person's sense of identity is central to how they function in the world. Moreover, because identities derive their meanings from society, every identity comes with values attached to it. The ways we communicate may reflect these values. If you wish to be sensitive to other people's identities, you should be aware of at least three key ethical issues that can impact your communication with others.

One issue you might consider is how you communicate with people whose identities are more, or less, valued. What do we mean by more or less valued? You probably already know. In the United States, for example, which of the following identities is more highly valued: White or multiracial? Male or female? Lawyer or school bus driver? Still, these rankings are not necessarily consistent across cultures. In Denmark, for example, work identities do not follow the same hierarchical pattern as those in the United States (Mikkelsen & Einarsen, 2001). Thus, Danes are more likely to view street sweepers and doctors as social equals because they don't place as high a value on the medical profession nor as low a value on service jobs as many U.S. Americans do. In the United States, in contrast, many service workers complain that most of the people they serve either ignore them or treat them rudely—even with contempt. Consequently, you might ask yourself, "Do I communicate more politely and respectfully with high- versus low-status people?" If you find yourself exhibiting more respect when you communicate with your boss than you do with the employees you manage, then you might want to consider the impact of your communication on your subordinates' identities.

The second ethical point to reflect on involves language that denigrates or puts down others based on their identities. Such language debases their humanity and shuts down open communication. Examples of unethical communication and behavior related to identity occur if men yell sexual slurs at women on the street, or straight people harass individuals they believe are gay, or when White people are disrespectful to people of color. Although you probably don't engage in such obvious insults to people's identities, do you denigrate them in other, more subtle ways? For example, have you ever referred to someone as "just a homemaker" or "only a dental assistant"?

Third, think about whether you tend to reduce others to a single identity category. As we pointed out previously, each of us is composed of multiple identities, and even within a specific identity group, individuals may differ widely from one another. Thus, individuals may be offended when others respond to them based on only one of their identities, especially one that is not relevant to the situation at hand. For example, managers in some organizations will not promote mothers of small children to highly demanding positions. They justify this by claiming the women won't be able to fulfill both their family and their professional roles competently. Although these women may be mothers, their identities as mothers likely are not relevant to their workplace identities and performances—just as men's identities as fathers are rarely seen as relevant to their jobs. Each person is a complex of identities, and each person desires others to recognize their multiple identities. You are more likely to communicate ethically if you keep this fact in mind.

Journal Prompt 2.5:
Ethics and Identity
What are three key ethical concerns related to identity?

Skills for Communicating about Identities

2.6 Explain three ways to communicate more effectively about identities.

Related to our discussion about ethical issues, we offer three guidelines for communicating more effectively about identities. The first guideline concerns the self-fulfilling prophecy we discussed previously: How you communicate *to* someone and *about* someone can influence how they perform their identity or how it develops. If a parent continually communicates with the child as if she were irresponsible, then the child is likely to act irresponsibly. To communicate effectively, be aware of the ways you create self-fulfilling prophecies through your own communication.

Second, there are many ways to perform a particular identity. You can improve your ability to communicate if you are tolerant of the many variations. For example,

ALTERNATIVE VIEW
Catfishing

Sometimes people invoke identities that are not their own to gain something from others, and this practice is often called "catfishing." People will engage others in their fabricated network of identities and social relationships to get them into a relationship. Manti Te'o, who played football at Notre Dame, and Thomas Gibson, an actor on *Criminal Minds*, were both purported to have been snared in catfishing games. Country music singer Brad Paisley and his wife were also catfished.

In *Digital Trends*, Molly McHugh identifies five different types of catfish:

- Revenge Catfish: This catfish feels they were wronged by you (or someone or something you're tied to) and is pathologically creating this online romance simply to get back at you.
- Bored Catfish: This catfish has an Internet connection and too much time on their hands.
- Secretly-In-Love-with-You Catfish: This catfish harbors an unrequited crush on you and for some reason doesn't find themselves good enough in real life to go for it.
- Scary Catfish: This catfish is simply out to break hearts and cause chaos.
- Lonely Catfish: This catfish usually has some sort of sob story and needs someone to talk to, and with a pretty picture and a Facebook profile, you've become that person.

Although the motives for engaging in catfishing may be even more complex than these five categories, what are the communication signs of catfishing?

- Bad grammar and spelling in messages despite them claiming they are from your country.
- The person asks for money.
- The conversation becomes romantic quickly.
- The person claims to have an illness or is struggling in some other way.
- They won't speak on the phone or webcam chat.
- The person has very few or no friends on Facebook.
- They claim they do not have a permanent address as they are working or traveling overseas (Waring, 2018).

McHugh raises an important ethical challenge for all of us to consider when she asks:

Really, we're all catfish. Have you ever edited your profile picture to look a little better? Do you untag? Have you ever faked a location check-in? We're all guilty of bending the truth with our profiles to some degree—hell, it's what all these platforms want us to do. Social media is a very aspirational beast and it's not very surprising that it's led to a catfishing epidemic.

SOURCES: McHugh, M. (2013, August 23). It's catfishing season! How to tell lovers from liars online, and more. *Digital Trends*. http://www.digitaltrends.com/web/its-catfishing-season-how-to-tell-lovers-from-liars-online-and-more/#ixzz2uvnrrkOx

Waring, O. (2018, March 18). What is catfishing and how can you spot it? *Metro* (UK). https://metro.co.uk/2018/03/18/catfishing-can-spot-7396549/

---

even if you believe that "real men" should act in certain ways, you are likely to communicate more effectively if you do not impose your beliefs on others. For example, you should not assume that because someone is male, he enjoys watching football, baseball, and other sports; wants to get married and have children; or eats only meat and potatoes. If you do, you are likely to communicate with some men in ways they will find less interesting than you intend.

Third, remember that people change over time. If you have been out of touch with friends for a period of time, when you encounter them again you may find that they have embraced new identities. Sometimes people change religious identities, or sometimes they change occupations. You can increase your communication effectiveness if you recognize that people change and that their new identities may be unfamiliar to you.

Journal Prompt 2.6: Communicating Identity
What are three strategies you can use to communicate more effectively with regard to identities?

SUMMARY

2.1 Identify six reasons identity is important to communication.

- We bring our identities to each communication interaction.
- Communication interactions create and shape identities.
- Identity plays a key role in intercultural communication.
- Much of our life is organized around specific identities.
- Identity is a key site in which individual and societal forces come together.
- We invoke our identities to help others understand our communication.

2.2 Define *identity*.

- Primary identities (race, ethnicity, age) are the focus in this chapter and have the most consistent and enduring impact on our lives.
- Secondary identities, such as occupation and marital status, are more changeable over the life span and from situation to situation.
- Our identities exist at both the individual and social level, are both fixed and dynamic, and are created through interaction.
- Identities must be understood within larger historical, social, and cultural environments.

2.3 Clarify how reflected appraisals, social comparisons, self-fulfilling prophecies, and self-concept contribute to identity development.

2.4 Identify examples of racial, national, ethnic, gender, sexual, age, social class, disability, and religious identities.

- Individuals perform their identities, and these performances are subject to social commentary. Straying too far from social expectations in these performances can lead to disciplinary action.
- People have multiple identities that come together and intersectionality asks that we consider these multiple identities.

2.5 Discuss three ethical considerations for communicating in a sensitive manner to and about others' identities.

- Learn to value and respect people within all identity groups.
- Avoid using denigrating language or put down people based on their identity.
- Avoid reducing people to a single identity category.

2.6 Explain three ways to communicate more effectively about identities.

- Being aware of the ways you create self-fulfilling prophecies through your communication.
- Being tolerant of different ways of enacting various identities.
- Being aware that people's identities may change over time.

KEY TERMS

identity p. 26
symbolic interactionism p. 28
reflected appraisals p. 28
looking-glass self p. 28
particular others p. 29
generalized other p. 29
reference group p. 30
self-fulfilling prophecy p. 30
stereotype threat p. 31
self-concept p. 32
self-esteem p. 32

self-respect p. 33
performance of identity p. 33
self-presentation p. 33
enacting identities p. 33
role expectations p. 35
mutable p. 35
racial identity p. 37
multiracial identity p. 38
national identity p. 38
ethnic identity p. 39
gender identity p. 40

BIPOC p. 40
enby p. 40
cisgender p. 41
transgender p. 41
sexual identity p. 41
gender fluid p. 41
age identity p. 42
social class identity p. 42
disability identity p. 44
religious identity p. 45
intersectionality p. 46

APPLY WHAT YOU KNOW

1. **People Have Many Different Identities**

   Some of your identities are more visible than others. Communication messages are often interpreted in the context of some of these identities. You might send a message that could be interpreted quite differently if someone with different identities sent the exact same message. Think about how your visible identities influence how you construct and send messages. Give some examples of messages that you typically send in light of your visible identities as well as messages that you don't feel comfortable sending that someone else might send.

2. **Majority Identities**

   Which of your identities are shared by a majority of people in society? What are some of the stereotypes of those identities? To answer this question, you may need to ask people who do not share that identity.

Communicating, Perceiving, and Understanding

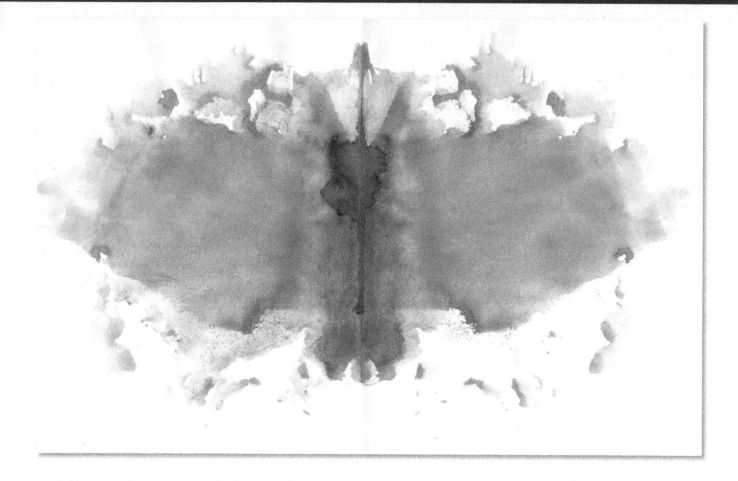

LEARNING OBJECTIVES

3.1 Explain why understanding perception is important.

3.2 Describe the three procedures people use to understand information collected through the senses.

3.3 Name three individual factors that affect one's perceptual processes.

3.4 Articulate how power, culture, social comparisons, and historical period influence perception.

3.5 Explain why ethics is relevant to the perception process.

3.6 Identify three ways you can improve your perception skills.

CHAPTER TOPICS

The Importance of Perception

What Is Perception?

Perception and the Individual

The Individual, Perception, and Society

Ethics and Perception

Improving Your Perception Skills

> *"No one should assume that what they perceive
> is the same as what others perceive."*

*After the first meeting of their research methods class, Charee and Mateo went out for coffee.
They soon found themselves sharing their impressions of the instructor.*

CHAREE: *What did you think of Professor Wolfe?*

MATEO: *I suppose she's okay. She made the class seem kind of hard, and I am worried
she will be difficult to talk to if I need help.*

CHAREE: *Really? I liked her a lot. I thought she was funny and would be really easy to
talk to. I think I am going enjoy taking this class.*

MATEO: *She seemed kind of unapproachable to me. I guess we'll have plenty of chances
to find out what she is really like during the semester.*

As the conversation between Charee and Mateo illustrates, our perceptions of others strongly influence how we respond to and communicate about them. If we perceive people as friendly and approachable, typically we are drawn to them and want to interact with them. If we view individuals as distant and unfriendly, we may try to minimize contact. However, not everyone perceives and responds to people and events the same way. Our perceptions are affected by individual factors, such as age, gender, genetics, and experience, as well as by societal forces including culture, historical events, and social roles.

For instance, on average, females experience pain more intensely than do males (Hurley & Adams, 2008), so a touch that feels slightly uncomfortable to a man may feel painful to a woman. Women and men also can differ in their perception of shades of color. To learn more about this difference, see *Communication in Society: The Grass Is Almost Always Greener to Women Than to Men*. But how do societal forces affect perception? Among other things, societies teach us what foods and beverages are tasty, how they should be served, and what constitutes a portion or size. One example of this is the difference in how people perceive soft drinks around the world. In many parts of the United Kingdom, cold beverages include a few pieces of ice, whereas in the United States a glass of soda may be half ice. Because of their varied perceptions of what a cold drink should taste like, people can be unhappy if they don't get what they expected. Similarly, what constitutes a large McDonald's soda can differ around the world. A medium-sized drink in the United States (21 ounces) is an ounce more than Japan's large-sized drink, and a U.S. large size (30 ounces) is 1.5 times bigger than the large-sized drink in Japan (20 ounces)!

In this chapter, we will first explore the importance of perception and the perception process. Next, we'll examine how individuals' attributes and experiences affect their perceptions, and we will explore societal influences on perception. We also will discuss how people can evaluate their perceptions through an ethical lens. Finally, we will end with suggestions for sharpening your perception skills.

▼ Depending on where you live, this cup of soda would be considered a small, medium or large size.

COMMUNICATION IN SOCIETY
The Grass Is Almost Always Greener to Women Than to Men

Biological sex is an individual characteristic that affects how people perceive the world. Did you know that women are better at detecting colors, particularly blues, greens, and yellows, than are men? Males, on the other hand, are more adept at tracking fast-moving objects and discerning detail from a distance (Abramov et al., 2012a, 2012b). These differences may be one reason men and women tended to fill different roles in hunter-gatherer societies. Women's increased skill allowed them to separate healthy plants from poisonous ones, and men's abilities improved their success at capturing game.

Researchers conducted experiments with college-age males and females and discovered that they assigned different shades to the same object. Women identified more different shades of green than did men, who were more likely to perceive a given shade of green as blue-green. Men also perceived orange shades as redder than did women (Owen, 2012). In addition, the study determined that men could "detect quick-changing details from afar and thinner, faster-flashing bars" in the context of an array of blinking lights (SciTechDaily, 2012).

Researchers attribute these perceptual variances to differences in neuron development in the visual cortex due to hormonal differences. Of course, not all people who identify as male or female have identical development in their visual cortex or have equal levels of estrogen and testosterone. What is true of individuals as a group is not necessarily true of a given person. In groups, however, this combination of strengths allowed humans to thrive by increasing their access to protein and decreasing the likelihood they would be poisoned.

SOURCES: Abramov, I., Gordon, J., Feldman, O., & Chavarga, A. (2012a). Sex and vision I: Spatio-temporal resolution. *Biology of Sex Differences, 3*(21). https://bsd.biomedcentral.com/articles/10.1186/2042-6410-3-20

Abramov, I., Gordon, J., Feldman, O. ,& Chavarga, A. (2012b). Sex and vision II: Color appearance of monochromatic lights. *Biology of Sex Differences, 3*(21). https://link.springer.com/article/10.1186/2042-6410-3-21

Owen, J. (2012). Men and women really do see things differently. *National Geographic.* https://www.nationalgeographic.com/news/2012/9/120907-men-women-see-differently-science-health-vision-sex/

SciTechDaily. (2012). Females distinguish colors better while men excel at tracking fast moving objects. *Biology News.* https://scitechdaily.com/females-distinguish-colors-better-while-men-excel-at-tracking-fast-moving-objects/

The Importance of Perception

3.1   Explain why understanding perception is important.

How individuals respond to people, objects, and environments depends largely on the perceptions they have about them. Although we tend think what we see, hear, and taste is "real," perceptions actually shape our understanding of the world. Thus, what we perceive as true or accurate may not reflect another person's reality. If you live with someone or are someone on the autism spectrum, you likely understand that you and others don't necessarily share similar perceptions. For example, some people on the spectrum struggle with filtering specific sensory stimuli, so sounds or lighting that are common in public settings are uncomfortable, even confusing, for them (Morton-Cooper, 2004). If what you perceive is different from others' perceptions, you may be tempted to assume that you are correct and that others are wrong. However, thinking this way not only is unfair, it negatively affects your ability to interact effectively with others.

Communication and perception are intertwined. When we communicate, we don't just respond to others' words; we respond to our perceptions of the way others look, sound, and smell and sometimes how they behave. For example, when we perceive people as being polite, we are more likely to agree to their requests (Kellerman, 2004). Recognize, however, that others may view what you see as "polite behavior" as overly formal or perhaps rude.

We noted in Chapter 2 that identities play an important role in communication. They also influence and are influenced by perception. Thus, just as our perceptions of others influence how we communicate with them, our perceptions and communication affect how they see themselves. Let's take our previous scenario as a case in point. How might Mateo's or Charee's perceptions affect Professor Wolfe's perception of herself? If most people perceive Professor Wolfe as Charee does—as amusing and open—and therefore respond to her by laughing and spending time with her, then she probably sees herself positively. On the other hand, if most people respond as Mateo did and consequently choose to have little contact with her, Professor Wolfe may perceive herself more negatively. As you might expect, then, perception and identity are also interwoven. On the one hand, Mateo's perceptions of Professor Wolfe affect her identity. At the same time, how the professor views herself and others influences how she perceives and responds to the world around her. If she has a positive self-image, Professor Wolfe may perceive that others like her and become more outgoing, she might be more optimistic and see the positive aspects of a situation more readily, and she could be less aware of others' negative reactions to her.

As you read this chapter, you are receiving considerable sensory input. An air conditioner or heater might be running, people may be moving past you, and the temperature where you sit likely fluctuates over time. In addition, you may feel hungry or tired, you might detect the scent of cleaning products, and the chair you are sitting on could be uncomfortable. How are you able to manage all the information your senses bring to you so that you can focus on your reading? How are you able to make sense of all this sensory input? The answer is that you continuously engage in a variety of processes that limit and structure everything you perceive (Kanizsa, 1979; Morgan, 1977). Let's look at how this works.

> **Journal Prompt 3.1: Perception and Communication**
> How does perception affect the communication process?

What Is Perception?

3.2 Describe the three procedures people use to understand information collected through the senses.

Perception refers to the process we use to understand our environment so we can respond to it appropriately. For example, if you see a small animal, before you reach down to pet it, you will seek to determine what type of animal it is and whether it is friendly. Perception is composed of three procedures: **selection**, **organization**, and **interpretation**. Together, these procedures help us understand the information we collect through our senses—what we see, hear, taste, smell, and touch. The sensory data we select, the ways we organize them, and the interpretations we assign to them affect the ways we communicate (Manusov & Spitzberg, 2008). Although these processes tend to happen concurrently and unconsciously, researchers separate them to better explain how they function.

> **perception**
> A sense-making process in which we attempt to understand our environment so we can respond to it appropriately.
>
> **selection**
> The procedure of choosing which sensory information to focus on.
>
> **organization**
> The procedure by which one recognizes what sensory input represents.
>
> **interpretation**
> The act of assigning meaning to sensory information.

Selection

Because people experience more sensory information than they can process, they selectively focus on and remember only part of it. In every interaction, each communicator has a field of perception. In this field, some objects, symbols, or words are at the center, others are on the periphery, and still others are outside the field altogether. Consciously or unconsciously, we attend to just a narrow range of the full array of sensory information available and ignore the remainder. This process is called **selective attention**.

Suppose your roommate is telling you an interesting story about a mutual acquaintance while the two of you sit on your apartment patio. Although cars may be driving by and people walking along the sidewalk, most likely your roommate will have your full attention. Peripherally you may notice the sights and sounds of people moving through your environment, the smell of car exhaust, and the glare of sunlight on your glasses; however, none of this will distract your focus. You probably will not even notice if someone you know walks by or storm clouds gather in the sky. Your attention will be devoted to the center of your field: your friend.

The sensory input we select, however, is not random (Goldstein, 2010a; Greenough et al., 1987). When a range of sensory experiences accost you, various factors affect your

> **selective attention**
> Consciously or unconsciously attending to just a narrow range of the full array of sensory information available.

selection, including your identity, features of the person or object you have encountered, and your experiences and values. For example, as you walk across campus, you are likely to attend to only one or a few people also going to class because you cannot focus on everyone at once. Who captures your focus depends on:

- aspects of your identity (e.g., if you are Native American, you may find your attention drawn more to students on campus who are also Native American)
- features of the person (e.g., someone dressed differently from everyone else will likely attract your attention)
- your goals (e.g., if you would like to meet a potential romantic partner, you may pay special attention to attractive men or women hurrying to class)

Research shows that people are most likely to pay attention to and remember information based on when it is heard and whether it is positive or negative. Specifically, our opinions are influenced more by information we learn first, called the **primacy effect**, or most recently, which is referred to as the **recency effect**. The primacy effect occurs when we evaluate a person, source, or event based on the first information we hear about them. Thus, if your professor is engaging, funny, and energetic during the first week of class, you will probably be more forgiving of them when they have a bad day. Recency operates similarly, except in this case our judgment is influenced more significantly by something we have learned recently. If you have seen three films by the same director, for instance, the likelihood that you will see their fourth movie typically is influenced more by how much you liked their third film than your reactions to their previous ones.

In addition, individuals are more attentive to and remember information that is negative, violates their expectations, and is said in situations that are important to them (Siu & Finnegan, 2004). For example, a comment such as "What on earth did you do to your hair?" is more likely to remain prominent in your mind and to influence your mood than "Nice haircut." Similarly, when an instructor says, "This will be on the test," students usually pay close attention to what the instructor says next. Comments that violate our expectations grab our attention and are more memorable. Suppose you meet someone new and ask, "How are you?" and instead of the expected, "Fine, thanks," they explain in detail all the misfortunes that have befallen them in the past year. You not only will be surprised, you will remember the event.

Organization

After selecting the sensory input we will attend to, we need to be able to recognize *what* it represents. To do this, we organize the information into a recognizable picture that has meaning. If you are awakened in the middle of the night by a loud noise, you will certainly attend to that noise and little else. However, you also must be able to make sense of the sound to respond. Is it a mechanical sound or an animal one? Is it human? You can make judgments such as these because you possess organizational structures or templates that tell you what information belongs together and how to "read" or understand what you perceive (Kanizsa, 1979). How does this work? In this section, we examine two primary cognitive principles—cognitive representation and categorization—which help people organize and respond to their perceptions.

Cognitive Representation   **Cognitive representation** describes the human ability to form mental models, or cognitive maps, of the world they live in (Levinthal & Gavetti, 2000; Weick, 1995). We create these maps and then refer to them later when circumstances call for them. For example, people know that a fire alarm communicates danger; furthermore, they know how to respond to a fire alarm because they have a cognitive map for alarms. Schools and workplaces have fire drills, in fact, to help people create cognitive maps that are familiar and enable them to act appropriately in an emergency. And research has shown that people who rehearse a plan—or develop a cognitive map—for specific crises are more likely to survive (Sherwood, 2009).

primacy effect
The tendency to form a judgment or opinion based on the first information received.

recency effect
The tendency to form a judgment or opinion on the most recent information received.

cognitive representation
The ability to form mental models of the world.

People also develop and use cognitive maps when they communicate. As we grow up, we learn cognitive maps or models for engaging in many types of communication acts, such as complaining, apologizing, and asking for a favor. Many people learn quite early that it is useful to be nice to someone before asking them for a favor, and this information becomes part of the map for requesting favors. Remember that maps are *representations* of things, not the things themselves. Thus, cognitive maps consist of general outlines; they are not fixed sets of utterances that are memorized. Three specific types of cognitive representations, or maps, that individuals use to organize their perceptions about people and communication are schemas, prototypes, and interpersonal scripts.

▲ Schools and workplaces have fire drills to help people create cognitive maps that are familiar and enable them to act appropriately in an emergency.

Schemas are cognitive maps that help us organize information. They are composed of preconceived ideas and frameworks representing an aspect of the world. People have more complex schemas for topics they know a lot about. For instance, if you are very interested in cars, you will not only be familiar with the specific cars sold by different manufacturers, but you will be able to identify what year a specific model of car was released based on details such as the grille, taillight shape, and body design. Schemas are important because they influence both what we pay attention to and how well we retain and integrate new knowledge. That is, we are more likely to notice and remember information that fits into our schema. In addition, we tend to reinterpret contradictions to the schema by viewing them as exceptions or by distorting the contradictions so they fit the schema. For instance, if you are afraid of dogs, you probably have developed a schema that positions them as dangerous, unpredictable, and perhaps repellent. As a result, you probably are more aware of dogs in your environment, even if they are some distance away. If you happen to meet a friendly dog, you may believe the dog is an exception to the general rule that dogs are dangerous, or you may decide that the dog is friendly now, but that does not mean it won't be vicious at any moment.

schemas
Cognitive maps that help us organize information.

prototype
A representative or idealized version of a concept.

Communication behavior also is influenced by idealized maps called prototypes. A **prototype** is the most representative example of a person or concept. For example, many people's prototypical idea of a professor is a person who is male, has white hair (and perhaps a beard), and wears a tweed jacket with leather patches. Although a few professors fulfill this prototype, many more do not. (Just look around your campus.) Nonetheless, this prototype persists, in part, because of how media depict college professors. We also possess prototypes for "ideal" best friends, romantic partners, and family members.

▼ Like many female politicians, Vice President Kamala Harris's behavior, appearance and communication style are compared to traditional ideals of feminism by people around the world.

Prototypes are important because people compare specific individuals, events, and experiences to their prototypes and then respond to them based on the degree to which they perceive the individual person or activity conforms to that prototype. This often happens when it comes to the issue of gender. People have prototypical ideas of what a "man" or a "woman" is. These prototypes represent idealized versions of masculinity and femininity. The degree to which an individual resembles one's prototype influences how one perceives and communicates with that person. Studies have found that how feminine a female political candidate appears is associated with how likely she is to win an election (Hehman et al., 2014). For these voters, women who display traditionally feminine characteristics reflect their idealized version or prototype of women, and they, therefore, favor them.

In addition to gender prototypes, people often have racial ones. We can have specific ideas regarding who makes a good marital partner or who is likely to be a good physician, CEO, or server based on the individual's race or ethnicity. Many executives of color tell stories about attending events where guests ask them to get them a drink or park their car. This is not to say that working as waitstaff or a valet is unimportant work but rather to point out the prototypes many of us have regarding who "looks like" a CEO. Having prototypes like these affects how we feel about others and the opportunities available to them. If we see someone with many tattoos, for instance, and assume they don't "look" like a good job candidate, we are less likely to hire them—which results in fewer opportunities for those who don't fit our prototypes.

An interpersonal **script** is a relatively fixed sequence of events expected to occur; it functions as a guide or template for how to act in particular situations (Burgoon et al., 2000; Pearce, 1994). We develop scripts for activities we engage in frequently (Fehr et al., 1999). Most people have a script for how to meet a new person. For example, when you first encounter a student you'd like to get to know, you probably introduce yourself, tell the person a basic fact about yourself such as "I'm from Texas," and then ask a question such as "How do you like living on campus?," "What is your major?," or "Where is your hometown?" Thus, you follow a routine of sorts.

We enact scripts because we find them comfortable, they are efficient, and they keep us from making too many social mistakes. Although many of the scripts we use will be familiar to others, we also tailor them to fit our own expectations for a situation. Our choice of script or the way we alter a script depends on our perceptions of others. We may use a different script to initiate a conversation with someone we perceive as friendly and outgoing than the one we use with someone we perceive as shy, quiet, and withdrawn.

script
A relatively fixed sequence of events that functions as a guide or template for communication or behavior.

▼ How do you perceive these two versions of the same person? Do any stereotypes come to mind?

As this discussion suggests, cognitive representations help people navigate the physical and social world. These maps provide guidelines that shape how we communicate with others through the schemas, prototypes, and interpersonal scripts we develop as we grow up and mature.

Categorization   Another type of cognitive process we use to organize information is **categorization**. Categorization is inherent to all languages. The linguistic symbols (or words) we use represent the groupings we see around us. Because it is impossible to remember everything, we use groupings that represent larger categories of information or objects (Goldstein, 2010b; Lakoff, 1987).

For example, we lump a lot of information under the category of *restaurant*. What did you think of when you read the word *restaurant*? You probably envisioned a subcategory, such as a café or a pancake house. However, the concept of *restaurant* has certain features that apply to all subcategories, so that you know what is meant and what to expect when you go to one. You understand that *restaurant* refers to a place to eat and not a place to worship or attend classes. Forming and using categories allows us to understand and store information and makes us more efficient communicators.

Although grouping is a natural cognitive and perceptual procedure, it also can lead to misperceptions. Categorizing can cause one to reduce complex individuals to a single category or to expect them to behave in ways consistent with the category, regardless of the circumstance. For instance, you might categorize an individual based on your perception that the person is either interesting or dull. Once you reduce people to a category, you may communicate with them as if they possess no other characteristics. If you categorize one of your coworkers as dull, you may only interact with them over tasks and never invite them to join you after work, where they might be able to show you how interesting and fun they can be.

When people categorize others, they typically also assign them a **label**. The two activities tend to go hand in hand. Thus, groups of people and the individuals within those groups often are labeled and treated as if they are exactly alike and no more than their labels. You may have heard of people described as jocks, sorority girls, or nerds. Perhaps you have heard someone called a "Karen" as a way to describe someone who abuses their privilege. Though labeling others can function as a useful shortcut, it also can lead to negative outcomes (Link & Phelan, 2001). When we label people, we run the risk that we, and others, will view them only through the lens of the label. The label also influences our expectations, evaluations, and responses to them. Labeling can cause problems even when the labels are positive, as was the case in *It Happened to Me: Lin Sue*.

When you were growing up, did your family have a label they used to describe you? Were you the smart one, the well-behaved one, or the goof-up? If you were labeled the goof-up, you may not have been given many opportunities to disprove the label, and your ideas may have been discounted even when they were valid. Because of such a label, you may have come to discount the value of your own ideas.

The negative effect of labels is magnified when entire groups of people are described in ways that generate hate and anger, such as labeling Black men as dangerous. In the 2020s, more people have become aware that U.S. Americans' perceptions, and resulting labels, regarding Black men and women have caused great harm to them. For example, on August 5, 2014, John Crawford III, a Black man, was shot and killed

categorization
A cognitive process used to organize information by placing it into larger groupings of information.

label
A name assigned to a category based on one's perception of the category.

It Happened to Me
Lin Sue

Because I am Chinese American, people often assume that I am some kind of whiz kid in academics. Well, I'm not. I was hit by a car when I was little, and I have residual brain impairment because of it. I have to study hard just to make passing grades. I get both angry and embarrassed when people assume I am this great student and imply that I will surely go to graduate school. I will feel fortunate if I just get out of undergraduate school. I really wish people wouldn't do this to me. They think they are being nice and complimentary, but they are still stereotyping me.

at a Walmart store while holding a BB gun that was for sale at the store. The video reveals that the officer shot him without giving any warning (*The Guardian*, 2014). In contrast, on May 14, 2020, White armed protestors who stormed the Michigan House of Representatives chamber over the COVID-19 stay-at-home order were unharmed (Solender, April 30, 2020). These and many similar examples show us that viewing a group of people as dangerous, problematic, or troublesome often leads to harsh or unfair treatment. By now, we know that it is not true that "sticks and stones may break our bones but words will never hurt us."

stereotyping
Creating schemas that overgeneralize attributes of a specific group.

As you may have guessed, labeling is related to stereotyping. **Stereotyping** occurs when schemas overgeneralize attributes of a group to which others belong (Cox et al., 2012; Operario & Fiske, 2003). A stereotype is an assumption that every member of the group possesses certain characteristics. For example, a female graduate who developed a technologically sophisticated presentation was told that her "boyfriend" had done a good job creating it. In assuming that all females have male romantic partners and that women are not capable of using creative technology, the speaker stereotyped the student in two ways.

Although grouping individuals makes it easy to remember information about them, it often leads to inaccurate beliefs and assumptions. Overgeneralizing a group's attributes makes it difficult to see the individuality of the people we encounter. Thus, a reliance on stereotypes can get those who use them into trouble.

Interpretation

As we perceive and organize sensory information, we assign meaning to it (Goldstein, 2010b). Returning to our previous example, imagine that you are awakened late at night. You hear a loud noise, which you determine is caused by a banging on your bedroom window. You now have to interpret what this means. Is it a tree branch? A loose shutter? Is it someone trying to break in?

We all assign meaning to the information we perceive, but we do not all necessarily assign the same meaning to similar information. One of the factors that influences how we interpret information is the frame through which we view it.

frame
Assumptions and attitudes that we use to filter perceptions to create meaning.

Frames   The assumptions and attitudes we use to filter perceptions to create meaning are called **frames**. An individual's understanding of an event depends on the frame used to interpret it (Dillard et al., 1996). For example, if you are someone who frames the world as a dangerous place rife with criminals, you are likely to interpret that banging on your window as an indication of someone trying to break in. Similarly, if your friend frames the world as a place full of rude people, they may interpret your failure to say hello as a deliberate snub, whereas if their view is that people are nice, they may interpret your behavior as a failure to see them. In essence, individuals view the world through interpretive frames that then guide how they make sense of events (Dijk, 1977; Durfeel, 2006).

Individuals' frames develop over time, based on experience, interaction with others, and innate personality (Neale & Bazerman, 1991; Putnam & Holmer, 1992). Because we cannot perceive every aspect of an experience, frames also direct our attention toward some features of an episode and away from others. A bad mood, for example, directs attention to the negative aspects of an event. Usually, people don't become aware of frames until something happens to force them to replace one frame with another. If a friend points out that you are focusing only on the negative, you will become more aware of how your mood is framing, or focusing, your perceptions and interpretations. Your frame can change, then, as new information is introduced.

How should you use this information about framing? Now that you are aware that interpretations of people, events, and objects are influenced by an individual's specific frames, you should be more critical of your own interpretations. It is helpful to recognize that your interpretations (as well as others') do not necessarily represent the "truth"—but simply represent a particular way of viewing the world at a particular moment in time.

Frames are important elements of interpretation because they function as lenses that shape how observers understand people and events. Bear in mind, however, that interpretation involves more than just framing; when individuals interpret events, they also offer explanations for them. When we develop explanations for our own and others' behaviors, we are engaged in making attributions. Let's see how this process works.

Attribution   How often do you wonder, "Why did she (or he) do that?" As we observe and interact with others, we spend considerable energy attempting to determine the causes of their behavior. For example, if your friend ignores you before class, you try to figure out why. At heart, most of us are amateur psychologists who search for the reasons people behave as they do. How confident are you regarding your attributions about specific others, such as your best friend or one of your parents?

Attribution theory explains the cognitive and verbal processes we use to judge our own and others' behavior (Manusov & Spitzberg, 2008). Fritz Heider (1958, 2013), a psychologist and professor, said that attribution is the process of drawing inferences. When individuals observe others, they immediately draw conclusions that go beyond mere sensory information. When someone cuts you off in traffic, what conclusion do you usually draw? What attribution would you make if you called your romantic partner at 3 A.M. and they weren't home? Although we're constantly being told we shouldn't judge others, attribution theory says we can't help it (Griffin, 1994).

One attribution we often make is whether the cause of an individual's behavior is internal or external. An *internal* cause would be a personality characteristic, whereas an *external* cause would be situational.

We are particularly likely to make internal attributions when the behavior is unexpected—that is, when it is something that most other people would not do (Kelley, 1973). For instance, if someone laughs during a sad scene in a movie, people are more likely to attribute this unexpected reaction to a personality trait—for example, rudeness or insensitivity. But when the behavior fits our expectations, we are likely to attribute it to external causes. Therefore, if someone cries during a sad movie scene, people are likely to attribute the behavior to the content of the movie.

In addition to expectations, attributions may also depend on whether we are the actor or observer of the behavior. A common mistake that occurs when we explain behavior is called **attributional bias**. Attributional bias describes the systematic errors people make when they evaluate or try to find reasons for their own and others' behaviors. For example, we are more likely to attribute our own negative behavior to external causes and our positive actions to internal states (Harvey & Martinko, 2010). This is referred to as a **self-serving bias**. If you are polite, it is because you have good manners; if you are rude, it is because others mistreated you. Operating under this bias, we tend to give ourselves more credit than is due when good things happen, and we accept too little responsibility for those things that go wrong.

Most individuals are harsher judges of other people's behavior than they are of their own. We tend to attribute others' negative behavior to *internal* causes (such as their personality) and their positive behavior to *external* causes (such as the situation). This tendency is referred to as the **fundamental attribution error** (Schwarz, 2006). For example, when you are driving during rush hour traffic and someone cuts in front of you abruptly as two lanes merge, what attribution do you make about the other driver? According to fundamental attribution error, people are more likely to attribute the behavior to some trait internal to the other driver ("That driver is a jerk and is deliberately trying to get ahead of me") rather than to something external ("That driver is distracted by a child in the car and doesn't realize the lane is merging"). But if the other

Critical Thinking Prompt
Are you an optimist or a pessimist? Do you think people are inherently generous or self-serving? The answers to these questions, and others like them, reveal how your beliefs help shape the frames you use and how, in turn, those frames influence the way you see—and respond to—the world. What other frames do you use that influence your perceptions?

attribution theory
Explanation of the processes we use to judge our own and others' behavior.

attributional bias
A cognitive bias that refers to the systematic errors made when people evaluate or try to find reasons for their own and others' behaviors.

self-serving bias
The tendency to give one's self more credit than is due when good things happen and to accept too little responsibility for those things that go wrong.

fundamental attribution error
The tendency to attribute others' negative behavior to internal causes and their positive behaviors to external causes.

driver slows down to let you enter the merged lane first, most people might assume the driver was simply following the rules of the road rather than deliberately attempting to be thoughtful.

A third type of attribution error people engage in is called **overattribution**. Overattribution occurs when you select one or two obvious characteristics (such as an individual's sex, race, ethnicity, or age) and use them to explain almost anything that person does (Olivier et al., 1999). If your professor forgets a meeting with you and you attribute it to the fact that they are an "absent-minded professor," you likely are engaging in overattribution. Overattribution occurs because we use mental "shortcuts" to understand events around us. However, doing so has consequences. For example, you may have read about a White woman from New York, Amy Cooper, who called the police to say that a Black man was threatening her—after he asked her to put her dog on a leash. In the incident, Ms. Cooper's words served to invoke societal overattributions based on cultural stereotypes. Her claim that she was "threatened by a Black man" cast her as a vulnerable White woman who was afraid of a potentially dangerous Black man. Fortunately, the video revealed that Ms. Cooper was not threatened, and police charged her with making a false report (NBC News, 2020).

Amy Cooper's utterance exemplifies how overattribution operates—we see a person, we select one characteristic and make attributions about that person based on our preconceived, often stereotyped, beliefs about that characteristic. Our attributions don't always result in negative consequences. However, in recent years many people have become more aware of the potential harm that can occur when they engage in overattributions. We see that when people who have power make overattributions about people of color, women, or those with disabilities, it can result in unemployment, housing discrimination, and even violence for members of those groups. When we make overattributions about others, we can hurt others even if we don't intend to.

Attributional biases have implications for the way people communicate and conduct relationships. For example, the types of attributions spouses make are linked to their feelings of marital satisfaction (Sillars et al., 2000, 2002). Those in unhappy relationships tend to assume the spouse's negative behaviors are internal, or personality based, and difficult to change. Unfortunately, they also tend to view their spouse's positive behaviors as situational and temporary (Bradbury & Fincham, 1988). Thus, unhappy spouses often feel helpless to change their partner's negative characteristics. This pessimistic outlook can then increase negative communication within the relationship—which leads to greater marital dissatisfaction—and the cycle repeats itself.

Interestingly, when people make attributions about others, they tend to trust the negative information they hear more than the positive information (Lupfer et al., 2000). If you hear both positive and negative information about a classmate, you tend to remember and rely on the negative rather than the positive information to formulate your attributions. However, you are not confined to these faulty attributional processes; you can work to overcome them.

overattribution

Selecting an individual's most obvious characteristic and using it to explain almost anything that person does.

▼ You are likely to attribute an internal cause to unexpected behavior—such as laughter during a sad movie.

First, remember that none of us is a mind reader and that the attributions we make are not always accurate. Remain aware that attributions are just guesses (even if they are educated guesses). It also helps if one remains aware of the self-serving bias and works to minimize it. Recognize that we all have a tendency to attribute our own positive actions to ourselves and others' negative actions to themselves. Look for alternative explanations for your own and others' behavior. Last, avoid overemphasizing the negative. People have a tendency to remember and to highlight the negative, so try to avoid the negative in your own comments and balance the positive against the negative in your evaluations of others. For an example of a mistaken attribution, see *It Happened to Me: Luis*.

It Happened to Me
Luis

I was at a party recently where I knew hardly anyone; I went up to this guy, stood next to him. When he didn't seem to notice me, I introduced myself and tried talking to him. But he completely ignored me! I was so put off that I stomped away and started complaining to my friend. I told her that the guy was so rude! She looked puzzled. "Oh, were you standing on his left side?" she asked. When I told her yeah, she explained that he was deaf in his left ear and probably hadn't heard me. I felt bad that I had jumped to a negative attribution so quickly. Later, I approached him on his right side and talked to him; I found out he was a really nice guy.

Perception and the Individual

3.3 **Name three individual factors that affect one's perceptual processes.**

Thus far, we have explained how perceptions form: Individuals engage in selective attention, use a variety of organizational procedures, and assign meaning to their perceptions. Therefore, if you hear a loud noise in the street, you will turn your attention to the street; and if you see a car stopped and a person lying in the road with their motorcycle, you will categorize the event as an accident. Finally, you likely will decide (interpret) that the car hit the motorcycle rider. You may even "decide" who is at fault for the accident. As we've discussed, a variety of individual factors influence people's perceptual processes and affect their selection, organization, and interpretation of sensory input. For example, those who often ride motorcycles may attribute fault for the accident to the car driver (because they have frequently experienced inattentive auto drivers), whereas people who only drive cars may attribute blame to the motorcyclist (because they observed cyclists driving between lanes of cars on the road). The individual factors that influence our perceptual processes generally fall into three categories: physical, cognitive, and personality characteristics.

Journal Prompt 3.2:
Perception and
Interpretation
What are the three procedures people use to understand information collected through the senses? How do they affect how we see the world?

Physical Differences

Each person's unique physical capabilities affect what they perceive and how they understand it. Some people have more acute hearing than others do, whereas some have more acute sight, or taste. For example, professional wine tasters have a highly developed sense of taste, pilots are required to have 20/40 vision in each eye, and musicians must possess the ability to identify various pitches and notes. People also experience differences in their physical endurance, ability to navigate indoor and outdoor settings, and ability to move easily. Because of these issues what is "easy" or "hard" to accomplish varies. A person in a wheelchair may find it difficult, even impossible, to access some buildings and parks, and anyone who is hearing or sight impaired could have problems finding their way through poorly marked settings. And all of these people may find it difficult to communicate with people who have not learned to adapt to individual differences.

DID YOU KNOW?
The Ringtone Adults Cannot Hear

Are you familiar with mosquito ringtones? What are the implications of the Mosquito teen repellent and mosquito ringtone for communicating, perceiving, and understanding?

The mosquito ringtone is based on technology created by Britain Howard Stapleton, who developed a device described as the Mosquito teen repellent. The device emitted a high-pitched frequency tone that adults could not hear but that teenagers found annoying. It was used by shopkeepers to disperse teenagers from public spaces where they congregated.

Later, inventive students converted the same technology into a ringtone that adults could not hear. This allowed them to receive phone calls and text messages while in class without their teachers being aware of it—that is, provided their teachers were old enough.

To test your ability to hear mosquito ringtones at different frequency levels, go to http://www.freemosquitoringtone.org.

Personality and Individual Characteristics

Each person's unique mix of personality, temperament, and experience also influences how they interpret and respond to sensory information. Elements that make up this mix include emotional state, outlook, and knowledge.

Emotional State If you are feeling happy or optimistic, you will tend to interpret and respond to sensory input differently than if you are feeling depressed, angry, or sad (Planalp, 1993). For instance, if you feel angry, you may perceive music, other people's voices, or background noise as irritating. By contrast, if you are in a positive mood, you may behave more helpfully toward others. In one experiment, researchers tested 800 passersby (Gueguen & De Gail, 2003). In half of the cases, researchers smiled at the passersby, and in half they did not. A few seconds after this interaction, the passersby had the opportunity to help another researcher who dropped their belongings on the ground. Those exposed to the smile in the first encounter were more likely to be helpful in the second. Thus, even a small impact on your emotional state can influence how you perceive and interact with others.

Outlook One's outlook refers to a tendency to view and interpret the world in consistent ways. Research shows that people tend to have a natural predisposition to either optimism or pessimism, based on genetics and experience (Seligman, 1998). People who are optimistic by nature expect more positive experiences and make fewer negative attributions. These positive expectations can influence their behavior—but not always for the best. For example, young people with an optimistic bias tend to believe that they are less likely than others to experience negative consequences from health behaviors. Therefore, they may be more likely to engage in sexual risk-taking (Chapin, 2001). This difference in outlook became particularly noticeable during the COVID-19 pandemic. Some people vigilantly wore masks and practiced social distancing, likely because they believed they were vulnerable or hoped to protect other people who were vulnerable to the virus, while others refused to use masks and frequented bars, restaurants, and gatherings, probably because they believed it was unlikely they would contract the virus or spread it to others. This difference in perception affected the spread of the virus and led to a number of conflicts between those who believed masks were needed and those who didn't. Thus, perceptions have real-world consequences for all of us.

Knowledge People frequently interpret what they perceive based on what they know of an event. If you know that your friend has a big exam coming up, you may interpret their irritability as the result of nervousness. Our knowledge of specific topics also influences our perceptions, communication, and decision-making. For instance, a study on organ donation revealed that members of families that discussed the subject were twice as likely to donate their organs as were members of other families (Smith et al., 2004). The researchers concluded that once people communicate and know more about the topic of organ donation, they perceive it in a more positive light.

Cognitive Complexity

As we discussed previously, categorization helps us to organize information. Scientists refer to the categories we form as **constructs**. **Cognitive complexity** refers to how detailed, involved, or numerous a person's constructs are (Burleson & Caplan, 1998; Granello, 2010). How does cognitive complexity affect perception?

First, people tend to be more cognitively complex about—and have more constructs for—those things that interest them or with which they have had experience. If you enjoy music, you likely have a wide range of constructs regarding types of music, such as rap, hip-hop, alternative, progressive, and neo-traditional country, and others may not possess these constructs at all. This high number of constructs affects your perceptions of music. As you listen, you can distinguish between multiple types of music, and you recognize when an artist is employing a specific form or fusing two or more genres.

One important purpose of education is to help you expand your constructs related to specific topics. As you progress through the chapters in this book and listen to your instructor's lectures and class discussions, you will develop more constructs for communication. When you began this course, you may have had just one broad construct you labeled "communication" that included all types of communication in which you engaged. By the time you finish this course, you will have many categories or constructs to describe different types of communication, such as rhetoric, small group communication, interpersonal communication, and intercultural communication. Once you have these constructs, you will then be able to more easily develop them and increase your understanding of them and, ultimately, the communication process as whole. As you acquire new information about each of these constructs, you will have a structure in which to place and organize this new information, which in turn will help you understand and remember that information. It might be helpful for you to think of constructs as folders that you use to organize information, and to which you refer later to help you understand a topic better.

In addition to these sets of personal constructs that help you interpret the world, you also possess *interpersonal constructs* that you use to make decisions and inferences about other people (Deutsch et al., 1991). From an early age, everyone possesses simple constructs that help organize their perceptions of others. These constructs tend to be bipolar, or based on opposing categories of characteristics—such as funny or serious, warm or cold, and responsible or careless. One's age, intellectual ability, and experiences influence how complex or detailed such constructs are. For example, very young children typically describe others with only a few constructs, such as nice or mean; most adults, however, have a much more involved set of constructs that allows them to describe others in more varied and specific ways, such as thoughtful, amusing, argumentative, quirky, or kind.

When you have cognitively complex construct systems, you tend to have many ways of explaining and understanding interpersonal interactions. Suppose, for example, that your friend Laura was almost an hour late meeting you for a dinner date. If you are cognitively complex, you might come up with a number of reasons to explain this behavior: Laura (a) was in a traffic accident, (b) forgot about the date, (c) was detained by an unforeseen event, (d) decided not to keep the date, and so on. These are all plausible explanations; without further information you will not know which one is correct. The point is that cognitively complex individuals can develop a large set of alternative explanations while they wait for more information to clarify the situation.

constructs
Categories people develop to help them organize information.

cognitive complexity
The degree to which a person's constructs are detailed, involved, or numerous.

Critical Thinking Prompt
Do you wonder how cognitively complex your interpersonal constructs are? To find out, think of a person you know well. Then for the next 60 seconds, write down as many terms as you can think of to describe that person. How many terms were you able to generate? How many different categories of terms were you able to list? (For example, *nice, kind, thoughtful* would group into one category as would *athletic, physically fit, sporty.*) Typically, the more terms and categories of terms you can generate, the more cognitively complex your interpersonal constructs for that person are believed to be.

▲ Cognitively complex individuals can develop a large number of explanations for the late arrival of a dinner date.

Journal Prompt 3.3: Cognitive Complexity
What three individual factors affect your perceptual processes the most?

In turn, your degree of cognitive complexity influences your perceptions and thus your communication behavior. For example, if you can only explain Laura's lateness by deciding that she is thoughtless, you will likely perceive her negatively and use a hostile communication style when you meet. Individuals' levels of complexity influence a broad range of communicative issues, such as how many persuasive messages they can generate (Applegate, 1982) and how well they can comfort others (Holmstrom & Burleson, 2010; Samter & Burleson, 1984).

Your perceptions strongly shape your communication and your actions. If you strike up a conversation with someone new who is physically attractive but who reminds you of someone you dislike, you may choose to end the conversation and move on. However, if you meet someone who reminds you of someone you like, you might invest energy in getting to know that person. If you interpret a new friend's teasing as a sign of affection, you may decide to increase your involvement with them. In these ways, your perceptual processes influence your interactions and relationships. In addition, broader societal factors also play a role in what you perceive, how you organize it, and the meanings you attach to it.

The Individual, Perception, and Society

3.4 Articulate how power, culture, social comparisons, and historical period influence perception.

How do societal factors affect perception? As we explain in this section, the position individuals hold in society and the cultures in which they live affect what they perceive and how they interpret these perceptions. As you read this section, we encourage you to consider the societal forces that affect your perceptions as well as how they might affect the perceptions of others.

The Role of Power

Every society has a hierarchy, and in a hierarchy, some people have more power than others do. Your relative position of power or lack of power influences how others perceive you, how you perceive others, and how you interpret events in the world. Moreover, those in power largely determine a society's understandings of reality. For example, in the United States, the dominant perception is that everyone can move up in society through hard work and education ("Middle of the class," 2005). However, individuals who are born poor and who live in areas with low-quality schools and few resources can find upward mobility to be difficult, no matter how hard they try to follow the path to "success" as defined by mainstream U.S. culture.

Thus, the perceptual reality of low-power people is likely to differ from that of those higher in the power hierarchy. Nonetheless, a specific view of reality dominates U.S. culture because it is communicated both explicitly and implicitly through media messages, public speeches, schools, and other social institutions. Whose reality do you think is communicated in these ways? As you probably guessed, it is people with power—because they are more likely to have access to media messages, to have their speeches heard, and to control the messages communicated in and by schools and cultural institutions.

One's individual experiences within a hierarchy may lead one to accept or reject dominant perceptions. For example, during the COVID-19 pandemic, White people were more likely to protest when businesses, parks, and schools closed (Branson-Potts et al., 2020) and therefore seemed to view the virus as less contagious than did people of color. Why did these groups' perceptions differ? They did so, in part, due to their relative awareness of the impact of the virus on people. That is, they observed different numbers of people falling ill from it.

Most White people, especially those who were middle and upper class, did not know anyone

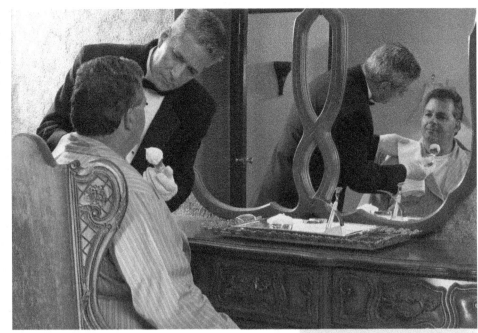

▲ Power differences affect people's perceptions of how easy or difficult it is to attain financial success.

who became ill during the early months of the pandemic. People of color, however, saw more acquaintances and family members become infected by the virus, so they were more aware of the effects of the disease. Specifically, non-Hispanic American Indian and Alaska Native persons had an infection rate approximately five times larger than that of non-Hispanic White persons, non-Hispanic Black persons had a rate approximately five times that of non-Hispanic White persons, and Hispanic or Latinx persons had a rate approximately four times that of non-Hispanic White persons (CDC, 2020). Thus, individuals' personal experiences influenced their perceptions.

The Role of Culture

Culture strongly influences individual perception. One way it does so is through its *sensory model*. Every culture has its own sensory model, which means that each culture emphasizes a few of the five senses (Classen, 1990). Moreover, what a culture emphasizes affects what its members pay attention to and prefer. People in the United States, for example, tend to give primacy to the visual; thus, we have sayings such as "seeing is believing," and students almost demand that professors provide PowerPoint slides for their lectures. By contrast, people living in the Andes Mountains of South America tend to place more emphasis on what they hear than on what they see. In their culture, important ideas are transmitted through characters in stories and narratives (Classen, 1990). Knowing this, how do you think students in the Andes prefer to learn? You might imagine that they would prefer vivid and detailed stories rather than a list of brief terms and concepts on PowerPoint slides.

A culture is composed of a set of shared practices, norms, values, and beliefs (Brislin, 2000; Shore, 1996), that helps shape individuals' thoughts, feelings, perceptions, and behaviors. For example, individuals in East Asian cultures often are highly interdependent and emphasize the group over the individual. Consequently, they don't approve of bragging and encourage greater self-criticism than some other cultures. By encouraging self-criticism (and then working on self-improvement), the thinking goes, people contribute to the overall strength of the group (Heine & Lehman, 2004; Markus et al., 1997). In the United States, however, the emphasis often is on the individual, and most people are encouraged to distinguish themselves from others. Therefore, the dominant culture in the United States encourages people to talk about their success and to refrain from self-criticism. As a result, someone from East Asia may see U.S. Americans as braggarts,

▲ Some travelers become upset when their cultural expectations about what is "food" are not fulfilled.

whereas a person from the United States may see East Asians as overly modest (Kim, 2002).

Cultural background also influences how people expect to talk to one another (Scollon & Wong-Scollon, 1990). In some Native American cultures, for example, individuals perceive strangers as potentially unpredictable, so they may talk little—if at all—until they have established familiarity and trust with newcomers (Braithwaite, 1990). This approach differs considerably from the customs of some European American cultures, in which people view strangers as potential friends and strike up conversations to become acquainted with them (Krivonos & Knapp, 1975).

Now imagine a Native American and a European American from these different communication cultures meeting for the first time. How is each likely to behave? The Native American may remain relatively quiet while observing the new person. The European American will most likely try to engage in a lively conversation and may ask a number of questions to draw out the other person. As a result, the Native American may view the European American as nosy, pushy, and overly familiar, whereas the European American may see the Native American as unfriendly or shy (Braithwaite, 1990). Each perceives or evaluates the other based on expectations shaped by their own cultural perceptions, their values, and the meanings typical for their own culture (Scollon & Wong-Scollon, 1990).

Cultural norms, values, and expectations provide a backdrop of familiarity. When we travel or when we meet people from other cultures, we can learn from exposure to our differences. However, sometimes these differences are upsetting, frustrating, or baffling. For example, one of our students, Simone, was taken aback when she was offered *chapulines* (fried grasshoppers) during her trip to Oaxaca, Mexico. U.S. Americans often are surprised by other cultures' perceptions of their food—many other cultures perceive peanut butter and jelly sandwiches to be disgusting. How would you respond if someone offered you haggis, a Scottish dish made with animal entrails and internal organs mixed with suet and oatmeal and boiled in a bag? How much does your own ethnocentrism factor into your personal reaction to each of these foods? Interestingly, most of us not only value the ways of our own culture, we often feel that others' cultural norms are less desirable—or even wrong—an issue we discuss next.

The Role of Social Comparison

As we discussed previously, categorizing groups of objects, information, or people is a basic quality of perception. *Social* categorization—or categorizing people—leads us to specific expectations about how others should or should not behave. These social categories and the expectations associated with them typically arise out of our culture and where we are positioned in the culture. Every culture has rules and expectations that its members take for granted. Because we become socialized to our culture and its rules at a very young age—so much so that most of it is absorbed subconsciously—we are not aware that our rules and expectations are learned. Instead, we feel as if they are simply "right" and that other rules and expectations are "wrong." For example, in the United States, people in different social classes have varying expectations or understandings for why people receive government subsidies for food or housing. Individuals who are middle and upper-middle class often perceive those who receive these subsidies as people who do not want to work hard, and they may therefore categorize them as lazy or dependent. However, people who are in the working class or among the working poor may have different perceptions, asserting that those who rely on these government subsidies work hard but are underemployed or have to live on a salary that is not a living wage (Ehrenreich, 2001; "Middle of the class," 2005). Similarly, in the United States, youth is typically valued over age, so older people may be seen as less competent or valuable. As a result, elders often are perceived as poor job candidates and as a burden on families and societies. In other cultures, such as Korean, Greek, and Native American, aging is celebrated and elders are respected. If you are from one of these cultures, you may perceive that U.S. Americans are misguided or even wrong in their treatment of the elderly. As you can see, the perceptions and categories that we develop often are tied to stereotypes and prejudice, which both flow from ethnocentrism, the perceptual concept at the core of social comparison.

Ethnocentrism   Most people view their own group as the standard against which they evaluate others. Thus, one's own ethnic, regional, or class group is the one that seems right, correct, or normal. This tendency to view one's own group as the standard against which all others are judged is described as **ethnocentrism**. It comes from the Greek words *ethnos*, which means nation, and *kentron*, which refers to the center of a circle (Ting-Toomey, 1999). People behave ethnocentrically when they view their own values, norms, or modes of belief and behavior as better than those of other groups.

ethnocentrism
The tendency to view one's own group as the standard against which all other groups are judged.

Although it is normal to be proud of one's national, cultural, racial, or ethnic group, one becomes ethnocentric when they engage in polarized thinking and behavior. This occurs when people believe that if "we" are right, correct, normal, and even superior, then "they" must be wrong, incorrect, abnormal, and inferior. Such thinking can seriously interfere with our ability to communicate effectively with those outside our group.

Stereotypes   Previously we described stereotypes as broad generalizations about an entire class of objects or people, based on some knowledge of some aspects of some members of the class (Brislin, 2000; Stephan & Stephan, 1992). When you stereotype computer programmers as smart but socially inept, you likely are basing your beliefs on your interactions with a few programmers—or perhaps on no interactions at all. Stereotypes may be based on what you have read, images in the media, or information you have obtained from others, as you'll see was the case with one college student in *It Happened to Me: Damien*.

If you develop a stereotype, it tends to influence what you expect from the stereotyped group. If you believe that someone is a lesbian, you may also believe she engages in specific types of communication behavior, dress, or interests. When you hold these types of beliefs and expectations, they tend to erase the stereotyped person's individual characteristics. In addition, you are likely to communicate with her as if your stereotypes were accurate rather than basing your messages on her actual interests and behavior (Snyder, 1998).

Stereotyping is an understandable and natural cognitive activity; in fact, stereotypes can serve as useful shorthand to help us understand the world. If you are interviewing for a job in the southern United States, it may be helpful for you to know that many Southerners prefer to engage in social interaction before getting down to business (though this is certainly not always true). However, when stereotyping

It Happened to Me
Damien

Shortly after school started, I decided to join a fraternity and began going to parties on the weekends. Often when people heard me mention that I was a part-time computer programmer, they would first look shocked and then crack some kind of joke about it, like "Bill Gates, Jr., eh?" I guess it surprises people that I don't have glasses, that I am a person of color, and that I engage in some social activities! I realize that their preconceived notions about "techies" have come from somewhere, but since at least half of my fellow "computer geeks" are far from the nerdy stereotype, it would be nice if people would recognize that we aren't all pale, glasses-wearing, socially awkward nerds!

leads to polarized understandings of the world as "between me and you, us and them, females and males, Blacks and Whites," then it can cause problems (Ting-Toomey, 1999, p. 149). In turn, polarized thinking frequently leads to a rigid, intolerant view of certain behavior as correct or incorrect (Ting-Toomey, 1999). For example, do you believe it is more appropriate for adult children to live on their own than with their parents while unmarried? People with polarized thinking assume that their own cultural beliefs regarding this issue are right or correct instead of recognizing that cultures differ in what is considered appropriate.

prejudice
Experiencing aversive or negative feelings toward a group as a whole or toward an individual because they belong to a particular group.

Prejudice   Stereotypes and feelings of ethnocentrism often lead to prejudice. **Prejudice** occurs when people experience aversive or negative feelings toward a group as a whole or toward an individual because they belong to a particular group (Rothenberg, 1992). People can experience prejudice against a person or group because of their physical characteristics, perceived ethnicity or race, age, national origin, religious practices, and a number of other identity categories.

Given the negative associations most people have with the concept of prejudice, you may wonder why it persists. Researchers believe that prejudice is common and pervasive because it serves specific functions, the two most important of which are *ego-defensive functions* and *value-expressive functions* (Brislin, 2000). Let's explore these concepts.

ego-defensive function
The role prejudice plays in protecting individuals' sense of self-worth.

The **ego-defensive function** of prejudice describes the role it plays in protecting individuals' sense of self-worth. For example, an individual who is not financially successful and whose group members tend not to be financially successful may attribute blame to other groups for hoarding resources and preventing them from becoming successful. The less financially successful individual may also look down on groups that are even less financially successful as a way to protect their own ego. These attitudes may make people feel better, but they also prevent them from analyzing the personal and structural reasons for their own situation. Moreover, they negatively affect the ways people talk to and about the targeted groups. People who look down on groups that are less financially successful may describe them and talk to them as if they were lazy, incompetent, or not very bright.

value-expressive function
The role played by prejudice in allowing people to view their own values, norms, and cultural practices as appropriate and correct.

Prejudice serves its **value-expressive function** by allowing people to view their own values, norms, and cultural practices as appropriate and correct. By devaluing other groups' behavior and beliefs, people maintain a solid sense that they are right. Unfortunately, this same function causes group members to denigrate the cultural practices of others. You may have seen many examples of the value-expressive function of prejudice, as when individuals engage in uncivil arguments and personal attacks over issues such as men's and women's roles, abortion, and politics.

The Role of Historical Period

In addition to a person's place in the power hierarchy, their culture, and their awareness of social comparison, the historical period in which one grows up and lives influences perception and communication (U.S. National Research Council, 1989). For example, anyone living in the United States who was older than five or six and lived through the coronavirus pandemic likely has had their perceptions altered by what they experienced. They may perceive air travel as riskier, be more scrupulous about washing their hands, and feel more uncomfortable when others sneeze and cough. These perceptions may in turn influence how they behave and react to other people.

Other historical events have affected the perceptions of individuals who lived through them. For instance, those who were young during the Vietnam War likely believe that collective action can influence political policy, while those who grew up watching *The Bachelor* and other reality TV programs probably view privacy differently than do prior generations. Another recent event that has influenced people's perceptions is the #MeToo movement.

The #MeToo movement started through a tweet that encouraged women to tweet about their experiences with sexual assault and harassment using the hashtag #MeToo. It sparked a movement that spread to multiple countries across the world. Between October 2017 and October 2018 #MeToo was used 19 million times on Twitter (*Columbia Journalism Review*, 2019). The movement not only brought attention to the prevalence and severity of the dangers women face on a daily basis, but it also called out many men in powerful positions who had used their power to hide their behaviors (Starkey et al., 2019). After centuries of sexual abuse being ignored and denied, women were able to reshape the conversation about power and sex in part because of the communication technologies available to them in the 2010s.

Social Roles

The roles one plays socially also influence one's perceptions, and consequently, communication. **Social role** refers to the specific position or positions that an individual holds in a society. Social roles include job positions, familial roles (such as mother or father), and positions in society. For example, Rosario holds a variety of roles, including mother, religious leader, soccer coach, and community activist. The fact that she holds these social roles affects how people perceive and communicate with her in several ways. First, society defines specific expectations for her various social roles (Kirouac & Hess, 1999). Many people, for example, expect religious leaders to be especially moral, selfless, and well intentioned. In turn, these expectations affect the ways that religious leaders interact with others. If you expect Rosario, as a religious leader, to be highly moral, she may work to communicate with you in ways that fulfill your expectations.

Second, the education, training, and socialization Rosario undergoes for her social roles influence her perceptions. In much of U.S. culture, people often expect that women will become mothers and that they will behave in specific ways as they fulfill that role. As girls grow up, they are socialized and taught—by both word and example—how mothers are supposed to communicate. Because Rosario is a parent, she may perceive different issues as important. For example, she may be more concerned with the quality of schools, the safety of her neighborhood, and access to health care than a nonparent might. Similarly, when individuals receive education and training, their perceptions of the world around them are affected. A person trained as an emergency medical technician may perceive the world as riskier because of the many accident victims they have treated, while an epidemiologist may be more aware of cleanliness and the potential for infection from everyday objects.

Each individual's perceptions are unique, based on their own roles and characteristics. However, individuals also share certain perceptual realities with others in their power position in society's hierarchy as well as with others in their cultures and social role groups. Because of these differing realities and power positions, your perceptions may lead you into prejudicial and intolerant thinking and communication. In the concluding section of this chapter, we suggest strategies for improving your perception processes and communication.

social role
The specific position or positions one holds in a society.

**Journal Prompt 3.4:
Social Comparison**
How do power, culture, social comparisons, and historical period influence how you perceive the world?

Ethics and Perception

3.5 Explain why ethics is relevant to the perception process.

As we've discussed throughout this chapter, the ways people communicate to and about others are connected to their perceptions and cognitions about them. That is, what we select to attend to, what categories we put people in, and the attributions we make about them all strongly influence what we believe, say, and do. For example, Dev was driving home late one night and stopped at a traffic light when he noticed a young White woman in the car next to his. She reached over and locked her door. As she looked up, Dev smiled slightly and then leaned over and locked *his* door. In this case, Dev was gently reminding the other driver that she was responding based on stereotypical perceptions and cognitions.

A common example of a time when perception, ethics, and communication intersect occurs when speakers perceive and label other groups of people negatively and then use derogatory terms to refer to them. Unfortunately, using such terms can reinforce and even intensify one's own, as well as others', negative responses to these groups. In addition, if what individuals attend to and perceive about people first is their skin color, their sex, or their relative affluence, they may find themselves communicating with those people stereotypically and failing to recognize other roles they fulfill. Doing so may lead one to assume and communicate as if all adult women are mothers (or there is something wrong with them if they are not) or to refer to a physician as nurse because she happens to be female. Each of these behaviors is problematic in that it denies others their right to legitimate identities. Consequently, such behaviors are ones that need to be examined through an ethical lens. That is, when tempted to create stereotypes of others and to communicate with them based on that stereotype, it helps to ask if doing so fits within your own ethical framework or how you would feel if someone stereotyped and assigned a negative label to you.

Although social factors such as power and position can influence many aspects of your life, you do have control of and responsibility for your perceptions and cognitions. Even though your social circle and your family may engage in problematic perceptual, cognitive, and communicative processes, once you become an adult, you are responsible for how you interpret the world. To help you think about your perceptions and cognitive procedures through an ethical lens, we discuss some guidelines to assist you in this process.

**Journal Prompt 3.5:
Ethics in Perception**
How are ethics relevant to the perception process?

Improving Your Perception Skills

3.6   Identify three ways you can improve your perception skills.

You probably realize now that perceptions are subject to variance and error because of the variety of steps one goes through in forming them (selection, organization, and interpretation) and the range of factors that influence the perception process (individual characteristics, cognitive complexity, power, culture, historical time period, and social roles). However, certain cognitive and communication behaviors can improve one's ability to perceive and understand the world.

First, one can engage in *mindfulness* to improve perception and understanding. Mindfulness refers to a clear focus on one's current activity, with attention to as many specifics of the event as possible (Langer, 1978). People tend to be most mindful when they are engaged in a new or unusual activity. Once an activity becomes habitual,

▼ One communication act that can improve your perception skills is checking with others to see if their perceptions are similar to yours.

we are likely to overlook its details. Mindfulness requires that one bring the same level of attention and involvement to routine activities as one does to novel ones.

In addition, before assuming your perceptions are accurate, you might ask yourself a few questions to help you check those perceptions:

- Have you focused too narrowly and missed relevant information because of selective attention? For example, did you focus on what the person was wearing rather than on what they were saying?
- What type of organizational pattern did you use? For example, just because two people are standing next to one another does not mean they are together.
- To what extent have you considered all possible interpretations for the information you perceived, using the full range of your cognitive complexity? For example, if you did poorly on a test, was it due to poor test construction, your lack of sleep, the teacher's failure to prepare you, or your own failure to study sufficiently?
- How might your physical condition have influenced your perceptions? For example, are you tired, hungry, or frightened?
- How has your cultural background influenced your perceptions? For example, are you perceiving politeness as deception?
- How has your social role influenced your perception? For example, have you begun to perceive all elderly people as infirm because you work in a nursing home?
- How has your social position influenced your perception? For example, have you considered how others with different positions might perceive the same issue?

Another way to improve one's perception and understanding is to clearly separate *facts* from *inferences*. Facts are truths that are verifiable based on observation. Inferences are conclusions that we draw or interpretations we make based on the facts. Thus, it may be a fact that Southerners speak more slowly than do people from other regions of the United States, but it is an inference if you conclude that their slow speech indicates slow thought processes.

Finally, one communication act in particular will greatly improve anyone's perception skills: *perception checking*. You engage in perception checking by communicating with others to determine if their perceptions match your own. If they do not, you may need to alter your perceptions. Perception checking is a way of communicating that allows you test your assumptions about what another person has said or done. When you engage in second-person perception checking, you seek feedback directly from the person you have spoken with or observed. In this situation, you may find this four-step procedure to be helpful:

- Describe the other person's behavior as you saw it. *When I texted you yesterday, you didn't respond.*
- State your interpretation of that behavior. *It made me wonder if you are angry with me.*
- Ask if your interpretation is accurate. *Are you mad at me?*
- If not, ask why your interpretation was inaccurate. *Why didn't you respond?*

Another type of perception checking occurs when you ask one or more people how they perceive a third party or an event. For example, Henderson once had an extremely negative reaction to a job candidate who interviewed at his company. He perceived the candidate as conceited and sexist. However, when he talked with his colleagues, he discovered that no one else had a similarly strong negative response. He decided that his perceptions must be influenced by something in his own background; for example, the candidate may have reminded him of someone he had once known who did display those negative traits. In revising his opinion of the candidate, Henderson demonstrated a well-developed sensitivity to the perception side of communication. All of us can benefit from greater awareness of the assumptions and attributions we make.

Journal Prompt 3.6: Perception Skills
What one skill could you develop that would most improve your perception processes? Why would it help?

SUMMARY

3.1 Explain why understanding perception is important.

- Perception plays an important role in everyday communication.

3.2 Describe the three procedures people use to understand information collected through the senses.

- People use three perceptual procedures to manage the vast array of sensory data in their environments: selection, organization, and interpretation.

3.3 Name three individual factors that affect one's perceptual processes.

- The sensory data we select to attend to, how we organize it, and the interpretations we assign are all influenced by our individual characteristics, such as physical abilities and differences, cognitive complexity, and personality and individual differences.

3.4 Articulate how power, culture, social comparison, and historical period influence perception.

- Perception processes are affected by one's position in the power hierarchy, culture, social comparisons, historical events during one's lifetime, and social roles.

3.5 Explain why ethics is relevant to the perception process.

- Perception, ethics, and communication intersect when speakers perceive and label other groups of people negatively and then use derogatory terms to refer to them.
- Using such terms can reinforce and even intensify one's own as well as others' negative responses to these groups.

3.6 Identify three ways you can improve your perception skills.

- You can improve your perception skills by engaging in mindfulness, separating facts from inferences, and concentrating on perception checking.

KEY TERMS

APPLY WHAT YOU KNOW

1. **Examining Stereotypes**
   For each of the following words, write down your beliefs about the group represented. In other words, provide a list of specific characteristics you believe are typically displayed by members of these groups.
   a. Fraternity members
   b. Politicians
   c. Models
   d. Rap stars
   e. Body builders
   f. Religious leaders
   g. Cannabis dispensary owners

   After you have done so, compare your list to the lists created by other members of your class. What characteristics for each group did you have in common? What characteristics differed? Can you think of at least one person from each group who does not display the characteristics you listed? What information and perceptions helped shape your stereotypes? How valid do you think your stereotypes are?

2. **Attributional Biases**
   As this chapter explains, people have a tendency to attribute their own positive behavior to internal traits and their negative behavior to external factors. However, they are also more likely to attribute others' positive behavior to external conditions and others' negative behavior to internal traits. In this exercise, we want you to indicate how the attributional bias would cause you to describe each of the following behaviors, depending on who had performed it.

   Example: *Forgetting to make a phone call*
           I'm busy. You're thoughtless.

   Example: *Earning a good grade*
           I'm intelligent. You were lucky.

   Do the exercise for each of the following behaviors/events:
   a. Receiving a raise
   b. Breaking a vase
   c. Arriving late
   d. Winning an award
   e. Burning a meal
   f. Making a group laugh

   Compare your responses with those of others in your class. What terms did others use to describe their own experiences? What terms did they use to describe others' experiences? What is it about the perception process that makes attributional bias so common?

   Although this is just an exercise, remember that attributional bias is quite common. Pay attention to your own thoughts and comments the next time something bad happens to you or others.

3. **Ethics and Perception**
   The authors argue that ethics is relevant to our perceptual processes. To what extent do you agree or disagree with this statement? Provide three arguments for each position. Now that you have considered arguments for both positions, is your opinion the same as it was before or has it altered?

Verbal Communication

LEARNING OBJECTIVES

CHAPTER TOPICS

4.1	Identify three reasons for learning about verbal communication.	The Importance of Verbal Communication
4.2	Describe the functions and components of language.	What Is Verbal Communication? Functions and Components of Language
4.3	Identify examples of several major influences on verbal communication.	The Individual and Verbal Communication: Influences
4.4	Describe the relationships between language, perception, and power.	The Individual, Verbal Communication, and Society: Language, Perception, and Power
4.5	Identify examples of confirming communication, disconfirming communication, and hate speech.	Ethics and Verbal Communication
4.6	Discuss ways to improve your own verbal communication skills.	Improving Your Verbal Communication Skills

> *"The verbal elements of communication are the foundation on which meaning is created."*

When Charee texts her friends, she knows that her verbal communication changes from when she speaks to them face-to-face. She uses "lol," gifs, emojis, and other such "NetSpeak" abbreviations, and she doesn't always use complete sentences. This is true as well when she is using Twitter, which limits her to 280 characters. Even with other social media sites, she keeps her messages brief. But when she writes a paper for class, she knows that she needs to change the way she uses her verbal communication skills. She needs to use complete sentences and formal language without using NetSpeak.

When we think of "communication," we tend to think about the verbal elements of communication: the words people choose, the accents they speak with, and the meanings they convey through language. We frequently don't consider the ways in which verbal communication assists or hinders relationship development, the technology we use, or its effect on the creation of identities.

In this chapter we will explore the verbal elements of communication and how people use verbal communication to accomplish various goals. First we discuss the importance of verbal communication and its value as a topic of study. We then describe how individuals use verbal communication, including the functions it serves and the components of language that make it possible. Next we explore individual characteristics that influence verbal communication, such as gender, age, regionality, ethnicity and race, and education and occupation. We investigate the societal forces that influence verbal communication by examining the relationships among language, perception, and power. Finally, we provide suggestions for communicating more ethically and more effectively.

The Importance of Verbal Communication

4.1 Identify three reasons for learning about verbal communication.

Although the nonverbal aspects of communication are important, the verbal elements of communication are the foundation on which meaning is created. If you doubt that this is the case, try this simple test. Using only nonverbal communication, convey this message to a friend or roommate: "I failed my exam because I locked my keys in my car and couldn't get my textbook until well after midnight." How well was your nonverbal message understood? If you have ever traveled in a country where you didn't speak the language, no doubt you already knew before trying this experiment that nonverbal communication can only get you so far. Similarly, although you may try to incorporate emoticons or other devices to mimic nonverbals, the verbal elements of messages are vital in texting, email, and many social networking sites. We will touch on the

▼ Children from families who converse and eat meals together on a regular basis have higher self-esteem and interact better with their peers.

importance of nonverbal communication here and discuss it in depth in Chapter 5. In this section we propose that to be a highly effective communicator you need to understand the verbal elements of communication.

Verbal communication is also important because of the role it plays in identity and relationship development. As you might remember from our discussion in Chapter 2, individuals develop a sense of self through communication with others. More specifically, the labels used to describe individuals can influence their self-concepts and increase or decrease their self-esteem. People's verbal communication practices also can impede or improve their relationships, which is a topic we will discuss further in Chapter 8. Research by four psychology professors at Emory University supports our claims about the relationship between verbal communication and an individual's identity development and relationship skills. These scholars found that families that converse and eat meals together on a regular basis have children who not only are more familiar with their family histories but also tend to have higher self-esteem, interact better with their peers, and are better able to recover from tragedy and negative events (Duke et al., 2003). Some research has shown the importance of family dinners and the role of parents in asking and listening to their children. Conversations between parents and children can build self-esteem in children by parents demonstrating they value what the children think and feel ("Why the family meal is important," 2020).

In addition, the very language people speak is tied to their identities. Studies of bilingual and multilingual speakers show that their perceptions, behaviors, and even personalities alter when they change languages (Ramírez-Esparza et al., 2006). Why does this occur? The answer is that every language is embedded in a specific cultural context, and when people learn a language, they also learn the beliefs, values, and norms of its culture (Edwards, 2004). So speaking a language evokes its culture as well as a sense of who we are within that culture. Thus the language you use to communicate verbally shapes who you are, as you will see in *It Happened to Me: Cristina*.

It Happened to Me
Cristina

I was teaching an adult education class composed primarily of Mexican immigrants when I first noticed that the language people speak affects how they behave. I'm bilingual, so even though we normally spoke English in my class, sometimes we switched to Spanish. Over time, I noticed that several male students were respectful and deferential when we spoke English; however, when we switched to Spanish, they became more flirtatious and seemed less willing to treat me as an authority figure. Now I understand that these differences probably were related to how men and women interact in the two cultures.

Journal Prompt 4.1: Studying Verbal Communication
What are three reasons for learning about verbal communication?

What Is Verbal Communication? Functions and Components of Language

4.2   Describe the functions and components of language.

Verbal communication generally refers to the written or oral words we exchange; however, as our opening example shows, verbal communication has to do with more than just the words people speak. It includes pronunciation or accent, the meanings of the words used, and a range of variations in the way people speak a language, which depend on their regional backgrounds and other factors.

Language, of course, plays a central role in communication. Some argue that it is our use of language that makes us human. Unlike other mammals, humans use symbols that they can string together to create new words and with which they can form infinite sets of never-before-heard thought, or read sentences.

This ability allows people to be creative and expressive, such as when they take ordinary words and use them in new ways. For example, the word *robo sapiens*—nominated by the American Dialect Society as one of the most creative words for 2013—refers to a class of robots with human intelligence. This is a play on the words *homo sapiens* for humans and *robo* for robot. Even small children who are unschooled in grammar create their own rules of language by using innate linguistic ability together with linguistic information they glean from the people around them. For example, young children often say "mouses" instead of "mice" because they first learn, and apply broadly, the most common rule for pluralizing—adding an *s*.

To help you better understand the role of language in the communication process, the next section explores seven communicative functions of language as well as four components of language use.

Functions of Language

We all use language so automatically that we usually don't think about the many roles it plays. However, language helps us do everything from ordering lunch to giving directions to writing love poems. Moreover, a single utterance can function in a variety of ways. For example, a simple "thank you" not only expresses gratitude, it also can increase feelings of intimacy and liking. Consequently, understanding the ways language functions can help you communicate more effectively. As we discuss next, language can serve at least seven functions: instrumental, regulatory, informative, heuristic, interactional, personal, and imaginative.

- The most basic function of language is **instrumental**. This means we can use it to obtain what we need or desire. For instance, when you send an e-vite to your friends to a party to celebrate a birthday, the invitation is instrumental in that you want your friends to come to the party and the invitation helps make that happen.

  instrumental
  Use of language to obtain what you need or desire.

- A second (and closely related) language function is **regulatory**, meaning that we can use it to control or regulate the behaviors of others. In your invitation, you may ask your friends to bring a bottle of wine or a dessert to the party, as a way of regulating their behavior.

  regulatory
  Use of language to control or regulate the behaviors of others.

- Another basic function of language is to **inform**—to communicate information or report facts. When you invite your friends to the party, you usually include the date and time to inform them of when you want them to come.

  informative
  Use of language to communicate information or report facts.

- We also use language to acquire knowledge and understanding, which is referred to as a **heuristic** use. When you want to invite friends, you may ask them to respond to indicate if they are available at that date and time to learn if your party is going to occur as scheduled or if you need to make some changes.

  heuristic
  Use of language to acquire knowledge and understanding.

- When language is used in an **interactional** fashion, it establishes and defines social relationships in both interpersonal and group settings. Thus, when you invite your friends to a celebration, you engage in a behavior that helps maintain your relationship with them as friends.

  interactional
  Use of language to establish and define social relationships.

- **Personal language** expresses individuality and personality and is more common in private than in public settings. When you invite your friends to the party, you might jokingly add a private message to one, "Don't bring a cheap bottle of wine, like you did last time." In this way, you use language to express your sense of humor.

  personal language
  Use of language to express individuality and personality.

- A final way you can use language is imaginatively. **Imaginative** language is used to express oneself artistically or creatively, as in drama, poetry, or stories. Thus, if your e-vite says "Screw cake, let's drink!" or "Let Them Eat Cake," you would be using the imaginative function of language.

  imaginative
  Use of language to express oneself artistically or creatively.

Speakers use these seven basic functions of language to accomplish specific goals or tasks. Note that these functions overlap and that one utterance can accomplish more than one function at the same time. For example, when inviting your friends to a party, if you jokingly said, "James, our butler, will be serving bubbly and cake promptly at eight, so

Critical Thinking Prompt
As a student, which functions of language do you use most frequently? Which do you use most often in your professional life? If you use different functions in each of these roles, why do you think this is true?

don't be late!" your utterance would both be imaginative (unless you actually have a butler named James) and regulatory. That is, you would be using language creatively while also attempting to regulate your guests' behavior to ensure that they arrived on time.

Now that we have summarized the essential functions that language can serve, let's examine the basic components that allow us to use language as a flexible and creative tool of communication.

Components of Language

Scholars describe language use as being made up of four components: *phonology* (sounds), *syntax* (structure or rules), *semantics* (meaning), and *pragmatics* (use). Every language has its own rules of **grammar**—the structural rules that govern the generation of meaning in that language. See *Did You Know? Prescriptive versus Descriptive Approaches to Language* to read about the different ways that French and German deal with these issues. In this section, we examine the role each plays in the communication process.

grammar
The structural rules that govern the generation of meaning in a language.

DID YOU KNOW?

Prescriptive versus Descriptive Approaches to Language

As you read the following description of how different languages approach the question of how to properly use each language, decide what you think of each approach. Do you prefer the prescriptive or descriptive approach? Can the approaches be combined?

French and German require different approaches to understanding the proper use of each language. A prescriptive approach guides the use of French in France. This means that the rules for correct usage are prescribed, or rigidly formalized and dictated.

In France, the French language is guided by the Académie Française (or French Academy). This institution is the authority on the French language and determines what is and is not proper French. In 2016, a number of changes to the French language were rolled out in schools, creating an uproar in France. Although these changes were voted on in 1990 by the French Academy, they were largely unnoticed at the time. About 2,400 French words have changed their spelling. For example, the French word for "onion" can now be spelled *ognon* or the more traditional *oignon*. The circumflex (^) is also being dropped from many words, such as in *paraître*, which becomes *paraitre* ("to appear"), and some hyphens disappear in words such as *porte-monnaie*, which becomes *portemonnaie* ("wallet").

When COVID-19 appeared, French speakers needed to communicate about it, but they didn't know if it was proper to use the masculine *le* or the feminine *la* for *COVID-19*. In May 2020, the French Academy declared that *COVID-19* is feminine, as the French word for "disease" is a feminine word (Asmelash, 2020).

Part of the French Academy's charge is to guard the French language against the intrusion of other languages, especially English, but also Arabic, German, Tahitian, and others. So instead of saying, "un restaurant en self-service" (a self-service restaurant), the correct French is "un restaurant en libre-service" as posted on February 2, 2017.

In contrast, in Germany, German takes a *descriptive approach* to language. The Duden dictionary is published every four or five years and describes the German language as

it has been changed by German speakers. Thus, Duden has added "blog" to its dictionary as German speakers use that word instead of the more German equivalent: *digitale Netztagebücher*. Although the German Language Society was upset that so many new words borrowed from English appeared in Duden, others see the German language changing as it incorporates these new terms. For Duden, how German speakers use language should determine which terms it includes. Duden takes a descriptive approach because it attempts to describe common usage instead of dictating what usage is correct. German speakers prefer to say "apps" rather than "Anwendungen für mobile Endgeräte," and so Duden recognizes this difference by including the English word. With the coronavirus pandemic, many Germans are using both the masculine *der* and the neuter *das* when communicating about the coronavirus. When the SARS virus was prevalent in 2013, Germans used *das*, and COVID-19 is a related virus. Yet some Germans are using *der*, and when the next Duden is published, we'll find out which is prevailing ("'Covid-19' bald im Duden?," 2020).

SOURCES: Académie Française. (2017, February 2). *Self-service.* http://www.academie-francaise.fr/dire-ne-pas-dire

Asmelash, L. (2020, May 16). Arbiters of the French language say "Covid" is feminine. *CNN.* https://www.cnn.com/2020/05/16/world/academie-franciase-covid-feminine-trnd/index.html

"Covid-19" bald im Duden? (2020, May 9). *Taggeschau.de.* https://www.tagesschau.de/inland/corona-duden-101.html#:~:text=Social%20Distancing%2C%20Corona%2DParty%20oder,einigen%20Wochen%20noch%20unbekannt%20waren.&text=%22Hei%C3%9Fer%20Kandidat%20f%C3%BCr%20die%20Aufnahme,Redaktion%2C%20Kathrin%20Kunkel%2DRazum

Sauerbrey, A. (2013, September 25). How do you say "blog" in German? *New York Times.* http://www.nytimes.com/2013/09/26/opinion/how-do-you-say-blog-in-german.html?_r=0

Willsher, K. (2016, February 5). Not the oignon: Fury as France changes 2,000 spellings and drops some accents. *The Guardian.* https://www.theguardian.com/world/2016/feb/05/not-the-oignon-fury-france-changes-2000-spellings-ditches-circumflex

Phonology: Sounds **Phonology** is the study of the sounds that compose individual languages and how those sounds communicate meaning. Basic sound units are called *phonemes*. They include vowels, consonants, and diphthongs (pairs of letters that operate as one, such as *th*). Different languages can use different phonemes. For example, French does not have the *th* sound. As a result, many native French speakers find it difficult to pronounce "this" or "that." Similarly, in Japanese, a phoneme that is between *r* and *l* is the closest equivalent to the English *r* sound. For more information about phonology, see https://www.internationalphoneticassociation.org, the home page of the International Phonetic Association.

Syntax: Rules **Syntax** refers to the rules that govern word order. Because of the English rules of syntax, the sentences "The young boy hit the old man" and "The old man hit the young boy" have different meanings, even though they contain identical words. Syntax also governs how words of various categories (nouns, adjectives, verbs) are combined into clauses, which in turn combine into sentences. Whether or not we are conscious of them, most of us regularly follow certain rules about combining words—for example, that the verb and subject in a sentence have to agree, so people say "the pencil *is* on the table," not "the pencil *are* on the table." Because of these rules, people combine words consistently in ways that make sense and make communication possible.

Semantics: Meaning **Semantics** is the study of meaning, which is an important component of communication. To illustrate the effect of syntax compared with the effect of meaning, Noam Chomsky (1957), an important scholar in the field of linguistics, devised this famous sentence: "Colorless green ideas sleep furiously" (p. 15). This sentence is acceptable in terms of English grammar, but on the semantic level it is nonsensical: Ideas logically cannot be either colorless or green (and certainly not both!), ideas don't sleep, and nothing sleeps furiously (does it?).

As you remember from Chapter 1, a central part of our definition of communication is the creation of shared meaning. For any given message, a number of factors contribute to the creation of its meaning. Perhaps most important are the words the speaker chooses. For example, did you have a friend in high school who always gave the right answer in class, got excellent grades, and always seemed to have a wealth of information at his fingertips? What word would you use to describe this friend: *smart*, *hardworking*, *well-read*, or *intelligent*? Because each word has a slightly different meaning, you try to choose the one that most accurately characterizes your friend. However, in choosing the "right" words, you have to consider the two types of meaning that words convey: *denotative* and *connotative*—terms that we also discussed in Chapter 1.

The **denotative meaning** refers to the dictionary, or literal, meaning of a word and is usually the agreed-on meaning for most speakers of the language. Referring back to our description of your friend, a denotative definition might describe *kind* as benevolent and *considerate* as empathetic for another's emotions or circumstances. Does either word exactly capture how you would describe your friend? If not, which word does?

Words also carry **connotative meanings**, which are the affective or interpretive meanings attached to them. Using the previous example, the connotative meaning of the word *considerate* implies being mindful and caring about someone else's feelings, so it might not be the best choice to describe someone who is self-centered and inconsiderate in communicating with others.

Pragmatics: Language in Use Just like phonology, syntax, and semantics, the field of **pragmatics** seeks to identify patterns or rules people follow when they use language appropriately. In the case of pragmatics, however, the emphasis is on how language is used in specific situations to accomplish goals (Nofsinger, 1999). For example, scholars who study pragmatics might seek to understand the rules for

phonology
The study of the sounds that compose individual languages and how those sounds communicate meaning.

syntax
The rules that govern word order.

semantics
The study of meaning.

denotative meaning
The dictionary, or literal, meaning of a word.

connotative meaning
The affective or interpretive meanings attached to a word.

pragmatics
Field of study that emphasizes how language is used in specific situations to accomplish goals.

communicating appropriately in a sorority, a faculty meeting, or an evangelical church. They would do this by examining communication that is successful and unsuccessful in each setting. They might also ask what this communication does in specific contexts and its purpose or goal. The three units of study for scholars of pragmatics are *speech acts, conversational rules,* and *contextual rules*. Let's examine what each contributes to communication.

speech act theory

Branch of pragmatics that suggests that when people communicate, they do not just say things, they also *do* things with their words.

Speech Acts   One branch of pragmatics, **speech act theory**, looks closely at the seven language functions described previously and suggests that when people communicate, they do not just say things, they also do things with their words. For example, speech act theorists argue that when you say, "I bet you ten dollars the Yankees win the World Series," you aren't just saying something, you actually are doing something. That something you are doing is making a bet, or entering into an agreement that will result in an exchange of money. You are also performing the act of challenging the other person to engage in the bet, or put their money where their mouth is.

One common speech act is the request. A recent study examined one type of request that occurs primarily in U.S. family contexts—the common practice of "nagging" (Boxer, 2002). Nagging (repeated requests by one family member to another) often concerns household chores and is usually a source of conflict. The researcher found that nagging requires several sequential acts. First, there is an initial request, which is usually given in the form of a command ("Please take out the garbage") or a hedged request ("Do you think you can take out the garbage this evening?"). If the request is not granted, it is repeated as a reminder (after some lapse of time), which often includes an allusion to the first request. ("Did you hear me? Can you please take out the garbage?") When a reminder is repeated again (the third stage), it becomes nagging and usually involves a scolding or a threat, depending on the relationship—for example, whether the exchange is between parent and child ("This is the last time I'm going to ask you, take out the garbage!") or between relational partners ("Never mind, I'll do it myself!").

▼ Nagging is one common type of speech act that occurs in U.S. family contexts.

The researcher found that men were rarely involved in nagging, and she suggests that this is because men are perceived as having more power and are therefore able to successfully request and gain compliance from another family member without resorting to nagging. She also notes that children can have power (if they refuse to comply with a request despite their lack of status) and a parent can lack power despite having status. The researcher also found that nagging mostly occurs in our intimate relationships. She concludes that, by nagging, we lose power—but without power, we are forced into nagging; thus, it seems to be a vicious cycle! The study shows that what we *do* with words affects our relationships.

Understanding the meaning of various speech acts often requires understanding context and culture (Sbisa, 2002). For this reason, people may agree on what is *said* but disagree on what is *meant*. For example, the other day Katy said to her roommate Mike, "I have been so busy I haven't even had time to do the dishes." He replied, "Well, I'm sorry, but I have been busy, too." What did he think Katy was "doing" with her utterance? When they discussed this interaction, Katy explained that she was making an excuse, whereas Mike said he heard a criticism—that because *she* hadn't had time to do the dishes, *he* should have. Thus, messages may have different meanings or "do" different things, from different persons' viewpoints. This difference lies in the sender's and receiver's interpretations of the statement. Most misunderstandings arise not around what was said—but around what was done or meant.

As we have seen, speech acts may be direct or indirect. That is, speech acts such as requests can be framed more (or less) clearly and directly. Let's suppose that you want your partner to feed the dog. You may directly ask: "Would you feed the dog?" Or you could state an order: "Feed the dog!" On the other hand, you may communicate the same information indirectly: "Do you know if the dog was fed?" or "I wonder if the dog was fed." Finally, you may make your request indirectly: "It would be nice if someone fed the dog" or "Do you think the dog looks hungry?"

Which do you think is better—to communicate directly or indirectly? This is actually a trick question. The answer is: It depends—on the situation and the cultural context. Consider what you do with words to get someone else to act. Although direct requests and questions may be clearer, they also can be less polite. Ordering someone to feed the dog makes one's desire clearly and unequivocally known, but at the same time, it can be seen as rude and domineering.

Research shows that U.S. Americans tend to be more indirect in their requests when compared to Mexicans (Pinto & Raschio, 2007) but probably not as indirect as many Asians (Kim, 2002). However, when expressing disagreement, most U.S. Americans tend to be more direct than most Asians. A study investigated how Malaysians handled disagreements in business negotiation and concluded that the Malays' opposition was never direct or on record but always indirect and implied. Despite their disagreements with the other party, they honored the other, always balancing power with politeness (Paramasivam, 2007). A pragmatic approach reminds us that how language is used always depends on the situation and cultural context. We'll discuss more cross-cultural differences in communication practices further in Chapter 7.

Conversational Rules Conversational rules govern the ways in which communicators organize conversation. For example, one rule of conversation in U.S. English is that if someone asks you a question, you should provide an answer. If you do not know the answer, others expect you to at least reply, "I don't know" or "Let me think about it." However, in some cultures and languages, answers to questions are not obligatory. For

▼ Conversational rules—such as turn-taking—govern the way we communicate and vary somewhat from context to context.

example, in some Native American cultures, such as that of the Warm Spring Indians of Oregon, questions may be answered at a later time (with little reference to the previous conversation) or not answered at all (Philips, 1990).

Perhaps the most researched conversational rules involve turn-taking. The most basic rule for English language speakers, and many others, is that only one person speaks at a time. People may tolerate some overlap between their talk and another's, but typically they expect to be able to have their say without too much interruption (Schegloff, 2000). Still, as a refinement of this point, Susanna Kohonen (2004)

found in her cross-cultural study of turn-taking that conversationalists were more tolerant of overlaps in social settings, such as at parties or when hanging out with friends, than in more formal settings. Also, in computer-mediated communication, turn-taking is influenced by face-to-face interactions but uses strategic pauses more to regulate speech (Anderson et al., 2010). In other words, although computer-mediated communication is not face-to-face, the communication interaction rules mimic face-to-face interactions; however, the different context results in slightly different rules. Different cultures may recognize different turning points, or appropriate places for another speaker to resume communication. Whereas English speakers focus on grammatical stops, Korean speakers focus on a lexical boundary where action completion occurs (Park, 2016). Thus, sometimes the context influences conversational rules. We discuss contextual rules next.

Other rules for turn-taking determine who is allowed to speak (Sacks et al., 1978). For example, if you "have the floor," you can generally continue to speak. When you are finished, you can select someone else. You can do this either by asking a question—"So Sue, what is your opinion?"—or by looking at another person as you finish talking. If you don't have the floor but wish to speak, you can begin speaking just as the current speaker completes a turn.

The turn-allocation system works amazingly well most of the time. Occasionally, however, people do not follow these implicit rules. For example, the current speaker could select the next speaker by directing a question to her, but someone else could interrupt and "steal" the floor. Also, some speakers are quicker to grab the talk turn, which allows them more opportunities to speak. Then speakers who are slower to begin a turn or take the floor have fewer opportunities to contribute to the conversation. They may feel left out or resent the other speakers for monopolizing the conversation.

Contextual Rules   No matter what language or dialect you speak, your use of language varies depending on the communication situation (Mey, 2001). For example, you probably wouldn't discuss the same topics in the same way at a funeral as you would in a meeting at your workplace, in a courtroom, or at a party. What would happen if you did? For example, telling jokes and laughing at a party are typically acceptable, whereas those same jokes and laughing might be interpreted negatively in a courtroom or at a funeral. One challenge for pragmatics scholars, then, is uncovering the implicit communication rules that govern different settings. As noted previously, communication pragmatics also vary by culture. For example, in some houses of worship, appropriate verbal behavior involves talking quietly or not at all, acting subdued, and listening without responding, but in others, people applaud, sing exuberantly, and respond loudly with exclamations like "Amen!" Neither set of communication rules is "right"; each is appropriate to its own setting and cultural context.

As you can see, verbal language is far more than the words people use; it also includes the sounds and meanings of those words and the rules individuals use for arranging words and for communicating in particular settings. Moreover, speakers differ in the ways they use language to communicate. They also differ in the ways they enunciate

▼ Pragmatics involves understanding the implicit communication rules that apply in one setting or another.

their words and how they present their ideas. For example, Southerners "drawl" their vowels, whereas New Englanders drop the *r* after theirs; some speakers are extremely direct, and others are not. What accounts for these differences? We explore the answers in the next section.

**Journal Prompt 4.2:
Functions of Language**
What are the seven functions of language? Give an example that illustrates how each works.

The Individual and Verbal Communication: Influences

4.3 Identify examples of several major influences on verbal communication.

As we saw in Chapter 2, our communication is influenced by our identities and the various cultures to which we belong. In turn, our communication helps shape these identities. When identities influence several aspects of language, we say that speakers have a distinct **dialect**, a variation of a language distinguished by its **lexical choice** (vocabulary), grammar, and pronunciation. In other instances, the influence of identity is less dramatic, and speakers vary only in some pronunciations or word choices. In this section we examine how identities related to gender, age, regionality, ethnicity and race, and education and occupation shape language use.

dialect
A variation of a language distinguished by its vocabulary, grammar, and pronunciation.

lexical choice
Vocabulary.

Gender

Growing up male or female may influence the way you communicate in some situations because men and women are socialized to communicate in specific ways. In fact—as exemplified in the popularity of books like *Men Are from Mars, Women Are from Venus* (Gray, 2012)—many people believe that English-speaking men and women in the United States speak different dialects. These beliefs are reinforced by media depictions that tend to present stereotypical depictions of men and women in magazines, on television, and in movies. For example, one team of researchers reviewed how journal articles talked about gender differences in the past 50 years and found that because people are more interested in hearing about differences than similarities, shows and books that emphasize these differences tend to sell better and receive wider recognition (Sagrestano et al., 1998).

Even scholarly research tends to focus on, and sometimes exaggerate, the importance of sex differences; some researchers have reported that women's verbal style is often described as supportive, egalitarian, personal, and disclosive, whereas men's is characterized as instrumental, competitive, and assertive (Mulac et al., 2001; Wood, 2002), and as we saw in Chapter 2, there is some evidence that differences exist in social media "talk." But other research refutes this claim. A review of studies comparing males and females on a large array of psychological and communication differences, including self-disclosure and interruptions,

▼ Televisions shows, such as *The Real Housewives of Orange County*, tend to present stereotypical depictions of men and women.

revealed few significant differences (Hyde, 2006). How can these contradictory findings be explained? To begin, many studies of gender differences ask participants to report on their perceptions or ask them to recall men's and women's conversational styles (e.g., Aylor & Dainton, 2004). This approach can be problematic because people's perceptions are not always accurate. For example, Nancy Burrell and her colleagues (1988) argue that persistent, stereotypical, gender-based expectations likely influence people's perceptions that men and women behave or communicate differently even when few behavioral differences exist. More recently, Heilman et al. (2010) found that gender stereotypes were invoked even more strongly when workers were told they would communicate using computer-mediated communication rather than face-to-face.

How do these faulty perceptions arise about communication differences between men and women? Two important contributors are a person's perceptions of their own gendered communication and media representations of men's and women's communication. Experts assert that gender-based perceptions are hard to change, whether or not the perceptions are true. For example, the negative stereotype of the talkative woman is persistent. In a 2007 study, students were shown a videotaped conflict between a man and a woman and were asked to rate the two on likability and competence. In different versions of the video, the researchers varied how much the man and woman each talked. As the researchers expected, viewers rated the couple as less likable when they saw the woman doing more of the talking. And the man who talked more was rated as most competent (Sellers et al., 2007). Even though this negative stereotype persists, many studies have shown that not only do women generally *not* talk more than men, actually the opposite is true—men tend to be more talkative in many situations (Leaper & Ayres, 2007). In addition, the stereotype persists that women are more "kind, helpful, sympathetic, and concerned about others," whereas men are seen as "aggressive, forceful, independent, and decisive" (Heilman, 2001, p. 658). Furthermore, these gender stereotypes can create differential treatment in the workplace and in social situations.

When people adapt to a specific audience, they are often adjusting to the communication style of the more powerful members of that audience. Thus, if powerful members of the audience use more direct or task-focused language, so might the speaker. In addition to adapting their communication style, people also often use more deferential or tentative language when communicating with more powerful people. Both men and women adapt to these power differences; thus both groups are more likely to use tentative language with their bosses than with their siblings. Women use language that is more tentative overall because generally they have lower status, and people with lower status are not typically expected to make strong, assertive statements (Reid et al., 2003). Similarly, women tend to use more "filler words" (such as *like* or *well*) and more conditional words (*would, should, could*) (Mehl & Pennebaker, 2003).

Researchers have wondered whether gender differences in conversations are a consequence of interacting with a partner who uses a particular style of communication. For example, if you encourage another person to talk by nodding your head in agreement, asking questions, etc., you are using a facilitative style of communication. To explore this question, social psychologists Annette Hannah and Tamar Murachver assigned male and female partners who were strangers to each other to meet and talk several times. After the first conversation, their communication styles were judged by outside observers to be either facilitative or nonfacilitative; and the researchers found that, regardless of gender, participants responded to each other in ways that mirrored their partner's style (Hannah & Murachver, 2007).

Over time, however, in subsequent conversations, the women and men shifted their speech toward more stereotypically gendered patterns; that is, the men talked more, for longer times, whereas women increased their use of minimal responses, reduced the amount they spoke, and asked more questions. In other words, the women increased their facilitative style of speech while the men decreased theirs. Discussing their findings, the researchers pose several questions: Why are women more facilitative in their speech? Why do they talk less when talking with men? Do they feel threatened or insecure? Are they less comfortable in talking more than men? Perhaps women feel that dominating conversations with men has negative social consequences and, therefore, they encourage men to do the talking—an explanation that would be confirmed by the previous study we mentioned, where students negatively evaluated couples in which the women talked more than the men. The researchers provide no definitive explanation, but note, as do we, that gender differences are complicated (Hannah & Murachver, 2007).

In conclusion, women and men do show differences in their communication styles, and much of this difference likely is attributable to differences in power, status, and expectations in communication situations.

Age

You may not think of age as affecting language use, but it does, particularly when it comes to word choice. For example, you might have talked about "the cooties" when you were a child, but you probably don't now. Moreover, children have a whole vocabulary to describe "naughty topics," especially related to bodily functions. Yet, most adults do not use those words. Adolescents also develop vocabulary that they use throughout their teenage years and then drop during early adulthood. Adolescents have described highly valued people and things as "cool," "righteous," "bad," "hot," "lit," "lewk" and "phat," depending on the generation and context. This distinct vocabulary helps teenagers feel connected to their peers and separate from their parents and other adults. For other examples of teen slang terms, see *Did You Know? Contemporary Slang.*

The era in which you grew up also influences your vocabulary. As you age, you continue to use certain words that were common when you were growing up, even if they have fallen out of use. This is called the **cohort effect** and refers to common denominators of a group that was born and reared in the same general period. For example, your grandparents and their contemporaries may say "cool" or "neat" and your parents may say "awesome" when referring to something they really like. What do you say? Recent research suggests that young girls (particularly young, urban, upwardly mobile) are the trendsetters in language use both for their own and other cohorts. The most recent examples are their use of "I can't even . . ." and the "vocal fry" or "creaky voice" (made by compressing the vocal chords and reducing the airflow through the larynx, makes speech to sound rattled or "creaky"). Zooey Deschanel and Kim Kardashian slip in and out of this register, as does Britney Spears, but it has been observed in college-aged women across the country. Women have long tended to be the linguistic innovators. Linguists say that if you want to see the future of a language find a young, urban woman. We have women to thank for "up-talk"—the rising intonation at the end of a sentence that has spread into mainstream speech—the discourse marker "like," and now, vocal fry (Arana, 2013; Cohen, 2014).

cohort effect
The influence of shared characteristics of a group that was born and reared in the same general period.

DID YOU KNOW?
Contemporary Slang

While we are accustomed to hearing many of the new slang words that appear as abbreviations in texting and other Internet usage, there are many others that that we might not recognize. For example, you are probably familiar with "bff" or "best friends forever" or "kk" for "okay, okay" or "it's cool." But have you ever seen 770880? In Chinese, this is equivalent to XOXO. What about AMHA? This is the French equivalent to IMHO or "in my humble opinion." Different languages have developed different slang to communicate with others, and these slang terms may not be distinguishable beyond their language group. Other languages have adapted to new technological environments, just as English has.

People's communication skills and the meanings they attribute to concepts also vary because of their age. Why? Older people are more cognitively developed and have had more experiences; therefore, they tend to view concepts differently than do younger people, especially children (Pennebaker & Stone, 2003). For example, children typically engage in egocentric speech patterns (Piaget, 1952). This means that they cannot adapt their communication to their conversational partners nor understand that others may feel or view the world differently. Children lack the number of constructs adults have. For example, young children have little concept of future or past time, so understanding what might happen next week or month is difficult for them. Consequently, parents usually adapt their communication when trying to help children understand some event in the future.

Regionality

Geographical location also strongly influences people's language use. The most common influence is on pronunciation. For example, how do you pronounce the word "oil"? In parts of New York it is pronounced somewhat like "earl," whereas in areas of the South it is pronounced more like "awl," and in the West it is often pronounced "oyl" as in "Olive Oyl." Sometimes regionality affects more than just accent, leading to regional dialects. Why do these differences arise?

Historically, verbal differences developed wherever people were separated by a geographical boundary—whether it was mountains, lakes, rivers, deserts, oceans— or some social boundary, such as race, class, or religion (Fromkin & Rodman, 1983). Moreover, people tended to speak similarly to those around them. For example, in the eighteenth century, residents of Australia, North America, and England had relatively little contact with one another; consequently, they developed recognizably different dialects even though they all spoke the same language. Typically, the more isolated a group, the more distinctive their dialect.

In the United States, dialectical differences in English originally arose because two groups of English colonists settled along the East Coast. The colonists who settled in the South, near present-day Virginia, primarily came from Somerset and Gloucestershire—both western counties in England—and they brought with them an accent with strongly voiced *s* sounds and with the *r* strongly pronounced after vowels. In contrast, the colonists who settled in the north, what we now call New England, came from midland counties such as Essex, Kent, and London, where people spoke a dialect that did not pronounce the *r* after vowels, a feature still common to many New England dialects (Crystal, 2003). See Figure 4.1 for an interesting outgrowth of U.S. local dialects.

Other waves of immigration have occurred over the past four hundred years, increasing dialectical diversity in the United States. Each group of immigrants brings a distinctive way of speaking and culture-specific communication rules. Some groups, especially those who have remained somewhat isolated since their arrival, maintain much of their original dialect; an example is the inhabitants of Tangier Island in the Chesapeake Bay (Crystal, 2003). Other groups' dialects have assimilated with the dialects of their neighbors to form new dialects. Thus, the seventeenth-century "western" English dialect of Virginia has become the southern drawl of the twenty-first century.

Today the world is a global village, so people all over the country (and, for that matter, all over the world) are able to speak frequently with one another and have access to similar media. Nonetheless, according to a recent comprehensive study, local dialects are stronger than ever (Labov, 2005; Preston, 2003). Language professor Julie Sedivy (2012) notes that: "It may seem surprising, but in this age where geographic mobility and instant communication have increased our exposure to people outside of our neighborhoods or towns, American regional dialects are pulling further apart from each other, rather than moving closer together." Do you have a recognizable regional linguistic dialect?

Figure 4.1 Generic Names for Soft Drinks by County

The terms we use to refer to soft drinks also vary by region in the United States.

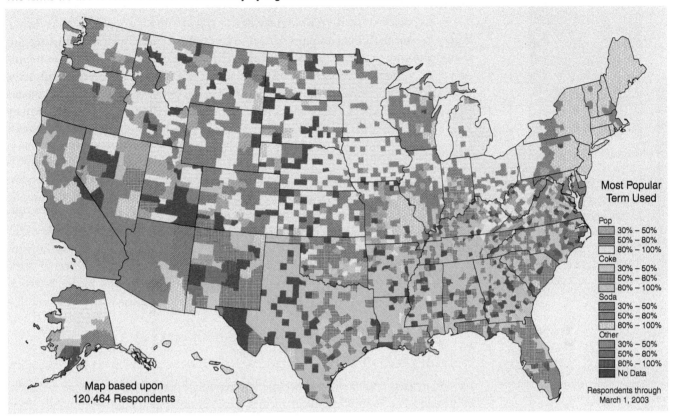

Most Popular Term Used

Pop
- 30% – 50%
- 50% – 80%
- 80% – 100%

Coke
- 30% – 50%
- 50% – 80%
- 80% – 100%

Soda
- 30% – 50%
- 50% – 80%
- 80% – 100%

Other
- 30% – 50%
- 50% – 80%
- 80% – 100%
- No Data

Map based upon 120,464 Respondents

Respondents through March 1, 2003

Ethnicity and Race

One's ethnicity can influence one's verbal style in a number of ways. In the United States, English is a second or colanguage for many citizens. This, of course, influences syntax, accent, and word choice. For example, if one is Latino, Latina, or Latinx and learns Spanish either before or at the same time as one learns English, one may use the same syntax for both. Thus, Spanish speakers may place adjectives after nouns (*the house little*) when they are speaking English because that is the rule for Spanish. The reverse can also occur: When English speakers speak Spanish, they have a tendency to place adjectives before nouns (*la pequeña casa*), which is the rule for English but not for Spanish.

Speakers' ethnicity can also influence their general verbal style. For example, Jewish Americans may engage in a style of talking about problems that non-Jews perceive as complaining (Bowen, 2012); some Native American tribes use teasing as a form of public rebuke (Shutiva, 2012); and some Chinese Americans who live in the southern United States are particularly likely to let other speakers choose conversational topics (Gong, 2012). When two ethnic or racial groups speak the same language but use different syntax, lexical items, or verbal style, one or both of the groups may view the other's verbal style as incorrect, as a failed attempt at proper speech rather than as a dialect with its own rules (Ellis & Beattie, 1986). Sometimes nonstandard ways of communicating can create important bonds with others in a cultural group (see *It Happened to Me: Luca*).

These views can have important real-life implications—political and monetary. Take the controversy about **African American Vernacular English**—a version of English that has its roots in West African, Caribbean, and U.S. slave languages. There is no agreed-on definition of African American Vernacular English; some linguists emphasize the international nature of the language (as a linguistic consequence of the African slave trade); others stress that it is a variety of English (e.g., the equivalent of Black English) or as different from English and viewed as an independent language.

African American Vernacular English

A version of English that has its roots in West African, Caribbean, and U.S. slave languages.

Yet we should also keep in mind that "there is no single and correct way to be 'African American.' These identities are negotiated in context and situationally emergent" (Hecht et al., 2003, p. 2).

In his book *You Are An African American, so Why Are You Talking Like a White Person,* Jeffrey Walker (2010) encourages African Americans to practice **code switching**—or change the way that they speak in different situations. Code switching is an important linguistic practice that helps speakers of different languages and dialects to change the way that they speak to communicate more effectively in mainstream culture, while also demonstrating cultural group membership in other situations. For example, some African Americans may use African American Vernacular English when speaking in social settings with other African Americans to demonstrate

It Happened to Me
Luca

I grew up in South Philadelphia, which was an Italian American area. Like many other Italian American families, my parents moved to the suburbs later. We spoke a type of Italian, but the Italians that I've met from Italy don't understand our way of speaking Italian. If people ask, I always say that I don't speak Italian. I think we speak a regional dialect in Italian, but maybe we've changed the language over time as we lived in Philadelphia. I know others who are from South Philadelphia because we communicate with each other in South Philadelphia Italian. There's a bond there.

their community membership, but use a more standard English when speaking in a professor context.

code switching
The practice of changing language or dialect to accommodate to the communication situation.

Education and Occupation

We will discuss education and occupation together because they are often mutually influencing. For example, medical doctors speak a similar language because they share a profession, but also because they were educated similarly. Typically, the more educated people are, the more similarly they speak (Hudson, 1983). Thus, larger dialect differences occur between Easterners and Midwesterners if they have not been to college than if they have doctoral degrees. This does not mean that all lawyers talk the same or that all professors speak similarly; rather, it suggests that differences become less pronounced as people receive more education.

Education affects dialect in part because any given university or college attracts people from different parts of the country. Therefore, college students have contact with a variety of dialects. At the same time, as students attend college they develop similar vocabularies from their shared experiences and learn similar terms in their classes. For example, you may never have used the term *dyad* to refer to two people before you went to college, but this is a term you might encounter in a range of courses, including psychology, sociology, anthropology, and communication.

To sum up, then, various features of language—phonology, syntax, semantics, and pragmatics—contribute to the development of meaning in verbal communication. These features combine with individual influences in language use, such as gender, age, and level of education, to create one's specific communication style. However, we have not yet covered every aspect of verbal communication. We now turn to the influence of societal forces on verbal communication.

Your occupation also influences the specialized terms you use to communicate. The specialized terms that develop in many

▼ Physicians, like members of other professions, develop specialized terms called *jargon.*

DID YOU KNOW?
Argot

Often minority communities have developed their own languages to communicate with each other. In England, gay men developed a language called Polari to communicate with other gay men as well as identify other men as gay. When homosexuality was legalized in England and Wales in 1967, Polari lost its usefulness and slowly disappeared.

Today, Lubunca serves a similar purpose in the Turkish language. In Turkey, "the rise in popularity of a secret language, Lubunca (pronounced looboonja), that is spoken by people from within the queer community is no luxury, but a necessity" (Wissing, 2020). This way of speaking Turkish is used by sex workers and trans people as well as cis-gendered gay men and others who identify as LGBTQIA+ or sexual minorities.

These are not separate languages, but function as ways of communicating in the dominant language that connect members of a marginalized community. The technical term for these other ways of speaking a language is **argot**. Typically, argot is not understood outside of that community. Unlike jargon, argot serves important communication functions for marginalized or stigmatized groups that need ways of communicating to survive in a hostile environment.

SOURCES: Polari: The secret language gay men used to survive. (2018, February 12). *BBC News*. Retrieved July 27, 2020 from https://www.bbc.com/culture/article/20180212-polari-the-code-language-gay-men-used-to-survive

Wissing, R. (2020, Summer). The secret language used by LGBTQ people in Turkey. *Attitude*. https://attitude.co.uk/article/the-secret-language-used-by-lgbtq-people-in-turkey-1/23524/?s=09

professions are called **jargon**. Lawyers routinely speak of *torts*, *depositions*, and *ex parte*. Physicians speak of *contusions* (bruises), *sequelae* (results), and *hemorrhagic stroke* (a stroke where a blood vessel bursts). In fact, most occupations have their own jargon. In addition to influencing your lexical choices, your occupation may also influence your overall communication style—including tone of voice and some nonverbal behaviors. For example, nursery school teachers are often recognizable not only by their vocabulary but also by the rhythm, volume, and expressivity of their communication style. Sometimes jargon is developed by marginalized or stigmatized cultural groups to help them survive in a hostile environment. See *Did You Know? Argot*.

jargon
The specialized terms that develop in many professions.

argot
A type of jargon used by marginalized or stigmatized communities.

Journal Prompt 4.3: Influences on Dialect
How do our region, gender, age, ethnicity and race, and education and occupation influence the way we speak?

The Individual, Verbal Communication, and Society: Language, Perception, and Power

4.4 **Describe the relationships between language, perception, and power.**

How do societal forces influence verbal communication? Culture and power are two of the most important influences. Culture impacts verbal communication primarily through its influence on language and perception. As we saw in Chapter 3, perception plays a key role in communication. Power is connected to verbal communication because within society, some language styles are viewed as more powerful, with consequences for both the powerful and the powerless.

Language and Perception

Scholars have long argued about the influence of language and culture on perception. The central issue they have debated is whether the words a culture has available to it influence how its members see and perceive the world around them. For example, the English language expresses action in the past, present, and future. Thus, English speakers may say, "Alan went to the library" (past), "Alan is at the library" (present), or "Alan will be going to the library" (future). In contrast, Japanese makes no distinction between the present and future. Although the verb for "went" is *ikimashita*, the verb used for both "is" and "will be going" is the same, *ikimasu*. Because English and Japanese have two different verb structures, scholars have questioned whether English speakers and Japanese speakers think about present and future actions in different ways. Scholars who have debated this relationship between language and perception generally fall into two camps: the *nominalists* and the *relativists*.

Nominalists claim that any idea can be expressed in any language and that the structure and vocabulary of the language do not influence the speaker's perception of the world. According to nominalists, English and Japanese may express present and future in different ways, but English speakers and Japanese speakers still understand the distinction.

In contrast, the **relativists** argue not only that language serves as a way for us to voice our ideas but that, in addition, it "is itself the shaper of ideas, the guide for the individual's mental activity" (Hoijer, 1994, p. 194). This idea is the basis for the **Sapir-Whorf hypothesis**. The Sapir-Whorf hypothesis argues that the language people speak determines the way they see the world. Adherents to this hypothesis believe language is like a prison because it constrains the ways individuals can perceive the world (Deutscher, 2010). According to this hypothesis, the distinction between the present and the future is not as clear-cut for Japanese speakers as it is for English speakers. Ignor Krupnik, an anthropologist at the Smithsonian Natural History Museum, was able to identify "more than 100 terms for sea ice alone in the Yupik language" (Panko, 2016). Yupik is largely spoken in western and south central Alaska. As another example, surfers have many more words for the types of waves in the ocean than do nonsurfers (Scheibel, 1995); the Sapir-Whorf hypothesis argues that, because of this, surfers perceive more types of waves than do others.

So how much does language influence perception? The Sapir-Whorf hypothesis position has been challenged by a number of scholars who investigate the connection between language and how we think. They represent a modified relativist position on the relationship between language and perception. For example, Steven Pinker (2007), a renowned cognitive scientist, cautions against assuming a simplistic connection between language and thought and rejects the Sapir-Whorf assumption that the particular language we speak compels us to perceive the world in a particular way or prevents us from thinking in different ways. By looking at language from the perspective of our thoughts, Pinker shows that what may seem like arbitrary aspects of speech (such as "hunk" versus "goo") aren't arbitrary at all but rather are by-products of our evolved mental machinery. In sum, all languages have the formal and expressive power to communicate the ideas, beliefs, and desires of their users. From this vast range of possibilities, human communities select what they want to say and how they want to say it. This view allows for more freedom than indicated by the Sapir-Whorf hypothesis.

Language and Power

In many ways, language and power are inextricably connected. People in power get to define what languages and communication styles are appropriate. In addition, people who use language and communication according to the rules of the powerful may be able to increase their own power. This view of the relationship between language and power is explained by *cocultural theory*.

nominalists
Those who argue that any idea can be expressed in any language and that the structure and vocabulary of the language do not influence the speaker's perception of the world.

relativists
Those who argue that language not only serves as a way for us to voice our ideas but "is itself the shaper of ideas, the guide for the individual's mental activity."

Sapir-Whorf hypothesis
Idea that the language people speak determines the way they see the world (a relativist perspective).

Critical Thinking Prompt
Which viewpoint makes more sense to you—nominalist or relativist? Why?

▼ In the Yupik language, spoken by a Native Alaskan cultural group, there are more than 100 words for sea ice.

Cocultural theory explores the role of power in daily interactions using the five following assumptions:

cocultural theory

Explores the role of power in daily interactions.

1. In each society, a hierarchy exists that privileges certain groups of people; in the United States, these groups include men, European Americans, heterosexuals, the able-bodied, and middle- and upper-class people.

2. Part of the privilege these groups enjoy, often subconsciously, is being able to set norms for what types of communication are acceptable or not acceptable (Orbe, 1998). Consequently, communication patterns of the dominant groups (in the United States, rich, male, White, educated, straight) tend to be more highly valued. For example, the preferred communication practice in many large corporations is that used by White males—direct, to the point, task oriented, and unemotional (Kikoski & Kikoski, 1999).

3. Language maintains and reinforces the power of these dominant groups, again, mostly subconsciously. Thus, people whose speech does not conform to what is valued in society may be excluded or negatively stereotyped. As we noted previously, commentators sometimes characterize women's speech as sounding more tentative than male speech. Because society values male speech styles at work, women aspiring to corporate leadership positions may undertake a special effort to make their speech direct or tough enough, or to avoid being too cooperative or nurturing in their communication practices.

4. In the relationship realm, society tends to value a more female communication style, and men may be criticized for failing to communicate appropriately with their intimates. Remember that none of these language variations is inherently good or bad, powerful or powerless; it is the societal hierarchies that teach us how to view particular communication practices. Of course, not every White male is direct, to the point, and task oriented, nor does every woman speak tentatively at work. Nor is every woman supportive and self-disclosive and every man distant and terse in close relationships. These generalizations can help explain communication practices, but they should not solidify into stereotypes.

5. These dominant communication structures impede the progress of persons whose communication practices do not conform to the norms. For example, what are the consequences for women who do not conform to "male" communication norms in a corporation? Or for African Americans who do not conform to "White" communication norms of the organizations in which they work? Or for students who do not conform to the "middle-class" communication norms at a university? They may risk being labeled negatively ("not serious enough," "soft," "doesn't have what it takes") and marginalized.

We explore these ideas further in Chapter 8. Now, let's look at how these societal hierarchies affect attitudes toward words, accents, and dialects and how they impact identity labels.

Power and Words

Attitudes about power can be built into language by certain roots or by the structure of the language. Consider words such as *chairman* and *fireman* or the generic use of *he* and *man* to refer to people. In the past it was widely believed that it didn't matter whether we used masculine words to mean *human*, but in recent decades researchers discovered that people didn't think *human* when someone mentioned the word *man*—they thought about a man. Similarly, awareness of the inequality inherent in terms such as *Mr.* (not designating marital status) and *Mrs.* (which does) has resulted in the use of new, more equal terms such as *Ms.* and *he or she*. More recently, some have argued for the use of *they* instead of *he or she* to be more inclusive of all gender identifications (see Table 4.1), including the *Washington Post* and the American Dialect Society (Hess, 2016).

Although some languages, such as Japanese or Korean, are strongly gendered (meaning that traditionally, men and women used almost a separate language), English

Table 4.1   Gender-Neutral Language

Gender-Based	Gender-Neutral
he/she	they
congressman/congresswoman	member of Congress
policeman	police officer
mankind	humanity
Miss, Mrs.	Ms.
freshmen	first-year students
man the controls	take control
male nurse	nurse

androcentrism

The use of male experience as normative for humanity and female experience as emphasizing gender difference.

is less gendered, but it is still androcentric. **Androcentrism** is the pairing of maleness with humanity and the consequent attribution of gender difference to females—often to women's disadvantage. Scholars recently reviewed 50 years of psychology articles for androcentric bias. Although they found few uses of *he* for *human*, information was still portrayed in a way that emphasized male as the norm. Male data was placed first in tables, and gender differences were often described as female—subconsciously assuming that male is the norm and female is different. Researchers point out that being different is not necessarily harmful but probably reflects some of the underlying stereotypes (and societal hierarchies) we have discussed previously (Hegarty & Buechel, 2006).

What are the implications for students? We argue that it's not about freedom of speech or being overly politically correct but rather about audience and awareness. Gender-neutral language has gained support from most major textbook publishers and from professional and academic groups as well as major newspapers and law journals. As an English professor suggested, "You need to be able to express yourself according to their guidelines, and if you wish to write or speak convincingly to people who are influenced by the conventions of these contexts, you need to be conscious of their expectations."

Power and Accent

Where did people learn that a British English accent sounds upper crust and educated? Or that English as spoken with an Asian Indian accent is hard to understand? Why do communicators often stereotype Black English as sounding uneducated? Although these associations come from many sources, they certainly are prevalent in the media. People have become so accustomed to seeing and hearing these associations that they probably don't even question them. In fact, William Labov, a noted sociolinguist, refers to the practice of associating a dialect with the cultural attitudes toward it as "a borrowed prestige model." For example, until the 1950s, most Americans thought that British English was the correct way to speak English (Labov, 1980); even today, people continue to think that an English accent sounds refined and educated. By contrast, Southern drawls and Black English have become stigmatized so that today, people who speak them are often perceived negatively. For similar reasons, people often find the English accent of people from India (where English often is a first language) difficult to understand—as reported by our student in *It Happened to Me: Bart*.

Such language stereotypes can be "set off" in one's head before a person even speaks, when one *thinks*, generally because of the person's appearance, that the person will not speak standard English (Ruben, 2003). This is probably

It Happened to Me

Bart

I recently had a course taught by an Asian Indian professor, and it took me some time to understand his accent and form of speaking. Sometimes I thought he was mumbling, and sometimes his speech sounded so fast that I couldn't understand it. After a couple of classes, my hearing disciplined itself to understand him better. In the end, I realized he was a fine teacher.

DID YOU KNOW?
Language Discrimination

Should language discrimination be illegal? Are there jobs where speaking English with an accent would impair someone's ability to do the job? Does language discrimination happen outside employment as well?

Language discrimination includes interlanguage discrimination and intralanguage discrimination. Interlanguage discrimination happens when people are treated differently because of the languages that they speak. In countries with an official language, discrimination can occur against those who do not speak the official language(s). Intralanguage discrimination happens when people are treated differently because they speak in a way that is not considered "proper" or the dominant language. In the United States, for example, someone who speaks Hawaiian pidgin or African American Vernacular English may be treated differently than someone who speaks standard American English. Both kinds of discrimination can happen in job situations where someone is not hired or promoted because of an accent or is treated differently from other employees. Language discrimination can also happen in schools when students are forbidden to speak certain languages. In the United States, for example, some schools require students to speak English, not only in class but also outside class. Language discrimination can also happen in social settings when someone is rebuffed because of the way they speak.

In the United Kingdom, there is no "British accent" but many different accents. Much more than in the United States, these accent differences reflect people's social class backgrounds. In 2017, the Social Mobility Commission, a British government organization, released a report that showed that people from working-class backgrounds are paid an average of £6,800 (approximately $8,500 USD), or 17 percent, less than similar professionals from more-privileged backgrounds. This social class pay gap exists across the workforce, but the pay gap is highest in "finance (£13,713), medicine (£10,218), and IT (£4,736)" (or over $17,000 USD, $12,700 USD, and $5,900 USD, respectively). The chair of the commission noted that this study again demonstrates that British society remains very elitist and some accents are much preferred over others. "This report provides powerful new evidence that Britain remains a deeply elitist society." In a more recent study of attitudes toward 38 different British accents, a British sociolinguist found that the high-prestige accents have retained their status.

When we discriminate against people who speak in certain ways or speak certain languages, we are discriminating against the individuals, not just the accents or languages.

SOURCES: Social Mobility Commission. (2017, January 26). New research uncovers "class pay gap" in Britain's professions. https://www.gov.uk/government/news/new-research-uncovers-class-pay-gap-in-britains-professions

Sharma, D. (2019, November 25). British people still think some accents are smarter than others—what that means in the workplace. *The Conversation*. https://theconversation.com/british-people-still-think-some-accents-are-smarter-than-others-what-that-means-in-the-workplace-126964

what happened to our student, Bart. Once he adjusted to the Indian English accent, he found he could understand his Indian professor just fine. (For examples of accents from many different language backgrounds, go to http://accent.gmu.edu/index.php.)

How does language cause one group to become elevated and another denigrated? The answer lies partly in understanding the social forces of history and politics. The positive and negative associations about African American, White, and British English developed during the nineteenth and twentieth centuries when European Americans were establishing themselves as the powerful majority in the United States while passing legislation that subjugated African Americans and other minority groups. Thus, it is not surprising that the languages of these groups were viewed so differently. Similarly, the English spoken by people from India was negatively stereotyped as the aberrant language of the colonized because England was the colonial power in India until the mid-twentieth century. Similar attitudes can be seen toward immigrant groups today; their accented English is often stigmatized, sometimes leading to language discrimination and lawsuits, as illustrated in *Did You Know? Language Discrimination*.

Power and Identity Labels

The language labels that refer to particular identities also communicate important messages about power relations. Members of more powerful groups frequently invoke labels for members of other groups without input from those group members. For example, straight people label gays but rarely refer to themselves as "straight". White people use ethnic and racial labels to refer to others (*people of color, African American,* or *Black*) but rarely refer to themselves as *White.* This power to label seems "normal," so most people don't think twice about specifying that a physician is a "woman doctor" but never describing one as a "male doctor." Or they might identify someone as a gay teacher but not a White teacher (even if this teacher is both). People usually don't think about the assumptions that reflect societal power relations; in sum, individuals feel the need to mark minority differences, but they tend not to identify majority group membership.

Not only do the more powerful get to label the less powerful, but they may also use language labels to stigmatize them. However, the stigma comes from the power relations, not from the words themselves. For example, in the Polish language, the word *Polack* simply means "a man from Poland," but the stigma associated with the term comes from the severe discrimination practiced against Eastern Europeans in the early twentieth century, which led to jokes and stereotypes that exist to this day. The term *Oriental* originated when Western countries were attempting to colonize, and were at war with, Asian countries—and the connotative meaning was *exotic* and *foreign.* Today, many Asians and Asian Americans resent this label. Read about one of our student's opinions on the topic in *It Happened to Me: Hiroko.*

This resentment can make communication more difficult for Hiroko and those who use this term to refer to her. As this example reveals, understanding the dictionary meanings of words does not always reveal the impact of identity labels. Members of minority communities are the best informants on the communicative power of specific labels.

It Happened to Me
Hiroko

I get really tired of people referring to me as "Oriental." It makes me sound like a rug or a cuisine. I refer to myself as Asian American or Japanese American. I know people probably don't mean anything negative when they use it, but it makes me uncomfortable. If it's somebody I know well, I might ask them not to use that word, but usually I just don't say anything.

World English
English in its many forms internationally.

ALTERNATIVE VIEW
Do English Speakers Need to Learn Other Languages?

Today, English is the most widely spoken language in the world with slightly more speakers than Mandarin Chinese, but most people do not speak English as a native language. There are about 1.5 billion people who can speak English. This also means that there are billions more who do not.

As the most widely spoken language, English is spoken in many different ways, and, collectively, these ways of communicating in English are called **World English**. World English refers to the many ways that English is spoken around the world. For example, in countries where English is an official language, such as Australia, Ireland, Singapore, and South Africa, there are many differences in the ways English is spoken. Despite these differences, English is a powerful way of communicating in many places around the world. Today, among countries where English is not the native or official language, the ability to speak English can vary. The Netherlands is the most fluent in English.

Given the value that other people place on the ability to speak English, should native English speakers, such as U.S. Americans, learn other languages? Those who favor learning other languages point to a report by the American Council on Teaching Foreign Languages that notes that about one-fourth of U.S. employers have lost business opportunities because of language barriers. Advocates of U.S. Americans learning other languages also argue that knowing other languages enriches your life, especially in the twenty-first century. What do you think? If many people speak English around the world, is it important for English speakers to learn other languages?

SOURCES: Abbott, E. (2020, January 9). Why learning another language can change your life. *The Hill.* https://thehill.com/changing-america/enrichment/education/477414-why-learning-another-language-can-change-your-life

Where are the world's best English-speakers? (2019, December 4). *The Economist.* https://www.economist.com/graphic-detail/2019/12/04/where-are-the-worlds-best-english-speakers

Not everyone in an identity group has the same denotative meaning for a particular label. For example, some young women do not like to be called "girl"; they find it demeaning. Others are comfortable with this term. Some people view these calls for sensitivity in language as nothing more than unnecessary political correctness.

We can think about the nuances of our communication in English by learning other languages, but learning another language is a considerable effort. As English speakers, should we learn other languages? See *Alternative View: Do English Speakers Need to Learn Other Languages?* for a discussion of this issue.

Moreover, the power of labels can change over time. In an earlier age, many viewed the term *WASP* (White, Anglo-Saxon, Protestant) as a descriptor or even a positive label; now, however, it is seen as rather negative (Martin et al., 1999). The shift probably reflects the changing attitudes of Whites, who are now more aware of their ethnicity and the fact that they are not always the majority. Similarly, the term *Paddy* as in "paddy wagon" (a term for a police wagon) originally was a derogatory term; some older Irish Americans may still find it offensive. It reflected a stereotype, widely held 100 years ago, of Irish men as drunks who had to be carted off to jail. Now that discrimination (and stereotyping) against the Irish has all but disappeared, this term has lost much of its impact.

In summary, language, power, and societal forces are closely linked. The societal environment profoundly influences the way people perceive the world and the language choices available to them. Those in power set the language and communication norms, often determining what verbal communication style is deemed appropriate or inappropriate, elegant or uneducated. They frequently get to choose and use identity labels for those who are less powerful. Those whose language does not fit the standard, or who are the recipients of negative labels, may feel marginalized and resentful, leading to difficult communication interactions.

Critical Thinking Prompt
Think about labels and terms we have for males and females. Why do you think so many more negative terms exist for females than for males?

Journal Prompt 4.4:
Language and Power
How does power influence language, words, accent, and labels? Can you give examples of the role of power in language, words, accent, and labels?

Ethics and Verbal Communication

4.5 Identify examples of confirming communication, disconfirming communication, and hate speech.

We have already discussed a number of ethical issues related to verbal communication in this book. In Chapter 1, we argued that ethical communicators consider the benefit and/or harm associated with their messages. In this section, we examine one specific type of language whose use may harm individuals or relationships.

Hate Speech

In the United States, we place a high value on freedom of speech. We have codified this value into our legal system, beginning with the First Amendment to the Constitution. However, freedom of speech is always balanced by competing societal interests. As the familiar saying goes, freedom of speech does not include the right to shout "fire!" in a crowded theater. But what about the right to express negative opinions about others? In the 1980s and 1990s, as U.S. society became more aware

▼ Hate speech is legal in the United States, but many argue that it is unethical.

hate speech

Use of verbal communication to attack others based upon some social category.

of the ethics of minority rights, the term *hate speech* began to be used (American Civil Liberties Union, 1994). **Hate speech**, or the use of verbal communication to attack others based on some social category such as race, ethnicity, religion, or sexuality, is seen as threatening an entire group or inciting violence against members of these groups. In the United States, the First Amendment guarantee of free speech is generally used to protect against laws that would make hate speech illegal (Liptak, 2008). However, many argue that even if hate speech is legal, it is unethical.

Many countries view the use of verbal communication to attack, demean, and degrade other groups of people as not only unethical but also illegal. Canada's criminal code, for example, forbids speech, writing, and Internet postings that advocate genocide or that publicly incite hatred (Media Awareness Network, n.d.). As another example, in some European countries it is illegal to deny that the Holocaust occurred. In February 2017, an Austrian woman was found guilty of denying the Holocaust happened when she criticized a Facebook posting of the German soccer team commemorating the liberation of Auschwitz, stating they were "spreading lies" ("Austrian woman," 2017). Also in February 2017, Amazon came under attack for selling books that deny the Holocaust in countries where it is illegal to do so, but later took down the books from their sites in France and Germany; they are still available in the United Kingdom and the United States (Gamp, 2017; Holmes, 2017). Although it is not illegal to deny the Holocaust happened per se in the United Kingdom, in 2019, Alison Chabloz was convicted in the United Kingdom under the U.K. Communications Act of 2003 that makes it illegal to send any message "'that is grossly offensive or of an indecent, obscene or menacing character'" (quoted in Sharon, 2019).

Sometimes even speaking another language from others can invoke anger and even physical assault. In February 2020, a mother and her daughter in East Boston, a neighborhood that is more than half Latinx, were attacked by two women for speaking Spanish. According to the mother, "The two women yelled: 'This is America!

DID YOU KNOW?

Facebook and Hate Speech

In 2020, a boycott arose that called on companies to stop advertising on Facebook because of the perception that Facebook was unable to deal with hate speech, lies, and other misinformation. #StopHateforProfit focused on Facebook because of Mark Zuckerberg's refusal to take action against hate speech. Recently, Facebook's lack of dealing with President Trump's postings has inflamed activists and politicians as well as some Facebook employees.

When George Floyd was murdered by Minneapolis police officers in May 2020, protests broke out in the United States and other countries over the policing of racial minorities. For example, in "the protests prompted by Floyd's death, Trump again tested the boundaries, posting on Facebook and Twitter a message that 'when the looting starts, the shooting starts'" (Hern, 2020). Twitter pointed to the racist history of this phrase and marked it with a warning that it violated Twitter's rules. In contrast, Facebook did not intervene in the post on its site. Since then, Mark Zuckerberg has put together an oversight board to make recommendations about how to move forward.

For some, the boycott continues, as many people remain unsatisfied with Facebook's dealing with hateful posts. Facebook has lost millions of dollars in advertising revenue from companies such as Coca-Cola, HP, Levi's, and Verizon. In the wake of this public boycott, Facebook's reputation has been hurt. In this case, what are ethical choices that Facebook can make? How fragile is Facebook's reputation?

SOURCES: Bond, S. (2020, July 1). Over 400 advertisers hit pause on Facebook, threatening $70 billion juggernaut. *National Public Radio*. https://www.npr.org/2020/07/01/885853634/big-brands-abandon-facebook-threatening-to-derail-a-70b-advertising-juggernaut

Hern, A. (2020, June 29). How hate speech campaigners found Facebook's weak spot. *The Guardian*. https://www.theguardian.com/technology/2020/jun/29/how-hate-speech-campaigners-found-facebooks-weak-spot

Hsu, T., & Lutz, E. (2020, August 1). More than 1,000 companies boycotted Facebook. Did it work? *The New York Times*. https://www.nytimes.com/2020/08/01/business/media/facebook-boycott.html

Speak English!'" (Levenson, 2020). Earlier in January 2020, a nail salon worker, Tiffany Nguyen, was attacked by a woman in Oklahoma City. While asking her boss about her paycheck in Vietnamese, the nail salon worker was confronted by a woman who "yelled at them to stop speaking the language before slapping Nguyen in the face" (White, 2020). Then she threatened to kill Nguyen's family and punched her in the face. Although people are free to speak in any languages they wish, sometimes negative feelings and attitudes arise when people are not speaking the dominant language.

Critical Thinking Prompt
As ethical communicators, where should we draw the line between free speech and unethical verbal communication?

Whether illegal or unethical, the use of verbal communication to attack others based on their group membership is often seen as an attack on the whole group, not just the person who is the receiver of such messages. See *Did You Know? Facebook and Hate Speech* for another example of using verbal communication to attack others.

Confirming and Disconfirming Communication

Although hate speech may be obviously unethical, there are other, less obvious types of communication that can be unethical because of the harm they can cause. One of these is *disconfirming communication*. **Disconfirming communication** occurs when people make comments that reject or invalidate a self-image, positive or negative, of their conversational partners (Dance & Larson, 1976). Consider the following conversation:

disconfirming communication
Comments that reject or invalidate a positive or negative self-image of our conversational partners.

TRACEY: Guess what? I earned an A on my midterm.

LOU: Gee, it must have been an easy test.

Lou's response is an example of disconfirming communication because it suggests that Tracey could not have earned her A because of competence or ability. Consequently, his message disconfirms Tracey's image of herself. You can disconfirm people either explicitly ("I've never really thought of you as being smart") or implicitly (as Lou did).

How can messages such as these cause harm? Imagine that you received numerous disconfirming messages from people who are important to you. How might it affect you? Such messages not only can negatively influence your self-image, but they also can impair your relationships with the people who disconfirm you. For instance, Harry Weger Jr. (2005) and John Caughlin (2002) have found that when couples engage in disconfirming behavior, their marital dissatisfaction increases. Disconfirming messages can harm both individuals and relationships and may be considered unethical as well as ineffective because they focus on the person.

If you want to avoid sending disconfirming messages, what should you do instead? You can provide others with confirming messages. Confirming messages validate positive self-images of others, as in the following example of **confirming communication**.

confirming communication
Comments that validate positive self-images of others.

TRACEY: Guess what? I earned an A on my midterm.

LOU: That's great. I know it's a tough class; you deserve to be proud.

OR LOU MIGHT SAY: Congratulations! I know you were studying very hard and you deserve that grade.

Confirming messages not only are more ethical, they are usually more effective. Most people enjoy communicating with those who encourage them to feel good about themselves. Although engaging in confirming communication will not guarantee that you will be instantly popular, if you are sincere, it will increase the effectiveness of your communication and ensure that you are communicating ethically. If using confirming communication does not come naturally to you, you can practice until it does.

Journal Prompt 4.5:
Types of Communication
What are examples of confirming communication, disconfirming communication, and hate speech? Give at least one example of each type of communication.

You might be wondering how you can provide negative feedback to people without being disconfirming. We discuss how to do this in the next section.

Improving Your Verbal Communication Skills

4.6 Discuss ways to improve your own verbal communication skills.

When considering the ethics of language use, you should think about the effectiveness of your verbal choices. What are some guidelines for engaging in more effective verbal communication? We describe two ways in which you might improve: You can work on using "I" statements and also become more aware of the power of language.

"I" Statements

One type of disconfirming message involves making negative generalizations about others. Although you recognize that people are complex and variable, have you nevertheless found yourself making negative generalizations such as those listed here?

> "You are so thoughtless."

> "You are never on time."

As you can see, negative generalizations (which also are called "you" statements) are typically disconfirming. But, in the real world everyone lives in, some people *are* thoughtless, and some *are* consistently late. So is there an ethical and effective way to make your dissatisfaction known? Yes. You can use a type of message called an "I" statement. "I" statements allow you to express your feelings (even negative ones) by focusing on your own experiences rather than making negative generalizations (or "you" statements) about others.

"I" statements are conveyed through a three-part message that describes

1. the other person's behavior,
2. your feelings about that behavior, and
3. the consequences the other's behavior has for you.

Taking the examples just given and rewriting them as "I" statements, you could come up with:

> "When you criticize my appearance (behavior), I feel unloved (feeling), and I respond by withdrawing from you (consequence)."

> "I think I must be unimportant to you (feeling) when you arrive late for dinner (behavior), so I don't feel like cooking for you (consequence)."

"You" statements often lead recipients to feel defensive or angry because of the negative evaluation contained in the message and because the listener resents the speaker's position of passing judgment. "I" statements can lead to more constructive resolution of conflicts because they arouse less defensiveness. They also are more effective than "you" statements because the receiver is more likely to listen and respond to them (Kubany et al., 1995). In addition, to make "I" statements, speakers have to explore exactly what they are dissatisfied with, how it makes them feel, and what the consequences of the other person's behavior are. "I" statements prevent speakers from attacking others to vent their feelings.

Although many communication scholars believe in the value of "I" statements, a recent study found that people reacted similarly to *both* "I" and "you" statements involving negative emotions. However, the authors point out that their study involved written hypothetical conflict situations. They admit that their results might have been different if they had studied real-life conflict situations (Bippus & Young, 2005).

Although "I" statements can be effective in a variety of contexts, this does not mean they are *always* appropriate. Situations may arise where others' behavior so violates what you believe is decent or appropriate that you wish to state your opinions strongly. Thus, if your friend abuses alcohol or takes illicit drugs, you may need to say, "You should not drive a car tonight" or "You need to get help for your addiction." The effectiveness of one's verbal communication must always be evaluated in the context of the situation, the relationships one has with others, and one's goal.

Become Aware of the Power of Language

As we noted in Chapter 1, language is a powerful force that has consequences and ethical implications. Wars have been started, relationships have been ruined, and much anger and unhappiness has resulted from intentional and unintentional verbal messages. The old adage "Sticks and stones can break my bones, but words will never hurt me" is not always true. Words *can* hurt.

When a speaker refers to others by negative or offensive identity terms, the speaker not only causes harm, he or she also denies those labeled individuals their identities— even if it isn't intentional. For example, one of our students, Cynthia, told us how bad she felt when she realized that some of her gay coworkers were offended by her use of the term *homosexual* (instead of *gay*). They explained that *homosexual* was used as a description of a psychiatric disease by the American Psychiatric Association's list of mental disorders until 1973 and has a connotation of this sexual orientation as a cold, clinical "condition." Using her embarrassment as a learning experience, she initiated an enlightening discussion with her coworkers. She learned that often the best way to discover what someone "wants to be called" is to ask. However, a conversation of this nature can only occur in the context of a mutually respectful relationship—one reason to have a diverse group of friends and acquaintances.

Journal Prompt 4.6: Improving Verbal Communication
What are two ways you can improve your verbal communication skills?

SUMMARY

4.1 Identify three reasons for learning about verbal communication.

- Verbal communication plays a significant role in people's lives, assisting in relationship development, creating identities, and accomplishing everyday tasks.

4.2 Describe the functions and components of language.

- Language is the foundation of verbal processes and it functions in at least seven ways: instrumental, regulatory, informative, heuristic, interactional, personal, and imaginative.
- The four components of language study are *phonology*, the study of sounds; *syntax*, the grammar and rules for arranging units of meaning; *semantics*, the meaning of words; and *pragmatics*, the rules for appropriate use of language.

4.3 Identify examples of several major influences on verbal communication.

- Individual influences on language include speakers' memberships in various identity groups (gender, age, regionality, ethnicity and race, education and occupation).
- When identities influence several aspects of language (vocabulary, grammar, and pronunciation), these speakers have distinct dialects. In other instances identity groups' language variations may be minor, involving only some pronunciation or word choices.

4.4 Describe the relationships between language, perception, and power.

- Societal forces affect verbal processes because they shape our perceptions and the power relationships that surround us.
- The language used in a given society influences its members' perceptions of social reality, whereas power relationships affect how its members' verbal patterns are evaluated.

4.5 Identify examples of confirming communication, disconfirming communication, and hate speech.

- Communicating ethically means avoiding *hate speech* (verbally attacking someone based on race, ethnicity, religion, or sexuality).
- *Disconfirming communication* rejects or invalidates self-image, while *confirming communication* validates positive self-image.

4.6 Discuss ways to improve your own verbal communication skills.

- Learn to use *"I" statements* when expressing dissatisfaction.
- Recognize the power of language. Words can hold deeper meaning and ethical implications, so use them thoughtfully.

KEY TERMS

APPLY WHAT YOU KNOW

1. **Thinking about Contexts**
   For each scenario, write a paragraph describing a typical communication exchange. For each, think about the various elements of verbal communication: sounds, grammar, meaning (word choice), conversational rules, and contextual rules.

   - An informal family outing
   - A meeting with your advisor
   - A bar, where you are trying to impress potential partners

   Hint: Working in a small group, see whether you and your classmates can come up with some shared contextual rules for communication in these various situations. Give some reasons why you can or cannot come up with shared rules.

2. **Words and Feelings**
   Take three sheets of paper and write one of the following words on each sheet: *garbage, milk, mother*. Take the first piece of paper and crumple it up and then stomp on it. Do the same with the second and third pieces. How did you feel crumpling up and stomping on the first piece of paper? The second? The third? What does this say perhaps about the difference between denotative and connotative meanings?

3. **Using I-statements**
   For each of the examples that follow, create an "I" statement that expresses your feelings about the situation:

   - Once again, your roommate has borrowed some of your clothes without asking and has returned them dirty or damaged.
   - For the third time this semester, your instructor has changed the date of an exam.
   - Your good friend has developed a habit of canceling plans at the last moment.
   - Your romantic partner embarrasses you by teasing you about personal habits in front of friends.

   Form a group with two or three of your classmates. Take turns reading your "I" statement for each situation. Discuss the strengths and weaknesses of each statement. As a group, develop an "I" statement for each situation that best expresses the group's feelings without encouraging defensiveness in the receiver.

4. **Regional Differences in English**
   Locate five people who either grew up in different parts of the United States or who grew up in different countries. Try to include both men and women and people of different ages in your sample. Ask each person to answer the following questions:

   - What do you call a carbonated beverage?
   - How do you pronounce "roof"?
   - What expressions do you use that some other people have had trouble understanding?
   - What does the term *feminist* mean?
   - Who do you think talks "different"?

Nonverbal Communication

LEARNING OBJECTIVES

5.1 Describe the important role of nonverbal communication in social interaction.

5.2 Define *nonverbal communication*.

5.3 Define five nonverbal codes and explain the five functions of nonverbal messages.

5.4 Explain how nonverbal communication can both trigger and express prejudice and discrimination.

5.5 Explain how nonverbal communication can be used to communicate unethically.

5.6 Explain how you can improve your ability to interpret nonverbal behavior.

CHAPTER TOPICS

The Importance of Nonverbal Communication

What Is Nonverbal Communication?

Nonverbal Communication and the Individual

The Individual, Nonverbal Communication, and Society

Ethics and Nonverbal Communication

Improving Your Nonverbal Communication Skills

> *"Humans express a wide array of nonverbal behaviors, many of which can be quite subtle. Consequently, understanding nonverbal communication requires knowledge and skill."*

Charee took her four-year-old sister with her to a group project meeting at which some members argued about how to present their class paper. After observing the interaction for a few minutes, her sister Anna whispered, "When it's your turn to talk, you have to make your mad face."

Even though Anna is only four years old, she is sensitive to the nonverbal behavior of others. She readily reads others' facial expressions and assigns meaning to them. Children learn the basics of nonverbal communication quickly (Boone & Cunningham, 1998); in fact, infants from an early age imitate others' nonverbal behavior. For example, when newborns observe caregivers sticking out their tongues, they do the same (Als, 1977; Meltzoff & Prinz, 2002).

In this chapter, we take a close look at the intricacies of nonverbal communication and the many factors that shape nonverbal messages and their interpretation. First, we describe the importance of nonverbal communication, provide a definition, and explore how it differs from nonverbal behavior. We then give you an overview of the various types of nonverbal codes, and we examine the functions that nonverbal messages serve. We next explore how societal forces intersect with individuals' nonverbal communication. We conclude the chapter by discussing ethical issues in nonverbal communication and providing you with suggestions for improving your nonverbal communication skills.

The Importance of Nonverbal Communication

5.1 Describe the important role of nonverbal communication in social interaction.

Nonverbal communication plays an important role in social interaction. It helps us express and interpret verbal messages, navigate everyday life, and make policy decisions.

First, nonverbal communication allows us to communicate more complex messages—such as when we:

- smile to *reinforce* an expression of thanks;
- hold our hands with palms forward to *substitute* for saying "stop";
- laugh flirtatiously to *contradict* the words "I hate you";
- put our index finger and thumb close together to *illustrate* how thin our new computer is.

Second, nonverbal communication influences how individuals interpret messages, especially those related to feelings, moods, and attitudes. Nonverbal cues are important to the expression of emotion because communicators often are more comfortable expressing their feelings nonverbally (such as by smiling or glaring) than they are stating them more explicitly through words (Mehrabian, 2007). For example, how often do you flatly tell a friend or colleague, "I am mad at you"? If you are like most people, this is a relatively rare event; instead, you probably rely on some type of nonverbal cue to indicate your dissatisfaction. The ability to decode others' nonverbal communication effectively helps you interpret the nuanced meanings in others' messages as well as how they feel—and how they feel about you. It also helps you respond better to those messages and feelings. This ability is particularly important in close relationships. For instance, a study of nonverbal communication and marital satisfaction found that

▲ Usage of the term *side-eye* can be traced to a 1797 periodical, but it is used much more commonly today.

nonverbal behavior
All the nonverbal actions people perform.

couples' ability to correctly decode their partner's nonverbal communication affect was connected to their relational satisfaction, especially for husbands (Koerner & Fitzpatrick, 2002).

Nonverbal communication can be complex and ambiguous—both for senders of messages to convey and for receivers of messages to interpret. Even though we begin learning nonverbal communication as children, we often have difficulty interpreting others' nonverbal communication. Why is this so? One reason is the fact that humans express a wide array of nonverbal behaviors, many of which can be quite subtle. Consequently, understanding nonverbal communication requires knowledge and skill.

However, beware of books, websites, and magazine articles that promise to teach you to "read a person like a book": there is no such thing as a key to decoding or interpreting every **nonverbal behavior** in every context. Why not? Because understanding nonverbal communication requires interpreting behavior and assigning meaning to it, and we don't always have the information we need to do that. If you are sitting in the library and notice a stranger staring at you, what does the stare mean? Does the person think they know you? Are they interested in meeting you? Are they being aggressive? Or is the person simply lost in thought and only *appearing* to be gazing at you? Nonverbal cues can be ambiguous. Because the meaning of nonverbal behavior is determined by a variety of factors, including context, culture, and even intentionality, it can be tricky to interpret a specific behavior.

In addition, nonverbal cues are continuous, meaning that people exhibit nonverbal behaviors virtually all the time they are conscious, and multiple behaviors act in concert to create a given message—or different messages, even unrelated ones. For example, imagine that Joan is talking to her husband about their need to spend time together to strengthen their marriage. Just as her husband asks, "What do you want to do about our marriage?" Joan happens to look over his shoulder at her computer screen and sees it displaying an error message. In frustration, she throws up her hands and sighs heavily. Joan was responding to her computer failure, but her husband thought she was responding to his question. He became upset, assuming she was expressing a wish to give up on their marriage.

Nonverbal communication also can be difficult to interpret because nonverbal cues are multichanneled; that is, they can be transmitted in a variety of ways simultaneously. Speakers can convey nonverbal messages through their facial expressions, vocal qualities, eye gaze, posture, and gestures, among other ways. Moreover, because a variety of cues may occur at the same time, it can be difficult and confusing to keep up with everything (Schwartz et al., 1983). If, for example, you are focusing on someone's face, you may miss important messages conveyed by the body.

"Pop psychology" treatments of nonverbal communication typically assume that each behavior has one meaning regardless of the context or who is performing it. Such explanations don't distinguish between nonverbal behavior and nonverbal communication; nor do they consider context, culture, individual variations in behavior, or the relationship that exists between the people being observed. All of these factors, and more, can influence the meaning of a nonverbal behavior in a specific instance. So don't believe that just because someone has their arms crossed over their body it means they are closed off to you. It may simply mean they need a sweater.

Third, nonverbal skills can help individuals navigate everyday life. For example, humans rely on nonverbal cues to determine whether other humans are a threat. Some of these signals arose from inherent emotional responses, such as anger and threat displays. We still use some of these signals deliberately to communicate emotions and feelings. For example, when describing aggressive feelings, people may open their mouths and show their teeth to display how they felt. Interestingly, this is a nonverbal behavior

DID YOU KNOW?

When the "OK" Sign Is Not OK

The hand gesture described as the "OK" sign, or ring gesture, first occurred in the fifth century BCE, if not before, when Greeks displayed it as a symbol of love because they believed the touching fingers looked like kissing lips. First-century Romans used it to signal agreement or approval, and in most English-speaking countries, it has these meanings in addition to conveying "all is well." Similar signs were used to represent the number 3 in China and among Plains Indians. In contrast to these positive meanings, the "O" part of the gesture can represent zero or nothing in Turkey, Tunisia, and the Middle East, while in parts of Germany and Latin America it can have a vulgar connotation.

More recently, the OK gesture has become part of a popular school game or prank called "the circle game." The prank consists of a person making the OK sign below the waist with the palm facing their body and trying to trick someone else into looking at the circle. If the opponent looks, the initiator punches their arm. Given its popular culture status, the game has evolved; for example, among some groups if the "looker" puts their finger in the hole before the initiator can respond, then the opponent gets to punch the initiator.

More recently, the OK sign has taken on a more problematic meaning. In 2017, some users of 4chan, an anonymous online message board, started a prank called "Operation O-KKK" to see if they could trick the larger population, particularly liberals and the media, into believing that the OK gesture was a secret symbol of white power. Surprisingly, it tricked a lot of people—including neo-Nazis, Ku Klux Klansmen, and other white nationalists—and the gesture then became a way for white nationalists to identify themselves and recognize others who agreed with them. Because of the potential for the OK sign to be read as a sign of white power, some people have stopped using it, while many others are less sure of what it means when they see others displaying it.

The OK sign is one example of how the meaning of nonverbal signals can change, similar to how the meanings of words have altered over time. However, perhaps even more than changes to language, alterations to nonverbal communication signals can render them ambiguous and difficult to interpret.

SOURCES: Müller, C., Cienki, A., Fricke, E., Ladewig, S., McNeill, D., & Tessendorf, S. (2014). Ring-gestures across cultures and times: Dimensions in variation. In C. Müller, A. Cienki, E. Fricke, S. Ladewig, D. McNeill, & J. Bressem (Eds.), *Body–Language–Communication* (pp. 1511–1522). De Gruyter Mouton.

Swales, V. (2019, December, 15). When the o.k. sign is no longer ok. *New York Times*. https://www.nytimes.com/2019/12/15/us/ok-sign-white-power.html

Tuleja, T. (2012). In the wink of an eye: Gestures and posture. *Curious customs*. Stonesong Press.

used by many mammals, who use it to communicate both real and play threat. Another nonverbal behavior that individuals use to navigate the world is the "you go first" sign, where we sweep a hand from one side to the other across our bodies.

Similarly, on a daily basis people need to be able to read subtle nonverbal behaviors to assess how friendly or hostile others may be. This is especially true for individuals whose identities are less valued culturally or whose societal position makes them more vulnerable. Because of this vulnerability, such individuals tend to become quite adept at reading and interpreting nonverbal communication. For example, if Gary's boss walks into the office frowning and shaking her head, Gary may interpret this as meaning that she is in a bad mood; consequently, he may try to be especially helpful and avoid doing anything to provoke her. In a study that compared Black Americans' and White Americans' ability to read the nonverbal behaviors of Whites, researchers found that Black Americans were far better at detecting prejudicial attitudes as expressed in subtle nonverbal behavior than were Whites (Richeson & Shelton, 2005). Similarly, a study of heterosexual and gay men found that gay men were better able to identify the sexual orientation of unfamiliar men when watching videos of them (Shelp, 2002).

Finally, nonverbal communication also is important because it can affect public policy decisions. For example, many, if not most, U.S. public schools have a dress code. Although some schools primarily regulate clothing that they see as "inappropriate" or too revealing, others require school uniforms. The supporters of this latter policy argue that school uniforms "help erase cultural and economic differences among students" (Isaacson, 1998) and improve student performance and attendance. Regulating school

Journal Prompt 5.1:
Interpreting Nonverbal
Communication
What features of nonverbal communication make it challenging for us to interpret it easily?

nonverbal communication

The sending and receiving of information through appearance, objects, the environment, and behavior.

Critical Thinking Prompt
Which of these two positions regarding nonverbal communication/nonverbal behavior seems more reasonable to you, and why? What evidence or reasoning influenced your decision? Finally, what difference does this distinction make?

▼ Baseball coaches often develop nonverbal signals that have specific symbolic meaning known only to their teammates.

dress rests on the assumption that one form of nonverbal communication—attire—should be regulated because it can be distracting or even disruptive. Other examples of public policy attempts to regulate nonverbal expression include efforts to ban flag burning and to forbid women from going topless. Countries would not engage in efforts to control nonverbal expression if it were not so important.

What Is Nonverbal Communication?

5.2   Define *nonverbal communication*.

The nonverbal components of communication include all the messages that people transmit through means other than words. More specifically, communication scholar Valerie Manusov and psychologist Miles Patterson define **nonverbal communication** as "encompassing the sending and receiving of information through appearance, objects, the environment and behavior in social settings" (Manusov & Patterson, 2006, p. xi). Thus, they argue that we communicate nonverbally when we blow a kiss, scratch our arm, or wear clothing that signals our group membership. Even more frequently, nonverbal and verbal aspects of communication combine to convey messages, as when we indicate anger by turning our backs and saying, "I don't want to talk with you right now."

However, not every scholar believes that all nonverbal behavior is communicative. These researchers argue that nonverbal communication occurs only when nonverbal behavior has symbolic meaning and is communicated intentionally (Burgoon et al., 1996). That is, they believe nonverbal communication stands for something, whereas nonverbal behavior may not. For example, from this perspective, scratching one's arm usually isn't intended by the scratcher, nor understood by the observer, to convey a particular message. Although it may provide information (that one's arm itches), it doesn't necessarily signal an *intentional* message. Rather, it would be considered an involuntary bodily "output." However, these scholars would argue that in baseball when a manager scratches his arm to signal that a runner on base should steal home, scratching the arm is symbolic and, therefore, an instance of nonverbal communication.

Nonetheless, these scholars acknowledge that some nonverbal communication does lack the element of intentionality. For example, a smile may be understood as an expression of pleasure even if the smiler is unaware that they are smiling. Thus, if a behavior typically is used communicatively, then that behavior is understood to be part of our nonverbal "vocabulary" and will be interpreted as such, regardless of one's own conscious use of it (Burgoon et al., 1996).

However, scholars who prefer a broader definition of nonverbal communication argue that many actions one might consider just a "bodily output" can still convey messages nonverbally. For example, people usually cough because of a scratchy throat or yawn because they are tired, and when they engage in these behaviors, others interpret their meaning. Of course, they also believe that when a person coughs as a signal to capture someone's attention or deliberately yawns to indicate he is bored, he is engaging in nonverbal communication.

As our discussion thus far suggests, most nonverbal behaviors have a variety of

DID YOU KNOW?

How Much Does Nonverbal Communication Contribute to Meaning?

How much of the meaning of a message do you think is conveyed by its nonverbal components? Fifty percent? Seventy-five percent? One of the most common beliefs about communication is that more than 90 percent of the meaning of a message is transmitted by its nonverbal elements. However, in truth, we do not know! So where did this belief originate?

In 1967, psychologist Albert Mehrabian (along with Morton Wiener) wrote that 93 percent of the meaning of the utterances he examined was conveyed through the nonverbal aspects of communication. Specifically, he argued that 38 percent of meaning in his study was derived from paralinguistic cues (tone of voice, etc.) and 55 percent from facial expressions, leaving only 7 percent of meaning to be provided by the verbal message. After he published his findings, other people, researchers and nonresearchers alike, began to generalize his claims about his one study to all communicative interactions.

However, a variety of scholars have contradicted this claim, either arguing for a different percentage (Birdwhistell, 1985) or suggesting that one cannot accurately determine how much words, context, nonverbal messages, and other factors actually contribute to the meaning of an utterance.

Those who critique Mehrabian's analysis argue that his study exhibited several problems. First, it examined how people interpreted the meaning of single tape-recorded words, which is not how we naturally communicate. Second, he combined the results of two studies that most scholars believe should not be combined. Further, he did not consider the contributions to meaning made by gestures and posture. Also, he tried to estimate the contribution of particular nonverbal behaviors—for example, gesture versus facial expression. In practice, however, no one behavior is particularly useful in determining meaning. In other words, inferences made about the meaning of any given action are not all that reliable, nor are estimates of what percentage of the total message a single nonverbal cue communicates.

SOURCES: Birdwhistell, R. L. (1985). *Kinesics and context: Essays in body motion communication.* University of Philadelphia Press.

Mehrabian, A. (1971). *Nonverbal communication.* Aldine-Atherton.

Mehrabian, A. (2007). *Nonverbal communication.* Aldine de Gruyter.

Mehrabian, A., & Weiner, M. (1967). Decoding of inconsistent communication. *Journal of Personality and Social Psychology, 6,* 109–104.

meanings—just as scratching one's arm can have multiple meanings. Therefore, neither we nor anyone else can provide you with interpretations for specific nonverbal actions. Perhaps in part because of this difficulty, we cannot accurately estimate the amount of meaning that nonverbal communication contributes to the overall meaning in an interaction. This inability is revealed in *Did You Know? How Much Does Nonverbal Communication Contribute to Meaning?*, where you can see why it can be difficult to estimate how much meaning nonverbal components convey in any message.

Journal Prompt 5.2: Defining Nonverbal Communication
What is nonverbal communication? How do some scholars differentiate nonverbal behavior from nonverbal communication?

Nonverbal Communication and the Individual

5.3 Define five nonverbal codes and explain the five functions of nonverbal messages.

If a smile is viewed as communicating pleasure even when the smiler doesn't intend to do so, then why don't all behaviors that are part of our nonverbal vocabulary always convey the same meaning? The answer is that assigning one simple meaning to a nonverbal behavior ignores the multiple meanings that may exist, depending on the context in which the behavior occurs. For example, you will read in this chapter that when a person leans toward another (called *forward body lean*), this is often a sign of interest or involvement. Does that mean that forward body lean always indicates interest? Absolutely not! A person might lean forward for a variety of reasons: their stomach hurts, the back of their chair is hot, they are trying to intimidate someone, or their lower back needs to be stretched.

To understand the meaning of a nonverbal behavior you have to consider the entire behavioral context, including what the person might be communicating verbally (Jones & LeBaron, 2002). Therefore, interpreting others' nonverbal behavior requires that you consider a variety of factors that can influence meaning. To interpret nonverbal communication, you also need to know the codes, or symbols and rules, that signal various messages. Finally, you will benefit from a familiarity with the variety of ways that nonverbal messages function. These are topics we take up next.

Influences on Nonverbal Communication

Four factors that play a significant role in how we interpret nonverbal communication are: *culture, relationship, familiarity*, and *gender. Culture* is one of the more important factors that influence the meaning of nonverbal communication. This is not to say that many nonverbal cues and signals aren't shared; in fact, research shows that gaze, or where people focus their eyes during interaction, is used to communicate aggression, dominance, and power as well as connection and nurturance across cultures and even species (Matsumoto, 2006). However, the specific manner in which gaze is used to communicate these messages can vary. For example, in many Arabic cultures, eye gaze during social interaction is more direct than is typical in the United States (Watson & Graves, 1966); thus, eye gaze that might be interpreted as friendly and involved in an Arabic culture could be perceived as somewhat aggressive by a U.S. American. Similarly, within the United States, gaze and visual behavior differ across sexes and ethnic groups, with women tending to gaze more than do men (Briton & Hall, 1995) and African Americans often using more continuous eye gaze while talking and less while listening than do many Whites (Samovar & Porter, 2004).

Some nonverbal cues are used widely across cultures, such as nodding to mean yes. However, many nonverbal gestures have vastly different meanings in different cultures. In the United States, for instance, the "thumbs-up" signals success, and the "hitchhiker's thumb" asks for a ride, but these nonverbal signs carry potentially vulgar meanings in several other cultures. In East Africa, instead of pointing with fingers, people often point with their lips—a gesture that is completely unfamiliar to most people in the United States. Differences in gestures also occur across ethnic groups in the United States. For example, Korean Americans historically tended to reserve smiling, shaking hands, and saying hello for friends and family; however, many immigrants changed this pattern of behavior once they recognized its meaning and importance in the United States (Young, 1999). Thus, the meaning of any nonverbal behavior is defined by the cultures of those interacting and the positions of power they hold in those cultures (Axtell, 1993; Segerstrale & Molnár, 1997).

In addition to culture, *the relationship between the people interacting* affects the meaning of nonverbal behaviors (Manusov, 1995). If a husband takes his wife's arm as they are crossing the street, the meaning likely is viewed as some mixture of care and affection; if a police officer were to do so, one probably would interpret it as an aggressive or controlling gesture. However, if a boss were to do the same with a subordinate, the meaning is more complex and potentially confusing or

▼ This gesture, called *horn fingers*, is best known in the United States as the symbol for "rock on" and is used by fans of heavy metal, hard rock, and similar types of music. It also is used in some countries as a sign to ward off evil or bad luck and in other places, especially when moved back and forth, as a sign that one's spouse is unfaithful.

troubling. One might wonder whether they are being friendly, controlling, affectionate—or maybe too affectionate? How we interpret others' nonverbal behavior, then, is highly dependent on the type of relationship we have with them.

Third, the meaning we attribute to someone's nonverbal behavior varies based *on familiarity or how well we know the communicator*. For example, if a stranger smiles at you, you might interpret it as a gesture of friendliness because that is the meaning most often associated with this facial expression. However, if you know your best friend tends to smile when they are angry, then you will be more accurate at interpreting that their smile is a sign of displeasure than would someone who did not know them well. Once we know people, then, we can usually read their nonverbal behavior and interpret its associated messages with more accuracy. Finally, we tend to *interpret individuals' nonverbal behavior based on their sex*. For example, when women toss their hair, the behavior often is read as flirtatious—and therefore communicative. However, if a man does the same, we are more likely to believe he is just trying to get his hair out of his eyes—a nonverbal behavior that is not necessarily communicative. As we discuss throughout this book, sex differences in nonverbal and verbal communication are a result of biological as well as social and cultural influences.

Nonverbal Codes

Nonverbal codes or signals are distinct, organized means of expression that consist of both symbols and rules for their use (Cicca et al., 2003). For example, when you place your hand palm up and then curl your index finger toward yourself, you are using a symbol that in the United States is understood to mean "come here." Rules for the use of that symbol include that the palm is face up and the arm is straight in front of you. This symbol is part of the larger set of symbols that belong to the nonverbal code of kinesics.

nonverbal codes
Distinct, organized means of expression that consists of symbols and rules for their use.

Although we describe a range of codes in this section, we do not mean to imply that any one code occurs in isolation. Generally, a set of behaviors or codes together determines the meaning or significance of an action. For example, if people are smiling, can we interpret that they are happy? As you know, sometimes people smile when they are angry, to be polite, or to conceal their feelings. To better understand what a smile means, we typically pay attention to how tense or relaxed a person's body is, whether the person's eyes are also "smiling," how physically close or distant the other person is, and whether their voice sounds "happy" or "angry." Thus, we interpret others' nonverbal communication by looking at many types of codes. However, here we discuss the codes individually because it is easier to understand them that way. In the real world, without access to a variety of nonverbal codes and the context of the interaction, interpretations about any behavior may be questionable or even wrong (Patterson, 1983). In this section, we'll look at five types of nonverbal codes—*kinesics, paralinguistics, time and space, haptics,* and *appearance and artifacts*—to see how this system of nonverbal codes works.

kinesics
Nonverbal communication sent by the body, including gestures, posture, movement, facial expressions, and eye behavior.

Kinesics **Kinesics** is perhaps the largest nonverbal code; it describes a system of studying nonverbal communication sent by the body, including gestures, posture, movement, facial expressions, and eye behavior. For clarity, we group kinesics communication into two general categories, those behaviors involving the body and those involving the face.

gestures
Nonverbal communication made with part of the body, including actions such as pointing, waving, or holding up a hand to direct people's attention.

illustrators
Signals that accompany speech to clarify or emphasize the verbal message.

emblems
Gestures that stand for a specific verbal meaning.

adaptors
Gestures used to manage emotions.

regulators
Gestures used to control conversations.

posture and movement
Kinesics behaviors that communicate messages by how immediate or relaxed they are.

immediacy
How close or involved people appear to be with each other.

relaxation
The degree of tension displayed by the body.

▲ What nonverbal messages might be understood from this photo? Remember that a nonverbal behavior can have multiple meanings.

The Body Our bodies convey many nonverbal messages. For example, we use **gestures** such as pointing, waving, and holding up our hands to direct people's attention. Communicators use four types of nonverbal gestures: *illustrators, emblems, adaptors,* and *regulators.* **Illustrators** are signals that accompany speech to clarify or emphasize verbal messages. Thus, when people come back from a fishing trip, they hold their hands far apart to indicate the size of the fish that got away. **Emblems** are gestures that stand for a specific verbal meaning; for example, raising one's hand in class indicates one wishes to speak, while raising both hands at or above head level communicates "I give up." **Adaptors** are gestures we use to manage our emotions. Many adaptors are nervous gestures such as tapping a pencil, jiggling a leg, or twirling one's hair. Finally, people use **regulators** to control conversation; for example, if you want to prevent someone from interrupting you, you might hold up your hand to indicate that the other person should wait. In contrast, if you wish to interrupt and take the floor, you might raise a finger to signal your desire.

Gestures contribute a lot to our communication efforts; even their frequency can signal meaning. For instance, how much gesturing we do while speaking can indicate how involved we are in a conversation. Many people who are excited indicate their involvement by using many and varied gestures; those who have little involvement may indicate their lack of interest by their failure to gesture. However, frequency of gesturing is influenced by many factors, not just involvement, which is a reminder that we best understand nonverbal communication when we know a lot of information about the person making the gestures.

We also use our bodies to convey meaning through **posture and movement**. In general, posture is evaluated in two ways: by how *immediate* it is and by how *relaxed* it appears (Mehrabian, 1971; Richards et al., 1991). **Immediacy** refers to how close or involved people appear to be with each other. For example, when people like someone they tend to orient their bodies in the other person's direction, lean toward them, and look at them directly when they speak. How do people act when they wish to avoid someone? Typically, they engage in the opposite behavior. They turn their backs or refuse to look at them, and if they are forced to stand or sit near the person they dislike, they lean away from them. To understand this, imagine how you would behave if you were attempting to reject an unwanted amorous advance.

Relaxation refers to the degree of tension one's body displays. When you are at home watching TV, for instance, you probably display a relaxed posture: lounging in a chair with your legs stretched out in front of you and your arms resting loosely on the chair's arms. However, if you are waiting at the dentist's office, you may sit hunched forward, your legs pressed tightly together, and your hands firmly grasping the chair arms.

The way you walk or move also can communicate messages to others, particularly about your mood or emotional state. Sometimes you use movement deliberately to communicate a message—such as when you stomp around the apartment to indicate your anger. At other times, your movement is simply a nonverbal behavior—that is, you move naturally and unconsciously without any clear intentionality. Even when your movement is not intentional, observers can and do make judgments about you. One study found that observers could identify when pedestrians were sad, angry, happy, or proud, just from the way they walked (Montepare et al., 1987). However, some emotional states (anger) were easier to identify than others (pride), and some individuals were easier to classify than others. So although people consciously communicate a great deal with their body movements and gestures and observers interpret others' movements, some messages are more clearly transmitted than others. It should also be noted that many of the same factors discussed previously, such as culture, context, background knowledge, and gender, can affect the ability to interpret kinesic behavior.

The Face   *Facial expressions* communicate more than perhaps any other nonverbal behavior. They are the primary channels for transmitting emotion, and the eyes, in particular, convey important messages regarding attraction and attention. Some research suggests that facial expressions of happiness, sadness, anger, surprise, fear, and disgust are the same across cultures and, in fact, are innate (Ekman & Friesen, 1969, 1986), although not all scholars agree. Through observations of deaf, blind, and brain-damaged children, researchers have concluded that commonality of facial expressions among humans is not the result of observation and learning but rather genetic programming (Eibl-Eibesfeld, 1972; Ekman, 2003).

The ability to accurately recognize others' emotions gives individuals an edge in their interpersonal actions. For example, people with greater emotional recognition accuracy are effective in negotiations and are able to create more value for all parties and to achieve more favorable outcomes (Elfenbein et al., 2007). If you are not adept at recognizing others' emotions, however, you can improve your ability to do so. A variety of studies show that individuals who are trained in emotion recognition and then receive feedback on their performance can improve their ability to recognize others' emotional expressions, especially if their targets are from different cultures than their own (Elfenbein, 2006).

Of course, people don't display every emotion they feel. Individuals learn through experience and observation to manage their facial expressions, and they learn which expressions are appropriate to reveal in what circumstances. In many cultures expectations of appropriateness differ for men and women. For example, in the United States, males are often discouraged from showing sadness, whereas females often are criticized for showing anger. In addition, women are routinely expected to smile (Chemaly, 2018), no matter how they feel, while relatively few men receive the same message. Whether or not they are conscious of such cultural expectations, many men believe they shouldn't feel strong emotions or don't want others to see them express strong emotions.

Eye behavior is especially important in conveying messages for humans as well as animals. For example, both humans and dogs use prolonged eye gaze (a stare) to communicate aggression, and they avert their gaze when they want to avoid contact. Furthermore, eye behavior interacts with facial expressions to convey meaning. Thus, most people believe a smile is genuine only when the eyes "smile" as well as the lips. Actors such as Viola Davis and Bradley Cooper are particularly gifted at this; they can, at will, express what appears to be a genuine smile.

Like other types of nonverbal communication, context and culture shape the meanings people attach to eye behavior. For example, cultures differ significantly in how long one is supposed to engage in eye contact and how frequently. Many Native Americans such as Cherokees, Navajos, and Hopis engage in minimal eye contact and many Arabic people maintain more intense and prolonged eye contact when they are listening compared to most White U.S. Americans (Chiang, 1993). Swedes tend to gaze infrequently but for longer periods of time, whereas southern Europeans gaze frequently and extensively (Knapp & Hall, 1992, 2001). Your relationship with others also affects how you interpret their eye behavior. Thus, you may find it appealing when a romantic partner gazes into your eyes but find the same behavior threatening when exhibited by a stranger. For an example of how differences in eye contact and facial expression can affect communication, see *Communication in Society: When You Smile on the Job.*

Critical Thinking Prompt
Think back to the last time you encountered someone you could tell was truly happy to see you. How could you tell? What nonverbal behaviors communicated the other person's happiness to you?

▼ The face and the eyes are particularly important for conveying emotion.

COMMUNICATION IN SOCIETY
When You Smile on the Job

Do you think it is reasonable for a retail store to require women cashiers to smile and make eye contact with all customers? Why or why not?

Have you noticed the smiles and greetings you receive when you shop at major grocery store chains such as Walmart and Safeway? Grocery stores weren't always such welcoming places. This friendly behavior, often called the "supermarket mandatory smile," began in the United States in the late 1990s. Although many stores encouraged this behavior, at one point Safeway actually required its employees to greet customers with a smile and direct eye contact. However, some female employees lodged complaints over this policy because they argued that male customers repeatedly propositioned them and asked them out on dates when they acted so friendly. Although Safeway denied that its policy was the cause of the men's behavior, it did eventually end it. If the organization had consulted nonverbal research on flirting, it might never have instituted the policy in the first place. One of the most common behaviors women use to signal their interest in men is a smile combined with eye contact and a slight tilt of the head (Trost & Alberts, 2006).

SOURCE: Trost, M. R., & Alberts, J. K. (2006). How men and women communicate attraction: An evolutionary view. In D. Canary & K. Dindia (Eds.), *Sex, gender and communication: Similarities and differences* (2nd ed., pp. 317–336). Lawrence Erlbaum.

paralinguistics

All aspects of spoken language except for the words themselves; includes rate, volume, pitch, and stress.

Paralinguistics   The vocal aspects of nonverbal communication are referred to as **paralinguistics**. Paralinguistics are those aspects of language that are *oral* but not *verbal*. That is, paralinguistics describe all aspects of spoken language except the words themselves. For example, typically you recognize other speakers' voices in large part through their paralinguistics, or how they sound, rather than the specific words they say. For this reason, when you call a close friend or relative, you may expect them to recognize you just from hearing your voice on the telephone. If someone close to you fails to recognize your voice, you may feel hurt or offended because their failing to do so suggests that perhaps they don't know you as well as you think they do. Paralinguistics are composed of two types of vocal behavior—*voice qualities* and *vocalizations*.

voice qualities

Qualities such as pitch, rhythm, vocal range, and articulation that make up the "music" of the human voice.

Voice Qualities   **Voice qualities** include *speed, pitch, rhythm, vocal range,* and *articulation;* these qualities make up the "music" of the human voice. We all know people whose voice qualities are widely recognized. For example, former President Barack Obama's vocal qualities were frequently remarked on. One critic (Dié, 2008) described his voice as resembling that used by preachers, arguing that if you listen only to how the former president speaks (rather than what he says), you would feel as if you were sitting in a small church in any Black neighborhood in the United States. He uses the same "ebb and flow," or rhythms and intonations, that are common to ministers' rhetorical style. To compare the vocal qualities of various presidents, go to www.presidentsusa.net/audiovideo.html and listen to audio and video recordings of many presidents.

Speakers whose voices vary in pitch and rhythm seem more expressive than those whose voices do not. For example, actors Kate Bosworth and Keanu Reeves are criticized by some as boring and inexpressive because their delivery is perceived as monotonous and their faces as blank—in both movies and real life (Harrison, 2014). Speakers also vary in how they articulate sounds, some pronouncing each word distinctly and others blurring their words and sounds. We tend not to notice this paralinguistic feature unless someone articulates very precisely or very imprecisely. If you have difficulty understanding a speaker, usually the fault lies not with how fast the person talks but with how clearly they articulate. When combined, the qualities of pitch and rhythm make your voice distinctive and recognizable to those who know you.

vocalizations

Uttered sounds that do not have the structure of language.

Vocalizations   **Vocalizations** are the sounds we utter that do not have the structure of language. Tarzan's yell is one famous example. Vocalizations include vocal cues such as laughing, crying, whining, and moaning as well as the intensity or volume of one's speech. Also included are sounds that aren't actual words but that serve as fillers, such as "uh-huh," "uh," "ah," and "er."

The paralinguistic aspects of speech serve a variety of communicative purposes. They reveal mood and emotion; they also allow us to emphasize or stress a word or idea, create a distinctive identity, and (along with gestures) regulate conversation.

Time and Space   How people use time and space is so important to communication that researchers have studied their use and developed specialized terms to describe them. **Chronemics**, from the Greek word *chronos*, meaning "time," is the study of the way people use time as a message. It includes issues such as punctuality and the amount of time people spend with each other. **Proxemics** refers to the study of how people use spatial cues, including interpersonal distance, territoriality, and other space relationships. Let's see how these factors influence communication and relationships.

chronemics
The study of the way people use time as a message.

proxemics
The study of how people use spatial cues, including interpersonal distance, territoriality, and other space relationships, to communicate.

Chronemics   People often interpret others' use of time as conveying a message, which removes it from the realm of behavior and places it in the realm of communication. For example, if your friend consistently arrives more than an hour late, how do you interpret her behavior? Culture strongly influences how most people answer this question (Hall & Hall, 1987). In the United States, time typically is valued highly; we even have an expression that "time is money." Because of this, most people own cell phones, clocks, and/or watches. Events are scheduled at specific times and typically begin on time. Therefore, in the United States, lateness can be viewed as communicating thoughtlessness, irresponsibility, or selfishness. A more positive or tolerant view might be that the perpetually late person is carefree.

Not all cultures value time in the same way, however. In some Latin American and Arab cultures, if one arrives 30 minutes or even an hour after an event is scheduled to begin, one is "on time." When people come together from cultures that value time differently, it can lead to conflict and a sense of displacement. This happened when one of our colleagues taught a class in Mexico. On the first class day, she showed up at the school shortly before the class was scheduled to begin. She found the building locked and no one around. And even though she knew that people in Mexico respond to time differently than she did, during her stay she never was comfortable arriving "late" and routinely had to wait outside the building until someone showed up to let her in.

The timing and sequencing of events convey a variety of messages. For example, being invited to lunch carries a different meaning than being invited to dinner, and being asked to dinner on a Monday conveys a different message than being asked to dinner on a Saturday. Events also tend to unfold in a particular order, so we expect informal interaction to precede intimate interaction and small talk to precede task talk. When these expectations are violated, we often attribute meaning to the violations, as shown in *Did You Know? Expectancy Violations*.

In addition, some people use time **monochronically**, whereas others use it **polychronically**, and the differences can be perceived as transmitting a message (Hall, 1983; Wolburg, 2001). Individuals who use time monochronically engage in one task or behavior at a time—one reads *or* participates in a conversation *or* watches a movie. If you engage in multiple activities at the same time, you are using time polychronically. Historically in the United States, people have used time monochronically; however, now that technology is so pervasive, more people are using time polychronically as they send text messages, post pictures on Instagram, or read a few tweets as they interact with others. Unfortunately, people who use time monochronically may feel insulted by those who use it polychronically, leading to comments such as "Put down that phone and pay attention to me when I talk to you!"

monochronically
Engaging in one task or behavior at a time.

polychronically
Engaging in multiple activities simultaneously.

Whenever an individual's use of time differs from that of others, miscommunication is possible. If you tend to value punctuality more than others do, you may arrive at events earlier than expected and irritate your host, or you may be perceived as too eager. Similarly, if you don't value punctuality, you may discover that others won't schedule activities with you or are frequently annoyed with you for disrupting their plans. Relationships and communication benefit when the people involved understand how others value and use time.

DID YOU KNOW?
Expectancy Violations

Think of a time when someone violated your expectations for nonverbal behavior. How did you interpret the behavior? Did you see it as a positive or negative violation? Why? How did you respond? How can a person use expectancy violation theory to increase liking?

Our expectations are one factor that influences our interpretations of others' nonverbal behavior. *Expectancy violation theory* states that when people violate our expectations, we tend to notice, become aroused, and attribute meaning to the violation, resulting in increased scrutiny and appraisal of the violator's behavior. For example, if you expect a stranger to shake your hand on being introduced, you likely will search for an explanation if they hug you instead.

However, we don't necessarily interpret and respond to these violations negatively. Judee Burgoon and her colleagues repeatedly have shown that responses to another's violation of our expectations are influenced by how we perceive the violator. In other words, we judge a violation as positive or negative depending largely on whether we view the violator as someone with whom we'd like to interact. Thus, if the stranger who hugs you is attractive and you are single, you may evaluate this violation positively. This judgment shapes your response to the violation; in this case, if you interpret the hug positively, you may respond by hugging back (Burgoon & Hale, 1988; Burgoon & Le Poire, 1993).

SOURCES: Burgoon, J. K., & Hale, J. L. (1988). Nonverbal expectancy violations: Model elaboration and application to immediacy behaviors. *Communication Monographs, 55,* 58–79.

Burgoon, J. K., & Le Poire, B. A. (1993). Effects of communication expectancies, actual communication, and expectancy disconfirmation on evaluations of communicators and their communication behavior. *Human Communication Research, 20*(1), 67–96.

Proxemics   As we mentioned previously, proxemics is the study of how one uses space. People use variance in distance from others for two purposes: to create a sense of safety and comfort and to signal intimacy and closeness. First, individuals need to maintain sufficient space from others to feel safe in their surroundings. The more unfamiliar or uncomfortable one is with another person, the more space one requires. This is one reason we often feel uncomfortable riding on crowded buses or trains. In these cases, we are forced to maintain minimal space between ourselves and people we don't know. Interestingly, this psychological and physical need for safety also occurs in virtual space. An individual's avatar responds to space violations the same way a person would in real life (Phillips, 1998).

Disabled or medically incapacitated people often find their needs for space violated (McLaughlin et al., 2008; Ohl, 2012). Strangers and acquaintances are more likely to invade the personal spaces of individuals who are blind, deaf, and in wheelchairs because they assume that individuals with disability conditions don't need or require as much personal space as the able bodied. However, infringing on these individuals' spaces may be even more disruptive given that they often have to navigate situations and settings not designed for people with their bodies and needs.

It is important to recognize that needs for space are not static; rather, feelings of comfort and safety, as well as displays of intimacy closeness, are situationally determined. For example, during the COVID-19 pandemic, norms for appropriate social distancing changed radically. Whereas prior to the pandemic people might have felt comfortable being spaced about four feet apart, the risks of infection meant that individuals often felt comfortable only when they were six or more feet apart from strangers and acquaintances. In addition, even people who were very close before COVID-19 found themselves reluctant to shake hands with, hug, and kiss friends and family (Centers for Disease Control and Prevention, 2020).

Individuals' use of space also serves a communicative function. The distance people stand or sit from one another symbolizes physical or psychological closeness. For example, if you were sitting in an almost-vacant theater and a stranger entered and proceeded to sit right next to you, how would you feel? If you are like many people in the United States, you might feel uncomfortable. By contrast, if a longtime friend or your romantic partner walked into the theater and chose to sit rows away from you, how would you respond? You probably would be perplexed, perhaps even hurt or angry.

We respond to how close others sit or stand to us because how much space we require to feel comfortable with others suggests how close or intimate we are them. That is, our physical closeness with others typically communicates our psychological closeness with them. Research by Edward T. Hall, a well-known anthropologist, has delineated four spheres or categories of space that reflect people's comfort and closeness with others (Hall, 1966). Let's take a look at each.

Intimate distance (zero to eighteen inches) tends to be reserved for those whom one knows very well. Typically, this distance is used for displaying physical and psychological intimacy, such as lovemaking, cuddling children, comforting someone, or telling secrets. **Personal distance** (eighteen inches to four feet) describes the space we use when interacting with friends and acquaintances. People in the United States often use the nearer

distance for friends and the farther one for acquaintances, but cultures and personal preference strongly influence this choice. When others prefer closer distances than you do, you may find their closeness psychologically distressing; comedian Jerry Seinfeld has referred to these people as "close talkers." One of our students details her encounters with such a person in *It Happened to Me: Katarina*.

intimate distance
(zero to eighteen inches) The space used when interacting with those with whom one is very close.

personal distance
(eighteen inches to four feet) The space used when interacting with friends and acquaintances.

It Happened to Me
Katarina

I have a friend whom I like very much but who makes me uncomfortable sometimes. She tends to lean in very close when she talks, especially if she has been drinking. One night, we were sitting together at a party. I sat in the corner of a couch while she leaned in to talk with me; I kept trying to pull my face away from hers while she talked until I was almost leaning over the back of the couch.

Social distance (four to twelve feet) is the distance most U.S. Americans use when they interact with unfamiliar others. This distance has taken on new importance since the COVID-19 pandemic. Historically, impersonal business with grocery clerks, sales clerks, and coworkers occurred at about four to seven feet, and people in more formal situations, such as job interviews, used the greater distance of 10 to 12 feet. Now, however, some people feel more comfortable at distances greater than six feet when they are talking with anyone they don't know. **Public distance** (12 to 25 feet) is most appropriate for public ceremonies such as lectures and performances, though an even greater distance may be maintained between public figures (such as politicians and celebrities) and their audiences.

social distance
(four to twelve feet) The distance most U.S. Americans use when they interact with unfamiliar others.

public distance
(twelve to twenty-five feet) The distance used for public ceremonies such as lectures and performances.

One's culture, gender, relationship to others, and personality all influence whether one feels most comfortable at the near or far range of each of these spheres. In the United States, two unacquainted women typically sit or stand closer to each other than do two unacquainted men, whereas many men are more comfortable sitting or standing closer to unknown women than they are even to men they know (Burgoon & Guerrero, 1994). However, people in other cultures may prefer the closer ranges. Cultural disparities can result in a comedic cross-cultural "dance," where one person tries to get closer to the other and that person, made uncomfortable by the closeness, moves away.

What does the space between interactants in a given culture reveal? It can communicate intimacy or the lack of it; it also can communicate power and dominance. If person A feels free to enter person B's space without permission but refuses to allow B the same privilege, this lack of reciprocity communicates that A is dominant in the relationship. This situation is common between supervisors and subordinates and may exist in some parent–child relationships as well.

All humans, as well as animals, have strong feelings of territoriality. We exhibit territorial behavior when we attempt to claim control over a particular area. A primary way we attempt to claim and maintain control of a space is through personalization or marking, especially by use of artifacts. That is, we alter spaces to make them distinctly our own through activities such as placing a fence around a residence or displaying family photos in an office. These markers are a form of nonverbal communication that specifies territorial ownership or legitimate occupancy (Becker, 1973). Markers function mainly to keep people away, thereby preventing confrontational social encounters. An unexpected manifestation of territoriality is described in *Did You Know? Space Invaders*.

Primary territories (areas under private control, such as houses and the bedrooms within them) serve as extensions of the owner's sense of identity, so markers there often include personally meaningful symbols reflecting the owner's style and taste (name plates, art objects, flower gardens). Public territories are less central to our self-concepts, and therefore, we tend to mark them with objects that are

▼ When some men engage in a behavior called "manspreading," others in their environment may call them out for taking up too much space.

DID YOU KNOW?
Space Invaders

What do road rage and street harassment have in common? They are both responses to perceptions that one's space has been invaded.

Most articles on nonverbal communication and territory focus on how people "mark" their private and public spaces, such as when homeowners use fences to delineate their property lines or when students leave jackets on the seats they regularly occupy. Less often do we examine how invasions of space lead to antisocial behavior. However, like other animals, humans may respond aggressively when they believe their territory has been invaded.

A common type of space violation in the United States occurs when one driver cuts off another driver. When an individual pulls into the lane ahead and causes them to slow down, some drivers become angry. They may engage in acts of road rage, such as chasing after the offender, driving them off the road, or pulling a gun. Why would someone respond violently to a behavior that usually is only a minor inconvenience? People who do so typically have a strong sense of ownership over their cars and the spaces they occupy. They are likely to perceive that they have been disrespected and that the other person has willingly and arbitrarily invaded their territory. As a result,

they feel the need to establish dominance over "their" space by responding aggressively.

Another regularly occurring response to perceived territory invasion is street harassment. Street harassment is a form of verbal and/or nonverbal harassment that has a sexual component. It is typified by debasing, objectifying, or threatening behavior designed to intimidate. Many cisgender women, transgender individuals, and gay men and women have experienced it. How is this behavior a response to space invasions? Social control theory argues that street harassment is at least in part an effort on the part of some cisgender men to mark the public domain as their territory. In these cases, women without male partners, transgender individuals, and gay men and women are seen as violators of cisgender men's territory, and street harassment is viewed as a way to discourage them from intruding into this space alone (Lord, 2009). This behavior appears to be successful. A majority of women as well as many transgender people and gay men report that they have changed where they walk or live to avoid street harassment.

SOURCE: Lord, T. L. (2009). *The relationship of gender-based public harassment to body image, self-esteem, and avoidance behavior.* Unpublished dissertation. Indiana University of Pennsylvania. ProQuest.

less personalized or that represent explicit claims to the space (for example, "reserved parking" signs). When someone violates a public territory, we tend to react with verbal retaliation, for example, asking the violator to leave. In contrast, we are likely to react strongly when someone violates our primary territory, for example, by seeking physical retaliation and legal sanctions (Abu-Ghazzeh, 2000).

haptics
The study of the communicative function of touch.

Haptics   Although researchers in communication know that touch, or **haptics**, is important, it is among the least studied forms of nonverbal communication. Nonetheless, research does indicate that infants and children need to be touched to be physically and psychologically healthy (Field, 2002). Also, although people vary considerably in how much or what type of touch they prefer, most enjoy being touched by those they care about. To understand how differences in preferences for touch affect relationships, see *It Happened to Me: Alondra.*

> ## It Happened to Me
> ### Alondra
>
> I grew up in upper Michigan, where people rarely touch unless they know each other very well. Then I started working with a guy from the South. From the beginning, he touched me whenever we talked; he touched my arm, put his hand on my shoulder, or even put his arm on the back of my chair. This infuriated me! I thought he was being condescending and too familiar. Later, I realized that he does this with everybody. I understand he doesn't mean anything by it, but I still don't like it.

Touch can be categorized into several general types (Givens, 2005), but people rarely notice the types unless a discrepancy occurs between their expectations and their experience. **Professional touch**, or **functional touch**, is the least intimate; people who must touch others as part of their livelihood, such as medical and dental caregivers, hairstylists, tattoo artists, and tailors, use this type of touch. Because touch often conveys intimacy, people who must use professional touch have to be careful of their interaction style; for example, they may adopt a formal or distant verbal communication style to counteract the intimacy of their touch. **Social-polite touch** is part of daily interaction. In the United States, this form of touch is more intimate than professional touch but is still impersonal. For example, many U.S. Americans shake hands when greeting acquaintances and casual friends, though in many European countries, such as France and Italy, hugging and kissing are appropriate forms of social touch. Even within the United States, people have different ideas about what types of touch are appropriate socially.

professional touch
The least intimate type of touch used by certain workers, such as dentists, hairstylists, and hospice workers, as part of their livelihood; also known as *functional touch.*

social-polite touch
Touch that is part of daily interaction in the United States; it is more intimate than professional touch but is still impersonal.

Friendship touch is more intimate than social touch and usually conveys warmth, closeness, and caring. Although considerable variation in touch may exist among friends, people typically use touch that is more intimate with close friends than with acquaintances or strangers. Examples include brief hugs, a hand on the shoulder, or putting one's arm loosely around another's waist or shoulders. **Love-intimate touch** most often is used with one's romantic partners and family. Examples are the long kisses and extended hugging and cuddling we tend to reserve for those with whom we are closest.

friendship touch
Touch that is more intimate than social-polite touch and usually conveys warmth, closeness, and caring.

love-intimate touch
The touch most often used with one's romantic partners and family.

As is true of other forms of nonverbal communication, sex, culture, and power strongly influence patterns of touch. In the United States, heterosexual males are more likely to reserve hand-holding for their romantic partners and small children, whereas females touch other women more frequently and hold hands with older children, their close female relatives, and even female friends. In general, women tend to touch other women more frequently than men touch other men, and in cross-sex interactions, men are more likely to initiate touch than are women (Hall & Hall, 1990). However, in cross-sex interactions, the nature of the relationship influences touch behavior more than does the sex of the participants. Across all stages of heterosexual romantic relationships, partners reciprocate touch, so they do not differ in amount of touch (Guerrero & Andersen, 1991). However, men respond more positively to their partners' touch than do women (Hanzal et al., 2008). In addition, men initiate touch more in casual romantic relationships,

▲ People can have different definitions for what constitutes social-polite touch.

demand touch
A type of touch used to establish dominance and power.

artifacts
Physical objects including cars, clothing, and other material items.

▼ Demand touching is often used to establish dominance and power.

whereas women do so more often in married relationships (Guerrero & Andersen, 1994).

Each form of touch we have discussed thus far has a "positive" quality, but, of course, people also use touch to convey negative messages. For example, one study revealed that individuals (especially parents) use aggressive touch and withdrawal of affectionate touch with children to signal their displeasure (Guerrero & Ebesu, 1993). Aggressive touch can include grabbing, hitting, and pinching, whereas withdrawal of affection involves rejecting the touch attempts of others, as when one pushes another's arm away or refuses to hold hands. Both children and adults use aggressive touch with their peers as well, though in none of these instances is aggressive touch considered an appropriate or competent way to communicate.

Demand touch is a type of touch that can be perceived negatively and is used to establish dominance and power. Demand touching increases in hierarchical settings, such as at work. One significant characteristic of demand touching is that touchers typically have higher status and have more control over encounters than do receivers; this allows them more freedom of movement and more visual contact. An everyday example of demand touch occurs when a supervisor stands behind a subordinate and leans over to provide directions, placing their hand on the subordinate's shoulder. The subordinate can't move easily or look directly at the supervisor, and the subordinate may feel both physically and psychologically constrained (Kemmer, 1992).

Appearance and Artifacts   In all cultures, individuals' appearance matters, as do their **artifacts**, or the clothing and other accessories they choose. Let's first consider appearance and how it operates as a nonverbal code.

In general, people's looks are believed to communicate something about them, and people develop expectations based on how others look. Hairstyle, skin color, height, weight, clothing, accessories such as jewelry, and other aspects of appearance all influence how we are perceived and how we perceive others. And in the United States, appearance is seen as especially important (Newport, 1999).

What is considered attractive, however, is influenced by one's culture and the time period in which one lives (Grammer et al., 2003). Many people find it hard to believe that the Mona Lisa was considered a great beauty in her day, and even more people wonder who could ever have liked the clothes and hairstyles their own parents wore when they were young. Although the global village we live in now means the media transmit images that can be seen all over the world, cultures still vary in what they consider most attractive. The current ideal body type for women in the United States, as portrayed in the media, for example, is considered too thin and unfeminine by many African Americans (Duke, 2002). Although some American women get collagen injections to achieve full lips, our Japanese students tell us that such thick lips are not considered attractive in Japan. Some Europeans also dislike the defined musculature favored for males in magazines and television ads in the United States.

In the United States, people invest considerable time, money, and energy adapting their appearance to cultural ideals of attractiveness. For example, the U.S. American weight loss industry earned approximately $72 billion in 2019 (Marketdata LLC, 2019). Americans don't just diet; they color and style their hair, frequent gyms and tanning booths, and even undergo extreme makeovers to be more attractive. People engage in all these efforts because the U.S. culture generally equates beauty with happiness, success, goodness, and desirability.

▲ Ideals of what constitutes beauty differ according to time period, culture, class, and other factors.

Although people face certain limits in reshaping their bodies and other physical attributes, they also have great flexibility in using clothing and other artifacts to convey important messages about themselves. In most business contexts, a suit is perceived to be authoritative and an indication of status. This is especially true of men; evaluations of their status often are based on their appearance and clothing (Mast & Hall, 2004). People also use artifacts to signal their occupations and identities. Nurses, flight attendants, and police officers wear uniforms to help others identify them and to send specific messages about their jobs (Gundersen, 1990). Thus, nurses wear scrubs to help others identify them as competent medical professionals and to signify their status as members of hospital staff.

Individuals also choose their accessories and artifacts, such as purses, watches, jewelry, sunglasses, and even cars, to communicate specific messages about status, personality, success, or group membership. A student who carries a leather briefcase on campus creates a different image than one who carries a canvas backpack. On a typical college campus, it is fairly easy to differentiate the communication professors from the business professors and the engineering students from the theater majors based on their dress and artifacts. We might argue that in the United States, where it is not considered polite to announce one's status or success, people often use artifacts to make those announcements for them (Fussell, 1992).

As you can see from the preceding discussion, multiple categories of nonverbal behavior influence communication; these include kinesics, paralinguistics, chronemics and proxemics, haptics, and appearance and artifacts. These categories are, in turn, influenced by multiple individual and cultural factors. In the next section, we explore how these categories work together to influence how we send and interpret messages.

Critical Thinking Prompt
What artifacts are important to you in terms of communicating your identity or status? If you had only one means of communicating high status, would you drive an expensive car, wear designer clothes, or live in an upscale neighborhood? What do you think your choice reflects about you?

The Functions of Nonverbal Messages

As mentioned previously, when people interpret nonverbal behaviors, they don't isolate kinesics from haptics or proxemics from appearance; rather, they observe an integrated set of behaviors, consider the context and the individual, and then attribute meaning. If you see two people standing closely together in a public place, you wouldn't necessarily assume they were being intimate. Rather, you would examine how relaxed or tense their bodies appeared, evaluate their facial expressions and eye gaze, and consider the appropriateness of intimate displays in this public space (for example, a bar versus a church). Only then might you make an attribution about the meaning or function of the couple's behavior.

In general, scholars have determined that nonverbal behaviors serve five functions during interaction (Patterson, 1982, 2003). Those five functions are communicating information, regulating interaction, expressing and managing intimacy, establishing social control, and signaling service-task functions. The most basic function is to communicate information, and this is the one we examine first.

communicating information

Using nonverbal behaviors to help clarify verbal messages and reveal attitudes and motivation.

Communicating Information   Most fundamentally, nonverbal messages are used to **communicate information**. From the receiver's point of view, much of a sender's behavior is potentially informative. For example, when you meet someone for the first time, you evaluate the pattern of the sender's behavior to assess a variety of factors. First, you might evaluate the sender's general disposition to determine if it is warm and friendly or cool and distant. You likely will also assess their more fleeting nonverbal reactions to help you decide if they seem pleased to meet you or are just being polite. Finally, of course, you evaluate the person's verbal message. For example, does the speaker say, "I've really been looking forward to meeting you," or do they say, "I'd love to chat, but I've got to run"? You then combine all these pieces of information to ascribe meaning to the encounter.

Nonverbal communication helps individuals convey and interpret verbal messages. They can do this in five ways:

regulating interaction

Using nonverbal behaviors to help manage conversational interaction.

expressing and managing intimacy

Using nonverbal behaviors to help convey attraction and closeness.

1. By repeating a message (smiling while saying "I'm just kidding");
2. By highlighting or emphasizing a message (pointing at the door while saying "Get out!");
3. By complementing or reinforcing a message (whispering while telling a secret);
4. By contradicting a message (saying "I love your haircut" while speaking in a sarcastic tone and rolling one's eyes);
5. By substituting for a message (shaking one's head to indicate disagreement).

As these examples illustrate, using nonverbal communication effectively can make you a better *verbal* communicator.

▼ Various nonverbal behaviors regulate the interaction that occurs in a conversation.

Regulating Interaction   Nonverbal communication also is used to **regulate interaction**. That is, people use nonverbal behaviors to manage turn-taking during conversation. Thus, if you want to start talking, you might lean forward, look at the current speaker, and even raise one finger. To reveal that you are finished with your turn, you may drop your volume and pitch, lean back, and look away from and then back toward the person you are "giving" your turn to. The regulating function tends to be the most automatic of the five, and most of us rarely think about it. The behaviors you use in this way include the more stable ones such as interpersonal distance, body orientation, and posture as well as more fluid behaviors like gaze, facial expression, volume, and pitch, which are important in the smooth sequencing of conversational turns (Capella, 1985).

Expressing and Managing Intimacy   A third function of nonverbal communication, and the most studied, involves **expressing and managing intimacy**. The degree of your nonverbal involvement with another usually reflects the level of intimacy you desire with that person. If you meet someone new and notice your partner is leaning toward you, gazing into your eyes, nodding their head, and providing many paralinguistic cues such as "uh-huh" as you talk, they are revealing a high degree of nonverbal involvement, which often signals attraction and interest. Of course, people can manipulate these behaviors to suggest attraction and involvement even if they are not experiencing these feelings. For example, in the workplace when subordinates talk with their supervisors, they often display fairly high levels of nonverbal involvement, regardless of their true feelings for their bosses.

Establishing Social Control   People also use nonverbal communication to exert or **establish social control**, or to exercise influence over other people. Individuals engage in the social control function when they smile at someone they want to do them a favor or when they glare at noisy patrons in a theater to encourage them to be quiet. You can use either positive or negative behaviors (or both) in your efforts to control others. People who are "charming" or very persuasive typically are extremely gifted at using nonverbal behavior to influence others.

establishing social control
Using nonverbal communication to exercise influence over other people.

When expressing and managing intimacy, people tend to respond in similar, or reciprocal, ways to one another's nonverbal behavior. On the other hand, when engaging in social control, people tend to respond in complementary ways to one another's nonverbal behavior. To better understand the role of these responses in nonverbal interactions, see *Alternative View: Nonverbal Reciprocity or Nonverbal Complementarity?*

Signaling Service-Task Functions   Finally, nonverbal communication has a **service-task function**. Behaviors of this kind typically signal close involvement between people in impersonal relationships and contexts. For example, golf pros often stand with their arms around novice golfers to help them with their golf swing, and massage therapists engage in intimate touch as part of their profession. In each of these cases, the behavior is appropriate, necessary, and a means to a professional end.

service-task functions
Using nonverbal behavior to signal close involvement between people in impersonal relationships and contexts.

Accurately interpreting nonverbal messages is a complex endeavor, requiring awareness of a number of elements—factors that influence individuals' communication patterns, nonverbal communication codes and signals, and the communicative

---

ALTERNATIVE VIEW
Nonverbal Reciprocity or Nonverbal Complementarity?

Which of the following explanations seems more accurate to you? In what situations do you believe people are more likely to engage in nonverbal reciprocity? In nonverbal complementarity?

Nonverbal Reciprocity

Numerous studies provide evidence that many people unconsciously mimic their partner's postures, gestures, and other movements in social settings. Furthermore, this mimicry, or reciprocity, seems to increase liking and rapport between speakers. In turn, increased liking and rapport lead to more frequent mimicry. However, status or dominance affects who is likely to mimic whom. Lower-status individuals are more likely to reciprocate the behaviors of higher-status people, which may be unconsciously designed to increase liking and rapport (Chartrand & Bargh, 1999; Dijksterhuis & Smith, 2005).

Nonverbal Complementarity

A set of studies found that people respond to another's nonverbal power moves with complementary responses; that is, they respond to dominant behaviors with submissive ones and submissive behaviors with dominant ones (Tiedens & Fragale, 2003). Thus, if one person stares aggressively at another (a dominant behavior), the recipient of the stare is likely to look away

(a submissive behavior). Furthermore, participants reported feeling comfortable with complementarity.

These studies specifically examined how people negotiate status in relationships with no prior hierarchy. Thus, in groups and relationships in which everyone is on equal footing, the first dominant or submissive display by an individual may result from a random movement or a tactical strategy. Whatever the cause of the display, a hierarchical relationship can then result if an observer responds in a complementary fashion. Moreover, because people prefer to complement dominance with submissiveness, and vice versa, they are likely to promote that differentiation. Thus, nonverbal complementarity and the comfort associated with it may encourage hierarchical relationships and help maintain them. This phenomenon, then, may be one reason why hierarchies are so common and widespread.

SOURCES: Chartrand, T. L., & Bargh, J. A. (1999). The chameleon effect: The perception-behavior link and social interaction. *Journal of Personality and Social Psychology, 76*, 893–910.

Dijksterhuis, A., & Smith, P. K. (2005). What do we do unconsciously? And how? *Journal of Consumer Psychology 15*(3), 225–229.

Tiedens, L. Z., & Fragale, A. R. (2003). Power moves: Complementarity in dominant and submissive nonverbal behavior. *Journal of Personality and Social Psychology, 84*, 558–568.

**Journal Prompt 5.3:
Nonverbal Communication
Functions**
What five functions does nonverbal
communication serve?

functions nonverbal messages fulfill. However, in some senses, we have only shown you one piece of the picture, as we have thus far focused primarily on nonverbal communication as performed by individuals. In the next section, we expand the frame to explore how societal forces influence both the performance and interpretation of nonverbal messages and behavior.

The Individual, Nonverbal Communication, and Society

5.4   Explain how nonverbal communication can both trigger and express prejudice and discrimination.

Nonverbal communication, like all communication, is strongly influenced by societal forces and occurs within a hierarchical system of meanings. One's status and position within the societal hierarchy, as well as one's identity, are all expressed nonverbally. However, the more powerful elements in society often regulate these expressions. In addition, nonverbal communication can trigger and express prejudice and discrimination. Let's see how this operates.

Nonverbal Communication and Power

Nonverbal communication and power are intricately related—especially via the nonverbal codes of appearance and artifacts. In the United States, power is primarily based on an individual's access to economic resources and the freedom to make decisions that affect others. Economic resources are typically revealed or expressed through nonverbal codes. At one point, style blogs commented on the $3,800 Chanel "graffiti" purse that Gwyneth Paltrow sported. Stylists found the beat-up, deconstructed bag to be "hideous." So why would Paltrow carry an expensive bag that most people agree is ugly? She likely did so because people display wealth through the clothing and accessories they wear (as well as the quality of their haircuts and the values of their homes and cars). What better way is there to signal wealth than by showing that one has so many purses that one can afford to carry an expensive, unattractive bag on occasion? Whether one can afford to buy the latest designer fashions or only to shop in discount stores typically communicates one's social class and power. English professor Paul Fussell (1992) provides an extensive description of how nonverbal messages communicated in our everyday lives reveal class standing. Consider, for example, the messages communicated by one's home. Fussell notes that the longer the driveway, the less obvious the garage, and the more manicured the grounds, the higher is one's socioeconomic class.

People use nonverbal cues to communicate their own status and identities and to evaluate and interpret others' status and identities. Based on these interpretations, people—consciously and unconsciously—include and exclude others and approve or disapprove of others. For example, in wealthier communities, people who don't look affluent may be stopped and questioned about their presence. Because of cell phones, we have seen more examples of this behavior, in which people, especially people of color,

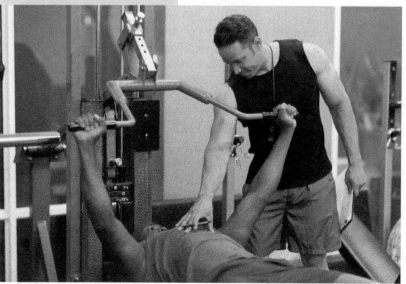

▼ Personal trainers often use the service-task function of nonverbal communication.

are asked to justify that they belong in their apartment complexes or neighborhoods or at specific businesses, community swimming pools, and other public areas. More overtly, gated communities offer clear nonverbal messages about who belongs and who does not belong to a community. Of course, it isn't just the wealthy who use artifacts to convey their identity and belonging. Gang members, NASCAR enthusiasts, football fans, and many others also use attire as well as gestures to signal their individual and group identities.

The use of nonverbal cues to communicate social class extends beyond the use of appearance and artifacts. For example, psychology professors Michael Kraus and Dach Keltner (2009) examined individuals' use of nonverbal communication while interacting with a stranger. In these interactions, they found that people with high socioeconomic status were more likely to display nonverbal signs of disengagement, such as doodling, and fewer signs of engagement, such as smiling and nodding, than were people with lower socioeconomic status. In addition, people who observed these interactions could correctly guess the participants' social class from their nonverbal behavior. Thus, nonverbal communication reproduces—or recreates—the society and social classes in which we live.

Although all groups use nonverbal communication to convey identity, more powerful segments of society typically define what is allowed. For example, many corporations have dress codes designed to communicate a particular professional image to the public. For the same reason, they may also have rules that regulate nonverbal expression of men's facial hair and men's and women's hairstyles. Companies like Disney not only strictly control what their employees wear, they also dictate the types of facial expressions they should display at work. Because these organizations are hierarchical, the decisions made by those in power in the organization must be followed by those who wish employment there.

In 2005, the National Basketball Association issued rules governing the off-court dress of NBA players: They were to dress in "business casual" whenever engaged in team or league business, and they are specifically excluded from wearing sleeveless shirts, shorts, T-shirts, headgear of any kind, chains, pendants, and sunglasses while indoors. Through these dictums, the organization attempted to regulate not only the players' clothing but also their expression of their identities. Of course, not all players supported these regulations (Wise, 2005). Some NBA players felt that the ban on chains and other jewelry was racially motivated. In June 2020, the NBA slightly modified the dress code to allow players "to go without a sports coat on the bench, and for them to wear short- or long-sleeve polos for 'team/league business'" during "bubble games"—that is, games without audiences in the stands (Wolf, 2020). The number and range of dress codes and regulations on appearance underscore the powerful impact that nonverbal cues can have. The more powerful segments of society also define what is most desirable and attractive in our culture. For example, cosmetic corporations spend billions annually on the development of beauty products and advertising to persuade consumers to buy them, and they expect to grow by $38 billion over current expenditures between 2020 and 2024 (Business Wire, 2020). The largest cosmetic companies have expanded to China, where the nation's 451 million women are of great interest to the cosmetics market. The media broadly communicate to us the definitions of beauty. This is why many

▼ The NBA issued rules governing NBA players' off-court dress to help shape the images they present to the public.

U.S. Americans believe that blonde hair is better than brown, thin is better than fat, large breasts are better than small, and young is better than old—beliefs that are not shared universally. Messages promoting a specific type of youth and beauty might seem rather harmless, until one considers the consequences for those who are not thin and blonde, especially those who have no possibility of meeting the dominant standards of beauty.

Aspects of dress are important in the United States at cultural events, particularly for women. The outfits worn to the Academy Awards and other "show business" honor ceremonies are reviewed and evaluated and are a topic of great interest for many people. Similarly, what the president's wife wears on Inauguration Day and at subsequent parties is a subject of conversation; in fact, the First Lady's wardrobe is discussed and critiqued regularly on TV, in blogs, and in magazines. The interest (and evaluation) of these nonverbal expressions, such as clothing, is driven by societal forces. In all of these cases, women know that their nonverbal messages will be carefully scrutinized and evaluated.

Nonverbal Communication, Prejudice, and Discrimination

At the intersection of societal forces and nonverbal communication are prejudice and discrimination. Both can be triggered by nonverbal behavior and are also expressed through nonverbal behavior. Let's look at how this works. First, one's race and ethnicity, body shape, age, or style of dress—all of which are communicated nonverbally—can prompt prejudgment or negative stereotypes. How often do people make a snap judgment or generalization based on appearance? Second, prejudice and discrimination are expressed nonverbally. In some extreme cases, nonverbal signals have even triggered and perpetrated hate crimes. For example, one night in Phoenix, Arizona, Avtar (Singh) Chiera, a small-business owner and a Sikh, waited outside his business for his son to pick him up. Two White men pulled up in a small red pickup truck, yelled at him, and then opened fire on him. Because of anger over the terrorists attacks of September 11, 2001, the two men likely targeted him as an Arab because of his turban and beard, even though Sikhs are neither Arab nor Muslim (Parasuram, 2003). In this encounter, nonverbal messages were the most important; the words spoken (if any) were of minimal impact.

Although the example of Chiera's shooting is extreme, there are many other more subtle ways prejudice can be communicated nonverbally—for instance, averting one's gaze or failing to reciprocate a smile. It can be as subtle as shifting your gaze, leaning your body away, or editing your speech. Sociologist A. G. Johnson (2001, pp. 58–59) created a list of specific nonverbal behaviors that can be interpreted as prejudicial or, as we call them now, microaggressions. "**Microaggressions** is a term used for brief and commonplace daily verbal, behavioral, and environmental indignities, whether intentional or unintentional, that communicate hostile, derogatory, or negative prejudicial slights and insults toward any group, particularly culturally marginalized groups" (Wing Sue, 2010, p. xvi). They are mostly noticed only by the person experiencing them and often happen unconsciously and unintentionally:

- Not looking at people when we talk with them;
- Not smiling at people when they walk into the room or staring as if to say, "What are you doing here?" or stopping the conversation with a hush they have to wade through to be included in the smallest way;
- Not acknowledging people's presence or making them wait as if they weren't there;
- Not touching their skin when we give them something;
- Watching them closely to see what they're up to; and
- Avoiding someone walking down the street, giving them wide berth, or even crossing to the other side.

Critical Thinking Prompt
How does this hierarchy of attractiveness affect communication with others? Do people respond to others negatively because of their appearance? Might they feel marginalized and resentful—even before they interact with others who more clearly meet the dominant standards?

---

microaggressions
Brief and commonplace daily verbal, behavioral, and environmental indignities, whether intentional or unintentional, that communicate hostile, derogatory, or negative prejudicial slights and insults toward any group, particularly marginalized groups.

Given the potential consequences of nonverbal communication, you may find it helpful to consider how your nonverbal communication reflects your own ethical stance. To guide you in making appropriate and ethical choices, in the next section we explore the ethics of nonverbal communication.

Ethics and Nonverbal Communication

5.5 **Explain how nonverbal communication can be used to communicate unethically.**

The ethics of nonverbal communication are actually quite similar to the ethics of communication in general. When people engage in behavior such as deceiving or threatening others or name-calling, their nonverbal behavior typically plays a central role in their messages. For instance, liars use nonverbal behavior to avoid "leaking" the deception, and they may also use it to convey the deceptive message. Moreover, deceivers may feel that lying nonverbally—for example, by remaining silent—is less "wrong" than lying with words. In the Old Testament of the Bible, Joseph's brothers were jealous of their father's affection for him, so they sold Joseph into slavery. When they returned without him, however, they didn't "tell" their father what happened; instead they gave him Joseph's bloody coat and let their father draw the conclusion that wild animals had killed Joseph. In this way, they deceived their father without actually speaking a lie. What do you think? Is it better, or less unethical, to lie nonverbally than it is to do so verbally?

When communicators use nonverbal cues that ridicule, derogate, or otherwise demean others, they run the risk of their behavior being viewed by others as unethical. For example, if someone speaks in a patronizing vocal tone, screams at the less powerful, or touches others inappropriately, would you view this behavior as unethical? What if people respond to others' communication in a way that misrepresents how they actually feel? For instance, if they laugh at a racist or sexist joke even though they dislike it, would you see that behavior as unethical?

Because these are the types of decisions you have to make routinely throughout your life, here are some guidelines for ethical nonverbal communication to help you make those decisions. Consider whether:

- Your nonverbal behaviors reflect your real attitudes, beliefs, and feelings;
- Your nonverbal behaviors contradict the verbal message you are sending;
- Your nonverbal behaviors insult, ridicule, or demean others;
- You are using your nonverbal behavior to intimidate, coerce, or silence someone;
- You would want anyone to observe your nonverbal behavior; and
- You would want this nonverbal behavior directed to you or a loved one.

Although there is no litmus test for evaluating the ethics of every nonverbal message in every situation, if you keep these guidelines in mind, they will help you make better, more informed decisions.

Improving Your Nonverbal Communication Skills

5.6 **Explain how you can improve your ability to interpret nonverbal behavior.**

By now you may be wondering how to decide what a set of behaviors means. How do you decide, for example, if your sports coach's touch is appropriately intimate (service-task) or just intimate? In the workplace, how can you determine whether your

Journal Prompt 5.4: Power and Nonverbal Communication
How does power influence nonverbal communication norms? How does status influence a person's nonverbal communication?

Journal Prompt 5.5: Unethical Nonverbal Communication
What are some ways in which it is possible for people to engage in unethical nonverbal communication?

▲ The meaning of this nonverbal behavior is strongly affected by the context.

congruent
Verbal and nonverbal messages that express the same meaning.

contradicting
Verbal and nonverbal messages that send conflicting messages.

subordinate genuinely likes you and your ideas (nonverbal involvement) or is merely trying to flatter you (social control)?

One way you can assess your own and others' nonverbal communication is to examine how it interacts with verbal messages (Jones & LeBaron, 2002). That is, how congruent (similar) are the two sets of messages? When the two types of messages are **congruent**, they are often genuine (or we assume them to be so). For example, a positive verbal message ("I like you") combined with a positive nonverbal message (smile, forward body lean, relaxed posture) usually conveys a convincing positive message. However, it is also possible that people who are good at deception are able to offer congruent messages while lying, and those who are less adept at communicating may unintentionally offer contradictory messages when telling the truth. Given all of this, what other factors could you rely on to help you decide whether a congruent message is truthful?

Of course, verbal and nonverbal messages can also purposely **contradict** one another. When using sarcasm, people intentionally combine a positive verbal message ("What a nice pair of shoes") with a contradictory or negative nonverbal message (a hostile tone). However, at other times people offer contradictory messages unintentionally or carelessly. Caretakers often confuse children (and encourage misbehavior) by telling a child to stop a particular behavior while smiling or laughing. How does a child interpret this message? Most children will accept the nonverbal aspect of the message and ignore the verbal (Eskritt & Lee, 2003).

In addition to assessing the congruence of the verbal and nonverbal components of a message, you improve your comprehension of nonverbal messages by analyzing the context, your knowledge of the other person, and your own experiences. For example, if you are playing basketball and a teammate slaps you on the rear and says, "good going," the message may be clear. Given the context, you may read it as a compliment and perhaps a sign of affection or intimacy. But what if the slap on the rear occurs at work after an effective presentation? Given that such behavior is generally inappropriate in a business context, you probably will (and should) more closely assess its meaning. You might ask yourself whether this person simply lacks social skills and frequently engages in inappropriate behavior. If so, the message may be inappropriate but still be meant in a positive fashion. In contrast, if the person knows better and has touched you inappropriately at other times, the behavior may be intentionally designed to express inappropriate intimacy or social control.

Here are a few more suggestions to keep in mind:

- Recognize that others' nonverbal messages don't always mean the same as yours.
- Be aware of individual, contextual, and cultural factors that influence meaning.
- Ask for additional information if you don't understand a nonverbal message or if you perceive a contradiction between the verbal and nonverbal messages.
- Remember that not every nonverbal behavior is intended to be communicative.
- Don't place too much emphasis on fleeting nonverbal behaviors such as facial expression or vocal tone; rather, examine the entire set of nonverbal behaviors.

**Journal Prompt 5.6:
Improving Nonverbal
Communication**
What are some specific strategies you can use to improve your ability to communicate nonverbally?

SUMMARY

5.1 Describe the important role of nonverbal communication in social interaction.

- It helps us express and interpret verbal messages and, in doing so, helps us more effectively navigate everyday life.

5.2 Define *nonverbal communication*.

- Nonverbal communication is defined as all the messages that people transmit through means other than words.

5.3 Define five nonverbal codes and explain the five functions of nonverbal messages.

- Nonverbal communication occurs through five codes or types of signals: kinesics, paralinguistics (vocal qualities), chronemics and proxemics (time and space), haptics (touch), and appearance and artifacts.
- These codes can combine to serve one of five functions: communicating information, regulating interaction, expressing and managing intimacy, exerting social control, and performing service-task functions.

5.4 Explain how nonverbal communication can both trigger and express prejudice and discrimination.

- Race and ethnicity, body shape, gender, age, or style of dress—all of which are communicated nonverbally—can prompt prejudgment or negative stereotypes.
- Prejudice and discrimination are expressed nonverbally through behaviors such as eye rolling, ignoring, smirking, and turning one's back on others.

5.5 Explain how nonverbal communication can be used to communicate unethically.

- You communicate unethically when you use nonverbal cues to demean others by speaking in a patronizing tone, screaming at the less powerful, and touching others inappropriately.

5.6 Explain how you can improve your ability to interpret nonverbal behavior.

- You can improve your ability to interpret nonverbal messages by assessing the congruence of the verbal and nonverbal components of a message, analyzing the context, asking for additional information if you don't understand a nonverbal message, and remembering that not every nonverbal behavior is intended to be communicative.

KEY TERMS

nonverbal behavior p. 106
nonverbal communication p. 108
nonverbal codes p. 111
kinesics p. 111
gestures p. 112
illustrators p. 112
emblems p. 112
adaptors p. 112
regulators p. 112
posture and movement p. 112
immediacy p. 112
relaxation p. 112
paralinguistics p. 114
voice qualities p. 114

vocalizations p. 114
chronemics p. 115
proxemics p. 115
monochronically p. 115
polychronically p. 115
intimate distance p. 117
personal distance p. 117
social distance p. 117
public distance p. 117
haptics p. 119
professional touch p. 119
functional touch p. 119
social-polite touch p. 119
friendship touch p. 119

love-intimate touch p. 119
demand touch p. 120
artifacts p. 120
communicating information p. 122
regulating interaction p. 122
expressing and managing intimacy p. 122
establishing social control p. 123
service-task functions p. 123
microaggressions p. 126
congruent p. 128
contradicting p. 128

APPLY WHAT YOU KNOW

1. **Waiting Times**
   How long is the "appropriate" amount of time you should wait in each of the following situations? Specifically, after how long a period would you begin to feel angry or put out? Estimate waiting times for:

   a. Your dentist

   b. A checkout line in a department store

   c. A movie line

   d. A friend at lunch

   e. A friend at dinner

   f. Being on hold on the telephone

   g. Your professor to arrive at class

   h. A stoplight

   i. Your romantic partner at a bar

   j. Your professor during office hours

   Do you see any patterns in your expectations for waiting times? What influences your expectations most—your relationship with the other party? The comfort of the waiting area? Your ability to control events? Compare your waiting times with others' to see how similar or different they are.

2. **Kinesics and Emotion**
   For this activity, observe at least five individuals as they move about in public spaces. You might watch people as they walk across campus between classes, on the street, and in your classrooms, or you could watch videos of people if they are filmed walking and interacting naturally. As you conduct your observations, look for nonverbal behavior and communication that convey the target's emotions or states of mind. For example, is the person's body relaxed or tense? Are they engaging in immediate or distant behaviors? Do they seem happy, sad, angry, proud, or something else? How confident are you about your observations? Why might your assessments be incorrect?

Conversational
Interaction

 ## LEARNING OBJECTIVES

6.1 Describe how in-person conversations differ from mediated conversations.

6.2 Define *conversational interaction*.

6.3 Explain the fundamental skills necessary for effective in-person conversations.

6.4 Explain the role society plays in conversational interaction.

6.5 Explain why manipulative conversational strategies are unethical.

6.6 Describe the characteristics of an effective apology.

> *"Face-to-face conversation is the most human and humanizing thing we do."*
>
> *Sherry Turkle (2015)*

Charee and her best friend, Troi, enjoy texting and using FaceTime to talk almost every day. In fact, sometimes Charee thought this was the reason they were so close and had so much fun together. But recently, she discovered Troi was going to spend a semester abroad in Spain and was surprised at how sad she felt; after all, they could still text and catch up on FaceTime. The news, however, made her realize how important their in-person conversations were and that she was going to miss them much more than she could have imagined.

People communicate through many channels, and communication textbooks devote chapters to most of them. We consider in-person conversation to be an essential and important way we interact, yet textbooks typically do not address this channel in a standalone chapter. Because many people, especially those who grew up with communication technology, say they aren't as comfortable with in-person conversations as they are texting and other forms of mediated communication, we believe it is vital that we offer in-depth instruction on how individuals can understand and enact meaningful conversations. In this chapter, we do so by addressing the many important skills necessary for you to become a highly effective conversationalist.

The Importance of Conversational Interaction

6.1 Describe how in-person conversations differ from mediated conversations.

Conversation serves many purposes, the most important of which is teaching us to be competent not only as communicators but as humans. Through conversing with others, we learn how to regulate our emotions, listen meaningfully, handle difficult situations, and read others' nonverbal cues. We also learn to communicate important feelings such as warmth, love, affection, and respect—along with a host of other important life skills (Turkle, 2015). Finally, because we learn all of these skills, we are able to create and sustain shared understanding with others and develop and maintain relationships (Galinsky et al., 2005). For these reasons, conversation may be the most important communication competency you can cultivate.

Although we can communicate in many ways, none of the mediated methods substitute for in-person conversation. You may wonder, don't interactive media like FaceTime, Skype, and Zoom accomplish the same thing? The answer is resoundingly no! When we communicate via interactive media, we don't receive all of the information we acquire when we talk in person. First, in these contexts, we don't see all or even very much of the other person; sometimes we just see faces, other times we can see people from the torso up, and occasionally we see all of someone's body. Even more rarely do we see people's bodies in motion. Therefore, typically we have to rely on facial cues, which are much easier to control than bodily cues (Azvier et al., 2012). You may be able to control nonverbal signs of your nervousness, excitement, or distress facially, but other parts of your body may be "leaking" this information, such as when you tap your finger or a pen, swing your leg under the desk, or tighten up your body as you become tense. This is why when we judge someone's character we generally prefer to talk to them in person, much like law enforcement professionals prefer to interview suspects or persons of interest in person. We intuitively understand bodily cues such as perspiration, fidgeting, and eye gaze can be more revealing than words or facial expressions. Second, as we discussed in Chapter 5 on nonverbal communication, the more verbal and nonverbal information we have, the better we can understand and communicate effectively with others. Interactive media, however, often impair our ability to observe the more nuanced aspects of conversation. For example, micro expressions, a subtle but influential nonverbal behavior we did not discuss in Chapter 5, is rarely visible through communication media. **Micro expressions** are unconscious and fleeting involuntary facial expressions that convey suppressed emotions (Ekman, 2004). Although we cannot control these brief expressions and typically observers are not consciously aware that they occur, many of us perceive and are influenced by them. Can you remember a time when you were talking with an individual and had a strong impression that they were withholding something? Have you observed someone smiling and thought, "That person is actually angry"? If so, it is likely that the other party's micro expressions influenced your reactions. While we can pick up this information when in person, micro expressions are difficult to see, hard to focus on, and often blurred by video resolution quality. Thus, when we use interactive media to converse, we are losing important nonverbal information provided by the body and, especially, the face.

> **micro expressions**
> Unconscious and fleeting facial expressions that convey suppressed emotions and feelings.

A third reason in-person conversation is so important is that, as of yet, we cannot smell others via interactive media. You may be asking, "Why do we need to smell someone?!" One of the nonverbal codes we didn't talk about in Chapter 5 but that is especially relevant in this chapter is olfactics. **Olfactics** refer to the communicative functions associated with the sense of smell. Most often, we aren't consciously aware of an individual's olfactics unless they smell very good—or not at all good—to us. However, we can detect and respond to odors of which we are not consciously aware. For example, people who are frightened, excited, or aroused emit particular smells that convey their emotional states, and our bodies may respond to these "scent signals" even when we do not consciously recognize what is occurring (de Groot et al., 2014). The smell of fear is somewhat acrid and unpleasant, and even if you don't exactly recognize what it means, if you smell it on another person, you may respond by becoming uncomfortable with the person or situation.

> **olfactics**
> The communicative functions associated with the sense of smell.

More importantly, perhaps, research suggests that natural body scent strongly influences sexual attraction (McCoy & Pitino, 2002; Singh & Bronstad, 2001). A number of studies indicate that people are sexually attracted to others whose scent they find appealing and that this attraction serves to help them locate mates likely to be a good genetic match. That is, scholars argue that people whose natural smell we find sexually attractive often have different genetic strengths and weaknesses than we do and that this difference can protect potential offspring from genetic disorders. The role of scent in sexual attraction may be one reason why being highly compatible with a potential romantic partner you meet online does not guarantee a successful "match." In addition, since we cannot smell another person through mediated communication, we may overlook partners who might be very attractive to us or overinvest in someone whom we, ultimately, don't find sexually attractive. So, the next time someone breaks off a relationship by saying, "It's not you; it's me," they may be telling the truth. You just may not smell right to that person! Interestingly, females are more likely to make this statement than are males because a variety of research has found that, on average, women have a keener sense of smell than do men (Herz & Inzlicht, 2002; Thornhill & Gangestad). Overall, women may be more positively influenced by smells they find attractive and negatively by smells they dislike. For more information on the influence of smell on perception, see *Communication in Society: Sex Differences in Sense of Smell*.

COMMUNICATION IN SOCIETY
Sex Differences in Sense of Smell

Have you noticed a difference in sense of smell between the sexes? Why do you think women typically have a keener sense of smell?

Did you know that scientists often use all-female panels when they look for objective descriptions of food based on sensory perception, such as taste, smell, and appearance? They do so because on standard tests of smelling ability—including odor detection, discrimination, and identification—women consistently outscore men. One researcher has claimed that this difference is evident even in newborn babies.

Age also influences an individual's sense of smell. A study that tested 3,282 participants found that, overall, one's sense of smell was most acute between the ages of 19 and 35 and was the least acute when one is older than 55. However, in all of the three tests conducted, women outperformed men. Other studies have shown that women also rate the sense of smell as being more important to them than do men.

Experiments that have examined men's and women's scent ability reveal that both sexes are able to recognize others from their body odor alone. In an experiment at Hebrew University, Jerusalem, childless women held an unrelated baby in their arms for an hour. When tested later to see if they could recognize the baby they had held by scent, most of them were successful. This study did not test men, so it isn't clear if men possess similar smell recognition ability for unfamiliar others. However, other tests have determined that men and women both can recognize their own children or spouses by their scent. Typically in these studies, participants' children or spouses wore a T-shirt for several days, and then the participants were asked to use scent to recognize the T-shirt belonging to their family member.

SOURCES: Croy, I., Buschhüter, D., Seo, H. S., Negoias, S., & Hummel, T. (2010). Individual significance of olfaction: Development of a questionnaire. *European Archives of Oto-Rhino-Laryngology, 267*(1), 67–71. https://doi .org/10.1007/s00405-009-1054-0

Hummel, T., Kobal, G., Gudziol, H., & Mackay-Sim, A. (2007). Normative data for the "Sniffin' Sticks" including tests of odor identification, odor discrimination, and olfactory thresholds: An upgrade based on a group of more than 3,000 subjects. *European Archives of Oto-Rhino-laryngology, 264*(3), 237–243.

Korneliussen, I. (2012). Women smell better than men. *Science Nordic.* http:// sciencenordic.com/women-smell-better-men

Maccaby, E. E., & Jacklin, C. N. (1978). *The psychology of sex differences.* Stanford University Press.

Finally, evidence suggests that in-person interaction is beneficial to both employees and employers. For example, one study found that moments of conversation between coworkers increase performance by 20 percent, and another study determined that 72 percent of employees who have a best friend at work are more satisfied with their job (Schawbel, 2017). *Forbes* also reported that business leaders were encouraging more person-centered communication in their organizations before the pandemic. For example, Apple had developed an innovative facility designed to promote worker relationships, idea sharing, and collaboration. Similarly, Google Cafés were designed to encourage interactions among employees across departments and teams, and IBM had stopped its remote-working program. These changes occurred because the companies found that when employees encounter each other in physical environments, it sparks creativity and relationship building that leads to positive outcomes.

▼ In-person conversations at work—in the breakroom, hallway, or water station—increase employee productivity, creativity, and satisfaction.

In sum, communicating in person can be qualitatively different from communicating through interactive media; furthermore, in-person conversations provide benefits and opportunities that are not available elsewhere. If conversation is so important, then why do many people choose to engage in text messaging instead? As one young woman explained, texting is so *rewarding* and easy. She said that she can spend a few minutes writing a message and text or tweet it to a group of people, and in just 10 or 15 minutes, she has many responses. When this occurs, for a little while she feels gratified and satisfied. Unfortunately, the pleasures of instant messaging can be somewhat superficial and short-lived, so she finds herself reaching out to others again and again. Conversely, when we have conversations, both deep and relatively mundane, with people we know and care about, we often feel a deep sense of satisfaction, and the conversations can stay with us for hours, days, weeks, and even years.

To enjoy the benefits of in-person conversations, however, it helps if we have a wide range of conversational skills that help us perform competently. If someone has poor skills—such as doing all of the talking and not listening to the other person—they likely won't have the meaningful conversations that lead to intimacy, warmth, and connection. In this chapter, we address a wide range of skills that can increase the quality and frequency of meaningful conversations. We begin by discussing what constitutes a conversation and how it differs from other forms of communication. Next we address the communication fundamentals of perspective taking, conversational and contextual awareness, and communication strategies for important, and sometimes challenging, conversations. We then move to discussing how society influences the ways we converse and the ethics of conversational interaction. We end by discussing how you can improve your conversational skills by learning how to apologize effectively.

Journal Prompt 6.1:
Conversational Interaction
How do in-person conversations differ from mediated conversations?

What Is Conversational Interaction?

6.2 Define *conversational interaction*.

If you search for the term "conversation" on Google or Bing, you will discover a variety of definitions for what constitutes a **conversation**; however, most include the following elements: it is spoken, it is interactive, and it involves an exchange of information. The English language includes a number of words that describe ways of sharing information, such as *discussing*, *talking*, *debating*, and *communicating*, but *conversation* stands alone in at least one respect. Only conversation, by definition, requires that we talk *with* one another.

conversation
Informal, in-person, spoken interaction in which participants exchange ideas, information, and feelings through talking with one another.

Communication, for example, is an overarching term that includes conversation along with all of the many ways we can convey information, including texting, giving speeches, and interacting nonverbally. A debate is different from a conversation because it is adversarial by nature (American Debate League, n.d.). It is an "organized argument or contest of ideas" on a selected topic in which each side presents arguments to an audience but rarely talks to, let alone interacts with, one another. Even the term *talk* is not the same as *conversation* (Nofsinger, 1991), though we use the terms interchangeably. Talk certainly can include interacting, but it also describes types of communication in which one person communicates and other people present are not expected or allowed to talk. For example, have you ever received a "talking to"? In the case of "talking to," generally the speaker addresses a lower-status person (child, employee, student) who is not invited to contribute much to the interaction. You may also have been required to attend a "talk" in which a speaker expounded on their area of expertise but you weren't invited to contribute. Importantly, you can talk without anyone else offering input, but you cannot have a conversation alone.

You might say, but what about discussing? Discussing is very similar to conversing, but most often, it represents a formal type of talk that focuses on one issue. Conversation, on the other hand, is informal talk that involves give-and-take

▲ In-person conversations can bring us joy, strengthen our relationships, and help us cope with difficult times.

among its participants and may address a wide range of topics. Therefore, we define conversation as informal, in-person, spoken interaction in which participants exchange ideas, information, and feelings through talking with one another. Inherent in this definition is that during conversations people speak directly with one another, back and forth, as they communicate together to create the interaction.

Because of the focus on conversation as a spoken interaction, your authors don't view text messages as a form of conversation. Text messages are communicative, of course, but they lack the spontaneity of a conversation occurring in real time. You may send text messages quickly, but you can choose to take time out to consider what you want to say. You can just quit communicating and explain later that someone walked into your space or you received a call you needed to take. In contrast, being physically present with another person lends a sense of urgency to your need to respond. Rarely do we have more than a few seconds to think before replying; it is difficult to stop talking for five or more minutes while we consider what we say or pretend that we have been interrupted!

Even though our definition of conversation includes those on the telephone and through interactive media like FaceTime and Skype, we focus on in-person conversation in this chapter for the reasons we have discussed—in-person conversation provides more information and is qualitatively different from other forms of communication.

Furthermore, we want to help you become effective conversationalists, and this requires more than learning how to phrase sentences correctly or make eye contact (though they are important). Skillful communicators don't respond only to spoken words, they also respond to nonverbal behavior and the emotions and intentions of the speaker as well as how these affect what is being communicated. Though most of us instinctively learn to hold a conversation as we grow up, we soon discover that all too often something goes astray. Throughout the remainder of this chapter, we will discuss how you can become a better conversationalist overall and how to engage in specific types of conversation more effectively. To understand some of the behavioral skills that enhance conversational interactions, see *Did You Know?: Becoming a More Effective Conversationalist.*

**Journal Prompt 6.2:
Defining Conversation**
What communication characteristics are specific to in-person conversational interaction?

The Individual and Conversational Interaction

6.3 Explain the fundamental skills necessary for effective in-person conversations.

In this module, we introduce fundamental skills you need to be successful in any conversation, and then we discuss conversational strategies speakers use to initiate and sustain important, and sometimes difficult, conversations. Together, these skills

DID YOU KNOW?

Becoming a More Effective Conversationalist

Becoming an effective conversationalist requires a lot more than becoming clearer or more concise. Great communicators are effective at conveying information, but more than that, they are exceptional in their ability to understand other people by paying close attention to what they say, don't say, and feel as well as how they respond to the interaction.

Find your motivation. People have to be motivated to invest the energy necessary to become an excellent conversationalist. We don't learn new behaviors without having a strong desire to change. Once we learn new skills, we also have to be motivated to use our skills in a specific interaction. For example, you might know someone who displays great conflict skills at work but then comes home and blows up at members of their family. A person behaving like this had the motivation to work hard and learn the skills, but they aren't motivated to use them in all settings. To converse effectively, you need to be willing to learn new skills and to use them when needed.

Hone your listening skills. You can't understand what someone is saying, let alone what they aren't saying, if you are not listening to them. In Chapter 7, we offer an in-depth explanation for how you can be a better listener. Learning these skills will help you focus on what people are meaning as well as what they are saying.

Become attuned to others' nonverbal communication. You also must observe the other party's nonverbal behavior and pay attention to how they respond moment by moment during your conversation. As we discussed in Chapter 5, people often convey their emotions and reactions through subtle nonverbal behavior, such as eye gaze, gestures, body tension, and movement. You have to be aware of these behaviors and interpret them as they apply to the person to whom you are speaking if you want to understand the full meaning of what they are doing with their words.

Become self-aware. Part of learning any new skill is reflecting on what you have done, what worked, and what you can improve upon. To do this, you have to be willing to be self-critical and listen to feedback from others. Accepting negative feedback, even from yourself, can be uncomfortable, but as you probably have learned, any skill—whether playing a sport, learning a new instrument, cooking a complicated dish, or conversing better—requires that you tolerate some discomfort and frustration as you work to become proficient.

Express empathy. The ability to understand how others feel and convey that understanding is central to being a good conversationalist. If you are talking with a client about their dissatisfaction with your service or listening to your best friend talk about their breakup, you need to understand what it feels like for them to have these experiences and talk with them in ways that show that you understand and want to hear them. How would it feel if you went to your professor to discuss your poor performance in class and they responded, "Well, this an introductory class, and if you just work hard enough, you should be able to pass this class"? On the other hand, how would you feel if your professor said, "I want you do well in this class, too. It probably feels frustrating to work hard and not earn the grades you want. Why don't you tell me more about your study habits and where you think you are missing the mark so I can help you find strategies that help you be more successful?"

help you understand why some of your conversations are successful while others fall flat. They also can enhance your ability to confidently initiate conversations and talk more easily about sensitive topics both positive ("I love you!") and challenging (hurtful messages).

Fundamentals of Conversational Interaction

Most of us find some people, situations, and topics engaging and easy, but even for the most talented conversationalists among us, occasions arise when we find it difficult to talk about issues that are important to us. For example, while many people want to initiate romantic and sexual relationships, a lot of them are unsure how to negotiate sexual contact or, on the other hand, to say that they are not ready for a sexual relationship yet. Similarly, we may easily confide in our friends when something we try doesn't work out but find it harder to tell our parents the same thing. The ability to deliver messages effectively and easily depends in part on fundamental conversation skills such as perspective taking and conversational and contextual awareness.

perspective taking
Understanding the world from another's point of view.

Perspective Taking   All great conversationalists share an important skill—they excel at **perspective taking**. You probably have come across this term before and may have heard it described as being similar to empathy. While perspective taking is essential for us to feel empathy, the terms are not the same. Empathy is the ability to understand and share the *feelings* of others; perspective taking involves understanding the world from another's point of view (Ku & Brewis, 2017). In order to share someone's feelings (empathy), we must be able to understand their experience *as they experience it* (perspective taking).

Perspective taking, therefore, is more than just feeling as others feel. It includes understanding how others think and interpret their experiences. Though you may have never done manual labor for a living, likely you can understand something about the perspective of people who do so. For example, you can imagine that a person who performs physical labor every workday is very tired at the end of the week, why they might not want to go on long hikes during their vacation, and how they would respond if someone criticized them for being "lazy" on the weekend.

As psychologist Jocelyn Duffy (2019) writes, "How we see our lives is how we live our lives." She means that we respond to events and people based how we, individually, view the world. If you view the world as a safe and friendly place, for example, you are likely to take more risks and worry less than someone who views the world as dangerous and unsafe. No matter how much you try to persuade someone that traveling solo across Europe is a good idea, if they see the world as unsafe, they will perceive your trip as dangerous. Thus, a person's perspective is the lens that defines what makes sense to them, which is different from how others see and interpret the world. Essentially, then, our perspective is our version of reality.

Perspective taking is important to conversations in two ways: it improves our ability to understand others' conversational contributions, and it allows us to frame messages that are clearer and more meaningful to others (Franzoi et al., 1985). First, it is important to conversational partners that we try to understand their point of view, but we cannot comprehend it if we don't understand how their reality is shaped. For example, have you tried to explain something important to a friend, such as that you dislike your job and dread going to work? How would you react if they listened to and validated your perspective by saying they understood why you felt that way and asked questions about your experiences? When this occurs, we tend to feel understood, are more open and honest, and feel good about ourselves, the conversation,

▼ The ability to listen empathetically to others helps them cope with distress and is greatly appreciated.

and the other party. But how would you respond if your friend said you were lucky to have your job, should quit whining, or were exaggerating how bad it was? You might feel misunderstood or insulted and wish to leave. When we are heard and supported, even if the other person doesn't agree with our perspective, we find interactions, and the people who participate in them, to be more enjoyable.

Perspective taking is equally important to our ability to clearly convey ourselves to others. One of the questions your authors ask their students at the beginning of the semester is "How many of you are communication majors?" We don't do this because we prefer having communication majors in class but rather because it lets us know how much information about communication our students likely already know, which allows us to skip over very basic information if it is not needed. Since messages are designed to be understood by specific people and audiences, speakers need to take into account what their listener does and does not know (Krauss & Fussell, 1991). Did you know that each fall, news organizations provide a list of "facts about" first-year students to help people, including university instructors, understand them? For example, the article might say, "The class of 2020 was three years old when YouTube launched" (Wilson, 2020). (For more examples, go to https://www.insider.com/facts-about-the-graduating-class-of-2020.) Knowing this information provides a framework for professors to understand the events that helped form students' worldview and, thereby, improves their ability to explain concepts to their classes.

Effective perspective-taking skills also serve to improve conversation in a variety of contexts. Research shows that co-workers (Park & Raile, 2010), mothers and daughters (Martini et al., 2001), romantic partners (Schroder-Abe & Schutz, 2011), and even dental patients (Blatt et al., 2010) report greater relationship satisfaction with conversational partners who successfully engage in perspective taking. Perspective-taking skills also increase creativity in teams and organizations (Grant & Berry, 2017; Hoever et al., 2012) and reduce racial bias in a variety of areas (Galinsky & Moskowitz, 2000; Todd et al., 2011). Thus, improving your perspective-taking skills can increase your success at work, with romantic partners and family, and in society.

Most communicators want to accurately perceive and understand other people, but we fall short because of two natural biases—a desire to think and respond efficiently and a desire to enhance our sense of ourselves (Gehlbach et al., 2012). That is, typically it is easier for us to take shortcuts in our thinking, so we rely on stereotypes or a small number of personal experiences when making judgments about other people, and in doing so we fail to consider others' uniqueness. We also like to think that our way of the world is the "right" or correct way and is superior to others' views because it increases our self-esteem. To overcome these tendencies, we have to learn to think differently.

Improving Your Perspective-Taking Skills   Knowing what perspective taking is and why it is important prepares to you to improve your skills in understanding others and communicating more effectively with them. However, improving one's perspective-taking skills requires practicing a number of behaviors that allow you to see the world through different lenses than the ones you habitually use. Research shows that you can improve these skills in five ways: (1) examining and overcoming your own biases, (2) experiencing new viewpoints, (3) generating more explanations for others' behavior, (4) being open to changing your views when faced with new information, and (5) being humble (Gehlbach et al., 2012).

- **Examine your own biases.** A fundamental bias we all have to overcome is "**naïve realism**," which is the human tendency to believe that we see the world objectively and that those who disagree are uninformed, irrational, or biased. Before we can understand other individuals' perspectives, we must accept that multiple ways exist of viewing and interpreting the world. As tempting as it is to believe in one objective reality, the fact that billions of intelligent, informed, and accomplished people see it differently suggests there is more than one way to view and interpret reality. To overcome your biases, you need to identify what they are. For example, what beliefs do you have about groups of other people that shape how you see them both as a group and as individuals? Do you believe, for instance, that the viewpoints people in the United States hold are superior to or more correct than

naïve realism
The human tendency to believe that we see the world objectively and that those who disagree are uninformed, irrational, or biased.

those held by people in other countries, or perhaps just to those in non-Western cultures? If you hold a belief like this, you need to work to suspend it and remind yourself that you want to learn about groups, not judge them.

- **Experience new viewpoints.** Once we accept that multiple views or realities exist, we can begin to understand why people hold the views they do. First, we can push ourselves to have new experiences and to talk to people with whom we usually don't speak. For example, talking to persons of different faiths allows us to see how their beliefs formed and permits us to see similarities we share. The same is true of other differences, including political, race and ethnicity, nationality and regionality, and many more.

  In addition, we can immerse ourselves in others' worlds through reading literature, plays, and essays, watching diverse movies and television shows, and listening to podcasts created by individuals who are different from us. You may not be able to talk in person with people from different countries or parts of your home country, but you can learn about them through their narratives of firsthand experiences and explanations of how everyday life functions for them. The wide reach of the Internet allows us to expose ourselves to many varying viewpoints without leaving home, and it would be a loss if we didn't seize the opportunity. It is important to point out, however, that approaching someone who is different from you in an attempt to persuade them that your perspective is the correct one will not change your effectiveness in perspective taking. For that to happen, you need to engage in the important conversation skill of listening and set aside any preconceived ideas or biases you may have.

- **Generate multiple theories.** A third practice we can use to improve our perspective taking is to create multiple theories or explanations for why the person in question is thinking or behaving in a particular way. For example, do you ever experience anger or frustration when you are driving because you perceive that another person has "cut you off" or interfered with your driving in some way? What do you think when that occurs? One of your authors handles their own irritation at this behavior by thinking of different (more positive) reasons for why other drivers act as they do. Instead of saying to themselves, "That person is a jerk," they choose to consider whether the "offending" driver is late to work, is being distracted by a child in the car, is suffering the loss of a loved one, didn't see them, or is hurrying to the hospital. When you find yourself judging others for their choices or behaviors, creating alternate theories or explanations for their actions helps remind you that a multitude of reasons, experiences, and constraints can influence an individual's behaviors and beliefs, and it can help you understand their perspective. As long as you try to create thoughtful and compassionate theories, you will find yourself reevaluating your own responses to others and recognizing that people typically react in ways that make sense from their point of view.

  Another strategy that you can try is "taking the opposite perspective" (Lord et al., 1984). For instance, if your friend doesn't show for a planned meeting, you might automatically think, "I can't believe Chris stood me up and wasted my time," or you could try out the opposite perspective: "Chris really wanted to be here and is probably just stuck in traffic." Thinking the opposite allows you to consider that your initial reaction could be wrong and encourages you to think about Chris's behavior from another perspective—which is likely to be more positive than yours.

- **Collect new information.** A fourth way we can practice perspective taking is to collect more information about the person or group we are interacting with by accessing information we don't already have. You can do this by asking the person/group questions to help you understand their formative experiences and worldview. You also can pay attention to their verbal and nonverbal behavior when you converse. For example, if you are talking with someone, you can observe their reactions to particular topics, when they choose to become silent, and subtle hints to their experiences or perspective. Based on these cues, you can make better guesses as to someone's perspective. However, keep in mind that directly asking the person is the best way to understand their perspective because the more information you have, the easier it will be for you to understand others' perspectives.

- **Be humble.** The biggest impediment to effective perspective taking is having confidence in one's perspective-taking skills. This may sound counterintuitive, but when we assume we know the other person well or think we are highly perceptive, we are most likely to engage in poor perspective taking. Several studies reveal that we are not the best judges of our perspective-taking skills. For instance, Park and Raile (2010) found no relationship between how people rated their own perspective-taking skills with how other people rated them. In addition, because we think we know people well, we ask them fewer questions about their perspective, which can make our efforts at perspective taking less accurate. Finally, when we try to understand others' perceptions, we often undervalue the power of a situation to explain their behavior, and this can be even more true for people we know well. We need to remember that understanding an individual's perspective requires knowing information about them and the situation. Just because your partner doesn't enjoy hugging your family members doesn't mean they don't like hugging anyone.

Conversational Awareness Good conversationalists are aware of the conversational rules a culture has as well as how to adhere to those rules. In Chapter 5, we introduced conversational rules as part of verbal communication, and here we discuss them in more detail. **Conversational awareness** refers to expectations speakers have for how people should communicate during conversation, and part of being a competent conversationalist is meeting these expectations. Turn taking is the most basic of these rules and is one many people overlook. Conversation is composed of "turns," which describe the individual contributions parties make as they interact with each other. Conversational turn-taking rules focus on the need for participants to contribute to a conversation while also giving others a chance to participate. When we refuse to engage actively in a conversation or neglect to allow others an opportunity to talk, we fail as conversationalists.

conversational awareness
Familiarity with the conversational rules a culture has as well as how to adhere to them.

According to our definition, you cannot have a conversation if one person doesn't contribute or if one person does all of the talking. Since conversation requires give-and-take, if only one person is participating, you have something closer to a lecture than a conversation—and most individuals become irate if they have to carry a conversation entirely on their own or they are "talked to" rather than with. Thus, effective communicators pay attention to how much or little they are talking and seek to fulfill their responsibilities as conversationalists by talking less if they are dominating the interaction or talking more if they are not adding to the conversation. This rule does not mean conversations don't include periods where one party is doing more talking and the other does more listening but that one needs to be sensitive to achieving a comfortable balance during conversations.

As you can see, listening is as much a part of conversing effectively as is talking. However, simply being quiet and letting the other person talk is not enough—we need to listen actively and respond to others when they speak. This requires nonverbally signaling that you are paying attention by looking at the person (and not your phone or somewhere else) and that you provide verbal evidence of your engagement through asking questions and offering feedback, such as "Really?" "Then what happened?" "That is interesting!" A related skill is listening for details as the other party talks. When you pay close attention to what others are saying, you understand what they are saying better, and it permits you to ask for clarification when needed. It is difficult to contribute to a conversation if you don't know what has just been said. In addition, you can use the details to connect to points you want to add or to extend the conversation. We discuss active listening more extensively in Chapter 7.

▲ Listening actively and carefully to others is a skill that we often forget to use.

A third conversational rule related to both listening and turn taking is the appropriate use of eye gaze. Like other conversational rules, what constitutes appropriate eye gaze varies across cultures. English speakers in the United States typically engage in a pattern in which the person listening looks somewhat steadily at the speaker while the speaker moves their gaze to and away from the listener while talking. This pattern is perceived as respectful, appropriate, and a sign of engagement in many, but not all, interactions. Exceptions include when lower status people maintain eye gaze with higher status people who are rebuking them or when staring intensively at another person. In these cases, eye gaze can be perceived as rude or threatening.

Adapting one's communication and language choices to one's audience is yet another guideline for conversing effectively. To be adept at talking with others, speakers need to adapt the formality of their utterances, select topics that are appropriate and of interest to conversational partners, use words and phrases familiar to listeners, and display emotions that fit the situation and nature of the conversation. Your ability to do this, however, relies on your perspective-taking skills. For example, when speaking to a six-year-old, you likely need to simplify your vocabulary, consider what they might find interesting (dinosaurs yes, tax code no), speak informally, and display emotions they can understand.

It can be easiest to understand adaptation strategies by looking at times people fail to accommodate their conversational partners. Perhaps this has happened to you. You may know someone who has a large vocabulary composed of words of many syllables who insists on speaking like a lecturer even when you are just hanging out and having fun. Or you might be familiar with a person who talks almost exclusively about their pet interest (the history of the railroad industry) even when no one is interested, or have a friend who continues to make jokes even though you are trying to talk about something serious. These all are examples of conversationalists who ignore what is relevant, interesting, or of value to their audience. People who are considered "charming" are often experts at adapting their conversation to specific audiences in ways that make them feel special and included. People who fail to adapt to their audience often are considered "bores."

Contextual Awareness   In addition to being aware of the relevant conversation rules, competent speakers also are familiar with **contextual awareness,** or how context influences conversations. Every conversation occurs within a specific context, and conversational effectiveness is determined, in part, by the context in which it occurs. The contextual factors that affect how appropriate conversation is include participant variables, the social situation, and social norms for appropriate language use.

Participant variables refer to the characteristics of the people involved in the conversation. A prevailing participant characteristic that affects how conversationalists interact is their relationship to one another, particularly as it relates to each person's status. Although people in the United States are not as status conscious as people in some other countries, we do have implicit expectations regarding who should be polite or respectful to whom. For many groups, age is an important variable that influences who should defer to whom. For example, in the United States there is some expectation that people will be more respectful of people who are older than they are, particularly if the older people are relatives or supervisors. Thus, children often are expected to be more polite

contextual awareness

Sensitivity to the circumstances in which a conversation occurs, including participant variables, the social situation, and social norms.

to their parents and grandparents than their siblings, and organizational members often act more politely to people higher in the organization. This practice is more common in some families and some industries, but where it exists, people who fail to follow these norms can be ostracized or punished. Generally, we speak most normally and casually when we are with people who roughly have the same status as we do, and we speak more formally when we converse with people who have a different level of status.

Perhaps the variable that most consistently influences conversational behavior and style is the social situation. Can you think of specific social contexts where you were taught to be behave more formally, politely, or respectfully? For many of us, one of the situations where we were encouraged to behave "better" was at places of worship. Other situations that often call for more formal behavior are funerals, weddings, visits with famous or politically connected individuals, and other situations perceived as serious or important. On the other hand, if we act seriously in situations that are fun, lighthearted, or for entertainment, we may be criticized as well. We also learn that specific types of conversation are appropriate for job interviews, talking to our teachers, going to a restaurant or movie, and many others. The important consideration here is that many norms exist for how to talk in specific situations and that others respond to us based on how well we conform to them.

A third and final context that influences conversation is social norms for appropriate language. One language norm that can be confusing for college students is what to call their professors. Unfortunately, the expectations for what name or title to use with your instructor can vary from institution to institution—or across departments within one university. For example, at one university it may be appropriate to call your instructors "Professor Smith," while at another you are expected to refer to them as "Dr. Smith," and there might be programs or colleges where students use their teacher's first names. Norms exist for many other types of language, including cursing, talking about sexual matters, or using terms of endearment. In the southern part of the United States, there are areas where communicators routinely use the terms *honey*, *dear*, or *sweetheart* to refer to a wide range of people, while in other parts of the United States such terms may be reserved only for romantic partners and very close relatives. Depending on where you are and with whom you are conversing, strong norms against specific topics can exist. In some families or social classes, it may be off-limits to talk about money, and in others, talking about politics might be perceived as rude. Because of the variation in language norms, it is helpful to learn the specific expectations that individuals and groups hold before you converse with them.

Critical Thinking Prompt
Have you unintentionally violated language norms in a new context or observed someone else doing so? How did you realize your (or the other person's) language violated norms? What did you learn from this experience?

Perspective taking and conversational awareness alone are not sufficient for us to communicate effectively in every instance, yet you must possess them before you can successfully converse on any topic, with any person, in any context. In addition to skills, you need to learn a variety of conversational routines and strategies that you can use across a variety of relationships and situations. This is the topic we take up next.

Conversational Routines

Conversation can seem random and unstructured, but this is not true. Conversations follow particular patterns. For example, we have conversational routines for how to begin and end a conversation, how to offer condolences, and how to apologize. We don't have strict utterances that we memorize, but we use basic formulas that allow us to improvise according to the situation, the audience, and our goals. However, if we haven't been explicitly instructed in these routines, we can feel nervous or uncertain when we try to implement them. We'll explain basic conversational routines, such as initiating a conversation, as well as strategies you can use for relationally important interactions like giving negative feedback to a friend or family member or negotiating sexual consent.

Initiating Conversations   One of the most common conversational actions is starting a conversation. However, many people feel uncomfortable beginning a conversation, such as at a party or social event. The process of initiating a conversation follows a few patterns. Fundamentally, you can begin conversations in six general ways.

1. **Approach someone and introduce yourself.** Although this is a simple strategy, some—if not a lot of—individuals feel uncomfortable just walking up to a stranger.

2. **Ask the person how they are, which you can combine with introducing yourself.** An effective way to do this is to look around and locate someone who is standing alone and approach them. Chances are, they are looking for someone to talk with and are feeling nervous about starting an exchange.

3. **Ask the person a question.** This technique and the next are useful when you are standing in line or sitting with other people, such as entering a crowded venue like a concert or at the beginning of a class ("What is the best concert you have attended?"). Frame your question or comment in a way that encourages the other party to respond. In other words, don't ask a yes or no question.

4. **Make a comment on something in the environment.** It is important to choose a neutral topic that the other person is familiar with. Your comment doesn't have to be inherently fascinating or clever; it just needs to provide an invitation for the other person to talk with you (e.g., "I heard this teacher is really funny.").

5. **Make a general complaint.** That is, complain about something most people are unhappy with—bad weather, a long wait, the temperature of the room, or poor acoustics. Again, your purpose is to encourage the other person to chime in so you can begin to chat.

6. **Offer a "social line."** Comment favorably on the social event you and the other party are sharing. For example, you might say, "The Halloween costumes at this party are amazing" or "I love this band and have followed them for years."

In sum, the best way to open a conversation is to say or do something (sometimes a smile is enough) to let the other person know that you are friendly and available to have a chat. For more ideas on beginning conversations, see *Did You Know?: Initiating Conversations*.

DID YOU KNOW?
Initiating Conversations

Although individuals can begin any conversation with an observation or general question, sometimes they want an opener that is more interesting or better suited to the other conversationalist. Here are five specific ways you can initiate a conversation.

1. **Tell me about you.** Almost everyone likes to chat about themselves, so this is a great way to encourage someone else to talk. This opener allows people to choose what part of their lives they want to discuss, but it may not be effective with someone who is shy or introverted.

2. **What was the highlight of your day (or week)?** This is a more interesting way to ask "How are you?" and it may elicit more specific information and spark a more in-depth conversation. A general opening like this is good for meeting people in anonymous places like airports and conferences or after being introduced to someone by friends or acquaintances.

3. **What are you doing this weekend?** Most people who have plans for the weekend are happy to talk about them. But if the other person responds, "Nothing," you can follow up with "What's your favorite activity on the weekend?" or "What would you do if you could choose anything?" This

opener can work well with acquaintances, coworkers, and the family and friends of people you already know.

4. **What was it like where you grew up?** People tend to have strong feelings, either positive or negative, about the place where they lived as children. If they reply that they lived a number of places, you can follow up by asking what is was like to move around when they were young. This question can be useful for initiating conversation with acquaintances, coworkers, and friends and family of people you know.

5. **I'm making a coffee/going to grab a drink—does anyone else want one?** This opener is a good one because you can direct your comment to a group of people and it can open up a conversation about favorite beverages. It also can start a conversation with anyone who chooses to go with you. It can be used at most social events and has the added bonus of helping you make a good first impression.

SOURCE: Van Edwards, V. (2014). 57 killer conversation starters so you can start a conversation with anyone, anytime. *Science of People*. https://www.scienceofpeople.com/conversation-starters-topics/

Exiting Conversations   At the other end of an interaction is finding a way to exit a conversation. Sometimes it can be even harder to get out of a conversation than to get into one. We can't just stop talking or say goodbye and walk away, so communicators typically use "pre-closings" and closing formula that prepare the other person for the conversation to end. Some examples include, "I've enjoyed talking with you, but I am afraid I have to go," "Well, I don't want to keep you from your work," or "This has been fun; let's get together sometime." The exact words you choose are not as important as that you end the conversation on an upbeat note indicating that you don't necessarily want to leave the interaction but that you must because of a pressing issue for yourself or the other party.

Shifting Conversations   Two other important conversational patterns concern changing the topic you are currently discussing and interrupting. Shifting the topic without forewarning can seem impolite or selfish. However, sometimes you do need to change the topic or reclaim it if someone has abruptly changed the topic before you have finished. When this happens, signal that you plan to alter the topic or that you are returning to the previous topic by making comments like "Oh, by way . . . ." That reminds me . . . ," "Going back to my point . . . ," or "Yes, as I was saying . . . " These remarks signal a change in the conversation topic and help listeners make sense of how the conversation is unfolding. These signals also help you return to a topic that was interrupted.

In general, interruptions are considered at least a little bit rude, so if you need to insert a comment while someone else is talking, it is best to apologize as you do so. Typically, the interrupter makes comments like "I am sorry to interrupt, but . . . ," "I apologize for interrupting," "If I may say something," or "Please forgive me, I need to say something." Comments such as these acknowledge that one's behavior is not polite and tacitly ask for permission or forgiveness for violating a conversational rule, which reduces the awkwardness of trying to talk when someone is already doing so.

Having Difficult Conversations   All of us have occasions where we need to discuss something important to us but aren't sure how to do it. Here we talk about two specific conversations—conveying hurtful messages and talking about sexual consent—that occur frequently in college students' lives but that can be difficult to express in a way that is comfortable and affirming for their conversational partners.

hurtful messages
Conversations in which one criticizes, teases, rejects, or otherwise causes an emotional injury to another person.

Hurtful Messages   The closer people are to one another and the more regularly they interact, the more opportunity they have to hurt one another (Vangelisti, 2007). One way they can harm each other is through **hurtful messages**. Hurtful messages occur when a person criticizes, teases, rejects, or otherwise causes an emotional injury to another (Folkes, 1982). Such messages often involve criticism of another person's behavior, physical appearance, abilities, personality traits, self-worth, or identity, and they suggest that the individual is deficient in some way. They are hurtful because they convey negative feelings and rejection (Vangelisti, 1994).

Unfortunately, hurtful messages are relatively common. Researchers have discovered that hurtful messages occur regularly between friends (Jin, 2013), siblings (Myers & Bryant, 2008),

▼ Carefully planning how you deliver a hurtful message can reduce the recipient's pain.

parents and children (Mills et al., 2002), and romantic partners (Zhang, 2009). For example, one study found that regardless of whether the couple was casually dating, seriously dating, engaged, or married; whether the relationship was long distance or not; the length of the relationship; or the couples' ethnic background, 95 percent of participants could recall a conversation in which their current romantic partners delivered a hurtful message (Zhang, 2009). When handled poorly, hurtful messages can negatively impact relationships, and in relationships where frequent hurtful messages occur, the members are less satisfied, more distant, and less emotionally close (Vangelisti & Young, 2000).

Most hurtful messages focus on relationships, personality, and appearance. However, messages that convey dissatisfaction or lack of regard for the relationship are especially painful. Comments such as "We don't really have anything in common anymore" or "I think we should start seeing other people" are perceived as the most distressing. Relationship messages are probably more upsetting because they signal a fundamental shift in the partner's feelings and because recipients may believe that while they might be able to change their personalities or appearance, they cannot change their partner's feelings.

Hurtful messages don't only include what one *says*; they can also include what one *doesn't say*. If you say "I love you" for the first time and your partner changes the topic, you are likely to be hurt and to perceive this as a rejection or proof that you are unloved. Similarly, if you get a new haircut and your best friend doesn't say anything, you may be upset because you believe your friend doesn't like it—or didn't even notice.

intentional messages

Messages that are perceived as purposely causing harm to the recipient.

Hurtful messages can be intentional or unintentional. **Intentional messages** are perceived as purposely causing harm to the recipient. When people make hurtful comments to one another while angry, their messages typically are viewed as intentional. Hurtful messages can also be unintentional—that is, not intended to hurt the recipient. People can utter unkind comments accidentally, out of thoughtlessness, or from insensitivity, as when a stranger asks a woman who isn't pregnant when her baby is due (Myers et al., 2006). Although **unintentional messages** may be somewhat less painful than those perceived as intentional (Mills et al., 2002), both can wound the recipient and the relationship.

unintentional messages

Messages that are not intended to hurt the recipient.

intensity

Degree of emphasis with which a speaker makes their claim.

How hurt one feels depends on whether they believe the message was said intentionally to hurt them and how satisfied they are in the relationship. Other factors that affect the hurtfulness of a message are how the message is delivered, one's self-esteem, how competent one feels to respond to the message, and the context in which the conversation occurs (Vangelisti, 2007). Partners who are more satisfied with their relationships and those who are in relationships where hurtful messages are infrequent are less likely to believe their partners do not care about the relationship (Vangelisti et al., 2005). Similarly, those who perceive the message as unintentional experience less hurt. Thus, if you confront your best friend to express your concern that his drinking is negatively affecting his grades and his relationships, he is likely to feel less hurt if he perceives that you are doing so because you care about him. To read about one student's experience with hurtful messages, see *It Happened to Me: Meredith.*

The way in which a message is framed also influences how it affects the recipient. The intensity of a message impacts the degree to which the recipient feels hurt. **Intensity** refers to the degree of emphasis with which a speaker makes their claim (McEwen & Greenburg, 1970). For example, "I am miserable in our relationship" is more intense than "I am not as happy as I once was in our

It Happened to Me
Meredith

I still can't believe I was so thoughtless, but recently I really hurt my friend Pepper. I was trying to joke with her, but I teased her about something she is sensitive about—her weight. I was talking about this study I read that said that people's weight tends to be heavily influenced by their friends' weight, and while telling this story, I made a joke that I was going to have to stop hanging out with her. She got upset, her face turned red, and then she stormed out of the room. I felt terrible. I was just kidding, but I should have known better than to say something so hurtful. Fortunately, later we talked, I apologized, and she forgave me. I don't know what I would have done if she had stayed mad at me.

relationship." In addition, the harsher or more negative the language ("I can't stand the sight of you"), the more painful the message is likely to be (Tracy et al., 1987). On the other hand, when a hurtful message is framed in a humorous manner, it is perceived as less intentional, and recipients experience less intense feelings and less hurt than when a message is offered seriously (Young & Bippus, 2001).

Finally, the context in which the message is delivered can impact the recipient's feelings of injury. Hurtful speech that occurs when two friends or family members are alone may be painful, but if it occurs when others are present, the pain and discomfort is often intensified (Miller & Roloff, 2005). Hurtful comments, by definition, are attacks on the recipient's identity, so the presence of an audience can worsen the feeling of being denigrated and add feelings of embarrassment.

Thus, there are better and worse ways to deliver a hurtful message. As mentioned above, when planning a message like this, consider lighthearted ways you can convey your feelings. For example, if you want to talk to a roommate about not keeping your shared bathroom clean, instead of saying "We need to talk about how messy you are," when they come out of the bathroom, you could say "It looks like you had a party in there." Also, remember that you want to use neutral language, so instead of saying "I really hate how you trash the bathroom," try "I need your help in keeping the bathroom clean." In addition, make clear that you are bringing up the issues because you like the person and want to stay friends with them. While using these strategies will not remove all of the sting from your comment, it can minimize how hurt your roommate feels and lead to a conversation where the two of you can solve your problems and remain friends. For more ideas, see *Did You Know?: Delivering Potentially Hurtful Messages*.

Sexual Consent   Conversations about **sexual consent** are among the most important ones we have. This is true for a variety of reasons. First, most people want their partners to willingly agree and actively participate in sexual activity with them; second, virtually none of us wishes to feel forced to have sex when we aren't willing to participate.

sexual consent
An agreement between participants to engage in sexual activity.

DID YOU KNOW?
Delivering Potentially Hurtful Messages

Think of a time when you needed to tell someone something that might hurt their feelings. How did you handle the situation? Are there ways in which you might have handled it better?

Occasionally, almost everyone has to deliver a message that has the potential to cause the recipient emotional pain. Though you might not be able to avoid delivering such messages, you can learn how to minimize others' pain. To help you accomplish this, we offer the following guidelines for how to deliver hurtful messages more effectively:

1. **Plan your message.** If you become irritated, you may be tempted to blurt out a hurtful message, which is likely to sound more negative than you would like. Instead, think about how you can deliver a message that minimizes how hurt the other party will feel. You have many ways to express yourself, and spending time to think through a variety of options will help you select one that is the most thoughtful.

2. **Use more specific and kinder language.** You want to avoid saying "always" and "never," using harsh words (e.g., "you look ridiculous"), and using extreme language (e.g., "I hate it when you do that"). Instead, mitigate your statements ("Sometimes you . . . "), use softer language (e.g., "I worry that others won't see how wonderful you are"), and select more reasonable word choices (e.g., "I prefer it when . . . "). Overall, be polite.

3. **Express your intentions.** You should express your concern, caring, and desire to help the other person. Let them know that you are making the comment because you want to help or bring out the best in them.

4. **Offer fewer rather than more criticisms.** Everyone finds friends and partners to be less than ideal. However, instead of offering frequent critiques, save your potentially hurtful comments for when they are most needed.

5. **Use humor, if it is appropriate.** Do not make fun of the other person, and be sure to avoid sarcasm. However, if offering the comment humorously softens the blow, consider doing so.

Third, having sex with an unwilling partner can constitute sexual assault legally, and violating another's boundaries and body is ethically and morally indefensible. Finally, sexual experiences are better for most individuals when their partners assent and do so enthusiastically. However, many people feel uncertain about how to have a conversation about sexual consent in a way that feels comfortable and protects all of the parties from feeling coerced. To learn more about how men experience sexual coercion, read *Alternative View: Men Are Sexually Coerced as Well.*

How sexual consent is conceptualized has changed over the past 50 years. In the 1970s and '80s, the idea that "no means no" was introduced, and at the time, it was considered a radical idea ("Consent conversations," n.d.). To a large degree, up until that point people (usually women) were expected to avoid situations where sexual activity might take place if they were not ready to consent. Thus, a person's presence constituted "evidence" of one's willingness to participate in sexual contact. In addition, because one's presence was believed to equal consent, if one said "no" or indicated they didn't want to be sexually active, the more willing person regularly viewed the comment as "token resistance," that is, as their partner not "really" meaning they didn't want to participate. As you can imagine, these assumptions led to incidences of

sexual coercion

Unwanted sexual activity that occurs when one is pressured, tricked, manipulated, threatened, or forced in a nonphysical way.

ALTERNATIVE VIEW
Men Are Sexually Coerced As Well

When people write about **sexual coercion**, they typically review research on the experiences of girls and women who were coerced by boys and men. Unfortunately, because of myths and misunderstandings about sexual behavior, relatively few people study men's experiences of unwanted sex. Although it is true that significantly fewer males experience rape than do women, a surprisingly large number of men are subjected to coercive sex.

Sexual coercion is unwanted sexual activity that occurs when one is pressured, tricked, manipulated, threatened, or forced in a nonphysical way (U.S. Department of Health and Human Services, n.d.). It also can include forced sexual conduct from someone who has power over an individual, such as a teacher, boss, or landlord, and seduction, particularly where a younger person is coerced by an older partner (French et al., 2015).

Since the 1970s, the number of men who report they have experienced sexual coercion has risen. As few as 10 percent of men indicated that they had been coerced into sexual activity in the early '70s, while more recently 34 to 43 percent of men acknowledge that they have been pressured into unwanted sexual conduct (Struckman-Johnson & Struckman-Johnson, 1994; French et al., 2015). Although men can be sexually coerced by other men, 95 percent of male college student respondents to a 2015 survey stated that they had been coerced by women.

It isn't clear if the increase in the number of men reporting unwanted sex is due to changing attitudes such that men now feel more comfortable talking about their experiences or if women have become more sexually aggressive—or both. Even if men are more willing to acknowledge female aggression, disbelief about men's reports of sexual assault continue to persist. Many people, for example, believe that because men often are physically stronger than women, they cannot experience coercion. The belief, or myth, that men always want sex indiscriminately also undermines

public recognition of men's sexual coercion. However, by definition, sexual coercion occurs not due to physical, but rather to psychological and emotional factors. Researchers have discovered that women are most likely to use psychological pressure, pleading and arguments, deception, and blackmail when they engage in coercion. Some men, for instance, have reported that women threatened to divulge damaging information about them to family, friends, and romantic partners if the men refused them (Struckman-Johnson & Struckman-Johnson, 1994).

Men who are sexually coerced also suffer many of the same negative effects as do women. They can experience psychological distress, higher rates of substance abuse, and increased sexual risk taking (Bates, 2016). In addition, they may suffer depression, suicide, and a variety of potential deadly side effects (French et al., 2015). Despite these effects, men are unlikely to report the incident to police, don't reveal their assault if they seek medical assistance, and rarely seek psychological support or treatment for the emotional issues they experience. Men might be more likely to seek help, however, if cultural norms viewed them as victims and recognized that women also engage in sexual coercion.

SOURCES: Bates, T. (2016, January 17). Sexual coercion of men often unreported, misunderstood. *Rome Sentinel.* https://romesentinel.com/stories/sexual-coercion-of-men-often-unreported-misunderstood,37366

French, B. H., Tilghman, J. D., & Malebranche, D. A. (2015). Sexual coercion context and psychosocial correlates among diverse males. *Psychology of Men & Masculinity, 16*(1), 42–53. https://doi.org/10.1037/a0035915

Struckman-Johnson C., & Struckman-Johnson, D. (1994). Men pressured and forced into sexual experience. *Archives of Sex Behavior, 23,* 93–114. https://doi.org/10.1007/BF01541620

U.S. Department of Health and Human Services. (n.d.). *Sexual coercion. Office of women's health.* https://www.womenshealth.gov/relationships-and-safety/other-types/sexual-coercion

sexual contact where one party felt assaulted, and law courts were not well prepared to handle these cases. "No means no" was intended to alter the belief that people said "no" when they meant "yes" and to provide a guideline for respecting individuals' bodily autonomy.

In the 1990s and 2000s, "only yes means yes" became the guiding principle for determining consent ("Consent conversations," n.d.). This form of consent was meant to respond to beliefs that saying "no" didn't really mean no by changing the focus from whether an individual said/meant "no" to whether they agreed or said "yes" to sexual interaction. In addition, requiring a person to say "no" had created an environment in which "yes" was the de facto or assumed response and the unwilling partner was responsible for stopping an action that likely was already in progress. In addition, the phrase was coined because sex educators were aware that some people didn't say no even when they wanted to because they didn't feel safe or comfortable enough to say it. This language change also served to recognize the nonverbal and indirect ways someone can communicate "no" without saying it.

Today we are moving toward a perspective that consent should entail enthusiastic agreement. This principle moves beyond a simple verbal "yes" by requiring that one's partner show engagement or interest ("Consent conversations," n.d.). Under this definition, one cannot give consent where manipulation, pressure, threat, and deception occur since one is not in a position to offer enthusiastic agreement. It also means that one needs to check in with one's partner and acknowledge their sexual and emotional signals to ensure they continue to consent. Further, this position recognizes that people can feel ambivalent about their desires and that consenting and wanting to have sex are not always the same thing (Muehlenhard et al., 2016). For example, one might want to have sex with a specific partner but not consent to it for a variety of reasons—they have a relational partner, they are worried about sexually transmitted diseases or other health issues, they don't have birth control that they trust, or they don't feel clear minded enough to make an informed decision. At the same time, one can consent to sex and not want it; for instance, one might not desire sexual interaction but be happy to accommodate their partner. Finally, this view communicates that a partner has the right to withdraw consent if they desire.

Critical Thinking Prompt
Have you ever felt ambivalent about having sexual contact with someone? If so, why did you feel ambivalent—that is, what were your reasons for thinking you might want to do so, and for what reasons did you consider declining?

Another issue that enthusiastic sexual participation addresses is the nature of consent. People often act as if consent is a single event, but the truth is that consent is a *process*. If it were just one event, then once consent was given, it could not be withdrawn, and this assumption does not fit with viewing consent as enthusiastic agreement. Thus, each partner should engage willingly in sexual interaction at every step of the act, and if for any reason one is no longer willing, it must be clear that they can withdraw their consent and have their decision honored. Again, people withdraw consent for a number of reasons, including that sex is painful, they do not feel safe with their partner, they do not find sex enjoyable, or they are bothered by something in the situation or context. Thus, it is not OK to try to persuade, cajole, threaten, or insult someone who no longer desires sex with you.

▼ Talking with your partner about sexual consent can increase satisfaction for both of you.

Studies that examine undergraduate students' perceptions and experiences of consent reveal that many students believe that consent is important but don't know how to communicate it. For example, Beres (2014) found that most respondents in her study saw consent as the minimum standard for ethical sexual relationships, but they also believed that consent was a single event rather than a process, and they were not sure how to solicit or convey it. Later, Muehlenhard and her colleagues (2016) found college students could identify a variety of ways individuals could express consent but that respondents did not report using these behaviors in their own real-life situations. In contrast, a large study of gay, lesbian, and heterosexual students determined that same-sex couples were significantly more likely to engage in explicit consent interactions (McLeod, 2015). These findings likely reflect the fact that cross-sex individuals often rely on a traditional sex-stereotyped script—where men initiate sex and women primarily respond nonverbally—to determine consent. Same-sex couples, on the other hand, don't rely on just one partner initiating sex, so they have developed conversational scripts that allow them to express consent and negotiate their sexual activity.

An effective way to communicate consent is to embrace it as a process that involves partners:

1. paying attention to one another's responses;
2. using both verbal and nonverbal strategies to convey interest and to determine the other's interest, enthusiasm, and willingness to engage in sexual conduct; and
3. checking in with one another throughout the process.

When some individuals hear that potential sexual partners need to show affirmative consent, they imagine that for this to happen the couple is doomed to having an awkward conversation that involves a script that reads:

Partner 1: I would like to have sex; would you like to have sex?

Partner 2: Yes, I would like to have sex with you.

We can assure that while nothing is wrong with having a conversation like this one, there are many other ways to express consent that may feel more comfortable for you. One strategy is to talk about expectations and attitudes about sex *before* you are in a position to consider initiating sex. That is, as you are getting to know one other and talking about previous experiences with romantic relationships—or discussing your views on romantic relationships generally—you can mention what you typically prefer. For example, you might mention that you only feel comfortable having a sexual relationship with someone you know well or when you are in a committed relationship. Or you might say that you prefer that you and your partner not have sex until you are ready to be exclusive. You could say that you are open to having sex whenever it feels right for you. If you are asexual or not looking to have a sexual relationship, you may find it easier to communicate that before you are in a sexual situation. Having a general conversation about your preferences for when sex occurs will help you understand one another and will make it easier for the two of you to negotiate consent when the need occurs.

When you feel ready to engage in sexual activity, you have three strategies for determining consent:

- **Listen for verbal cues.** This includes a willingness to understand and accept the messages your partner is sending. For instance, if you start initiating sex or seem to be moving toward initiating it, listen for cues that your partner is not interested. They may indicate this by saying they don't want to have sex, of course, but they also can do so by changing the topic, making an excuse, or suggesting another behavior ("Consent conversations," n.d.). At that point, you should follow your partner's lead by talking about something else or accepting their excuse, and/or you can say that you understand and you are fine with their choice. Also, listen to their voice. If someone says yes but they sound hesitant or as if they are not interested or they are not enthusiastic about what is happening, then they aren't freely giving consent, so you should stop.

- **Ask prompting questions.** You also can ask prompting questions. Doing so allows you to determine what your partner likes and is comfortable with happening. You can do this by asking, "Do you like this (e.g., having your neck kissed, being touched)?" or saying "Are you OK to keep going, or would you rather stop or pause for a while"? You can use a series of these prompting questions as you become more intimate with your partner ("Consent conversations," n.d.). At the same time, you should be paying attention to your partner's nonverbal behavior; if they are saying yes, do they also seem relaxed and to be experiencing pleasure, or are they saying yes but their body is tense and they won't make eye contact? If it is the latter, you should pause and take time to discuss how your partner is feeling.

- **Talk with your partner.** If you can't read your partner's cues, the cues seem mixed to you, or you would feel more comfortable having an explicit statement of consent, please talk to your partner. You can tell them you are interested in having sex but aren't sure how they are feeling and don't want to proceed until you are certain they also want to have sex. It is much better to seek explicit consent than to unwittingly have sex with someone who didn't want to have sex with you.

As these strategies indicate, consent occurs not through one word or sentence but over time as you and your partner communicate verbally and nonverbally. Therefore, throughout your interaction, you and your partner should be checking in with each other to determine if you are OK with what is happening and you understand what you each find pleasing and displeasing. If you are not tuned in to your partner's verbal and nonverbal communication, you will have difficulty determining whether they are offering consent.

**Journal Prompt 6.3:
The Individual and
Conversational Interaction**
Identify the fundamental skills
necessary for effective in-person
conversations.

The Individual, Conversational Interaction, and Society

6.4   Explain the role society plays in conversational interaction.

Rarely do people consider the effect societal expectations and norms have on conversation, and when they do, they probably imagine that everyday interactions are influenced primarily by our own and the other party's beliefs, attitudes, and conversational style. However, virtually every exchange is shaped by **social norms**. For example, do you talk the same way to your professor as you do to friends your own age? Have you ever thought someone's conversational style seemed "immature" or "too formal"? Perhaps you have seen a male ridiculed for talking like a female or been criticized for the way you spoke to someone. Incidents like this occur when someone perceives that a speaker has violated norms for conversational interaction—norms based on the parties' relationship to one another, their sex and gender, and their positions of power in the status hierarchy.

social norms
The informal rules or expectations that
govern behavior in groups.

We are taught to follow conversational norms and are corrected if we don't because an important function conversation serves is to reflect and support current social structures and relationships. That is, people are expected to converse in a way that reflects their gender (people tend to believe women talk one way, men talk another), their status (low-status people should be deferent, high-status individuals can be dismissive), and the type of relationship they have to one another (romantic partners can say, "I love you," while acquaintances probably should not). By policing individuals' conversational style, we attempt to maintain existing patterns of talk and reveal how we think different groups of people in society should behave. Although people rebel against these expectations and sometimes norms change, change tends to happen slowly and sometimes only partially.

▲ Fraternities and sororities are just two of the many groups that use gatekeeping to determine their membership.

gatekeeping
The practice of admitting some people but not others to a societal group.

Gatekeeping is a second way that conversations function socially. **Gatekeeping** refers to the practice groups use to decide whom they will allow to be a member of their group. Sororities and fraternities, corporations, social organizations, and friend networks are some of the groups that engage in gatekeeping. One of the ways we differentiate who "belongs" from who is an "outsider" is the way the person talks. Humans have used conversational patterns to determine who is an "insider" since Biblical times, and people around the world and across status levels of society still do so. However, gatekeeping can lead to inequality when people who have power purposefully or inadvertently use it to preserve their advantage and prevent others from having the same opportunities as they have.

To test the effects of gatekeeping, a group of researchers developed a series of studies to examine whether participants could determine others' social class from their speech patterns (e.g., pronunciation and accent) and, if so, whether that ability affected hiring decisions. In four studies, the authors found that participants could recognize individuals' social class by listening to brief clips of their speech. They then conducted a follow-up study where they asked people with hiring experience to pre-interview potential job candidates by listening to recordings of their conversations. After that, participants chose which candidates were most competent and the best fit for a specific position and assigned the potential new hires starting salaries and signing bonuses. What happened? The investigators found that study participants' decisions inadvertently were biased in favor of applicants whose speech marked them as being of a higher social class. Participants were not only more likely to hire people with higher-class conversational styles, they also offered them larger salaries and bonuses. The findings confirmed the researchers' theory that conversation and conversational style affect individuals' access to valuable social positions, such as jobs, and other positions of power.

As we discussed in Chapter 4, cocultural theory posits that people who have power attempt to hold onto their power advantage, and one of the ways they do so is through communication broadly and conversation specifically. People with power accomplish this by using specific conversational styles and specialized vocabulary or phrases—such as those used by lawyers and physicians—to signal their membership in the group. Because of their power and influence, the dialects of dominant groups become more highly valued. In the United States, dominant groups are composed primarily of White, educated males, and perhaps unsurprisingly, the dialect they use is called **standard American English (SAE)**. Since this dialect is defined as *the* standard, every other dialect by comparison is viewed as inferior.

standard American English (SAE)
American English dialect spoken by most White conversationalists.

For the remainder of this module, we discuss how specific status markers—such as sex and gender, socioeconomic class, and race—influence conversational styles, how these styles are compared to SAE, why some people choose to adapt their conversational styles, and the consequences that can arise for people who don't—or can't—adapt.

Influence of Sex and Gender

When conversational styles are perceived as reflecting one's gender—that is, when specific types of talk are seen as inherently female or male—they serve to maintain individuals' gender identities and help create structural-level inequality. To state this a bit differently, if you are female and you follow the conversational norms deemed appropriate to your gender (a style considered inherently inferior), you cannot speak like nor will you be identified as a member of the dominant groups. Thus, your everyday interaction patterns will position you as a member of the "outgroup" (women), not the "in-group" (men) (Smith-Lovin & Robinson, 1992).

Investigators have conducted a large number of studies on the relationship between gender and conversational style to determine which strategies are more typical of females or males. The most consistent findings about how women interact suggest that they converse more frequently and in greater depth about topics involving themselves and close relationships with their friends (Johnson & Aries, 2012), use verbal expressions of emotion more often and across a wider variety of settings (Goldschmidt & Weller, 2011), and are more affiliative conversationalists (Shinn & O'Brien, 2008). **Affiliative conversationalists** focus on the other person in the conversation, encourage others to participate more in the conversation, and attempt to elicit ideas and involvement from their partners. In addition to women's style being viewed as more affiliative, their style is viewed as more relational and emotional. Males, on the other hand, have been found to converse more often and in greater depth about activity-oriented topics (Johnson & Aries, 2012), ask more disruptive questions that challenge speakers (Holmes & Stubbe, 1997), and speak more assertively (Shinn & O'Brien, 2008). Since **assertive conversationalists** direct attention to themselves, seek to control the conversation, and attempt to influence their partners' ideas or actions, men's style is considered more active and confident.

Although men and women speak much more similarly than differently (Schlamp et al., 2020), they may vary in the frequency with which they use specific strategies. For instance, men and women both use affiliative and assertive conversational strategies, but differences in how often they enact these strategies means that, overall, women's speech is perceived as polite and more subordinate and men's is viewed as more direct and powerful. If women already use direct and powerful strategies at times, why don't they simply use them more often?

There are two reasons why they do not and cannot. First, a variety of studies provides strong evidence that people are socialized to use specific conversational patterns and styles based on their gender. We learn sex-specific ways of talking by watching how the boys and girls and men and women in our lives talk as well as how each sex converses in movies and television shows, on YouTube and TikTok, and through advertisements. Authority figures, peers, and others tell us to "speak like a man" or "to talk like a lady," and we read novels, magazines, and textbooks that reinforce how males and females are supposed to converse. But the primary place we learn to use gendered conversational strategies is in our homes. Evidence for this is provided by a number of studies that find that mothers use a more affiliative (other-focused) conversation style with their children and that fathers use a more assertive (self-focused) style when parenting (Leaper & Ayres, 2007; Merrill et al., 2015; Shinn & O'Brien, 2008). Interestingly, Shinn and O'Brien found that although mothers in their study were more affiliative and fathers more assertive, both parents were more affiliative with their sons and more assertive with their daughters. For example, at dinner parents might ask their son what he wants to do after college but tell their daughters what they think she should do. Based on these findings, it appears that from an early age men are taught to be self-focused and direct when they speak and to expect that others will focus on them. On the other hand, women learn that their conversation should be polite and focused on others and that they can't expect others to focus on them.

affiliative conversationalists
Style of conversation that focuses on the other person, encourages others to participate in the conversation, and attempts to elicit ideas and involvement from the speaker's partners.

assertive conversationalists
Style of conversation that directs attention to themselves, seeks to control the conversation, and attempts to influence the speaking partner's ideas or actions.

Powerful women who speak confidently and directly often experience very negative reactions from others.

Critical Thinking Prompt
Why do you think that some people dislike women who speak directly and are self-focused in their conversations?

socioeconomic status
One's position in the economic hierarchy of society based on a combination of annual income, educational attainment, and occupational prestige.

A second reason that women can't just "talk more like a man" is that socially there are expectations or norms regarding how men and women are supposed to talk, and those who fail to meet these expectations can be sanctioned, often severely. For example, from an early age boys who are perceived to use a more feminine conversational style are teased, bullied, and even shunned. While girls are given more latitude to talk like boys, by adulthood women who talk like men often find themselves criticized and insulted by romantic partners, family members, and work colleagues for not being "womanly" or for being "bitchy" (Guadagno & Cialdini, 2007; Heilmen et al., 2004; Oakley, 2000). Studies examining the relationship between biological sex and job hiring and employment salary negotiations have found that women who are direct and self-focused are penalized for their conversational style and for being "unlikeable" (Bowles & Babcock, 2007). A concrete example of this is how some people, especially men, criticize and insult Representative Alexandria Ocasio-Cortez for her direct and forceful conversational style.

Influence of Socioeconomic Class

Given that biological sex and—to a certain extent—gender are obvious during in-person interactions, it makes sense that sex and gender significantly influence how conversationalists are perceived and evaluated. It also seems reasonable that **socioeconomic status**, or one's position in the economic hierarchy, would be easier to hide and would have less effect on social equality. However, studies show that verbal indicators of socioeconomic class are easily recognized and have an even larger effect on how speakers are viewed than do sex and gender (Kraus et al., 2019).

It may seem odd that conversational style contributes significantly to economic inequality in the United States. The beliefs that anyone in the country can become president and that equal opportunity is available to everyone are cherished ideals in the United States. However, considerable evidence proves otherwise. Many people are locked out of the opportunity for well-paying jobs, quality housing, and adequate health care due to the way they talk. As we discussed earlier, people signal their social class membership, including their likely income, education level, and occupation, whenever they interact with others through vocal style, including word choice, linguistic and paralinguistic patterns, and accent. Verbal identifiers of social class are important because perceptions of one's social status influence one's experiences and opportunities. For example, evaluations of others' social class influence perceivers' judgments of their traits, including personality, fit for a job position, and desirability as a social contact (Cote et al., 2014).

Furthermore, we often judge interaction partners differently, depending on our own and the partner's social class, and these evaluations affect our desire for social affiliation or connection. For example, one study discovered that participants' desire to affiliate or befriend their conversational partners depended on that person's social class (Cote et al., 2014). It found that both higher- and lower-class participants wished to affiliate with interaction partners when the partner was higher class. Why are so many people interested in others' social class and prefer higher-class friends and colleagues? They do so because they inherently recognize that higher-class people have more resources, including money, but also increased connections to people and places that can benefit them.

One of the ways social class and preference for higher-class connections contribute to inequality is that many, if not most, new company hires are recommended by someone within the organization. Generally, people recommend their friends for jobs and other benefits. If your dialect is perceived as not being higher-class, you may have

▲ One's social class influences one's opportunities for well-paying jobs, quality housing, and adequate health care.

fewer friends in a position to recommend you for desirable career positions and other opportunities. While it makes sense that we recommend and provide benefits to people with whom we affiliate, doing so means people with non-SAE dialects and potentially fewer connections likely have a much smaller chance of accessing good jobs, investments, and services. Therefore, people have developed an "ear" for befriending people who can benefit them.

Social class preferences affect our lives in many ways besides our choice of friends. We also interact with people from different classes in gatekeeping situations—such as in education settings, the workplace, and health institutions. Gatekeepers can intervene to help or hinder our success in these contexts (Ridgeway, 2014). Unfortunately, whom they help may depend on the individual's social class. For example, a study of faculty–student interactions discovered students from upper-class families were more likely than those from lower- or middle-class families to assist faculty with research for course credit, communicate with faculty by email or in person, and interact with faculty during lecture class sessions. Further, researchers found that students who assisted with faculty research earned higher GPAs and were more likely to express a desire to earn advanced degrees (Young & Sax, 2009). Thus, according to studies like this, being higher class increases the likelihood that you will receive more attention and have more interactions with your teachers, which in turn is likely to better prepare you for graduate school and professional occupations.

A wide range of research studies also establish that socioeconomic status and conversation style influence the quality of health care individuals receive. Communication between patients and physicians strongly affects patients' compliance with doctor's orders. The factors that most strongly affect compliance are increased physician information giving, positive talk, and a participatory conversational style—all of which influence overall health outcomes (Willems et al., 2005). However, Street and colleagues (1992) found that physicians' information giving is positively influenced by features of the patient's conversational style, such as question-asking, emotional expressiveness, and opinion giving. While this style was common among higher-social-class patients, it was rare among lower-class patients and, thus, likely affected the quality of their health care.

Other evidence, however, reveals that physicians give more information to particular types of patients than others regardless of the patients' interaction style. That is, more-educated patients receive more diagnostic and health information than do their counterparts even when both groups use the same conversation style. Furthermore, physicians acknowledged that they explained and listened more to patients from higher social classes than to patients from lower social classes but argued they gave the latter more "other help," which they did not specify. Physicians also said they spent more time examining lower-class patients but gave them less advice, in part, because they perceived that the patients did not want more information and were less able to take part in the care process (Street et al., 1992). See *Communication in Society: Vocabulary, Social Class, and Educational Opportunity* for more on how socioeconomic status impacts society.

COMMUNICATION IN SOCIETY
Vocabulary, Social Class, and Educational Opportunity

For years, critics of the Scholastic Aptitude Test (SAT) complained to The College Board, an educational association that develops and administers the test, that its product was deeply flawed. They argued that the SAT didn't measure a student's aptitude but measured their socioeconomic status instead. The vocabulary portion of the test was a particular point of contention for these detractors. They argued that the vocabulary words chosen for the subtest were relatively obscure and not words college students likely would ever use.

Further, critics claimed that students with wealthier, more educated parents had an advantage in that they were exposed to more advanced vocabulary and had parents who could afford tutors and pay for test prep courses. Some also believed that the test was biased against students from lower-social-class backgrounds because the tests were written and evaluated by higher-social-class individuals who unknowingly may have been assessing class-based knowledge. For instance, the test creators may have written questions that relied on background knowledge about golf rather than baseball or basketball.

Following is a chart from a report on SAT scores from 2009 detailing students' scores based on their parents' income (Goldfarb, 2014).

As you can see from the chart, parental income was strongly associated with students' SAT scores. Because most colleges and universities use SAT scores as a criterion for admission, it is very likely that students from wealthier families were accepted to a larger number and more competitive higher education institutions. Because of their scores, these students also were more likely to receive scholarships and grants to help pay their educational expenses.

Due to findings like these, in 2016, The College Board revised the SAT by changing its vocabulary list and dropping the essay portion of the exam, thereby providing a fairer test and, perhaps, more opportunity to applicants with lower-class socio-economic status.

SOURCES: Goldfarb, Z. A. (2014). *Economic policy.* https://www.washingtonpost.com/news/wonk/wp/2014/03/05/these-four-charts-show-how-the-sat-favors-the-rich-educated-families/?arc404=true

Subtirelu, N. (2014). *Shibboleths of social class: On the obscurity of SAT vocabulary.* https://linguisticpulse.com/2014/04/18/shibboleths-of-social-class-on-the-obscurity-of-sat-vocabulary/

Wade, L. (2012). The correlation between income and SAT scores. *The Society Pages.* https://www.washingtonpost.com/news/wonk/wp/2014/03/05/these-four-charts-show-how-the-sat-favors-the-rich-educated-families/?arc404=true

SAT Scores by Family Income

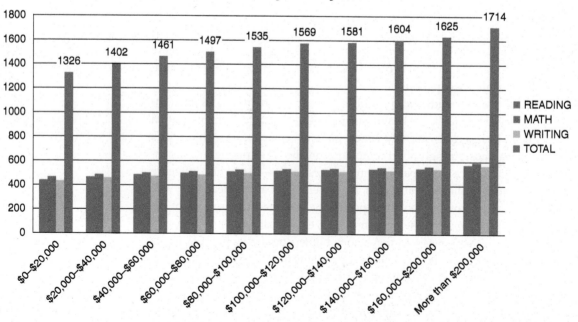

Influence of Race and Ethnicity

As we discussed in Chapter 4, across the United States people use many different dialects, depending on the region they live in, the groups they belong to, and the race and ethnicities with which they identify. Although stereotypes exist about a number of these dialects, none are as pervasive—and problematic—as the ones associated with racial and ethnic ways of speaking. People from around the world live and work in the United States and bring with them dialects associated with their countries of origin, but it is the dialects of African American and Mexican American citizens that evoke the most biases and, therefore, scholarly interest.

Many forms of bias and discrimination exist, but some are difficult to detect, identify, and prosecute. One type of such discrimination occurs due to **linguistic profiling**, a term coined by Professor John Baugh to refer to the act of using conversational style to attribute specific characteristics to a particular group (Baugh, 2003; Nour, 2019). Sometimes positive linguistic profiling occurs. For example, many U.S. Americans perceive British speakers who use an upper-class dialect (called *received pronunciation*) as intelligent and sophisticated, qualities they also associate with French accents. Perhaps more often, negative profiling happens. This arises when listeners identify speakers as less intelligent, trustworthy, or hard-working based on their dialects.

Dialects vary based on a number of factors, including speech rate and rhythms, word choice, pronunciation, and grammatical rules as well as accent. Research reveals that people frequently can identify a speakers' race based on their dialect (Baugh, 2003; Perrachione et al., 2010). For example, one study found listeners were 83.6 percent accurate at identifying White and 77.1 percent at recognizing Black communicators from samples of their conversations (Groggin, 2010). However, for us to be able identify an individual's race accurately from their dialect, we need to be familiar with the specific dialect, and even then, errors occur (Perrachione et al., 2010). Why is it important that people identify speakers by their dialects? First, since we usually are less familiar with other groups' dialects, we are more likely to commit errors of recognition. It is also problematic because speakers have an inherent bias in favor of their own dialects (Perrachione et al., 2010) such that they typically perceive their own way of speaking as superior to others'. Furthermore, listeners not only recognize other groups' dialects, they often attribute negative characteristics to the speakers who use them, and those attributions can significantly affect speakers' lives.

The most prominent dialects in the United States include standard American English (SAE), which is spoken by most White conversationalists; **Chicano English (ChE)**, spoken predominantly by Mexican Americans; and **African American English (AAE)**, used primarily by African American communicators. Conversationalists who use a dialect other than SAE often experience discrimination in real estate transactions, job interviews, and, occasionally, even legal matters. In a series of studies, native speakers of each of these three dialects called potential employers, real estate agents, loan officers, and service providers to determine how they responded to callers' different dialects. Researchers found that speakers of ChE and AAE dialects received fewer return calls overall, were more likely to be steered away from looking at properties in prominently White neighborhoods, were denied opportunities to request loans, and received fewer invitations for job interviews (Purnell et al., 1999).

Because racial discrimination in housing is against the law, researchers have studied bias in the real estate market extensively. In a study of the effect of dialect on apartment rentals (Purnell et al., 1999), callers who used SAE, AAE, and ChE dialects contacted rental agents in apartment buildings with units for lease in five communities that varied in their racial and ethnic diversity. Researchers found that the percentage of SAE callers who received confirmed viewing appointments was the same across all five neighborhoods. However, the percentage of AAE and ChE speakers who received confirmed appointments was equal to the percentage of the Black and Hispanic populations in

linguistic profiling
The act of using conversational style to attribute specific characteristic to a particular group.

Chicano English (ChE)
American English dialect spoken predominantly by Mexican American conversationalists.

African American English (AAE)
American English dialect used primarily by African American conversationalists.

▲ Members of cocultural groups often speak in dialects that remind them of the people and communities important to them.

each area. In a neighborhood with a higher White and lower Black population, 70.1 percent of SAE callers received viewing appointments while only 28.7 percent of Black callers did. In another area with a higher Black population and a low White population, 68.7 percent of SAE and 70.1 percent of Black callers received viewing appointments.

Similarly, scholars have examined the effect of dialect on bias in employment opportunities. Jeffrey Grogger (2019) found evidence that dialectal differences were responsible for job discrimination. Specifically, he found an association between a speaker's perceived race, based on their dialect, and their total earnings. African American speakers who were identified as Black earned 12 percent less than those who were not identified as Black, and those individuals who were not identified as Black earned as much as White workers. Other researchers who explored how non-SAE accented conversation influences interview judgments and decisions (Purkiss et al., 2003) found similar results. This study revealed that non-SAE accented speakers were viewed less positively by interviewers, while another determined that as non-SAE speakers' accents become stronger, evaluations of them became proportionately less favorable (Dragojevic et al., 2017).

Finally, people who speak in non-SAE dialects confront additional problems in courts of law. They are affected in two ways. First, since a ruling in 1985, a number of courts allow witnesses to identify offenders based on their dialects, even if the witness did not see the accused and despite the fact that erroneous identifications have been made. Second, at a criminal trial, *Florida v. Zimmerman*, a young Black woman speaking with an AAE dialect had her testimony disregarded because the judge believed people attach negative stereotypes to the way she spoke (McNeal et al., 2019). Although linguistic profiling is not inherently discriminatory, the many examples of discrimination based on bias and prejudice against non-SAE dialects detailed in this chapter and elsewhere reveal that both inside and outside courts of law linguistic profiling can result in negative consequences for non-SAE speakers.

"Show Me How You Speak, and I'll Tell You Who You Are"

As we have discussed throughout this chapter, power, privilege, and influence are communicated and perpetuated through conversation and perceptions of conversational style (Popp et al., 2003). For these reasons, we need to understand and push back against the fact that individuals' personal characteristics—such as sex/gender, socioeconomic class, and race and ethnicity—and conversational style can impede their success and well-being. Historically, efforts to change this situation have focused on "teaching" people to speak more "powerfully"—that is, more like White, educated males—but they have not proven to be effective. This strategy has failed because changing one's dialect does not remove all of the prejudices that give rise to discrimination; the speakers will still be female, economically disadvantaged, and not White.

Furthermore, a person's dialect is important to them for many reasons. The heading of this section comes from the title of an article whose author believes one's dialect is deeply entwined with one's identity (Schneider, 2000). He argues conversational style is not merely a habit or learned behavior; we also use it to signal who we are and who we want to be. Often, dialects are learned from and represent people we have been closest to throughout our lives, and the way we talk identifies us as members of groups that are important to us. Altering one's dialect can feel like a betrayal of one's family, community, and racial and ethnic identity. Thus, a more reasonable approach is to teach everyone that dialectical differences are valuable, interesting, equally valid ways of talking that enrich the English language and are not indicative of an individual's intelligence, character, and work ethic. They are merely ways of talking that remind us of home.

Journal Prompt 6.4:
The Individual, Conversational Interaction, and Society
How does society affect conversational interaction?

Conversational Ethics

6.5 Explain why manipulative conversational strategies are unethical.

A fundamental challenge all individuals face in their relationships is influencing the people who are important to them. In all types of relationships, people want to be able to persuade, or influence, others. For example, you want to be able to persuade friends to join you for a night of fun or to help you move into a new apartment. If you find you can't influence your friends and romantic partners, you may find those relationships dissatisfying and unfulfilling. Similarly, if it is difficult or impossible for you to refuse friends' and romantic partners' persuasion attempts, you will probably find those relationships frustrating or distressing.

When we talk about **persuasion** or influencing others, we are discussing occasions when people exert effort to cause an individual to do or believe something through reasoning or argument. Persuasion also is referred to as social influence. Since your authors are writing about persuasion in a module on ethics, it would be reasonable for you to think that we believe persuasion is unethical, but we definitely do not. However, at times people engage in efforts to influence others through manipulative conversational strategies, which we do believe are unethical. Most of us do not think of ourselves as being manipulative, but it is highly likely that many of us have acted this way without carefully considering what we are doing or the consequences it has.

In this context, **conversational manipulation** refers to persuasion attempts that intend to fool, control, or convince a conversational partner into doing or believing or buying something that causes them harm or provides no benefit (Fields, n.d.). In essence, manipulation occurs when we try to influence other people's behavior in a way that benefits us but not them. For example, if I sell you a product or cure for a disorder you have but I lie about its effectiveness to enrich myself at your expense, then I have manipulated you. A well-known literary example of manipulation occurs in *The Adventures of Tom Sawyer* when Tom persuades a dozen of his friends to whitewash a fence he was charged with painting. In the story, he spins an elaborate story whereby the boys come to believe

persuasion
Exerting effort to cause another person to do or believe something through reasoning or argument.

conversational manipulation
Persuasion attempts that intend to fool, control, or convince a person into doing, believing, or buying something that provides no benefit.

▼ When people lie or pretend to be someone they are not, they engage in conversational manipulation.

that Tom is doing *them* a favor rather than the other way around. While this is amusing in fiction, when we feel tricked into doing or buying something that offers us no benefit, we often feel angry, abused, and hostile toward the person who misled us.

Although persuasion and manipulation are similar in that we are trying to influence or convince another party, they are quite different. The difference between them lies in (1) your intent, (2) your truthfulness and the transparency of the interaction, and (3) who benefits by your efforts. In persuasion, our intent is to influence another to do something because we believe it is good for them or something they would enjoy; we tell the truth in our persuasive arguments, and the other party or even both of us benefit. Thus, trying to influence someone is not the problem; the issue is the purpose and manner of how we accomplish our effort. For example, if an instructor tries to influence you to enroll in their classes because they believe it will prepare you for your upper-division classes and enhance your ability to acquire a prestigious internship, then they have behaved ethically and have engaged in persuasion. On the other hand, if the instructor attempts to persuade you to enroll in one of their classes because the department will cancel the class unless one more student enrolls and the class doesn't count toward course requirements or directly benefit you, the instructor has manipulated you.

Lest you think that manipulation is a rare occurrence, a survey of 351 employees found that 5 percent to 14 percent of respondents felt that they were manipulated by malicious means on a weekly basis while 3 percent to 11 percent reported that they experienced manipulation every day (Hyde et al., 2016). If those numbers seem bad, think of all of the people who were being manipulated by unethical conversationalists and didn't realize it. Respondents in the study also admitted using malicious conversational strategies, such as making a colleague feel guilty or anxious or using flattery and deception by giving fake compliments. Thus, manipulation is relatively common, and many people might not think about their behavior as being unethical. Nonetheless, most of us have felt "used" or manipulated at some time in our lives.

How do you know if you have been manipulated conversationally—or that you engage in this behavior? You can begin by understanding these five primary conversational strategies manipulators use to persuade you to do what they want.

Critical Thinking Prompt
Has someone attempted to manipulate or successfully manipulated you? How did you feel when this happened? What strategies did the person use?

lying
Concealment, distortion, or dishonesty in communication.

minimization
Denying one's behavior or intent and trying to rationalize it.

evasion
Giving irrelevant, rambling, or vague responses.

1. **Lying.** Lying is probably the most prevalent tactic used to manipulate others. Liars can lie by commission, which occurs when someone provides information or "facts" that they know are not true, or by omission, which happens when a person knows you are misinformed but doesn't tell you the truth. It is difficult to tell when someone is lying to us, so our best protection is seeking confirmatory information whenever possible before committing to a course of action.

2. **Minimization.** Minimization occurs when a speaker denies their behavior or intent and tries to rationalize it. For example, it happens when you call someone out for insulting or hurting you and they argue that the problem is that you are too sensitive, not that they were unkind, or they claim that you are "overreacting" and what they have done isn't a violation or as serious as you believe. This behavior can go even further, such as when someone tries to persuade you that you don't feel as you say you feel.

3. **Evasion.** This occurs when a person gives an irrelevant, rambling, or vague response. A common tactic in this situation is for the manipulator to change the topic or make a joke so they don't have to address the issue.

4. **Feeling guilt.** Another common and often distressing way people manipulate others is by trying to make the other person feel guilty. They try to make their conversational partners feel bad by suggesting they are uncaring, selfish, spoiled, or otherwise at fault for the manipulator's behavior. For example, if a friend loses their temper and demeans you, they will tell you that they wouldn't behave this way if you were more loving or were less demanding. When people behave this way, the target may feel guilty, anxious, and unsure of themselves and the relationship.

5. **Bandwagon.** Finally, manipulators try to persuade others by using the **bandwagon effect**. This occurs when a person argues that many or even most people—or most "normal" people—have done what they want you to do. They often argue that your refusal is due to some flaw or problem within you. This strategy often arises in situations that we describe as involving "peer pressure," such sexual coercion, influencing a target to drink alcohol, or inducing someone to engage in risky behavior. Sometimes the manipulator will try to entice you into agreeing to their wishes, or they might insult you by saying you are too uptight, scared, or boring to do what they want.

If you discover that someone is attempting to talk you into or out of something or you find that you are using these conversational strategies, it is important that you recognize that the behavior is unethical. Honest persuaders provide truthful arguments and let other people make their own decisions. We often think we know what is best for other people, but they know themselves better than we do, and they have a right to make informed decisions. To do otherwise is an effort to trick someone, which is not what friends, colleagues, romantic partners, and family members expect.

bandwagon effect
Arguing that many or even most people have done what the manipulator wants you to do.

Journal Prompt 6.5: Conversational Ethics
Describe the five conversational strategies used to manipulate others.

Improving Your Conversational Interaction Skills

6.6   Describe the characteristics of an effective apology.

Though most people have been apologizing since they were very young (perhaps insincerely and because their parents forced them to), they still often find it difficult to ask for forgiveness. Apologizing is challenging because it can be uncomfortable to admit one is at fault and it can be hard to convey that one is truly sorry. Yet a heartfelt apology can go a long way toward repairing a relationship and persuading others to forgive you. Therefore, we offer three behavioral requirements and three conversational strategies to help you convey apologies effectively (Dunleavy et al., 2009).

Behaviors to display before the offended party will be open to hearing your apology:

- **Don't wait.** Waiting too long can be perceived as negatively as not apologizing at all. It is best to apologize as soon as possible after your transgression. A delayed apology suggests that you are only doing so because you feel coerced, which leads to our next point.

- **Be genuine.** Injured people tend to be very sensitive to any suggestion that you are being insincere. An insincere apology does not repair the damage or your relationship. If you are truly sorry, it will be easier to make a successful apology.

- **Accept the other person's anger.** Just because you are now sorry doesn't mean the other person automatically and immediately forgives and forgets. You need to listen to the injured party, discuss how your behavior has hurt them, and you need to give them time to get over their pain. It is the least that you owe someone whom you have hurt.

Conversational strategies for effectively expressing remorse:

- **Identify what you did wrong.** Make it clear that you know exactly how you injured the other party, and under no circumstance utter the statement "I am sorry if you feel bad" ("got hurt," "were disappointed," etc.). This is *not* an apology. Such a statement suggests that the other person is responsible for feeling hurt or injured, and it does not acknowledge what you did wrong.

- **Don't offer justifications or excuses.** As tempting as it may be, do not try to justify your behavior or offer an excuse (e.g., "I was drunk or angry or stressed"). And certainly do not excuse your behavior by blaming the other person (e.g., "If you didn't work all the time, I wouldn't have been so lonely that I cheated on you").
- **Explain how you will ensure the injury does not occur again.** It is not enough to feel bad about the past; you also need to offer assurances that you have learned your lesson and will not repeat the offense again. Apologies that are not accompanied by a commitment to change are of little value.

Developing the ability to offer sincere, effective apologies can enhance your life in several ways. First, it can help repair or strengthen relationships that are important to you. Everyone engages in behaviors that hurt or injure those they love, but people who show that they are truly sorry and will not reoffend can often minimize the long-term effects on their relationships. Second, apologizing shows that you take responsibility for your behavior and that you have integrity, both of which are likely to influence others to forgive you and trust you again. Third, as you gain experience with admitting you are wrong, you will find that—contrary to what many people believe—doing so actually makes you stronger and more respected. Finally, if you follow these suggestions, in time you will find it easier to apologize and perhaps even discover that you have fewer reasons to do so.

**Journal Prompt 6.6:
Improving Your Conversational
Interaction Skills**
Summarize and explain three
conversational strategies necessary
for an effective apology.

SUMMARY

6.1 Describe how in-person conversations differ from mediated conversations.

- In-person conversations provide more information than mediated conversations by allowing us to see a wider range of nonverbal cues, including micro expressions and bodily and olfactic cues. They also offer personal and professional benefits and opportunities that are not available elsewhere.

6.2 Define *conversational interaction*.

- Conversations are informal, in-person, spoken interactions in which participants exchange ideas, information, and feelings through talking with one another.

6.3 Explain the fundamental skills necessary for effective in-person conversations.

- Perspective taking, conversational awareness, and contextual awareness are the fundamental skills needed for one to be an effective conversationalist.

6.4 Explain the role society plays in conversational interaction.

- Societal norms and expectations shape the rules for how we talk with one another and how others evaluate us and our conversational styles.

6.5 Explain why manipulative conversational strategies are unethical.

- Conversational manipulation is unethical because it deprives us of the information we need to make decisions that are informed and beneficial to us.

6.6 Describe the characteristics of an effective apology.

- Effective apologies are timely and genuine and identify the wrongdoing that occurred. Furthermore, the apologizer accepts the other person's anger, refrains from offering justifications and excuses, and explains how they will ensure that the injury does not happen again.

KEY TERMS

micro expressions p. 133
olfactics p. 133
conversation p. 135
perspective taking p. 138
naïve realism p. 139
conversational awareness p. 141
contextual awareness p. 142
hurtful messages p. 145
intentional messages p. 146
unintentional messages p. 146

intensity p. 146
sexual consent p. 147
sexual coercion p. 148
social norms p. 151
gatekeeping p. 152
standard American English (SAE) p. 152
affiliative conversationalists p. 153
assertive conversationalists p. 153
socioeconomic status p. 154

linguistic profiling p. 157
Chicano English (ChE) p. 157
African American English (AAE) p. 157
persuasion p. 159
conversational manipulation p. 159
lying p. 160
minimization p. 160
evasion p. 160
bandwagon effect p. 161

APPLY WHAT YOU KNOW

1. **Take Another Person's Perspective**

   To help you practice taking another person's perspective, think about a recent conversation in which you and another person disagreed or argued. Describe the conflict from *the other person's perspective*. That is, explain how the other person saw the conflict and why they interacted as they did.

   After you complete your explanation, write down any biases you have about the other person, the topic, the situation, or yourself. Next, generate at least three explanations or theories for why the other person spoke and acted as they did. Then examine how accurately you think you captured the other person's perspective. After doing this, revise your description, and contact the other person to hear how they would describe the conflict. Finally, explain what you have learned from this activity.

2. **Plan a Potentially Hurtful Message**

   For this activity, think about a hurtful message you need to express to someone. Next, review the five suggestions for creating messages that are potentially hurtful and follow them to restate the hurtful message to create a new message that you could deliver in the future.

3. **Create an Effective Apology**

   Based on the three behaviors and three conversational strategies that help people apologize more effectively, write an apology that you could deliver to someone you know. You may choose an event from the past where you didn't apologize or didn't apologize effectively, or you can plan an apology that you feel you should offer in the near future.

Listening and Responding

 LEARNING OBJECTIVES

CHAPTER TOPICS

7.1 Identify six reasons why listening is important.

7.2 Describe the four stages of listening.

7.3 Describe the influences on listening and barriers to effective listening.

7.4 Understand the role of societal forces (hierarchy, contexts, and community) in listening.

7.5 Describe ethical challenges in listening.

7.6 Discuss two ways to improve your own listening behavior.

The Importance of Listening

What Is Listening? Four Stages

Listening and the Individual: Influences and Barriers

The Individual, Listening, and Society: Hierarchy, Contexts, and Community

Ethics and Listening

Improving Your Listening Skills

> *"Listening retains its position as the most widely used daily communication activity."*

Charee wonders if her listening skills are deteriorating. After taking a class in communication and learning about both bad listening habits and effective strategies for listening, she realized that she often doesn't listen to what others are saying because she's busy thinking of the next thing she's going to say. She also started thinking about the impact of what her professor calls "chronic earbud attachment syndrome"—the "addiction" that she and many of her fellow students have to their earbuds and to their almost-constant "listening" on social media. Although this doesn't impact their ability to listen, she thinks it probably affects their opportunities to listen, perhaps meaning she misses out on little things that humans hear throughout the day that help make sense of the world and maybe also sends a negative message to others. She thinks about the fact that when she's in an elevator with her professor, she doesn't have to converse or stand in silence; she can avoid the interaction. She says it was hard, and it took conscious effort, but she's been trying to take more listening opportunities and also to listen to what others say and acknowledge their thoughts before she responds. She thinks it has helped because now she even finds the discussions in classes more productive and interesting.

Listening may be the single most important skill in the communication process because communication doesn't exist without a listener (Lacey, 2013, p. 168)! But most of us, like Charee, don't really think about it very much. Why is this? Perhaps it's because we confuse hearing and listening. As we will discover later in this chapter, hearing is passive; it occurs when listeners pick up the sound waves directed at them. Listening, however, like speaking or writing, is a more active communication process and involves understanding and evaluating messages. Or perhaps we think that listening can't be taught or learned. After all, few college courses teach listening theory and practice. However, as we'll discover in this chapter, a great deal of academic research focuses on the listening process, which includes not only hearing what others say but also critically evaluating messages and responding. Communication experts have shown that by being aware of the dynamics of listening and working on being better listeners, we can become better communicators overall.

In this chapter, we will first identify six important reasons for improving listening and responding skills. We will then describe the process of listening as well as some of the influences and barriers to effective listening. Finally, we'll discuss the role of societal forces in listening, ethical issues related to listening, and suggestions for becoming a more effective listener.

The Importance of Listening

7.1   Identify six reasons why listening is important.

You might not understand why it is important to learn about listening. After all, it seems rather automatic, something we don't think about often. As this section shows, improving our listening skills can lead to many personal and professional benefits.

The first important reason for learning more about listening is that we spend so much time doing it! Listening is the primary communication activity for college students (Janusik & Wolvin, 2009), and experts estimate that they spend 55 percent of their total average communication day listening. About half that time is spent in interpersonal listening (class, face-to-face conversations, phone, listening to voice messages) and the other half in media listening (Emanuel et al., 2008). In fact, media listening, in the broadest sense, encompasses a variety of online activities, including social media such as Facebook, Instagram, TikTok, and Twitter, which provide a steady stream of messages (Perrin & Anderson, 2019).

Second, having better listening skills can improve your memory, give you a broader knowledge base, and increase your attention span (Pasupathi & Billitteri, 2015). The brain is like any other muscle; you have to use it to improve it. The more you exercise it, the better you'll be able to process and remember information. The first step in exercising the brain is to pay better attention when others are speaking. You can't remember something if you never learned it, and you can't learn something—

▲ Learning to be a better listener can boost academic performance.

that is, encode it into your brain—if you don't pay enough attention to it.

A third, related reason to learn more about listening is that good listening skills can enhance academic performance. Not surprisingly, a number of research studies have shown that college students who have good listening skills are better students than those who are less effective listeners (Ferrari-Bridgers et al., 2017a). Recent research shows that one of the most important outcomes of classes on listening is that students become more aware of what constitutes good listening (Ferrari-Bridgers et al., 2017b). Although this indicates that a college course can help you identify the skills needed to be a good listener, you may need a lot of practice and attention to skill building on your own to become an effective listener. This is what Charee, in the opening vignette, realized.

Better listening is also linked to enhanced personal relationships—a fourth reason to learn more about listening. In earlier chapters, we have discussed how effective communication skills can lead to enhanced personal relationships. This is also true for listening skills. It's easy to understand how better listening can lead to fewer misunderstandings, which in turn can lead to greater satisfaction, happiness, and a sense of well-being for us and those we care about (Floyd, 2014; Manusov et al., 2020).

A fifth reason to improve listening skills is because leaders in many professions have long emphasized that effective listening is a highly desirable workplace skill; in fact, listening is "extremely important to almost all jobs that require an employee to work in hierarchical teams or to serve customers" (Carnevale, 2013, p. 8), from physicians and nurses (Shafran-Tikva & Kluger, 2018) and social workers but also beauticians (Hanson, 2019), engineering and math professionals (Ferrari-Bridgers et al., 2017a), and many others. This is especially important given that several business studies report that recent undergraduate students tend to lack the effective communication skills to survive in twenty-first-century jobs (Ramos Salazar, 2017). Poor listening skills can be costly; the consequences include wasted meeting time; inaccurate orders/shipments; lost sales; inadequately informed, misinformed, confused, or angry staff and customers; unmet deadlines; unsolved problems; wrong decisions; lawsuits; and poor employee morale (Battell, 2006). In contrast, people with good listening skills are perceived to be more trustworthy, which is important to a variety of work relationships, including physician–patient, salesperson–customer, and supervisor–employee (Lloyd et al., 2015).

People who are perceived to be good listeners in work settings are likely to be perceived as having leadership qualities (Kluger & Zaidel, 2013), and listening seems to play an interesting role in career advancement as well. One study showed that as workers move into management positions, listening skills become more important (Welch & Mickelson, 2013), particularly listening that involves close attention to the verbal and nonverbal aspects to the message. As more and more organizations expand internationally, managers and nonmanagers find that listening plays an even more important role in their intercultural interactions. As we discuss later in the chapter, effective listening behaviors may vary from culture to culture, and individuals need to understand the influence of culture on listening patterns (Roebuck et al., 2016).

Finally, good listening can actually lead to improved physical health. Some studies show that when we listen attentively, heart rate and oxygen consumption are reduced, which leads to increased blood and oxygen to the brain—a healthy cardiovascular condition (Diamond, 2007). Psychologists and spiritual leaders point out that listening well is critical to our collective emotional health, especially during a pandemic when many people are frightened, sad, grieving, or angry, and need attentive and supportive listeners (Klein, 2020). We'll discuss these strategies later in the chapter.

Now that we've discussed the importance of learning about listening, the next section describes the process of listening, which shows that listening is much more than just hearing what others are saying.

Journal Prompt 7.1: Listening and Responding
What are six reasons for learning about listening and responding? Why are good listening and responding skills so important in professional contexts?

What Is Listening? Four Stages

7.2   Describe the four stages of listening.

The first step in striving to improve listening skills is to understand exactly what we mean when we talk about listening. Thus, we first provide a definition and then describe the process of listening.

Although there are various definitions for **listening**, the one we'll use is provided by the International Listening Association. Listening is "the process of receiving, constructing meaning from, and responding to spoken and/or nonverbal messages" (International Listening Association, 1995, p. 4; Wolvin, 2013, p. 104). As you can see, this definition includes the concept described in Chapter 1 as the decoding phase of the communication process. While most people think of listening as a holistic activity (Lipetz et al., 2020), it is useful to consider it in four stages: *hearing, understanding, evaluating,* and *responding* (Rosenfeld & Berko, 1990).

Let's see how this might work. **Hearing** occurs when listeners pick up the sound waves directed toward them. Suppose you're sitting in your apartment deep into Instagram and you hear sounds in the kitchen; it's your roommate, Makeva, returning from her part-time job as a delivery driver. She yells out, "Guess what happened at work today." For communication to occur, you must first become aware that information is being directed at you. In other words, you have to hear the sounds. But, of course, hearing something is not the same as understanding or evaluating the information—the next steps. This means that hearing is not the same as listening. Hearing is really only the first step.

Once you sense that sounds are occurring, you have to interpret the messages associated with the sounds—that is, you have to **understand** what the sounds mean. The meaning you assign affects how you will respond—both physiologically and communicatively. In the example of your roommate, Makeva, you understand her words—she's asking you to guess what happened to her at work that day.

After you understand (or at least believe you understand) the message you have received, you **evaluate** the information. When you evaluate a message, you assess your reaction to it. For example, what do you think Makeva is really asking you? Did something incredibly important happen to her at work? Or does she ask you this every time

listening
The process of receiving, constructing meaning from, and responding to spoken and/or nonverbal messages.

hearing
The stage when listeners pick up the sound waves directed toward them.

understanding
Interpreting the messages associated with sounds or what the sounds mean.

evaluating
Assessing your reaction to a message.

she returns from work, so you know it doesn't matter what you answer because she is going to tell you some long, drawn-out story about people to whom she delivers who you don't know? Or is she trying to engage you in conversation because you have both been busy and haven't seen each other much lately? As you can see, critical thinking skills are important in evaluating what you have heard—what are the possible interpretations of the message sent? What are the logical interpretations?

Finally, you **respond** to messages. Maybe you decide that you really want to hear what Makeva's going to tell you or at least want to have a conversation with her and you tell her so—"No, I can't imagine what happened at work today. Tell me!" Your response provides the most significant evidence to others that you are listening. Responding means that you show others how you regard their messages. For example, you could have responded to Makeva in a sarcastic tone, letting her know that you'll listen but you're not really interested; or you could have just said "hmmm," telling her you don't even want to engage in a conversation. Even failing to respond is a type of response! Not answering a text message or not replying to a tweet or not responding to (liking) a good friend's TikTok video is a response of sort. You can respond in numerous ways; however, your response will be influenced by *how* you listen. In his recent book on communication tips (*If I Understood You, Would I Have This Look on My Face?*), actor Alan Alda encourages readers to respond in conversations based on what they see in another person's behavior. He explains that this type of listening is "responsive listening . . . [because] real conversation can't happen if listening is just my waiting for you to finish talking" (p. 10). In other words, he is encouraging readers to be *active*, rather than passive, listeners, actively focusing on the speaker and ignoring all distractions.

In addition to these phases of listening, we need to recognize that the total process of listening as a communication process is complex, involving motivations (we have to want to listen), cognitions, emotions, and behaviors (Bodie et al., 2008). In addition, some communication experts expand the definition of listening to include lurking—following tweets and Instagram and Facebook posts without responding (see *Alternative View: Lurkers as Listeners*).

responding
Showing others how you regard their message.

Critical Thinking Prompt
Think of a recent conflict you had, and describe how listening behaviors might have influenced the outcome. How might it have been different if those involved had spent more time listening instead of talking?

ALTERNATIVE VIEW
Lurkers as Listeners

Some listening experts think we should broaden our definition of listening, suggesting that just by attending to the many new messages we see each day—streaming TikTok videos, seeing Facebook and Instagram posts, following tweets—we are listening, even if we just "lurk" and don't respond. However, there are varying viewpoints about the merits of this type of listening.

On the one hand, some TikTok users clearly express hostility toward lurking listeners (https://www.tiktok.com/tag/lurkers?lang=en), especially directed at exes or "stalkers" (e.g., "kill the b*** that's lurking," "to the girls lurking for my ex, tell him I'm doin great"). And some research suggests that lurking, especially for adolescents with "peer problems," can have negative psychological effects, including depression (Underwood & Ehrenreich, 2017). Also, there is evidence that regular exposure to the "very bad, hateful, awful things" one encounters while lurking is bad for the brain (Lange, 2018).

However, others see it more positively. Writer Joanne McNeil (2020) sees online space as a library, "a civic and independent body" where "everyone is welcome . . . just for being." And lurking then can be an act like reading, for work or research or general curiosity.

In this view, lurker listeners have an important role, as every public forum needs listeners as well as speakers; every publishing platform needs readers as well as writers. Lurking listeners are necessary to provoke the senders to keep speaking. And anonymity is part of the deal—we can publish our opinions, photos, and texts without knowing exactly who will see them "and that's part of what makes publishing online a hopeful experience" (Lange, 2018).

SOURCES: Lange, J. (2018). Let us lurk. *theweek.com*. https://theweek.com/articles/804466/let-lurk

McNeil, J. (2020). *Lurking: How a person became a user*. MCD.

Underwood, M. K., & Ehrenreich, S. E. (2017). The power and the pain of adolescents' digital communication: Cyber victimization and the perils of lurking. *The American Psychologist, 72*(2), 144–158.

Journal Prompt 7.2:
Defining Listening
What is a definition of listening?
What are the four stages of listening?

Now that you understand the process of listening, the next section shows how an individual's personal characteristics influence listening and responding. We also describe how different situations require different types of listening skills.

Listening and the Individual: Influences and Barriers

7.3 Describe the influences on listening and barriers to effective listening.

Do you have any friends who are especially good listeners? Any who are not so good? Do you find it easier to listen in some situations than in others?

Although some studies have identified general listening skills (see *Communication in Society: The "Big Five" of Listening Competency*), there are many factors that influence whether listening in any particular situation is easier or more difficult. In this section, we describe some of these factors, including individual listening styles and individual characteristics such as gender, age, and nationality. Finally, we discuss physical and psychological barriers to listening.

Influences on Listening

Not everyone listens in the same way; our personal listening habits may be influenced by gender, age, ethnicity, or even certain idiosyncratic patterns. These influences can then affect how we respond to others. Let's look first at the various listening styles and then turn to other characteristics that may influence how we listen and respond.

listening style

A set of attitudes, beliefs, and predispositions about the how, where, when, who, and what of the information receiving and encoding process.

Listening Styles   According to experts, a **listening style** is a set of "attitudes, beliefs, and predispositions about the how, where, when, who, and what of the information reception and encoding process" (Watson et al., 1995, p. 2). To put it more simply, it is "the way people prefer to receive oral information" (Watson et al., 1995, p. 9). Researchers have identified four listening styles used in various situations (Bodie et al., 2013a) and find that a given individual will tend to prefer to use just one or two of these styles, depending on the situation, of course (Gearhart et al., 2014).

Each listening style emphasizes a particular set of skills that are useful for responding to others in particular situations. The point of this is not that you should strive to

COMMUNICATION IN SOCIETY
The "Big Five" of Listening Competency

An online questionnaire asked 1,319 students to describe what it means to be an effective listener. The results revealed the following top or "Big Five" dimensions of effective listening.

Notice how each of these dimensions is associated with the phases of listening (hearing, sensing, and so on). Are there other skills that you would add?

1. Openness or willingness to listen
2. Ability to read nonverbal cues
3. Ability to understand verbal cues
4. Ability to respond appropriately
5. Ability to remember relevant details

Although these skills are important and confirm findings from previous studies, the authors of the study note that other factors, such as age, maturity, and personal experiences, influence an individual's listening competence. In addition, they note that the study design did not address the influence of context or interpersonal relationship.

SOURCE: Cooper, L. O., & Buchanan, T. (2010). Listening competency on campus: A psychometric analysis of student listening. *International Journal of Listening, 24*(3), 141–163.

develop a particular style or that having a particular style ensures you will be a good listener but that your listening style should vary somewhat by context or situation. And, indeed, studies have shown that most people do vary their listening style from situation to situation, as we'll discuss later in the chapter.

Critical Listening Style   The **critical listening style** focuses on the accuracy of the content and reflects a preference for error-free and well-organized speaking. If the speech is rambling and disorganized, people using this style may be mentally taking notes and second guessing the truth or legitimacy of what is being discussed.

> **critical listening style**
> Listening style that focuses on the accuracy of the content and reflects a preference for error-free and well-organized speaking.

The following are listening skills that are useful in situations requiring attention to the veracity and organization of the content:

- **Consider the speaker's credibility.** Is this speaker qualified to make these arguments? Is this speaker trustworthy?
- **Listen between the lines.** Are the words spoken and the body language consistent? Are the content and the emotion in harmony?
- **Weigh the evidence.** Does what is being said make sense? Are the opinions presented supported by fact?

Task-Oriented Listening Style   The **task-oriented listening style** reflects an interest in listening as a simple transaction, focusing on the *substance, the point* of the content. People who use this style attend to details and appreciate efficiency and clarity. They may get impatient, check their email, or send a text when they think someone is taking too long to get to the point.

> **task-oriented listening style**
> Listening style that reflects an interest in listening as simply a transaction, focused on the substance, the point of the message.

The task-oriented style requires **informational listening** skills. For example, at work you probably listen primarily for content, to make sure you understand the instructions of your boss, supervisor, or coworkers. Informational listening skills are also useful at school during course lectures or when professors give detailed instructions about assignments. How can you improve your informational listening skills? Here are some suggestions:

> **informational listening**
> Listening skills that are useful in situations requiring attention, in general, to content.

- **Attend to what the speaker is saying.** Maintain eye contact, face the person, and lean toward them.
- **Paraphrase.** Reflect the speaker's words back to make sure you understand and let the speaker know you are listening—for example, if your professor is describing instructions for an assignment, you might say, "You're saying that the five-page paper needs to cite at least 10 different research sources."
- **Clarify.** Ask questions to clear up any confusion or seek more information. For example, if you don't completely understand your professor's instructions about a paper assignment, you might ask, "Can we email it to you or do you want us to hand it to you in class?"
- **Review and summarize.** Summarizing captures the overall meaning of what has been said and puts it into a logical and coherent order but should not add any new information. After your summary, you might also ask, "Is that correct?"

Analytical Listening Style   The **analytical listening style** focuses on the facts and involves a tendency to engage in systematic thinking as opposed to mere enjoyment of complex, error-free information. People using this style withhold judgment about another's ideas until they have heard the whole message, listening to all sides of an issue before responding.

> **analytical listening style**
> Listening style that systematically focuses on the facts and the logical consistency of a speaker's message and withholds judgment until all information is presented.

This style involves the task-oriented listening skills detailed previously and an additional set of systematic analytical skills that are particularly useful in situations involving persuasive speaking—for example, when you are listening to a political speech or a sales pitch—or even in more informal settings, such as when friends or

Relational listening involves listening not only to words but also to others' feelings.

acquaintances try to persuade you to see their point of view about an issue or activity. Here are some suggestions for developing analytical listening skills:

- **Listen between the lines.** Note the nonverbal messages as well as the verbal messages in order to understand more completely what the speaker is saying,

- **Don't judge the speaker prematurely.** Making mental judgments can prevent you from understanding the content of the speaker's message.

- **Evaluate the messages being sent and their implications.** Ask yourself, "What conclusions can be drawn from what is being said? Where is this leading?"

- **Periodically review and summarize.** As with informational listening, you need to periodically check to make sure you understand the message. Ask yourself, "Do I have it straight? Do I understand the speakers' arguments and main points? Do I understand well enough to draw some conclusions and, if appropriate, respond to the speaker?"

relational listening style

Listening style that is associated with friendly, open communication and an interest in establishing ties with others.

active-empathic listening (AEL)

Listening skills that involve active engagement with the speaker and listeners putting themselves emotionally in the speaker's shoes, not only on understanding information but also "listening" to others' feelings.

Relational Listening Style   People using this style are interested in hearing about others' experiences, thoughts, and feelings. The **relational listening style** is often associated with friendly, open communication and an interest in establishing ties with others. This style is useful in many different contexts; a research study found that most people prefer empathic, person-centered listeners who are sensitive to their emotions (Itzchakov et al., 2014).

Relational listening involves **active-empathic listening (AEL)** skills, focused not only on understanding information but also "listening" to others' feelings—which they may communicate nonverbally, as we saw in Chapter 5. It turns out that people with good AEL also tend to be more open and agreeable in personal relationships (Sims, 2017).

Consider the following suggestions for active-empathic listening. Notice also how many of them involve nonverbal behaviors on the listener's part:

- **Put the other person at ease.** Give space, time, and permission to speak. Do this by showing that you *want* to hear the speaker. Look at them. Nod when you can agree. Encourage the speaker to talk.

- **Remove distractions.** Be willing to take out your earbuds, close a door, and stop texting or checking your phone. Let the speaker know they have your full attention.

- **Empathize with the other person.** Take a moment to stand in the other person's shoes, to look at the situation from their point of view, especially if they are telling you something personal or painful. Empathy can be expressed by allowing the person to talk while maintaining a nonjudgmental, noncritical manner. Don't discount the person's feelings (e.g., "it's not really that bad" or "you'll feel better tomorrow") and paraphrase what you think the person really means or feels to communicate that you understand the emotions and feelings involved.

- **Be patient.** Some people take longer to find the right word, make a point, or clarify an issue.

- **Be aware of your own emotions.** Active-empathic listening can sometimes be challenging. It may cause stress on the part of the listeners (Sims, 2017), and as we'll discuss later in the chapter, emotions can be a barrier to effective listening. A religious leader described how she meets the challenges of her emotions when she is experiencing the same losses and uncertainty during the pandemic: "At work, I take more breaks to breathe and reflect to remain present to others. In my personal life, I consider my capacity to listen well and make adjustments, perhaps letting a loved one know I need to change the subject or asking for time to express my feelings" (Klein, 2020).

In conclusion, to become a more effective listener in a variety of personal and professional contexts, identify your preferred style(s) and then work on developing the skill sets that accompany the other styles. For example, if you tend to be a relational listener, you might improve your task-oriented and critical listening skills. On the other hand, if you tend to prefer the task-oriented style, you might work to develop your relational listening skills. You might also improve particular skills key to your profession. For example, social workers, medical paraprofessionals, and beauty professionals require relational (as well as task-oriented) listening skills (Hanson, 2019). Engineers and math professionals require critical and analytic skills (Ferrari-Bridgers et al., 2017a).

A recent study found that individuals often adapt their preferred style to particular situations, depending on the context and goals for the interaction. One study participant identified their preferred style as relational but reported an interaction (on the job at a department store) when they chose the analytical listening style. In this instance, a customer disclosed intimate personal details and opinions about relational infidelity, and the participant felt it was more important to withhold judgment and opinions (analytical listening) than to try to understand the feelings of the customer, as the topic seemed inappropriate for the professional department store context (Gearhart et al., 2014, pp. 13–14).

Individual Identity Characteristics   Now let's turn to other individual influences on listening behaviors. How do individual identity characteristics such as gender, age, and ethnicity affect listening behaviors? Do males and females tend to listen differently? Do older people listen in a different way than do younger people? And a related set of questions: Should we adapt our listening behaviors depending on who we are listening to? For example, should we listen to children differently from adults? Let's look at how the experts weigh in on answers to these questions.

Gender   Some scholars think that in general men and women not only differ in their listening styles, but that women tend to be better listeners than men. Other researchers have found no gender differences in listening behavior (Imhof, 2004; Pearce et al., 2003). Before looking at the research on this topic, let's discuss the issue of gender stereotypes— that is, the common perceptions people have concerning gender and listening.

Two communication scholars have identified common gender-based listening stereotypes: Men, they say, are supposedly logical, judgmental, interrupting, inattentive, self-centered, and impatient, whereas women are stereotyped as emotional, attentive, empathetic, other-centered, responsive, and patient (Barker & Watson, 2000). And there is some evidence to suggest that women are better at empathic listening (Welch & Mickelson, 2020). For example, one study, asking 500 staff workers and managers in a variety of industries to rate themselves on a Listening Competency Scale, found that both female staff and managers rated themselves as more competent at therapeutic (active-empathic) listening than males, and overall, female managers scored higher than the male managers (Welch & Mickelson, 2013). Similarly, two more recent self-report studies found that women scored higher than men on several aspects of active-empathic listening (e.g., sensing and responding) (Pence & James, 2015) and communicating engagement in conversation nonverbally (Sims, 2017).

As we've discussed in earlier chapters, most behavioral scientists believe that although some innate gender differences may exist, most behavioral differences between men and women are influenced more by cultural norms than biology (Sims, 2017). To sum it up, there do seem to be a few gender differences in listening behaviors, but both men and women can demonstrate feminine and masculine listening behaviors (Bodie & Fitch-Hauser, 2010). Remember, too, that gender differences are not fixed and given; people of both genders can learn to be effective listeners.

Critical Thinking Prompt
Consider the various listening styles and think about which style(s) you tend to use. Which are you less likely to use? Which sets of skills might you need to work on to become a more effective listener?

▲ Listening to children involves adjusting one's listening style and being tolerant of children's "breaking" conversational rules.

Age   Do you listen differently to your parents than to your younger siblings? The fact is that people have different communication capacities and skill levels during various life stages, which means that we often adapt our listening behaviors depending on the age of the speaker (Brownell, 2015). We can and should adapt our listening behaviors for children (Clark, 2005). Because young children are in the process of developing their communication skills, we need to be patient when they "break" conversational rules or are struggling to say something; children have more to say than they can express. Give them your undivided attention, maintaining eye contact when they're speaking and asking questions; in other words, be a good listening role model (Brownell, 2015).

As we get older, listening may become more difficult if hearing ability is an issue. We'll discuss hearing disability in the next section, under barriers to listening. However, not everyone who is old is deaf or has diminished mental abilities. Assuming that they are—that is, yelling or treating listeners like children—can be hurtful and insulting (Froemming & Penington, 2011).

Nationality   Do people in all cultures consider listening equally important? The answer is no. Generally speaking, people in Western countries (the United States and Europe) tend to place more emphasis on speaking skills, whereas many Asians consider listening to be the most important communication skills and are taught early that they *must* be good listeners (Beall, 2010, p. 233). In addition, there are cultural differences in what people consider appropriate nonverbal expressions of listening and responding (Imhof & Janusik, 2006). In most Western cultures, good listening is demonstrated by eye contact, head nods, and some back-channeling vocalizations such as "hmmm" and "oh." However, in some countries, such as Vietnam and Thailand, good listening behavior (listening respectfully) involves avoiding eye contact. In other countries, such as Japan, good listening may involve responding with lots of head nods, back-channeling, and even saying "yes, yes," which actually means, "I hear you," not "I agree with you" (Fujii, 2008).

A recent study comparing listening style perceptions in Bulgaria, Finland, Germany, Japan, and the United States found that while participants in all countries judged listening concepts in a similar way, there were some differences in specific behavior expectations (e.g., as described earlier). The authors conclude that "when individuals from different cultural backgrounds interact, they might be communicating based on quite distinct assumptions which—when they remain implicit—may cause misunderstanding and confusion" (Janusik & Imhof, 2017, p. 93). We'll explore more cross-cultural differences in communication patterns in the following chapter.

Here, however, to summarize, factors that can influence an individual's listening behavior include gender, age, and nationality as well as one's own listening style preferences and the particular situation. Still, one cannot assume that an individual will listen in a particular way just because they belong to a certain gender, age, or nationality group. Listening is a complex behavior, and numerous factors beyond these kinds of identity characteristics can serve as barriers, the topic we turn to next.

Barriers to Listening

Like Charee in the opening vignette, people have many reasons for not listening to others. Some typical ones include physical and physiological barriers, psychological barriers, conflicting objectives, and poor listening habits (Robertson, 2005). Let's explore in more detail how these factors can interfere with effective listening.

Physical and Physiological Barriers Physical barriers to listening include a noisy environment or physical discomforts that make it difficult to concentrate. We have all had

▲ Fatigue is a common barrier to listening.

the experience of trying to listen to someone in a noisy bar or in a room with a loud television or while standing outside with traffic whizzing by on a busy highway. Physical barriers are the most elemental; if we can't hear because of the noise around us, it doesn't matter how refined our listening skills are.

Another physical barrier is fatigue. Whether a listener is tired from lack of sleep or from high stress, it can be a barrier to good listening. For example, it's difficult for students to listen effectively in class when they are exhausted, and it's difficult for parents to listen to children when they are stressed out from working hard and managing their many responsibilities. As we hope you understand by now, listening well takes effort and requires alertness and focus—both of which may be absent when one is tired.

Another type of listening barrier is physiological—for example, a hearing disability. Good listening is a skill, but it is also strongly affected by a person's physical ability to hear. The Hearing Loss Association of America estimates that more than 48 million people in the United States (and 466 million worldwide) have a hearing loss that could be treated, and in fact, an increasing number of younger people have hearing problems due to listening to loud music at concerts or cranking up the volume on their earbuds (Sagon, 2017). (See *Did You Know? Statistically, How Many People Are Deaf or Hard of Hearing?*) Unfortunately, many people with hearing loss do not treat it—whether because of vanity (not wanting to wear a hearing aid), lack of funds, or lack of knowledge about the disability. Getting over this barrier may mean recognizing and treating the disability or, in the case of mild impairment, asking people to enunciate more clearly and use adequate speech volume. On the other hand, hearing assistance is getting more effective and less visible, as earbuds that function as hearing aids are now available (Gilmore, 2019).

Psychological Barriers Common psychological barriers that prevent us from listening effectively are boredom and preoccupation. The human mind can process information at a rate of about 600 words per minute, about three times faster than the typical speaker can talk. This phenomenon is sometimes labeled the "thought-speech differential" (Brownell, 2015, p. 89). Consequently, as Charee discovered, your mind has plenty of time to wander, and you can easily become distracted or bored, which will certainly undermine the amount that you listen to and retain.

DID YOU KNOW?

Statistically, How Many People Are Deaf or Hard of Hearing?

How often do you assume that the person listening to you has good hearing? How might this assumption influence how you respond and, ultimately, the outcomes of your communication encounters? How might you modify your way of speaking if you knew you were speaking to someone with a hearing loss?

Statistically, how many people are deaf or hard of hearing? It is actually difficult to estimate because some people may not wish to identify themselves as having a hearing loss, or the questions may not ask directly if a person has a hearing loss. The term *hard of hearing* refers to people with hearing loss ranging from mild to severe. They usually communicate through spoken language and can benefit from hearing aids, captioning, and assistive listening devices, including Apple AirPods that function as hearing aids (Gilmore, 2019). People who are deaf mostly have profound hearing loss, which implies very little or no hearing. They often use sign language for communication.

Here are some interesting facts about hearing loss:

- About two to three out of every 1,000 children in the United States are born with a detectable level of hearing loss in one or both ears. More than 90 percent of deaf children are born to hearing parents.

- One in eight people in the United States (13 percent, or 30 million) age 12 years or older has hearing loss in both ears.
- Hearing loss increases with age. About 2 percent of adults ages 45 to 54 have disabling hearing loss. The rate increases to 8.5 percent for adults ages 55 to 64 and nearly 25 percent of those ages 65 to 74, and 50 percent of those who are 75 and older have disabling hearing loss.
- Men are more likely than women to report having hearing loss.
- Approximately 18 percent of Americans between the ages of 20 and 69 have high-frequency hearing loss due to five or more years of exposure to very loud noise at work.

Hearing loss can have important academic, social, and emotional impacts. Hearing loss can delay spoken language development and academic performance. Hearing loss affects an individual's ability to communicate and can lead to loneliness, isolation, and frustration, particularly among older people with hearing loss.

SOURCES: Gilmore, J. (2019). Design for everyone: Apple AirPods and the mediation of accessibility. *Critical Studies in Media Communication*, *36*(5), 482–494.

Hearing Loss Association of America. (2016, December 15). *Quick statistics.* https://www.hearingloss.org/hearing-help/hearing-loss-basics/

▼ Strong emotions can interfere with listening by making people defensive, overly sensitive, or hostile.

Preoccupation, or distracted listening, is a related psychological barrier. During an interaction, people often think of other things and thus do not listen to what is being said. Preoccupation can be caused by many things. For example, many students are preoccupied with cell phones and other digital devices, leading scholars to investigate the phenomenon of "distracted students" and how professors cope with students who are not really listening to classroom discussions (Cheong et al., 2016). Of course, the same distraction can occur in informal conversations. Perhaps you've experienced being distracted in conversations because you're thinking of other things you need to do and other places you need to be. It seems that listeners are often distracted and constrained by time in today's society (Wolvin, 2017).

Another source of preoccupation comes from strong emotions. For example, some older

Americans identify emotional triggers that cause them to tune out (e.g., "false familiarity," for example, someone calling them by their first names) (Froemming & Penington, 2011). Or when we hear something we strongly disagree with, figuratively we reach up and mentally turn off what we do not want to hear. By contrast, even joy, for example, can make a person too preoccupied to listen and can also influence how they understand and react to messages, so if something wonderful has just happened to you, you may be concentrating on your good news and how you are going to celebrate rather than focusing on the speaker. Thus, a wide variety of emotions can distract you and influence how you listen and respond in communicative interactions (Nichols, 2009).

Emotions can also make people defensive and thus impair their listening abilities. Defensive listening occurs when someone perceives, anticipates, or experiences a threat (Nichols, 2009). In such cases, the listener often puts up a "wall" for protection. These walls can distort incoming messages, leading to misinterpretation. For example, one of our colleagues described how her emotional reactions to her father hindered her ability to listen to him: "We had such a rotten relationship that every time he even opened his mouth to speak, I was so defensive, so sure he was going to criticize me or yell at me that I never even heard a word he said." Some people are more defensive than others; their personalities and experiences have influenced them to respond defensively to many messages. However, certain types of messages are more likely to elicit defensive listening. Preconceived ideas about issues or participants can also trigger strong emotions. For example, sometimes we allow negative past experience with a person to interfere; that is, if you expect your sibling (or father) to be angry at you, you will likely interpret any comment as hostile—as was the case with our colleague and her father. The psychological barriers discussed here can act as "filters that allow only selected words and ideas into our consciousness . . . [they can also] screen out the less comfortable and uncomfortable messages, [so that] only pieces of the message are received—the comfortable pieces" (Shafir, 2003, p. 46). The end result is that these barriers can stifle the potential for developing meaningful relationships and new ideas. For one example of how people can manage emotional reactions and practice effective listening and dialogue, see *Communication in Society: Listening and Civil Dialogue*.

COMMUNICATION IN SOCIETY
Listening and Civil Dialogue

The current extreme polarization of political views reveals that many people listen only to ideas and opinions that agree with their own and reject any with opposing views. This polarization has resulted in fracturing of family and personal relationships, leading experts to call for communication strategies that enable people to be able to speak honestly with each other without resorting to attack or criticism. One of these strategies is Civil Dialogue.

Civil Dialogue®, developed by Clark Olson and colleagues at Arizona State University, is a structured method of public conversations designed to engage people with differing opinions on a controversial topic (see https://www.civil-dialogue.org/). Civil Dialogue has been used to build bridges between individuals on divergent sides of topics, including climate change, evolution, sexual violence, presidential elections, and more. It has been used in both local communities and the classroom, engaging communities as diverse as homeless populations to Arab communities.

In a "Civil Dialogue," groups of citizens or students are invited to describe their positions from "strongly agree" to "strongly disagree" on a topic while seated in front of an audience. The participants (and later audience members) are encouraged to communicate their personal opinions and experiences without trying to change each other's minds or demonize one another. A core element of these dialogues is *active* or *intentional* listening, and facilitators stress the importance of letting voices be heard, the impact of narrative story in listening to the "other" point of view, and the opportunity to model civility.

The reasoning behind listening to the narrative story is while it's easy to shoot down an opinion or a position alone, *listening* to someone's life experience can help us see how a formative experience is never wrong, even if we don't agree. It's just another shade of reality.

SOURCES: Genette, J., Olson, C. D., & Linde, J. (2017). *Hot topics, cool heads: A handbook on Civil Dialogue®*. Kendall Hunt.

Linde, J., Genette, J., & Olson, C. D. (2014). *Civil Dialogue: Producing civility through the process of dialogue*. https://www.civil-dialogue.org/publications.html

▲ It is easier to identify poor listening habits in others than in ourselves.

Conflicting Objectives A third barrier to listening involves conflicting objectives. How people understand and react to others' communicative attempts depends in part on their objective(s) for the conversation. For example, how do you listen to a lecture when your instructor announces, "This will be on the midterm"? How do you listen when told the material will *not* be on a test? Your different objectives for these situations are likely to influence how well you listen.

Sometimes participants in a conversation differ in their objectives for an interaction. For example, during a business meeting Ignacio's objective was to explain a new procedure for evaluating employees, whereas Roberta's objective was to get a raise. Consequently, the two focused on different aspects of their conversation, assigned different meanings to what occurred, and remembered different aspects of their meeting. Of course, people may have multiple objectives for an interaction, each of which will influence how they listen and respond.

Poor Listening Habits   As it turns out, people can more easily define poor listening than effective listening. Similarly, people can more easily identify the listening habits and flaws of others than they can their own. In our opening story, Charee saw other students' poor listening behaviors—although she also recognized her own.

Here are five common ineffective listening behaviors, which result in not really getting the speaker's message.

1. **Wandering:** Probably the most common. The listener's mind wanders from time to time, not really focused on what the speaker is saying. The words go in one ear and out the other.
2. **Rejecting:** The listener "tunes out" the speaker at the beginning of the message, often because of a lack of respect or a dislike for the speaker.
3. **Judging:** The listener focuses on what the speaker says but makes a hasty evaluation of the speaker's message, ignoring the remainder of the message.
4. **Predicting:** So common—the listener gets ahead of the speaker and finishes their thoughts, again missing at least some of the speaker's message.
5. **Rehearsing:** The listener is thinking about what they are going to say next.

Journal Prompt 7.3: Listening Styles
Which of the four listening styles do you find the most challenging? Which of the four common barriers do you encounter most often?

Are there other annoying habits you would like to add to this list? Are you guilty of any of these? Most of us are. Perhaps the most important way to avoid these bad habits is to first become more aware of our own listening behavior and to really focus on the speaker rather than on our own thoughts and feelings and what we're going to say next. As we've mentioned, however, societal factors can have an important impact on one's ability to listen effectively, and this is the subject we turn to next.

The Individual, Listening, and Society: Hierarchy, Contexts, and Community

7.4   **Understand the role of societal forces (hierarchy, contexts, and community) in listening.**

As emphasized throughout this book, communication behaviors do not exist solely on the individual level but are a complex interaction of individual and societal factors, reflected in our Synergetic Model of Communication. Let's examine listening as it's affected by three levels of societal forces: social hierarchy, context, and community.

Social Hierarchy

Societal norms and social hierarchy influence much of our communication behaviors, and listening is no exception. Let's look more closely at how this works. Every society transmits messages about who is most powerful and important, and these are the people who set the communication norms. How do these messages affect our listening and responding?

Each time we meet someone for the first time, we immediately evaluate whether that person is worth listening to. We mentally go through our personal (influenced by society's) criteria. If the person doesn't meet the criteria, the person's words "become fainter and fainter until only our thoughts fill our attention" (Shafir, 2003, p. 57). Some of the most crucial information to be gained as listeners—like people's names—gets lost while we process acceptability checklists. Three important "filters" are social status, physical appearance, and vocal cues.

Social Status   One criterion on many people's acceptability checklist is social status. We ask ourselves: Is this person worthy of my time and attention? Most of us are more attentive and listen more closely to those we consider equal to us or higher in society's hierarchy. For example, we listen closely to the words of physicians, teachers, successful businesspeople, and celebrities. Do we listen with as much attention to people who have less education? Perhaps not, as Danny found out in *It Happened to Me: Danny*. Regardless of the positions we hold, most of us are similarly influenced by systems of hierarchy, and these systems are sometimes tinged with prejudice. After George Floyd was killed by Minneapolis police, there was much discussion about social justice and the systemic racial inequities in the United States. We might ask in these discussions, "Who is listened to, and who should be listened to?" Algeria K. Wilson (2020), director of public policy at the National Association of Social Workers, says it's time for White people, of all ages and backgrounds, "to listen . . . to the requests that have come from Black people for so long . . . and act . . . in a manner that is long term and systemic, not brief and for optics."

It Happened to Me
Danny

Being in college, I'm a part of a culture that's very different from the culture where I grew up. In college, people value talking about ideas, learning new information, and working toward becoming more "educated." When I go home, however, I have to remember that not everyone in my family and not all of my friends went to college. They don't understand a lot of the jargon I use, and they don't know about the things I've studied. I try to be mindful of this when I visit; I don't want to sound condescending. I also try to remember that their opinions are equally valid and that I need to listen as attentively to them as I do to my college friends.

Physical Appearance   One of the most common obstacles to listening relates to physical appearance. Societal forces set the norms for physical attractiveness, which include being physically able-bodied, having symmetrical features, and embodying certain weight and height norms. This means that many people hold stereotypes about people with disabilities or physical challenges, and they often find it difficult to listen to them, avoiding eye contact or ignoring the person entirely. One of our colleagues, Tanya, had a stroke as a young adult and uses a walker or wheelchair. She describes a common situation she encounters:

> It really irritates me sometimes when I'm in public and people avoid looking at me, look at my husband instead, and ask him what I want. Why can't they listen to what *I'm saying* and respond to *me*?

In sum, social hierarchies can act as a filter that, in turn, influences people's listening behaviors.

Vocal Cues   In addition to social status and appearance, vocal cues (the *way* a person talks) can also be a filter that influences how people listen to others. Sometimes these judgments are factually accurate. For example, people can often tell by hearing someone's voice whether the speaker is male or female, young or old. However, one study showed that people make other judgments about a person, in addition to gender and age, based on the pitch and sound of their voice (Imhof, 2010). In this study, the researchers found that people with higher-pitched voices were judged by others to be more outgoing and open but less conscientious and less emotionally stable. The judgments stem from societal cues and assumptions that link people's vocal cues to personality. Another study found that college students tended to avoid talking with international students with strong accents—contributing to the fact that many international students have very little contact with U.S. American students on their campuses (Wang et al., 2017).

The important question is how do we listen to people we consider "less conscientious" or "less emotionally stable" or foreign? Something to keep in mind is whether we are making unwarranted judgments that then influence how we listen.

The point here is that these "filters," based on social hierarchy, can prevent us from listening to others with openness and in a nonjudgmental manner that is usually thought of as part of effective listening. However, several experts have pointed out that it is probably not really possible to "set aside prejudices" and "consider all people as equal," so that setting these goals as a necessary and sufficient condition for effective listening means almost certain failure. Rather, they suggest that we see them as ideals—goals to strive *toward*. In so doing, certainly becoming aware of our "filters" is a first step (Bodie, 2010; Floyd, 2010).

Listening in Context

As discussed previously, different contexts may call for different listening styles and behaviors. For example, in professional contexts we generally focus on content or critical listening, whereas in social contexts we generally focus more on people and relationship affirmation (Bodie et al., 2013b). With friends, we are often called on to listen sympathetically and with little judgment, establishing empathy and communicating a recognizable *"feeling* of being heard" (Shotter, 2009, p. 21).

In professional contexts, too, whether one is working on an assembly line or as a manager, listening with empathy is important because it enables people to understand each other and get the job done (Battell, 2006; Imhof, 2001). At the same time, employees must be cautious about letting their work relationships get too personal. For example, when Donna's new boss, Lena, asked Donna to be Facebook friends, Donna was flattered. However, when Lena posted nasty messages about her divorce and aired problems she was having with her children and continued these conversations at work,

Donna soon found that Lena's personal issues were taking lots of time and keeping her from getting work done. In addition, she discovered that her coworkers were critical of her for being unable to keep things on a professional level. The lesson, then, is that colleagues need to balance task and relational listening skills (Nichols, 2009).

Societal forces may affect listening behavior in any context. For example, some individuals are the victims of prejudice, discrimination, or even bullying in social or workplace contexts because of gender, age, race, ethnicity, or sexual orientation. When this happens, they may not be able to easily adapt their listening behavior. Others' bullying or discriminatory reactions to them may completely undermine their attempts to demonstrate good communication skills. Deborah Tannen's (1994) influential work showed how women's contributions in office meetings were often not listened to, and similarly, a disabled person might display good listening skills in a conversation by making eye contact, leaning forward, and paying close attention, but these good communication skills can be undermined if the speaker expresses prejudice toward the listening disabled person by *avoiding* eye contact in return or by ignoring the disabled person's contribution by not listening when that person becomes the speaker. We'll address the role of prejudice and discrimination in communication further in Chapter 8.

Listening and Community

Communication scholar David Beard (2009) reminds us that in addition to all the voices in various hierarchies and contexts we listen to every day, we also listen to **soundscapes**— the everyday sounds in our environments. Instructors "listening" in the classroom to understand students better—hearing the cough, the fidgeting, the scraping of chairs, the nonverbal movements (Ahern & Mehlenbacher, 2019). Sound can also build community, since uniting people in a sound experience creates an "acoustic community" where shared auditory perception is a framework for coming together (Holba, 2019). For example, communication scholar Deondre Smiles (2019) describes how Native Americans and White people come together, forming a hybrid listening community through listening to Native Radio—a network of radio stations, usually owned and operated by Native Americans on reservations or in urban areas (https://americanindian.si.edu/explore/film-media/native-media-topics/native-radio). Smiles (2019) describes how these two communities come to understand each other a little better through this shared listening.

> **soundscape**
> The everyday sounds in our environments.

Community-specific soundscapes can also vary with generational differences. Contrast the technological soundscapes of your parents' and grandparents' generation—the hiss of the needle on a record player, the sound of rotary phone dialing (and perhaps even a live operator's voice), the chimes of the NBC logo, the screech of dial-up Internet access—with your own soundscapes. What were the soundscapes of the neighborhood where you grew up? What sounds do you hear every day that may represent your generational identity and communities? Perhaps more importantly, how do these affect you? Are they comforting? Irritating? Are there some that you tune out? Perhaps they are so much a part of the sound "background" that we don't consider their effect on us.

Although, as you've seen, the quality of one's listening is subject to powerful social forces as well as individual factors such as listening style, gender, and age, we do have some latitude for making choices about our own behavior. In other words, we do make ethical decisions about listening—the topic we turn to next.

> **Journal Prompt 7.4:**
> **Listening and Context**
> How do contexts affect how we listen and respond to others?

Ethics and Listening

7.5 Describe ethical challenges in listening.

People have several ethical decisions to make about listening. These decisions include choosing what you will listen to and when, as well as how you will respond when listening to other people or to the soundscapes that surround you.

▲ Ethical listening involves knowing how to handle confidentiality if you receive a message not intended for you.

To begin, choosing to listen or not is an ethical decision, in both face-to-face and mediated communication contexts (Beard, 2009; Lacey, 2013). Just because someone wants to tell you something doesn't mean you have to listen. And sometimes the act of listening—or refusing to—means taking a moral stand. For example, let's say a friend of yours tweets a vicious rumor about another person or tells a racist joke. You have an ethical decision to make. How are you going to respond? Are you going to retweet it? Ignore it?

You can tell your friend you don't want to hear any more or even gently explain why you don't want to. Or you can do nothing, sacrificing honesty to avoid making yourself (and others) feel uncomfortable. What are the consequences of each of these decisions? If you listen to something offensive and pass it on, you are in effect agreeing with the tweet. It may be awkward to tell your friend (either at the moment or later) that you don't want to listen to such remarks, but the friend may think twice before sending similar tweets in the future. Obviously, there are no easy answers; you need to consider the consequences and possible outcomes in each situation as you make these ethical decisions.

Let's say you overhear some information or see a text message not intended for you. What are some guidelines for dealing with this information? As we suggested in Chapter 1, you might first consider the expectations of the individual who sent the message. Perhaps this person has made it clear that they want this information kept private. Or you might consider that if you were in this person's position, you would want the information to be kept private. Or perhaps you know that the sender does not mind if the information is shared more widely—but what about the person to whom the message is addressed? You need to consider their wishes, too. Depending on the privacy expectation, the ethical decision might be to listen to or read the message—or not. Would the sender or addressee feel harmed? Would any benefit result from your listening to the message? The answer to these questions probably depends a great deal on your relationships with the sender and addressee. A close friend may not mind your listening in on messages; someone you don't know very well may object strenuously.

Mediated communication contexts also can pose ethical issues with regard to listening. Communication expert Kate Lacey says we need a special set of listening skills to help us cope with this barrage of messages and to be selective in our listening choices; we train in "public speaking," but not "public listening" (2013, p. 190). She notes that, on the one hand, we have an ethical responsibility to "grant right of audience" to those who would otherwise not be heard because they present opportunities to expand our horizons, as we noted in those who encourage White people to listen to voices previously unheard on social justice issues and solutions (Wilson, 2020), and of course we need to balance openness with critical thinking. On the other hand, much of our social media listening is increasingly narrowed—device settings/apps that program what we hear (music, talk, TV, newsites) to our idiosyncratic preferences (Gottfried & Shearer, 2016).

How to counter this narrowed exposure to listening opportunities? Some companies have tried some strategies: Facebook modified the algorithm of the "Trending" page so users would see more news sources on a specific topic; BuzzFeed News has "Outside Your Bubble," a module showing various reactions/comments at the bottom of social media articles. And some communication scholars say that the echo chamber is a bit overstated, that yes, if one only consumes news from social media, one is likely to encounter those with similar ideas, but in a complex, multimedia environment—which is the way people live now because of the Internet—you don't find that, you find people consuming a lot of media (Dubois & Grant, 2018).

Here are some choices we make, as listeners, to become more or less ethical beings, in our mediated world:

1. **The choice to cut ourselves off from listening to our immediate environments.** As Charee discussed in the chapter opening, we can choose to listen alone (putting on the headset/earbuds), which sometimes might be a positive, self-constructive act. At other times, however (e.g., in a work situation or at home when our relational partner wants to talk), doing so can be isolating and damaging to relationships.

2. **The choice to listen selectively.** For example, we can choose to listen to media "candy" or to media that enhance and inspire us as people. We can choose to listen to a friend's choice of media, so we can discuss it together, or we can listen only to our own choices.

3. **The choice not to listen.** For example, in the public arena, we can decide to listen (or not listen) to a political speaker who espouses ideas we oppose. Our choice has a potential impact on us and our thinking because listening implies the possibility of change in attitudes and behavior. Listening to a political speaker (or even a friend) promoting ideas and beliefs that we disagree with may open us up to ideas previously unexplored or may reinforce our own beliefs. Choosing never to listen to opposing views ensures that we won't alter our beliefs or learn to defend them in a logical and constructive way.

4. **The choice to listen together.** For example, when we attend a music concert or a political rally, we open ourselves to being part of a community of music fans or political sympathizers (Beard, 2009). The consequences of the decision to listen with a particular community may open up opportunities for new experiences that may alter our future thinking or behavior.

The point is that all these choices are just that—choices. Although we don't usually consider these types of choices when we think of listening, the decisions we make regarding them do influence our communication life—influencing our communication identity and relationships with those important to us.

Journal Prompt 7.5:
Ethical Listening
What are some ethical choices you have encountered in listening and responding?

Improving Your Listening Skills

7.6   Discuss two ways to improve your own listening behavior.

As we have shown in this chapter, listening (including responding appropriately) is an important communication skill. As is the case with all communication skills, however, there are no surefire, easy recipes for becoming a more effective listener. Still, two guidelines might help you improve.

Identify Poor Habits

As noted, most people have some poor listening habits, particularly in our close and intimate relationships, where partners often develop irritating practices such as finishing the other person's sentences, interrupting, and "tuning out" the other person. These irritating behaviors crop up especially if you are an action- or task-oriented

▲ For White people, an ethical decision might involve listening to voices previously unheard on social justice issues and solutions.

listener. Ask yourself, then: What keeps you from really listening? Which filters block your ability to hear and understand what others are saying? Overcoming listening barriers—especially those that are reinforced by social hierarchies—can be challenging.

Perhaps one way to overcome those societal messages is through awareness that our listening behaviors play an important role in the outcome of communication encounters. A number of research studies have shown that when people listen attentively to one another, the speaker is more likely to speak coherently. On the other hand, when listeners do not pay careful attention, speakers tend to be less coherent and less engaged and may even feel under-valued (Pasupathi & Billitteri, 2014). Put another way, regardless of who they are or their social location, when speakers feel they are listened to with respect and attentiveness, they become better communicators and vice versa.

Strive for Mindful Listening

Applying the concept of mindful listening, described by renowned listening expert Rebecca Z. Shafir (2003), can help. We defined mindfulness in Chapter 3. Mindful listening, which is a specific kind of mindfulness, is based on Eastern philosophy and Zen Buddhism; it is defined by focus, concentration, and compassion, and it can bring health, peace, and productivity to our everyday lives. This holistic approach requires that we listen with the heart, body, and mind, and for most of us, that means a major change in attitude. Mindful listening focuses on the *process* of listening versus the *payoff*.

Shafir suggests that to be a better listener to each of our friends, family, and acquaintances, we need to understand their "movie." What does that mean? Shafir compares listening to movies with listening to people. Most of us don't have trouble focusing on and paying attention while watching a movie; we get caught up in the plot, the emotion, and the characters. Why, she asks, should listening to people be any different? To continue the comparison, if we approach a listening opportunity with the same self-abandonment as we do a movie, think how much more we might gain from those encounters (Shafir, 2003). Actor Alan Alda agrees, citing neuroscientist Uri Hasson's description, "when you tell me a story, our brains get coupled in a very real way" (cited in Alda, 2017, p. 168). He elaborates about how the brain is acting as if it is really watching the movie.

Being a mindful listener requires three elements:

1. The desire to get the whole message,
2. The ability to eliminate the noisy barriers discussed previously, and
3. The willingness to place your agenda lower on the priority list than the speaker's.

Mindful listening is based on empathy—the ability to identify with and understand someone else's feelings. As listening expert Michael Nichols states it, listening is not just taking in information; it is also "bearing witness" to, validating, and affirming another's expression. The core of listening, he says, is "to pay attention, take an interest in, care about, validate, acknowledge, be moved . . . appreciate" (2009, p. 14).

Journal Prompt 7.6: Improving Listening
What are two ways you can improve your own listening behavior?

SUMMARY

7.1 Identify six reasons why listening is important.

- Listening is considered to be one of the most important communication skills, partly because we spend so much time doing it!

- Better listening skills can lead to improved cognition, improved academic performance, enhanced personal relationships, enhanced professional performance, and better health.

7.2 Describe the four stages of listening.

- *Listening* is defined as "the process of receiving, constructing meaning from, and responding to spoken and/or nonverbal messages" and occurs in four stages: hearing, understanding, evaluating, and responding.

7.3 Describe the influences on listening and barriers to effective listening.

- Our own personal listening habits may be influenced by our gender, our age, our ethnicity, or even our own predominant listening style.

- There are four listening styles: *Critical listening style* focuses on the accuracy of the content, watching for errors and inconsistencies in others' speech. *Task-oriented style* involves informational listening skills; *analytical style* involves informational listening skills plus systematic thinking/listening to evaluate messages, withholding judgment until all sides are heard; *relational style* involves active-empathic listening skills.

- People have many reasons for not listening to others, but some typical ones include physical or physiological barriers, psychological barriers, conflicting objectives, and poor listening habits.

7.4 Understand the role of societal forces (hierarchy, contexts, and community) in listening.

- Listening habits and preferences are influenced by societal forces: contexts, and hierarchies.

7.5 Describe ethical challenges in listening.

- Ethical decisions with respect to listening behavior include choosing what to listen to and when and how to respond when listening to other people or to the soundscapes around us, including media.

7.6 Discuss two ways to improve your own listening behavior.

- Although we can offer no surefire, easy recipes for becoming a more effective listener, two guidelines might help: identify your poor listening habits or barriers and practice mindful listening.

KEY TERMS

listening p. 168
hearing p. 168
understanding p. 168
evaluating p. 168
responding p. 169

listening style p. 170
critical listening style p. 171
task-oriented listening style p. 171
informational listening p. 171

analytical listening style p. 171
relational listening style p. 172
active-empathic listening (AEL) p. 172
soundscape p. 181

APPLY WHAT YOU KNOW

1. **Evaluate Others' Listening Skills**
   When you are in class or in a group, whether online or in person, notice how people listen to each other and respond. Reflect on what you think is more or less effective about others' listening skills. Then apply what you observed to your own listening skills.

2. **Evaluate Your Listening Skills**
   Ask someone to observe your listening skills over a period of time. This person can be a parent, friend, teacher, or romantic partner. Ask the observer to give you constructive feedback on how you can improve your listening skills. Try to implement those suggestions.

Communication across Cultures

 LEARNING OBJECTIVES

> *"Many, if not most, of your daily interactions are intercultural in nature."*

Charee has become good friends with Kaori, a Japanese exchange student. Kaori's English is really good, but sometimes they misunderstand each other when they send messages. For example, Charee recently learned that when she used terms like brb and ttyl or made sarcastic remarks such as "What a great idea, Einstein!" Kaori didn't understand. Kaori didn't tell Charee that she didn't understand, she just didn't respond to the messages. She only explained later when Charee became concerned about the lack of response and pressed Kaori to tell her if something was wrong.

Kaori's story illustrates several points about intercultural communication. First, intercultural contact is a fact of life in today's world; and second, although intercultural contact can be enriching, it can also bring challenges and misunderstanding, especially in mediated communication such as messaging. In Kaori's case, communicating in English in writing messages is especially challenging because of the lack of nonverbal cues. She explained to Charee that she doesn't always feel comfortable telling people when she doesn't understand. She said that in Japan, people generally avoid direct communication and prefer to be more indirect, as we will discuss later. Kaori is an example of someone living "on the border"—between two cultures—having to negotiate sometimes conflicting sets of languages and cultural values.

In today's world, we typically have many opportunities to meet people from different cultures. You may sit in class with students who are culturally different from you in many ways—in nationality, ethnicity, race, gender, age, religion, sexual orientation, and physical ability. In addition, today's widespread access to communication technologies and foreign travel provides many opportunities for intercultural encounters beyond the classroom. On the other hand, the increasing number of terrorist attacks in many countries, the tightening of national borders in response to global migration and COVID-19, conflicts between police and communities of color in the United States, and the racist and hateful content posted online may inspire doubt about the ability of people from different cultures to coexist peacefully and may lead to the belief that cultural differences necessarily lead to insurmountable problems. However, we believe that increased awareness of intercultural communication can help prevent or reduce the severity of problems that arise due to cultural differences.

In this chapter, we'll first explore the importance of *intercultural communication* and define what we mean when we use this term. Next, we will describe the increasingly common experience of individuals who must negotiate different cultural realities in their everyday lives. Then we'll examine how culture influences our communication and discuss how society affects communication outcomes in intercultural interactions. Finally, we provide suggestions for how one can become a more ethical and effective intercultural communicator.

The Importance of Intercultural Communication

8.1 Explain why it is important to learn about intercultural communication.

How many reasons for studying intercultural communication can you think of? If you are like many students, entering college has given you more opportunities than ever before for intercultural contact, both domestically and internationally. You will communicate better in these situations if you have a good understanding of intercultural communication. In addition, increased knowledge and skill in intercultural communication can improve your career effectiveness, intergroup relations, and self-awareness. Let's look at each of these reasons more closely.

Increased Opportunities for Intercultural Contact

diaspora
The movement, migration, or scattering of a people away from an established or ancestral homeland.

Experts estimate that more than a billion people travel each year. People leave their countries for many reasons, including national revolutions and civil wars (Syria and Sudan) and natural disasters (droughts in Latin America and Africa, hurricanes in Puerto Rico and the Bahamas). Experts estimate there are now a record number of displaced people in the world, 79.9 million, and almost 1 percent of the earth's population is displaced (United Nations High Commissioner for Refugees, 2020). Sometimes, in a process called **diaspora**, whole groups of people are displaced to new countries as they flee genocide or other untenable conditions or are taken forcefully against their will. Diasporic groups often attempt to settle together in communities in the new location while maintaining a strong ethnic identity and a desire to return home. Historically, diasporic groups include slaves taken from Africa in the 1700s and 1800s, Jews persecuted throughout centuries and relocating around the world, Chinese fleeing famine and wars in the nineteenth and twentieth centuries, and Armenians escaping Turkish genocide in early 1900s (Pendery, 2008; Waterston, 2005). More recent diasporas include Albanians from Kosovo and Chechens from Russia, and some experts refer to the current Latino diaspora, the increasing numbers of Latin Americans who settle outside their homelands, or the Syrian diaspora, the thousands of who have fled civil war in that country (Balachandran, 2016). Some migrants travel to new lands voluntarily for economic opportunities (to make a better life for themselves or their families) or personal reasons (to join family or friends abroad).

Although influenced by the pandemic, many people have in the past and will again travel overseas for pleasure, with more than a billion international arrivals in 2019 (UNTWO, 2020). Many people, like the student Kaori in the opening story, also travel for study. According to the Institute of International Education (2020), more than a million international students study in the United States each year, and more than 300,000 U.S. students study overseas (USA Study Abroad, 2020). Many students study abroad because of the exciting opportunities that exist for intercultural

---

DID YOU KNOW?

Meeting Other Travelers Adds Depth to Argentina Visit

Have you had experiences with people from other cultures that changed how you saw the world or the United States? If so, what was it about those interactions that changed your views? If you could change other countries' views of the United States, what would you want to tell them?

Allison, from the United States, is an exchange student in Argentina. Here's an excerpt from her travel blog:

We went to the North West last week; four of us stayed in a youth hostel there. I felt like I had discovered a secret that had been hidden from me all my life. I IMMEDIATELY felt at home. It was just a bunch of kids all traveling from all parts of the world just hanging out and meeting people and sharing all their stories. Our first friends we met were two Canadian kids who had been backpacking through South America the past two months. We spent a lot of time with them drinking mate (the traditional Argentine tea) and chatting about all their experiences in South America. There was a Venezuelan girl and a Japanese girl. It was a pleasure sharing a room with them. In talking to everyone I became

even more aware of how misinformed about international news we are in America and how uncommon it is for us to actually be interested enough to really be concerned about what's going on in the rest of the world.

I had a really intriguing conversation with an Israeli soldier who had been traveling through South America during his time off. Hearing his stories was absolutely heartbreaking . . . all that he was forced to see and to do was absolutely awful! No one of any age should have to endure those things, and he's been doing it since he was 18. I guess that's how it is for people that live in countries where that's just their reality. They become accustomed to falling asleep with gun shots outside their window and getting up to go to work not having any idea what their day will hold and whether or not they'll die. It's awful and such a foreign concept to us; maybe we should make it more of a reality. . . .

SOURCE: Allison Nafziger Travel Blog. Reprinted by permission of Allison Nafziger.

encounters, as exchange student Allison describes in *Did You Know? Meeting Other Travelers Adds Depth to Argentina Visit.*

Another source of increased opportunity for intercultural contact exists because of the increasing cultural diversity in the United States. According to U.S. census figures, there are continuing dramatic increases in ethnic and racial diversity, and in the next several decades the United States will become a "plurality nation" in which no group is in the majority. In fact, there are now 109 counties that are "majority-minority"—where there is no one majority ethnic group and minority groups account for more than 50 percent of the population (Schaeffer, 2019). Racial and ethnic minorities are now growing more rapidly in numbers than Whites. The fastest growth is among multiracial Americans, followed by Asians and Hispanics. Non-Hispanic Whites make up 60 percent of the U.S. population; Hispanics make up 19 percent; Blacks, 13 percent; Asians, 6 percent; and multiracial Americans, 3 percent (U.S. Census Bureau, 2019). This trend is expected to continue, as shown in Figure 8.1. The Hispanic population will more than double in size and constitute approximately 30 percent of the population by 2060; in the same time period, the Asian American population will also double in size and will constitute about 9 percent of the total population. Blacks will remain approximately the same in numbers and comprise almost 13 percent of the population; Whites will continue to be a smaller majority as minority populations increase in number. The nation's elderly population will increase considerably, as the baby-boom generation enters the traditional retirement years. The number of working-age Americans and children will grow more slowly than the elderly population and will shrink as a share of the total population (Colby & Ortman, 2015).

Of course, communication technologies also provide increased opportunity for intercultural encounters. You can play video games with students in China, get acquainted with a former exchange student's friends and family on Instagram, debate rock climbing techniques with climbers from Norway to New Zealand on a sports blog, or collaborate with students from around the country for a virtual team project in one of your classes. In the next sections of this chapter, we will discuss the opportunities that these types of contacts offer—and the benefits to be had from learning more about the intricacies of intercultural communication.

Critical Thinking Prompt
How multicultural is your circle of friends? How many of your friends differ from you in nationality, religion, class, gender, age, sexual orientation, or physical ability?

Figure 8.1 **How the Racial Makeup of the United States Is Projected to Change by 2060**

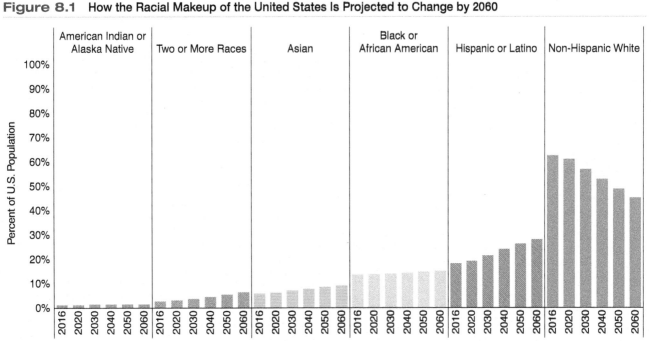

SOURCE: Adapted from https://www.apmresearchlab.org/blog/the-united-states-will-soon-be-bigger-older-and-more-diverse, based on U.S. Census Bureau's 2017 US Population Projections.

Enhanced Business Effectiveness

Studying intercultural communication can lead to greater success in both domestic and international business contexts. In the domestic context, the U.S. workforce is becoming increasingly diverse as the general population does the same. In fact, a growing number of research studies show that being around people who are different can make us more creative and more diligent and make us work harder, especially for groups that value innovation and new ideas. Specifically, these types of organizations that have gender and racial diversity have more diverse ideas and outperform less diverse groups (Phillips, 2014). One study showed that close intercultural work relationships can actually spark creativity and innovation (Lu et al., 2017). Furthermore, virtual communication, increased by the pandemic, makes global business communication faster and cheaper to collaborate with overseas vendors and customers. A primary cause for international business failures is still lack of attention to cultural factors. For example, eBay, the successful American e-commerce giant, copied its American model to China and got completely destroyed by local competitor Taobao. Why? Because Taobao understood that in China, shopping is a social experience and people like talking and even haggling with sellers and building relationships with them. Taobao had a chat feature that allowed customers to easily talk to sellers (Custer, 2015). Other failures include Mattel's Barbie (Barbie is popular in China, but it is not a cultural icon like in the United States, so the Chinese wouldn't buy all the other pricey Barbie-themed clothing, foods, and goods) and Home Depot (Chinese are not typically a DIY culture, so there was no market for weekend DIYers) (Carlson, 2013).

Improved Intergroup Relations

Although we cannot blame all the world's political problems on ineffective intercultural communication, the need for better communication and understanding between countries and ethnic groups is clear. Sometimes tensions can be created by (and be the result of) world events and government policies. After devastating terror attacks in France, Germany, and the United States, people and governments had heightened concerns about security posed by Middle Eastern refugees moving into Europe and the United States. For some, this concern translated to anti-immigrant/refugee attitudes and legislation. While immigrants in the United States have generally more easily assimilated into the larger U.S. society, tensions between communities of color and police and anti-immigrant attitudes, particu-

▼ Intercultural contact is a fact in today's world. Many, if not most, of our daily interactions are intercultural in nature.

larly directed at Muslims and more recently toward Latin immigrants, have led some to question our ability to realize a peaceful multicultural society. Recent restrictions on legal immigration and refugees, more barriers on the U.S.-Mexico border, and the suspension of the DACA program (Shear & Kanno-Youngs, 2019; Zoppo et al., 2017) have led to heightened tensions among cultural groups in the U.S. While some feel that these are reasonable measures, others feel that they pave the way for increased prejudice and discrimination against foreigners, particularly those from the Middle East and Latin America. Some question these restrictions given the fact that terrorist attacks by Islamist groups comprise only 7 percent of attacks in the West, while twice as many (18 percent) were committed by far right groups (including white nationalists) (Brzozowski, 2019).

Intercultural communication expertise can facilitate interethnic relations, which have frequently involved conflict. Consider the ethnic struggles and religious struggles in India and Pakistan; the continued strife between Shia and Sunni in the Middle East; and the racial and ethnic struggles and tensions in neighborhoods of many U.S. cities. These conflicts often call for sophisticated skills of intercultural communication and **peacebuilding**, or working toward equilibrium and stability in a society so that disputes do not escalate into violence and war. For example, communication scholar Benjamin Broome (2004, 2014) has successfully facilitated interethnic relations on the island of Cyprus, which was one of the most heavily fortified regions in the world. Through his efforts and implementation of intergroup dialogues over many years, small groups of Greek and Turkish Cypriots have worked together to identify communication barriers and propose suggestions for improved relations between their two groups (Broome, 2013; Broome & Hatay, 2010). It should be acknowledged, however, that even with sophisticated intervention, miscommunication and intercultural conflicts can persist: witness the long-standing conflicts in the Middle East, where peacebuilding efforts have long been part of the attempts at resolution. In some cases, people are not motivated to resolve these "intractable conflicts," which are "exceptionally complex, usually involving issues of identity, meaning, justice, and power, often resisting even the most determined attempts at resolution" (Broome & Collier, 2012, p. 1). Experts also tell us that current political divisions (also considered cultural groups) far overshadow conflicts between other groups in American society—rich and poor, Black and White, and so on (Schaeffer, 2020); thus, learning how to communicate across these cultural divides is needed more than ever. Although we must admit that there is no easy cure-all for intercultural tensions and misunderstandings, intercultural communication skills are certainly valuable in this area.

> **peacebuilding**
> Working toward stability in a region to prevent conflicts from escalating into war.

Enhanced Self-Awareness

The final reason for studying intercultural communication is to increase self-awareness. This may seem like a contradiction, but it is not. Intercultural exploration begins as a journey into the cultures of others but often results in increased self-knowledge and understanding (Braskamp et al., 2009). People often learn more about themselves and their own cultural background and identities by coming into contact with people whose cultural backgrounds differ from their own, as our student discovered during her stay in South Africa (see *It Happened to Me: Susan*).

What you learn about intercultural communication may depend on your social and economic position. For example, individuals from minority racial and ethnic groups in the United States may learn to be a bit wary of intercultural interactions and expect some slights, such as a Chinese American colleague who is sometimes approached at professional meetings by White communication professors who assume she is a waitress and ask her to take their drink order!

It Happened to Me
Susan

I rarely ever thought about being White or an American until my family and I spent a year in South Africa. Then I thought about both every day, especially about my being White. The official language of South Africa is English, but even though we technically spoke the same language as the South Africans, my family and I had problems. It started when we were to be picked up from the airport in a *combie*, but I didn't know what that was. It turned out to be a van! Small pick-up trucks were *bakkies*, traffic signals were *robots*, and friends wanted to collect my *contact details*, which meant that they simply wanted the number of my *mobile*, better known as a cell phone, and our address. I felt that every time I opened my mouth, everyone *knew* I was American. The Black/White thing was even more pronounced. When we went down to the flea market or to the Zulu mass at the church we attended, we stood out like "five white golf balls on a black fairway," as my husband liked to say. I wondered if the self-consciousness I felt being White was the same as an African American has walking down the street in America.

Journal Prompt 8.1: Studying Intercultural Communication
What are four reasons for studying intercultural communication? Of the reasons given, which do you think are most important? Can you think of other reasons?

If you are White and middle class, intercultural learning may mean an enhanced awareness of your privilege. White friends tell us that they became more aware of their racial privilege after George Floyd was killed by a white police officer in Minneapolis. In the midst of the nationwide protests, the legal protections afforded by the police came into view. That is, many in the country became aware of the myriad ways that police (and other social institutions) are protected and empowered by laws and court cases that create an unequal field that helps and hurts us in different ways. With these reasons for studying intercultural communication in mind, we need to define precisely what we mean by intercultural communication and culture and give examples of intercultural interaction, the subjects we turn to next.

What Is Intercultural Communication?

8.2   Define intercultural communication and describe three types of border dwellers.

intercultural communication
Communication that occurs in interactions between people who are culturally different.

Generally speaking, **intercultural communication** refers to communication that occurs in interactions between people who are culturally different. This contrasts with most communication studies, which focus on communicators in the same culture. Still, in practice, intercultural communication occurs on a continuum, with communication between people who are relatively similar in cultural backgrounds on one end and people who are extremely different culturally on the other. For example, your conversations with your parents would represent a low degree of "interculturalness" because you and your parents belong to two different cultural (age) groups and you probably have much in common—nationality, religion, and language. On the other hand, an interaction with a foreign teaching assistant who has a different nationality, language, religion, age, socioeconomic status, and gender would represent a high degree of interculturalness. Although these two examples represent different ends on the continuum, they are both intercultural interactions. So you can see that many, if not most, of your daily interactions are intercultural in nature.

The two essential components of intercultural communication are, of course, culture and communication. Having read this far in your text, you should have a good understanding of communication. However, we think it is worthwhile to review our definition of **culture**. In Chapter 1, we defined culture as *learned patterns of perceptions, values, and behaviors shared by a group of people*. As we also mentioned, culture is dynamic (it changes) and **heterogeneous**, it operates within societal power structures (Martin & Nakayama, 2018, p. 89), and we can explore how features of culture impact individuals' intercultural interactions. But consider this cautionary note—not all cultural differences have equal impact on one's interactions. For example, although your parents may sometimes seem to come from a different culture, age differences generally have a less dramatic effect on people's interactions than do ethnic and national differences.

culture
Learned patterns of perceptions, values, and behaviors shared by a group of people.

heterogeneous
Diverse.

border dwellers
People who live between cultures and often experience contradictory cultural patterns.

Because of increased opportunities for cultural contact, many people today are **border dwellers**, who engage in intercultural communication on a daily basis and often experience contradictory cultural patterns, as they move between ethnicities, races, religions, languages, socioeconomic classes, or sexual orientations. One can be a border dweller in three ways: through travel, through socialization (co-cultural groups), and through participation in an intercultural relationship. Let's look at each in turn.

Border Dwellers through Travel

Individuals travel between cultures both voluntarily and involuntarily and for both long and short periods. Voluntary travelers include study-abroad students, corporate personnel, missionaries, and military people and immigrants who settle in other locations, usually seeking what they perceive is a better life, as is the case for many immigrants who come to the United States. Involuntary travelers include refugees forced into cultural migration because of war, famine, or unbearable economic hardship or those who are forced to permanently migrate to a new location, including the many diasporic groups referred to previously.

When people think of traveling or living in a new culture, they tend to think that learning the language is key to effective intercultural interaction; however, intercultural communication involves much more than language issues. Most sojourners find there are two types of challenges: (1) dealing with the psychological stress of being in an unfamiliar environment (feeling somewhat uncertain and anxious) and (2) learning how to behave appropriately in the new culture, both verbally (e.g., learning a new language) and nonverbally, for example, bowing instead of shaking hands in Japan (Kim, 2005).

The first of these two challenges is often called *culture shock*. **Culture shock** is a feeling of disorientation and discomfort resulting from the unfamiliarity of surroundings and the lack of familiar cues in the environment. Sometimes people even experience culture shock when they move from one region of the United States to another (e.g., relocating from Boston to Birmingham or from Honolulu to Minneapolis), or minority students attending predominantly white universities (Orta et al., 2019). When travelers return home, they may experience similar feelings, known as **reverse culture shock** or **re-entry shock**, which is a sort of culture shock in one's own home location (Pitts, 2016). After being gone for a significant amount of time, aspects of one's own culture may seem somewhat foreign, as the student Maham discovered on his return home to Pakistan after living in the United States for four years (see *It Happened to Me: Maham*).

There are many reasons why an individual may be more or less successful at adapting to a new culture. Younger people who have had some previous traveling experience seem to be more successful than older people and first-time travelers. By contrast, if the environment is hostile or the move is involuntary, adaptation may be especially difficult and the culture shock especially intense. For example, Asian, African, and Latino students in the United States tend to have a more difficult adaptation because of experiences of discrimination and hostility based on their race/ethnicity (Gareis, 2012; Hanasono et al., 2014). Although we may think that anti-immigrant attitudes are a recent phenomenon in the United States because of the number of immigrants or where they come from, historians remind us that today's immigrants have much in common with previous immigrants—including anti-immigrant attitudes (Jaret, 1999).

For diasporic groups, whether relocated within their own country or in a foreign country, the culture shock and disorientation can be complicated and even extended because of their strong desire to return home and a feeling of rootlessness. As one Iraqi refugee said, after fleeing war and terrible violence, only to encounter unemployment and poverty in the United States, "We came to this country for the future of our children. We have no future" (Yako & Biswas, 2014, p. 143).

One thing that can ease culture shock is having a social support network. This can come from organizations such as an international student office or a tourist bureau that can assist with housing, transportation, and so forth. Close relationships with other travelers or host-country acquaintances, as in the case of Charee and Kaori, can also provide support in the form of a sympathetic ear; through these relationships sojourners can relieve stress, discuss, problem solve, acquire new knowledge, or just have fun (Geeraert et al., 2014; Sobré-Denton, 2011). The role

culture shock
A feeling of disorientation and discomfort as a result of the lack of familiar environmental cues.

reverse culture shock/re-entry shock
Culture shock experienced by travelers on returning to their home country.

It Happened to Me
Maham

I would say that I experienced culture (re-entry) shock when I visited Pakistan after moving away from there four years ago. In those four years, I had basically forgotten the language and became very unfamiliar with the culture back home. Even though I enjoyed my visit to Pakistan a lot, I had problems adjusting to some of the ways of life. I was not familiar with the bargaining system . . . where people can go to the store and bargain for prices. I felt very out of place. . . . As I spent more time there, I got adjusted and used to how people did things there.

Critical Thinking Prompt
How important is it to reject your own home culture in adapting to a new culture? How can immigrants use their own cultural traditions to help make a smooth transition to the new culture? What could we in the host country do to help immigrants transition successfully to the United States?

of social support is even more crucial for immigrants, although some, like LGBTQIA+ migrants, avoid asking for help because they assume that they won't get it because of discrimination and rejection (Kahna et al., 2017). Instead, they and some diasporic individuals maintain strong relationships with other members of their own group for much needed social support, sometimes through cyber communities or in in-person interaction (Kim & McKay-Semmler, 2013). If there is little social support or the receiving environment is hostile, immigrants may resist assimilation, finding that their own culture is "a source of comfort and strength, a source of rational survival, persistence, and positive self-identity" (De La Garza & Ono, 2015, p. 281).

Another option for immigrants is to adapt in *some* ways to the new culture, which means accepting some aspects, such as dress and outward behavior, while retaining aspects of the old culture. For many immigrants to the United States, this has been a preferred option and seems to lead to less stress. For example, Asian Indians constitute one of the largest immigrant groups in the United States. Many have successfully adapted to U.S. life both professionally and socially. Still many retain viable aspects of their Indian culture in their personal and family lives—continuing to celebrate ethnic or religious holidays and adhering to traditional values and beliefs (Hegde, 2012). However, this integration of two cultures is not always easy, as we'll see later in the chapter. Families can be divided on the issues of how much to adapt, with children often wanting to be more "American" and maybe date interculturally and parents wanting to hold onto their native language and cultural practices (Ward, 2008; Shenhav et al., 2017). For a discussion about current immigrants in the U. S., see *Alternative View: Immigrants*.

Border Dwellers through Socialization

A second group of border dwellers is composed of people who grow up living on the borders between cultural groups. Examples include ethnic groups, such as Latinos, Asian Americans, and African Americans, who live in the (currently) predominantly White United States, as well as people who grow up negotiating multiple sexual orientations or religions. For example, those who identify with two or more ethnic/racial

---

ALTERNATIVE VIEW

Immigrants

Some people seem to think that immigrants in the United States come here to obtain government benefits, bring disease and crimes, and don't want to learn English. Consider the following facts regarding current immigrants. Does this information make you think differently about immigrants? How might this information impact communication between citizens and recent immigrants?

According to a recent survey . . .

Most U.S. Americans actually have a positive view of immigrants; 62 percent said that immigrants strengthen the country because of their hard work and talents, and about half say that the United States should accept refugees. The exception are White evangelical protestants, of whom only 25 percent say the United States should accept refugees (Hartig, 2018).

According to other statistics, current immigrants living in the United States . . .

- Are less likely than native-born citizens to commit crimes or become incarcerated.

- Are not eligible for federal public benefits such as Social Security, Medicaid, Medicare, and food stamps. This is limited to undocumented immigrants, though with very few exceptions, such as access to medical care for victims of human trafficking.
- Have never been the source of any modern disease outbreaks in the United States. In fact, many Latin American countries have higher vaccination rates for one-year-olds than the United States.
- Have better English language skills than immigrants of the past. Learning English is an important aspect of becoming an American.

SOURCES: Hartig, H. (2018, May 24). Republicans turn more negative toward refugees as number admitted to U.S. plummets. *pewresearch.org*. https://www.pewresearch.org/fact-tank/2018/05/24/republicans-turn-more-negative-toward-refugees-as-number-admitted-to-u-s-plummets/

Landgrave, L. (2019, September 17). Immigrants learn English. *cato.org*. https://www.cato.org/publications/immigration-research-policy-brief/immigrants-learn-english-immigrants-language

cultures (e.g., biracial, multiethnic individuals) are the fastest-growing racial/ethnic group between 2010 and 2020 with a 36 percent increase (Mather & Lee, 2020).

There are many famous multiracial U.S. Americans, including singers Rihanna (Afro-Bajan, Irish, and Afro-Guyanese) and Nicki Minaj (East Indian and Afro-Trinidadian), actor Ezra Miller (identifies as non-binary gender, queer, with an Ashkenazi Jewish father and a German-Dutch mother), and U.S. vice president Kamala Harris (Indian-American mother and Jamaican-American father). Members of minority groups sometimes find themselves in a kind of cultural limbo—not "gay" enough for gay friends, not "straight" enough for the majority; not Black enough or White enough. However, many recognize their unique positions, in limbo between but also potential bridges between two cultures. For example, children raised in biracial homes find they are often able to, as adults, relate easily with individuals of both races. They can fit in with both Whites and Blacks and often have diverse friendship networks.

▲ Border dwellers through socialization include many multiracial individuals and families. How might the concept of border dwellers change as these many children grow up?

Border Dwellers through Relationships

Finally, many people live on cultural borders because they have intimate partners whose cultural background differs from their own. Within the United States, increasing numbers of people cross borders of nationality, race, and ethnicity in this way. In fact, in one study, 50 percent of college students surveyed said they were currently in intercultural relationships (fewer were in interracial relationships), and they were more open to intercultural relationships than older people (Shenhav et al., 2017). It was illegal in Virginia and 13 other states for Whites and Blacks to marry until June 12, 1967, when the Supreme Court declared bans on interracial marriage unconstitutional in all states. Attitudes toward intercultural relationships have changed significantly in the ensuing decades, and now one in six newlyweds (17 percent) are married to someone of a different race or ethnicity. However, some relationships are more accepted/common than others. Asian Americans and Hispanics are most likely to intermarry, and Whites are the least likely to date and marry across ethnic and racial lines (Geiger & Livingston, 2019; McGrath et al., 2016; Shenhav et al., 2017).

Intercultural relationships are not without their challenges. The most common challenges involve negotiating how to live on the border between two religions, ethnicities, races, languages, and, sometimes, value systems. A recent study of intercultural marriages, some based on religious and some on racial and ethnic differences, found that communication played an important role in the success of these relationships. That is, open communication about the differences helped

▼ Americans are now more accepting of interracial and *gay* marriages.

promote relationship growth. If partners were able to understand, appreciate, and integrate each other's similarities and differences, they would be able to use these in an enriching manner (Reiter & Gee, 2009).

The balancing act between cultures can be especially challenging when friends, family, and society disapprove. A Jewish professor who married a Muslim woman reflects on how people would react if he decided to convert to Islam:

> What a scandalous action! My family would be outraged and my friends startled. What would they say? How would I be treated? What would colleagues at the university do if I brought a prayer rug to the office and, say, during a committee meeting, or at a reception for a visiting scholar, insisted on taking a break to do my ritual prayers? (Rosenstone, 2005, p. 235)

Journal Prompt 8.2: Defining Intercultural Communication
What is a definition of intercultural communication? What is meant by the phrase "culture is dynamic and heterogeneous and operates within societal power structures"?

Intercultural Communication and the Individual: Cultural Values

8.3   Describe how cultural values influence communication.

In Chapters 5 and 6, we described how culture influences verbal and nonverbal communication. You might think that these differences would be important to understanding intercultural communication; however, just as important is understanding **cultural values**, which are the beliefs that are so central to a cultural group that they are never questioned.

cultural values
Beliefs that are so central to a cultural group that they are never questioned.

The Influence of Cultural Values on Communication

Cultural values prescribe what *should* be. Understanding cultural values is essential because they often lie below consciousness and are unquestioned and yet so powerfully influence people's behavior, including their communication. Intercultural interaction often involves becoming aware of, confronting, and responding to an entirely different set of cultural values. Let's see how this works.

Social psychologist Geert Hofstede (2010) and his colleagues conducted a massive study, collecting 116,000 surveys about people's value preferences in approximately 80 countries around the world. Psychologist Michael Bond and his colleagues conducted a similar, although smaller, study in Asia (Chinese Culture Connection, 1987). Although these studies identify value preferences of national cultural groups, they can also apply to religious and ethnic or racial groups, socioeconomic class groups, and gender groups. For example, anthropologists Florence Kluckhohn and Fred Strodtbeck (1961) conducted a study that identified the contrasting values of three cultural groups in the United States: Latinos, Anglos, and American Indians. Recently, communication scholars have identified cultural values of other racial groups: African Americans and Asian Americans. Together, all these studies identified a number of cultural values.

As you read about these cultural value orientations, please keep three points in mind. These guidelines reflect a common dilemma for intercultural communication scholars—the desire to describe and understand communication and behavior patterns within a cultural group and the fear of making rigid categories that can lead to stereotyping:

1. The following discussion describes the *predominant* values preferred by various cultural groups, not the values held by *every person* in the cultural group. Think of cultural values as occurring on a bell curve: Most people may be in the middle, holding a particular value orientation, but many people can be found on each end of the curve; these are the people who *do not go along* with the majority.

2. The following discussion refers to values on the cultural level, not on the individual level. Thus, if you read that most Chinese tend to prefer an indirect way of speaking, you cannot assume that every Chinese person you meet will speak in an indirect way in every situation.

3. The only way to understand what a particular individual believes is to get to know the person. You can't predict how any one person will communicate. The real challenge is to understand the full range of cultural values and then learn to communicate effectively with others who hold differing value orientations, regardless of their cultural background.

▲ In individualistic cultures, the nuclear family household is most common [just parent(s) and children]: children are raised to be autonomous and to live on their own by late adolescence, whereas parents are expected to not "be a burden" on their children when they age.

Now that you understand the basic ground rules, let's look at seven key aspects of cultural values.

Individualism and Collectivism   One of the most central value orientations identified in this research addresses whether a culture emphasizes the rights and needs of the individual or that of the group. For example, many North American and northern European cultural groups, particularly U.S. Whites, value individualism and independence, believing that one's primary responsibility is to one's self (Bellah et al., 2007; Hofstede et al., 2010). In relationships, those with this **individualistic orientation** respect autonomy and independence, and they do not meddle in another's problems unless invited. For example, in cultures where individualism prevails, many children are raised to be autonomous and to live on their own by late adolescence (although they may return home for short periods after this). Their parents are expected to take care of themselves and not "be a burden" on their children when they age (Triandis, 1995). A recent example of individualism/collectivism is the differing cultural responses to COVID-19, with many U.S. Americans refusing to wear facial masks and practice "social distancing." Experts suggest these behaviors reflect a cultural belief in individualism, "Let me live my life and make my own choices about what risks I'm willing to take" (Linker, 2020).

individualistic orientation
A value orientation that respects the autonomy and independence of individuals.

In contrast, many cultures in South America and Asia hold a more **collectivistic orientation** that stresses the needs of the group, as do some Hispanic and Asian Americans in the United States (Ho et al., 2004). Some argue that working-class people tend to be more collectivistic than those in the middle or upper class; in the United States, for example, working-class people donate a higher percentage of their time and money to help others (Piff et al., 2010). For collectivists, the primary responsibility is to relationships with others; interdependence in family, work, and personal relationships is viewed positively. Most Asians' initial response to COVID-19 was to wear facial masks in order to protect the health of those around them (Linker, 2020). Collectivists value working toward relationship and group harmony over remaining independent and self-sufficient. For example, giving money to a needy cousin, uncle, or aunt might be preferable to spending it on oneself. Or sharing belongings, such as cars, computers, and mobile phones, may be expected in collectivist communities. In many collectivist cultures, too, children often defer to parents when making important decisions, like accepting a new job or choosing a spouse.

collectivistic orientation
A value orientation that stresses the needs of the group.

Critical Thinking Prompt
As you were growing up, in what ways were you reared to be individualistic? Collectivistic? Which orientation was the predominant cultural value of your family?

▲ In many collectivist cultures, adult children often defer to parents when making important decisions.

As noted previously, however, not all Japanese or all Indians are collectivistic, nor are all U.S. Americans individualistic. In fact, journalist Colin Woodard (2012) maintains that there are significant regional differences here in the degree of commitment to individual freedom or conversely, sacrifice for the good of the community. In addition, generational differences may exist within countries where collectivism is strong. Young people in many Asian countries (e.g., Korea, Vietnam) are increasingly influenced by capitalism and individualism and are now expressing individuality in making their own personal decisions rather than following their family's wishes.

For example, young men and women in Korea are now getting body tattoos—a practice unheard of 50 years ago (Park, 2015). In addition, not all cultures are as individualistic as U.S. culture or as collectivistic as Japanese culture. Rather, cultures can be arranged along an individualism–collectivism continuum (Ting-Toomey, 2010) based on their specific orientations to the needs of the individual and the group.

preferred personality

A value orientation that expresses whether it is more important for a person to "do" or to "be."

Preferred Personality   In addition to differing on the individualism–collectivism spectrum, cultural groups may differ over the idea of the **preferred personality**, or whether it is more important to "do" or to "be" (Kluckhohn & Strodtbeck, 1961). In the United States, researchers have found that *doing* is the preferred value for many people, including European Americans, Asian Americans, and African Americans (Ting-Toomey, 1999). In general, the "doing mode" means working hard to achieve material gain, even if it means sacrificing time with family and friends. Other cultural groups, for example, many Latinos, prefer the *being* mode—which emphasizes the importance of experiencing life and the people around them fully and "working to live" rather than "living to work" (Hecht et al., 1993).

Some scholars suggest that many African Americans express both a doing mode, fighting actively against racism through social activity for the good of the community, and a being mode, valuing a sense of vitality and open expression of feeling (Hecht et al., 2002). Cultural differences in this value orientation can lead to communication challenges. For example, many Latinos believe that Anglos place too much emphasis on accomplishing tasks and earning money and not enough emphasis on spending time with friends and family or enjoying the moment.

Critical Thinking Prompt

What kinds of communication problems might occur when members of a diverse work team hold different value orientations toward being and doing? How might someone who usually uses a being mode view someone with a doing mode, and vice versa?

---

view of human nature

A value orientation that expresses whether humans are fundamentally good, evil, or a mixture.

Human Nature   A third value difference concerns the **view of human nature**—in particular, whether humans are considered fundamentally good, evil, or a mixture. The United States, for example, was founded by early White settlers who believed that human nature was fundamentally evil (Hulse, 1996). In the years since the founding of the country, a shift occurred in this view, as evidenced in the U.S. legal and justice systems. It emphasizes rehabilitation, which suggests a view of humans as potentially good. In addition, the fact that the U.S. justice system assumes people are innocent until proven guilty indicates that people are viewed as basically good.

In contrast, cultural groups that view humans as essentially evil, such as some fundamentalist religions, emphasize punishment over rehabilitation. Some evidence indicates that U.S. Americans in general are moving again toward this view of human nature. For example, state laws such as the "three-strikes rule" emphasize punishment over rehabilitation by automatically and significantly increasing the prison sentences of persons convicted of a felony who have been previously convicted of two or more violent crimes or serious felonies. Also, incarceration rates in the United States have increased by more than 500 percent since the early 1970s, and among developed countries, the United States now has the highest percentage of incarcerated individuals—more than China, Cuba, and Russia (Robertson, 2019). As you might imagine, people who differ on the question of human nature can have serious disagreements on public policies concerning crime and justice.

Human–Nature Relationship   A fourth value that varies from culture to culture is the perceived relationship between humans and nature, or the **human–nature value orientation**. At one end of this value continuum is the view that humans are intended to rule nature. At the other extreme, nature is seen as ruling humans. In a third option, the two exist in harmony. Unsurprisingly, the predominant value in the United States has been one of humans ruling over nature, as evidenced in the proliferation of controlled environments. Phoenix, Arizona, for example, which is in a desert, has more than 200 golf courses—reflecting the fact that Arizonans have changed the natural environment to suit their living and leisure interests. In other parts of the United States, people make snow for skiing, seed clouds when rain is needed, dam and reroute rivers, and use fertilizer to enhance agricultural production. Such interventions generally reflect a belief in human control over nature (Trompenaars & Hampden-Turner, 2012).

> **human–nature value orientation**
> The perceived relationship between humans and nature.

In contrast, many in the Middle East view nature as having predominance over humans. This belief that one's fate is held by nature is reflected in the common Arabic saying "*Enchallah*" ("Allah willing"), suggesting that nature will (and should) determine, for example, how crops will grow. A comparable Christian saying is "God willing," reflecting perhaps a similar fatalistic tendency in Christianity. Interestingly, many Spanish-speaking Christians express the same sentiment with the word "*Ojalá*," which is rooted in "*Enchallah*" and originates from the centuries when southern Spain was a Muslim province.

Many American Indians and Asians value harmony with nature. People who hold this cultural orientation believe that humans and nature are one and that nature enriches human life. For many traditional American Indians, certain animals such as buffalo and eagles are important presences in human activity (Porter, 2002). For example, the use of feathers can be an important part of the sundance, a religious ceremony practiced by many different American Indian groups. In this ceremony, the eagle is viewed as the link between humans and creator. When people see an eagle in the sky during a ceremony, they are especially thankful because the eagle flies highest of all birds and the moment it disappears into the skies, people's prayers are heard. These traditions show high regard and utmost respect for these animals and reflect a belief in the close and important relationship between humans and nature ("Eagle aviary allows American Indians to continue heritage," 2005).

In the United States, differences arise between real estate developers, who believe that humans take precedence over nature, and environmentalists and

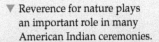
▼ Reverence for nature plays an important role in many American Indian ceremonies.

many Native American groups, who believe that nature is as important as humans. This conflict has surfaced in many disagreements; for example, in controversies over water rights in Oregon where Indian tribes want to maintain water levels for endangered fish they traditionally harvest, thus denying water to farmers downstream (Barboza, 2013). There are also value conflicts between loggers and environmentalists over the endangered spotted owl, which is now also threatened by the more aggressive barred owl in the southwestern United States (Sahagun, 2014).

power distance

A value orientation that refers to the extent to which less powerful members of institutions and organizations within a culture expect and accept an unequal distribution of power.

Power Distance   **Power distance**, the fifth value orientation, refers to the extent to which less powerful members of institutions and organizations within a culture expect and accept an unequal distribution of power (Hofstede et al., 2010). In Denmark, Israel, the United States, and New Zealand, many people value small power distances. Thus, most people in those countries believe that inequality, although inevitable, should be minimized, and that the best leaders emphasize equality and informality in interactions with subordinates. In many situations, subordinates are expected to speak up and contribute.

Societies that value large power distance—for example, Mexico, the Philippines, and India—are structured more around a hierarchy in which each person has a rightful place, and interactions between supervisors and subordinates are more formal (Hofstede et al., 2010). Seniority, age, rank, and titles are emphasized more in these societies than in small power distance societies. In addition, a preference for informal communication tends to go along with small power distance orientation.

People who are used to large power distances may be uncomfortable in settings where hierarchy is unclear or ambiguous and communication tends to be informal. For example, international students who come from countries where a large power distance value predominates may initially be uncomfortable in U.S. college classrooms, where

It Happened to Me
Nagesh

I was amazed when I took my first online class at an American university. The students seemed very disrespectful toward the teacher and toward each other. In discussions, they addressed the teacher very informally, just like "Hey, I have a question!" They didn't address the professor by title, and they would openly disagree with each other. In my country (India), students would never behave this way toward a teacher. I found it difficult to speak up in this kind of online classroom situation.

relations between students and teachers are informal and characterized by equality, especially in online classes, a situation described in *It Happened to Me: Nagesh*.

In contrast, U.S. Americans abroad often offend locals when they treat others too informally—calling them by their first names, treating them as if they were friends. For example, former First Lady Michelle Obama shocked the Queen and the British media when she threw her arm around Her Majesty the Queen, as a classic British rule is that you never touch the Queen (Collman, 2018). Note that value orientations often represent a cultural ideal rather than a reality. Although many Americans say they desire small power distance, the truth is that rigid social and economic hierarchies exist in the United States. Most Americans are born into and live within the same socioeconomic class for their whole lives (Telford, 2019).

long-term versus short-term orientation

The dimension of a society's value orientation that reflects its attitude toward virtue or truth.

Long-Term versus Short-Term Orientation   The research identifying the five values we've described has been criticized for its predominately Western European bias. In response to this criticism, a group of Chinese researchers developed and administered a similar, but more Asian-oriented, questionnaire to people in 22 countries around the world (Chinese Culture Connection, 1987). They then compared their findings to previous research on value orientations and found considerable overlap, especially on the dimensions of individualism versus collectivism and power distance. These researchers did identify one additional value dimension that previous researchers hadn't seen— **long-term versus short-term orientation**.

This dimension reflects a society's attitude toward virtue or truth. A **short-term orientation** characterizes cultures in which people are concerned with possessing one fundamental truth, as reflected in the **monotheistic** religions of Judaism, Christianity, and Islam. Other qualities identified in the research and associated with a short-term orientation include an emphasis on quick results, individualism, and personal security and safety (Hofstede et al., 2010).

In contrast, a **long-term orientation** tends to respect the demands of virtue, reflected in Eastern religions such as Confucianism, Hinduism, Buddhism, and Shintoism, which are all **polytheistic** religions (belief in more than one god). Other qualities associated with a long-term orientation include thrift, perseverance, and tenacity in whatever one attempts, and a willingness to subordinate oneself for a purpose (Bond, 1991, 2010).

Indulgence versus Restraint Based on recent research by Michael Minkov, one of Hofstede's associates, there is now a seventh value dimension, **indulgence versus restraint** (Hofstede et al., 2010). This dimension is related to the *subjective* feelings of happiness. That is, people may not actually *be* happy or healthy but they report that they *feel* happier and healthier. National cultures that are categorized as more indulgent (Mexico, Nigeria, Sweden, Australia) tend to allow relatively free gratification of needs related to enjoying life and having fun. In these cultures, having lots of friends (e.g., Facebook) is important, as is active participation in sports, and there is less moral regulation. Societies that emphasize restraint (Russia, Egypt and other Islamic countries, China, India) tend to suppress gratification of needs and regulate it by means of strict social norms. Having many friends is reportedly less important, there is more watching of sports, but less participation, and a strong work ethic. Countries with a predominant indulgent orientation emphasize freedom of speech over maintaining order; countries with more restraint orientation tend to value maintaining order over allowing freedom of speech.

Although knowing about these value differences can help you identify and understand problems that arise in intercultural interactions, you might be concerned that this approach to the study of intercultural communication leads to generalizing and stereotyping. One strategy for counteracting this tendency is the **dialectical approach**. Dialectics has long existed as a concept in philosophical thought and logic. In this book we introduce it as a way to emphasize simultaneous contradictory truths. Thus, a dialectical approach helps people respond to the complexities of intercultural communication and to override any tendencies to stereotype people based on cultural patterns. This concept may be difficult to understand because it is contrary to most formal education in the United States, which often emphasizes **dichotomous thinking**, in which things are "either/or"—good or bad, big or small, right or wrong. However, a dialectical approach recognizes that things may be "both/and." For example, a palm tree may be weak *and* strong. Its branches look fragile and weak, and yet in a hurricane it remains strong because the "weak" fronds

short-term orientation
A value orientation that stresses the importance of possessing one fundamental truth.

monotheistic
Belief in one god.

long-term orientation
A value orientation in which people stress the importance of virtue.

polytheistic
Belief in more than one god.

indulgence versus restraint
A value orientation that reflects a subjective feeling of happiness. The indulgence orientation emphasizes relatively free gratification of basic and natural human drives related to enjoying life and having fun. Restraint emphasizes suppressing gratification of needs and regulates it by means of strict social norms.

dialectical approach
Recognizes that things need not be perceived as "either/or" but may be seen as "both/and."

dichotomous thinking
Thinking in which things are perceived as "either/or"—for example, "good or bad," "big or small," "right or wrong."

▼ Although being White involves cultural advantages, being poor involves disadvantages.

can bend without breaking. Similar dialectics exist in intercultural communication and emphasize the fluid, complex, and contradictory nature of intercultural interactions. Dialectics exist in other communication contexts such as relationships, which we explore in Chapter 9.

This dialectical approach helps us resist making quick, stereotypical judgments about others and their communication behavior. One individual can have individualistic and collectivistic tendencies, can be both culturally similar and different from us, and can be culturally privileged in some situations and culturally disadvantaged in others (Ting-Toomey, 2010). We provide more specific detail on how the dialectic approach can be used to avoid stereotyping others later in the chapter.

Journal Prompt 8.3: Cultural Values
What are seven common core values that differentiate various cultural groups? How might these values influence intercultural communication?

The Individual, Intercultural Communication, and Society: Politics, History, and Power

8.4 Explain the roles that politics, history, and power play in communication between people from different cultural backgrounds.

As you have probably gathered by now, intercultural communication never occurs in a vacuum but must be understood in the context of larger societal forces. In this section, we first focus on social, political, and historical forces; second, we turn our attention to the role of power in intercultural communication.

Political and Historical Forces

That societal forces can affect intercultural encounters is exemplified by the varying reactions toward some ethnic groups during the pandemic. Turns out that Asian Americans experienced reactions from others that caused them to question their "American" identity. Before the pandemic, they considered themselves well adapted to U.S. culture. Consider Tracy Wen Liu, a student living in Austin, Texas; pre-pandemic nothing in her life felt un-American. She went to football games, watched *Sex and the City*, and volunteered at food banks. "Honestly, I didn't really think I stood out a lot," she says (Cheung et al., 2020). As she reported to a journalist, that changed with the pandemic: "Being Asian in America can make you a target . . . a Korean friend was pushed and yelled at by several people in a grocery store, and then asked to leave" (Cheung et al., 2020). The journalist went on to note how in other states East Asians have been spat on, punched, kicked, and in one case even stabbed. Thus, they are reminded that they are different; they are not completely accepted as Americans, and, in fact, there were 1,700 hate crimes against Asian Americans reported between March and May 2020 (Lee, 2020). This makes interactions between Asians/Asian Americans (or those who are perceived as Asian) and some other Americans more difficult.

Historical forces also can influence contemporary intercultural interaction in a dialectical relationship. For example, although slavery is long gone in the United States, one could not understand contemporary Black–White relations in this country without acknowledging its effect. Author James Loewen (2010) describes the twin legacies of slavery that are still with us: (1) social and economic inferiority for Blacks brought on by specific economic and political policies from 1885 to 1965 that led to inferior educational institutions and exclusion from labor unions, voting rights, and the advantage of government mortgages and (2) cultural racism instilled in Whites. Some thought that the election of Barack Obama as the first African American U.S. president demonstrated significant progress in interracial relations. The intense political and social conversations that have occurred since then, often centering on race (e.g., the killing of unarmed Black men by police, including Michael Brown, Alton Sterling, Freddie Gray, Walter Scott, Eric Garner, Laquan McDonald, and George Floyd), as well as the largest protest in U.S. history led by the Black Lives Matter movement in 2020 demonstrate that the historical legacies of racism impact interracial encounters and show a need for a continuing national conversation about race ("America's reckoning on racism," 2020; Buchanan et al., 2020).

Current demographic statistics also indicate that Americans remain fairly racially segregated in their schools and neighborhoods (Massey, 2016; Scott, 2016) and results in interactions between Whites and Blacks in the United States that are often limited and sometimes challenging. For example, a Pew Research poll found that 70–80 percent of both Black and White Americans report that all or most of their close friends are of the same race (Parker et al., 2015). As a society, which institutions or contexts now promote the best opportunities for interracial contact? Neighborhoods? Educational institutions? Churches, synagogues, and other places of worship? The workplace? Neighborhoods and workplaces do not seem to provide opportunities for the *type* of contact (intimate, friendly, equal-status interaction) that facilitates intercultural relationships (Johnson & Jacobson, 2005). By contrast, it appears that *integrated* religious institutions and educational institutions provide the best opportunities for intercultural friendships and the best environment to improve interracial attitudes (Johnson & Jacobson, 2005). For example, a study of six California State University campuses found that the students on these campuses interacted equally, in interracial and intraracial encounters (Cowan, 2005). These campuses are diverse; no single ethnic or racial group is a majority. However, a more recent study cautions that sometimes students in multicultural campuses assume that they have intercultural relationships just by virtue of being surrounded by cultural diversity and may not make the effort to actually pursue intercultural friendships (Hudson, 2018).

Intercultural Communication and Power

As we noted in Chapter 4, the more powerful groups in society establish the rules for communication, and others usually follow these rules or violate them at their peril (Orbe, 1998). A number of factors influence who is considered powerful in a culture. For example, being White in the United States has more privilege attached to it than being Latino. Although most Whites do not notice this privilege and dominance, most minority group members do (DiAngelo, 2018; Moon, 2016). Being male also has historically been more valued than being female, and being wealthy is more valued than being poor. Further, being able-bodied is traditionally more valued than being physically disabled (Allen, 2011; Johnson, 2017), and being straight and cisgender is more valued than being gay or trans. Every society, regardless of power distance values, has these kinds of traditional hierarchies of power. Although the hierarchy is never entirely fixed, it does constrain and influence communication among cultural groups.

How do power differences affect intercultural interaction? They do so primarily by determining whose cultural values will be respected and followed. For example, even though the United States is increasingly diverse culturally, faculty, staff, and students in most U.S. universities adhere to the values and communication norms set by the White, male-dominant groups. These values and communication norms emphasize individualism. Thus, although group work is common in many courses, professors usually try to figure out how to give individual grades for it, and most students are encouraged to be responsible for their own work. Moreover, the university is run on monochronic time (see Chapter 5), with great emphasis placed on keeping schedules and meeting deadlines—and these deadlines sometimes take precedence over family and other personal responsibilities. The communication style most valued in this culture also is individual-oriented, direct and to the point, and extremely task-oriented, as is the case in many organizations in the United States (Sanchez-Burks et al., 2003).

What is the impact for those who come from other cultural backgrounds and do not fit into this mold—say, for those who have collectivistic backgrounds and value personal relationships over tasks and homework assignments? Or for those, like Kaori, whose preferred communication style is more indirect? They may experience culture shock; they also may be sanctioned or marginalized—for example, with bad grades for not participating more in class, for not completing tasks on time, or for getting too much help from others on assignments.

To more fully consider these problems we need to refer to cocultural theory (described in Chapter 4 and Chapter 6) and reintroduce the concept of the **cocultural group**, meaning significant minority groups within a dominant majority (e.g., White U.S. culture) that may not share dominant group values or communication patterns, e.g., some Native American, Mexican American, and Asian American individuals. Researcher Mark Orbe (1998) suggests that cocultural group members have several choices as to how they can relate to the dominant culture: They can assimilate, they can accommodate, or they can remain separate. He cautions that each strategy has benefits and limitations. For example, when women try to assimilate and "act like men" in a male-oriented organization, they may score points for being professional, but they also may be criticized for being too masculine. When African Americans try to accommodate in a largely White management, they may satisfy White colleagues and bosses but earn the label "oreo" from other African Americans. In contrast, resisting assimilation or remaining apart may result in isolation, marginalization, and exclusion from the discussions where important decisions are made (Orbe & Roberts, 2012). Again, it is important to note that there is a great deal of diversity within co-cultural groups. Some question whether this diversity is adequately represented in television and film (See *Communication in Society: African American TV Families: Diverse Enough?*).

cocultural group
A significant minority group within a dominant majority that does not share dominant group values or communication patterns.

Journal Prompt 8.4: Politics, History, and Power
What roles do politics, history, and power play in communication between people from different cultural backgrounds?

COMMUNICATION IN SOCIETY
African American TV Families: Diverse Enough?

How important do you think it is that television shows, especially reality TV, reflect or critique social reality?

One author describes the debate over the role of reality television shows—whether they reflect or shape our views on racial and economic diversity—and also explores the question of whether diversity matters in reality TV. Tamar Braxton of *Braxton Family Values*, on WEtv, explained why her family chose to do a reality show: she noted that it was important "especially for our black community" to show audiences people to whom they could relate. And it makes sense for the network's bottom line—attracting a large diverse audience.

[However,] it should also be noted that the families on some reality television can't be used to generalize about families of any race; they're really rich: for example, *Braxton Family Values*, where one sister is singer Toni Braxton, and *The Real Housewives of Atlanta*, part of a franchise where affluence is the common experience.

So although there may be racial diversity, is the lack of socio-economic diversity of African American TV families, scripted and unscripted, a problem? As Cynthia Bailey, of *The Real Housewives*

of *Atlanta*, says, she couldn't identify with the *Cosby Show* when she was growing up. "That wasn't what my family was like," she says. "In my mind, that was almost a rich black family."

Some experts think this is a problem. Communication professor Catherine Squires, author of *African Americans and the Media*, says that because television shows, especially reality television, are supposed to reflect reality, "[l]ooking at rich, black people acting out after you've looked at rich, white people acting out, does that give people who aren't rich and black any sense of what the black people closer to their lives are like?" And even a show like *Real Housewives*, which is relatively diverse across the franchise, represents each racial group as largely cut off from the others. Squires says that while the monoracial nature of television does reflect ongoing segregation everywhere from schools to Hollywood, such mirroring means it's all the more important to notice.

SOURCE: Rothman, L. (2012, July 8). Essence Fest 2012: Is reality TV still not diverse enough? *Time.com*. http://entertainment.time.com/2012/07/08/essence-reality-tv-family-panel/

Ethics and Intercultural Communication

8.5 Give three guidelines for communicating more ethically with people whose cultural backgrounds differ from your own.

How can you communicate more ethically across cultures? Unfortunately, no easy answers exist, but a few guidelines may be helpful.

First, remember that everyone, including you, is enmeshed in a culture and, thus, communicating through a cultural lens. Recognizing your own cultural attitudes, values, and beliefs will make you more sensitive to others' cultures and less likely to impose your own cultural attitudes on their communication patterns. Although you may feel most comfortable living in your own culture and following its communication patterns, you should not conclude that your culture and communication style are best or should be the standard for all other cultures. Such a position is called **ethnocentrism**, which you learned about in Chapter 3. Of course, appreciating and respecting other cultures does not mean you don't still appreciate and respect your own.

Second, as you learn about other cultural groups, be aware of their humanity and avoid the temptation to view them as an exotic "other." Communication scholar Bradford Hall (1997) has cautioned about this tendency, which is called the "zoo approach."

When using such an approach, we view the study of culture as if we were walking through a zoo admiring, gasping, and chuckling at the various exotic animals we observe. One may discover amazing, interesting, and valuable information by using such a perspective and even develop a real fondness of these exotic people but miss the point that we are as culturally "caged" as others and that they are culturally as "free" as we are (Hall, 1997, p. 14). From an ethical perspective, the zoo approach denies the humanity of other cultural groups. For example, the view of African cultures as primitive and incapable led Whites to justify colonizing Africa and exploiting its rich resources in the nineteenth century.

Third, you will be more ethical in your intercultural interactions if you are open to other ways of viewing the world. The ways that you were taught about the world and history may not be the same as what others were taught. People cannot engage in meaningful communication if they are unwilling to suspend or reexamine their assumptions about the world. For example, some Europeans believe that the United States becomes involved in other countries' affairs so that it can control its oil interests, whereas many U.S. Americans believe that concern over human rights is the motivation. If neither group will consider the opinion of the other, they will be unlikely to sustain a mutually satisfying conversation.

▲ It is difficult to engage in meaningful communication if people are unwilling to suspend or reexamine their deeply held assumptions.

ethnocentrism
The tendency to view one's own group as the standard against which all other groups are judged.

Journal Prompt 8.5: Ethical Intercultural Communication
What three strategies can you use to help you respond ethically during intercultural interactions?

Improving Your Intercultural Communication Skills

8.6 Discuss ways to improve your own intercultural communication skills.

How can you communicate more effectively across cultures? As with ethics, no magic formula exists, but here are several suggestions.

Increase Motivation

Perhaps the most important component is *motivation*. Without the motivation to be an effective communicator, no other skills will be relevant.

Part of the problem in long-standing interethnic or interreligious conflicts—for example, between the Israelis and the Palestinians—is the lack of interest, on both sides, in communicating more effectively. Some parties on both sides may even have an interest in prolonging conflict. You might reflect on what stops you from reaching out to cultural others and/or improving your intercultural skills. For some, it's a reluctance out of fear of being misunderstood or making mistakes. For others, it may be complacency or simply no desire (Holmes & O'Neill, 2012). Perhaps a review of the first section of this chapter can provide some motivation by reminding you of the benefits gained by learning more about intercultural communication.

Increase Your Knowledge of Self and Others

In addition to being motivated, you become a more effective intercultural communicator if you educate yourself about intercultural communication. Having some knowledge about the history, background, and values of people from other cultures can help you communicate better, both face to face and online. When you demonstrate this type of knowledge to people from other cultures, you communicate that you're interested in them and you affirm their sense of identity. Obviously, no one can know everything about all cultures; nonetheless, some general information can be helpful, as can an awareness of the importance of context and a dialectical perspective. Just a note of instruction to White students interested in learning more about the experience of people of color in the United States: people of color are not obligated to teach you. As one Black journalist explains it: Asking Black people in the United States to discuss race is asking them to relive every moment of pain, fear, and outrage they have experienced. "Too often the white friends who want their black friends to educate them about race don't do that work, and don't accept that being uncomfortable with Black anger is part of that work . . . Few things are more off-putting to a black person than being subjected to Socratic questioning by a white person over seemingly trivial matters that may actually be deeply personal and painful. No can do" (Wilson, 2020). Another Black author compares it to learning about rules of baseball: if you want to call yourself a baseball fan, you don't interrupt the players to ask about basic rules—that's rude. You consult the tons of information already out there. You educate yourself (Holloway, 2015). There are tons of articles, books, and movies about the experiences of people of color in the United States.

Self-knowledge also is important. If you were socialized to be individualistic and direct in your communication style, you may initially have a hard time understanding collectivistic tendencies or indirect communication. Once you become aware of these differences, however, you can more easily communicate with someone who holds a different perspective. Growing up in a middle-class family may also influence your perceptions. Many middle-class people assume that anyone can become middle class through hard work. But this view overlooks the discrimination faced by people of color, members of religious minorities, and LGBTQIA+ individuals. How can you increase your cultural self-awareness? Perhaps the best way is to cultivate intercultural encounters and relationships.

Developing facility in intercultural communication occurs through a cyclical process. The more one interacts across cultures, the more one learns about oneself, and then the more prepared one is to interact interculturally, and so on. However, increased exposure and understanding do not happen automatically. Being aware of the influence of culture on oneself and others is essential to increasing one's intercultural experience and competence (Ting-Toomey, 2010).

Where should you start? You can begin by examining your current friendships and reach out from there. Research shows that individuals generally become friends with people with whom they live, work, and worship. So your opportunities for intercultural interaction and self-awareness are largely determined by the type of people and contexts you encounter in your daily routine.

Avoid Stereotypes

Cultural differences may lead to stereotyping and prejudices. As we discussed in Chapter 3, normal cognitive patterns of generalizing make our world more manageable. However, when these generalizations become rigid, they lead to stereotyping and prejudices. Furthermore, stereotyping can become self-fulfilling (Guéguen et al., 2009). That is, if you stereotype people and treat them in a prejudiced or negative manner, they may react in ways that reinforce your stereotype.

On the other hand, we must note, overreacting by being "sweet" can be equally off-putting. African Americans sometimes complain about being "niced" to death by Whites (Yamato, 2001). The guideline here is to be mindful that you might be stereotyping. For example, if you are White, do you only notice bad behavior when exhibited by a person of color?

As we noted earlier, taking a dialectical approach is a useful strategy to avoiding stereotyping others. Here are six dialectics that can assist you in communicating more effectively in intercultural interactions.

1. **CULTURAL–INDIVIDUAL**

   What it is: It emphasizes that some behaviors are determined by our culture, whereas others are simply idiosyncratic, or particular to us as individuals. Taking this approach means that one does not immediately assume that someone's behavior is culturally based.

   Example: *Robin twists her hair while she talks.* This idiosyncratic personal preference should not be mistaken for a cultural norm. She doesn't do it because she is female or young or Protestant or African American.

2. **PERSONAL–CONTEXTUAL**

   What it is: This dialectic focuses on the importance of context or situation and the personal in intercultural communication. Reducing an interaction to a mere meeting of two individuals means viewing intercultural communication too simplistically.

   Example: *An Italian and a German exchange student strike up a conversation in a gym where they are both exercising.* The immediate situation has an impact, so their conversation would probably differ dramatically if it occurred at a party or at a funeral service. The larger situation, including political and historical forces, also plays a role. The two might be wary of engaging in conversation due to recent events surrounding the economic problems in Italy. Some Germans felt that the Italian government and people were irresponsible in their failed financial policies and resented having the EU (led by Germans) "bail out" their economy again. Likewise, many Italians felt that the Germans were unfair, that these demands were an expression of long-standing German prejudice toward Italians and other southern European cultures. At the same time, the characteristics of the specific individuals also affect the exchange. Some Italians (or Germans) would ignore the larger situation and reject the antipathy toward the other group. Others would attach great importance to the larger context and view the other student negatively.

3. **DIFFERENCES–SIMILARITIES**

   What it is: Real, important differences exist between cultural groups; we've identified some of these in this chapter. However, important commonalities exist as well.

   Example: One of our students summed up this point nicely in *It Happened to Me: Angelina.*

4. **STATIC–DYNAMIC**

What it is: Although some cultural patterns remain relatively stable and static for years, they also can undergo dynamic change. A static–dynamic dialectic requires that you recognize both traditional and contemporary realities of a culture.

Example: Many people form impressions about American Indians from popular films such as *Smoke Signals* or even children's movies like *Pocahontas* or *The Indian in the Cupboard*, which portray Indians living the rural life they lived centuries ago, even though the majority of Indians in the United States today live in urban areas (Infoplease Staff, 2020).

5. **HISTORY/PAST–PRESENT/FUTURE**

What it is: This dialectic focuses on the present and the past.

Example: One cannot fully understand contemporary relations between Arabs and Jews, Muslims and Christians, or Catholics and Protestants without knowing something of their history. At the same time, people cannot ignore current events. For example, the conflict over where Yasser Arafat was to be buried in the autumn of 2004 flowed from a complex of historical and contemporary relations. His family had resided for generations in Jerusalem and wanted him laid to rest there. Israel, having current control of Jerusalem and viewing Arafat as a terrorist leader of attacks against Israel, refused.

6. **PRIVILEGE–DISADVANTAGE**

What it is: In intercultural interactions, people can be simultaneously privileged and disadvantaged (Johnson, 2017).

Example: Although U.S. Americans may be privileged in having more money and the luxury of travel, they can also feel vulnerable in foreign countries if they are ignorant of the local languages and customs. Poor Whites in the United States can be simultaneously privileged because they are White and disadvantaged because of their economic plight (Engen, 2012). As a student, you may feel privileged (compared to others) in that you are acquiring a high level of education, but you may also feel economically disadvantaged because of the high cost of education.

Strive for Empathy

In addition to being motivated, learning about others, and avoiding stereotypes, striving for intercultural empathy can also increase your cross-cultural competence. Empathy refers to the ability to know what it's like to "walk in another person's shoes." However, empathic skills are culture bound, meaning that we cannot really view the world through another person's eyes without knowing something about their experiences and life (DeTurk, 2001). Communication scholar Broome (2015) stresses that, rather than trying to achieve absolute accuracy in predicting someone else's thoughts (which is impossible), people should forge strong relationships and strive for the creation of shared meaning in their intercultural encounters—accepting that understanding another's point of view and their feelings is not an all or nothing proposition—it is a *process* and relational empathy is a goal one strives for in intercultural encounters.

> ### It Happened to Me
> **Angelina**
>
> In my first year of college, I had the most memorable friendship with a person from the Middle East. Through this friendship I learned a lot about the way people from the Middle East communicate with friends, family, and authority. My new friend and I differed in many ways—in religion, culture, nationality, race, and language. However, we were both female college students the same age, and we shared many interests. She dressed like I did and styled her hair similarly, and we shared many ideas about the future and concerns about the world.

Navigating the Borderlands

If you are one of those individuals who lives on the borderlands and engages in intercultural communication in everyday life (e.g., through travel or an intercultural relationship, or circumstances), how can you improve your intercultural competence? How can you successfully negotiate the tensions between often-contradictory systems of values, language, and nonverbal behavior of two or more cultures? In some cases, people in such situations can feel caught between two systems; feeling as if one were swinging on a trapeze, a metaphor that captures the immigrant's experience of vacillating between the cultural patterns of the homeland and the new country, or between two ethnic or religious groups (Hegde, 1998). Typically, cultural minorities are socialized to the norms and values of both the dominant culture and their own; they may be pressured to assimilate to the dominant culture and embrace it, yet those in the dominant culture may still be reluctant to accept them as they try to do so. As one Black woman expressed, "Immediately when I step into a setting where I'm the only Black, I'm feeling like all eyes are upon me, for my entire race, especially Black women. My tone changes, the way I speak, following the rules of language—not that I don't do it anyway, but I'm more alert, making sure that I don't stumble over certain words" (Scott, 2013, p. 319).

Managing these tensions while living on the border and being multicultural can be both rewarding and challenging. Based on data from interviews she conducted, Janet Bennett (1998) described two types of border dwellers or, as she labeled them, "marginal individuals": *encapsulated marginal people* and *constructive marginal people*.

Encapsulated marginal people feel disintegrated by having to shift cultures. They have difficulty making decisions and feel extreme pressure from both groups. They try to assimilate but never feel comfortable or at home.

In contrast, **constructive marginal people** thrive in their "border" life and, at the same time, recognize its tremendous challenges. They see themselves as choice makers. They recognize the significance and potential of being "in between." For example, communication scholar Lisa Flores (1996) shows how Chicana feminist writers and artists acknowledge negative stereotypes of Mexican and Mexican American women—illiterate Spanglish-speaking laborers, passive sex objects, servants of men and children—and transform them into images of strength—as strong, clever bilinguals, reveling in their dual Anglo-Mexican heritage. In so doing, they also gain strength by reaching out to other women (women of color and immigrant women), and together strive to achieve more justice and recognition for women who live "in the middle" between cultural worlds.

Although border dwelling can be challenging and frustrating, it also can lead to cultural insights and agility in navigating intercultural encounters.

encapsulated marginal people
People who feel disintegrated by having to shift cultures.

constructive marginal people
People who thrive in a border-dweller life, while recognizing its tremendous challenges.

Journal Prompt 8.6: Improving Intercultural Communication
What are three suggestions for communicating more effectively across cultures? Which do you think is the most important? Why?

SUMMARY

8.1 Explain why it is important to learn about intercultural communication.

- Four reasons for learning about intercultural communication are increased opportunity, increased business effectiveness, improved intergroup relations, and enhanced self-awareness.

8.2 Define intercultural communication and describe three types of border dwellers.

- *Intercultural communication* is defined as communication between people from different cultural backgrounds.

- Increasing numbers of individuals today live on cultural borders—through travel, socialization, or relationships.

- *Culture* is defined as learned patterns of perceptions, values, and behaviors shared by a group of people. It is dynamic and heterogeneous, and operates within power structures.

8.3 Describe how cultural values influence communication.

- Seven core cultural values differentiate various cultural groups, and these value differences have implications for intercultural communication: Individualism/collectivism, preferred personality, human nature, human–nature relationship, long-term versus short-term orientation, indulgence versus restraint.

8.4 Explain the roles that politics, history, and power play in communication between people from different cultural backgrounds.

- Power is often an important element in that those who hold more powerful positions in society set the rules and norms for communication. Those individuals who do not conform to the rules because of differing cultural backgrounds and preferences may be marginalized.

- Societal forces, such as political and historical structures, play an important role in intercultural communication because intercultural encounters never occur in a vacuum.

8.5 Give three guidelines for communicating more ethically with people whose cultural backgrounds differ from your own.

- To ensure that you are communicating ethically during intercultural interactions, avoid ethnocentric thinking, recognize the humanity of others, and remain open to other ways of understanding the world.

8.6 Discuss ways to improve your own intercultural communication skills.

- You can become a more effective intercultural communicator in at least five ways: increase your motivation, acquire knowledge about self and others, avoid stereotyping, strive for intercultural empathy, and navigate the borderlands.

- There are six dialectics that can help you improve your intercultural communication: cultural-individual, personal–contextual, differences–similarities, static–dynamic, history/past–present/future, and privilege–disadvantage.

KEY TERMS

diaspora p. 188
peacebuilding p. 191
intercultural communication p. 192
culture p. 192
heterogeneous p. 192
border dwellers p. 192

culture shock p. 193
reverse culture shock/re-entry
  shock p. 193
cultural values p. 196
individualistic orientation p. 197
collectivistic orientation p. 197

preferred personality p. 198
view of human nature p. 198
human–nature value orientation p. 199
power distance p. 200
long-term versus short-term
  orientation p. 200

APPLY WHAT YOU KNOW

1. **Cultural Profile**
   List all the cultural groups you belong to. Which groups are most important to you when you're at college? When you're at home? Which groups would be easiest to leave? Why?

2. **Intercultural Conflict Analysis**
   Identify a current intercultural conflict in the media. It can be conflict between nations, ethnic groups, or gender. Read at least three sources that give background and information about the conflict. Conduct an analysis of this conflict, answering the following questions:

   - What do you think are the sources of the conflict?
   - Are there value differences?
   - Power differences?
   - What role do you think various contexts (historical, social, and political) play in the conflict?

Communicating in Close Relationships

LEARNING OBJECTIVES

CHAPTER TOPICS

9.1 Describe the importance of close relationships.

The Importance of Communication in Close Relationships

9.2 Explain five communication theories of relationship development.

Close Relationships and the Individual

9.3 Identify tactics for initiating, maintaining, and terminating friendships and romantic relationships.

Communicating in Friendships and Romantic Relationships

9.4 Explain the role that society plays in the formation and maintenance of interpersonal relationships.

The Individual, Relationship Communication, and Society

9.5 Explain how to ensure that interactions with close others are authentic.

Ethics and Close Relationships

9.6 Articulate how to recognize passive-aggressive communication.

Improving Your Close Relationship Communication Skills

> *"Communication is the foundation on which all relationships are built."*

Charee and her friend Cristina were at a club one weekend when Charee spotted a man who had hit on her earlier in the evening. As he walked toward the two women, Charee leaned over to Cristina and said, "There's that jerk I was telling you about." Eighteen months later, Cristina and the "jerk" were married.

How is it that one person's jerk is another person's ideal mate? On more than one occasion, you may have wondered why your friends pick the romantic partners they do. Perhaps you even have questioned your own choices. Though relationship researchers haven't unraveled all the mysteries of love and friendship, they have made considerable progress in explaining how and why relationships develop, are maintained, and sometimes fail—and the role communication plays at each stage.

To help you understand communication in close relationships, we begin by describing the importance of these relationships and providing a definition for them. Next, we address the role of the individual in close relationships and explore the factors that increase the likelihood that you will become involved with another person. We then examine five theories and two models that explain how communication influences relationship development between friends and romantic partners. We conclude our focus on individuals in relationships by discussing problems that can occur in friendship and romance, such as aversive communication, jealousy, aggression, and sexual coercion. Finally, we explore the societal forces that influence relationships and the communication within them and present you with guidelines for communicating more ethically and effectively in your own relationships.

The Importance of Communication in Close Relationships

9.1 Describe the importance of close relationships.

Friends play an important role in people's lives. Close relationships are a source of much happiness (and some distress) and serve as a significant context within which a person's interactions take place (Donaghue & Fallon, 2003). As illustrated in *It Happened to Me: Olivia*, friends can come to the rescue in a crisis by providing both emotional and physical support. Relationships with friends, lovers, and family members also offer a sense of belonging, help alleviate loneliness, and are central to psychological and physical health.

Researchers have found that loneliness, or a lack of close relationships, is associated with psychological disorders such as depression and anxiety (Miller, 2002). People with even a few close relationships experience greater well-being than those who are lonely (Gierveld & Tilburg, 1995). People with satisfying relationships also experience better physical health. For example, an examination of 148 studies found that the quantity and quality of individuals' social relationships were linked both to their mental health and to their longevity. The authors found that high-quality social relationships were associated with a 50 percent increased likelihood of living longer (Holt-Lunstad et al., 2010).

It Happened to Me
Olivia

I was at a friend's house, eating junk food and watching TV, when someone knocked on the door. Standing there in the rain, with tears running down her face and sobbing, was one of our friends. She told us that her mom had hit her and thrown her things out her bedroom window. We sat with her for ages until she calmed down; then we asked her to stay the night. Without us, she would have had nowhere to go and no one to talk to.

▲ Friends are an important source of comfort.

Similarly, studies of marital relationships reveal that people in happy marriages are less likely to experience high blood pressure and serious heart episodes (Holt-Lunstad et al., 2008). Thus, close relationships can improve not only our satisfaction with life but also our health.

The importance of close relationships in people's lives is one reason the incidence of anxiety and depression increased during the COVID-19 pandemic (Zarefsky, 2020). At one point, even former First Lady Michelle Obama revealed that she was experiencing low-level depression (Zarefsky, 2020). Why is being quarantined difficult for so many people? As you have learned throughout these chapters, our relationships are integral to who we are—so much so that our interactions with others shape our identities. You may remember that in Chapter 2 we discussed that one of the ways we know who we are is through how other people communicate with us. In addition, people we are close to provide love, affection, and much-needed support. Of course, being socially isolated because potentially one could become seriously ill is difficult, but being lonely because one lacks important communication skills is even more difficult.

The relationships we develop with friends, family, and romantic partners are qualitatively different from other types of interpersonal relationships, such as those relationships people have with their mail carriers or Starbucks's barista (LaFollette, 1996). Close relationships are distinguished by their frequency, intensity, and diversity of contact (Kelley et al., 1983) as well as by their level of intimacy, importance, and satisfaction (Berg & Piner, 1990). These relationships also require considerable time to develop. For example, communication professor Jeffrey Hall (2018) found that it takes around 30 hours of interaction for individuals to become casual friends and about 20 more hours for them to transition to being friends. Becoming good friends (more than 140 hours) and best friends (after 300 hours) takes even longer. Thus, creating and sustaining close, satisfying relationships requires both skill and considerable investment of time.

People in close relationships see each other as unique and irreplaceable. They are more open in their communication with each other than with other people, and they tend to disclose more personal details (Janz, 2000). In addition, the communication in these relationships is influenced more by individual factors (as opposed to social factors) than is usually true of casual relationships. That is, people in close relationships know each other better and share more experiences, so they are better able to adapt their own communication and more effectively interpret their partner's communication. This can lead to greater ease in communicating as well as increased understanding and intimacy. For these reasons, people in close relationships expect their relationships to endure over time because they are committed to them (Wright, 1999).

Casual relationships, in contrast, involve little disclosure or affection and are perceived as interchangeable because they are usually role-based, as between a salesperson and a customer (Janz, 2000). For example, although you might like your mail carrier and would miss seeing her if she quit her job, you probably would be perfectly content to receive your mail from someone new. But if your fiancé or best friend terminated your relationship, it's unlikely you would be content with a substitute. Because casual relationships are not based on the participants' knowledge of each other as individuals, the communication that occurs within them tends to be influenced more by social norms for interacting and, therefore, are less personal and more superficial.

Journal Prompt 9.1: Close Relationship Communication
How does the communication in your close relationships differ from your communication in casual relationships?

Close Relationships and the Individual

9.2 **Explain five communication theories of relationship development.**

Because relationship development is an important aspect of life and because the process sometimes goes awry—for example, approximately one-third of first marriages end in divorce or separation within 10 years (Bureau of Labor Statistics, 2013)—scholars have devoted considerable effort toward creating theories and models to explain it. No single theory can explain how all human relationships develop; however, the following theories offer insight into how relationships develop and change over time as people communicate with one another.

▲ Close relationships can be a source of happiness, comfort, and even distress.

Theories of Relationship Development

Do you ever question why you form friendships and romantic relationships with some people but not others? Many social science scholars have, so they studied close relationships extensively, and based on those studies, they have developed a variety of theories to explain why we choose whom we choose. Why should you be interested? When you understand the factors that predict and explain the successful initiation and development of relationships, you can use that knowledge to help you begin relationships and communicate in them so they are more successful and enduring. Here we discuss several communication theories that help explain why some interactions lead to relationships and some don't as well as why some of those relationships last longer than others.

Attraction Theory   For any relationship to develop, you must first notice that a particular person exists and be interested enough to initiate contact. Zheng still remembers meeting Rob during their first year of college. A mutual friend introduced them, and he became interested in sustained interaction with Rob when he discovered they shared a passion for all things Star Wars and enjoyed cosplay. They spent most of the evening talking with each other even though 30 other people were at the party.

Attraction theory explains the three primary forces that draw people together to form relationships. These three forces—*proximity, interpersonal attractiveness*, and *similarity*—were all operating the evening Zheng and Rob met. They were students at the same university, they found each other easy to talk to, and they discovered that they had similar interests.

Of course, proximity, interpersonal attractiveness, and similarity don't guarantee a lasting friendship or romance, but they do set the stage for relationships to develop. Let's see how these three factors influence relational development and the role that communication plays in each.

Proximity   Most people are not aware of it, but **proximity**—how physically close you are to others—plays an important role in relationship development. Historically, proximity referred to physical closeness between people. Typically, people became friends with or dated those who lived in their apartment complexes, neighborhoods, or dorms; those who were in their classes; or those with whom they worked (Sias & Cahill, 1998; Sprecher, 1998). Now, however, technologies such as FaceTime, Snapchat, and Zoom have made it easier for people to create the feeling of proximity even with individuals who are not physically nearby.

attraction theory
Theory that explains the primary forces that draw people together.

proximity
How physically close one is to others.

Proximity has a strong impact, at least initially, on individuals' interactions and relationships. One of the ways proximity affects relationship development is that it facilitates informal, relatively unplanned communication that provides the opportunity for people to notice others' attractive qualities, learn about their similarities, and develop a relationship (Berscheid & Reis, 1998).

Once people graduate from college, however, they often find that their romantic and friendship options dwindle significantly because proximity to other young, available individuals decreases. In response, companies such as Her, Grindr, and Hinge have developed apps that make it easier for users to find potential romantic partners in their area without having to rely on chance proximity. A variety of apps also have been created to help people make friends and find others who share their interests, including BumbleBFF, Friends, and Atleto (Pugachevsky & Andrews, 2020). (We discuss the influence of social media and dating apps on interpersonal relationship in more detail in Chapter 14.)

Usually, the easier it is to interact with someone, the easier it will be to develop and sustain a relationship. Of course, some people do develop and maintain long-distance relationships, though this may be more common for romantic relationships than friendships. Recent statistics suggest that approximately 3 million married couples live apart for reasons other than dissatisfaction with their relationship and that up to 75 percent of college students will engage in long-distance relationships at some time during college (Stafford, 2010). Most of these people, however, likely were physically close to one another at some point in their relationships.

Attractiveness   Obviously, proximity is not enough to launch a relationship. Most of us have daily contact with dozens of people. How is it that you form relationships with some and not others? One of the more obvious answers is **attractiveness**. Although most of us are attracted to those we find physically appealing (Buss et al., 2001), we also tend to develop relationships with people who are approximately as attractive as we are. This tendency is called the **matching hypothesis**. Interestingly, researchers have found that the matching hypothesis applies to friendships (Bleske-Rechek & Lighthall, 2010), romantic relationships (Sprecher & Hatfield, 2009), marriage (Hinsz, 1989), and even choosing roommates (Kurt & Sherker, 2003).

Fortunately, attractiveness is a broad concept. It is composed of physical attractiveness, social attractiveness, and task attractiveness (McCroskey et al., 2006). Social attractiveness refers to how friendly, outgoing, warm, and sociable one is perceived to be, whereas task attractiveness refers to how desirable people are as coworkers or task partners (Burgoon & Bacue, 2003). People are attracted to others not only because of their physical appearance but also for their contributions to mutual tasks, wonderful personalities, or charming ways. Most of these qualities are revealed through communication; therefore, individuals with good communication skills are often perceived as more attractive than they might be otherwise (Burleson & Samter, 1996). Consequently, improving your communication skills can increase others' desire to form relationships with you.

Similarity   It may be equally obvious that most people are attracted by **similarity**; they like people who are like them, who enjoy the things they enjoy, who value what they value, and with whom they share a similar background (Byrne, 1997). In many cases opposites *do* attract, but when it comes to background, values, and attitudes, "birds of a feather [more often] flock together." For example, Buss (1985) found that the more similar the participants in his study were, the more likely they were to report increased levels of attraction. This makes sense. If you like to socialize, enjoy the outdoors, and are involved in a religious community, you may find it difficult to develop a relationship with someone who is introverted, prefers to stay home to read and listen to music, and avoids organized religion. No matter how open-minded you are, you probably view your orientation to the world as preferable, especially concerning values such as religion, politics, and morality.

attractiveness

The appeal one person has for another based on physical appearance, personality, or behavior.

matching hypothesis

The tendency to develop relationships with people who are approximately as attractive as we are.

similarity

Degree to which people share the same values, interests, and background.

You may wonder how individuals determine whether they are similar in values, attitudes, and background. Generally, they discover this during the early stages of conversational interaction in either face-to-face or online contexts (Berger & Calabrese, 1975; Berger & Kellerman, 1994). Researchers also have found that individuals are attracted to people, especially friends, whose communication skills are similar to their own (Burleson & Samter, 1996). This is true whether one possesses low or high levels of communication skills. It's important to note that friendship pairs who have low levels of

▲ We are attracted to people who like the same activities we do.

communication skills are just as satisfied with their friendships as are those who have high levels of skills. All of these findings suggest that the type of people who might be attracted to you are people who are similar to you in terms of communication skills, interests, and attractiveness and that spending time with them can provide opportunities for friendship or romance to develop. This is why the best advice for meeting compatible others is to engage in organized activities you enjoy, such as volleyball or video game–playing clubs, and make the effort to attend these activities regularly.

Attractiveness and similarity in communication competence as well as similarity in attitudes and values are revealed through communication. You can see, then, why communication is considered the foundation on which all relationships are built.

Uncertainty Reduction Theory   One communication theory that examines how communication impacts relationship development is uncertainty reduction theory. According to **uncertainty reduction theory** (Berger & Calabrese, 1975), when we first meet someone, much of our interaction is dedicated to reducing uncertainty and determining whether we wish to interact with the person again. This theory argues that relationship development is facilitated or derailed by participants' efforts to reduce their uncertainty about each other. It assumes that people are uncomfortable with uncertainty about others and seek to reduce it to decide if the other person is safe, interesting, and desirable—or dangerous, boring, and undesirable.

uncertainty reduction theory
Theory that argues relationship development is facilitated or derailed by participants' efforts to reduce their uncertainty about each other.

Uncertainty reduction theory explains much of the behavior we engage in when we first meet people. For example, if introduced to someone new at a party, what do you do? If you are like most people, you probably provide a bit of information about yourself or ask questions about the other person. You might ask how your new acquaintance knows the host, what they do for a living, or whether they like the music that is playing. If you like the other person based on this relatively superficial interaction, you will probably continue to talk with them. If, however, you find the person is quite unlike you or uninteresting, you're likely to excuse yourself and find someone new with whom to talk.

This explains why our initial interactions with others are so important. To initiate new relationships, we have to be able to communicate in a way that helps others reduce their uncertainty about us in a positive and pleasant manner. If we find others desirable based on our initial attempts to reduce uncertainty and continue to have opportunities to interact, we tend to increase our levels of disclosure and to solicit more personal disclosure from the other person. This process continues until the two participants either form a relationship or cease to have opportunities to interact. An important assumption of uncertainty reduction theory, however, is that as we reduce our uncertainty about someone, we like the person more because we dislike uncertainty. Although uncertainty reduction is central to forming relationships, there is at least one type of relationship in

COMMUNICATION IN SOCIETY
Why Can't Couples Talk about Their Friends with Benefits Relationships?

Have you or anyone you know been in a friends with benefits (FWB) relationship? How hard was it for you or your friend to communicate about the relationship? Do you think that communicating clearly about boundaries and expectations would have improved the relationship?

We all have been told many times that communication is essential for good relationships. However, one relationship most people don't want to talk about is their FWB relationship. Most FWB relationships would benefit from a good talk, yet according to communication professor Kendra Knight, such communication is rare. Why? The college students she interviewed offered four reasons why they don't feel comfortable talking about their FWB relationships with their partners.

1. **Talking about the relationship is at odds with the view that FWBs are casual and easy.** Maintaining relationships can be effortful and emotional, which is what many participants want to avoid. FWBs are supposed to be fun and not carry the baggage of a "real" relationship.
2. **Talking about the relationship can be face-threatening.** A basic premise of FWBs is that the partners

are not exclusive or committed to one another. Even talking about the relationship suggests one wants more from the relationship, which some participants feel makes a person look needy.

3. **Talking about emotions in the relationship violates the rules of the relationship.** Though FWBs are supposed to be "just friends," in reality many people have strong emotions about their relationships. They may feel jealousy, possessiveness, and insecurity—feelings that are antithetical to a FWB relationship.
4. **Talking about the relationship threatens the status quo.** Even when one person is willing to discuss the relationship, the other partner may be fearful that talking about the relationship will disrupt it or change it somehow. Not talking about the relationship, then, is seen as a way to maintain the relationship as it is.

SOURCE: Knight, K. (2014, September). Communicating dilemmas in adults' friends with benefits relationships: Challenges to relational talk. *Emerging Adulthood*. http://eax.sagepub.com/content/early/2014/09/19/2167696814549598

which couples may be willing to tolerate uncertainty. To understand how this process works, read *Communication in Society: Why Can't Couples Talk about Their Friends with Benefits Relationships?*

Predicted Outcome Value Theory   Have you ever liked someone initially but over time, as you learned more about the person, you discovered you didn't like the person after all? How can this be explained by uncertainty reduction theory? According to communication researcher Michael Sunnafrank, it can't. Consequently, he developed **predicted outcome value theory** (1986), an adaptation of uncertainty reduction theory that attempts to explain how reducing uncertainty can lead to attraction *or* repulsion. Sunnafrank argues that during initial conversations with others we attempt to determine whether continuing to interact with another person is of value, that is, whether it is worth our time and energy. If we predict that future interactions will be valuable, we continue to talk with the person, and if we continue to predict positive outcomes, we will form a relationship. However, if at any point we begin to predict negative outcomes for our interactions, then we will de-escalate or end the relationship.

predicted outcome value theory
Theory that attempts to explain how reducing uncertainty can lead to attraction or repulsion.

What do these theories tell us about developing our own relationships? First, they can help us better understand why some relationships catch fire—or die out—quickly. From our first moments of meeting someone, both we and the other party are attempting to determine how safe, competent, and interesting the other is. If something goes wrong at the beginning—a mistimed joke, a comment that suggests we are boastful, or nonverbal behaviors that indicate disinterest—the interaction can immediately end and cut off any potential relationship. Second, all of us make quick assessments of others based on their conversations, and if we want to attract others, we need to communicate in ways that suggest we will be interesting, fun, or even useful to know. If you have difficulty developing relationships, you might want to pay attention to your initial interactions with others to see if you are unintentionally communicating a negative image.

Social Exchange and Equity Theories   The three theories we have discussed thus far focus on the earliest stages of relationship development; the next two, social exchange and equity theories, examine the characteristics of relationships as they develop past the initial stages. Social exchange and equity theories are similar in that they both propose that relationship development, satisfaction, and longevity are related to how "rewarding" individuals find their relationships to be. **Social exchange theory** (Thibault & Kelley, 1959) argues that in U.S. society, people attempt to maximize the rewards and minimize the costs of their relationships. The rewards of such relationships include companionship, being cared for, and, in some cases, sex. The "exchange" part of the theory argues that in exchange for these rewards, people provide similar or complementary rewards to their relationship partners. Of course, providing rewards for others counts as a "cost," so the belief is that people seek relationships where perceived rewards outweigh perceived costs. Based on this theory, individuals are satisfied in and committed to their relationships when they feel they are receiving sufficient rewards and not too many costs. Although the fundamental ideas of social exchange may make sense, many people object to it because they see as it as calculating.

> **social exchange theory**
> Theory that explains the development and longevity of relationships as a result of individuals' ability to maximize the rewards and minimize the costs of their relationships.

Equity theory (Walster et al., 1973) offers a refinement of social exchange theory. It argues that rather than focusing purely on rewards and costs, people are most interested in achieving fairness in their relationships. That is, individuals are satisfied when they perceive their relationships as equitable and dissatisfied when they perceive them as inequitable. Equity describes the desire for one's costs (or inputs) to be balanced by one's rewards (or outputs). According to equity theory, both people who are **underbenefitted** (those whose inputs exceed their outputs) and those who are **overbenefitted** (those whose outputs exceed their inputs) may feel dissatisfied with their relationships. Underbenefitted people may feel angry or taken advantage of, whereas overbenefitted people often feel guilty. According to this theory, dyads are happiest when fairness occurs, that is, each person gets out what they put into the relationship.

> **equity theory**
> Theory that argues that people are more satisfied in relationships they perceive as fair, that is, where their costs are balanced by their rewards.

> **underbenefitted**
> Underbenefitted people perceive that their costs exceed their rewards.

> **overbenefitted**
> Overbenefitted people perceive that their rewards exceed their costs.

Equity is not the same as equality; the theory doesn't argue that each partner should receive the same amount of rewards for satisfaction to occur. Instead, it suggests that whoever contributes more should benefit more from the relationship. Some research supports this theory. For example, a study of 200 couples found that satisfaction was highest for people who perceived their relationship to be equitable. Overbenefitted partners were the next-most satisfied, followed by those who felt underbenefitted (Canary & Stafford, 1992). If the ratio of costs and rewards is dissatisfying for one or both partners, then the two of you should discuss how you can change that ratio. If, for example, you feel angry and underbenefitted, you could reduce your costs. This happened to Aaron. He and his roommate Matt became friends during their first semester living together, and Aaron really enjoyed hanging out with him. Over time, he realized that he was picking up the tab far more often when they went out and that Matt never returned favors that Aaron routinely granted, such as loaning Matt his car and taking him to the airport. Eventually Aaron decided that he wasn't enjoying their friendship anymore, so he decided to cut his costs and get a new roommate for sophomore year.

> **equity**
> Perception that one's costs (or inputs) are balanced by one's rewards (or outputs).

Models of Relationship Development

Thus far, we have discussed five theories that attempt to explain why and how voluntary relationships such as romantic relationships and friendships develop. Because they are theories, these explanations tend to be somewhat general and do not focus on the particular types of interactions that occur during relationship development.

Table 9.1 Knapp's Stages of Romantic Relational Development

Stage	Goal	Example
Initiating	Appear pleasant, likeable	"Hey, that's an awesome bike. Where did you get it?"
Experimenting	Learn about each other	"Do you like to travel?"
Intensifying	Increase intimacy, connectedness	"I can't imagine being with anyone else."
Integrating	Establish dyad as a couple	"I love you. I feel like you are a part of me."
Bonding	Public commitment	"Will you marry me?"
Differentiating	Increase interpersonal distance	"I'm going; you can come if you want to."
Circumscribing	Discuss safe topics	"Did you pick up the dry cleaning?"
Stagnating	Prevent change	"Let's not talk about it right now, okay?"
Avoiding	Decline to interact with partner	"I'm too busy now. I'll get back to you later."
Terminating	End the relationship	"It's over."

SOURCE: Knapp, M. L., & Vangelisti, A. (1997). *Interpersonal communication and relationships* (2nd ed.). Allyn & Bacon.

Knapp's stage model
Model of romantic relationship development that views relationships as occurring in stages and focuses on how people communicate as relationships develop and decline.

initiating
Stage of romantic relational development in which both people behave so as to appear pleasant and likeable.

experimenting
Stage of romantic relational development in which both people seek to learn about each other.

intensifying
Stage of romantic relational development in which both people seek to increase intimacy and connectedness.

integrating
Stage of romantic relational development in which both people portray themselves as a couple.

bonding
Stage of romantic relational development characterized by public commitment.

differentiating
Stage of romantic relational dissolution in which couples increase their interpersonal distance.

circumscribing
Stage of romantic relational dissolution in which couples discuss safe topics.

stagnating
Stage of romantic relational dissolution in which couples try to prevent change.

avoiding
Stage of romantic relational dissolution in which couples avoid interaction with each other.

terminating
Stage of romantic relational dissolution in which couples end the relationship.

Therefore, several scholars have developed models of relationship development that seek to explain more specifically the ways that communication promotes or inhibits relationship development and maintenance.

Stage Models of Romantic Relationship Development   The best-known stage model of romantic relationships was developed in 1978 by Mark Knapp, a communication scholar (Knapp, 1978; Knapp & Vangelisti, 1997). **Knapp's stage model** conceptualizes relationship development as a staircase. The staircase depicts relationship development as being composed of five steps that lead upward toward commitment: **initiating, experimenting, intensifying, integrating,** and **bonding**. It also portrays relationship dissolution as occurring in five steps that lead downward: **differentiating, circumscribing, stagnating, avoiding,** and **terminating**. In this model, couples at the relationship maintenance level of development move up and down the staircase as they move toward and away from commitment as a result of the fluctuation of their relationships.

Knapp's stage model is a *communication* model because it explores how individuals' communication practices affect relationship development and decline. For example, *circumscribing* is identified by the fact that couples' conversations focus mostly on "safe" topics, such as household tasks, whereas *experimenting* is defined by couples' communication efforts to learn more about one another. This stage model assumes one can determine what stage a couple is in by observing what the two people say and do. For example, if couples spend most of their communication interactions discussing the ways in which they are different, they are at the *differentiating* stage. As Table 9.1 reveals, each stage is based on the types of communication couples perform within it.

As you might have noticed, Knapp's model includes a *terminating* stage. This does not suggest that all relationships end, but it does recognize that many relationships do (Weber, 1998). Relationships that end are often treated as "failures," and the people who experience them often feel that they have done something wrong. But, in fact, as people grow and mature, it is not unusual for them to change their social networks (Dainton et al., 2003). This is not to say that you won't have long-lasting or permanent relationships, but not every relationship termination should be viewed as a mistake.

Critics of Knapp's stage model point out that people don't move from one stage to the next in an orderly fashion, and many couples experience a "repair" stage where they try to improve their relationship prior to moving on to termination (which Knapp does not mention). Importantly, critics also argue that people who meet online may not move through the stages he details or may do so in a different order. The potential romantic partners one meets in a public place, they argue, may reveal their goals and preferences gradually over the course of multiple dates, but users of online sites often reveal personal information early in their interactions to avoid over-investing time and energy in pursuit of less-than-ideal matches (Lever et al., 2008).

Knapp has responded to this critique by arguing that dyads can skip stages but that they have to go back at some point and move through the skipped stages. For example, when two people "hook up," they may move from initiation to integration in a matter of hours. However, if they go on to form a relationship and stay together, they will have to go back and experience the experimenting and intensifying stages. Knapp also argues that over the course of a relationship, dyads move up and down the staircase as people and events change.

A stage model for friendships also has been developed. Communication professors Rawlins and Holl (1987) suggest that friendships are created through six steps. They call these steps *limited interaction, friendly relations, moving toward friendship, nascent friendship, stabilized friendship,* and *waning friendship.* As you can see, like Knapp, Rawlins and Holl include a step describing relationships in decline (see Table 9.2).

▲ The bonding stage of romantic relationships is characterized by public commitment, such as moving in together or becoming engaged.

As you read about the stage model of relationship development, you may have thought that these models don't describe your own experiences very well. If so, you are not alone. Indeed, some researchers believe that relationships can follow a number of paths: Some may be fairly straight like a sidewalk, whereas others may be like winding mountain paths, as described by **relational trajectory models** (Baxter & Bullis, 1986; Surra, 1987).

Turning Point Model of Relationship Development The most popular model that emerged from research on relational trajectory research is the **turning point model for romantic couples** (Baxter & Bullis, 1986). It is a nonlinear model that best captures the fact that relationship development can be bidirectional—that is, couples and friends move both toward and away from commitment (couples) or closeness (friends) over the course of their relationships. The original communication model proposed that romantic couples engage in approximately 14 types of "turning points" that influence the direction of their relationship trajectory (see Table 9.3). For example, the turning point "passion" (first kiss or saying, "I love you") tends to be an event that increases couples' commitment to their relationship, whereas the turning point "external competition" (such as a rival lover) decreases commitment to the relationship.

relational trajectory models
Relationship development models that view the development process as more variable than do stage models.

turning point model for romantic couples
Model of relationship development in which couples move both toward and away from commitment over the course of their relationship.

Table 9.2 Stages of Friendship Development

Stage	Description	Example
Role Limited Interaction	Communicating with others based on your social roles	You communicate with a group member in your class about issues related to completing your group project.
Friendly Relations	Communicating with others to determine if there are common interests and a desire to get to know one another	You ask the group member about themselves and their interests while revealing information about yourself and your interests.
Moving toward Friendship	Communication attempts to develop a more personalized relationship	You are more open with your potential friend, and you each disclose more personal information about yourselves.
Nascent Friendship	Committing to spend more time together	You expect to spend time together in the future and may set up specific times that you will meet regularly.
Stabilized Friendship	Taking each other for granted in the sense that you know the other person will continue to be in your life	You know your friend is available to be with you when you both find the time to do so.
Waning Friendship	Communicating less frequently and intimately as the relationship comes to an end	You begin to text and call your friend less and less often, and when you talk, you discuss superficial topics.

SOURCE: Rawlins, W. R., & Holl, M. (1987). Communicative achievement of friendship during adolescence: Predicaments of trust and violation. *Western Journal of Communication,* 51(4), 345–363.

Table 9.3   Turning Points in Developing Romantic Relationships

Turning Point	Description	Effect on Relationship
Get-to-know time	Events and time spent together learning about one another	Increases commitment
Quality time	Special occasions for appreciating the other or the relationship	Increases commitment
Physical separation	Time apart as a result of school breaks, etc.	Little effect on commitment
External competition	Competing for partner's time/attention because of others or events	Decreases commitment
Reunion	Coming back together after physical separation	Increases commitment
Passion	Physical/emotional expression of affection	Increases commitment
Disengagement	Ending the relationship	Decreases commitment
Positive psychic change	Acquiring a more positive outlook on partner/relationship	Increases commitment
Exclusivity	Decision to date only each other	Increases commitment
Negative psychic change	Acquiring a more negative outlook on partner/relationship	Decreases commitment
Making up	Getting back together after a breakup	Increases commitment
Serious commitment	Moving in with one's partner or getting married	Increases commitment
Sacrifice	Providing support or gifts to one's partner	Increases commitment

SOURCE: Baxter, L. A., & Bullis, C. (1986). Turning points in developing romantic relationships. *Human Communication Research, 12,* 469–493.

▲ One turning point in romantic relationships is the presence of external competition.

turning point model of friendship

Model of relationship development where friends move toward or away from closeness over the course of their relationship.

Although we know more about heterosexual relationships than we do about gay and lesbian relationships, what we do know suggests that these relationships may follow different relational development paths. In heterosexual relationships, friendship and romantic sexual involvement traditionally have been mutually exclusive; therefore, the termination of romantic intimacy usually meant the end of the friendship as well (Nardi, 1992, 2007). In contrast, gay male friendships often start with sexual attraction and involvement but evolve into friendship with no sexual/romantic involvement, whereas lesbian relationships may begin with friendship and evolve into romantic relationships (Nardi, 1992, 2007; Peplau, 2009). However, this difference between heterosexual and gay and lesbian couples may be less true than it once was; more heterosexual young people appear to be combining the categories of friendship and sexual involvement.

A slightly different **turning point model of friendship** also has been developed by scholar Amy Johnson and her colleagues (2004) (see Table 9.4). The authors interviewed males and females regarding the development of friendships that had ended. The turning points that they determined were most often associated with increased closeness between friends included participating in activities together and sharing common interests. Decreased closeness most often occurred when friends stopped living together, had conflicts, experienced interference from one person's romantic partner, moved so that they no longer lived near one another, or underwent change (Johnson et al., 2004). A similar study (Becker et al., 2009) where researchers interviewed participants who had longtime, ongoing friendships found the same turning points as the previous study; however, they discovered that long-term friends were more like romantic couples in that their closeness varied and changed over the years as dyads move closer, then apart, and closer again.

Table 9.4   Turning Points in Friends' Relationships

Turning Point	Description	Effect on Relationship
Personality traits	See friend as having similar or attractive personal characteristics	Increases closeness
Activities—positive	Participate in activities together; spend time together outside the context where they met	Increases closeness
Activities—negative	Stop participating in activities together; spend less time together	Decreases closeness
Channels	Contact one another through email, phone calls, visits, taking trips together	Increases closeness
Share living quarters	Live together in a house, apartment, or dorm room	Increases closeness
Stop sharing living quarters	Move away from shared living spaces	Decreases closeness
General talking/hanging out	Engage in self-disclosure, offer support, do favors	Increases closeness
Solve a conflict	Confront a problem and resolve it	Increases closeness
Meet/interact with others	Spend time with other's friends, romantic partner, family members	Increases closeness
Geographical distance—positive	Live nearer to one another	Increases closeness
Geographical distance—negative	Live further away from one another	Decreases closeness
Contact change not due to geographical distance—positive	Increase in interaction	Increases closeness
Contact change not due to geographical distance—negative	Decrease in interaction	Decreases closeness
Common interests	Share similar sports, activities, and conversational topics	Increases closeness
Few common interests	Share few activities, sports, and conversational topics	Decreases closeness

SOURCE: Johnson, A. J., Wittenberg, E., Haigh, M., & Wigley, S. (2004). The process of relationship development and deterioration: Turning points in friendships that have terminated. *Communication Quarterly, 52,* 54–68.

How does understanding stage and relational trajectory models help you understand your relationships? First, they explain the types of interactions that lead to and reflect where you are in your relationships with others. Second, they can help you understand your own relationship patterns by letting you see where your relationships commonly terminate, where they are strongest, and how you can change patterns that aren't working for you.

In the next section, we examine the specific communication processes that individuals use to develop, maintain, and terminate their relationships.

> **Journal Prompt 9.2: Relationship Theories and Models**
> Which of the five theories of relationship development have you observed in your own life? Which of the two models better describes your relationship? Why?

Communicating in Friendships and Romantic Relationships

9.3 Identify tactics for initiating, maintaining, and terminating friendships and romantic relationships.

People tend to see friendship as being a different type of relationship than a romance. If that is true, how do you think communication differs between friendship pairs and romantic couples?

In the following, Jeff describes how he sees the difference between friendship and romantic relationships:

> You're more likely to let your friends see you warts and all. There's no fear of rejection, for me anyway. . . . In a romantic relationship, you don't want them to see you at your worst. . . . You want them to think you're very well adjusted. And your friends know that's a total crock so there's no use even pretending. (Reeder, 1996)

As Jeff's description illustrates, friendships can differ markedly from romances in how much we reveal, especially in the early stages. But other differences exist as well. For example, we typically expect exclusivity from our romantic partners but not from our friends. Also, people often have higher expectations for their romantic partners,

▲ Most flirting, though not all, is nonverbal.

especially with regard to physical attractiveness, social status, and a pleasing personality (Sprecher & Regan, 2002). And we may require greater expressions of commitment and caring from romantic partners than from friends (Goodwin & Tang, 1991). In the following sections, we explore in more detail the similarities and differences between friendships and romances.

Initiating Relationships

An individual's ability to begin a conversation is essential to the development of any relationship. Although many people disparage small talk, there can be no "big talk" if small talk does not precede it. But even before you engage in small talk, you need to be able to signal your interest to others. (See Chapter 6 for specific information on how to initiate conversations.)

Initiating Romantic Relationships   Meeting romantic partners and establishing relationships can be a problem for many people for a variety of reasons. LGBTQIA+ individuals, for example, may find it difficult to identify and meet potential partners in their day-to-day lives, depending on where they live. In addition, dating anxiety is pervasive among almost all adolescents and young adults—regardless of sexual orientation (Essau et al., 1999).

How can people initiate interaction to show they are interested in a potential relationship? Frequently, budding partners "test the waters" by flirting. Considerable research has been conducted on flirting in heterosexual relationships, both because of its crucial role in the initiation of romantic relationships and because of its ambiguity. Much flirting (though not all) is nonverbal because nonverbal communication entails less risk: if the other person does not respond, you can pretend you weren't flirting after all.

When initiating a potential heterosexual romantic/sexual relationship, women are typically more active than men; they use more eye contact, smiles, brief touches, and self-grooming behaviors to signal interest and attraction. Although men do use gazing, smiling, and grooming behaviors, the only behavior they engage in more than women do is intimate touching (hugging, hand holding). Thus, in heterosexual relationships, women engage in more flirtation at the onset of the interaction; then, men tend to escalate the relationship through touch (McCormick & Jones, 1989).

There is an important caution about flirting, however. Men and women don't always agree on what flirting means. A review of 15 research articles on flirting revealed that men are more likely to interpret flirting as sexual while women were more likely to see flirting as something that is fun or a signal they want to change or intensify the relationship (Henningsen, 2004). For these reasons, people need to be careful about the assumptions they make when someone flirts with them—don't assume that what it means for you is what means for someone else. To learn more about the "science of flirting," visit the website for the Social Issues Research Centre at http://www.sirc.org/publik/flirt2.pdf.

The problem of initiating romantic relationships can be challenging for LGBTQIA+ individuals. It is not just a matter of fear of rejection or anxiety. Gay men have been assaulted or killed because heterosexual men believed they were being flirted with.

Critical Thinking Prompt
Think back to the last time you were aware that someone was interested in you romantically. How did you know? What verbal and nonverbal behaviors suggested that romance was a possibility?

This is one reason that more LGBTQIA+ individuals use social networking sites (e.g., Instagram or Snapchat) and dating apps (e.g., Grindr for gay and bisexual men and women; Her for bisexual women and lesbians) created specifically for them to meet potential romantic partners.

Once couples successfully convey their interest and initiate a conversation in person or online, if their interest continues they may begin dating. Or do they? Some scholars, journalists, and college students suggest that dating no longer exists. They argue that traditional dating has been replaced by group dates, hookups, friends with benefits, and celibacy. To explore this idea further, see *Communication in Society: The Truth about Hookup Culture on Campus*. Initiating romantic and dating relationships is not always easy. People often lack confidence in their social and communication skills. Many people aren't sure how or where to approach others, and they worry about being rejected.

In general, successful relationship development appears to be related to effective communication skills. For example, individuals who self-disclose a little as they initiate relationships are more successful than those who disclose a lot (over-sharers) or none at all. Competent daters know that one should disclose primarily positive information early in relationships. They also act interested in what others have to say, help others out, and are polite and positive. Finally, those who successfully initiate relationships are more able to plan and ask for dates. In contrast, ineffective behaviors include trying too hard to make an impression, disclosing too much information too soon, being passive (waiting for the other person to initiate conversation and activities), and acting too self-effacing or modest (Young, 1981).

As is true of all communication interactions, we need to be aware of the cultural expectations of the people involved when pursuing a romantic relationship. In some cultures, being open, asking people out, and flirting are normative, so engaging in these communication behaviors is expected and rewarded. However, in some other cultures, spending a lot of time in a potential romantic partner's presence or meeting their family is expected before you escalate the relationship. Cultural awareness is important in every communication interaction, and it is even more so when we are entering—or trying to enter—a romantic relationship.

COMMUNICATION IN SOCIETY
The Truth about Hookup Culture on Campus

What is a hookup? No one really knows. Most college students have their own definition of the term, and according to Dr. Kathleen Bogle, author of *Hooking Up: Sex, Dating, and Relationships on Campus*, it's deliberately vague. "The point is that it involves sexual activity, ranging from kissing to intercourse, outside of an exclusive relationship," she tells *Teen Vogue*. The hookup is nothing new—Bucknell sociologist William Flack has been studying it since 2001, and casual sex has been happening on campus for decades—but the dominance of explaining your encounter with a romantic venture as "hooking up" has become widely accepted as something that everyone in college does, but it's not really as campus-wide as most people think. The hookup culture is, in fact, more of a subculture. It hasn't replaced dating; it's just changed how we think about it.

Professor of sociology at New York University, Dr. Paula England has conducted research about college students' sexual behavior. "When I go out and visit colleges and talk to students, they'll all say the date is dead and hardly anyone dates here, but

in reality if we just look at seniors, most of them have been on a number of dates," Dr. England says. Her research shows that while the average college senior has hooked up with eight people over four years, they have also gone on an average of seven dates and had an average of two relationships. Sixty-nine percent of college seniors also report being in a relationship lasting more than six months. And while 67 percent of respondents told Dr. England that they hooked up and dated before their most recent relationship became a "relationship," 26 percent dated without hooking up beforehand.

But because of the widespread myth that everyone is hooking up all the time, it sometimes seems like the date is dead. It's pretty safe to say that society's ideas about dating have changed since the age of the dance card, but nowadays, there is no universally accepted norm—we just think there is.

SOURCE: Adapted from Dwyer, L. (2015, September 9). The surprising reality of hook-up culture on campus. *Teen Vogue.* http://www.teenvogue.com/story/hookup-culture-myth-dating-college

At times, initiating a romantic relationship may seem like a rather complicated dance. Each person has a part, but the dance steps vary from one couple to the next. Fortunately, initiating friendship can seem a bit more straightforward.

Initiating Friendships   In any relationship, even friendships, initiating conversation can be difficult because people may fear being rebuffed. In fact, many people assume that the other person's failure to initiate a conversation is because of a lack of interest (Vorauer & Ratner, 1996). If everyone felt this way, however, no relationship would ever begin! Therefore, you may need to begin the conversation if you wish to meet new people.

What is the best way to approach a new person? A nonthreatening comment such as "This sure is an interesting class" usually works, as does a question expressing interest in the other person, such as "Are you a communication major?" If the other person is receptive, you will feel more comfortable continuing the conversation. And if the person doesn't respond in a way that furthers the conversation, you can easily move on.

Once you begin a conversation, you can keep it going by asking a broad, open-ended question. For example, you could ask, "Why did you choose this university?" or "What do you enjoy doing when you're not working?" The idea is to ask questions that can't be answered with a yes or no or with only a brief response. Your goal is to get the other person talking and to learn more about them. (See Chapter 6 for a more detailed discussion of conversation starters.)

Of course, initiating a conversation isn't enough to move you from meeting someone to having an established relationship. A key skill for successfully moving a relationship forward is the ability to share and elicit communication that is appropriate for the stage of your relationship—neither revealing all the intimate details of your life nor withholding all of your thoughts, values, and experiences. Both of these approaches can lead to problems as we try to develop and maintain relationships. **Social penetration theory** describes how the process of disclosing, or revealing, ourselves through communication shapes relationships (Altman & Taylor, 1973, 1987). According to this theory, people gradually increase their self-disclosure as they get to know one another, and through a process of reciprocal disclosure, strangers become friends (or lovers). The authors propose that self-disclosure occurs across three dimensions: breadth, depth, and frequency:

social penetration theory
Theory that proposes that relationships develop through increases in self-disclosure.

- *Breadth* describes the number of different topics dyads willingly discuss. For example, you probably discuss only a few general topics with strangers, such as movies, what you do for a living, or hobbies; however, as you become more intimate with others, you likely discuss a wider range of topics, including how you feel about the people in your life or dreams you have for the future.

- *Depth* refers to how deep or personal communication exchanges are; people tend to provide superficial disclosures to strangers (e.g., I like Thai food) and reserve more personal revelations for their intimates (e.g., I am disgusted if the different foods on my plate touch each other). The depth of your conversations increases as you learn more about others and they learn about you.

- *Frequency* is how often self-disclosure occurs; individuals usually are more disclosive to people with whom they are close and come in contact more often.

Altman and Taylor propose that through increases in communication breadth, depth, and frequency people become more familiar with and trusting of one another, and as they become closer, they feel comfortable revealing more of themselves. Through this circular process, relationships of increasing intimacy are developed. This process seems relatively clear and possibly easy, so why do some people have difficulty forming relationships? Often, the problem such people encounter is that either they don't understand that disclosure is a process that occurs over time or they do not understand the norms of disclosure for their relationships.

As discussed in Chapter 8, what is considered "disclosure" can differ across cultures. In the United States, for example, people may disclose problems in their families or personal stories about their lives. In China, by contrast, revealing that a relative is ill or that one is not fond of one's sibling is considered impolite in any but the closest of relationships. If you don't know the norms for disclosure, you might reveal more than others are comfortable hearing, and they may consider you odd, inappropriate, or someone to avoid. Similarly, if you are in a culture that discloses a lot of information easily, and you don't reciprocate that disclosure, you may be seen as secretive, unfriendly, or hard to talk with. Learning how much disclosure is appropriate at different times in a relationship affects how people perceive strangers and acquaintances and how likely they will be to strike up a relationship with them.

Making new friends requires both skills and motivation, but the rewards of casual, good, and best friends are many. Sometimes friendships turn into romantic relationships, and most of the skills you have developed as friends will work in your new relationship as well. However, once you and your partner successfully navigate the process of meeting and developing a friendship (or romantic) relationship, you will then need to develop a way to maintain your relationship.

Maintaining Relationships

Effective communication is, of course, essential to developing and maintaining relationships. In fact, a strong association exists between people's communication skills and their satisfaction with their relationships, particularly romantic ones (Emmers-Sommers, 2004; Noller & Fitzpatrick, 1990). It appears that effective communication and relationship satisfaction operate in a circular process in which effective communication increases couples' happiness with their relationships and satisfaction with the relationship leads to more effective communication. Communication also is essential to developing friendships. Most of the important functions that friends serve—providing companionship and a sense of belonging, offering emotional and physical support as well as reassurance, and giving feedback on self-disclosures—are communication-based (Duck, 1991).

Although initiating friendships and romances can produce anxiety, it can also be exhilarating and fun. When relationships are new, we tend to focus on their more positive aspects. However, as relationships endure, we have a harder time ignoring others' shortcomings. Consequently, maintaining relationships over time can be challenging.

▼ A strong association exists between people's communication skills and their satisfaction with their relationships.

However, communication can help us meet these challenges in two essential ways: through helping us manage common tensions that arise in our relations and by allowing us to engage in interactions that sustain our connections to each other.

Dialectics in Relationships
Communication professor Leslie Baxter and her colleagues have proposed relationship dialectics to explain how relationships develop and are maintained. As you may remember from Chapter 8, *dialectic* refers to the tension people experience when they have two seemingly contradictory but connected values or

needs. As you will see, developing close relationships is associated with the ability to manage these contradictory but connected desires.

For example, perhaps you feel lonely when you are separated from your romantic partner, but sometimes you feel suffocated when you're together. You want to be able to tell your best friend anything, but at times you feel the need for privacy. These types of feelings arise when you experience a dialectical tension, and they are common in all types of relationships. How you respond to and manage these tensions impacts how successfully you can develop and maintain relationships.

Three primary dialectical tensions exist in relationships: autonomy/connection, expressiveness/privacy, and change/predictability (Baxter, 1988). Autonomy/connection refers to one's need to connect with others and the simultaneous need to feel independent or autonomous. For example, early in romantic relationships people typically have a high need to feel connected to their partners and can barely tolerate being separated from them. But as the relationship develops, most people need time away from their partners so they don't feel stifled or overwhelmed.

Friends also can struggle with managing the autonomy/connection dialectic. One person may have more friends than the other does or have less need for interaction, and therefore, the two may have different expectations about how often they will interact. Once this occurs, friends must manage the autonomy/connection dialectic both as individuals and as members of a dyad. That means that if they wish to continue the relationship, they have to find a balance between their needs. Otherwise, one person may feel overwhelmed or the other neglected, and the relationship may end (see *It Happened to Me: Laurel*).

It Happened to Me
Laurel

I started seeing this guy a few weeks ago, and finally I understand why I've been feeling the way I do. Although I enjoy being with him, I have started to feel smothered. He texts me constantly when we are apart and gets upset if I don't respond right away, and he wants to spend more evenings together than I do. I enjoy hanging out with my friends and being alone; he wants to be with me all the time. I was beginning to think there was something wrong with him, and then I read Baxter's article on relationship dialectics. Now I think we just have different needs for autonomy. However, I don't know if we will be able to manage this so that we'll both be happy.

The second tension, expressiveness/privacy, builds on social penetration theory. It describes the need to be open and to self-disclose while also maintaining some sense of privacy. For example, although Warren may reveal his feelings about his romantic partner to his closest friend, he may want to keep private that his boss fired him from his first job. To maintain their relationships, dyads need to respond to this tension effectively. Both partners need to feel comfortable with their own level of disclosure as well as their partner's. For instance, you may be okay with talking about your exes and past relationships and listening to your romantic partner do the same, but your partner may not feel the same way. However, if you fail to open up and reciprocate your friend's disclosure, they may perceive you as aloof or cold and may not wish to continue the relationship. Thus, this dialectical tension is important to relationships in the initiating stage of development as well as during the development and maintenance stages.

Finally, the change/predictability tension delineates the human desire for events that are new, spontaneous, and unplanned while simultaneously needing some aspects of life to be stable and predictable. For example, you probably want your partner's or friend's affection for you to be stable and predictable, but you might like them to surprise you occasionally with a new activity or self-disclosure. Relationships that are completely predictable (that is, certain) may become boring, but those that are totally spontaneous are unsettling; either extreme may render the relationship difficult to sustain.

Dialectics are constantly in process. Each day, couples and friends manage their individual and relationship needs for autonomy/connection, expressiveness/privacy, and change/predictability; the manner in which they manage these tensions influences

Table 9.5 Couples' Relationship Maintenance Behaviors

Behavior	Description	Example
Positivity	Acting cheerful, positive; upbeat; doing favors for one another	Giving compliments, speaking positively about the future, running errands for one's partner
Openness	Sharing one's feelings and encouraging one's partner to do the same; talking about one's concerns and listening to one's partner	Telling someone "I love you" for the first time or discussing your fear of clowns
Assurances	Reminding a partner about one's love and commitment to the relationship	Saying "I love you," talking about the future, stressing one's commitment to the relationship
Sharing tasks	Helping equally with tasks, performing household responsibilities	One person cooks dinner, and the other cleans up afterward
Social networks	Spending time with friends; engaging in routine events and rituals	Inviting friends over to socialize; celebrating birthdays and holidays
Joint activities	Spending time with one another	Watching television together, going to movies, hiking with each other
Cards/letters/calls	Using mediated communication	Texting, telephoning, emailing each other
Avoidance	Spending time apart; refusing to discuss particular issues	Spending time with friends instead of one another; changing the topic when unwanted issues arise
Anti-social	Engaging in behaviors that seem unfriendly or unpleasant	Acting temperamental, moody, or critical to create distance in the relationship
Humor	Being funny in positive or negative ways	Making jokes, teasing, and being sarcastic

SOURCE: Canary, D., Stafford, L., Hause, K., & Wallace, L. (1993). An inductive analysis of relational maintenance strategies: Comparisons among lovers, relatives, friends, and others. *Communication Research Reports, 10,* 5–14.

the continuance of their relationships. Understanding dialectical tensions is useful because it can help you recognize the sources of disagreement in your relationships and assist you in responding to the competing feelings you and your partner/friend may experience within them.

Maintaining Romantic Relationships through Communication   To understand how couples maintain successful relationships, communication researchers Dan Canary and Laura Stafford conducted some of the earliest studies of how couples keep their relationships satisfying. Based on their research, they created a typology of **relational maintenance** behaviors that heterosexual, gay, and lesbian couples use (Canary & Stafford, 1994; Haas & Stafford, 1998; see Table 9.5). Like most researchers who study this topic, they asked couples to describe or list the tactics they used to maintain their relationships. Because participants responded about the strategies they were aware of and chose to use, the findings are described as "strategic," meaning they were used to accomplish a goal.

relational maintenance
Behaviors couples perform that help maintain their relationships.

Although research shows that straight, gay, and lesbian couples use similar strategies to maintain their romantic relationships and friendships, this does not mean that straight and LGBTQIA+ dyads face similar issues regarding maintenance of their relationships. It is true that some heterosexual romantic couples start out as friends or maintain a friendship after the romance is over, but LGBTQIA+ individuals typically have much more crossover between their friendship and romantic relationships for several reasons. First, because LGBTQIA+ communities often are small, individuals may experience pressure to remain friends with former romantic partners to preserve

▼ Couples maintain their relationships through routine as well as strategic behaviors.

harmony within their social circles (Peplau, 2009). In addition, partners in LGBTQIA+ relationships often receive significantly less social and practical support from their families, so their friends are major providers of support and more central to their lives. Consequently, when couples break up, they likely are more invested in their joint friendships and have a stronger desire to maintain some of the social support they have developed as a couple (Fingerhut & Peplau, 2013). Finally, because their networks are smaller, LGBTQIA+ people have smaller pools from which to select friends and romantic partners. For these reasons, LGBTQIA+ individuals may have stronger incentives and more need to maintain their relationships.

Communication scholar Jess Alberts and her colleagues examined the nonstrategic, routine behaviors couples perform that help maintain their relationships. Based on audiotapes of the couples' interactions in their homes, they found that individuals use 12 types of conversational behaviors in their daily lives, including humor/joking, self-report (or self-disclosure), positivity (attempts to make interactions pleasant), and talking about television. Moreover, these couples tended to engage in more conflict, humor, household task talk, and planning on weekends than during the workweek (Alberts et al., 2005).

Maintaining Friendships through Communication   As you learned in Chapter 6, conversations are central to our relationships with others, and they play a significant role in friendship as well. One study determined that many conversations with friends last only about three minutes and that these conversations were mostly small talk. Nonetheless, people rated these conversations as highly significant (Duck, 1991). Thus, intimate disclosures may be important, but so are daily, routine interactions, which connect friends and reaffirm or maintain their relationships.

▼ Communication is key to maintaining friendships.

What are some maintenance behaviors that friends use to keep their relationships alive? Not surprisingly, they use similar strategies to those used by romantic couples: positivity, joint activities, social networks, and openness (Johnson et al., 2008). For their friendship relational maintenance study, rather than asking participants what types of behavior they use to maintain their friendships, the authors collected 226 emails students had sent and examined them for the naturally occurring maintenance behaviors they use. As shown in Table 9.6, the participants' emails revealed a more restricted use of relationship maintenance strategies than occurred when people were asked to list the tactics they used.

Table 9.6   Friends' Relationship Maintenance Behaviors

Behavior	Description	Example
Positivity	Efforts to make interactions pleasant	Good luck on your test! It was great to see you today.
Openness	Direct discussions; self-disclosure	How did you do on the midterm? I'm starting to worry about my grades.
Social networks	Relying on friends (e.g., for information, support)	That TA in bio is a tough grader. Do you know if Taylor is going to the game?
Joint activities	Spending time together to maintain the relationship	Let's grab lunch tomorrow before class. Do you want to head to Mill Avenue on Friday night?

SOURCE: Johnson, A .J., Haigh, M. M., Becker, J. A. H., Craig, E. A., & Wigley, S. (2008). College students' use of relational management strategies in email in long-distance and geographically close relationships. *Journal of Computer-Mediated Communication, 13*(2008), 381–404.

As you can see, communication is essential to both friendship and romantic relationship maintenance. However, sometimes we find ourselves unable, or unwilling, to invest energy in maintaining previously valued friendships or romances.

Ending Relationships

Not all relationships endure. When couples consistently engage in behaviors that are not satisfying, one or both partners likely will exit the relationship. Some courtship relationships end after the first date, whereas others end after months or years. Friendships end as well. Relatively few people retain all the friends they make over the course of their lives (Rawlins, 1992). Despite this, relationship termination can be an awkward stage—both to experience and to study.

People generally are much more willing to answer questionnaires and speak with researchers about developing or maintaining a relationship than about ending one. Studying this process is also difficult because relationship de-escalation and termination typically occur over an extended period, with no easy way to say when exactly the process began. Some relationships do end abruptly and decisively, however. The two basic trajectories for ending romantic relationships as well as friendships are called *sudden death* and *passing away* (Duck, 1982; Hays, 1988).

Sudden death refers to relationships that end without prior warning (at least for one participant). Some people are shocked to discover their partners are leaving. Although the ending is unexpected for the one partner, the other may have been thinking about their departure for some time. Occasionally an event occurs, such as infidelity or betrayal, that so damages the relationship that the partners terminate the relationship relatively quickly.

More typically, relationships experience a **passing away**, or decline over time, and the partners are aware that problems remain unresolved. During this period, the partners may vacillate between attempts to improve the relationship and efforts to de-escalate it. Over months or even years, romantic couples may seek counseling, take trips together, or try other methods to improve the relationship, whereas friends may sporadically try to renew their friendship. At the same time, they may develop outside interests or friends as they withdraw from the relationship. It can be a difficult period, especially for romantic couples.

To help you understand this often-confusing stage of relationship development, we next explore the reasons that relationships end and the communication strategies people use to terminate them.

Reasons and Strategies for Romantic Relationship Dissolution When asked why their relationship terminated, gay and heterosexual couples provide similar reasons: lack of autonomy, lack of similarity/compatibility, lack of supportiveness, and infidelity. Heterosexual couples also indicated that insufficient shared time, inequity, and the absence of romance contributed to the demise of their relationships (Baxter, 1991; Kurdek, 1991).

People also terminate relationships because characteristics they thought they liked in a partner become less appealing over time. One study determined that in almost one-third of the romantic relationships examined, the qualities individuals initially found attractive became the

sudden death
Process by which relationships end without prior warning for at least one participant or due to a betrayal.

passing away
Process by which relationships decline over time.

▼ Romantic relationships may end due to a lack of autonomy, compatibility, and supportiveness as well as infidelity.

qualities that led to the end of the relationship (Felmlee, 1995), a concept called *fatal attractions*. For example, one woman liked her relational partner because he had a "don't-care" attitude and liked to have fun, but later she found him to be irresponsible (Felmlee, 1995).

When relationships end, everyone looks for explanations. People blame themselves, they blame the other person, and they may even blame people outside the relationship. Sometimes no one is to blame (Duck, 1991). For example, relationships may end because the partners live too far apart or the timing is wrong. You might meet Ms. or Mr. Right, but if you meet immediately following a painful breakup or just as you are beginning a new and demanding job, you won't have the emotional stability or time needed to develop a successful relationship. In sum, relationship termination is normal, though it can be difficult.

Researchers have identified five general categories of disengagement strategies for dissolving romantic relationships (Cody, 1982):

1. Surprisingly (or perhaps not), the most frequent strategy romantic couples use to end their relationships is **negative identity management**, which means communicating in ways that arouse negative emotions to make the other person upset enough to agree to break off the relationship, e.g., criticizing one's romantic partner or conveying indifference to their feelings and desires.

2. **De-escalation strategies**, a broad category, were used next most often and included behaviors such as promising some continued closeness ("We can still be friends") and suggesting that the couple might reconcile in the future. Thus, these were conversations that attempted to reframe or change the definition of the relationship.

3. **Justification strategies** occurred third most frequently. As the label implies, justification strategies attempt to provide a reason or excuse for why the relationship has failed and should end. Examples include explaining the positive consequences of ending the relationship ("We can devote more time to our careers"), the negative consequences of not ending the relationship ("We will come to hate each other"), or addressing the feelings and concerns of the partner ("I care for you, but you deserve someone who can commit to you").

4. **Positive tone strategies** were next most often used. These strategies expressed caring, sadness about the termination of the relationships, and a desire to be fair. For example, one might say, "I really care about you, but we may just not be right for each other. I'm sure you're going to find someone who makes you truly happy."

5. **Behavioral de-escalation** strategies, which have traditionally occurred the least frequently, involve avoiding the partner. However, with the rapid development of technology, "ghosting," or having someone you view as a friend or a romantic partner suddenly cease communicating with you without warning, is on the rise. According to Vilhauer (2015), **ghosting** is a phenomenon that around 50 percent of those dating today experience at some point. It still remains to be seen if this means that "behavioral de-escalation" is happening more than other strategies as a way to dissolve romantic relationships, but the prevalence of ghosting could indicate that these strategies may be influenced by the times in which they are studied.

Reasons and Strategies for Friendship Dissolution   Why do friendships end? Friendships are particularly vulnerable to termination because few societal pressures encourage their continuance (Blieszner & Adams, 1992) and because friends may not expect to have consistent contact. Some friendships decline without either person being aware of it. Once the friends recognize the decline, it may no longer be possible for the relationship to recover. Thus, friendships, unlike romantic relationships, can end without either person being dissatisfied with the relationship.

---

negative identity management
Communicating in ways that arouse negative emotions to make the other person upset enough to agree to break off the relationship.

de-escalation strategies
A broad category that includes promising some continued closeness and suggesting that the couple might reconcile in the future.

justification strategies
Providing a reason or excuse for ending the relationship.

positive tone strategies
Communicating concern for the rejected partner and trying to make the person feel better.

behavioral de-escalation
Avoiding the partner.

ghosting
Having someone you view as a friend or have been dating suddenly cease communicating with you without warning.

Friendships end for a range of reasons, based on how close the friendship was. Casual friends are more likely to report that their relationships ended because of a lack of proximity, whereas close and best friends more often state that their relationships terminated because of decreased affection. In addition, best and close friends report that their friendships dissolved as a result of interference from other relationships, such as one person's romantic partner (Johnson et al., 2004).

Critical Thinking Prompt
What rules do you have for close friendships? That is, what could a friend do that would be such a significant violation of your expectations that you would terminate your friendship?

Scholars have identified five specific factors that can contribute to the termination of a friendship: lack of communication skills, rule-breaking, deception, boredom, and other reasons (Duck, 1988). With regard to the first factor, if you wish to maintain relationships you must display appropriate communication skills. We know that poor conversationalists tend to be lonely (Duck, 1988) and that lonely people are not perceived to be competent communicators (Canary & Spitzberg, 1985).

Friendships also end because one or both members violate fundamental, often unspoken, rules of the relationship that have been established over the course of the friendship (Argyle & Henderson, 1984; Bowker, 2004). For example, most friends believe that good friends don't gossip about each other, flirt with each other's romantic partners, or lie to each other. Successful relationship partners discern the rules of the relationship and adhere to them.

Because friendships are generally less formal than romantic relationships, the termination strategies used in them may be more subtle and less obvious (Hays, 1988). Thus, ghosting may be even more frequent in friendships than romantic relationships.

When friends desire relationship dissolution, they are likely to use one or more of the following disengagement strategies: withdrawal/avoidance, Machiavellian tactics, positive tone, and openness (Baxter, 1982). As with behavioral de-escalation among romantic couples, when friends engage in **withdrawal/avoidance** they spend less time together, don't return phone calls, and avoid places where they are likely to see the other. **Machiavellian tactics** involve a different type of avoidance; they use a third party to communicate one's unhappiness about the relationship and one's desire to de-escalate or end it. Positive tone strategies are similar to positive tone tactics used by romantic couples; they communicate concern for the rejected friend and try to make the person feel better. Thus, you might tell a friend that you wish to end your friendship because school and work take up too much time rather than admitting you do not enjoy their company anymore. Finally, **openness** means that one straightforwardly explains to one's friend why the relationship is ending.

withdrawal/avoidance
Friendship termination strategy in which friends spend less time together, don't return phone calls, and avoid places where they are likely to see each other.

Machiavellian tactics
Having a third party convey one's unhappiness about a relationship.

openness
Straightforwardly explaining why the relationship is ending.

Destructive Behaviors in Close Relationships

Although this section has focused on how and why friendships and romances end, relationship termination isn't the only difficulty friends and romantic partners face. Individuals face relationship problems at all stages. In the next section, we discuss two types of destructive communication-related behaviors that can occur in friend and romantic relationships.

Interpersonal Aggression **Interpersonal aggression** refers to a variety of behaviors that attempt to inflict physical and psychological/social harm on family, friends, romantic partners, and acquaintances. Physical harm encompasses relatively mild (pushing) to severe (beatings, using weapons) forms of aggression. **Psychological/social aggression** is designed to cause harm to another by attacking their psychological and/or social well-being. Examples include revealing private information, using insulting and derogatory language, humiliation, obsessive monitoring, and threats (Bennet et al., 2011). Though psychological/social aggression does not involve direct physical injury, it can cause significant psychological and physical damage to a person and their social network. For example, bullying can lead to health problems and even suicide (Lutgen-Sandvik et al., 2007). We begin by discussing one of the most pervasive and harmful forms of physical aggression in the United States, intimate partner violence.

interpersonal aggression
Behaviors that attempt to inflict physical and psychological/social harm on family, friends, romantic partners and acquaintances.

psychological/social aggression
Behavior designed to cause harm to another by attacking their psychological and/or social well-being.

intimate partner violence
Physical violence against one's romantic partner.

Intimate partner violence involves physical aggression against one's relational partner(s), and most of this violence is directed at females, 76 percent, compared to males at 24 percent (Bureau of Justice Statistics, 2014). More specifically, approximately 25 percent of women and about 10 percent of men will experience sexual violence, physical violence, and/or stalking by an intimate partner during their life (Centers for Disease Control and Prevention, 2019). Research indicates that intimate partner violence among same-sex couples occurs at similar rates as among straight couples (Rohrbaugh, 2006). The enactment of same-sex intimate partner violence also is similar in many ways to that in heterosexual couples. Both experience the following: patterns of abuse that include physical (along with emotional and psychological) harm, the abuser blackmails them into silence, and physical abuse and sexual abuse co-occur.

However, notable differences exist as well. LGBTQIA+ abusers may threaten to "out" their partners, which can have negative consequences for their family lives, friendships, and employment status. Similarly, LGBTQIA+ targets may be more reluctant to contact law enforcement because doing so will reveal their sexual identity. In addition, in LGBTQIA+ relationships, abusers can threaten to take away their partners' children because in some states a non-birth parent has no legal parental rights. Another difference is that research suggests gay and lesbian victims are more likely to fight back than are heterosexual women (Center for American Progress, 2011).

Two types of intimate partner violence can occur in gay, straight, and lesbian romantic relationships: battering and situational couple violence. *Battering* describes relationships in which one individual uses violence as a way to control and dominate their partner (though most batterers are male). *Situational couple violence* is characterized by less intense forms of violence and tends to be more mutual in its performance, although women usually suffer more serious injuries than do men. During situational couple violence, couples may engage in pushing, shoving, slapping, or throwing objects, but they typically don't engage in beating one another severely or using weapons, in contrast to battering.

Research reveals that couples who engage in situational couple violence lack fundamental communication and problem-solving skills, and they appear unable to let even small matters slide (Lloyd, 1990). These couples are more likely than nonabusive couples to attack each other's character, curse, and threaten their partners. They also make few attempts to de-escalate the conflict or facilitate their conversations calmly (Cordova et al., 1993; Sabourin, 1996). In addition, husbands in aggressive relationships attribute hostile intent to their wives' communication and behavior and respond negatively when their wives attempt to influence them (Anglin & Holtzworth-Munroe, 1997). Thus, the communication of couples who engage in situational violence appears to contribute significantly to their hostility and abuse.

Social aggression among peers and friends frequently takes place online. A study of college students found that 92 percent of participants had experienced some type of electronic victimization in the past year (Bennet et al., 2011). In this context, perpetrators engaged primarily in four types of aggression: hostile and intrusive comments and questions and attempts to exclude or humiliate their targets. While both males and females are subject to these behaviors, women tend to have stronger, more negative reactions to them.

Psychological/social aggression is common for several reasons. First, when making the choice of an aggressive strategy, people are aware of the "effect/danger" ratio. That is, perpetrators are aware that physical aggression is highly associated with their getting hurt as well. Perpetrators recognize that psychological/social aggression can be just as effective as or even more effective than physical aggression, and the danger to themselves is much lower. In addition, the pervasiveness of different types of social and communication technologies means that it is easy to aggress against someone and for the target's hurt and humiliation to be seen by a wider audience. Finally, this type of aggression often is used to position oneself as being of higher status than the target.

Sexual Coercion   Sexual coercion is another type of negative, potentially violent, interaction in which the participants' communication is of importance (Willan & Pollard, 2003). People often find it difficult to discuss sexual coercion. Part of the problem arises from lack of clarity on what it is. **Sexual coercion** is most effectively defined as "the act of using pressure, alcohol or drugs, or force to have sexual contact with someone against their will, (including) persistent attempts to have sexual contact with someone who has already refused" (Struckman-Johnson et al., 2003). Some people believe that a person who "gives in" to such pressure is equally to blame; however, people tend to engage in unwanted sex because of concern for the relationship, difficulty with resisting pressure, or real concern for personal safety (Spitzberg, 1998).

sexual coercion
Unwanted sexual activity that occurs when one is pressured, tricked, manipulated, threatened, or forced in a nonphysical way.

Sexual coercion occurs among friends, family, acquaintances, and romantic couples. Individuals of all sexes and sexual orientations experience unwanted sexual behaviors, though the degree to which groups experience it differs. One of the more comprehensive studies on unwanted sex was conducted by the Centers for Disease Control and Prevention in 2020. Researchers there found that over their lifetimes approximately one in three women and one in four men experience sexual violence. "Nearly 1 in 5 women and 1 in 38 men have experienced completed or attempted rape, and 1 in 14 men was made to penetrate someone (completed or attempted) during his lifetime" (Centers for Disease Control and Prevention, 2020).

Other studies have determined that lesbians and bisexual women experienced unwanted sex at rates similar to heterosexual women. However, the unwanted sex experienced by gay and bisexual men is markedly different from that of heterosexual men (Menning & Holtzman, 2014). In one study, 11.6 percent of gay men and 13 percent of bisexual men reported being raped (Balsam et al., 2005).

As these studies suggest, sexual assault is pervasive, and men as well as women suffer from abuse. How is sexual assault a communication issue? Although some sexual assaults are perpetrated by strangers, the majority of them are committed by friends, acquaintances, and romantic partners. In these cases, communication can play a significant role, especially when sexual coercion occurs. Perpetrators of sexual coercion use a variety of verbal tactics to pressure individuals into sexual acts. Some badger the person or beg until they relent; others use bribes, persuasion, economic leverage, or the threat of withdrawing their affection or themselves from the relationship. In addition, the targets of coercion often are people who have difficulty defending themselves and their positions or who have been taught to be compliant and overly considerate of others.

What can you do to prevent yourself from becoming a target—or a perpetrator? The ability to discuss consent is one important way. The ability to talk about what each party wants and would willingly participate in needs to be articulated and respected. Don't discount your partner's refusal. That is, don't assume that your partner is using *token resistance*, that is, saying no then giving in (Muehlenhard & Hollabough, 1988); any indication of reluctance or refusal should be honored. If anyone tries to persuade you into sexual contact that you do not want, do not engage in arguing or explaining your position. Once you begin to explain your position, you provide information for the other party to use to persuade you that your "reasons" are not valid. You are better off simply stating what your position is (No, I don't want to . . .). When asked why you won't do something, simply say, "Because I don't want to." Here are some specific ways you can respond to sexual pressure (McCoy & Oelschlager, 2011):

- "I really like you. I'm just not ready to have sex."
- "If you really care about me, you'll respect my decision."
- "I said no. I don't owe you an explanation."

Other ways you can protect yourself from being a target or a perpetrator is to avoid drinking or being around people who are drinking and not isolating yourself from other people in your environment. Most importantly, be clear to yourself about what you want. Indecisive people can be coerced or persuaded to engage in behavior they will later regret.

How can you tell if you are being coerced? If your partner makes comments such as "If you value me and our relationship, you'll have sex with me" or "We've had sex before, so you can't say no" or attempts to make you feel that you "owe" them sex because of money your partner has spent, then you are probably experiencing sexual coercion (McCoy & Oelschlager, 2011). (See Chapter 6 for a more detailed discussion of communication and sexual coercion.) If you would like additional information on preventing unwanted sex, the health clinics and security departments of most colleges and universities can provide pamphlets, books, and other resources.

The effectiveness of individuals' communication plays an important role in how enduring and rewarding their relationships are. Thus, individuals are at the center of relationships, and what they say and do affects their relationships at every stage. However, societal norms and pressures shape relationships as well. In the next section, we examine relationships within this broader frame.

Journal Prompt 9.3: Flirting and Communication
What strategies do women use to initiate a relationship through flirting? How do men and women compare in their understanding and interpretation of women's flirting communication?

The Individual, Relationship Communication, and Society

9.4 Explain the role that society plays in the formation and maintenance of interpersonal relationships.

Most heterosexuals are unaware of the effect cultural norms have on their romance choices (O'Brien & Foley, 1999) and on how they express affection and commitment in them. Until 50 years ago, partners of different races could not legally have intimate relationships in the United States; until the year 2000, Alabama still had a law against interracial marriages (Root, 2001; Sollors, 2000). Unsurprisingly, the vast majority of marriages in the United States are still racially homogeneous. Moreover, they occur primarily between people of similar religious backgrounds (Watson et al., 2004), economic status (Kalmijin, 1994), age (Watson et al., 2004), education (Bennhold, 2012), weight (Schafer & Keith, 1990), and appearance (Little et al., 2006). Such a high degree of similarity, or **homogeneity**, suggests that individual preference is not the only factor influencing our choices.

Commonly held stereotypes also influence choices about whom one should or should not date and marry. For example, some interracial pairings are more common than others. In 75 percent of Black–White marriages, the husband is Black, and in 75 percent of White–Asian couples, the husband is White (Sailer, 2003). The frequency of these pairings reflects strong societal norms about who is attractive as a partner (and who is not).

As discussed earlier (in Chapter 8), communication norms vary across cultures, and the romance context is no exception. For example, in some cultures (e.g., Japan, Indonesia, Kuwait), romantic couples rarely express their feelings or affections in public (Chung, 2016). Other cultures, as in Indonesia,

homogeneity
High degree of similarity.

▼ People are drawn to others who are highly similar to themselves.

would be shocked by kissing in public or other public displays of affection. If you were to do so, you could face social backlash or even legal consequences, depending on what area of the country you are in (Starmer-Smith, 2004). Thus, every relationship is situated within a set of societal and cultural norms and expectations, and what occurs within that relationship is likely to be affected by those norms.

Cultural norms and legal policies also impact the ways in which LGBTQIA+ individuals can communicate with and about their romantic partners. They often can't express affection in public without fear of negative, even violent, responses. For this

▲ Societal institutions, such as synagogues, influence our communication and relationships.

reason, they may refer to their lovers as "friends" or "roommates" or attempt to conceal their romantic partner's sex by never using pronouns such as *him* or *her*. Having to alter one's verbal and nonverbal behavior to conform to society's norms may seem a small matter if you are heterosexual. But imagine what life would be like if in many contexts you could never acknowledge your partner or you had to pretend that you were "just friends." Not only would this be exhausting, it would significantly inhibit your ability to be close to others. Unfortunately, this is the life that many LGBTQIA+ live.

The practices of specific institutions (e.g., religions) impact our communication and relationships. For example, many faiths have long prescribed whom their members should marry, how many spouses they could have, and even if they should date. For example, the Mormon faith once permitted men to have more than one wife (although it no longer does), Muslim men are instructed to marry Muslim women, and Hindus often discourage young people from dating and selecting their own marital partners. Although over time religions can and do alter their positions on these issues (e.g., the Church of Jesus Christ of Latter Day Saints' position on polygamy), they may be slower to change than other social institutions. For example, a recent Pew Research Center (2015) survey found that although some Catholics are open to nontraditional families, 9 in 10 U.S. Catholics still believe that a household headed by a married mother and father is ideal for child-rearing. In these ways, religious institutions and beliefs influence how we view relationships as well as how we act within them and communicate about our relationships.

Similarly, business organizations create policies and practices that affect the types of relationships and communication practices their employees can have. Some examples include bans against "affectional relationships," at work, fraternization—or relationships that cross the organizational hierarchy—in the military, and limits on nepotism (hiring one's family members). They also express their views on same-sex relationships and the institution of marriage by providing, or not providing, domestic-partner benefits or even firing employees who marry same-sex partners. Organizations often create rules that attempt to control and influence employees' communication through sexual harassment policies, secrecy clauses, and dictates on what can be communicated to others outside the organization. Yet another way organizations influence employee communication is by firing those whose communication—on social media or in person—they do not wish to have associated with their company.

In addition to shaping relationships in the ways already discussed, societal factors influence negative aspects of romantic relationships, such as violence and rape. For

Critical Thinking Prompt
What cultural factors—whether familial, religious, social, or organizational—have the greatest influence on your relationships?

example, most talk about violence in romantic relationships focuses on the behavior of individual aggressors rather than on the social structures that allow abuse (Payne & Smith, 2013). Most people assume that men and women experience equity in their relationships (Ferraro, 1996; Lloyd & Emery, 2000) and that men are not abused by their partners. However, the facts are that women typically earn less money than men, are more responsible for children, and often are faced with social institutions, such as the police, that do not believe their stories of intimate partner violence or sexual violence (American Civil Liberties Union, 2015; Walzer, 1996).

These factors seriously compromise how equal women can be in heterosexual relationships and likely account for the fact that far more women are severely injured and murdered by their partners than vice versa (National Coalition Against Domestic Violence, 2015). At the same time, little conversation occurs about violence against men; in fact, men who are abused are often ridiculed and stigmatized so that they have few places to turn for help and support (Kimmel, 2002).

In addition, the ways we talk about romance can encourage acceptance of aggression in relationships. For example, popular media frequently portray male aggression as normal and acceptable, as in movies, television shows, and novels, where male aggression is often a central and recurrent plot point. The popular image that men have urgent and difficult-to-control sexual drives implies that women are responsible for controlling sexual contact. Thus, more attention is paid to how *women* behave during unwanted sexual encounters than how men behave.

Finally, people frequently blame the victim. For example, people often ask, "What was she doing out late at night by herself?" When we blame victims, we ask what they could have done to prevent the violence rather than focusing on what we should do as a culture to minimize relational aggression. Lloyd and Emery argue that how we define aggression is important; when we make statements such as "He just slapped her around a bit," we diminish the real emotional and physical trauma associated with assault. Overall, these researchers propose that if we truly wish to reduce the violence in relationships, we must examine and alter the ways we talk about relational aggression.

Unlike marriage, friendships are not governed by laws and institutions. However, social norms still affect our choice of friends or our behavior within friendships. Take a moment to think about your closest friends over the past five years. How similar are they to you? Do you have any friends who are decades older than you? How many of your friends are from a different ethnic group than you are? Clearly some people do have friends who differ from themselves on demographic factors such as race, age, income, and education, but this is more often the exception than the rule (Aboud & Mendelson, 1996). As we discussed in Chapter 8, these multicultural relationships, though potentially rewarding, sometimes take more "care and feeding" than relationships in which two people are similar. Intercultural friends may receive pressure from others, particularly from majority group members, to stick with people who are similar to them (Pogrebin, 1992).

Thus, friendship is not only an individual matter, but it also is a social event that occurs in contexts that exert a powerful influence on its development (Allan, 1977). In the United States, it is understood that friendships play an extremely important role in the lives of adolescents. In this culture, parents are encouraged to understand that their adolescent children will turn away from talking and spending time with them (Rawlins, 1992). By contrast, married adults are expected to place their romantic partners and families before their friends (Dainton et al., 2003).

Journal Prompt 9.4: Society and Relationships
What are some other ways in which society affects individuals' romantic relationships? How does society influence individuals' friendships?

Ethics and Close Relationships

9.5 Explain how to ensure that interactions with close others are authentic.

Although communicating ethically is important in all contexts and relationships, it is nowhere more important than in the context of close relationships. If we communicate unethically with our friends, family, and romantic partners, the consequences may be severe. Certainly relationships have ended as a result of deception, secrecy, and even the truth, too harshly expressed. All the ethical considerations we have discussed throughout this book are important in close relationships, but here we will focus on authentic communication.

Authentic communication is particularly important in close relationships for two reasons: We expect our closest friends and family members to be authentic, or "real," with us, and authentic communication is connected to intimacy. Why is authenticity in communication an ethical issue? Because inauthentic communication attempts to manipulate the interaction or the other person for one's own goals, it can be considered a type of deception, given that during inauthentic communication, one hides how one really feels and misrepresents one's feelings and beliefs. In addition, inauthentic communication denies people the information they need to make an informed choice about their relationships with others.

▲ To maintain an authentic relationship, you need to confront issues that are important to the relationship.

For most people, intimacy is based on the feeling that one knows and is known by another. When we feel intimate with others, we believe that we are connecting with their "true" selves and that we are able to be our truest selves in the relationship. However, when people are not authentic in their communication with those close to them or deny them the right to communicate authentically, it can decrease intimacy and even lead to termination of the relationship. And if we discover that an intimate friend or partner was being inauthentic and manipulative, we may feel not only deceived but betrayed. For example, if you discover that your friend has been pretending to like your romantic partner while making negative remarks about them on the sly, you might feel angry and betrayed. In addition, if you want to continue the relationship, you now have to deal not only with your friend's feelings about your romantic partner but also with your friend's deceit.

How can we ensure that our interactions with close others are authentic? We can do so by being open to others' communication efforts, being open in our own communication, taking responsibility for what we say, and respecting the rights of others to speak. In effect, we need to avoid the three "pitfalls" of inauthentic communication: topic avoidance, meaning denial, and disqualification.

1. **Topic avoidance.** To maintain an authentic relationship with another, it is vital to confront issues that are important to the relationship and to the other person. If one or both people in a relationship prohibit the other from discussing issues that are important to either of them, it can be difficult for them to maintain intimacy and commitment. For example, if a good friend wishes to discuss their sexual identity and the person they are speaking to refuses to do so, they risk damaging the closeness and relationship with the other person by shutting down communication on this topic.

2. **Meaning denial.** In addition, authentic communication involves taking responsibility for what we say and mean. If one is angry and teases a friend harshly because of it, it is inauthentic to deny that one is angry and trying to be hurtful.

gaslighting
A tactic used to exert power or control over another person by encouraging them to question their reality.

Journal Prompt 9.5: Authenticity in Communication
Why is authenticity considered an ethical issue? What communication strategies can you use to ensure that you engage in authentic communication?

passive-aggressive communication
Indirectly communicating negative feelings and reactions instead of openly talking about them.

Even worse, if one puts the onus on the friend for being "too sensitive," they may be compounding the problem. This behavior is also an example of "**gaslighting**," which is a tactic used to exert power or control over another person by encouraging them to question their reality (Sarkis, 2017). Repeated interactions such as this can undermine trust and intimacy.

3. **Disqualification.** Finally, authentic communicators allow others to speak regardless of their positions or experiences. If a single friend attempts to give relationship support and advice, they may feel disqualified if their friend refuses to listen because they aren't married. We also engage in disqualification when we deny a romantic partner the right to speak on a topic because we perceive ourselves to be more expert on the topic. If a person finds themselves saying, "What could you know about this?" then they may be disqualifying the other party and potentially engaging in inauthentic communication.

Engaging in authentic communication can help people develop and maintain their relationships more effectively. To help you begin the process, we conclude this chapter with suggestions for how you can communicate more effectively by being open and direct with others.

Improving Your Close Relationship Communication Skills

9.6 Articulate how to recognize passive-aggressive communication.

Do you know what it means to communicate passive-aggressively? You may have heard someone call another person "passive-aggressive," but can you identify the behavior in others—or yourself? We use **passive-aggressive communication** when we indirectly communicate our negative feelings and reactions instead of openly talking about them. For example, have you asked a friend for a favor that they agreed to do, but then they repeatedly "forgot" to do it? Of course, sometimes we do just forget things, but if you sense your friend is reluctant rather than has a poor memory, they may be communicating that they regret agreeing but also aren't willing to talk about it openly.

Social worker Signe Whitson calls passive-aggressiveness "hostile cooperation" (Long et al., 2016). By this, she means that people who are passive-aggressive appear to be cooperative in that they agree to others' requests, but fundamentally, their behavior is hostile or uncooperative because they don't follow through and/or nonverbally express negative feelings. These mixed signals can frustrate and upset others because they can't solve the problem. That is, they can't just let the issue go because they sense the other's anger, but they can't retract the request because the offending party says it is not a problem. In addition, they can't get the angry party to talk about it. What type of behavior does this sound like? If you guessed gaslighting, you are correct!

How do you know if you or someone else is being passive-aggressive? You or they might be if:

- You/they agree to do something reluctantly and feel resentment about it.
- You/they are unwilling to be truthful about negative feelings.
- You/they complain to third parties about being taken advantage of or cheated.
- You/they make repeated excuses regarding why the task agreed to hasn't been done.
- You/they use email, texts, and social media to avoid having to be open with another person.

You may have seen passive-aggressive behavior play out if you have lived in an apartment complex or neighborhood where people disagree on appropriate behavior. This occurs when one person lodges a complaint against another secretly or anonymously to the neighborhood association or apartment supervisor but then acts friendly with the person they have complained about. People who call the police on their acquaintances or neighbors because they are unhappy with something they have done are engaging in passive-aggressiveness and potentially causing more severe harm than they ever intended.

Why is being passive-aggressive bad for our relationships? It is for many reasons. First, feeling resentful toward one's friends, family, and romantic partners increases our anger, decreases our patience, and erodes our feelings for one another. Also, strong relationships are built on feelings of closeness and acceptance. When one partner feels resentful, it inhibits their feelings of love and affection, and since generally we can tell when our partners are angry or upset with us, we don't feel loved and accepted when they exhibit it. Finally, it is very difficult to feel close to someone when we are unable to be truthful with them or trust that they are truthful with us.

What should you do if you think you communicate passive-aggressively at times?

- First, determine when you are most likely to engage in passive-aggressive communication. Does it occur with specific people in your life? Does it happen when you are asked to agree to something you don't want to do? To change a behavior, you must be able to identify that you are engaging in it and when.

- Accept that your behavior needs to change. It will not only improve your relationships; clearly stating how you feel and what you want will make you happier.

- Don't agree to something until you have time to think it over. If your romantic partner asks if it is okay if they go on a weekend getaway with friends on your birthday, don't say yes (or no) immediately. Take time to explore how you feel now and how you are likely to feel in the future.

- If you don't want to agree, then you need to tell your partner honestly and calmly how you feel and why you feel that way.

- If you agree to something and later regret having agreed or disagreed to it and are feeling upset or angry, again you need to tell you partner how you are feeling. It is true that being open and honest can lead to hurt feelings on occasion, but we can work through those moments. Agreeing with your partner and then punishing them because you now feel resentful only creates a negative environment and can lead to anger, conflict, and dissatisfaction.

Journal Prompt 9.6: Addressing Passive-Aggressive Communication
To prepare yourself to respond to someone who has communicated passive-aggressively, develop a brief script you can use to communicate that you would like for the other party to tell you honestly and openly how they feel.

SUMMARY

9.1 Describe the importance of close relationships.

- Close relationships are important because they affect our health and emotional well-being.

9.2 Explain five communication theories of relationship development.

- Attraction theory explains the influence of three factors—proximity, physical attractiveness, and similarity—on an individual's likelihood of forming a relationship with another person.
- Two theories—uncertainty reduction theory and predicted outcome value theory—explain how communication serves to increase or decrease intimacy and commitment in relationships.
- Two theories—social exchange theory and equity theory—explain how individuals evaluate their relationships based on the costs and rewards they accrue. Social exchange theory focuses on individuals' desire to maximize rewards and minimize costs in their relationships while equity theory argues that people are more satisfied in relationships they perceive as fair—where their costs are balanced by their rewards.

9.3 Identify tactics for initiating, maintaining, and terminating friendships and romantic relationships.

- Strategies for initiating relationships include opening with impersonal questions, listening attentively, being polite, expressing approval, and asking open-ended follow-up questions.

- Relationship maintenance strategies and behaviors include being open, expressing positivity, and offering assurances.
- The relationship termination strategies people are likely to use include negative identity management, positive tone strategies, justification, and de-escalation strategies.

9.4 Explain the role that society plays in the formation and maintenance of interpersonal relationships.

- Societal laws and norms influence whom we marry or befriend, how we communicate with relational partners, and how we communicate with the rest of the world about these relationships.

9.5 Explain how to ensure that interactions with close others are authentic.

- Authentic communication requires that one is open to others' communication efforts, open in one's own communication, takes responsibility for what one says, and respects the rights of others to speak.

9.6 Articulate how to recognize passive-aggressive communication.

- An individual likely is engaging in passive-aggressive communication if they are unwilling to express negative feelings; they complain to third parties that they are being mistreated; they offer repeated excuses for why they haven't fulfilled commitments they have made; and they use email, texts, and social media to avoid open communication with others.

KEY TERMS

attraction theory p. 215
proximity p. 215
attractiveness p. 216
matching hypothesis p. 216
similarity p. 216
uncertainty reduction value
    theory p. 217
predicted outcome value theory p. 218
social exchange theory p. 219
equity theory p. 219
underbenefitted p. 219
overbenefitted p. 219

equity p. 219
Knapp's stage model p. 220
initiating p. 220
experimenting p. 220
intensifying p. 220
integrating p. 220
bonding p. 220
differentiating p. 220
circumscribing p. 220
stagnating p. 220
avoiding p. 220
terminating p. 220

relational trajectory models p. 221
turning point model for romantic
    couples p. 221
turning point model of
    friendship p. 222
social penetration theory p. 226
relational maintenance p. 229
sudden death p. 231
passing away p. 231
negative identity management p. 232
de-escalation strategies p. 232
justification strategies p. 232

APPLY WHAT YOU KNOW

1. **Maintaining Friendships and Romantic Relationships**

   Interview two people and ask them how they maintain their closest friendship. What conscious, deliberate strategies do they use to ensure that they will stay close with their good friends? Also, what routine behaviors do they use to maintain closeness (for example, using nicknames, emailing funny stories)? Then interview two people and ask them the same questions about how they maintain their current romantic relationship. Finally, compare the four sets of responses. Do your interviewees use similar or different strategies for maintaining their friendships and their romances?

2. **Societal Influences on Relationships**

   Choose six magazines or popular lifestyle blog websites. Be sure to select a wide range of sources, including those directed toward men and women as well as some focused on political, social, and health issues. Skim through your choices, first looking at the advertisements. What can you tell about the way friendships and romances are viewed in the United States? Ask yourself these questions:

   a. To what degree do the people in the ads "match" by ethnicity, age, attractiveness, height and weight, and other factors?

   b. How many romantic couples depicted?

   c. How many of the friendship pairs depicted are female? Male?

   d. In the ads depicting friends, what are female friends doing? What are male friends doing?

   e. How many ads picture people who are overweight? Physically unattractive? What products are they advertising?

   f. What population of readers does the source target?

   After answering these questions, look for patterns that exist within the sources by their target audience. What does this reveal about society's views of friendships and romantic relationships?

Small Group Communication

LEARNING OBJECTIVES

10.1 Identify four reasons for learning about small group communication.

10.2 Define *small group communication* and *virtual small groups*.

10.3 Identify examples of task, relational, and disruptive small group roles.

10.4 Describe five theories of group leadership.

10.5 Describe the characteristics of communication that occur during the four phases of small group decision making.

10.6 Discuss how diversity influences small group processes.

10.7 Give three types of guidelines for communicating more ethically in small group communication.

10.8 Discuss ways to improve your small group communication skills.

CHAPTER TOPICS

The Importance of Small Group Communication

What Is Small Group Communication?

Small Group Communication and the Individual: Roles

Small Group Communication and the Individual: Leadership

Effective Small Group Communication

The Individual, Small Group Communication, and Society: Power and Diversity

Ethics and Small Group Communication

Improving Your Small Group Communication Skills

> *"The quality of a group depends on the contributions of individual members."*

Charee had an interesting group experience in her Business Communication class. One of the assignments involved working in groups with students from another campus. Each group had six students (half from her campus and half from the other campus). As a group, they were assigned to select one team on a reality show—for example, judges on The Voice *or* RuPaul's Drag Race, *teams on* Hell's Kitchen, *or investor panels on* Shark Tank, *and so on. Using concepts learned in class, they evaluated the effectiveness of the group communication on the chosen show. They had to show their analysis in a multimedia presentation to be posted on Google Sites.*

Charee enjoyed the project because her group could select a show that most group members were interested in and use creativity in the analysis and presentation. Most of the group members worked well together; they exchanged messages on Snapchat or Instagram, sometimes collaborating on Google Docs, and some actually became friends. They had discussed the task guidelines and the group expectations at the beginning of the project. All but one of the group members completed the tasks on time, helped each other, and always knew what the other members were doing. However, there was one member who never posted his work on time, rarely communicated with others, and in general didn't do a good, thoughtful job. He never knew what was going on because he never communicated with other group members. Charee and her group members found that part of the project frustrating even though they tried to work around him.

Charee's group experience illustrates many of the issues we will discuss in this chapter. First, almost any job these days involves cooperation—and often working in virtual groups—where members rarely or never work in person, and effective communication is a critical determinant of successful group work (Eisenberg et al., 2019). Second, as Charee discovered, group work can be productive and even enjoyable when members are motivated and get along in addition to having clear guidelines and expectations for the project. However, it can be frustrating if one or more group members communicate poorly or, as in Charee's group, fail to participate altogether. It is easy to imagine that their group presentation would have been better if the entire group had worked together as assigned.

In this chapter, we begin by discussing reasons for studying small group communication; we explain what a small group is and define small group communication and also describe characteristics of virtual small groups. We then identify the benefits and challenges of small group work, some of which are illustrated in Charee's experience, and discuss the various communication roles and behaviors that help make groups effective and satisfying for group members. Next, we turn to a discussion of group leadership and describe decision-making processes in a common type of group: problem-solving groups. Finally, we discuss the impact of society on small group communication, addressing the issues of power, cultural diversity, and technology in small group communication. We conclude the chapter with suggestions for how you can communicate more effectively and ethically in small groups.

The Importance of Small Group Communication

10.1 Identify four reasons for learning about small group communication.

Small groups seem to be an integral part of life. You probably belong to a number of groups—social groups, course project groups, work groups at your job, or perhaps support or interest groups in your community. However, you might be surprised to discover that learning how to communicate better in groups can actually enhance your academic and professional achievements. Let's see why this is so.

Reasons to Study Small Group Communication

There are at least four reasons to study small group communication: small groups are a fact of life, and they enhance your college performance, your career success, and your personal life.

A Fact of Life   If you have mixed feelings about working in small groups, you are not alone. In fact, a term exists, **grouphate**, which describes the distaste and aversion that some people feel toward working in groups (Keyton et al., 1996). As one of our students told us, "I would rather just do the whole group project myself than try to get together with a group of students I don't know and might not trust to do a good job." One study found that students (in a small group communication course) who reported an active dislike for working in groups (grouphate) also reported experiencing less group cohesion, consensus, and relational satisfaction in their group work (Myers & Goodboy, 2005). Thus, it is possible that by actively disliking group work, students are negatively influencing how they experience working with a group.

Regardless of how you feel about working in groups, groups are everywhere. Social groups, many online, fill an important function, especially during a pandemic, and there are as many groups as there are interests: scooters, salsa dancing, book clubs, and so on. The purpose of these groups is simply to socialize and enjoy each other's company, whether in person or online.

However, this chapter's focus is on groups that meet principally to solve problems or achieve goals, such as support groups or work groups. These groups can involve long-term commitments, as in the case of support groups that meet regularly for months or even years. Long-term work groups also include standing committees in business and civic organizations. However, probably most common are short-term project groups—for example, groups that students belong to in various classes as well as work groups in business organizations. Increasingly, most of these groups accomplish their work virtually, which we'll discuss throughout the chapter.

Enhanced College Performance   Considerable research indicates that college students who study in small groups perform at higher intellectual levels, learn better, and have better attitudes toward subject matter than those who study alone (Allen & Plax, 2002). This is probably because studying with others allows you to encounter different interpretations and ideas. As we'll see in the next section, group work can also lead to higher-quality thinking and decision making. Thus, learning how to interact more effectively in groups and seeking out learning groups to participate in can lead to enhanced college performance.

Enhanced Career Success   According to a *Forbes* article, the top skills employers say they seek are the ability to work in a group structure and the ability to make decisions and solve problems (Adams, 2014). These skills are particularly important in today's global workplace—where you may be working, in person or online, with people from different countries/cultural backgrounds. Whether you are in business or another profession, organizations tend to hire and promote those who have proven they can work well with others (Hansen, 2011; Phadnis & Caplice, 2013). Thus, your career advancement prospects could very well depend on your success in a collaborative work environment.

Enhanced Personal Life   Most people also participate in at least some small groups outside work. For one thing, most people communicate with family and friends on a

grouphate
The distaste and aversion that people feel toward working in groups.

regular basis. In addition, many people serve on committees in religious or political organizations, and increasing numbers of people join support groups to deal with crises, life transitions, or chronic health conditions. So learning how to communicate better in small group settings, both in person and online, can serve you personally, academically, and professionally. Despite its prevalence and importance, group work has both advantages and disadvantages.

Advantages and Disadvantages of Group Work

Working in small groups brings many advantages in addition to those already described. Research shows that groups often make more creative and higher-quality decisions than do individuals. First, a group can produce more innovative ideas than can an individual working alone. The small group discussion itself actually stimulates creativity as research shows that people tend to work harder and do better when others are around, particularly if the work group is cohesive and other group members are modeling effective group behavior (Park & Shin, 2015).

Second, some evidence indicates that small group work can promote critical thinking, leading to better decisions. A group of people offers more collective information, experience, and expertise than any single person can. For example, if a group member offers an opinion or makes a claim, collectively, other group members may offer evidence that supports or refutes it; they may also contribute alternative opinions or suggestions. However, some experts caution that critical thinking and cognitively complex ideas are not automatic consequences of small group discussion. Rather, it may take some leadership to elicit diverse ideas and to then facilitate the type of discussion described previously that promotes critical analysis, interpretation, and critiquing (Jobidon et al., 2016).

Of course, group work also has disadvantages: it can be time-consuming because group decisions take more time than do individual ones; it can lead to too much closeness and agreement, resulting in premature decisions; and it can silence divergent opinions—particularly from minority group members (Jaeger, 2020).

Finally, a fourth disadvantage is that group discussion can be less than satisfying when some group members dominate or withdraw, as happened with Charee's group in our opening vignette. Such communication behaviors can cause frustration and conflict, preventing members from working productively and cohesively (de Wit et al., 2012).

Given that most of us need to work in small groups from time to time and that learning how to communicate better in small groups can enhance critical thinking as well as lead to academic and professional success, what do you need to know to be a successful group member? To answer this question, we first must clarify what we mean by *small group communication*.

> **Journal Prompt 10.1:**
> **Studying Small Group**
> **Communication**
> What do you think is the most important reason for you to learn about group communication? Why?

What Is Small Group Communication?

10.2 Define *small group communication* and *virtual small groups*.

To acquire a clear idea of what we'll be discussing in this chapter, let's consider two types of groups: (1) a group of people waiting in line for a movie and (2) a group of students working on a semester-long research project. The first type of group is not the focus of this chapter, whereas the second is. We define **small group communication** as "communication among a small number of people who share a common purpose or goal, who feel connected to each other, and coordinate their behavior" (Arrow et al., 2000, p. 34). Let's look more closely at who the small group in this definition is.

> **small group communication**
> Communication among a small number of people who share a common purpose or goal, who feel connected to each other, and who coordinate their behavior.

A Small Number of People

Most experts agree that three is the fewest number of people that can constitute a small group and that five to seven people is the optimum upper limit for working groups. This general guideline may vary depending on whether the small group is working in person or virtually. In general, small groups of three (whether working in direct contact or virtually) experience better communication in terms of openness and accuracy than do larger groups of six. As group size increases, people may feel more anonymous, and discussions can become unwieldy and unfocused as members tend to break into smaller groups. However, size seems to have less impact on groups that are working virtually (Lowry et al., 2006). Under this portion of our definition, people waiting in line for a movie would not likely be considered a small group because any number of people can wait for a movie.

A Common Purpose

Although a group of people waiting for a movie fulfills the second requirement of our definition—they share a purpose—that purpose is rather limited. Here we focus on communication in small groups that are working together toward a common purpose. Sometimes the purpose may be assigned by an instructor or employer—a semester-long course project, completing a marketing research study for a client, or working together to recommend a candidate for a job. Having a clear purpose or goal is important and is directly (positively) related to group productivity and increased group performance (Crown, 2007).

A Connection with Each Other

People waiting for the movie don't generally feel any sense of group connection, nor do they need to. In contrast, people in work groups need to experience a group identity and recognize their interdependence because—as we saw in Charee's experience—when members do not feel a sense of connection, the group won't function as it should. The challenge for the small group is to find ways to create a sense of group identity for all members, and communication is often the key to making this happen.

▼ We define small group communication as "communication among a small number of people who share a common purpose or goal, who feel connected to each other, and who coordinate their behavior."

An Influence on Each Other

Members of small groups need to coordinate their behavior, and in doing so, they may exert influence on each other. People waiting for a movie do not need to exert influence on each other, but members of a work group do. This influence can be positive or negative, and each group member contributes to the success or failure of the whole group. Most groups aren't successful without the positive contribution of all members. In Charee's experience, the negative influence of one member detracted from the success of all.

In sum, a collection of people waiting in line for a movie rarely constitutes a small group because they typically don't influence one another, they don't feel connected to each other or develop a shared identity, and they share a common purpose only in the most limited way. We should also note that the word *team* is sometimes used interchangeably with the word *group*, but experts distinguish the two. While they both require collaboration and shared goals, teams generally require a higher level of cooperation and commitment, have greater resources, require complementary—not identical—skills from

▲ Groups separated by time or distance rely on a variety of technologies, including videoconferencing.

their members, and have a stronger group identity. So all teams are groups, but not all groups are teams. Members of student project groups, a neighborhood hospitality committee, or a fraternity new member selection committee, for example, have members who are often the luck of the draw, not chosen for complementary skills; have some degree of commitment for periods of time; and probably don't have huge resources. Contrast these groups with NFL teams, Cirque de Soleil teams, industry product design teams—all have a strong sense of identity (often with specific names, e.g., New England Patriots), strong commitment to the team goals, and substantial resources, and members are selected for specific (complementary) expertise. Of course, there can be overlap. Some groups may become teams over time, and some groups may have some of the features of a team (Rothwell, 2019). Since all teams are groups, most of what we discuss in this chapter can apply to both groups and teams. Both team and small group work is being carried out increasingly virtually, the topic we turn to next.

Critical Thinking Prompt
Think about all the groups you belong to. Which could help you be more successful personally? Academically? Professionally?

Virtual Small Groups

According to experts, participation in virtual business teams grew by 25 percent between 2010 and 2018 (Bakken, 2018), and with more employees working remotely during the pandemic, the trend is only increasing. It is likely that you already have been working in virtual groups in some of your college courses and/or in your job/career.

A **virtual small group** is simply a group whose members interact primarily "through electronic communication media" (Handke et al., 2020, p. 4). With increased use of technology in most organizations, we now view **virtuality** as a continuum, and small group work can range from low to high virtuality. Highly virtual groups communicate entirely by electronic media and are usually geographically dispersed—spread across geographical regions and sometimes many different time zones. Members of less virtual groups may be geographically dispersed or separated only by a few cubicles or building floors, and group members may communicate by electronic means sometimes but meet occasionally in person.

One of our students, Marek, is a member of a *highly virtual* group working for an international pharmaceutical company and often collaborates on projects with group members whom he has never met. Members of his group are scattered around the globe

virtual small group
A small group whose members interact through electronic communication media.

virtuality
The degree to which groups work through electronic communication media.

in multiple time zones. Thus, he may be online with Luc in Montreal, Caroline in London, Liana in Buenos Aires, Ahmed in Riyadh, Setsuko in Osaka, and Giles in Melbourne. Although he may not have met his group members in person, their tasks are well defined, and this enables the group to complete their projects with few problems. Moreover, their diverse cultural backgrounds enhance the group's ideas and produce a stronger product. Another student, Lucia, has more experience working in less virtual groups in her job in the Phoenix, Arizona, office of a national insurance company, headquartered in Chicago, Illinois. She's the director of the local marketing sector and often communicates with her group members virtually even though they are in the same building; she occasionally meets virtually with other marketing directors located around the country.

Do virtual small groups have any communication challenges that differ from those faced by groups working in person? As virtual work becomes more commonplace and people are increasingly comfortable with communication technology tools, some see little difference between virtual and in-person work. This is especially true for groups who often use videoconferencing, which approximates in-person (face-to-face) encounters in that members can see/hear both verbal and nonverbal communication cues. This is the case for Lucia. She rarely meets in person with any of her group members and uses Microsoft Teams software to set up meetings; this software allows her to see everyone's schedule and invite them to meetings. During the video meetings, they use screensharing so all members can view the same documents. Or if her group members are unavailable to meet at the same time, they then use asynchronous tech tools, like the Teams Channel function, to upload files and exchange messages through a social networking platform, like Yammer.

There are at least three challenges that are unique to small groups who are working virtually to some degree: time zone differences, technology access, and technology use choices. Some experts suggest that the communication problems between virtual group members are related to the number of time zones that separate them. If only a few time zones apart, as is Lucia's situation, members can come to work earlier or later and still have overlapping workdays. If members are separated by many time zones, as in Marek's work, it becomes a much bigger challenge, particularly on Fridays and Mondays, but most groups find a way to work with the geographical distance and time differences. For example, one company with team members in the United States and Australia (a difference of 15 time zones) has a policy that members from each country take turns getting up at 2 a.m. once a month for videoconferencing with members from the other country. The rest of the time, they rely on their social networking platform, like Slack, and email.

Second, virtual small groups may face technology access issues. Lucia has access to very sophisticated communication technology and a full-time IT department in her office. Members of other small groups may have varying access to software tech tools or hardware (computers) or may not have consistent and reliable access to the Internet and, thus, may experience more challenges. This is the case for Marek's small group; Liana in Buenos Aires and Ahmed in Riyadh occasionally have trouble with Internet connections and speed, which makes videoconferencing a bit more challenging. Similarly, college students working in online small group projects report similar concerns and frustration when they encounter communication technologies that are unfamiliar or that malfunction from time to time, experienced by many during the Zoom classes of the pandemic (Blum, 2020).

Third, with increasing variety and sophistication of communication technology tools available, virtual groups often need to make decisions about which media tool to use at particular phases of a project and may even use different tools for similar

DID YOU KNOW?
Virtual Team Technology Tools

Here is a list of eight types digital technologies that can assist virtual groups in communicating, information exchange, scheduling, planning, collaborating, and sharing. Which of these have you used? If you have participated in a virtual group, did any of the tools listed here facilitate the team's work? Can you think of other tools a virtual group could use that are not listed here?

1. **Collaborative suites:** a collection of data management tools that enables info sharing, exchange, and collaboration, such as Google's G Suite (Gmail, Docs, Drive, and Calendar), Microsoft World, and Office365 (Word, Excel, Teams, Outlook, and OneDrive).

2. **Communication tools:** facilitate team member communication including text-based messages, like Slack and Microsoft Teams, as well as video conferencing and face-to-face conversations using tools like Zoom, Microsoft Teams, and Google Chat.

3. **Instant messaging tools:** provide for real-time chats among team members, with tools like Jabber, Grape, Rocket.Chat, Skype, and Mattermost.

4. **Social network tools:** allow for collaborating and interacting with group members, such as Yammer, Chatter, and Jive.

5. **Cloud storage and file sharing tools:** enable secure exchange among group members, such as with Google Drive, OneDrive, and DropBox.

6. **Project management tools:** facilitate group task assignment and scheduling, as with Jira, Trello, Monday, and Asana.

7. **Document co-creation tools:** enable group members to co-create and co-edit documents or visuals in real time via Google Docs, Prezi, Conceptboard, Scribblar, ONLYOFFICE, or Xtensio.

8. **Scheduling tools:** enable groups to schedule common meeting times with group members, using tools like Calendly, Doodle, ScheduleOnce, TimeandDate, HubSpot, and Scheduling.

Adapted from: *Thecouchmanager.com.* (2020, September). https://www.thecouchmanager.com/the-ultimate-list-of-virtual-team-technology-tools/; 10 Essential Tools to Support Your Digital Transformation (N.D.). https://www.lumapps.com/solutions/digital-transformation/digital-transformation-tools/

---

tasks (see *Did You Know?: Virtual Team Technology Tools*) (Handke et al., 2019). Individual group members may prefer one tool over others. For example, Belén, one of Lucia's coworkers, prefers to send iMessages rather than respond to a video call. Some experts suggest that too much video time can be tiring, and for groups working only virtually, once initial goals/expectations are established, later tasks can be accomplished effectively through asynchronous communication, project management tools, and screencasts (Blum, 2020; "Virtual work trends," 2020). Accordingly, it is a good idea for groups to brainstorm on possible communication media, their use, and their effectiveness at the start of their collaboration. Establishing group norms—such as when meetings are particularly desirable, if possible (i.e., at the beginning of the project)—and member preferences for media tools can help manage expectations and guide group member communication (Handke et al., 2019). We will discuss some of the communication challenges of virtual groups throughout the rest of the chapter.

In sum, while these virtual problems may seem only technical (hardware, software issues, time differences), they can present communication challenges. Communication technology issues can hinder smooth communication and lead to misunderstandings and frustrations that can negatively impact group processes like decision making, cohesion, and ultimately group outcomes. We will address these communication issues for both face-to-face and virtual group work in the remainder of the chapter.

With these definitions and distinctions in mind, in the next section we will look at individual communication in small groups.

Journal Prompt 10.2: Defining Small Group Communication
What is a definition of small group communication? What are some differences of a small group and a virtual small group?

Small Group Communication and the Individual: Roles

10.3 **Identify examples of task, relational, and disruptive small group roles.**

The quality of a group depends on the contributions of individual members—so much so that one reason for ineffective groups is the poor communication skills of individual members. Lack of communication among group members can even be disastrous. Poor communication between pilot and copilot has been cited as the primary cause of several deadly airplane crashes. Fortunately, poor teamwork doesn't usually have such disastrous consequences; nevertheless, communication scholar Lawrence Frey (1994) points out that "communication *is* the lifeblood that flows through the veins of groups" (p. x).

To better understand communication processes in small groups, it is helpful to think of its two primary dimensions: task communication and relational communication. Task communication focuses on getting the job done and solving the problem at hand—for example, requesting information or asking for clarification. Relational communication focuses on group maintenance and interpersonal relationships, such as offering encouragement or mediating disagreement. These two types of communication are thoroughly mixed during group interaction; in fact, one statement can fill both functions. When a group is getting bogged down in discussion, one member might encourage the group *and* focus on the task by saying something like "All of these ideas show how creative we are. Which do you think would be the most useful in helping us solve our problem?"

To help you understand how individuals can contribute to (or detract from) the performance of task and relationship communication, we explore the various communication roles that members of small groups perform. We then discuss another important ingredient of small groups—leadership—and in so doing, we present several important theories of leadership. Finally, we'll look at principles and processes that can make small groups effective.

Types of Communication Roles

group roles

The shared expectations group members have regarding each individual's communication behavior in the group.

Every group member plays a variety of roles within a group. **Group roles** describe the shared expectations group members have regarding each individual's communication behavior in the group. These roles can involve task communication or relational communication or both. When you join an established group, you learn these expectations through communication with current members. If all members are new to the group, they rely on their perceptions and beliefs, as well as their group skills and previous group experience, as they work out various role behaviors (Bernier & Stenstrom, 2016).

For example, our friend Mitchell works for a software company. Although the employees of this company are scattered across the country and primarily work at home, they must work together to design software that meets a client's specific needs, meeting virtually from time to time, depending on the particular project goals. Because Mitchell is the expert at writing software programs, he assumes that role. Similarly, Mitchell and Giuliana make sure to follow the advice of Bob, the market researcher who has studied the client's market needs. In this case, each group member knows their roles; they have developed this understanding based on their individual and collective experiences in groups.

Although group roles often evolve as the members work together, sometimes roles are assigned as part of a job description or through group discussion. For example, LaKresha, the chair of her community's Animal Welfare League, always leads the group's discussions because this is one of her responsibilities as chair. Kristie, as secretary of the organization, always takes notes because that is her role. Effective group members contribute by filling roles that are of interest to them and compatible with their skills, but they also fill roles that the group needs at a particular time. Thus, successful small group work depends on task and relational communication, which in turn depends on individuals' effective performance of task and relational roles (Benne & Sheats, 1948). In addition, small group members may perform a third, less productive type of role, which is referred to as a *disruptive*, or *individual-centered role*. Let's look at these three types of roles and how they contribute to or detract from effective group communication.

Task Roles   **Task roles** are directly related to the accomplishment of group goals; they include behaviors such as leading the discussion and taking notes. These communication roles often involve seeking, processing, and evaluating information. A list of task roles is provided in Table 10.1.

Let's explore how task roles function within a group using a case study. Lenore and Jaime were part of a campus task force working to improve campus safety, meeting in person prior to the pandemic and then shifting to Zoom meetings toward the end of their group work. Their small group of seven members met twice a month for several months and discussed the problem and possible solutions. During the discussions, group members filled the various task roles, depending on their particular strengths and interests and the needs of the group, changing roles as needed.

For example, Karin tended to serve as initiator–contributor, proposing new ideas and suggesting that the group look at several dimensions of the problem, such as personal security and the protection of private property. Information seekers, in particular Aidan and Ralph, often asked for clarification of facts or information. Opinion seekers, such as Eliza and Wen Shu, asked how other group members felt about various proposals—say, the potential expense that would be incurred by implementing suggested solutions. In addition, opinion givers responded by sharing how they felt about the expense.

task roles

Roles that are directly related to the accomplishment of group goals.

Table 10.1   Small Group Task Roles

Task Role	Description	Example
Initiator–contributor	Proposes new ideas or approaches to group problem solving	"How about if we look at campus safety as issues of personal security *and* protection of private property?"
Information seeker	Asks for information or clarification	"How many instances of theft occur on our campus each year?"
Opinion seeker	Asks for opinions from others	"How do you feel about charging students a fee that would pay for extra police protection?"
Information giver	Provides facts, examples, and other relevant evidence	"My research showed that other campuses have solved similar problems by increasing numbers of campus police and improving lighting."
Opinion giver	Offers beliefs or opinions	"I'm often concerned about my personal safety when I walk to certain campus parking lots at night."
Elaborator	Explains ideas, offers examples to clarify ideas	"If the university had increased security patrols, my bike might not have been stolen last month."
Coordinator	Shows relationships among ideas presented	"Installing new light fixtures might improve personal safety and reduce thefts on campus."
Orienter	Summarizes what has been discussed and keeps group focused	"We've now discussed several aspects of personal safety; maybe it's time to turn our attention to issues of protection of private property."
Evaluator–critic	Judges evidence and conclusions of group	"I think we may be overestimating the problem of theft."
Energizer	Motivates group members to greater productivity	"Wow! We've gotten a lot accomplished this evening, and we only have a few more points to discuss."
Procedural technician	Performs logistical tasks—distributing paper, arranging seating, etc.	"If all four of us sit on the same side of the table, we'll be able to read the diagrams without having to pass them around."
Recorder	Keeps a record of group activities and progress	"We have 10 more minutes; let's see if we can get through our agenda in time to review any questions."

SOURCE: Benne, K. D., & Sheats, P. (1948). Functional roles of group members. *Journal of Social Issues, 4,* 41–49.

As information givers, several members provided statistics about the security problem so that the group could know the extent of the problem. They also provided information on how other campuses had solved similar problems—by installing better lighting, and having volunteer "security teams" patrol campus. Serving as elaborator, Lenore told about having her bike stolen and suggested that having an increased number of campus police might have prevented the theft. Jaime often served as coordinator and orienter, showing how various ideas related to each other, whereas other members filled the role of evaluator–critic, carefully evaluating various ideas. The procedural technician made sure that everyone had paper and pens when they met in person and, later when the group met virtually, issued the invites and hosted the meeting. A designated recorder took notes and posted them later, and one member often served as the energizer, infusing interest into the group when attention and focus lagged.

Not every group has members who can fill each of these roles and certainly not with the same level of skill. But the more effectively these roles are filled, the better the group will function and the more likely it is that goals will be met.

relational roles

Roles that help establish a group's social atmosphere.

Relational Roles   In contrast with task roles, **relational roles** help establish a group's social atmosphere (see Table 10.2). Members who encourage others to talk or mediate disagreements are filling relational roles. Group members can fill both task and relational roles, depending on the needs of the group. For example, in Lenore and Jaime's group, one member sent out emails to get the group organized (task role), and he also sent congratulatory texts after the group did a Zoom presentation to the student governing council (relational role). There is some evidence that relational roles are particularly important in highly virtual small groups (Abrams et al., 2015). How do you identify with or establish trust virtually with someone you've never seen or interacted with before? For this reason, some virtual groups also communicate via social media to increase the "getting to know you" phase of virtual group development. In addition, virtual group members may fail to pick up on subtle nonverbal cues from other group members (i.e., signals of confusion or dissatisfaction) during videoconferences (Blum, 2020); thus, sensitive observations and gatekeeper, harmonizer, and encourager roles (described in Table 10.2) become particularly important in virtual group work.

Table 10.2   Small Group Relational Roles

Role	Description	Example
Encourager	Offers praise and acceptance of others' ideas	"That's a great idea; tell us more about it."
Harmonizer	Mediates disagreement among group members	"I think you and Ron are seeing two sides of the same coin."
Compromiser	Attempts to resolve conflicts by trying to find an acceptable solution to disagreements	"I think both of you have great ideas. Let's see how we can combine them."
Gatekeeper	Encourages less talkative group members to participate	"Maria, you haven't said much about this idea. How do you feel about it?"
Expediter	Tries to limit lengthy contributions of other group members	"Martin, you've told us what you think about most of the ideas. Why don't we hear from some of the other members?"
Standard setter	Helps to set standards and goals for the group	"I think our goal should be to submit a comprehensive plan for campus safety to the dean by the end of this semester."
Group observer	Keeps records of the group's process and uses the information that is gathered to evaluate the group's procedures	"We completed a similar report last semester. Let's refer to it before we spend time working on this new one."
Follower	Goes along with the suggestions and ideas of group members; serves as an audience in group discussion and decision making	"I like that idea. That's a really good point."

SOURCE: Benne, K. D., & Sheats, P. (1948). Functional roles of group members. *Journal of Social Issues, 4,* 41–49.

During their discussion of campus safety, some members served as encouragers (praising and accepting others' ideas). Others served as harmonizers (mediating disagreement) or compromisers (attempting to find solutions to disagreements). As communication majors, Lenore and Jaime paid close attention to how the discussion was going and, when necessary, served as gatekeepers, encouraging participation from less talkative members, or as expediters, gently limiting the contributions of more talkative members. Overall, the group met its goal of addressing the problems of campus security partly because members effectively filled both task and relational roles as needed.

How can you apply this information to improve your own skills as a group member? First, try to keep these roles in mind during your own group work, whether in person or online, noting who is playing which roles and whether some essential role is missing. Once you've made this assessment, you can try to fill in the missing role behaviors. For example, if a group seems "stuck" and keeps rehashing the same ideas, you might try the role of initiator–contributor or information giver. Or if one person in the group is dominating the discussion and talking constantly, you might assume the expeditor or gatekeeper role and try to balance out the contributions of the various members.

Disruptive Roles   **Disruptive or individual-centered roles** tend to be dysfunctional to the group process (see Table 10.3). Group members serving in these roles focus more on their own *individual* interests and needs than on those of the group. Thus, they tend to be uninvolved, negative, aggressive, or constantly joking. A group member who consistently assumes one or more negative individual roles can undermine the group's commitment to goals and its sense of cohesion—ultimately resulting in decreased group performance and productivity. This is why it is so important for other group members to be aware of effective task and relational behaviors and to demonstrate them (Braun et al., 2020).

A common individual-centered role is the joker. When another member contributes, the joker always has to "one up" the comment with a joke or a story, constantly moving the group off-task. Here, a member filling the orienter role can help the group refocus on the task at hand. Another individual-centered role that often hinders effectiveness

disruptive or individual-centered roles

Roles that focus more on individuals' own interests and needs than on those of the group.

Critical Thinking Prompt
Think about group experiences you've had. Which task communication roles do you tend to fill? Which relational communication roles? Which communication roles would you like to fill? How flexible have you been in your ability to fill various task and relational roles?

Table 10.3   Small Group Individual Roles

Role	Description	Example
Aggressor	Attacks other group members, tries to take credit for someone else's contribution	"That's a stupid idea. It would never work."
Blocker	Is generally negative and stubborn for no apparent reason	"This whole task is pointless. I don't see why we have to do it."
Recognition seeker	Calls excessive attention to their personal achievements	"This is how we dealt with campus security when I was at Harvard."
Self-confessor	Uses the group as an audience to report non-group-related personal feelings	"I'm so upset at my boyfriend. We had a big fight last night."
Joker	Lacks involvement in the group's process, distracts others by telling stories and jokes	"Hey did you hear the one about . . . ?"
Dominator	Asserts control by manipulating group members or tries to take over group; may use flattery or assertive behavior to dominate the conversation	"I know my plan will work because I was a police officer."
Help seeker	Tries to gain unwarranted sympathy from group; often expresses insecurity or feelings of low self-worth	"You probably won't like this idea, either, but I think we should consider contracting out our campus security."
Special-interest pleader	Works to serve an individual need rather than focusing on group interests	"Because I only have daycare on Wednesdays, can we meet on Wednesday afternoons?"

SOURCE: Benne, K. D., & Sheats, P. (1948). Functional roles of group members. *Journal of Social Issues, 4*, 41–49.

in student projects is the dominator, who insists on doing things their way, and the blocker, a member who is negative for no apparent reason, as was the case for one of our students (see *It Happened to Me: Tiacko*).

You may also be familiar with the self-confessor, the help seeker, and the special-interest pleader; all these individual-centered roles take up a lot of airtime in unproductive conversation. How can you deal with these types of roles? As illustrated by Tiacko's experience, group members can deal with critical group members by assuming a relational communication role—complimenting other group members for their ideas (i.e., encourager role) and counteracting criticism with positive feedback, such as "I have to say I thought Tanya's idea was really intriguing. Let's look at how we might implement it in our project." A single member's

It Happened to Me
Tiacko

In one of my classes, we had to complete a group project. One of our members dominated the discussion and was always very critical. No matter what contributions we made to the project, he always found a way to criticize them. Nothing was good enough for him. Fortunately, we also had some very skilled communicators in our group, and they limited his impact on the group by always countering his negative remarks with more positive comments.

criticism has less force when several members note the high quality of a contribution. In general, probably the best strategies to deal with these disruptive roles come from those relational roles that help the group refocus on the task: the gatekeeper and expeditor roles. Several task roles may also prove helpful—for example, the initiator–contributor, who may start a new line of conversation; the orienter, who helps the group see where they are in accomplishing their task; or the opinion seeker, to solicit other supportive opinions, contradicting some individual roles' negativity.

Any group member may serve in any of these roles at any time. In a successful group, like Jaime and Lenore's task force, members play various roles as needed, with minimal indulgence in the individual roles. Some group members play only to their strengths and consistently serve in one or two particular roles. This is fine as long as all the needed roles are being filled. As we'll see, some of these challenges can be facilitated by a group leader, the topic we tackle next.

Journal Prompt 10.3: Task and Relational Roles
What is the difference between task and relational role behaviors in small group communication? How are they related to each other?

Small Group Communication and the Individual: Leadership

10.4 Describe five theories of group leadership.

A group or organization's success is often directly related to the presence of good leadership, online or in person, and leadership should be a concern for all of us because it is not just a quality for those with formal subordinates. Rather, leadership occurs in many forms and contexts; as one expert says, leadership can take place "during a sales call, a customer service response, a family decision or a meeting with friends" (Gollent, 2007). As we describe leadership characteristics and theories, think about the ways in which you may play leadership roles in the various groups and organizations in which you are a member.

Definition of Leadership

Organizational behavior scholar Richard Daft defines leadership as "an influence relationship among leaders and followers who intend real changes and outcomes that reflect their shared purposes" (2015, p. 5). Perhaps the most important element in this definition is the idea of an influence relationship. Influence does not just reside in one person but rather is a process that involves relationships between leaders and followers (Daft, 2015; Northouse, 2012).

The second element in Daft's definition of leadership involves the intention to change; this distinguishes it from the concept of management, which is more about order and stability. In addition, Daft refers to outcomes that reflect the shared purposes and vision of leaders and followers. For example, Martin Luther King Jr. built a shared vision of a society in which people would be judged by their character, not their color; he mobilized his followers to act via nonviolent protest in realizing this vision. Similarly, today's ordinary citizens and students can rally others around a strongly held idea of change.

It Happened to Me
Martha

I've worked at several different organizations in different sectors, but I have found that the most important thing that leaders, bosses, or supervisors can do is give their subordinates a sense of empowerment. When you're given a task by your boss, you want her to trust that you'll do a good job—you want her to believe in your abilities and give you the space to succeed. I couldn't work for someone who questioned everything I did or watched my every move.

Leadership experts describe the essence of good leadership as the capacity to "energize" potential followers by *connecting* with people at a personal, sometimes emotional, level so that they become motivated, engaged, and empowered to help achieve the shared vision (Denhardt & Denhardt, 2004; Matha & Boehm, 2008). These elements are exemplified by the story our student tells about her boss in *It Happened to Me: Martha*.

Because followers are individuals with their own differences and each leadership situation is unique, there is no one "right" way of communicating nor one way of leading. However, researchers have identified five theories that explain effective leaders: trait theory, functional theory, style theory, transformational leadership theory, and servant leadership theory.

Critical Thinking Prompt
Consider the definition of leadership provided in this chapter. In which of your relationships and everyday activities do you provide leadership? In which contexts (school, home, extracurricular activities) are you most likely to provide leadership?

Trait Theory

Probably the oldest theory concerning leadership in the communication field is **trait theory** (Stogdill, 1974). Trait theory suggests that leaders are born. For example, people associate height with leadership ability (Judge & Cable, 2004), some personality traits (extroversion, openness to experience, agreeableness), and intelligence (Judge et al., 2002, 2004).

trait theory
A theory that assumes leaders are born, not made.

A more recent advocate of trait theory, leadership expert Fred E. Fiedler, proposed the "Contingency Model" of leadership (Fiedler, 1981; Fiedler & Garcia, 1987). In his view, a leader's strength tended toward either relationship or task orientation, and he emphasized that each of these two types of traits was effective in particular situations. A task-oriented style is effective under extreme conditions—in natural disasters or in uncertain situations, like medical emergencies (Van der Haar et al., 2017). Relationship-oriented leaders are more effective when leader-member relations are good and members are able to work independently.

Many examples challenge the trait approach to leadership. In recent years, a number of people have developed leadership qualities out of a deep motivation to make the world a better place. For example, in 2018, Greta Thunberg, a young Swedish girl, inspired (led) thousands of people around the world, including world leaders, to fight for issues of climate change, which she feels requires international cooperation and collaboration (Sengupta, 2020). American undergraduate Sindhura Citineni, when confronted by the appalling statistics of world hunger, negotiated with her university to sell several simple food items in the cafeteria—called Hunger Lunch— and gave part of the revenue to hunger-relief work. She then led a group of students who expanded that project into Nourish International, now a nonprofit organization that connects college students from universities around the United States to development projects abroad (http://nourishinternational.org). As you see, although there are some personality characteristics associated with good leadership, most experts now reject the trait theory notion that leaders are born, not made.

It should also be noted that some of the world's most well-known leaders were reserved and rather introverted. See *Did You Know?: Introverts Can Be Leaders, Too.*

Functional Theory

functional (situational) theory
A theory that assumes that leadership behaviors can be learned.

A second approach to analyzing leadership, the **functional (situational) theory**, stands in direct contrast to the trait approach. Unlike trait theory, which assumes leadership is innate, this theory assumes that leadership behaviors can be learned, even by group members who are not "leadership types." Functional theory assumes that, in self-managed groups, whatever the group needs at a particular time can be supplied by a set of behaviors any group member can contribute (Benne & Sheats, 1948; Pavitt, 1999). Thus, this theory argues that the leader can change from time to time, depending on the changing needs of the group. And leaders can emerge by demonstrating skillful and effective task and relational behaviors. However, experts caution that any relational or task role leadership can be ineffective if excessive. For instance, an individual who takes charge of the decision making for the group or setting goals for others too much may be seen as too controlling. Similarly, excessive relational behaviors can become intrusive and unwelcoming, like constantly seeking input from group members who might not be willing to make or comfortable making important decisions for the group (Mitchell et al., 2019).

According to functional theory, a group does not need a designated leader; rather, any group member can serve as the leader at any particular time by filling the required role. For example, the leader can fill task roles when the group needs direction, then step into relational roles when group members understand the task but need encouragement. Occasionally, no leadership is needed, such as when the short- and long-term purpose is clear and group members are working well independently.

DID YOU KNOW?
Introverts Can Be Leaders, Too

Conventional wisdom holds that leaders should be outgoing and extroverted, enjoy meeting new people and making new friends. However, a book by author Susan Cain questions this view. What do you think? Do you think extroverts make better leaders? Have you encountered an effective leader who seemed introverted? Which category do you tend to fall into? Take the quiz at http://www.the-powerofintroverts.com/quiet-quiz-are-you-an-introvert/ to find out.

In her book *Quiet: The Power of Introverts in a World That Can't Stop Talking*, author Susan Cain argues that the belief that only extroverts make good leaders reflects a historical shift in early-twentieth-century society—from a culture of character to a culture of personality. She suggests that this belief is changing and that now, half the population—introverts—are viewed much more positively. In fact, she points out that the traits associated with extroversion sometimes lead to unproductive behaviors and poor leadership: risk taking, dominance, and thoughtless behavior. She encourages extroverts to tone it down a little and learn to listen, suggesting that everyone should "embrace the power of quiet." Business experts, building on her suggestions, note that some of the most influential leaders have been introverts: Abraham Lincoln, Eleanor Roosevelt, Warren Buffet, and Bill Gates. They suggest that introverts and extroverts can learn from each other, each contributing their strengths to make a stronger workforce. Introverted workers bring thoughtfulness and critique to issues, and they are more likely to listen to others and apply suggestions made by others, but they need time and quiet spaces to process. Extroverts are good at inspiring otherwise uninspired workers and need opportunities to mix it up with others.

SOURCES: Cain, S. (2013). *Quiet: The power of introverts in a world that can't stop talking.* Broadway Books.

Moore, K. (2012). Introverts no longer the quiet followers of extroverts. *Forbes.com.* http://www.forbes.com/sites/karlmoore/2012/08/22/introverts-no-longer-the-quiet-followers-of-extroverts/

A related notion is **shared leadership**, also called *collaborative* or *distributed leadership*. Here the functional leadership approach is extended to an organizational level where group relationships become more of a partnership in an organization (MacNeil & McClanahan, 2005). This style of leadership can occur either as an explicitly stated objective or may simply emerge if the designated leader is too passive or simply refuses to provide leadership (Kramer, 2006). However it occurs, the requirements for this kind of leadership are a balance of power in which:

- all members are equal partners;
- all share a common purpose or goal;
- all share responsibility for the work of the group (take an active role and are accountable for completing their individual contribution);
- all have respect for the person—and skills and ideas that each brings to the group; and
- all work together in complex, real-world situations.

Style Theory

A third approach to analyzing leadership asserts that a leader's manner or **style** of leading a group determines their success. Further, this theory describes three common styles of leadership: authoritarian, democratic, and laissez-faire.

An **authoritarian leader** takes charge and has a high level of intellect and expertise, making all the decisions and dictating strategies and work tasks. This type of leadership is appropriate in military, sports, or crisis situations, or when time for discussion is short or when the stakes are high. For example, military organizations have a highly authoritarian structure, and in battle, the chain of command must be rigorously followed because there's no time for discussion or trial and error. Similarly, medical teams in an emergency department generally follow authoritarian leadership—one person, the doctor, directs the others in what needs to be done (Van der Haar et al., 2017).

Democratic leadership is the style we are most familiar with, and the one that seems to work best in many group situations. A **democratic leader's** style is characterized by a great deal of input from group members; the qualities of this leader are best summarized by Lao-tse (550 B.C.E.): "A good leader is one who talks little; when his work is done, his aim fulfilled, they will all say 'We did this ourselves'" (cited in Foels et al., 2000, p. 677). In this style, group discussion determines all policies, strategies, and division of labor. Members are free to assume a variety of roles, to contribute when appropriate, and to share leadership.

In contrast, some small group situations call for a **laissez-faire** style. This style is characterized by complete freedom for the group in making decisions. The leader participates minimally and may supply materials and information when asked, but makes no attempt to evaluate or influence the discussion. The laissez-faire style may work well when little is at stake, as in some social groups like book clubs or gourmet clubs (Barge, 1989).

shared leadership
A type of leadership style in which functional leadership is extended to an organizational level; all members are equal partners and share responsibility for the work of the group.

style theory
Theory that asserts that a leader's manner or style determines their success.

authoritarian leader
Leader who takes charge, makes all the decisions, and dictates strategies and work tasks.

democratic leader
Leader whose style is characterized by considerable input from group members.

laissez-faire
A leadership style characterized by complete freedom for the group in making decisions.

▼ Tony Dungy served as a head coach for 13 seasons with the Tampa Bay Buccaneers and Indianapolis Colts and was the first African American coach to win a Super Bowl. As a leader, he had to make split-second decisions during football games.

Transformational Leadership Theory

transformational leadership
A leadership style that empowers group members to work independently from the leader by encouraging group cohesion.

A relatively recent theory, **transformational leadership** theory, emphasizes the importance of *personalized relationships* in leadership and group cohesion. That is, such leaders recognize unique strengths and capabilities of followers and, through their relationships with followers, inspire, motivate, and empower them to develop their full potential and work beyond standard expectations (Jung & Sosik, 2002). Transformational leaders also have high moral and ethical standards and a strong vision for the future, challenge the status quo, and encourage and inspire innovation (Bono & Judge, 2004). According to leadership experts, the style has been routinely praised and "recognized for its positive influence on group processes and performance for many years" (Eisenberg et al., 2019, p. 350).

charismatic leadership
A leadership style in which extremely self-confident leaders inspire unusual dedication to themselves by relying on their strong personalities and charm.

Transformational leadership is sometimes confused with **charismatic leadership**, a style proposed by scholars in political science and religious studies. Like transformational leaders, charismatic leaders have a strong belief in their vision. They are also extremely self-confident and able to inspire great dedication and loyalty in their followers. Followers of charismatic (and transformational) leaders are often willing to set high (sometimes unrealistic) objectives and often make tremendous sacrifices, ultimately achieving more than was expected or deemed possible (Rowold & Heinitz, 2007).

As you might imagine, strong communication skills (compelling vocal style, listening skills, ability to motivate and persuade) are central to both charismatic and transformational leadership (Levine et al., 2010). However, as shown in Table 10.4, there are important differences between charismatic and transformational leaders. Specifically, charismatic leaders rely on their strong personalities and charm to create loyalty to themselves, whereas transformational leaders build relationships and strive to create loyalty to the group or organization, not to the individual leader. Thus, when a transformational leader exits the group, the organization is more likely to thrive because member commitment is to the group. When charismatic leaders leave, the group may falter because the individuals' commitment is to the leader, not to one another. And unlike transformational leaders who manage to inspire their followers for a long time, charismatic leadership may be relatively short-lived because they may also be autocratic and self-serving, and followers may become disillusioned (Daft, 2015; Pavitt, 1999). In fact, charismatic leadership can have disastrous results: Hitler and Mussolini, for example, were charismatic leaders. Although such leaders inspire trust, faith, and belief in themselves, there is no guarantee that their vision or mission will be correct, ethical, or successful.

Servant Leadership Theory

servant leadership
A leadership style that seeks to ensure that other people's highest-priority needs are being served to increase teamwork and personal involvement.

The idea of **servant leadership** was introduced to organizations through Robert Greenleaf's 1970 essay "The Servant as Leader." The concept was further popularized by writers such as Stephen Covey, whose 1989 bestseller *The Seven Habits of Highly Effective People* made a major impact in the business world.

According to Greenleaf, a servant leader must excel at 10 characteristics:

* awareness
* listening

Table 10.4 **Transformational and Charismatic Leaders**

Transformational	Charismatic
Strong vision	Strong vision
High expectations for followers	High expectations for followers
Builds relationships	Relies on strong personality
Creates loyalty to organization	Creates loyalty to self
Enduring inspiration	Leadership may be short-lived

- empathizing
- persuasion
- conceptualization
- foresight
- stewardship
- healing
- commitment to the growth of others
- building community

You will notice that most of these 10 characteristics are communication skills. Servant leadership emphasizes collaboration, trust, and the ethical use of power. The theory proposes that at heart, the individual is a servant first and makes a conscious decision to lead to better serve others, not to increase their own power. The objective is to enhance the growth of individuals in the organization and to increase teamwork and personal involvement (Greenleaf, 1970/1991, 2016).

The servant leadership style has recently gained a great deal of credence, and its effectiveness has been studied in a variety of organizational settings (tourism, pharmaceutical, social work, sports industries) in various countries, including China, France, and Pakistan (Cater & Young, 2020). The studies have shown that servant leadership has many positive effects on group cohesion, task performance, creativity, and job satisfaction, leading multimillion- and multibillion-dollar companies, including Southwest Airlines, TDIndustries, and Starbucks, to embrace this leadership type (Stauffer & Maxwell, 2020). In addition, several studies have found that servant leadership may be more congruent and reflective of the leadership behaviors of women (Sims & Morris, 2018).

Leadership in Virtual Groups

Does leadership differ in virtual groups? Some evidence suggests that leadership is particularly important in some virtual groups: the effective leader needs to ensure that expectations are set and understood, combating the *out of sight/out of mind* problem of some virtual work (Bakken, 2018). That is, a leader needs to pay particular attention to the relational aspects of group processes in virtual groups that rarely use videoconferencing—and thus miss out on the rich verbal and nonverbal immediacy cues so important to facilitating interpersonal relationships and group cohesion. You may think, then, that leadership styles that are characterized by personal relationships would be less effective in these types of virtual groups, and at least one study found this to be true. This study hypothesized that transformational leaders' effectiveness would be diminished in virtual groups, since the core of transformational leadership—*personalized relationships*—would be difficult to achieve in some of these groups. The researchers studied 55 innovation teams ranging in geographic dispersion in 200 industrial R&D companies and discovered that indeed transformational leadership was less effective overall than other leadership styles in virtual teams. They suggested that transformational group leaders in virtual groups should not only consider being proactive in providing structure and a clear direction but also develop ways to enable group members *themselves* to be more involved in regulating group processes and performance (Eisenberg et al., 2019).

More specifically, experts suggest that leaders of highly virtual groups, with any leadership style, have several challenges that *may* be more difficult: establishing effective and high-quality relationships with group members, establishing a culture of communication, and ensuring that task goals are met. Establishing relationships of trust with group members can be realized by having regular one-on-one meetings with group members, by showing concern and empathy, and by encouraging each group member's development and self-expression. A culture of communication is achieved by making sure group members are communicating regularly, setting clear expectations about how

Journal Prompt 10.4: Group Leadership
What is the definition of group leadership, and why is leadership important in small group communication?

the group is to communicate (frequency and technology tools to be used), and encouraging consensus and a shared team cohesion (Eisenberg et al., 2019). Some of these challenges can be met by holding regular virtual meetings.

Effective Small Group Communication

10.5 Describe the characteristics of communication that occur during the four phases of small group decision making.

Now that we have described the important role of communication in effective leadership and various theories of group leadership, we are ready to ask the question: What communication behaviors are necessary for effective small group interaction? The answer seems to be that effective groups maintain a balance of task and relational communication, and the sequence of each appears to be more important than the relative amount of each. For example, after an intense period of task talk, group members might defuse their tension with positive social, or relational, talk and then return to task talk (Pavitt, 1999).

Effective Small Group Communication Practices

What types of communication lead to effective sequencing of task and relational communication? And how can members best use these skills when the primary goal of a small group is to solve a particular problem? Experts find that the following four communication processes lead to task effectiveness and member satisfaction (relational effectiveness) in small groups in many situations—whether a group project in a *Fortune* 500 company, a fund-raising committee for a charity organization, or a small group assignment in a communication course (Oetzel, 1998, 2001, 2005).

1. *Equal participation*: The fact is that if everyone participates, the group can consider a wider variety of ideas, attend to more aspects of the topic, and thus make better decisions. Furthermore, group members who do not contribute feel less commitment to the group outcomes and implementation and may ultimately sabotage the group effort (Lewis et al., 2010). It is especially important to encourage participation in online group work because quiet or silent members can go unnoticed and the cause of the nonparticipation may be the result of many different reasons. As a group member, you can monitor the participation of all members, playing the expeditor role to prevent talkative or domineering members from talking too much and the gatekeeper role in drawing out those nonparticipating members.

2. *A consensus decision-making style*: Members participate in and agree with the decisions made by the group. Although it is not always possible to have every group member agree with every decision, nonparticipating members and members who disagree with group decisions can have negative impacts on group outcomes—as described previously. Therefore, it is in the best interests of the group to get buy-in from as many members as possible. As a group member, you can facilitate agreement by encouraging participation of all members, by showing how ideas are related (coordinator role), and by encouraging a cooperative conflict style.

3. *A cooperative conflict style*: The group manages conflict by integrating all parties' interests. As we will see, some conflict is an inevitable part of small group discussion, and when handled well, it can be productive in sharpening issues and getting out various positions. For now, let's just say that effective groups approach conflict in a cooperative rather than a competitive, divisive manner. This means that the goal in a cooperative approach is to try to turn the conflict into a communal problem where all members work to their mutual benefit, making the task easier and less stressful (Lamberts-Berndt & Blight, 2016). A little later in the chapter, we will provide more specific strategies for dealing with group conflict in a cooperative manner.

4. *A respectful communication style*: Group members demonstrate that other members are valued and important. How is this accomplished? Most often, members show respect by communicating a sense of mutual support and acceptance. This means using the verbal and nonverbal strategies that strengthen interpersonal relationships—described in other chapters in this book.

How can members best use these skills when the primary goal of a small group is to solve a particular problem? One of the great communication challenges for groups is to pinpoint the problem and all its possible solutions. In this section, we'll first describe a five-step agenda that problem-solving groups have found useful. Second, we'll examine how decision making occurs in small groups, including a negative group process—groupthink. Finally, we'll describe the characteristics of discussions in small groups whose members are separated geographically and, in particular, the role technology can play in them.

Dewey Sequence of Problem Solving   A danger in problem-solving groups is jumping immediately to a solution, and one useful tool for avoiding a premature and incomplete solution is to develop and follow a sequence or agenda (Chahine et al., 2017); one of the best known is "Dewey's Reflective Thinking Model," developed by educator John Dewey (Cragan & Wright, 1999, p. 97). Two points are central to using an agenda effectively, and at first they may sound contradictory. First, researchers have found that most problem-solving groups have less conflict and a more consistent focus when they follow formal procedures (Klocke, 2007). Second, successful groups do not necessarily solve all problems in strict sequential order; they may take a variety of paths (Schultz, 1999). In general, then, groups benefit from keeping the agenda in mind, but members should realize that they may have to cycle back and forth between phases before reaching a solution.

We previously discussed the example of a campus task force working to improve campus safety. Let's return to that example and see how that group might follow the five-step problem-solving agenda and the recommendations for effective communication at each step.

Step 1. *Define and Delineate the Problem.* The first step in solving a problem is to make sure that everyone in the group understands it in the same way. After all, the problem can't be solved unless group members know what it is (and is not). On the campus security task force case study, the group members were successful in part because they agreed on the definition of the problem. They decided their problem was twofold: (1) the personal security of students in dorms and while walking on campus and (2) the protection of students' personal property. They decided that they would not address the security of classroom and office equipment because they were primarily a student group. This helped them narrow the focus and set limits for the discussion of solutions.

If you were a member of this problem-solving group, what communication roles might you use to improve the group's effectiveness?

Step 2. *Analyze the Problem.* In some ways, this is the most important phase of the agenda because it determines the direction of potential solutions (Hirokawa & Salazar, 1999). Group members must look at all sides of the problem. To do so, they answer questions such as "Who is affected by the problem? How widespread is it?" In the case of the campus security team, the group had to gather data on the exact nature of security problems—the frequency of burglaries, rapes, assaults, and robberies on campus; where and when these incidents were occurring; and what consequences the incidents had. However, a word of caution is in order. In some cases, too much analysis can result in **analysis paralysis** and prevent a group from moving toward a solution (Rothwell, 2019). Our campus security group, for example, could continue to gather statistics, interview people about the problem, and discuss the problem—and never move on to possible solutions.

Step 3. *Identify Alternative Solutions.* One challenge at this stage is to avoid rushing to premature solutions; instead, the group should consider several possible solutions. One way to make sure that many solutions are considered is to **brainstorm**, generating as many ideas as possible without critiquing them. However, it turns out that the types of ideas generated depend on the length of time devoted to brainstorming. That is, the most feasible, but not necessarily the most original, ideas are generated quite quickly (in one study in less than 2 minutes), whereas the more creative and original ideas take longer. Experts suggest that groups can save some time by deciding early on how they define the "best" ideas for their particular project—as most feasible or most creative (Johnson & D'Lauro, 2018). By brainstorming, the campus security group put forth a wide range of possible solutions, including putting up more lighting, increasing the number of campus police, and helping students to register their private property (bikes, computers, stereo equipment, and so on) so that stolen property could be traced. Some solutions were more creative, including suggestions to eliminate foliage where assailants could hide, to sell wristband tracking devices to students, to place guard dogs in dormitories, and to have 24/7 volunteer security details in the dorms.

Step 4. *Evaluate Proposed Solutions.* Evaluating proposed solutions involves establishing evaluation criteria. The campus security task force, for example, identified three criteria for its solutions: They had to be economically feasible, logistically feasible, and likely to solve the problem of campus security. With these criteria in mind, the task force had a basis for evaluating each solution. This stage is critical, but it can be difficult. If members are tired or frustrated by all the work they've already done, they may jump to conclusions. However, if they keep to the agenda and carefully consider each alternative, they will quickly reject some solutions and find others attractive. According to one study, a strong positive relationship exists between a group's decision-making performance and members' satisfaction with alternatives chosen (Hirokawa & Salazar, 1999).

Step 5. *Choose the Best Solution.* Although this step may seem redundant, choosing the best solution(s) is not the same as evaluating all proposed solutions. Here it is especially important that everyone participates and buys into the solution, and decision-making procedures are most critical.

The problem-solving agenda is a specific format or set of guidelines that task groups can follow to ensure high-quality solutions. As groups progress through the stages, however, they will need to make multiple decisions. For example, during stage four, the evaluation stage, the group will need to decide what the appropriate criteria are for evaluating proposed solutions, whether they will evaluate all, or just some, of the proposed solutions, and how they will manage differences of opinion regarding the value of proposed solutions. To help you understand the decision-making process that occurs throughout the problem-solving agenda, we explore the *process* of decision making in the next section.

analysis paralysis
Potential pitfall in small group interaction; occurs when excessive analysis prevents a group from moving toward a solution.

brainstorm
To generate as many ideas as possible without critiquing them.

Decision-Making Phases   How do small groups arrive at good decisions? Are there specific communication processes that can lead to good decisions? What are some warning signs of unproductive decision making? Is conflict a necessary part of the group decision-making process, or should it be avoided? These are questions we'll tackle in this section. As you can imagine, there is no one recipe for effective decision making. However, there are several phases that seem to represent the communication that occurs in effective problem-solving groups: orientation, conflict, emergence, and reinforcement (Wheelan et al., 2003).

Before describing these phases, we should note that most groups do not proceed through them in an orderly, linear fashion. Rather, they may cycle through the first phase twice before moving to the next phase, or they may revert back to the conflict phase after reaching the final, emergence phase (Poole, 1983). With these thoughts in mind, let's look at the four phases individually.

Phase 1. *Orientation.*   During this phase of decision making, group members usually orient themselves to the problem and to each other (if they have just met). Uncertainty at this stage is common and is referred to as **primary tension**. For example, as a group member, you might wonder how the group is going to function. As it turns out, setting positive expectations for group performance early on is very important as they have a self-fulfilling prophecy function—positive expectations here usually result in positive group outcomes (Sleesman et al., 2018).

primary tension
The uncertainty commonly felt in the beginning phase of decision making.

You may also wonder about the relational aspect of the group processes: Are you going to like the other members? Will you all get along, or will you clash? You may also experience uncertainty about the task you are to undertake: Will everyone contribute equally? Will the work get done efficiently and on time? In *It Happened to Me: Kirstin,* one of our students describes a relational problem that emerged at the beginning of her group project and that contributed to the tension the group felt as they began their talk. As you can see, she played an important relational role as a gatekeeper in encouraging the nonparticipating members to communicate and as a harmonizer in helping the group members work through a situation that seemed well on its way to becoming a conflict situation.

It Happened to Me
Kirstin

Being the only communication major in our group, I immediately noticed some problems. The nonverbal cues from two members contradicted their verbal messages. They rolled their eyes or turned their bodies away from the group when they were asked to do a task. When someone asked what was wrong, those two replied, "Nothing." I knew this did not bode well for the group, so I shared some of my communication skills and knowledge. I encouraged the two nonparticipating members to contribute and asked them if anything was wrong. They told us they were worried because they'd had a bad experience in an earlier group project. We talked about how we all needed to pull together. I was kind of a cheerleader for the group. So we got through this, and the group arrived at a decision and completed the task without any major conflict.

Communication at this phase is generally polite, tentative, and focused on reducing uncertainty and ambiguity through clarification and agreement. The importance of the orientation phase is that many relational and task norms are set for the future. Fortunately for Kirstin's group, she realized the importance of group communication and got the group off to a good start.

Regardless of norms that they establish, groups often experience recurring primary tension if they meet over an extended period. For example, at the beginning of each meeting, group members may need to spend time reconnecting and reviewing their views on the task. In response, then, a group member filling the orienter role might summarize what has been accomplished at the most recent meetings, and the recorder could read back minutes or notes from the last meeting.

Phase 2. *Conflict.*   The conflict phase in decision making is characterized by **secondary (recurring) tension**. This phase usually occurs after group members become acquainted, after some norms and expectations are set, and when decision alternatives are to be addressed.

secondary (recurring) tension
Conflict or tension found in the second or conflict phase of the decision-making process.

As members become more relaxed, this phase of their communication becomes more animated and honest. Members may interrupt each other, talk loudly, and try on group roles. Some may try to dominate, push their own agendas, and form coalitions in an effort to increase their influence; others may engage in side conversations as they lose their focus on the decision at hand. It is especially important at this time to follow the suggestions for effective group communication mentioned previously: equal participation, consensus decision making, and respectful communication. In fact, experts suggest assigning members explicit roles such as "decision-maker advisor," someone who monitors and encourages information giving (van Swol, 2009).

We should note here that concerning conflicts in a virtual group, the online environment is a double-edged sword. On the one hand, virtual groups can experience less bad relationship conflict because members are usually more focused on their work and less on interpersonal relationships. However, for virtual groups that have less video work (which can help build interpersonal relationships, trust, and empathy), task-related conflict may deteriorate into relationship conflicts, which are more likely to escalate (Ferrazzi, 2012), possibly because, as we will discuss in Chapter 14, people seem to have less restraint in their online messaging communication. (We've all probably experienced nasty exchanges on Instagram and TikTok that would not occur in person.) For these reasons, the owner of Mitchell's (software) company (described earlier) encourages his team to videoconference when possible and flies everyone out to Los Angeles periodically so they can work together offline and build trusting relationships (Martinic et al., 2012). They also have regularly scheduled virtual meetings with clear goals for each, which helps establish good group relationships. However, conflicts can arise; for some ideas for dealing with virtual conflicts, see *Did You Know?: Handling Conflicts in Virtual Groups*.

Of course, all groups experience some conflict, and a certain amount of constructive conflict can actually lead to better group performance; conflict can be both healthy and functional because it can increase member involvement and even lead to more innovative thinking (Klocke, 2007; Van der Haar et al., 2017). For example, innovation often comes about when the majority accepts an opinion advanced by a numerical minority (one group member). A productive way to handle group conflict is through using a cooperative conflict style; that is, a style that is open to minority opinion *and* integrates all members' interests (Oetzel, 2005; Poole & Garner, 2006). We should note that *task*-related conflict is more likely to lead to positive group outcomes than *relational* conflict (Koeslag-Kreunen et al., 2018).

DID YOU KNOW?
Handling Conflicts in Virtual Groups

As with any workplace conflict, a disagreement in virtual teams needs to be carefully managed. You may have fewer "tools" at your disposal than if you were together in an office, so it's important to nip disagreements in the bud early.

Therefore, virtual group expert Keith Ferrazzi suggests:

- Have an online discussion tool (e.g., Slack) that provides opportunities for people to communicate easily and discuss minor issues so they don't fester and that keeps conversations searchable. Members can read, take time to reflect, and then respond. Transparency builds trust when issues are dealt with openly and in a timely manner.

- Assign a "point person" for a particular problematic issue—that person keeps track, summarizes, and then submits ideas for an agenda item.
- "Diverge and then converge"—after all pros and cons are solicited, schedule a real-time discussion (e.g., teleconference) to select a course of action.

SOURCES: Ferrazzi, K. (2012, November 19). How to manage conflict in virtual teams. *HBR Blog Network*. http://blogs.hbr.org/2012/11/how-to-manage-conflict-in-virt/

Five ways to effectively handle conflict in a virtual team. (2020). *thevirtualhub.com*. https://www.thevirtualhub.com/blog/5-ways-to-effectively-handle-conflict-in-virtual-teams/

Phase 3. *Emergence.* In the **emergence phase**, the group has worked through the primary and secondary tensions, and members express a cooperative attitude. In successful groups, coalitions dissipate, and group members are less tenacious about holding their positions. Comments become more favorable as members compromise to reach consensus, discuss their problem at length, consider possible alternatives, and eventually generate a group decision. This is the longest phase, where information problem-solving skills (IPS) are important and depend on active participation of all members as well as the cognitive skills of analysis, evaluation, and information selection. These skills are important to obtain high-quality solutions, particularly in virtual groups (Garcia & Badia, 2017). Two biases to avoid are accepting the first information that is advanced and accepting only information that all agree on. As noted earlier, innovation and higher-quality decisions are more likely when unique information is advanced and accepted/discussed and when initial preferences are not accepted as final (Klocke, 2007).

Recurring and sustained bouts of secondary tension or conflict can be problematic. In response, members can fill relational roles that promote trust (assuring members that they can rely on each other to put forward their best effort) and cohesion (expressing a desire to remain in the group). Members can also reduce tension by articulating a positive attitude or feeling about their group, the task, or other members and by emphasizing group identity and pride in the group's effort. In short, strong relational bonds within a group promote high-quality decisions and problem solving (Keyton, 1999, 2000), and groups with high trust have fewer relationship conflicts (Peterson & Behfar, 2003).

Phase 4. *Reinforcement.* During the **reinforcement phase**, members reach consensus, the decision solidifies, and members feel a sense of accomplishment and satisfaction. If a small majority makes the decision, they spend phase 4 convincing other members of its value. In successful groups, members unify and stand behind the solution. Comments are almost uniformly positive. (See *Alternative View: A Reason to Notice Conflict in Small Group Work*).

emergence phase
The third phase of the decision-making process; occurs when group members express a cooperative attitude.

reinforcement phase
The final phase of the decision-making process when group members reach consensus and members feel a sense of accomplishment.

ALTERNATIVE VIEW
A Reason to Notice Conflict in Small Group Work

Experts agree that conflict, differences in viewpoints, ideas, and opinions are inevitable in problem-solving group processes, and researchers have studied the effects of and strategies for dealing with conflict in both virtual and face-to-face groups. Interestingly, most of the research investigates the impacts of conflict at the *group level* and not the perceptions of *individual* group members. An exception is recent research that focuses on variations in individual perceptions of group conflict. That is, some members don't seem to notice conflict in a group, while other high conflict perceivers do. Previous research seems to assume that high conflict perceivers will experience negative consequences such as negative emotions, low satisfaction, and absenteeism.

However, one group of researchers speculated that high conflict perceivers may be more effective than those who are oblivious to conflict in the group. They reasoned, based on previous theories and research, that the negative emotions may trigger feelings of uncertainty and doubt about whether the group will achieve its goals. This uncertainty may then motivate them to contribute more effort to the group effort.

The researchers tested their hypothesis in several studies on small group projects, measuring group members' perceptions of conflict during discussions regarding the group task; they also measured members' uncertainty about task completion and asked group members to rate the effectiveness of other members.

Their hypothesis was confirmed!

They concluded that the negative emotions of high conflict perceivers trigger feelings of uncertainty and that, paradoxically, these feelings of uncertainty propel them to contribute more effort, which is noticed by other group members, who then rate them as more effective group members.

Perhaps the lesson here is to be aware of the possibility of group conflict and not ignore it. If you see it, work harder to facilitate the discussion and the eventual achievement of group goals.

SOURCE: Wang, S., Homan, A. C., & Jehn, K. (2020). Individual task conflict asymmetry and peer ratings of member effectiveness. *Small Group Research*, 51(3), 402–426.

groupthink
A negative, and potentially disastrous, group process characterized by "excessive concurrence thinking."

Preventing Groupthink

One common and potentially disastrous group process is **groupthink**. This happens when groups arrive at a premature decision before all alternatives have been realistically assessed. What are the symptoms? Groupthink happens when members feel pressure to conform and do not speak up or they reject new information and may even react negatively to any information that contradicts the group decisions. Other symptoms are evidenced when group members have an illusion of invulnerability or unanimity. These symptoms produce pressure on group members to go along with the favored group position, assuming not only that the group preferences will be successful but also are just and right (Henningsen & Henningsen, 2006). This phenomenon can have disastrous consequences. The term was coined in an analysis of several foreign policy fiascoes, such as the Bay of Pigs Invasion in 1961 and the U.S. decision to invade Iraq in 2003.

Another example of the disastrous consequences of groupthink is the high number of climber fatalities (11) on Mount Everest in 2019. One mountaineer expert described the huge traffic jams of trekkers that caused climbers to be stuck for hours at the mercy of the weather and next to a thousand-foot drop. The jams, and ultimately the deaths, were caused by groupthink—a pack mentality that led most climbers to go for the summit when the first good weather was predicted—afraid of missing the weather window and not waiting for more information (Sharma et al., 2019).

What causes people to engage in groupthink? One reason may be a high level of cohesiveness. Although group cohesion is usually viewed as a positive thing, too much of it can lead to premature agreement. The same is true about conflict; too much can result in an ineffective group, but some dissent can help prevent groupthink. Leadership can also promote groupthink: either strong leadership, where one dominating person promotes only one idea, or the opposite—a lack of leadership, leaving the group without direction. Groupthink can also result from a failure to set norms for decision making or from a failure to follow a problem-solving agenda, perhaps due to an external threat that causes stress, like a deadline or a change in group purpose (Jaeger 2020). Finally, extreme homogeneity in the backgrounds of group members may also lead to rushed solutions rather than careful examination of alternatives (Henningsen & Henningsen, 2006).

Groupthink can be prevented in several ways. First, groups need to be aware of precursors to and symptoms of groupthink as they propose and enact important change. Second, following an established procedure and making sure adequate time is spent in discussion before reaching a decision are both helpful. Third, playing "devil's advocate" and arguing an opposing view to the majority opinion can play a legitimate role in thwarting and derailing the impulse to form a consensus too quickly without considering the alternatives. We discussed previously the important role that minority opinion can play in resolving conflict and producing innovative thinking. Minority opinions can also play an important role in preventing groupthink; this suggests that individual critiques of the majority point of view still need to be carefully considered and answered before the group treats an issue as settled. Third and perhaps most important, group members should be aware of the causes and consequences of groupthink and encourage critical evaluation (at the appropriate time) of ideas and some dissension to prevent premature decisions.

**Journal Prompt 10.5:
Effective Small Group Communication**
What are the four elements of effective small group communication? What are the five steps in the problem-solving agenda?

The Individual, Small Group Communication, and Society: Power and Diversity

10.6 Discuss how diversity influences small group processes.

Small group communication, like all communication, is influenced by societal forces. The world outside influences this form of communication in two important respects: (1) the way power is used inside and outside groups, and (2) the role cultural diversity plays.

Power and Group Communication

Small groups function within the influences of the societal forces we have discussed throughout the chapters: political, economic, and historical. People communicating in small groups bring with them their identities and the hierarchical meanings associated with those identities (see Chapter 2). Those group members who hold the values and follow the communication rules of the dominant group in society may more easily contribute to the group and dominate it, which may cause resentment among those who feel marginalized in society generally (Oetzel, 2005).

Groups also establish a power structure. For example, a group member may be elected or appointed to lead a group, which allows that person to wield *legitimate* power (French & Raven, 1959). Much of an individual's power is derived from their society/ social status and standing. For example, when an individual is appointed to lead a group, this usually occurs because of their position within the social hierarchy of the organization.

These power arrangements come with benefits and drawbacks. On the one hand, productive uses of power can facilitate group processes (Sell et al., 2004). On the other hand, leaders or group members may turn legitimate power into *coercive* power, or threats, to get others to do what they want. For example, they may threaten to withdraw or undermine the process if group members don't do what they want, as experienced by one of our students in *It Happened to Me: Sarah*. In dealing with this dominating member, Sarah's group might have tried some relational roles such as expediter or harmonizer to prevent the dominator from derailing the group discussions.

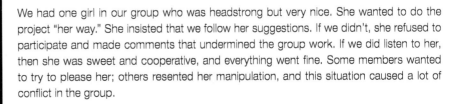

It Happened to Me
Sarah

We had one girl in our group who was headstrong but very nice. She wanted to do the project "her way." She insisted that we follow her suggestions. If we didn't, she refused to participate and made comments that undermined the group work. If we did listen to her, then she was sweet and cooperative, and everything went fine. Some members wanted to try to please her; others resented her manipulation, and this situation caused a lot of conflict in the group.

The use of coercive power is usually unproductive because, as you can see in Sarah's experience, group members resent the threats and may reciprocate by using coercive power when they get the chance. Thus, too much power or a struggle for power can lead to resentment and poor decision making. In contrast, researchers find that groups whose members share power equally exhibit higher-quality communication. When everyone participates and contributes to the discussion equally, power will more likely be distributed equally. In contrast, the unequal power of social hierarchies often occurs in the small group situation because members bring their identities and experiences to the group. Thus, members' cultural identities, which fall along a power hierarchy, can impact small group work.

Cultural Diversity and Small Group Communication

Given the changing demographics in the United States and abroad, small groups will increasingly include members whose backgrounds differ. As we discussed in Chapter 8, cultural backgrounds influence communication patterns, and small group communication is no exception. For example, people from countries where a collectivistic orientation dominates may be most concerned with maintaining harmony in the group, whereas members with an individualistic orientation may be more assertive and competitive in groups, and group members from countries where a direct communication style is preferred seem to have an easier time working in virtual groups. These differences can lead to challenges in accomplishing group goals. In addition, global multicultural groups working virtually face additional challenges—working

DID YOU KNOW?

Five Tips for Running Inclusive Virtual Meetings

1. Send all relevant materials early, considering different time zones, schedules, language and work style differences.

2. Establish an agreed-upon agenda and process, with one clear goal for meeting.

3. Allow for side conversations; non-native speakers can clarify/confer with colleagues in their native language, indirect speakers can share or reach consensus.

4. Use a variety of participation techniques (e.g., whiteboards, chat boxes, polling questions) so less vocal group members can participate more easily.

5. Check for agreement and understanding, especially at crucial points. Send a summary afterward and follow up with key members.

SOURCE: Five tips for running inclusive virtual meetings. *globesmart.com*. https://www.toolbox.com/hr/mobile-workforce/guest-article/inclusive-virtual-meetings/

---

across many time zones, languages, and varying access to communication technologies. These groups can benefit from a leader who is proactive in addressing these challenges, including facilitating virtual meetings. (See *Did You Know?: Five Tips for Running Inclusive Virtual Meetings*.)

How does cultural diversity affect small group processes? Does it result in poor communication, more conflict, lower productivity, and less satisfaction? Or can diverse groups, with their various viewpoints, make better, more effective, and more creative decisions?

Research indicates that even though interactions might be more complex, especially in the early stages of group work, diversity can lead to positive and productive outcomes. Let's look at how diversity influences four aspects of group communication: innovation, efficacy, group processes, and group enjoyment.

Innovation   Decades of research by organizational scientists, psychologists, sociologists, economists, and demographers show that socially diverse groups (that is, those with a diversity of race, ethnicity, gender, and sexual orientation) are more innovative than homogeneous groups (Phillips, 2014). For example, in one study, diversity in education and gender was found to be positively related to the likelihood of introducing an innovation (Ostergaard et al., 2011). Another study of 122 manufacturing firms showed that diverse top management teams had a strong impact on new product innovativeness (and ultimately enhanced performance) (Talke et al., 2010).

This makes sense because having different perspectives means also having a variety of information sources to apply to a problem or issue. This variety of information broadens people's views and their ability to evaluate; as one researcher noted, "Diversity jolts us into cognitive action in ways that homogeneity simply does not" (Phillips, 2014). So, ultimately, a diverse workforce operating in a rapidly changing world is better able to monitor, identify, and respond quickly and innovatively to external problems than a homogeneous one. What are the implications for you, as a potential group/team member in professional, academic, or social settings? If the group is a diverse one, know that the potential is there for innovative work. But also remember that for maximum innovation and effectiveness, you and other group members need to encourage equal participation. The Internet has provided opportunities for virtual groups working collaboratively to produce very innovative ideas and products (see *Communication in Society: COINs: Virtual Innovation*).

Performance (Efficacy)   Some research studies report that diverse groups work more effectively. For example, a 2017 study found that U.S. companies with more female directors reported higher earnings than those companies with no female directors

COMMUNICATION IN SOCIETY
COINs: Virtual Innovation

One type of virtual group phenomenon has changed the way people and businesses develop ideas—through collaboration on the Internet. Are you familiar with other examples of successful Internet collaborations?

Peter A. Gloor, a research scientist at Massachusetts Institute of Technology, and his colleagues have been studying Collaborative Innovation Networks, or COINs. Gloor defines a COIN as "a cyberteam of self-motivated people with a collective vision, enabled by the web to collaborate in achieving a common goal by sharing ideas, information and work" (2006, p. 4). These inspired individuals, working together spontaneously as a virtual group, often at great distances, are not motivated by financial gain. Rather, they collaborate because of their shared passion for innovation and a commitment to common goals or causes. Gloor describes their collaboration as "swarm creativity." As they spontaneously "swarm" together in cyberspace, they create an environment that promotes dynamic and innovative collaborative thinking.

The results of these virtual collaborations have been astounding. As Gloor notes, the Internet itself is an example of a successful COIN. It was started by a group of people working at a physics research lab and then developed and fine-tuned by various groups of students, researchers, and computer scientists, crossing conventional organizational structures and hierarchies. The rest, as they say, is history. Other examples of more recent COIN successes are wikis as well as open source software products and a number of other lesser-known commercial innovations. Gloor and colleagues stress that for COINs to be successful, the group members not only need to share a passion for the products they're developing but also need a certain level of trust in fellow group members, balanced communication, and a shared code of ethics guiding their collaboration. A latest project introduces a way to automatically measure a person's moral values through hidden "honest" signals in their email communication. The results explained 70 percent of the person's moral values measured later with the moral foundations survey. Specifically, they found that the more positive and less emotional people were in their language, the more they cared about others (Gloor & Colladon, 2020).

SOURCES: Gloor, P. A. (2006). *Swarm creativity: Competitive advantage through collaborative innovative networks.* Oxford University Press.

Gloor, P. A., & Colladon, A. F. (2020). Heart beats brain: Measuring moral beliefs through e-mail analysis. In A. Przegalinska, F. Grippa, & P. A. Gloor (Eds.), *Digital transformation of collaboration* (pp. 85–99). Springer.

(Posner, 2018), and another study found that diverse organizations outperform competitors by 35 percent (Westover, 2020). However, other studies report the opposite (Caya et al., 2013). This isn't surprising, given the many types of diversity and the fact that each group develops communication and processes that may help or hinder performance. Communication in diverse groups may be more challenging at the onset, so that cultural differences in attitudes and communication styles may lead to early conflict. However, if group members handle these differences well, the outcome may be as good as or better than in homogeneous groups (Nishimura, 2020).

There are several ways to accomplish this. One is by focusing the group's attention on the goal of the group, something shared by all, rather than on individual cultural differences. A second strategy is to explore commonalities among group members—for example, shared interests, activities, or experiences. In a college course, group members may discover that they

▼ Because diverse groups can outperform homogeneous groups, it is often wise to seek out opportunities to work with people who are different from you.

are enrolled in other courses together as well or that they participate in the same extracurricular sport or social activity. In a business setting, the group members may find that they have shared professional experiences or hobbies. Some discussion of these commonalities helps solidify relationships, leading to enhanced group cohesion. Third, establishing clear communication expectations and decision-making agenda also helps build early group cohesion in diverse groups and smoothes the way to managing differences in later discussions. These suggestions are also especially important in global virtual group work (Walker et al., 2018). As a group member, you can help a diverse group perform more productively by facilitating cohesion early on in the group effort.

group processes

The methods, including communication, by which a group accomplishes a task.

Group Processes   As we discussed in Chapter 8, one way that individuals differ across cultures is in their preference for individualism or collectivism, and these preferences have an impact on **group processes**. To understand these preferences, in one study, one group of researchers randomly assigned students to task groups so that each group had varying degrees of age, gender, and ethnic diversity. Their group task was a course assignment in which they analyzed conversations using various theories presented in class. The students then filled out a questionnaire measuring their communication processes in the group (e.g., participation rate, listening, respect, and conflict management), their own individualistic–collectivist tendencies, and their satisfaction with the group work (Oetzel, 1998).

Interestingly, ethnic, gender, and age diversity in this study had little effect on the communication process, but those who preferred more interdependent or collectivistic interaction participated more and cooperated more in the group, thus having a more positive impact on group processes. Group members who convey respect and participate in a cooperative manner are also likely to put forth substantial effort toward completing a task and to encourage the contributions of others. Why? Effective communication by some may reduce isolation and encourage effort of all group members. Not surprisingly, those members who participated more were more satisfied with the group outcome. Other studies have found that collectivistic values along with group member independence also stimulate creativity—probably because group members feel encouraged to speak up individually in this positive group climate (Choi et al., 2019). These studies suggest that groups that are diverse in terms of race, ethnicity, and gender don't necessarily experience more difficult processes. Moreover, because people are diverse and different in so many ways, one can't make assumptions about any collection of individuals based on physical attributes like age, race, or gender.

Group Enjoyment   Although diverse groups may be more innovative and effective, are they more enjoyable? To explore this question, another study examined the experience of college students who worked in groups that were composed of either (1) mostly Whites or (2) mostly ethnic minorities (Asians, Asian Americans, African Americans, Hispanics, and others of mixed ethnicity). The researchers found that minorities and White students all preferred minority-dominated groups to White-dominated groups. How can one explain these findings? The researchers suggest that some level of collectivism may have been working in the minority-oriented groups, and whether or not it was, members of these groups were more attentive to relational harmony (Paletz et al., 2004). In a more recent study, students working in multicultural virtual groups (with systematic guidelines for establishing group communication and group processes) reported significant cross-cultural bonding experiences and high trust with other group members (Walker et al., 2018).

What are the implications to be drawn from all these studies that have examined the effect of diversity on group work, whether working online or in person? First, it seems there are two types of diversity: demographic diversity (age, gender, ethnicity, and race) and deeper cultural differences in attitudes and values (individualism and collectivism preferences) that also play an important role. Second, culturally diverse groups *may* produce more innovative ideas, *may* be more enjoyable, and *can* be as productive as homogeneous groups. However, enjoyment and productivity do not occur automatically in these groups; they depend largely on group members setting expectations, following an agenda, and utilizing communication skills, which do not always come naturally. "Many people believe that good communication skills are 'common sense.' Contrary to expectations, the problem with common sense is that it is not all that common" (Oetzel, 2005, p. 366). Thus, leaders of culturally diverse groups need to focus on helping all group members, including reticent ones, learn to participate fully and to communicate respectfully in a way that promotes collaboration, group cohesion, and consensus building (Caya et al., 2013).

These findings also suggest that organizations need to develop systematic policies and programs allowing for and valuing the unique characteristics of each group, whether working face-to-face or online. Further, with proper education and development, diverse groups have the potential to experience higher levels of satisfaction and effectiveness. To summarize, communicating in groups occurs within societal structures—whether the groups are groups working in a small business, task forces in a nonprofit organization, or small problem-solving groups in a college course. These social structures establish power relations and status hierarchies that in turn come into play in group interaction. The cultural backgrounds of group members also influence group communication, and if handled well, cultural diversity can enhance group innovation, performance, communication processes, and enjoyment. However, the bottom line is that effective group work flows from effective and ethical communication skills, the topics we turn to next.

Critical Thinking Prompt
Think about a small group experience you've had recently. What did other group members say that made you (and others) feel a part of the group? What was said that made you (and others) feel excluded from the group?

Journal Prompt 10.6: Power in Small Groups
What is the difference between legitimate and coercive power in small groups?

Ethics and Small Group Communication

10.7 Give three types of guidelines for communicating more ethically in small group communication.

Ethical communication in small groups is especially important because the success of the group and the task depend on it. One might argue that being in a group carries additional ethical responsibilities because one's individual actions can affect how people think about and react to other members of the group and their ideas. In short, in groups, you are no longer responsible only for yourself but for other members as well. Consider three types of ethical guidelines: (1) those aimed at strengthening group relationships, (2) those dealing with specific communication practices, and (3) those related to group decisions.

Relational ethics involve demonstrating commitment to the group. For example, an ethical small group member attends group meetings and participates. As we've discussed, equal participation, buy-in, and establishing trust are all important aspects of group success that cannot be achieved when members are absent from or silent in group discussions. Another relational ethic involves doing your fair share of the group work because equal participation extends to sharing equally in the responsibilities for completing the tasks. A third ethical guideline to strengthen small-group relationships is to maintain open channels of communication (maintaining contact with other group members, contacting others when needed, and responding to others in a timely manner).

In considering ethical communication practices in small groups, it might be helpful to think about the ethical guidelines discussed in Chapter 1 and consider how they might apply to a small group context. First, being truthful in your communication is particularly important because you are making contributions that affect larger collective decisions (Hargrove, 1998). Truthfulness also includes being accurate and avoiding exaggeration.

For example, if you were reporting facts about crime on campus, you would offer statistics, not just say, "I found out that crime is really a huge problem." Although you should strive for accuracy and honesty in your language, there may be times when you should not say everything you know—for example, when you should respect the confidentiality of others, including group members. If your friend has been raped and you know this information might be helpful to your group discussion about campus security, you should ask for your friend's permission before divulging this information. Similarly, group members may disclose personal information in the group discussion that they may not wish repeated outside the group.

Secondly, ethical group members also work toward communicating authentically, as discussed in Chapter 1. Why is authentic communication essential? As we noted previously, group cohesion and trust are important to the performance and success of groups. Authentic communication that is open and free from pretense and language that is inclusive and not hurtful to others go a long way in promoting the kind of group cohesion necessary for group effectiveness. Finally, as a receiver, you must listen with an open mind while also evaluating others' contributions. Doing so will enhance the quality of discussions and help prevent groupthink, in which groups jump to premature conclusions and decisions.

A third area of small group ethics concerns the collective actions of the group members. For example, what if you find a project paper on the Internet that closely resembles the project you've been working on? Your group is running out of time at the end of the semester and it would be easy to copy portions of the paper, making only a few minor changes. What ethical guidelines apply here? Perhaps the ethics of fairness and taking responsibility for one's own actions apply. Submitting someone else's work instead of your own is not fair to other students in the course who did their own work, and taking responsibility for poor time management as a group is a more ethical action than using someone else's work.

Journal Prompt 10.7: Ethics in Small Groups
What are three areas of ethical guidelines for small group work? Which guidelines do you think are most important, and why?

Improving Your Small Group Communication Skills

10.8 Discuss ways to improve your small group communication skills.

Although no strategies will work in every group communication situation, two strategies can help you be more effective in many of them.

First, cultivate an interdependent or collectivist attitude, a "we" orientation instead of a "me" orientation, and work toward collaborative communication, whether working face-to-face or online (Lewis et al., 2010). This means that you must sacrifice some of your personal ambition, needs, and wants in favor of the group's needs and work to ensure buy-in from all group members. People who are extremely individualistic may find this difficult. Yet those with a more collectivist attitude can influence group processes toward more effective communication, more participation, and more satisfaction of all members. A related guideline is to be cooperative. Cooperativeness helps to establish group harmony in working conditions and can provide individuals with interpersonal help, making the job easier and less demanding and making individuals less likely to experience burnout in their group work. Thus, cooperative group members may be more satisfied with individual and group performance (Lambertz-Berndt & Blight, 2016).

In addition to cultivating an interdependent attitude and being cooperative, striving for cohesion is also important in successful small group relationships and task accomplishment. Cohesion occurs when group members trust each other.

Further, group success depends on the participation of each member, but members are unlikely to give their best to the group if they can't trust other members to do the same. Trust is particularly important in virtual groups, where members may have less face-to-face interaction that might otherwise provide important clues to the intent or attitude of fellow group members. Several strategies build trust and cohesion:

- Focus on the strengths of all group members and recognize their contributions to group goals. Be sure to acknowledge all group achievements.

- Remind the group of common interests and background experiences. Doing this can help build cohesion, prevent unnecessary conflict, and strengthen group identity.

- Be observant and notice when a member might be feeling unappreciated or uninvolved in the group. Encourage that person to participate. People gain trust and become more trusting as they participate, especially if their participation is encouraged. Fortunately, more trust leads to more cohesion and stronger group identity, which in turn leads to better communication, more satisfaction, and more cohesion.

In sum, the effectiveness of a small group depends in large part on the communication and the relationships established among the members. As a group member, you can promote (or inhibit) the productive communication needed. We believe that using the tools discussed in this chapter not only will make your small group work more effectively but also will make it more enjoyable.

Journal Prompt 10.8: Improving Small Group Communication
What are two general strategies for improving your small group communication? Why is cohesion so important in small group communication? What is a collectivist perspective and how does it enhance small group work?

SUMMARY

10.1 Identify four reasons for learning about small group communication.

- Small group communication is a fact of life, and learning to be a better small group communicator can enhance your academic performance, your career achievement, and your personal success.

10.2 Define *small group communication* and *virtual small groups*.

- Small group members share a common purpose, are interdependent, and exert influence on each other.

- The primary benefit of small groups is that they are more productive and creative than individuals working alone.

- The disadvantages are that decisions take longer; groups can silence minority opinions, get distracted, and make poor decisions; and relational problems and conflicts can make the experience less than satisfying.

- A virtual small group is a group whose members interact primarily "through electronic communication media."

10.3 Identify examples of task, relational, and disruptive small group roles.

- Twelve task and eight relational roles are required for effective group work. In effective groups, individuals fill these roles as needed at any given time during group work. Eight disruptive (individual-centered) roles also exist that group members may fill; these roles, however, tend to be dysfunctional and unproductive.

10.4 Describe five theories of group leadership.

- A group's or organization's success is often directly related to the presence of good leadership.

- Leadership is defined as an influence relationship among leaders and followers who intend changes and outcomes that reflect their shared purposes.

- Five theories of leadership—trait, style, functional, transformational, and servant—explain leadership effectiveness.

10.5 Describe the characteristics of communication that occur during the four phases of small group decision making.

- Successful problem-solving groups tend to follow agendas. The most common is a five-stage agenda: (1) defining the problem, (2) analyzing the problem, (3) identifying alternative solutions, (4) evaluating the proposed solutions, and (5) choosing the best solution.

- Related to the five-stage agenda are the four phases of decision making that most groups complete in every stage of the problem-solving agenda: orientation and primary tension, conflict and secondary tension, emergence, and reinforcement.

- Although group cohesion is generally beneficial, too much of it can lead to groupthink.

10.6 Discuss how diversity influences small group processes.

- Societal forces impact small group processes via the role of power in small group work and through cultural diversity.

- Although cultural diversity can present challenges for group processes, it can also produce innovative, efficient, and enjoyable group experiences if handled appropriately. Building cohesion and trust in early stages of group work is particularly important in diverse groups.

10.7 Give three types of guidelines for communicating more ethically in small group communication.

- There are three types of ethical guidelines that should guide small group work: (1) those aimed at strengthening group relationships, (2) those dealing with specific communication practices, and (3) those related to group decisions.

10.8 Discuss ways to improve your small group communication skills.

- Skills for achieving effective group communication include cultivating an interdependent attitude and striving for trust and cohesion.

KEY TERMS

grouphate p. 246
small group communication p. 247
virtual small group p. 249
virtuality p. 249
group roles p. 252
task roles p. 253
relational roles p. 254
disruptive or individual-centered
    roles p. 255

trait theory p. 257
functional (situational) theory p. 258
shared leadership p. 259
style theory p. 259
authoritarian leader p. 259
democratic leader p. 259
laissez-faire p. 259
transformational leadership p. 260
charismatic leadership p. 260

servant leadership p. 260
analysis paralysis p. 264
brainstorm p. 264
primary tension p. 265
secondary (recurring) tension p. 265
emergence phase p. 267
reinforcement phase p. 267
groupthink p. 268
group processes p. 272

APPLY WHAT YOU KNOW

1. **Group Roles**
   Think of a recent group experience you've had. Look at the lists of task, relational, and disruptive role behaviors in Tables 10.1 through 10.3. Record all behaviors and roles that you filled. Which behaviors (if any) were missing in your group? Which other roles might you have filled?

2. **Groupthink**
   Consider experiences you've had in group work. Answer the following questions concerning groupthink. After answering the questions, meet in person or virtually with several classmates and compare answers. Then, as a group, come up with suggestions for ensuring against groupthink.

   - Have you ever felt so secure about a group decision that you ignored all the warning signs that the decision was wrong? Why?

   - Have you ever applied undue pressure to members who disagreed to get them to agree with the will of the group?
   - Have you ever participated in a "we-versus-they" feeling—that is, depicting those in the group who are opposed to you in simplistic, stereotyped ways?
   - Have you ever served as a "mind guard"—that is, have you ever attempted to preserve your group's cohesiveness by preventing disturbing outside ideas or opinions from becoming known to other group members?
   - Have you ever assumed that the silence of the other group members implied agreement?

   For more information about how to spot and prevent groupthink, see https://www.mindtools.com/pages/article/newLDR_82.htm.

Communicating in Organizations

LEARNING OBJECTIVES

11.1 Explain the importance of understanding communication in organizations.

11.2 Define *organizations* and explain their communication functions and structures.

11.3 Understand the types of communication that occur among coworkers and explain their functions.

11.4 Discuss current social influences on organizations and organizational communication.

11.5 Distinguish between individual and communal perspectives on organizational ethics.

11.6 Identify four steps involved in a strategic approach to conflict management.

CHAPTER TOPICS

The Importance of Organizational Communication

Defining Organizational Communication

Organizational Communication and the Individual

The Individual, Organizational Communication, and Society

Ethics and Organizational Communication

Improving Your Organizational Communication Skills

> *"Much of our success within organizations is connected to our communication abilities."*

Charee's first assignment in her organizational communication class was to list all the organizations she interacted with for one day. As she went through her day—buying a cup of coffee at Starbucks, interviewing for a job, listening to class lectures, ordering lunch at Chipotle, and tutoring at a community center—she had a realization. Almost every interaction she had that day occurred either with representatives of organizations or within organizations.

We live in a society of organizations. You may not realize it, but organizations shape your life in many ways. For example, legislative bodies and law enforcement agencies implement formal codes—such as traffic laws—that constrain your daily behavior. Educational institutions shape what counts as knowledge, such as when schools determine whether evolutionary theory, intelligent design, or both will be taught in science classes. In addition, religious groups influence popular moral beliefs about issues such as gay marriage or abortion rights.

Business corporations also are major players in shaping our society. Some argue that because they control vast economic resources, huge transnational corporations have become even more powerful than governments and thus heavily influence government personnel and policy, educational content and practices, and international relations (Khanna & Francis, 2016). Corporations also affect our lifestyle desires and choices. For instance, why do consumers want and purchase new, "improved" cell phones, tablets, and televisions when their current ones work perfectly well?

Even though organizations cast a strong influence on individuals, individuals also affect organizations—as consumers, as supporters, as participants in religious and civic institutions, and as individuals who work for or against specific organizations. Although living in an organizational society generally means you can't escape the influence of organizations, you can have a profound effect on them, just as they do on you. For example, in 2020, African American TikTok users expressed frustration with TikTok's perceived racist practices, including discrimination against Black creators and allowing White supremacists to have platforms. They organized a protest, asking TikTok users to sign a petition, give the app a one-star review on June 19 (Juneteenth), and threaten to delete their accounts. With almost 100 million users, the TikTok company responded with an apology and declared its "commitment to support diverse voices and perspectives, Black creators, and communities." More importantly, it implemented organizational change; it established inclusive Community Guidelines and removed videos that violated the guidelines, established a Creator Diversity Collective to advise leadership, supported pages devoted to Black history and voices, and donated millions to Black community, educational, and artistic organizations (Onibada, 2020; Pappas & Chikumbu, 2020). Thus, individuals can influence organizational behavior; however, your ability to have this effect depends on your understanding of organizations and your skills communicating with and within them.

In this chapter, we explain what we mean by organizational communication and explore the types of communication that commonly occur within organizations. First, we look at how individuals communicate within organizations. Then we broaden the discussion to examine the ways society impacts the interactions between individuals and organizations as well as how organizations influence society and individuals. We wrap up with a discussion of ethical issues associated with communication in and by organizations and offer ways to improve your ability to manage conflict more effectively within organizations.

The Importance of Organizational Communication

11.1 Explain the importance of understanding communication in organizations.

Because you participate in organizations regularly, you will benefit from understanding how to communicate more effectively with and within them. Doing so will enhance your professional success, allow you to ask more informed questions about everyday organizational practices, and help you decide what organizations you wish to frequent and support.

Much of your success within organizations is connected to your communication abilities. For example, if you want an organization to hire you, you must first display good interviewing skills. If you want a promotion, it may be essential to understand your boss's goals and beliefs but also to effectively engage in what some business experts call "a series of continuing conversations" with your boss (Knight, 2018). And if you seek public or civic office, you must have strong public-speaking and social-influence skills to gain support from your political party and endorsements from influential organizations.

In addition to enhancing your professional success, understanding organizational communication will help you ask more informed questions about everyday organizational practices, such as how the corporation you work for determines pay raises, how a nonprofit charity you support can become a United Way organization, or how you can influence legislation in your community. Knowing what questions to ask and how to ask them will improve your ability to accomplish your goals. Finally, given that a wide variety of religious, corporate, and community organizations exist, there is a limit to how many you can support. Understanding how to question organizations and how to interpret their responses and policies can help you make informed choices regarding which ones to embrace. For example, you might decide not to purchase products or services from for-profit organizations that force their employees to work mandatory overtime at the expense of their home lives. Or you might decide that you are better off working for an organization whose goals and beliefs you support strongly because your agreement with those goals likely will influence your career success.

In sum, organizational communication is central to a person's ability to navigate successfully the myriad legal, educational, religious, corporate, and civic organizations one confronts across a lifetime.

Journal Prompt 11.1: Organizational Communication
What are the benefits of studying organizational communication?

Defining Organizational Communication

11.2 Define *organizations* and explain their communication functions and structures.

Next, we define what we mean when we say *organization*, and we explain the role communication plays in it. As part of this definition, we focus on two aspects common to all organizing efforts: communication functions and structures. We then conclude this section by examining the role of communication in establishing organizational cultures.

Organizations from a Communication Perspective

Scholars from a variety of fields, including sociology, economics, psychology, and business management, are interested in understanding organizational life. However, communication scholars bring a particular focus to the study of organizations. From their perspective, communication is not just another variable of organizational life. Thus, it is not merely the oil that lubricates other parts of the machine or the glue that binds parts together. Put bluntly, without communication, they argue, there are no "parts"; there is no "machine."

Consider the organization of a college classroom, for instance. Communication scholars argue that it is in the *process of interacting* as student and teacher—giving and listening to lectures, taking and grading exams—that the meaning of these abstract roles becomes real. In this view, then, communication is the process that calls organizations into being. Thus, communication scholars argue that *communication constitutes organizations*. It enables or creates them (Brummans et al., 2014).

From this perspective, then, **organizations** are defined as the set of interactions that members of groups use to accomplish their individual and common goals (Bisel, 2010; McPhee & Zaug, 2009). Two parts of this definition are important: that organizations are composed of group members' interactions and that organizational members pursue goals.

▲ Individuals join organizations such as Doctors without Borders because they can accomplish their goals more effectively if they work with others.

organizations
The set of interactions that members of purposeful groups use to accomplish their individual and common goals.

In Chapter 9, we explained how a dyad (a pair of individuals) creates and maintains a relationship through communication; this same process occurs within organizations. As individuals in organizations maintain, or alter, their communication practices, they influence the organization itself. For example, if a new store manager is hired who encourages employees to be more courteous in their interactions with each other as well as with customers, the nature of the organization is likely to change. Employee turnover may be reduced, employees may feel more positively about their jobs and therefore work harder, and the more positive interactions with clients could increase sales. Thus, just changing an organization's communication interactions can significantly affect the organization and its members.

In addition to being composed of communication interactions, our definition indicates that organizations are purposeful. Organizations are not random groupings of people; organizational members come together to accomplish individual and collective goals. For example, organizations such as the World Wildlife Fund, Doctors without Borders, and Habitat for Humanity exist because their individual members want to make positive changes in the world, and they can do so more effectively if they work together.

Communication Function and Structure

Organizational communication is interaction that organizes purposeful groups, and it generally exhibits several properties—two of which are especially relevant here. The first we will call **function**, by which we mean the goals and effects of communication. Traditionally, scholars recognized three major functions of organizational communication (Daniels et al., 1996). **Production** refers to communication that coordinates individuals' activities so they can accomplish tasks. For example, when a manager creates and posts the store opening and closing procedures along with monthly sales goals or develops a standardized process for assembling products, she allows employees to accomplish various tasks. The **maintenance** function of organizational communication serves to maintain existing aspects of the organization. Consider, for example, awarding an employee-of-the-month plaque, conducting a

function
The goals and effects of communication.

production
A function of organizational communication in which activity is coordinated toward accomplishing tasks.

maintenance
A function of organizational communication in which the stability of existing systems is preserved.

▲ The maintenance function of organizations serves to preserve existing systems, such as providing high performers with recognition to ensure that workers continue to strive for excellence.

innovation

A function of organizational communication by means of which systems are changed.

structure

Recurring patterns of interaction among organizational members.

downward communication

In a traditional conduit model of communication, communication with subordinates.

upward communication

In a traditional conduit model of communication, communication with superiors.

horizontal communication

In a traditional conduit model of communication, communication with peers.

hierarchy

A power structure in which some members exercise authority over others.

formal communication channels

Officially designated channels of communication, reflecting explicit or desired patterns of interaction.

informal communication channels

Patterns of interaction that develop spontaneously based on personal relationships and contacts.

performance review, and clarifying a vague set of workflow procedures—all of which enforce the status quo and keep the system running smoothly. A third function is **innovation**, which involves communication that encourages change in the organization. Examples might include creating a "digital suggestion box" where employees can post ideas to improve an organization's functioning (e.g., software to streamline accounting processes, practices to improve customer service).

You may have noticed that in most of these examples the three traditional functions overlap considerably. Let's take performance reviews as an illustration. As a manager, you may hope to reinforce the status quo (maintenance) by providing an employee with positive feedback, but you may also hope to instigate change (innovation) in that employee's behavior by offering suggestions for improvement. Also, most performance reviews involve other goals not adequately captured by the three-function model, such as negotiating trust, flexing egos, and so forth. With closer examination, you may see that at least some of these performance review goals are at odds with one another. In fact, most organizational communication serves multiple, even competing, functions.

The second major property of organizational communication is **structure**. Traditionally, communication structure referred to channels of communication, or a system of pathways through which messages flow. Such a conduit model of communication emphasizes *direction*: **downward communication**, with subordinates, **upward communication,** with superiors, and **horizontal communication**, with peers (Miller, 2015). Note that direction-based metaphors presume **hierarchy**, a kind of power structure in which some members exercise authority over others. Another way to define structure is as *recurring patterns of interaction among members* (Monge & Contractor, 2001). Rather than treating messages as literal objects moving through conduits, this definition points to communication networks that emerge among members. It recognizes that such networks may be hierarchical, though other possibilities exist.

Another important distinction exists between **formal** and **informal communication channels**. Formal communication follows the hierarchy of the official organizational chart, whereas informal communication "travels from person to person based on personal relationships and contacts" (Kramer & Bisel, 2017, p. 133). As an analogy, think of sidewalks on your campus as the official walkway (formal channels), whereas footprints worn in the grass represent the shortcuts and detours people take from the path they are given (informal channels). Thus, formal channels are explicit or desired patterns of interaction (that is, what the organization suggests we do). Informal communication are patterns of interaction that develop spontaneously. Most organizational members use both formal and informal structures, for example, following corporate procedures for requesting a leave of absence (formal) and asking a friend in a position of power to recommend their leave request to the boss (informal).

Of the many features of organizational communication we might choose to discuss, we highlight function and structure because they have surfaced continually in scholarly visions of organizational communication.

Organizational Culture

In addition to structure and function, each organization also develops distinct organizational cultural patterns. Remember our discussion about cultures in Chapters 1 and 8? **Organizational culture**, like national and ethnic/racial cultures, refers to a pattern of shared beliefs, values, and behaviors shared by members of the organization. More informally, organizational culture can be thought of as the "personality" of an organization (McNamara, 2008). However, organizational cultures are also dynamic and heterogeneous, meaning that these beliefs and values will probably not be shared by everyone in the organization (Cheney et al., 2004; Martin, 2002). As these definitions suggest, organizational cultures are created as people act and interact with one another and may change over time. Within any organization there may be subcultures; for example, at your university, the student culture may share some beliefs and behaviors that differ from those of the academic faculty or administrative employees.

organizational culture
A pattern of shared beliefs, values, and behaviors.

Like national/ethnic/racial cultures, organizational cultures are composed of the values, languages, rites and rituals, ceremonies, stories, and habits enacted by members of that group.

Languages in this sense refer to the types of phrases and words used to describe and talk about the organization and its relationships with others. For example, all of the authors of this book worked at Arizona State University (ASU). Here are some examples of languages used in the university: administrators routinely refer to ASU as "the new American University," the football stadium is called "Sun Devil Stadium," the university's mascot is "Sparky," and its archrival in sports is the University of Arizona (UofA). As you can imagine, the UofA has its own mascots, stadium names, and university catchphrase as well. All organizations develop these specific names, words, and phrases to describe common practices, experiences, and members in their workplaces.

Ceremonies are preplanned events that can be formal or informal. Generally, they serve a practical purpose as well as a symbolic one (Martin, 2012). For example, universities have graduation ceremonies that serve to recognize the work and success of the year's students who have completed their coursework. These events are largely symbolic in that most universities don't actually hand out diplomas to students during the ceremony. (In case you didn't know, usually students receive diploma covers at graduation and their actual diplomas arrive in the mail.) But they also serve a practical purpose in bringing together students, faculty, and staff as well as students' families so they can celebrate this achievement together.

The terms *rites* and *rituals* are often used interchangeably. Ceremonies are composed of rites and rituals; having faculty march into the auditorium at graduation, singing the school song, and having students move their graduation cap tassels from the right to the left are all examples of rites and rituals. But rites and rituals can occur during everyday activity as well.

For example, in Lucia's organization, employees meet up on a come-and-go-as-you-please basis anytime during the lunch hour in the office kitchen. Each month, the organization celebrates all employees' birthday that month, buying everyone lunch. They also have a digital "water cooler" channel where employees post info and photos marking significant personal events (new baby, prom, vacation). They also mark and celebrate anniversary dates for how long employees have been with the organization.

Habits refer to behaviors that people regularly perform at work but that are not part of the organization's formal or informal policies. Rather, habits are voluntary, casual actions that are accepted, ignored, or at least not commented on. For example, at some organizations, employees routinely arrive a few minutes late in the morning or when returning from lunch. Such behavior certainly is not part of a company's policies, but it

▲ A classic example of dysfunctional organizational culture is illustrated in the sitcom *The Office*.

may be tolerated. Because habits are informal behaviors that are implicitly agreed on by a company's membership, they adapt and change as new employees are hired—and especially as management of the organization changes.

Finally, stories are members' recounting of their experiences as a way of dramatizing organizational life. People tell three types of stories at work: personal, collegial, and corporate. Personal stories are ones that individuals tell about themselves; typically they are used to support a positive portrayal of oneself and may include a hint of bragging. Collegial stories are those that employees tell about others. They can be amusing or harrowing, but they tend to reveal how people feel about the organization. Finally, corporate stories represent how managers see the organization and are often used to justify organizational policy or to endorse behaviors they prefer. Stories offer a simple and entertaining way for people to express their beliefs and attitude about the organization (Pacanowsky & Trujillo, 1983).

Participating in an organization's culture is important to one's sense of belonging; consequently, at universities newcomers, students, faculty, and staff become familiar with and integrated into their organizations as they learn the specific languages, attitudes, stories, and so on enacted by that organization. A classic example of dysfunctional organizational culture is portrayed in the sitcom *The Office*. In this sitcom, the Scranton, Pennsylvania, branch of the Dunder-Mifflin Paper Company has an ineffective, clueless manager, sensitivity training that backfires, inappropriate office romances, and a stodgy organizational culture with no real traditions, the exception being an attempt at a Christmas celebration forever remembered as the Booze Cruise.

Organizational cultures develop as a result of organizations' attempts to integrate, or assimilate, new members and as they respond to internal and external feedback as well as external conditions. Thus, organizational culture is not static but changes over time. Organizational experts speculate on how organizations (and their cultures) may change long-term in response to the pandemic. As more people work remotely, will leaders/managers have to work harder to maintain morale? Will increased monitoring of employees digitally (e.g., virtual clocking in and out, tracking work computer usage, and monitoring employee communications/chats) lead to resentment? While some organizations prioritized the well-being of employees as people over employees as workers, others have pushed employees to work in conditions that are high risk with little support—treating them as workers first and people second (Baker, 2020). In addition, organizational cultures reflect larger cultural values as well as the beliefs, attitudes, and practices of the specific organizations, which can and do change over time.

Organizational culture doesn't happen by accident, and there is a reciprocal relationship between communication and culture. Research shows that when the organizational leadership emphasizes a people orientation, collaboration, sharing, and team orientation (i.e., supportiveness), employees perceive the communication of their organization to be symmetrical—which leads employees to have high levels of trust, satisfaction, and commitment toward their employers, reinforcing a healthy organizational culture (Men & Jiang, 2016). Thus, culture shapes communication and communication can reinforce culture.

Each organization develops its own culture, though some organizations may share similar cultural characteristics. One cultural characteristic that is common to a variety of organizations is gender. That is, organizational cultures often are classified as masculine or feminine based on the values they embrace. For instance, firefighters, the military, and high-tech entrepreneurs share a "masculine culture" that values risk taking, courage, and rugged individualism (Larson & Pearson, 2012; Thurnell & Parker, 2008; Van Gilder, 2019). By contrast, "feminine cultures" such as Mary Kay Cosmetics and nursing are described as sharing a value of family-friendly policies, open communication, and participative and egalitarian decision making (Everbach, 2007).

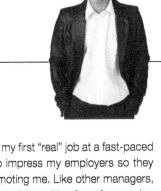

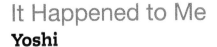

It Happened to Me
Yoshi

When I got promoted to project manager while working at my first "real" job at a fast-paced engineering firm, I was thrilled. I tried to do everything to impress my employers so they would know that they had made the right decision in promoting me. Like other managers, I often worked through lunch and stayed late. After I was in the position for a few weeks, I was discussing some project details with my supervisor, when he asked me what I was doing the coming weekend. I answered (truthfully) that I needed to get my car to a repair shop and was going to play in a tournament on my community soccer team. He just looked at me and said, "Oh, I thought you'd be coming to work." I soon learned that most of the project managers worked in the office at least one day of the weekend! I left this job about 6 months after this conversation, as I came to realize I was not a good fit for this particular company and job.

Nonetheless, organizations can be of a similar type or serve a similar function but still have aspects of their culture that differ considerably. Thus, although they are all restaurants, the organizational cultures of McDonald's, Applebee's, and Hooters differ. If you were to assess their cultural differences, you might think about who the employees are, the type of clothing employees wear, how they interact with patrons and each other, and what type of qualities are rewarded and valued. Even a brief visit to these establishments quickly reveals cultural differences.

The discussion thus far may suggest that organizational cultures are viewed positively by their members; however, that is not always the case. Some, many, or even most of the members of an institution may dislike their organization's culture. **Organizational climate** is the term used to describe how people feel about, or experience, organizational cultures (Schneider et al., 2005). If you have ever worked at a place you detested, it is likely that the organization had a culture you disagreed with or felt uncomfortable in (see *It Happened To Me: Yoshi*). Often when managers refer to whether a job candidate is a good "fit," they are describing whether they believe the person will like and participate in the company's culture.

organizational climate
How organizational members feel about, or experience, the organization's culture.

One challenge faced by organizations when they merge is how to integrate their respective cultures to form a new organizational culture. This is often not an easy task. (See *Did You Know?: Comparing Corporate Cultures.*) What type of organizational culture do you think you would find most compatible? Are you aware of any current organizations whose culture sounds appealing to you? When looking for a job, how can you find out about the corporate culture of an organization you're interested in?

Now that you have been introduced to the basic features of organizations, in the following section we discuss how individuals become members of organizations and the important role communication serves in supervisor–subordinate and coworker relationships.

**Journal Prompt 11.2:
Defining Organizational Structure**
What is the contemporary definition for organizational structure? How does it differ from the previous description of organizational structure?

DID YOU KNOW?
Comparing Corporate Cultures

You can imagine that integrating two very different corporate cultures during a corporate merger could be a daunting undertaking. This challenge was seen dramatically in Amazon's 2017 acquisition of Whole Foods.

Amazon's acquisition of Whole Foods was a partnership of "love at first sight." Amazon could expand beyond its online sales and sell groceries in stores while collecting shopper data. Whole Foods could recoup falling sales and reduce high prices. By 2020, no one, including customers and investors, seemed optimistic. Whole Foods employees were reportedly furious about Amazon's heavy-handed and punishing rules and were exploring unionizing. Organizational experts say the partnership problems were completely predictable and due to a clash between "tight" and "loose" corporate cultures.

Tight company cultures, like Amazon's, value consistency, routine, well-defined rules, and processes and have little tolerance for employee deviation. There is high priority on efficiency and predictability but less on adaptability. Amazon's employees know and operate within the hierarchy and guidelines, and their performance is constantly evaluated and surveilled, anonymously and overtly.

Loose cultures, like Whole Foods', are more fluid and adaptable, encourage innovation, avoid strict rules, but can be disorganized. Prior to the merger, the company structure was egalitarian with self-managed teams. Employees had significant decision-making power; store managers had autonomy to consider customer preferences in stocking products. This loose corporate culture may have contributed to inefficiencies that drove up prices and certainly led to Whole Food employees' unhappiness after the merger.

Experts say that with careful planning, flexibility, and organizational communication skills, these clashes can be avoided. Leadership teams should (1) (pre-merger) develop a cultural integration plan; (2) be culturally flexible, embracing the value of both tight and loose cultures; (3) address employees' underlying fear of change; and (4) be prepared to reevaluate their original integration strategy.

SOURCE: Gelfand, M., Gordon, S., Li, C., Choi, V., & Prokopowicz, P. (2018, October 2). One reason mergers fail: The two cultures aren't compatible. *hbr.org*. https://hbr.org/2018/10/one-reason-mergers-fail-the-two-cultures-arent-compatible

Organizational Communication and the Individual

11.3   Understand the types of communication that occur among coworkers and explain their functions.

If you wish to influence the organizations you interact with, you need to understand some of the basic types of communication that help create organizations and organizational life. It is important to be familiar with guidelines for how you might perform these types of communication most successfully. Although all the communication skills and abilities we examine in this book will definitely make you a better communicator in organizational contexts, here we focus on three types of communication that are integral to organizations: assimilation, supervisor–subordinate communication, and coworker communication. We also explore three types of organizational dilemmas or tensions that employees must manage.

Assimilation

assimilation

The communicative, behavioral, and cognitive processes that influence individuals to join, identify with, become integrated into, and (occasionally) exit an organization.

In the organizational context, **assimilation** refers to the communicative, behavioral, and cognitive processes that influence individuals to join, identify with, become integrated into, and (occasionally) exit an organization (Gailliard et al., 2010; Jablin, 2001). When you join an organization, you usually don't become an accepted member of the group automatically, nor do you immediately identify with the organization and its members. Instead, over time you go through a sometimes-complex process in which you and others begin to see you as an integral and accepted part of the organization that may include aspects of organizational life (e.g., getting to know coworkers and supervisors, participating in organizational activities, developing job competence, and learning organizational norms and standards) (Gailliard et al., 2010). The pledge process for sororities and fraternities is one highly ritualized form of assimilation.

Assimilation is a common experience for individuals who join any type of organization, whether it is a business, a religious group, or a social group. However, you probably most often think of assimilation as occurring when you begin a new job. Assimilation is similar to the process of cultural adaptation experienced when individuals enter a new culture, as we discussed in Chapter 8.

Organizational identification is a stage of assimilation that occurs when an employee's values overlap with the organization's values (Gioia & Patvardhan, 2012). For example, Arizona Public Service (a utility company) values community involvement, encourages its employees to volunteer, and even provides time off for workers to do so. Some new hires, however, may not inherently value volunteerism, and others may even resist the corporation's attempt to influence their behavior outside work. However, over time, some of these new hires will begin to identify more strongly with the organization and its values, and their attitudes will change. Those who had not given much thought to volunteering may now see it as a corporate responsibility, and those who were opposed may come to see time off for community service as a benefit.

organizational identification
The stage of assimilation that occurs when an employee's values overlap with the organization's values.

Developing an organizational identity is not necessarily a smooth one-way process. It can involve sometimes intense negotiation between individuals and the organization (Gioia & Patvardhan, 2012), and, of course, not every new employee experiences organizational identification. Some employees never come to accept their organization's values. For instance, if an employee values an environment in which coworkers become friends and socialize frequently, they likely will never identify with a highly competitive sales organization in which employees work independently and socialize only rarely. Such employees often leave their jobs, or if they remain, they never come to see themselves as part of the organization. Over time, most people do identify with the organizations they join, and they become increasingly integrated. While individuals usually adapt and change to their organizational culture, some may change some values of an organization. For example, a non-White woman who is hired as an accountant in an organization where the ideal employee/identity is White and male may, over time, be seen as a new "type" of employee—by showing commitment to other organizational values (e.g., civic responsibility) with positive coworker interaction—and thus change the ideal identity type. In fact, this organizational change in values may ultimately facilitate the entry of other "outsiders" into the organization (Thomson, 2020).

If and when members leave their organizations (voluntarily or involuntarily), they go through a process of decoupling their identities from the organization and move from being seen as insiders to once again being viewed as outsiders (Jablin, 2001). This leaving process can be difficult, especially if the exit is not voluntary and/or one does not have a new identity and organizational affiliation. For

▼ When these soldiers joined the U.S. Army, they were not immediately integrated. As they learned about the organizational culture and its rules, they became assimilated.

example, people who retire often feel sad and disconnected because they have lost an important identity.

The communication process most central to assimilation is information seeking, a reciprocal process in which individuals seek out information that helps them adapt to the organization and the organization attempts to convey information that will assist in this process. Two organizational communication scholars, Vernon Miller and Fred Jablin (1991), developed a typology of the information-seeking tactics that newcomers use to ascertain organizational roles, rules, and norms. These strategies take the same forms as other types of uncertainty-reduction techniques (see Chapter 9) and include active, passive, and interactive strategies (Berger, 1979).

The passive strategies new members use include observation and surveillance. These strategies involve watching others' communication and behavior or interpreting stories about past communication and behavior so that one can infer the rules and norms of the organization. For example, if you wonder what time employees typically arrive for work, you could go to work quite early one day and observe who arrives at what time, or you might attend to stories about people who arrived consistently late to work and what happened to them.

Active strategies include overt questioning, indirect questioning, disguising conversations, and questioning third parties. In these instances, the employee tries to discern organizational expectations by acquiring information from others. For example, a new employee might directly ask a more experienced coworker, "Are we expected to stay after 5 P.M.?" or she might pose the question more indirectly by saying, "How often do most employees stay past 5 P.M.?" Or she could engage in a disguising conversation by complaining about how late she had to stay in her previous job to see how her colleague responds. In addition, she might ask a third party (an administrative assistant) rather than a primary source (her supervisor) whether employees at her level are expected to stay past 5 P.M.

Finally, new employees seek information through the interactive strategy of "testing limits." A newcomer tests limits by seeing how far they can push specific boundaries. For instance, an employee might determine whether leaving at 5 P.M. is acceptable by leaving consistently at that time and then noting how people respond. To see a different perspective on organizational assimilation, see *Alternative View: What Is a "Real Job"?*.

Some experts suggest that individuals should start seeking information prior to joining the organization in an anticipatory socialization phase, learning about and evaluating general career options, or seeking information about potential organizations once a career has been chosen. For example, many students change majors during college—perhaps due to learning about potential or chosen majors. (Incidentally, changing majors correlates with higher graduation rates.) However, it turns out that few college students are seeking adequate career information, leading some employers to express concerns regarding college graduates' preparation for the professional workforce. These graduates often end up being underemployed or in jobs not requiring a college degree (Fetherston, 2017).

Critical Thinking Prompt
Which assimilation strategies do you think would be the most effective for a new employee to use?

The communication strategies that employees use throughout the assimilation process often set the tone for how they will interact with the organization. Another type of communication that influences how employees interact act at work is supervisor–subordinate communication.

Supervisor–Subordinate Communication

Supervisor–subordinate communication occurs when one person has the formal authority to regulate the behavior of another. In hierarchical organizations, virtually all employees engage in supervisor–subordinate communication, even CEOs—who must report upward to boards of directors (their supervisors) and downward to other organizational members (their subordinates).

ALTERNATIVE VIEW
What Is a "Real Job"?

How would you define what a "real job" is? What types of jobs do you think of as not being "real jobs"? Where have you heard the term *real job*, and who taught you its meaning?

In Robin Clair's work "The Political Nature of a Colloquialism, 'A Real Job': Implications for Organizational Assimilation" (1996), she critiques current models of organizational assimilation, such as Miller and Jablin's, for assuming that any work that occurs prior to or aside from working for an organization is not "real" work. To help us understand how individuals become socialized outside the context of organizations and to understand what constitutes work, she studied the popular expression *real job* by asking undergraduate students to write an essay about a time they encountered the term. She did so to examine what students mean by the term *real job* as well as to understand who was socializing them into a belief about what a real job looks like.

In their essays, Clair's respondents identified five dominant characteristics of a "real job":

- The money (i.e., one is well paid)
- Utilizes one's education
- Is enjoyable
- Requires 40 hours of work per week/8 hours per day
- Advancement is possible

Specific jobs that were identified as *not* being real jobs included serving in volunteer organizations such as the Peace Corps, working in a fast-food restaurant, working for one's family, or not making enough money to provide for a family. Overall, the respondents suggested that people with a college degree do not belong in unskilled labor positions, which for them did not constitute real jobs.

A number of respondents did acknowledge that the concept of a real job was a social construction, and some even rejected it. But even those who embraced jobs that others might consider not a real job continued to compare their own work to the societal standard and felt the need to justify their choices.

When asked who shaped their perceptions of what constitutes a real job, respondents pointed to family members (particularly fathers), friends, and coworkers. As Clair also points out, however, socialization is not a linear process in which society socializes young people into a particular belief about what constitutes a real job. Instead, she argues, those who are being socialized also serve to socialize themselves and others by the ways they talk about their own and others' employment plans and desires.

SOURCE: Clair, R. (1996). The political nature of a colloquialism, "A real job": Implications for organizational assimilation. *Communication Monographs, 63,* 249–267.

When organizational hierarchies exist, subordinates frequently attempt to please their supervisors to keep their jobs, receive raises and promotions, or perhaps even to become supervisors themselves someday. By the same token, successful supervisors must motivate and manage their subordinates. These sets of needs and goals impact how supervisors and subordinates communicate.

What are communication strategies supervisors can employ to increase employees' (as well as their own) satisfaction and success? As you might imagine, we suggest that they engage in effective communication. Although many communication strategies contribute to supervisor success, we highlight four: openness, supportiveness, motivation, and empowerment.

Openness occurs when communicators are willing to share their ideas and listen to others in a way that avoids conveying negative or disconfirming feedback (Cheney, 1995; Jablin, 1979). When supervisors are open, they create an environment of trust that increases the likelihood that upward communication will be perceived by employees as satisfactory.

Even though openness is a desirable characteristic, one can engage in *too much* openness. For example, if an employee is on leave to undergo rehabilitation for addiction, a supervisor typically should not share that information directly, or even indirectly, with others because doing so would be inappropriate. In addition, sometimes supervisors need to shield their employees from information. For example, informing subordinates of a possible layoff before the decision is final could cause unnecessary stress and panic.

Supportive supervisors provide their subordinates with access to information and resources. Thus, supportive supervisors explain roles, responsibilities, and tasks to those they manage; they also take the time to answer employees' questions. Further,

Critical Thinking Prompt
Think about supervisors you have had. What was it about their communication strategies that you liked or disliked? Which of the strategies we've mentioned here did they use?

openness
Sharing ideas as well as listening to others in a way that avoids conveying negative or disconfirming feedback.

supportiveness
Providing subordinates with access to information and resources.

managers are supportive when they give their subordinates the tools, skills, education, and time they need to be successful. Overall, supervisors who help their employees solve problems, listen actively, provide feedback, and offer encouragement are not only supportive, but they are also successful (Jia et al., 2017; Whetton & Cameron, 2002).

Productive and successful supervisors are able to motivate their subordinates. Workers experience **motivation** when they feel personally invested in accomplishing a specific activity or goal (Kreps, 1991). Many U.S. American supervisors and organizations focus on creating extrinsic or external motivators, such as pay raises, bonuses, promotions, titles, and benefits. However, supervisors who can instill intrinsic motivation in their subordinates are more successful. Intrinsic motivation occurs when people experience satisfaction in performing their jobs well, find their jobs to be enriching, and are, therefore, dedicated to their organizations or professions (Cheney et al., 2004).

Supervisors can create intrinsic motivation by setting clear and specific goals that are challenging but attainable and by engaging workers in the creation of those goals. In addition, they need to provide frequent and specific feedback, including praise, recognition, and corrections. Positive feedback is especially important because it encourages job satisfaction, organizational identification, and commitment (Larson, 1989). Finally, intrinsic motivation thrives in a positive work environment that stresses camaraderie or social relationships.

Empowerment, the fourth characteristic that improves communication, relates to the supervisor's ability to increase employees' feelings of self-efficacy. They do this by instilling the feeling that the subordinate is capable of performing the job and has the authority to decide how to perform it well (Eisenberg et al., 2019). In general, supervisors who empower their subordinates function more like coaches than traditional managers. They encourage employees to be involved in decision making, to take responsibility for their tasks, and to provide suggestions for improving their own and the organization's performance. Employees who feel empowered are more likely to develop intrinsic motivation and to communicate openly with their supervisors.

Communication is also central to subordinates' success on the job (Steele & Plenty, 2015). Subordinates who get along with their supervisors are much more likely to be satisfied and successful. Consequently, subordinates use a variety of means to manage and maintain the quality of their relationships with their supervisors. Studies of subordinate communication tactics determined that employees who use three specific upward communication tactics—ingratiation, assertiveness, and rationality—were most likely to positively affect their manager's perceptions of them (Dockery & Steiner, 1990; Wayne & Ferris, 1990).

Ingratiation refers to behavior and communication designed to increase liking. It includes friendliness and making one's boss feel important. Of course, one can be too ingratiating and come off as being insincere, but genuine respect and rapport can be effective. **Assertive** subordinates who can express their opinions forcefully without offending or challenging their bosses also tend to engender liking and approval. In addition, subordinates who can argue **rationally**—meaning that they communicate

motivation

Feeling personally invested in accomplishing a specific activity or goal.

empowerment

Feeling capable of performing a job and having the authority to decide how to perform it well.

ingratiation

Behavior and communication designed to increase liking.

assertiveness

Expressing one's opinions forcefully without offending or challenging others.

rationality

The ability to communicate through reasoning, bargaining, coalition building, and assertiveness.

▼ Positive communication between supervisors and their subordinates is characterized by openness, supportiveness, and the empowerment of subordinates.

with their bosses through reasoning, bargaining, coalition building, and assertiveness—are often adept at managing their supervisors. Finally, employees who understand their bosses' professional and personal goals as well as their strengths and weaknesses, and who can adapt to their preferred communication styles, can create positive working relationships.

While high-quality superior–subordinate relationships are linked with many positive outcomes for employees, such as job satisfaction, career progression, and motivation, the boundaries of these relationships are fluid. One possible consequence is job creep, in which supervisors may ask employees to accept and employees agree to accept extra-role tasks as reasonable, like frequently taking over the supervisor's responsibilities when the supervisor is absent. Supervisors tend not to make such requests of employees with whom they have lower-quality relationships. Thus, employees who have high-quality relationships with their supervisors are especially vulnerable to overextending themselves and to experiencing job stress. Of course, the frequency and tone with which the supervisor assigns the task make a difference. Assigning the tasks infrequently and with a question, an explanation, and expression of appreciation can lessen the stress (Sias & Duncan, 2019).

Another challenge supervisor–subordinate communication faces is **employee dissent**, which occurs when an employee perceives an inconsistency in what was promised by the organization and subsequently objects to, questions, or disagrees with circumstances. Dissent can also occur when an employee perceives the organization is behaving unethically. Dissent can affect job performance and satisfaction, organizational commitment, and turnover intentions, so it's important to understand the communication process involved; that is, how the employee expresses dissent can influence how the manager responds to initial dissent, which can then influence the employee's reaction, and so on. If each responds negatively, the result is a negatively escalating communication spiral (De Ruiter et al., 2016). Let's see how this might work in a real-life work context.

Alisha works in a customer service call center. She is bilingual and has small children at home. She was promised an extra bonus for bilingual calls and weekends off. She's been working for several weeks, and about 50 percent of calls require bilingual skills, but she's only received the bonus for three calls. She discovers that her supervisor is only counting a call as bilingual if the caller starts the conversation in Spanish, whereas most callers start off with a few English sentences and then switch to Spanish. In addition, she's been asked to work the last weekend of the month (as a special favor to her manager).

In such cases when an employee perceives an inconsistency in what was promised but not delivered by the organization, employees and managers have several communication options. It is important to view the issue from a dyadic viewpoint, as each has a communication choice to make at each point that can then influence subsequent interactions. Researchers De Ruiter, Schalk, and Blomme (2016) outline the possible responses and related consequences.

The employee's (e.g., Alisha's) potential responses are (1) to not say anything, (2) to voice dissent, (3) to neglect her work (e.g., waste time, perform poorly, frequent absences), (4) a more active response (e.g., verbal aggression against supervisors or coworkers or even theft), or (5) to leave the job/organization. Alisha's first response was to send a private message to her supervisor, voicing her dissent and asking about the reduced pay and required weekend work. Now, her manager had several potential responses to Alisha's voiced dissent. The supervisor might (1) delay responding, (2) give a favorable response (e.g., express sympathy and give an acceptable explanation), or (3) give an unfavorable response (e.g., become irritable, annoyed, angry).

From research findings we know that Alisha's first response (to voice dissent and try to discover the cause of the perceived inconsistency) is the typical initial response of most employees. We also know that if a supervisor then provides a favorable response (is sympathetic and provides a reasonable explanation), the issue does not escalate, and the pre-dissent situation returns.

employee dissent
When an employee perceives an inconsistency in what was promised by the organization and subsequently objects to, questions, or disagrees with circumstances.

However, if either side responds negatively, then with each interaction, the outcome is very different. For example, if Alisha's first response had been to aggressively confront her manager in front of other employees, perhaps threatening to sue, it is likely that the manager would have given an unfavorable response—delaying responding or becoming angry and yelling at Alisha—which may then cause Alisha to respond even more angrily, perhaps neglecting her work, and the communication escalates into a negative spiral.

De Ruiter and colleagues make two important points about this dissent interaction. First, dealing with the issue privately, for both employee and manager, is a good guideline. Embarrassing or humiliating the other person in public is likely to cause strong negative emotions, which in turn is likely to trigger more negative responses. Second, once a cycle of negative employee–manager communication exchanges gets established, it is likely to continue until the employee has had enough; after experiencing major frustration, decreased loyalty to the organization, or passive or active neglect of job responsibilities, the employee often exits the organization. The takeaway here is that both employee and employer should consider carefully the first few response choices once the dissent process is initiated.

An increasingly common situation is employee dissent regarding unethical organizational behavior, which we will discuss in more detail later in the chapter. Experts suggest that supervisors encourage this dissent, partly to prevent future harmful legal and/or economic consequences for the organization. For example, some U.S. military units have reportedly allowed sexual harassment and assault to occur unchecked within their ranks. This unethical behavior can result (and has resulted) in negative legal and public relations problems for these military units. As we will discuss later in the chapter, instances of sexual harassment are often not reported. That is, employees rarely voice dissent, allowing unethical behavior to continue.

How can managers/supervisors encourage dissent in situations of unethical organizational behavior? Communication scholars Bisel and Adame (2018) conducted an interesting study investigating strategies used by supervisors to encourage dissent. Specifically, they compared two styles of supervisor talk to discover which was more likely to encourage employee dissent (e.g., Does the supervisor regularly talk about the importance of *logical* thinking, encouraging workers to follow their *intellect* in carrying out responsibilities and making decisions, or do bosses regularly talk about the importance of "following your heart" and "going with your gut"?). Bisel and Adame asked their study participants (employees) which type of supervisor talk would encourage ethical dissent. Perhaps not surprisingly, they found that the more effective strategy was to encourage employees to trust their moral instinct (e.g., "going with your gut") rather than approaching issues from an intellectual or rational (or legal) fashion. In addition, this "following your gut" approach seems to reduce employee anxiety when expressing ethical dissent.

Communicating with Coworkers

Along with assimilation and supervisor–subordinate communication, communication with coworkers is fundamental to organizations and their employees. Sometimes the communication that occurs among coworkers or peers is described as *horizontal* because it is directed neither upward (to superiors) nor downward (to subordinates). No matter how they are described, workplace relationships are distinctive interpersonal relationships that influence both the individuals within them and the organization as a whole (Sias, 2005).

Employees become friends with their colleagues for many of the same reasons they develop other types of interpersonal relationships—proximity, attraction, and similarity. Some people, especially those who live alone, may spend more time with their colleagues than they do with anyone else. Even people who live with others may spend as much—or more—time with coworkers as they do with their families or housemates.

However, unlike other interpersonal relationships, friendship development at work is affected by an additional dimension—how supervisors treat individual employees. If supervisors are perceived to treat some employees more favorably and this treatment is perceived as undeserved, coworkers may dislike and distrust favored employees. On the other hand, if a manager is seen as treating a subordinate more negatively than others and the treatment is perceived as unwarranted, it can increase employee interaction and cohesiveness (Graen & Graen, 2006; Sias & Jablin, 1995).

▲ Coworkers engage in informal–personal as well as formal–professional interactions.

Coworkers in organizations engage in both formal–professional and informal–personal interactions. The formal–professional category includes communication about tasks, solving problems, making plans, and influencing one another's beliefs and decisions (Kram & Isabella, 1985). In addition, coworkers engage in considerable informal, or personal, interaction. In fact, adults draw many of their friends from the pool of people at work, and approximately 50 percent of employees state that they have engaged in a romance at work (Vault, 2003). Coworkers also can serve as an important source of emotional and social support (Rawlins, 1994).

The professional and the personal aspects of coworker communication and relationships are not distinct. Rather, professional interactions influence coworkers' personal relationships, and vice versa. Sias and Cahill (1998) found that more talk about more topics among coworkers not only resulted from increased closeness in their relationships but also contributed to it. Thus, coworkers who also are friends tend to communicate more intimately and about more topics, both professionally and personally, than those who are not (Sias et al., 2003). As you might expect, being isolated from employee networks can result in isolation from quality work-related information (in addition to loneliness) and cause one to be at an information disadvantage relative to one's colleagues (Sias, 2005). Research indicates that this information disadvantage has important consequences. Poor coworker communication and lack of access to information have been found to predict lower job satisfaction and commitment.

The presence of friendly relationships among coworkers has positive consequences for individuals and organizations. When employees feel connected to their colleagues, they provide each other with support and assistance that can increase their success. Such relationships also intensify workers' loyalty to the company and increase job satisfaction and organizational identification, which can help minimize job turnover. Friendly relationships with coworkers are particularly important when people are working remotely and can feel isolated. In fact, one study found that friendly communication among telecommuting coworkers even lessened the impact of employees' complaints on their organizational commitment (Fay & Kline, 2011).

Despite the ease, attractiveness, and advantages of forming close relationships at work, such relationships can require careful navigation. Friendship, by its nature, is egalitarian, but power differences often occur among coworkers. Even employees at the same level in the organization may have different levels of informal power, and the situation can become increasingly problematic if one of them receives a promotion and thereby acquires greater formal power in the organization. In addition, coworkers may find themselves torn between their loyalty to the organization and their loyalty to a friend. For example, how should one respond if a friend engages in unethical behavior at work, decides to become a whistleblower, or quits in protest over a denied promotion? It can be difficult for individuals to decide how to respond in a way that protects their own as well as their friends' interests. Finally, it can be more difficult to be objective with a friend, to withhold confidential information, and to provide honest feedback.

In addition, other employees can develop negative perceptions and interpretations of the friendships and courtship relationships of their colleagues (Cowan & Horan, 2014). Coworkers may question the motives of the partners, may believe that the individuals involved are conspiring to affect corporate policy, or may perceive that the relationship partners treat others unfairly in comparison. For instance, if two salespeople become close, their coworkers may perceive that they are sharing information or client lists that permit them to be more successful than those outside the relationship. In addition, because of the potential for trouble and bad feelings, some organizations have explicit policies that discourage "affectional" relationships, which may include friendships but most certainly include romances.

Organizational Dilemmas

Although organizations can provide many benefits to an individual, including status, money, a sense of belonging, and even a significant part of one's identity, they also can create physical and psychological distress. Thus, in addition to being proficient at the three key types of organizational communication, members of organizations may have to communicatively manage and respond to three types of organizational dilemmas: emotion labor, stress and burnout, and work–life conflict.

Emotion Labor   As we discussed previously, employees learn a variety of norms for organizational behavior during assimilation. Some of these norms pertain to emotion display rules (Scott & Myers, 2005). Emotion display rules are the explicit or implicit rules that organizations have for what emotions can be appropriately displayed and how those emotions should be communicated. For example, firefighters learn early in the assimilation process that they should not express strong negative emotions such as fear, disgust, and panic (Scott & Myers, 2005). Instead, they learn to speak in calm tones, to offer verbal assurances, and to suppress any comments that might distress the public. Similarly, the employees at the local grocery store have learned to show cheerfulness and helpfulness toward customers, even if they actually feel irritation, anger, or frustration.

When the organization expects or requires workers to display particular feelings, employees are engaging in emotion labor (Hochschild, 1983). Typically, organizations ask employees to alter their emotional behavior in three ways. First, they may ask employees to heighten or increase their expressions of joy (e.g., cruise ship and other tourism employees), to appear mean or indifferent (debt collectors and law officers, on occasion), or to convey "a vaguely pleasant professional demeanor" (nurses and receptionists) (Cheney et al., 2004, p. 68). For one student's experience with emotion labor, see *It Happened to Me: Sonya*.

It Happened to Me
Sonya

For a year, I worked on a cruise line as an assistant cruise director. My job was to organize activities and help entertain the passengers. I helped with bingo games, organized costume contests, and participated in various games with the passengers. In addition, I was expected to dance with the passengers in the evening at the nightclub. Unfortunately, I often had to deal with passengers who had had a few drinks and wanted to "get friendly" or invite me back to their rooms. No matter how the passenger behaved, I was expected to be polite, pleasant, and friendly without, of course, ever actually becoming involved with one! It was really difficult sometimes. I would be so angry, upset, or embarrassed at how a passenger behaved, but I could never show it. This is one of the major reasons I did not sign up again after my first year on the ship.

Some scholars believe that performing emotion labor benefits employees. They argue that when workers perform emotions they do not actually feel, they can better cope with stress (Conrad & Witte, 1994), and they are more able to interact in emotionally satisfying ways with their clients (Shuler & Sypher, 2000). These scholars suggest that social workers, emergency medical personnel, and other employees in the social services find their work easier and more meaningful when they perform emotion labor.

Others believe it can be harmful (Tracy, 2000; Waldron, 1994), especially when it is required and when it benefits the organization but not the employee. For example, Sarah Tracy (2005), an organizational communication scholar, studied correctional officers' emotion labor and its consequences. She found that the officers often were expected to manage contradictory emotional displays—for example, showing respect for inmates but not trusting them or nurturing them while also being tough. She discovered that performing these contradictory emotions led some of the officers to experience withdrawal, paranoia, stress, and burnout. Thus, consistently having to perform emotion labor, especially when the requirements are ambiguous and contradictory, may cause psychological and physical harm to some workers.

Recent research suggests that perhaps both these positions have some merit and requires a distinction between **surface acting** (where employees express the required emotion without the accompanying feeling) and **deep acting** (where employees work to actually *feel* the emotion required). A recent study investigated the emotional labor of lawyers, who are viewed as highly rational but at the same time are required to enthusiastically represent their clients regardless of how they feel about their client or their guilt. In addition, sometimes the process/outcomes have highly charged emotional or high-stakes implications. Turns out that for these lawyers, work-related emotional communication had both positive and negative effects—surface acting seemed to cause more exhaustion and cynicism and led to burnout (a topic we discuss later in this chapter), whereas being able to authentically feel the required emotion seemed to lead to improved performance and even a sense of well-being (Powers & Myers, 2020). Overall, deep acting seems to also contribute to higher job satisfaction, especially if there is perceived organizational support. Thus, employers in hospitality and other tourism industries, for example, could develop training that focuses on improving employees' ability to monitor and manage emotions and thus reduce the impact of bad emotions. The training might include ways that employees could show positive real emotions in order to provide high-quality customer service (Wen et al., 2019). In addition, employers should consider constantly improving the organizational support environment to their frontline employees. Individuals considering prospective careers or prospective organizations could benefit from learning about the emotional communication requirements and decide whether their own emotional needs are compatible (Powers & Myers, 2020).

Stress and Burnout As you just read, correctional officers often experience stress and burnout. But they are not the only employees who suffer in this way; stress and burnout have become widespread in the U.S. workplace, and the terms have become common in everyday speech. However, **burnout** includes a specific set of characteristics, including exhaustion, cynicism, and ineffectiveness (Maslach, 2003; Maslach & Leiter, 1997). It is a chronic condition that results from the accumulation of daily stress, where stress is defined as a common response to important and consequential demands, constraints, or opportunities to which one feels unable to respond (McGrath, 1976).

Exhaustion, which is a core characteristic of burnout, can include physical, emotional, or mental exhaustion. It expresses itself as physical fatigue, loss of affect (or emotion), and an aversion to one's job. Employees who are emotionally exhausted may try to reduce the emotional stress of working with others by detaching from them, a behavior called depersonalization, which is related to the second characteristic of burnout—cynicism. Cynicism is manifested as an indifferent attitude toward others.

surface acting
When employees express the required emotion without the accompanying feeling.

deep acting
When employees work to actually *feel* the emotion required.

Critical Thinking Prompt
Do you believe that performing emotion labor is beneficial or detrimental to employees? Why? Could it be beneficial in some jobs but not others? Why?

burnout
A chronic condition that results from the accumulation of daily stress, which manifests itself in a specific set of characteristics, including exhaustion, cynicism, and ineffectiveness.

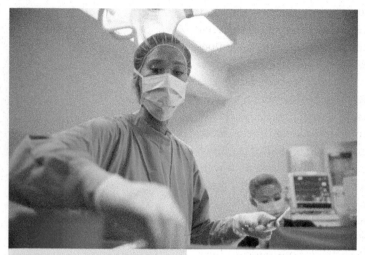

▲ Job stress tends to be high for healthcare workers because of the highly consequential demands inherent in the job and the fact that, in some cases, even the most highly skilled professionals are unable to save a patient's life.

A person with a cynical attitude may view others as objects or numbers and may also express hostility and harsh criticism toward them. Employees might feel ineffective, the third characteristic of burnout, which occurs when workers negatively evaluate their own performance. Ineffectiveness may result in absenteeism, decreased effort, and withdrawal (Richardsen & Martinussen, 2004).

Burnout arises as a result of a combination of personality factors (e.g., how well one manages ambiguity and stress) and organizational stressors. Organizational stressors are aspects of one's job that create strain. Some of the more significant organizational stressors include work overload; confusion, conflict, and ambiguity related to job roles; being undermined by a supervisor (Westman & Etzion, 2005); and low levels of social support (Koniarek & Dudek, 1996).

Workload refers to the amount of work an individual is expected to perform. Work overload occurs when employees feel they have more work than they can accomplish, and this is a major contributor to feelings of exhaustion. Despite expectations that technology, and especially mobile technology, would lessen the burden for workers in the United States, people today are working longer hours and dealing with heavier workloads than before the advent of these technologies. There are at least two areas of impact: communication technology used in the workplace and also at home. According to some workers, the introduction of mobile communication technologies in their workplaces has led to work disruption and overload. In a recent survey, almost 70 percent of employees said they toggle between mobile applications up to 10 times per hour, and searching for information from multiple sources is disruptive. At the same time, they agreed that these technologies allow them to handle very complex tasks and multitasking (Yin et al., 2018).

In addition, these technologies impact workers when they are at home, as they frequently find that because of mobile technologies, they are never "away" from the job, which can lead to increased stress. However, it turns out that how employees feel about this technology-linked stress seems to depend on employee perception. That is, in one study, employees who had less-firm boundaries between work and life viewed using communication technologies for work-related tasks at home as a convenience, had positive perceptions of the usefulness of these technologies, and experienced less stress and work–life conflict, whereas workers who prefer a more rigid separation between the two domains saw mobile communication technology use as more of an intrusion into their private lives and experienced increased stress and work–life conflict (Wright et al., 2014).

Work overload also is related to our second major organizational stressor—role confusion, conflict, and ambiguity. Role ambiguity occurs when employees do not understand what is expected of them. This is most likely to occur when one begins a new job, but it also occurs when organizations undergo change. Because today's workers are faced with continual change resulting from budget cuts, reorganizations, and new technologies, they frequently experience role ambiguity (Chambers et al., 1998).

To give some perspective on the role ambiguity and confusion play as work stressors, consider this. As recently as 20 years ago, newly hired engineers primarily needed to communicate with other engineers, most of whom were born in the United States and were native speakers of English. Since that time, however, U.S. companies have hired more engineers from other countries and have expanded their operations around the world. Consequently, many engineers now need to communicate with and supervise others who do not share their native culture and background. They have been required to develop intercultural communication skills they never expected would be necessary and to become conversant with cultures outside the United States. Some long-term employees are unsure of their ability to respond appropriately. Employees in many industries face similar challenges as organizations respond to changing market conditions, globalization, and new technology. Unfortunately, uncertainty about one's job duties and one's ability to perform those duties creates considerable stress for workers.

Role conflict arises when employees find it difficult to meet conflicting or incompatible job demands (Igbaria & Guimaraes, 1993). For example, the correctional officers we mentioned in our discussion of emotion labor experienced considerable role conflict. On the one hand, they were expected to act like social workers whose job it was to treat prisoners with respect, to nurture them, and to facilitate their well-being and rehabilitation; on the other hand, they were expected to function as paramilitary agents whose job it was to maintain order and safety, to mistrust the prisoners, and to be tough. Similarly, when managers are told to treat their employees fairly and humanely but also to meet tight production deadlines, they suffer from role conflict. Research indicates that being asked to perform such incompatible tasks on the job gives rise to considerable stress and ill effects (Rizzo et al., 1970). For example, role conflict and ambiguity can cycle into burnout, leading workers to experience feelings of ineffectiveness in their jobs.

To complete our discussion of organizational stressors and burnout, we focus squarely on communication issues. When employees feel undermined by their supervisors, whether through having information withheld, being denied the resources they need to do their jobs, or being treated unfairly, they are more likely to experience cynicism and a lack of efficacy (Maslach & Leiter, 1997). They may feel they cannot accomplish their work because they lack the resources to do so, and they may believe that even if they do perform well, they will not be rewarded.

Communication with coworkers can contribute to burnout when one's colleagues are unable to provide the social support one needs to cope with organizational stressors. Feelings of burnout then may spread from one employee to their colleagues. This fact, combined with the faster pace of most organizations, can lead to a breakdown of community within the organization and disconnect coworkers from one another (Maslach & Leiter, 1997).

Interestingly, research has established that communication itself can be an important moderator of employee burnout. Findings show that supervisor communication that includes active listening, effective feedback, participative decision making, and supportiveness can decrease the severity of subordinate burnout (Casey, 1998; Golembiewski et al., 1998). Similarly, communication with coworkers that conveys warmth and support and reaffirms the meaning of one's work can help employees cope with burnout (Casey, 1998).

If you would like to see if you are experiencing burnout, go to http://www.mind-tools.com/pages/article/newTCS_08.htm and take the Burnout Self-Test.

Work–Life Conflict   A third type of organizational dilemma that workers face is **work–life conflict**, defined by the difficulties individuals and families face as they try to balance job and home responsibilities. Since the 1990s, work–family balance has become an issue of concern and another type of role conflict, especially for dual-career couples (Kirby & Krone, 2002). As more women have entered the workforce and more families have become reliant on two incomes, people are finding it difficult to manage their competing demands. As we have seen, the pervasiveness of communication technologies such as email, cell phones, instant messaging, and Zoom technology has made it difficult for some workers to ever get away from work and focus on the other aspects of their lives.

In addition, the COVID-19 pandemic has added an additional stressor for many workers, especially women, who tend to be the more "essential" workers (service workers, healthcare workers), not able to stay home with their children but having to ensure childcare and at the same time risking their own health going to work every day. Also facing increased work–life conflict are those women who work remotely from home and try to manage a full-time job plus supervise their children's schoolwork. As one female

work–life conflict
Difficulty balancing job and home responsibilities.

▲ The widespread use of technology in many jobs has increased the conflicts people have in maintaining separation between their work lives and private lives.

professor expressed her frustration: "Managing four young children at home while trying to maintain productivity as an academic is challenging. Making the switch to working from home with the whole nuclear family unit in residence was tough, and the first week of confinement was a circus. . . . My husband became a permanent fixture at the dining room table on video calls as his company tried to stop losing clients. This was a palpable miasma of stress. My children approached the situation like a free-for-all screen fest" (Stephens et al., 2020, p. 431).

In response to work–life conflict, many organizations have developed family-friendly policies, such as flextime, family leave, and dependent-care benefits (Morgan & Milliken, 1992). However, studies have shown that many employees do not take advantage of these benefits (Kirby & Krone, 2002; Rapoport & Bailyn, 1996). The reality is researchers have found that some employees are discouraged from taking advantage of these benefits or are not informed about their existence. For example, managers may indirectly communicate that employees should not use the available benefits because it causes problems for them, their departments, and the organization (Rapoport & Bailyn, 1996).

A study of Corning, Xerox, and Tandem Computers determined that employees who used such benefits experienced negative career consequences (Rapoport & Bailyn, 1996). Once employees discovered that their coworkers suffered when they used the company's family leave or flextime benefits, they simply stopped requesting them. Kirby and Krone (2002) conducted another study whose title aptly describes this organizational policy: "The Policy Exists, but You Can't Really Use It." The irony is that some organizations receive credit for being family friendly while not having to actually implement their policies (Jenner, 1994; Solomon, 1994). When workers are not able to balance the many demands in their lives, they, their families, and society at large suffer the consequences.

Earlier, we discussed the impact of using communication technologies for *work-related activities* at home and at work. What about using them for *home-related* communication at work? A recent study of employees using private smartphones at work showed that workers who gave high priority to work over home viewed the interruptions as family life intrusions at work (e.g, learning about a daily hassle in the family domain, receiving an unpleasant message in a WhatsApp group) and experienced more exhaustion and work–life conflict (Derks et al., 2021).

Although both men and women must manage work–life issues, much of the research on work–life conflict has focused on the difficulties working women face as they try to manage paid and unpaid labor. Men are perceived to work as hard as or harder at paid work than women, but research indicates that women contribute at least twice as much unpaid labor to their families, resulting in high levels of work–life conflict (Alberts et al., 2011).

Organizational scholar Sarah Tracy and colleagues (2015) have proposed training to prepare college students to deal with work–life balance issues they will face later. For example, one training activity focuses on "doing" work–life balance by asking students to record their behavior (e.g., Am I returning emails during dinner? Am I complaining about work or my kids? When do I feel most alive?), estimate the number of hours they currently engage in various activities (e.g., paid work, domestic labor, leisure, etc.), and consider and propose preferences for future work–life balance. Through this training students can reflect on their priorities and their current patterns of work–life balance and prepare for future work–life challenges in personally relevant ways (Tracy et al., 2015, p. 325).

To summarize, communication is central to an individual's life within an organization, and individuals face many communication-related issues as they navigate organizations. Such challenges involve assimilation as well as communication with supervisors, subordinates, and coworkers. Inevitably, conflicts arise, as do a variety of potential organizational dilemmas, including emotion labor, stress and burnout, and work–life conflict. Thus, successful individuals are those who are able to communicate effectively as they negotiate the challenges, conflicts, and dilemmas of organizational life. However, as you've seen throughout this book, if you only consider individual forces or factors, you can't understand the whole picture. Individuals and organizations both are subject to numerous societal forces, the topic we turn to next.

Journal Prompt 11.3:
Supervisor Communication
What four communication strategies contribute to supervisors' success?

The Individual, Organizational Communication, and Society

11.4   Discuss current social influences on organizations and organizational communication.

In this section, we explore how organizations and the societies in which they are located exert influence on each other and the individuals within them. First, we examine two of the most significant societal forces that impact organizational communication—history and globalization. Next, we discuss three important recent organizational practices that influence individuals and society, including the development of a new social contract between organizations and employees, the rise of urgent organizations, and the blurring of boundaries between home and work. Finally, we examine power relations within organizations and their impact on employees. We address these topics to explicate how each has influenced beliefs about organizational communication and its performance.

Societal Influences on Organizations

Organizations are shaped in part by the societies in which they are located. As societies change over time, so do the organizations within them. In addition, as organizations spread their operations into new cultures, they must change and adapt to those cultures to be successful. In the next section, we focus on these two societal influences on organizations: (1) social change and its impact on organizations and the communication within them and (2) globalization and its effects on organizations and organizational communication.

Historical Forces   Prevailing beliefs about work, individuals, and knowledge creation have influenced what people expect of organizations as well as how they are expected to act within them. For example, until the early 1900s, popular talk about organizational techniques took a moral tone. Journalists, novelists, clergy, and other prominent figures often described business owners as men of superior character, which they were obligated to model for the betterment of the lower, working class (Barley & Kunda, 1992). During this time, managers' and owners' opinions and communication were considered important, whereas those of the working classes were not.

By the 1930s, a major change in thinking about organization and communication occurred. Resulting from cultural changes as well as researchers such as Mary Parker Follett (1942), people began to question the absolute right of managers to command and control employees and began to focus, instead, on the human relations function of organizations. That is, management began to be seen as needing to educate (through teaching and persuading), to interact with employees (by seeking input), and to integrate everyone's input. Thus, for the first time, organizational theorists and managers came to believe that workers needed to have a voice in the organization.

A variety of developments around the 1960s prompted another shift in thinking about organizations and communication (Barley & Kunda, 1992) toward what we might call a *systems mentality*. Military operations research began to find a home in industry, and the rise of computers fostered interest in organizational communication processes. Across many academic disciplines, researchers began a quest for general, even universal, theoretical principles. Biologist Ludwig von Bertalanffy (1968), for instance, developed a highly influential **general systems theory** that, he believed, applied as well to the social sciences as it did to the life and physical sciences. Many organization scholars agreed. They saw organizations as systems not only composed of many subsystems but also embedded in larger systems. Hence, they sought to develop strategies for communication that occur within the units or subsystems of the organization as well as for communication that occurs between the organization and its environment.

general systems theory
Theory that organizations are a system composed of many subsystems and embedded in larger systems, and that organizations should develop communication strategies that serve both.

Today, one of the most important societal factors to impact organizations, and the individuals who work within them, is globalization (Altman, 2020; Faiola, 2020). **Globalization** refers to the increasing connectedness of the world in economic, political, and cultural realms (Cheney et al., 2004). Although we typically think of globalization in economic terms, it also describes the ways in which political and cultural events affect people around the world. For example, terrorist attacks in Europe and the Middle East influence tourists' travel plans as well as governments' political alliances. From an economic perspective, conflict in the Middle East leads to fears that oil production will suffer and that higher energy costs will occur in the United States and other countries reliant on this source of oil. Because of globalization, people in the United States are connected intimately to other parts of the world; as a result, decisions and events in far-removed places can affect them.

globalization
The increasing connectedness of the world in economic, political, and cultural realm.

Although many scholars and experts agree on what globalization *is*, considerable disagreement exists concerning whether globalization, specifically economic globalization, is a positive or negative force in individuals' lives. Proponents believe that globalization leads to decreased trade barriers that result in increased prosperity and economic development across societies (Krugman, 2002). Critics, however, argue that globalization leads to a growing gap between the rich and the poor because transnational organizations can operate without oversight by national and international institutions that protect the interests of individuals (Ganesh et al., 2005). More specifically, these critics maintain that this lack of oversight leads to companies attempting to profit by ignoring worker safety, not providing fair compensation, and exploiting the environment.

▼ Starbucks is one of many global organizations.

What are the communication implications of globalization? First, it means that more people and businesses have intercultural contact and that they need to learn how to communicate more effectively across cultures, as we noted in Chapter 10. Many categories of individuals need to interact with support personnel around the world, even in their nonwork lives, and increasingly workers in multinational organizations must communicate and work with people from diverse cultures. Second, global forces such as market deregulation may have leveling or homogenizing effects on organizational practices all over the world. Learn more about this issue in *Communication in Society: Case Study: Antiglobalization Protests.*

COMMUNICATION IN SOCIETY
Case Study: Antiglobalization Protests

Do you think economic globalization, on the whole, improves individuals' lives in the United States and elsewhere? Why or why not? What terms would you use to refer to those in the movement opposing globalization? What do you predict the future of corporations and other organizations will be like with regard to globalization?

Most Americans first became aware of the so-called antiglobalization movement in 1999, when protests erupted in Seattle outside the meeting of the World Trade Organization (WTO); hundreds of demonstrators were arrested and thousands were injured. In subsequent years, antiglobalization demonstrations were organized in the United States and foreign cities outside meetings of the International Monetary Fund (IMF), World Bank, Group of Eight (G8), and other high-level global economic institutions.

Activists in the movement argue that "antiglobalization" is a misnomer because they are not against globalization as such. Instead, they use terms such as "antiplutocracy" and "anticorporate." Many consider themselves proponents of a global justice movement. In 2001, they organized the first World Social Forum in Porto Alegre, Brazil, as a counterevent to the World Economic Forum, which was taking place in Davos, Switzerland, at the same time.

The loosely organized global social justice movement includes a wide variety of organizations and individuals, among them Nobel Prize–winning economists Amartya Sen and Joseph E. Stiglitz. In general, what they oppose is "corporate personhood" and the unbridled capitalism inherent in "free trade" under agreements such as the North American Free Trade Agreement (NAFTA) and the Association of Southeast Asian Nations Free Trade Area (AFTA). They also oppose what they see as the exploitation of workers in free-trade zones (FTZ) such as the maquiladora zone in Mexico along the U.S. border—manufacturing centers, located primarily in developing countries, where raw goods can be imported, manufactured into finished goods, and reexported without having to pass through normal international trade barriers such as customs inspections.

The antiglobalization movement has been criticized for lacking a coherent set of goals. Critics also point to data indicating that poverty has decreased in developing countries since the early 1990s, when the globalization trend began. They argue that U.S. workers have benefited from increased opportunities to export goods to developing countries.

Influence of Organizations on Individuals and Society

Not only are organizations influenced by society and cultures, but they also influence them and the individuals who comprise them. In this section, we explore three trends in contemporary organizations and the ways in which they impact society and individuals' lives. These trends include the new social contract, urgent organizations, and blurred boundaries between work and life.

The New Social Contract   Over the past 25 years, a fundamental change has occurred in the relationship between individuals and their employers (Chilton & Weidenbaum, 1994; Jablin & Sias, 2001). Until recently, employees expected to spend years, if not their entire working lives, with a single company and to be rewarded for their service and loyalty with job security and good retirement benefits (Eisenberg et al., 2010). This is no longer the case. Along with globalization, an increase in organizations' willingness to lay off workers during economic downturns and corporate restructuring have led to a **new social contract** between employers and employees. Under this "new social contract," loyalty is not expected by workers or organizations and job security rarely exists (Eisenberg et al., 2010). This means that if it is deemed profitable, companies are quick to sell or merge with other corporations, and employees are willing to jump ship if the right opportunity arises.

A number of individuals have argued that the financial crisis of 2007–2009 worsened by recent economic problems brought on by the pandemic has led to a greater imbalance in the social contract between companies and employees. They argue that organizations used these crises as an excuse to engage in hiring practices that benefit organizations at great cost to employees. Although not everyone agrees, it is true that during the "Great Recession" and the pandemic millions of jobs were eliminated as

new social contract
Assumes that loyalty is not expected by workers or organizations and that job security is unlikely.

▲ Google and other technology companies manifest many of the behaviors typical of urgent organizations.

temporary layoffs became permanent or some jobs became part-time, as full-time work was not available (Coy et al., 2010; Thomas et al., 2020; Zuckerman, 2011). The rise of the sharing or "gig" economy, including companies such as Lyft, Airbnb, and Uber, likely is tied to this increase of unemployed workers who are willing to be contingent employees (Roose, 2014).

This change in the employee–employer relationship has resulted in job holders feeling more fearful of or unable to change jobs, so the unemployed now are willing to settle for low wages or no benefits. It also has led to an increase in job and career shifting as well as to an increase in the employment of contingent workers—workers who do not have a long-term commitment to their organizations nor their employers to them.

urgent organizations

Companies that try to shorten the time it takes to develop new products and respond to customer demands.

Competitiveness and Urgent Organizations   Another significant change is the rise of **urgent organizations**. Urgent organizations are companies that attempt to "shorten the time in which they develop new products and respond to customer demands" (Eisenberg et al., 2010, p. 17). Urgent organizations occur because of the intense time pressures related to global competition and the subsequent consumer demand for innovation and immediate fulfillment of wants and needs. Apple and other technology companies manifest many of the behaviors typical of urgent organizations. For example, the first iPhone was sold to the public in June 2007, and then just 10 weeks later its price was dropped $200 in response to customer demand (although doing so infuriated those "early adopters" who bought the phone in June and July). In July 2008, just one year later, the iPhone 3G was released, with the price once again reduced, this time by half. Similarly, Walmart attempts to compete globally by requiring all of its suppliers to abide by a policy that requires every vendor to either lower the price or increase the quality of each product every year (Fishman, 2006).

Urgent companies evolve and thrive because they are successful. Speed and quick response times provide them with an edge; companies that release products first tend to attract the most media and consumer attention, and clients and consumers are more likely to patronize companies that respond quickly to their requests for services and products.

Organizations, Communication, and Power

Organizations in the United States historically have been hierarchical, meaning that power, decision-making authority, and control have been held by a relatively small percentage of people within the organization, including managers, vice presidents, presidents, and CEOs. To a great extent this is still true today. Although a hierarchical structure seems natural and normal to most of us, it can lead to power differences and to communication behavior that negatively affects those workers who hold little or no power. In the discussion that follows, we examine three of the communication problems that can result from large power differences.

bullying

Repeated hostile behaviors that are or are perceived to be intended to harm parties who are unable to defend themselves.

Bullying   Organizational **bullying** refers to repeated, hostile behaviors that occur in the workplace over an extended period and that are intended, or are perceived as intended, to harm one or more parties who are unable to defend themselves (Lutgen-Sandvik et al., 2005). Although interpersonal conflict is common in organizations, and perhaps necessary, bullying is not necessary. Bullying differs from conflict in that conflict can be constructive and positive. In addition, intent to harm may not be present in typical interpersonal conflict, and the parties in an interpersonal conflict often are relatively equal in power. However, in bullying, the intent to harm is a defining element, and power differences are important. Bully targets lack the ability to defend themselves and have limited strategies with which to respond. During interpersonal conflict, participants both act and are acted on. In contrast, in bullying interactions, one party (or group) is the actor or perpetrator and one (or more) person(s) is the target.

You may wonder why we bring up the issue of bullying, since it may not seem like a prevalent problem. However, it probably is more common than you think. A 2017 study found that about 20 percent of the 1,000 respondents had been or were currently being bullied at work (Namie, 2017), and bullying is especially problematic for LGBTQIA+ individuals (Kenny, 2018). In addition, bullying is important because employers seldom take the issue seriously or respond to workers' complaints. (See *Communication in Society: Employer Responses to Workplace Bullying*.) We address bullying here because, fundamentally, it is a communication issue (Alberts et al., 2005). Of the 22 behaviors used to enact bullying, seventeen of them involve verbal interaction, such as ridicule, rumors, false allegations, insults, and threats of violence (Alberts et al., 2005).

A different type of bullying that is occurring in the workplace is **cyberbullying**, "repetitive and aggressive behavior transmitted through mediated channels aimed at directing malice toward a victim with a to-harm goal" (Palamares & Wingate, 2020). Perpetrators often attack targets with harmful, degrading, threatening, or sexually explicit messages or photographs through texting, email, social media, and personal profiles, among others (Madan, 2014). As mentioned, bullying in the physical workspace typically is related to the bully's organizational power; however, with cyberbullying this is not necessarily so. Because individuals can remain anonymous when targeting others, people with low power in the organization are able to engage in cyberbullying that they likely would not attempt if they were physically present with the target or had to make their real names known. We know relatively little about the frequency of cyberbullying at work, but one study of a manufacturing firm found that 34 percent of the organization's employees had experienced face-to-face bullying, whereas 10.7 percent had experienced cyberbullying. It is important to note that all of the respondents who were cyberbullied indicated that they also were bullied face to face (Privitera & Campbell, 2009). Thus, we don't currently know how many people in the workplace are only bullied online.

cyberbullying
Repetitive and aggressive behavior transmitted through mediated channels and intended to harm a victim.

COMMUNICATION IN SOCIETY
Employer Responses to Workplace Bullying

Have you ever been bullied at work or known someone who was bullied at work? How did others in your workplace, including your employer, respond? How do you think employers should respond when an employee makes a complaint about bullying?

Many U.S. organizations still do not treat workplace bullying as a serious issue according to a recent survey. As shown, the 2017 Workplace Bullying Institute survey of workplace bullying found that more than 70 percent of U.S. employers react to reports of abusive conduct in ways that harm targets, whereas

23 percent took action that resulted in positive change for the target.

Employer Responses to Bullying Complaint

Complaint filed, employer did nothing	26%
Employer investigated complaint inadequately, nothing changed	46%
Employer investigated complaint, positive changes for target	23%
Post-investigation negative outcomes for perpetrator	6%

SOURCE: Namie, G. (2017). *The 2017 WBI U.S. workplace bullying survey.* https://workplacebullying.org/research-wbi/

Because bullying does occur regularly and typically is related to one's power in the organization, scholars have sought to determine strategies that can help targets respond. However, because targets typically have low power in the organization, their options are limited. For example, a problem-solving approach involves discussing the issue and seeking resolution. It requires that all parties be able to participate openly. This is rarely true for the target of bullying. Similarly, compromising can occur only if one has leverage within the organization, meaning that each party must be able to offer something in return for a change in the other's behavior, which a low-power person may not possess. Obliging, or accommodating to the bully's demands, may be the only strategy if one wishes to remain in the organization. Withdrawing may be an option if one is willing to leave, and targets report that leaving the organization was the most effective, and often only, solution to the problem. Competing typically is not a useful strategy; it only intensifies the bully's abusive behavior. For a student's account of organizational bullying, see *It Happened to Me: Bob.*

It Happened to Me
Bob

I still can't believe it happened to me. About a year ago, I was transferred to a new branch of my credit union. Within a few months, my supervisor began to criticize everything I did and make sarcastic and mean comments about me in front of other people. I tried to talk to her about it, but she just told me I was too thin-skinned. I don't know if it was because I was one of only a few males in the office or what. Finally, it got so bad that I asked for a meeting with my supervisor and her supervisor. During our meeting, I became so upset that I started having chest pains. I thought I was having a heart attack and had to go to the hospital by ambulance. It turns out it was a panic attack. When I got back to work a few days later, my supervisor started ridiculing me for having a panic attack. I have asked for a transfer, but I am also looking for another job.

Sexual Harassment   Sexual harassment describes unwanted sexual attention that interferes with an individual's ability to do their job or behavior that ties sexual favors to continued employment or success within the organization (Equal Employment Opportunity Commission, 1980). Federal law recognizes two types of sexual harassment, quid pro quo and hostile work environment (Roberts & Mann, 2000). **Quid pro quo** is the request for sexual favors as a condition of getting or keeping a job or benefit. ("You do what I ask, and I'll help you advance in the organization.") A **hostile work environment** results when a coworker or supervisor engages in unwelcome and inappropriate, sexually based behavior and creates an intimidating, hostile, or offensive atmosphere. Indulging in inappropriate verbal and nonverbal behaviors; repeatedly asking someone for a date; calling coworkers or subordinates by affectionate names (e.g., honey, sweetie); touching, patting, and stroking; and displaying posters and objects of a sexual nature can all constitute acts of sexual harassment. This difference has led many organizations to take a legal-centric, and often inadequate, approach to sexual harassment (Clarke, 2020). Many organizations have sexual harassment training for legal reasons, and for many workers, cynicism about the organization's commitment to ending sexual harassment has a significant impact on these trainings (Cheung et al., 2018).

Even with this list of criteria, however, people could differ over what constitutes a hostile work environment. As a guideline, the U.S. Court of Appeals (Aeberhard-Hodges, 1996) ruled that sexual harassment should be examined from the perspective of what a "reasonable woman," not a "reasonable person," would find offensive. This led some to this central question: If a reasonable woman standard prevailed, would men, even "reasonable men," ever be sure how to behave? The court's ruling, however, rests on the understanding that women are the most frequent targets of sexual harassment and that their experiences in the workplace and around issues of sexuality often differ markedly from men's.

At this point, you might be wondering how bullying differs from sexual harassment. We see sexual harassment as a specific type of bullying behavior because it contains many of the same elements: It is rooted in power differences, the target typically is unable to defend themselves, and the target perceives it as hostile and intentional.

quid pro quo
Requests for sexual favors as a condition of getting or keeping a job or benefit.

hostile work environment
An intimidating, hostile, or offensive workplace atmosphere created by unwelcome and inappropriate sexually based behavior.

As you can see, sexual harassment primarily is a communicative behavior. Because of this, researchers have typically explored how targets can use communication to respond effectively. The typical strategies recommended include confronting the harasser and stating that the behavior must stop, complaining to one's boss or the human relations department, suing, or leaving the organization (Sigal et al., 2003).

However, three out of four people who experience sexual harassment in the workplace never report it (Zillman, 2017). Why not? Sexual harassment typically occurs between people of unequal power, so confronting the harasser may not be an option. Targets risk losing their jobs, seeing the harassment intensify, or losing out on promotions and raises.

▲ Sexual harassment is primarily a communicative behavior.

Complaining to a third party or reporting by a third party (who observed the behavior) does sometimes work, particularly in organizations with a clearly articulated sexual harassment policy (e.g., a zero-tolerance policy) and a human resources department empowered to handle these cases effectively (Jacobson & Eaton, 2018). However, some organizations do not wish to deal with these issues, or do not see them as important, so complaining to a third party does not always result in a benefit. Of course, suing the harasser and the organization that allows harassment is possible, but not every case is settled to the target's satisfaction, and the process can be long, painful, and ultimately unrewarding.

Although leaving the organization does tend to resolve some aspects of the problem, some employees lack the option of leaving or find that leaving takes considerable time and effort. In addition, leaving one's job may resolve the physical/behavioral aspect of the harassment, but it does not help targets manage the long-term physical or psychological effects of harassment, does not address the impact of the harassment on the target's career, and does not result in changes in the perpetrator or the organization.

None of this means that targets should tolerate inappropriate behavior, but it does mean that they should carefully consider their options before committing to a response strategy. Targets should consider what response will be most effective in their specific situations. To do so, targets of sexual harassment (or bullying) might consider the following options. First, a target should consider responding assertively the first time the harassment occurs. This strategy is most likely to be successful when the perpetrator and target have equal power or a relationship of trust. If direct confrontation does not seem to be an option or has not been successful, then the target should consider approaching their supervisor, human resources department, or an organizational ombudsperson. Many organizations want to and will respond to such complaints, recognizing that the organization as a whole is harmed by such behavior.

If confrontation and appealing to authorities have not succeeded, targets must assess their needs and options carefully. They might consider seeking social support from family and friends, seeking assistance from a counselor or therapist to help them manage the emotional distress, developing strategies to avoid the perpetrator (if possible), or requesting a transfer or another job.

Unfortunately, the most common strategy targets select is to do nothing. This is not a response that, in the long run, benefits the individual *or* the organization. Moreover, doing nothing is especially problematic if the target has not even determined what other options exist. Too often, targets assume their efforts will be unsuccessful before they even make an attempt. If you do become a target, we encourage you not to make this assumption.

In conclusion, organizations experience significant impact from the society and the historical time period in which they exist. Two societal factors currently influencing corporations in the United States are globalization and changing power relations in the workplace. Globalization has meant that many jobs have been transferred from the United States to other countries, and both consumers and employees now must increase their contact with workers around the world. This change has been accompanied by an increased focus on power relationships at work and their impact on employees. This tendency to critique organizational uses of power has also led to more discussion of organizational ethics, which we examine next.

Journal Prompt 11.4: Organizations, Communication, and Power
What are three communication problems that can result from large power differences? Identify one communication strategy to use for each of the three problems.

Ethics and Organizational Communication

11.5 Distinguish between individual and communal perspectives on organizational ethics.

As a result of organizational behavior such as providing bonuses to CEOs who lead failing financial companies and the Boeing 737 MAX jet crashes, U.S. Americans are paying more attention to business ethics than perhaps ever before (Holt, 2020; Matthews & Gandel, 2015), and organizations are being advised to solicit and listen to employee complaints regarding ethics breaches (Bisel & Adame, 2018). However, observers don't agree on where responsibility for ethical behavior and communication rests within the organization. For example, who should be held accountable for the engineering design flaws and lack of transparency at Boeing and the FAA's failure to adequately oversee the jet's design? Should only the engineers who designed the systems be prosecuted? Should the managers of the company be accountable? How about former Boeing CEO Matthias Muller? Is he responsible for the ethical standards within his company? When attempting to determine the ethical choices and decisions organizations should make, people usually view the process either from the *individual perspective* or the *communal perspective* (Brown, 1989).

Many U.S. Americans take an individualistic perspective, viewing ethical failures as resting on the shoulders of specific individuals within the organization. From this outlook, each person in the corporation is responsible for their own behavior. In the case of Boeing, then, only the managers themselves who ignored complaints and concerns raised by engineers about decisions that were being made are accountable.

▼ When corporations dump toxic and dirty water into rivers and lakes, who should be held responsible?

In the communal view, however, individuals are considered to be members of a community and are all partially responsible for the behavior of its members. The assumption here is that the ethical standards within an organization are created by and should be monitored and reinforced by all of its members. From this perspective, everyone within the Boeing organization, especially the managers and CEO, is responsible, because they had a duty to create and maintain high ethical standards within the company.

When ethics is discussed in organizational contexts, the focus typically is on the rights of the individual—such as the rights to free speech or privacy—and policies and behaviors that infringe on these rights are seen as unethical. However, a communal approach focuses on the "common good," or what is in the best interests of the entire community, and recent organization scholars emphasize the importance of an organizational climate that fosters ethical communication and behaviors (Teresi et al., 2019). Thus, the morality of an action is assessed based on its consequences for the group. In an individualistic approach, the responsibility for the Boeing 737 MAX's design flaws lies with the engineers who directly created the design. From a communal approach, the consequences of this design error are harmful to the organization as well as society, and the people responsible for that harm are the members of the organization collectively, that is, the organization itself.

Problems exist with both approaches. When we view individuals alone as responsible, they alone are punished, whereas the organization is left essentially unchanged. Yet, when we view corporations in a completely communal way and hold them responsible for their unethical practices, no individual may be held accountable or liable. Consequently, those responsible for the decision to engage in unethical and often illegal practices may not suffer any consequences—and may be free to continue these practices.

How should we balance these two approaches? Most likely, we need to hold both the organization and the individuals who lead them responsible for their practices—just as political leaders are tried in war courts for crimes against humanity, even though their subordinates performed the atrocities. At the same time, corporate leaders need to consider the impacts of their decisions on both individuals and society. To read about one student's experience with organizational ethics, see *It Happened to Me: Nichole.*

How is communication a factor in organizational ethics? Communication figures in organizational ethics in two ways (Cheney et al., 2004). First, many of the ethical issues in organizations revolve around communication. For example, organizations have to decide when to tell employees of impending layoffs, they develop advertising campaigns that communicate the identity of their corporation and its products to consumers, and they must decide how to communicate information regarding their profits and losses to shareholders and Wall Street. Second, the ways in which an organization defines, communicates about, and responds to ethical and unethical behavior shape how individuals within the organization behave. If corporate policy and organizational leaders are vague on the issue of ethics, or worse yet, fail to address it, employees may believe that ethics are not a central concern of the organization and may behave

It Happened to Me
Nichole

The chapter on organizational communication helped me better understand a problem I encountered with Residential Life at my college. It wasn't about drinking or drugs or letting in strangers or any of the usual problems that students have with the dorm; it was about my resident assistant (RA), who now is my boyfriend.

Just to clarify, there were no rules stated that I could not date my RA, and he was never told he couldn't date his residents. Plus, there is actual love involved, not just random friends-with-benefits hookups, and we really feel as though we have met the right person. But Residential Life has a huge problem with our relationship, and they called us into a meeting. We both felt as though it was a violation of our privacy. We had the meeting, he quit his job, and we are still dating, 10 months strong!

Now, though, when I look at the relationship through the eyes of the school, I can see their problems with it. What would have happened if an employee of the college got me pregnant? Also, he lived in my hall, and his duty was to keep us in line, but there was huge preferential treatment going on. I mean, would my boyfriend really write me up for anything? So now I see that they had a point. But I don't understand why nothing was ever said about this practice being against the rules.

accordingly. For example, in 2020, the *New York Times* published an article about the ethical decisions being made over who would get COVID-19 treatment if hospitals were overwhelmed with patients. Hospitals are organizations, but they don't operate in a vacuum. They know that the ethical decisions they make impact their employees and their public image (Teresi et al., 2019). The choices made by hospitals and public health officials in the states varied widely. Alabama put "persons with severe mental retardation" low on the list for treatment as well as those with AIDS. However, Alabama officials said they have replaced the plan with a different set of guidelines. Louisiana excluded people with severe dementia, and Maryland gave "lowest priority" to people over 85 years old. As hospitals grappled with these state ethical guidelines for treatment priority, they considered many issues, including the patient's age, pregnancy (Utah considers how far along the pregnancy is), dementia, and Alzheimer's (Baker & Fink, 2020).

Journal Prompt 11.5: Organizational Ethics
How do the individual and communal approaches to organizational ethics differ? What role does communication play in organizational ethics?

Improving Your Organizational Communication Skills

11.6 Identify four steps involved in a strategic approach to conflict management.

Much of the time, if not most, people are only willing to engage in conflict when they are angry or emotional. How often have you been involved with, or observed others engaging in, highly emotional conflict at work? As you probably have noted, this style of conflict engagement typically doesn't resolve anything and may cause long-lasting damage to one's relationships with others.

A better way to manage conflict with coworkers is to use a strategic approach to conflict management. People who use a strategic approach prepare for their conflicts and engage in **strategy control** (Canary & Lakey, 2012). When behaving strategically, one assesses the available information and options, which increases one's understanding of the conflict and the other party. In turn, these behaviors help people choose conflict behaviors that are responsive to the partner's as well as their own needs and increase the possibility for cooperation, collaboration, and compromise.

strategy control
Assessing the available information and options to increase one's understanding of the conflict and the other party.

When using a strategic approach, before you even initiate a discussion over an issue in conflict, you should know what you want to occur as a result of the interaction. If you wish to confront your coworker about not doing his fair share of a joint project, you should first decide what your goal is. Do you want your colleague to apologize? To stay late until the report is finished? To complete the project by himself? To take the lead on the next joint project? Or do you desire some combination of these outcomes? You will be far more successful and satisfied with your conflict interactions if you go into them knowing what you want.

Second, decide if the issue is worth confronting—or worth confronting now. You may know what you want, but do you have a reasonable chance of accomplishing your goals? That is, how likely is your coworker to apologize or to successfully take the lead on your next joint project? If the answer truly is "highly unlikely," you may choose not to engage in the conflict or to seek other solutions. For example, you might decide to ask your supervisor to assign someone else to work with you. Alternatively, you may decide you do want to have the conversation, but perhaps not right now, because both of you are hungry and tired.

If you decide that the conflict is worth confronting, you next want to try to understand the other party's goals, that is, what they want. What, for example, do you think your coworker's goal is? Does he want to receive credit for the work without having to do it? Does he want assistance with parts of the project he doesn't feel competent to complete? Is he busy with other projects and wants more time to finish the project? Depending on your understanding of his goals and interests, you will likely suggest different solutions. Please remember, however, the tendency for each of us to attribute negative motivations to others' behavior. If you are upset, you will be particularly likely to believe your colleague's goal is to avoid work but receive the rewards of it. Recognize that your attributions may be incorrect and that you probably will need to talk with your coworker to determine what his motivations really are.

You have one more step to complete before you are ready to talk with your colleague; you need to plan the interaction. More specifically, you should think about when and where the conversation should take place and what tactics you believe will be most effective. Typically, you

▲ People often are only willing to engage in conflict when they are angry or emotional.

will want to choose a time when neither you nor your coworker is angry, rushed, or stressed. In addition, you should probably have the conversation in private. If others are around, one or both of you may behave more competitively or avoid the interaction entirely because you are embarrassed to be observed by others. Finally, you should think through how you will explain your dissatisfaction with the current state of affairs neutrally and how you will frame your suggested solutions. Once you have done all of this, you are ready to talk with your colleague and discuss calmly what the two of you can do to reduce your feeling that you alone are working on the project. What are your options if you feel that another employee or a supervisor has committed an extremely serious infraction against you, perhaps betraying a serious confidence and spreading harmful misinformation about you? Perhaps attempts to discuss the issue have only resulted in worsening the relationship.

Communication scholars have recently discussed the important role of compassion and forgiveness in the workplace. For example, Sarah Tracy and colleagues (2017) describe the need for compassionate communication strategies in problematic work situations—supportive listening, positive language, and optimistic framing. Scholars Paul and Putnam (2017) identify four potential workplace forgiveness responses, acknowledging that a particular response may vary depending on the closeness of the personal relationship, the task involved, and one's own individual communication style: (1) moving on, a passive approach that is primarily task-focused; (2) not taking it personally, associated with task focus and closer relationships; (3) letting go, reflecting a higher degree of collaboration, intertwining relationships and task; and (4) conciliatory forgiving, less concern with task and reflective of close relationships and working through the conflict. Paul and Putnam also emphasize that while forgiveness is seen as an individual action, the organizational values and norms can play a role and influence whether (and how) any act of forgiveness may be enacted in the workplace context.

Journal Prompt 11.6: Strategic Conflict Management
What is meant by "a strategic approach" to managing conflict? What are the four steps to the "strategic approach" to conflict management?

SUMMARY

11.1 Explain the importance of understanding communication in organizations.

- Understanding how to communicate in organizations will enhance your professional success, allow you to ask more informed questions about everyday organizational practices, and help you decide what organizations you wish to frequent and support.

11.2 Define *organizations* and explain their communication functions and structures.

- Organizations are composed of interactions that members use to accomplish their individual and common goals.
- Organizational communication functions include production, maintenance, and innovation.
- Organization communication structures include formal structure and informal structure.

11.3 Understand the types of communication that occur among coworkers and explain their functions.

- Assimilation describes the processes that influence individuals to join, identify with, and become integrated into an organization.
- Supervisor–subordinate communication refers to communication that occurs when one person has the formal authority to regulate the behavior of another. One challenge of supervisor–subordinate communication is employee dissent.
- Coworker communication is composed of the formal–professional and informal–personal interactions employees have with one another.

11.4 Discuss current social influences on organizations and organizational communication.

- Two of the most significant societal forces that impact organizational communication are history and globalization.
- Three recent practices that influence organizations are the development of a new social contract between organizations and employees, the rise of urgent organizations, and the blurring of boundaries between home and work.
- Two power relations that influence organizations are workplace bullying and sexual harassment.

11.5 Distinguish between individual and communal perspectives on organizational ethics.

- An individual perspective views ethical failures as resting on the shoulders of specific individuals.
- A communal perspective of ethical failures argues individuals are considered to be members of the community and are all partially responsible for the behavior of its members.

11.6 Identify four steps involved in a strategic approach to conflict management.

- Decide what you want to occur as a result of the conflict interaction.
- Decide if the issue is worth confronting—or worth confronting now.
- Try to understand the other party's goals.
- Plan the interaction.

KEY TERMS

organizations p. 281
function p. 281
production p. 281
maintenance p. 281
innovation p. 282
structure p. 282
downward communication p. 282
upward communication p. 282
horizontal communication p. 282
hierarchy p. 282
formal communication channels p. 282
informal communication channels
   p. 282

organizational culture p. 283
organizational climate p. 285
assimilation p. 286
organizational identification p. 287
openness p. 289
supportiveness p. 289
motivation p. 290
empowerment p. 290
ingratiation p. 290
assertiveness p. 290
rationality p. 290
employee dissent p. 291
surface acting p. 295

deep acting p. 295
burnout p. 295
work–life conflict p. 297
general systems theory p. 300
globalization p. 300
new social contract p. 301
urgent organizations p. 302
bullying p. 302
cyberbullying p. 303
quid pro quo p. 304
hostile work environment p. 304
strategy control p. 308

APPLY WHAT YOU KNOW

1. **Understanding Emotion Labor**
   Think of five jobs that require employees to engage in emotion labor and delineate the emotions that these employees are "expected" to display. What emotions are they expected to suppress? What contradictory emotions and behaviors are they expected to perform? Which of the five jobs that you listed appears to have the heaviest emotion labor load?

2. **Understanding Relationships at Work**
   Form a group with one or more of your classmates. Assume that you are a work group that has been charged with developing a fraternization policy for your job. Develop a policy about the types of relationships that are appropriate in your workplace and how people who have these relationships should communicate and behave while at work.

Rhetorical Communication

 LEARNING OBJECTIVES

CHAPTER TOPICS

12.1 Describe some of the key issues in rhetorical communication.

The Importance of Rhetoric

12.2 Identify cultural and social influences on the development of rhetoric.

What Is Rhetoric? A Broader View

12.3 Identify and define the three artistic proofs of ethos, pathos, and logos.

The Rhetor: Rhetoric's Point of Origin

12.4 Explain four functions of rhetoric: reaffirming cultural values, increasing democratic participation, securing justice, and promoting social change.

The Individual, Rhetoric, and Society

12.5 Understand the ethical issues facing rhetors and audience members.

Ethics and Rhetoric

12.6 Identify the basic steps in preparing a speech.

Using Your Rhetorical Skills: Speaking in Public

> *"Rhetoric is essential to a vital democracy."*

Charee is familiar with the debates about Black Lives Matter, policing, immigration reform, deportations, and many other issues that are going on in the United States. She listens to speeches at rallies as well as political discussions on television, and she reads the discussions online. In all of these communication contexts, she is swimming in rhetorical communication from various perspectives that attempt to persuade her (and others) to their view on these issues. She knows that she needs to wade through the various arguments and emotional pleas coming from these other perspectives before she can decide how she feels. As the daughter of an Asian immigrant, how does that influence her political views on this issue? What evidence does she believe? Who has more credibility: someone speaking at a rally? Or someone who is anonymous and posting messages online? Which news sources are more reliable and accurate? Although it may feel overwhelming, Charee wants to have a reasonable way to guide herself through the ocean of rhetorical messages and make smart choices about how to do so, as she recognizes how important it is to her everyday life.

Charee knows the power of rhetoric, as she is now more careful about being alone at night. When she hears President Trump, ignoring the World Health Organization's guidance, refer to COVID-19 as the "China Virus," she sees the sudden rise in attacks on Asians and Asian Americans as connected to the anger that he is stoking. Although she is Vietnamese American, she knows that Korean Americans, Filipino Americans, and other Asian Americans are under attack "by a bigotry that does not know the difference" (Tavernise & Oppel, 2020).

Charee recognized the power of rhetorical communication to persuade and motivate people to action. **Rhetoric** is communication that influences the attitudes or behaviors of others; it is also called *the art of persuasion*. All of the messages that Charee is confronting—whether in person, in media outlets, or on the Internet—are rhetorical in that they are designed to influence how listeners and readers view COVID-19, Black Lives Matter, immigration reform, and deportation. On other occasions, communicators might use rhetoric to influence people to vote a particular way, to raise awareness about income inequality, or to participate in a protest for police reform.

rhetoric
Communication that is used to influence the attitudes or behaviors of others; the art of persuasion.

All of these rhetorical messages serve important cultural and personal functions, and gaining insight into such functions is, by itself, an important reason to study the art of rhetoric. But people study rhetoric, which comes from the ancient Greek word for speaking, for a variety of other important reasons as well, which we will explore throughout this chapter. Because most of us spend more time as receivers of rhetorical communication, this chapter also focuses on how to be a responsible rhetorical critic.

In this chapter, we explore rhetoric as it informs the study of communication today. We will first consider the definition and functions of rhetoric. We next examine how characteristics of public speakers, or *rhetors*, make them credible, influence what they say, and impact how they relate to their audiences. We then turn our focus to a broader topic, the intersection of society and rhetoric. And before providing a guide for preparing a rhetorical presentation, we consider the merits of being a rhetorical critic.

The Importance of Rhetoric

12.1   Describe some of the key issues in rhetorical communication.

The rhetorical tradition lies at the heart of communication studies. Since the days of Aristotle in ancient Greece, rhetoric has been considered the art of persuasion. Among the many ways that communication operates, the Greeks felt that the ability to influence how others view the world on various issues was paramount. Rhetoric's practice is contingent on culture, political arrangements, and social contexts and conventions. For example, how might courtroom rhetoric differ among people who believe in magic, witches, and the presumption of guilt from a courtroom rhetoric among people who believe in DNA, forensic science, and the presumption of innocence? Or in a political system with a dictator versus one with elected officials? We'll look at the changing notions of rhetoric as cultures and societies have differed. First, let's look at how rhetoric functions in our society.

Rhetoric's Functions in Society

Rhetorical communication serves at least three important social functions. First, as you may have surmised, rhetoric is essential to a vital democracy. For people to make informed decisions (and vote) about a range of issues, they must consume rhetorical messages critically and then advocate with care. By advocating for one's perspective and engaging with the perspectives of others, people can make decisions together regarding the common good. Hence, rhetoric can strengthen democratic society, and speeches or other types of communication to the public can serve important political and social functions.

Sometimes congressional representatives hold town hall meetings to listen to the concerns of their constituents, and many people attend those and express their concerns on a variety of issues. But formal government outlets are only one of the many ways that people use the Internet to engage in activism. Activism can be speeches at rallies and more, but it can also be online as in the case of change.org. Claiming to be "the world's largest platform for social change," change.org says "We believe that to create a world where no one is powerless, we need social and political systems that ensure people everywhere have a voice on the issues that they care about" (change.org, 2019, p. 7). Yet not everyone is convinced of the rhetorical power of online activism. For example, at its peak, the Save Darfur campaign "was one of the largest on the social network" (meaning activist social networking sites), but of the online activists (who numbered more than one million), "less than 3,000" moved on to contribute about $90,000 total to the cause. This level of engagement reflects "pitiful statistics compared to the wider Darfur campaign, which raised over $1m in 2008 alone" (Tostevin, 2014). What do you think about social media and the Internet more generally as a platform for rhetorical messages and democratic engagement?

Second, rhetoric helps people seek justice. Probably one of the most obvious sites of this rhetorical function is the courtroom. Not only lawyers but also jurors need rhetorical skills; they need to listen carefully and critically not only to what is said but also to how it is said, and they must be able to persuade other jurors of the proper verdict. Speakers also use rhetoric to persuade others to pursue social justice, for example, to support a moratorium on the death penalty or treat animals more ethically.

Justice can also be sought outside the courtroom. If people do not feel that justice is found in the courtroom, they can use social media and other outlets to try to persuade others that an injustice occurred. During and after the trial of Brock Turner, the former Stanford University athlete who was found guilty of sexual assault, some people felt that the relatively short prison sentence did not result in justice and tried to persuade others to their view. More recently, Black Lives Matter has highlighted a number of cases of police shootings of African Americans as unjust. In response, the *Washington Post* has posted an interactive webpage about the number of people killed by police since 2015 at https://www.washingtonpost.com/graphics/investigations/police-shootings-database/. On this webpage, you can get more information about each of these shootings. In these cases and in many others, people use the Internet to help shape how we view justice and injustice and actions that we can take to make things right that we are persuaded are wrong.

Third, rhetoric helps people clarify their own beliefs and actions. For example, after the many police actions that led to the deaths of so many African Americans and Latinos across the nation, many people, like our student in *It Happened to Me: Mark*, were not sure what to believe about why this is happening, how they should respond, or what can be done. People often look to our leaders to find direction and understanding. In addressing the unrest taking place across the nation, President Trump noted that "my supporters are wonderful, hard-working, tremendous people, and they turn on their television set and they look at a Portland or they look at a Kenosha . . . They are looking at all of this and they can't believe it. They can't believe it" (Blake, 2020). If you are a supporter of President Trump, you see yourself and the protests in one way. If you are not, you likely view things differently and view this kind of rhetoric as divisive rather than unifying.

It Happened to Me
Mark

I was really upset to watch the police action that led to George Floyd's murder in Minneapolis. I became more outraged as I watched the tragic deaths at the hands of police, such as Breonna Taylor in Louisville, Rayshard Brooks in Atlanta, and many more. When the protests over the shooting of Jacob Blake in Kenosha, Wisconsin, turned violent and Kyle Rittenhouse, a teenager from Illinois who is a supporter of "Blue Lives Matter," shot and killed two people, I was stunned. I was really disappointed when President Trump gave a divisive speech that praised Rittenhouse and further divided our country rather than finding important American cultural values that might unite us and bring calm in the face of such violence.

The Advantages of Studying Rhetoric

In addition to serving important functions in society, rhetoric is also an important area of academic inquiry. Studying rhetoric as a field of scholarship is useful for four reasons. First, the study of public communication generates findings that help people understand the range of viewpoints on social issues. For example, if you wanted to understand the reasoning behind the U.S. immigration policy, you could examine the rhetoric of people who are attempting to influence that policy. You might listen to the president's speeches on immigration; you could examine the Catholic Church's views on pending immigration legislation; you could review the public comments of various members of Congress, some of whom are themselves the children or grandchildren of immigrants; and you could listen to interviews and speeches of other people who support various changes to immigration policy. You can find many of these viewpoints online and in more traditional outlets, such as the *Congressional Record* and newspapers. By examining the rhetoric of these individuals and groups, you would be better able to understand how U.S. immigration policies respond to these varied perspectives as well as think through what you believe is the best course of action. It may also help you understand the barriers to immigration reform.

Second, the study of rhetoric helps people better understand culture. Both consciously and unconsciously, through listening to and analyzing public communication, people learn the expectations of their own cultures—what it means to be a good parent, how to present oneself, how to decorate one's home, and much more. Debates about same-sex marriage led to arguments about what marriage means and how it should be defined. You may find yourself drawn more to one vision and definition of marriage than another based on the rhetoric that you have heard. People can study and understand other cultures, too, by being attuned to how public communication sustains patterns of social life.

Third, studying rhetoric can help people critically evaluate messages designed to influence them, such as advertising. Other rhetoric tries to persuade people to support particular policies or to vote for or against certain politicians or propositions. As receivers of these persuasive messages, people can learn to listen critically, analyze these messages, and respond appropriately.

Finally, the study of public communication helps us become better public communicators or to understand what makes specific public communicators effective or ineffective. We can learn much about public speaking by analyzing instances of public speech. In addition, we can determine why some speakers are more successful or persuasive than others by comparing their public communication. We can also learn why some web postings are more persuasive than others and why we find them more persuasive and believable.

rhetorical critic
An informed consumer of rhetorical discourse who is prepared to analyze rhetorical texts.

Becoming a Rhetorical Critic　The term **rhetorical critic** refers to an informed consumer of rhetorical discourse who is prepared to analyze rhetorical texts. You may think that a critic's job is simply to be negative about whatever is under analysis. However, everyone is a critic in everyday life, and we have an ethical duty to think critically about the rhetorical texts we encounter. Although some people reserve the term *rhetorical critic* for those who work in academia, we see it differently. We consider anyone who pursues sustained and detailed analyses of rhetorical discourse to be a rhetorical critic.

We hope that you and your fellow citizens all become more attuned to the sensitivities of rhetorical discourse and that you become strong analysts of it because it has tremendous influence on the ways you conduct your everyday life and the way society functions. To give just one example, rhetorical discourse likely shapes your understanding of what it means to be a good parent. Do you think that good parents have to sacrifice everything for their children? Pay for their college educations? Their weddings? Do good parents expect their children to take care of them in their old age? Or should good parents do everything possible to avoid being a burden on their children? Are good parents married? What is the right way for good parents to deal with divorce? Of course, no "right" answer exists for any of these questions. But it's important to be aware that you do have some ideas about what constitutes good parenting. It's also important to be aware that these ideas came from a barrage of rhetorical messages from newspaper reporters, magazine writers, psychologists, religious organizations, movies, television shows, blogs, and others. Understanding how these messages rhetorically frame parenting can help you better understand how you have shaped your own vision of good parenting. Becoming more aware of your opinions and where they come from can make you a more effective rhetorical critic.

Being an informed rhetorical critic can also help one appreciate the artistic aspects of discourse (Darsey, 1994) as well as what makes a particular rhetorical message effective or persuasive. When you read the excerpt from a famous antislavery speech in *Did You Know?: Frederick Douglass*, consider what makes it effective. What are the artistic aspects of this speech? Why didn't Douglass simply say, "Slavery is wrong"?

Rhetorical criticism is a method for generating knowledge about historical sources of contemporary social problems, especially those that generate a significant amount of discourse. Through attentiveness to how rhetoric has functioned and continues to function in various contexts, you can build an understanding of your culture, your society, and the ideas that predominated during a given period. Hence, an analysis of any one rhetorical message should be seen as part of a much larger and ongoing dialogue.

A variety of approaches to rhetorical criticism exist. We cannot cover all the major approaches to rhetorical criticism in this introductory course. There are many courses and textbooks that focus on rhetorical criticism. Instead we hope to teach you to listen carefully to how rhetoric functions every day and to analyze what purposes it serves. As you listen to rhetoric from presidents, governors, mayors, church leaders, or others, ask yourself, how does this message reinforce the status quo? How does it argue for change? What ideas are mentioned, and what ideas are absent? How and why is the rhetoric persuasive, and how might it influence the public in making public policy decisions?

Because you can only consume a limited amount of the rhetoric generated and because the rhetorical environment is always changing, the ways in which you understand and think about the world will always be changing as well. By adopting a critical approach, you can empower yourself to better understand the messages and the issues at hand.

DID YOU KNOW?

Frederick Douglass

When Frederick Douglass began to speak out against slavery, many White Americans did not believe he had really been a slave or that he was African American. In her biography of Douglass, Sandra Thomas explains: "People gradually began to doubt that Douglass was telling the truth about himself. Reporting on a lecture that he gave in 1844, the Liberator wrote that many people in the audience refused to believe his stories: 'How a man, only six years out of bondage, and who had never gone to school could speak with such eloquence—with such precision of language and power of thought—they were utterly at a loss to devise.'" Unfortunately, this response to minority speakers may not be unusual.

Here is a famous excerpt from a speech Douglass gave about the Fourth of July. How do the appeals used in this speech help to move an audience?

> What, to the American slave, is your 4th of July? I answer; a day that reveals to him, more than all other days in the year, the gross injustice and cruelty to which he is the constant victim. To him, your celebration is a sham; your boasted liberty, an unholy license; your national greatness, swelling vanity; your sounds of rejoicing are empty and heartless; your denunciation of tyrants, brass-fronted impudence; your shouts of liberty and equality, hollow mockery; your prayers and hymns, your sermons and thanksgivings, with all your religious parade and solemnity, are, to Him, mere bombast, fraud, deception, impiety, and hypocrisy—a thin veil to cover up crimes which would disgrace a nation of savages. There is not a nation on

▲ Frederick Douglass was a powerful rhetor who spoke out against slavery in the United States.

the earth guilty of practices more shocking and bloody than are the people of the United States, at this very hour.

SOURCES: Douglass, F. (1852, July 5). *The meaning of July Fourth for the Negro.* http://www.pbs.org/wgbh/aia/part4/4h2927t.html

Thomas, S. (n.d.). *From slave to abolitionist/editor.* http://www.history.rochester.edu/class/douglass/part2.html

Truth and Rhetoric

Since the fifth century BCE, teachers and scholars of rhetoric have argued over its fundamental purpose. Does it help speakers and listeners discern truth, or is it only concerned with what an audience can be persuaded to believe? If persuasion is the goal, then truth plays a smaller, perhaps even nonexistent, role.

The first people to teach persuasive speaking skills in the Greek city-states were called **sophists**. Their approach to rhetoric was practical; they believed rhetoric's purpose was to persuade, especially on matters of urgency. Therefore, they taught speakers to adjust their notions of right or wrong, true or untrue, depending on their speaking situation, their audience, and their goals. Today sophistry is often associated with a focus on the ends justifying the means; in other words, use whatever means are expedient to get the desired results. Because anyone might use deception, invented "facts," and other problematic ways to persuade others, sophistry is largely seen as unethical in today's rhetorical environment. At the same time, sophistication is seen as a value in some speech contexts. So the debate between the sophists and Plato is ongoing two millennia later.

Some contemporaries disagreed with the sophists. One of the more prominent of these was Plato (429–347 BCE), who strongly opposed a relativistic approach to

sophists
The first group to teach persuasive speaking skills in the Greek city-states.

speech-making. In his well-known dialogue *Gorgias*, he disparagingly compared sophistic rhetoric to "cookery," in which a set of elements (or ingredients) were "mixed together" to create the final speech (or dish) for the sake of pleasure and not of the good, or health, of the body. Plato insisted that speakers only speak in favor of universal principles of truth and that these truths should then influence society's behavior for the better. Plato's position implies that access to universal truth is possible.

But there is reason to believe that Plato was not as critical of rhetoric as he was of sophistical rhetoric. In fact, Plato wrote dialogues, not philosophical treatises. Evidently, he thought that the best way to search for truth was through oral dialogue. In an eloquently written dialogue, the *Phaedrus*, Plato argued for a philosophical rhetoric based on truth and a philosophical truth spoken rhetorically (Conley, 1994; Infante et al., 1990). Whether he was critical or supportive, the irony between Plato's rhetorical choices and criticisms about sophists still captivates modern audiences. Looking back, some will judge President Obama's two presidential terms not as much by which policies he passed but by the hope that his rhetoric engendered in an upcoming generation. Persuasion, meaning the sweetness of words, evidently means that pleasure can sometimes have good effects.

Not unlike students today, Plato's student Aristotle (384–322 BCE) challenged his teacher's arguments. He did not agree with Plato's insistence on the relationship of absolute truth to rhetoric; instead he believed speakers needed to learn skillful persuasion so they could defend truth and justice. As you might guess, his position was more relativistic than Plato's but less so than the sophists'. However, some rhetorical historians argue that Aristotle could strike a middle-of-the-road position because he wrote about oratorical practices as theoretical. Theorizing practices into definitions as he did narrows the avenues future speakers take to express themselves. In effect, Aristotle's permutation of the sophists and Plato organizes a plurality of styles by prescriptions of what kinds of speech techniques are more effective than others (Haskins, 2006, 2013).

Aristotle defined rhetoric as "the art of discovering all the available means of persuasion in a given situation" (Aristotle, 1991, p. 42). With this perspective in mind, he sought to create general rules of rhetoric that could be applied to a variety of circumstances and occasions. He was so successful that his text, *The Rhetoric*, has been used as a handbook for public speaking for more than 2,000 years.

When the Romans conquered the Greeks in 146 BCE, they incorporated the writings of Greek rhetoricians into Roman education. Cicero (106–43 BCE), a prominent advocate and politician, is often considered the greatest Roman **orator**, or public speaker, and the most influential theorist of ancient rhetoric. Cicero believed speakers should use rhetoric for the public good and that eloquence without wisdom was feeble and even dangerous.

Cicero offered guidelines for organizing speeches and was a master of style; in fact, his speeches are still appreciated today for their rhetorical force. He is known best for identifying the three purposes or goals of public speaking: to instruct, to please, and to win over. Modern public speaking courses require mastery of these three types of speeches, which we now refer to as speeches to inform, to entertain, and to persuade.

As the Roman Empire declined, the Catholic Church replaced secular educational institutions as the leading disseminator of knowledge in the West. Once again, the issue of truth's relationship to rhetoric became important. First, because rhetoric had developed from a non-Christian tradition, concerns arose about its relevance and appropriateness to Christianity. The most prominent thinker and writer of this era was Augustine of Hippo (354–430 CE), whom you may know as St. Augustine. He was a professor of rhetoric before converting to Christianity, and he struggled to reconcile his rhetorical background with his religious beliefs. Augustine's view of truth was close to Plato's—that truth exists in an absolute way—and he promoted the idea that rhetoric could impart the divine truth (Conley, 1994). From this perspective, ethical decisions were not situation specific; choices were always right or wrong, good or evil.

Critical Thinking Prompt
How do you view the sophists' relativistic approach to rhetoric? Have you ever been in a situation in a class or debate where you were required to argue for a position that clashed with your personal values? How did it feel to make the argument?

---

orator
A public speaker.

Journal Prompt 12.1: Study of Rhetoric
What are some of the ways that the study of rhetoric has been influenced by its historical context?

What Is Rhetoric? A Broader View

12.2 **Identify cultural and social influences on the development of rhetoric.**

When you think of rhetoric, you may think about overblown statements, exaggerations, or even outright lies and misstatements—as in "Oh, that's just a bunch of political rhetoric." Unfortunately, this dismissive view of rhetoric is all too common today. However, as we saw in the preceding section, rhetoric has a rich history, and it serves important functions in a democratic society. As you saw in the opening example about debates regarding Black Lives Matter, rhetoric in its truest sense refers to communication that is used to influence others. Thus, rhetoricians would view the president's communication following September 11, 2001, not as simply an attempt to provide information but also as an attempt to guide U.S. Americans to view this topic in a way that suits his particular goals. In both the historical and the contemporary sense, rhetoric focuses primarily on public communication or messages designed to influence large audiences.

More than 50 years ago, communication professor Douglas Ehninger suggested that throughout history people have had different ideas of what rhetoric is and the purposes it serves (1967). Ehninger's thinking sparked interest in connecting rhetoric to the cultural, social, and historical forces that exist in any particular time and in exploring how these forces shape rhetoric. Therefore, scholars began to research the ways that rhetoric serves social needs in societies around the world. For example, they looked at how the uses of rhetoric in a religious state may differ from those in a secular one. In addition, their research showed that the methods and reasons that people speak out in public depend on how such communication is received. Although Ehninger focused on the European tradition, his argument stirred interest in understanding how non-Western cultures developed their own rhetorical traditions (Lucaites et al., 1999).

The European rhetorical tradition is only one of many in the world, and public communication functions in different ways in other places. It can, however, be difficult to research and study rhetoric historically or globally because the word *rhetoric* is not used in all cultures to describe that which is called "rhetoric" in the European tradition. The term comes to the English language from the Greek word *rhetorike*. However, it is important to note that the concept of "rhetoric" can likewise exist in non-Greek cultures whether or not a synonym for the specific word exists in other languages. A **rhetor** is a person or institution that addresses the public. Public address can happen without reference to the public speech forums of Greek democracy and Roman republicanism. George Kennedy, a scholar of the ancient world, focuses less on the word and more on the concept itself: "Rhetoric is apparently a form of energy that drives and is imparted to communication. . . . All communication carries some rhetorical energy" (1998, p. 215). In this sense, rhetoric is not a cultural phenomenon unique to the West, but it is a facet of communication across cultures; it is the motive for communicating.

rhetor
A person or institution that addresses a large audience; the originator of a communication message but not necessarily the one delivering it.

▼ Different cultures assign power to people based on different factors.

Culturally, the social position of the rhetor often determines their right to speak or to access civic speaking spaces. In some cultures, it is important that the rhetor is an elder or that he be male or come from a high-status family. In others, everyone is able to speak. These cultural differences influence who has the ability to speak and who needs to study rhetoric to be the most capable communicators.

To understand how these social positions differ across cultures, it is important to seek out the structures of different cultures and societies. In some cultures, people rise to leadership positions by being democratically elected, whereas in other cultures leaders gain and hold onto power through financial prowess, political intrigue, or military force. Religious leaders sometimes hold the most powerful positions. Some cultures are led by a group instead of a single leader. Relationships to certain families, credentials from certain schools, or even one's physical attractiveness can lead to empowerment (or dis-empowerment). Yet how one's rhetoric is received is dependent on one's social position.

Some rhetorical critics have strategically located rhetoric in spaces traditionally disassociated from civic forums. For example, the kitchen, and kitchen table talk specifi-cally, has been a domestic site of transformative dialogue for many women. This was especially so during America's twentieth-century civil activist history. Today, many Black feminist scholars feature the kitchen table as a metaphor for a place where rhetoric is in action. Even if it is not a location for legislation, women who have been excluded from public domains of political action have debated political issues and spread word about community at their hearths. In this way, rhetorical criticism can analyze classical modes of rhetoric by changing where we think rhetoric takes place.

As you think about the role of rhetoric around the world, consider how decisions are made in different societies. You might also contemplate how our own culture is changing as we take part in public debates over such far-reaching topics as same-sex marriage, immigration reform, retirement and pension plans, and more.

**Journal Prompt 12.2:
The Rhetor**
What is a rhetor, and how do the rhetor's social status and culture influence the ability to speak?

The Rhetor: Rhetoric's Point of Origin

12.3 Identify and define the three artistic proofs of ethos, pathos, and logos.

It is conventional to think about a rhetor as a specific public speaker; for example, when the president speaks to the nation, the president is a rhetor. As notions of rhetoric have expanded over time, however, corporations, organizations, and governments have also come to be thought of as rhetors. Thus, a rhetor is the originator of a communication message, not necessarily the person delivering it.

Like other areas of communication studies, the study of rhetoric acknowledges the relationship between individual forces and societal forces. In this segment of the chapter, we look at the individual forces that make for more or less effective rhetors. These forces include the rhetor's artistic proofs, position in society, and relationship to the audience.

Ethos, Pathos, and Logos

artistic proofs
Artistic skills of a rhetor that influence effectiveness.

ethos
The rhetorical construction of character.

In the *Art of Rhetoric*, Aristotle argued that there are three **artistic proofs**, or means through which a rhetor gains the trust of an audience and designs credible messages. They are ethos, pathos, and logos.

Ethos Aristotle considered **ethos**—usually translated as "character"—the most important of the three artistic proofs. Aristotle emphasized that rhetors create ethos, or a sense of their character, by displaying to their audience good sense, moral character, and goodwill. He also included family background, attractiveness, and athletic ability as valuable assets in persuasion through ethos. Advertising commonly exploits this aspect of ethos, using famous family names, attractive models, and celebrated athletes to promote products.

To communicate a certain aspect of their ethos, a rhetor can create and project a *persona*. **Persona** is related to the notion of identity that we discussed in Chapter 2. It describes the identity one creates through one's public communication efforts. A speaker's public persona may be quite different from their private one. In contrast, a speaker's social identities, such as race, ethnicity, age, and nationality, remain unchanged from situation to situation and are not under the speaker's control. The public persona a speaker projects can enhance their ethos if audiences find the persona credible, informed, or intelligent; it can diminish their ethos if audiences perceive the persona to be untrustworthy, deceitful, unintelligent, or misinformed.

Interpretations of ethos are influenced not only by how a speaker presents themselves but also by social factors such as stereotypes and assumptions. For example, sometimes people hear accents that increase or decrease their perceptions of the speaker's intelligence. British accents tend to increase credibility in the United States, whereas Southern accents may have the opposite effect, especially in the northern United States.

persona
The identity one creates through one's public communication efforts.

Critical Thinking Prompt
What characteristics do you think are important to a speaker's credibility, or ethos? Which of Aristotle's list apply today? Which characteristics are most important to you?

Pathos   **Pathos** refers to the rhetorical use of emotions to affect audience decision making. Speakers often use emotion to influence the audience to identify with a particular perspective. In a court case, the prosecuting lawyer may reenact the crime to help the jury see the case from the victim's point of view. An effective reenactment may influence the jury to emotionally identify, and thus side, with the prosecution rather than the defense.

pathos
The rhetorical use of emotions to affect audience decision making.

There are many different emotional appeals that can be made. Emotional appeals have been used many times throughout history. Fear can get people to support government actions that they otherwise would not, such as the USA PATRIOT Act, Transportation Security Administration (TSA) screening procedures, and other measures instituted in reaction to fears of terrorism.

Former President Trump tended to emphasize pathos in his political rallies. European communication expert Laura Westring observes that "he is a master of pathos—one of Aristotle's three modes of persuasion. Trump used pathos to appeal to the emotions of his audience to the point where the absence of Aristotle's other two modes, logos (logic) and ethos (character) barely feature as talking points among his supporters" (2019). One of his common rhetorical strategies was to get his audience to be angry about something: "Using slights to channel and rouse anger is a near daily strategy that Trump has used against the FBI, the news media, the Mueller investigation and other perceived enemies" (Arrigo, 2018). If you have watched a Trump rally, do you recognize how his rhetoric works?

Emotional appeals are often more subtle. For example, the athletic and alumni websites of many universities incorporate pathos to invite participation in their events and support for their organizations. Some of these emotional appeals may involve feelings of pride by associating with the university, as well as positive memories that alumni may have about their student days. You may have similar feelings some day.

Logos   Although the word **logos** looks like "logic," it is not as narrowly defined. Rather, *logos* refers to reasoning or argumentation more generally. As an artistic proof, logos refers to how rhetors construct arguments or present evidence so that audiences reach a particular conclusion. For example, a lawyer may use evidence such as fingerprints to build a case and explain how a crime occurred, or a politician may point to their voting record to establish their credibility as a conservative.

logos
Rational appeals; the use of rhetoric to help the audience see the rationale for a particular conclusion.

Aristotle felt that combining ethos, pathos, and logos was more effective than relying on only one kind of proof. For example, if a rhetor wanted to address the problem of obesity, it would be important to use ethos appeals to establish goodwill, avoiding mockery or mean-spiritedness. Logos, in turn, could offer the rationale for losing weight. Combining these appeals with the pathos-based approach of television shows like *The Biggest Loser* might enhance the impact on waistlines. The three artistic proofs work best synergistically.

Sometimes, the speaker may select to emphasize or subordinate one of the three artistic proofs. In early 2017, President Trump found a way to subordinate his usual high intensity emotional performance. Instead of focusing on emotional grandstanding, the president gave what the *Washington Post* called his "most presidential speech." In it, he calmly described which policies his administration had pursued in his first 100 days. Although he subordinated pathos to logos, emotion did punctuate in the middle of the address. When the president honored U.S. Navy Special Operator Senior Chief William "Ryan" Owens, the camera panned to Senior Chief Owens's widow. Forty-eight million Americans watched members of Congress give her a record-breaking stand of ovation as she cried. Later, CNN political analyst Van Jones argued that President Trump's speech had achieved the unprecedented. In part, it was because he had mitigated his direct appeal to pathos. Instead, he presided over an emotional connection between Congress and a citizen.

Social Position and Relationship to Audiences

Related to the concept of ethos is the social position from which a rhetor speaks. Aristotle noted that those who came from noble families were better positioned as rhetors. Yet **social position** refers to more than the prestige of one's family. One's social position comes from the way society is structured. Everyone is located in more than one position in the social structure as they speak—as a student, a customer, a friend, a voter, and so on. As a receiver of public communication, you should always consider the position or positions from which the rhetor is speaking.

What aspects of social position might help or hinder a speaker's ability to advocate a point of view? The answer is that it depends on the society and the situation. We expect certain people to speak in certain situations, such as family members at a funeral or the governor after a natural disaster. In these cases, the rhetor's authority comes from a combination of their position and the audience members' expectations. Yet these social positions are also hierarchical, meaning that some positions have more power than others. For example, if you, as a student, were to speak out about U.S. immigration policies, you would be less influential than the president when he speaks about the same topic. Even if you spoke well, you could not make up for the difference in social positions between a student and a president. Social positions and positions of power are deeply intertwined because social positions gain their power from the society that supports the structure. This power structure allows certain rhetors to be more effective than others in promoting a message.

In societies that have strong caste systems, such as India, lower castes have few rhetorical mechanisms for changing the rules that guide their lives. Compared with higher castes, fewer of them have access to the Internet, they are less able to garner media coverage of their issues, and they therefore have fewer opportunities to be heard by those in power. Furthermore, in her study of the use of Native Americans as sports mascots, Janis King (2002) concluded that Native Americans have few opportunities to change the use of these mascots, as "team owners and the majority of the fans are White. And it is these individuals who have the power to eliminate the mascots, clothing and actions" (p. 211). More recently, the controversy has been focused on the former Washington Redskins, who have now retired the name *Redskins* and are playing as the Washington Football Team. They intend to pick a new name and logo at a later date. The Washington Football Team is not the only team with a controversial mascot.

social position

Place in the social hierarchy, which comes from the way society is structured.

▼ If this officer were to testify against you in court, how might your different social positions influence how the officer's testimony and your testimony are heard? In the wake of discussions on police killings, police reform, and the Black Lives Matter movement, do police officers have the same credibility when they testify as they did before?

Social institutions, also considered rhetors according to our definition, have distinct social positions that contribute to the effectiveness or persuasiveness of their public messages. For example, when the U.S. Supreme Court issues a ruling, it sends a public message that—coming from its position of power within our social structure—has tremendous implications for the ways in which we live. Other social institutions, including those involved in medicine, religion, the military, and education, also exercise their power through rhetoric.

Just as different rhetors wield different amounts of influence, so do audiences differ in terms of cultural, social, and political assumptions and perspectives. Since the deaths of George Floyd, Breonna Taylor, Rayshard Brooks, Philando Castile, and many other African Americans in police encounters, the Black Lives Matter movement immediately gained majority support from U.S. adults. In June 2020, 67 percent supported the movement. After criticism from President Trump and escalating confrontations between police and protestors, a Pew Research Center study found the "recent decline in support for the Black Lives Matter movement is particularly notable among White and Hispanic adults" so that a majority of White adults do not support the movement. In contrast, "support for the Black Lives Matter movement has remained virtually unchanged among Black and Asian adults" (Thomas & Horowitz, 2020). One common mistake of speakers is to think only of the dominant culture, overlooking minorities who may also be part of the audience. The wide disparity in the ways racial groups view Black Lives Matter serves as an important reminder of the range of opinions that may be represented in any audience.

Who, then, is the rhetorical audience for any particular message? Rhetorical scholar Lloyd Bitzer (1968) argued that only those people who could take the appropriate action are part of the **rhetorical audience**. In other words, if a candidate for president of the United States wants to persuade a group of people to vote for her, only those people in the audience who are U.S. citizens and registered voters are part of the rhetorical audience. Although citizens of other nations or minors may be physically present for the campaign pitch, because they cannot vote for this candidate, they would not be part of the rhetorical audience. Thinking about the audience in this way may help the speaker design an appropriate, appealing, and potentially persuasive message.

rhetorical audience
Those people who can take the appropriate action in response to a message.

Yet this perspective on audience is quite narrow. As you may have noticed from following presidential elections, not all citizens who can vote do. In 2016, the United States saw the lowest voter turnout "in two decades" (Wallace, 2016) with only about 55 percent of the American electorate participating. But this does not necessarily mean that nonvoters weren't part of the rhetorical audience, especially those who understood their nonvote as a vote against an electoral system. Furthermore, U.S. citizens are not the only people who pay attention to campaign rhetoric. People around the world are also quite interested in who is elected and which policies—economic, military, cultural—this president will pursue. We live in a global environment in which the actions of the United States affect others around the world. Thus, the presidential candidate can use rhetoric to construct the desired rhetorical audience, perhaps including non-U.S. citizens and even people living in other countries.

In addition to being broader than a speaker might initially think, audiences are also fragmented. French theorist Michel Maffesoli (1996) has suggested that society consists of multiple "tribes," or identity groups, with their own ways of seeing the world. These groups are often marked by how they consume products, wear clothing, or participate in certain activities. These tribes might include NASCAR dads, soccer moms, or goths. This tribe theory can help illuminate the complexity of audiences and how rhetoric works in differing contexts with various groups. Much more work needs to be done on the use of specific rhetorical devices among diverse cultural audiences so that we can better understand their complex functions.

In summary, a rhetor's effectiveness depends on a configuration of characteristics such as artistic proofs—ethos, pathos, and logos—as well as social position and relationship to audiences. Many factors contribute to our impression that one speaker

Journal Prompt 12.3:
Characteristics of Rhetors
What are the most important characteristics of individual rhetors? What characteristics do you find most effective in some speakers versus others?

is more charismatic and powerful than another. Audience members may not always agree on which speaker is the best, but most can say which one moves them and which leaves them cold—or drowsy! Considering individual rhetor characteristics gives us only a partial view of rhetoric. In the next section, we will broaden our focus to examine the relationship between rhetoric and society and the roles rhetoric plays in giving meaning to major events, fulfilling democratic functions, and bringing about justice and social change.

The Individual, Rhetoric, and Society

12.4 Explain four functions of rhetoric: reaffirming cultural values, increasing democratic participation, securing justice, and promoting social change.

Because rhetoric always arises within a specific social context, its functions can vary considerably. The distinct cultural forces that influence a particular society should be considered when studying its rhetoric. In the United States today, rhetoric serves four important democratic functions that form the basis of how we come to decisions and work together collectively. We will look at these four functions next.

Reaffirming Cultural Values

rhetorical event
Any event that generates a significant amount of public discourse.

The term **rhetorical event** refers to any event that generates a significant amount of public discourse. Such "explosions" of rhetoric give insight into the ways meaning is constructed and rhetoric and cultural values are affirmed. For example, unusual weather or natural disasters incite a great deal of rhetorical discourse that attempts to explain what has occurred. Some of the discourse usually comes from scientists, who provide scientific explanations about the event. Other discourse may come from political commentators, who try to connect such natural disasters to a larger political or religious meaning. For example, during and after the devastating wildfires that consumed enormous amounts of land in the western U.S., especially California, Oregon, and Washington, people tried to find culprits to blame. President Trump blamed poor forestry management, former Vice President Biden blamed climate change, and others tried to blame (incorrectly) QAnon on the right and Antifa on the left for starting fires. All of these viewpoints emerge from different value systems. Should we be allowing more housing development in wooded areas? Should we pay more attention to our impact on the environment and how to mitigate our carbon footprint? This affirmation, as well as negation, of our relationship to the environment reflects our cultural values, and that kind of rhetoric is known as **epideictic rhetoric**.

epideictic rhetoric
The type of rhetoric that reaffirms cultural values through praising and blaming.

Part of the function of rhetorical events, then, is to reaffirm cultural values. Every four years, for example, the United States inaugurates a president, and the speeches given, particularly the president's inaugural speech, highlight important national values along with that president's goals. Holidays, sports events, weddings, funerals, retirement parties, campaign speeches, declarations of war, and protest marches are also rhetorical events. Such occasions often include speakers who celebrate cultural values relevant to and that resonate with their respective audiences.

Increasing Democratic Participation

As noted, among the ancient Greeks and Romans, rhetoric was valued for its use in civic life. The belief that advocating for one's ideas is in the best interests of society is a cornerstone of democracy. Not all societies are democracies, of course, and in those nondemocratic societies rhetoric has served different purposes. For our discussion we will examine aspects of rhetorical communication that influence citizen participation, which is a key part of the democratic process.

Deliberative rhetoric, the type of rhetoric used to argue what courses of action a society should do in the future, is deeply embedded in the democratic process. When legislators argue about raising taxes to pay for new roads or increasing funding for education, they are engaged in deliberative rhetoric. A speaker's ability to advocate effectively drives the open discussion and debate about what society should or should not do.

Also essential to a democracy is citizens' ability to evaluate the many important arguments they hear. In 2003, the United States argued in front of the United Nations Security Council that Saddam Hussein had weapons of mass destruction and, therefore, military intervention was needed. In hindsight, both government officials and citizens can see the errors made in arguments for the invasion. However, at the time, social position played an important role in the persuasiveness of the argument to go to war. Because Secretary of State Colin Powell was well respected nationally and internationally, he spoke from a position of power and credibility. Donald Rumsfeld, as Secretary of Defense, also spoke in favor of invading Iraq, as did President George W. Bush. In this instance, however, as well as in many others, citizens in a democracy benefit from listening to a variety of arguments and evaluating them based on the evidence available—without the undue influence of social position.

Another important area of inquiry within rhetorical studies as it relates to democracy focuses on the public sphere. The **public sphere** is the arena in which deliberative decision making occurs through the exchange of ideas and arguments. For example, legislative bodies such as Congress are places where decisions are made about a wide range of issues. Protests against the World Trade Organization, underground and alternative magazines and newspapers, and performance art that critiques social issues also constitute types of public sphere rhetoric but are sometimes referred to as *counter-publics* because they occur outside the mainstream media and institutions. This type of rhetoric is also central to the functioning of a democratic society because it typically includes the voices of marginalized or less powerful individuals and groups.

Bringing about Justice

As we noted previously in this chapter, a specific type of rhetoric is used in courts of law to bring about justice. Called **forensic rhetoric**, this form addresses events that happened in the past, as in "Where were you on the night of April 24?" The goal of forensic rhetoric is to set things right after an injustice has occurred. Another function of rhetoric in the context of justice is to allow citizens to exchange and negotiate ideas about what constitutes "just" and "unjust." As we look back over U.S. history, we can see how notions of justice have changed. In 1692, people in Salem, Massachusetts, felt that justice was served when they hanged 19 people and jailed hundreds more for practicing witchcraft. Today, we see those trials as examples of injustice. In 1872, Susan B. Anthony, along with a number of other women, voted in an election in Rochester, New York. Anthony was arrested and convicted of violating laws that prevented women from voting. Today, most people view her actions as not only just but also courageous.

As these examples illustrate, laws and court judgments can only determine what is just and unjust within specific situations at particular moments in history. For example, Dred Scott was a nineteenth-century slave who tried to buy freedom for himself and his wife, but when the owner refused, he sought freedom through the court system. The U.S. Supreme Court ultimately ruled that he was neither a citizen—and therefore could not bring a case in federal court—nor entitled to his freedom because he was someone's personal property. Today, we would be shocked at this kind of Supreme Court ruling. As a nation, we have decided that slavery is an injustice, but coming to this decision involved considerable public communication, or rhetoric, about slavery. It also involved a bloody civil war. Nevertheless, debates about citizenship and racial restrictions on who was eligible to be a U.S. citizen continued well into the twentieth century.

deliberative rhetoric
The type of rhetoric used to argue what courses of action a society should take in the future.

public sphere
The arena in which deliberative decision making occurs through the exchange of ideas and arguments.

forensic rhetoric
Rhetoric that addresses events that happened in the past with the goal of setting things right after an injustice has occurred.

Hindsight makes it easy to see that slavery or the denial of rights to women or Blacks is unjust. In many cases, however, considerable disagreement exists about what is just. For example, the United States has been grappling with the proper and just role of policing in society. Visual images of African Americans being shot by police or killed in other ways has ignited an important discussion about policing and the legal protections afforded police officers. Many people were outraged watching the Minneapolis police officer with his knee on George Floyd's neck, which resulted in his death. This outrage fueled the "defund the police" movement, which "does not mean abolish the policing" (Ray, 2020). Instead, it alleges that the financial resources devoted to policing would be better spent on other services, for instance, resources for mental health, drug abuse, and other social problems. See *Did You Know?: Visual Rhetoric*. How powerful are the images of people dying in encounters with the police? How persuasive is visual rhetoric?

In the effort to find justice, Ameneh Bahrami, an Iranian woman, asked that Islamic law be imposed on a man who threw acid on her face, disfiguring and blinding her. This man had wanted to marry Bahrami, but she declined his marriage proposal. At the trial, "an Iranian court ordered that five drops of the same chemical be placed in each of her attacker's eyes, acceding to Bahrami's demand that he be punished according to a principle in Islamic jurisprudence that allows a victim to seek retribution for a crime" (Erdbrink, 2008, p. A1). In late July 2011, she pardoned her attacker so that he did not end up being blinded (Dehghan, 2011). Although recognizing cultural and religious differences, is this justice? How do we determine what is just and what is unjust, except through public discussion and deliberation? As you contemplate these types of questions you will undoubtedly realize that many different kinds of punishments were (and are) acceptable in different periods and places. Questions of justice are neither easily settled nor universally agreed on, and they are negotiated rhetorically. Through our public discussions, we try to build a more just society.

DID YOU KNOW?
Visual Rhetoric

As you consider the image of a Confederate statue being taken down, how do these images function? Do they help the nation move past slavery and on a path toward racial reconciliation? Or do they erase a significant part of our national history? For different audiences, these statues are viewed differently: "For some, they've symbolized heritage, but for many, many others, the statues have been a symbol of past and present racism in the U.S." (Aguilera, 2020). What do you think when you see a Confederate statue?

SOURCE: Aguilera, J. (2020, June 9). Confederate statues are being removed amid protests over George Floyd's death. Here's what to know. *Time.* https://time.com/5849184/confederate-statues-removed/

Prompting Social Change

As you can see from the many police killings, especially of African Americans, across the nation, laws do not always ensure justice for all. Thus, people who want to bring about social change and promote their views of justice often use rhetoric to mobilize large numbers of people. If a mobilization succeeds, it can lead to a **social movement**, which is a mass movement of people motivated to create social change. Scholars have studied the public messages of social movements, such as the movement to abolish slavery, the women's suffrage movement, and the anti–Vietnam War movement. Social movement scholars also have tried to understand opposition to such movements and to evaluate the persuasiveness of that opposition.

Other social movements that have received attention from rhetoricians include the Chicano movement (Delgado, 1995), the environmental movement (DeLuca, 1999), and the gay/lesbian movement (Darsey, 1991). In this latter study, Darsey tracked the changing arguments of gay rights activists over time in relation to the changing contexts of sexual liberation, antigay legislation, and AIDS. The goals of his study and other similar ones are to understand the arguments that activists in social movements make, the social and historical context in which they put forth these arguments, the events that spark the emergence of social movement discourse, the resistance to the arguments, and why arguments on both sides are or are not persuasive. People arguing for change have also turned to new tools available, including Twitter. See *Alternative View: Twitter Activism*.

As you can see, public messages are deeply embedded in the culture of their times. In past eras, debates and speeches about slavery, women's suffrage, and U.S. involvement in the Vietnam War permeated the daily life of Americans. Today, far more rhetoric focuses on domestic terrorism, mass shootings, and racism. As people perceive wrongs that need to be corrected, social movements emerge, and people use rhetoric to argue for the desired changes. Because a social movement is typically controversial, those who prefer to maintain the status quo will oppose it and also use rhetoric to argue against change. This has been the case in every social movement mentioned.

Today, the uses of rhetoric extend far beyond the traditional medium of public speaking. People who desire to change our society use every available

social movement

A large, organized body of people who are attempting to create social change.

▼ Social movements emerge out of the wrongs people perceive in society that need to be corrected. Those people often use rhetoric to elicit change.

ALTERNATIVE VIEW

Twitter Activism

Twitter has been used as an important tool for social movements. Given the limited number of characters allowed per tweet, it may not be obvious that Twitter can be a site of significant rhetorical influence. While President Trump used it very effectively, marginalized groups have also used the platform to organize and empower social movements. In their research on Twitter, Sarah Jackson, Moya Bailey, and Brooke Foucault Welles (2020) examine how hashtags have become a powerful rhetorical tool for marginalized groups. They examine a range of hashtags, including #MeToo, #BlackLivesMatter, #SurvivorPrivilege, #SayHerName, and many more. Rhetoric is at work everywhere, and it is not only about speeches.

SOURCE: Jackson, S. J., Bailey, M., & Welles, B. F. (2020). *#HashtagActivism: Networks of race and gender justice.* MIT Press.

means of communicating. This means that rhetoric is a part of our everyday lives, relayed via advertising, blogs, emails, texts, television programming, and newspapers. Rhetoric is embedded in all manner of communicative media, which are themselves the topic of the next chapter. Various aspects of communication often overlap.

In sum, rhetoric plays an important role in a society. It can provide meaning and shape our thoughts about major events. It can also serve democratic functions in the political life of a society. Furthermore, rhetoric can bring about justice and provide momentum for major social changes, as it has in historical movements and as it continues to do today. But how can you use these ideas about rhetoric to become more ethical? This is the topic of the next section.

Journal Prompt 12.4: Rhetoric and Society
Why is rhetoric important in a democratic society? How can rhetoric bring about justice and social change?

Ethics and Rhetoric

12.5   Understand the ethical issues facing rhetors and audience members.

Concerns about ethics and rhetoric have been a mainstay in rhetorical studies since the origins of rhetoric. From ancient Greeks to contemporary thinkers, rhetoricians have wrestled with the best ways to be ethical in using and consuming rhetorical messages. There have been many debates over what is ethical and unethical in attempting to persuade others to view the world as the rhetor does. Although most would agree that the use of outright deception or lying would be unacceptable, there is no set list of rules that are universally agreed on to guide your ethical choices. In building a rhetorical case advocating a particular way of viewing a topic—for example, death penalty, abortion, financial reform—be aware of the choices that the rhetor is making. Is the best available evidence being used? Is the message adapted to the audience?

It is important to be aware of the language that is used. Obviously, pejorative terms for members of various cultural groups should be avoided because it is unethical to dismiss entire groups of people with negative terms. Sometimes rhetors demean or disparage particular social groups, either overtly or subtly. When someone engages in this communication behavior, much of the audience may turn against the rhetor. For example, when Mayor Barry Presgraves of Luray, Virginia, referred to Kamala Harris with a racist and sexist term, he felt the need to apologize: "Passing off demeaning and worn-out racial stereotypes as humor isn't funny. I now fully understand how hurtful it is. I can and will do better, and we can all do better. We must. From the bottom of my heart I am sorry and humbly ask for your forgiveness and your grace" (qtd. in VanHoose, 2020).

Aside from such obvious choices, you should also consider your use of what rhetorician Richard Weaver described as "god terms" and "devil terms" (1985). These terms too easily lead (or mislead) people without critical reflection. God terms are words such as *freedom*, *equality*, and so on. Devil terms are similar but negative, such as *communist*, *nazi*, and so on. God terms and devil terms must be used carefully because they can serve more as propaganda than rhetoric, and when we hear those terms, we should carefully consider what the rhetor is trying to persuade us to think or do.

Rhetorical ethics are also focused on the ends or goals of the rhetorical messages. For example, if someone is trying to convince people that we should undertake the genocide of a particular cultural group, does it matter if they do not lie or fabricate any evidence in making the argument? So, ethics in rhetoric include a consideration of the goals of the rhetoric. What do these rhetorical messages encourage us to do or to think?

Social media present new challenges to the need to think through how we attempt to persuade others to view the world as we do (and vice versa). The Internet not only reproduces and reflects larger social issues, but it can also shape the ways that the rhetorical discussions take place (Nakamura & Chow-White, 2012). You may have encountered many problematic comments online. This phenomenon is interesting in that it creates a space for people to try to align others to their world-views. Because of the rhetorical power of social media, there has been much pressure put on Facebook, Twitter, and other platforms to regulate what happens there. In response, Twitter has permanently banned white supremacist and former Ku Klux Klan member David Duke (Effron, 2020), and Twitter has also taken down thousands of accounts associated with QAnon, a group that promotes conspiracy theories, with one of their central beliefs that "Mr. Trump ran for office to save Americans from a so-called deep state filled with child-abusing, devil-worshipping bureaucrats" (Conger, 2020). Chapter 14 explores social media in more detail, but the rhetorical power of these platforms can shape how people view the world whether those views are true in Plato's sense or not.

Using what you know about rhetoric, then, what can you do to become an ethical receiver of rhetorical communication? Here are some guidelines:

- Be willing to listen to a range of perspectives on a particular topic. Although you may not initially agree with a particular rhetor, you should consider their perspective (Makau, 1997), including why you do or do not agree.

- Be willing to speak out if you know that a rhetor is giving misinformation or deceiving an audience.

- Don't be silenced by information overload. If a speaker gives too much information, focus on the main points and be critical of this kind of presentation.

- Listen critically to the rhetor; don't accept the arguments presented at face value.

- Be willing to speak out publicly if a rhetor communicates in a way that dehumanizes or demeans others (Johannesen, 1997).

- Listen to and fairly assess what you hear, which may require that you postpone judgment until you hear the entire message.

- Be willing to change your mind as more evidence becomes available.

Journal Prompt 12.5: Ethical Rhetoric
What are some of the major ethical issues facing rhetors and audiences?

Using Your Rhetorical Skills: Speaking in Public

12.6   Identify the basic steps in preparing a speech.

Throughout this chapter, we have discussed rhetoric primarily from the viewpoint of the receiver or critic. But we can also be rhetors by writing for an audience, by using other media such as video to reach audiences, and by practicing the art of public speaking. Becoming an effective rhetor is important because speaking in public is a cornerstone of our participatory democracy in the United States. Citizens need to become adept public speakers so that they can advocate for what they think is best (Gayle, 2004). Learning to speak up for your interests can also improve your satisfaction from participating in student organizations, as well as in local organizations such as a city council or a volunteer group. Public speaking skills are also important for success in most jobs. Increasingly, businesses want employees who can speak well in meetings and in public settings outside the organization (Osterman, 2005).

In the following sections, we introduce the basic elements of speech preparation. We'll look at the range of communication events in which people may be called to speak, the importance of understanding audiences, and the basics of constructing, organizing, and delivering a speech. These elements supply the foundations for effective public speaking.

Understanding the Communication Event:
The Synergetic Model

Recall from Chapter 1 that the Synergetic Model of Communication depicts communication as a transactional process that is influenced by individual, societal, and cultural factors. It is easy to see how this model applies to public speaking. Far from being a one-way communication in which the rhetor delivers a speech to the audience, effective public speaking is a transaction between the rhetor and the audience. You as an individual bring yourself to the speech—speaking is self-presentation as well as being the presentation of a message. A good speaker also relates to audience members as individuals, giving each listener the sense that the speaker is "talking to me." Finally, every speech event is influenced by the societal and cultural contexts in which it takes place.

In this section, we will examine the steps in understanding the communication event: identifying your general purpose, understanding your audience, selecting your topic, and identifying a specific purpose for your speech.

Identifying Your General Purpose   The great Roman orator Cicero identified three objectives for public speaking: to inform, to persuade, and to entertain. These three types of speeches are still taught in most public speaking courses today (McKerrow et al., 2003; O'Hair et al., 2004). However, the objective "to entertain" has been broadened to "to evoke feeling," which is a more accurate description of what this type of speech can do. For example, a halftime locker room speech does not aim to be entertaining but inspiring. Of course, inspiration motivates the team to win, so it remains a kind of persuasion, albeit indirect. For reference, watch Tony D'Amato, Al Pacino's character in *Any Given Sunday*, deliver a moving football halftime locker room speech. D'Amato doesn't have to persuade his team to win. They already want to win, but their morale is low. Sometimes, stirring emotion is the key to goading people to persevere and perhaps achieve their goals. We will refer to this third type as the *evocative speech*.

The *informative speech* explains, instructs, defines, clarifies, demonstrates, or teaches. The *persuasive speech* attempts to influence, convince, motivate, sell, preach, or stimulate action. Finally, the purpose of the *evocative speech* is to entertain, inspire, celebrate, commemorate, or build community (Sprague & Stuart, 2005, p. 65). A common type of evocative speech, including the wedding toast, celebrates aspects of a person or topic. Sometimes evocative speeches are also known as **special-occasion speeches**, and they include speeches given at retirement dinners, award ceremonies, weddings, graduations, and funerals.

Obviously, the three general purposes do not function in isolation. Speakers often persuade others by informing them about something, or they inform audiences by entertaining them. A speech by a politician might primarily aim to persuade voters to adopt a particular point of view, but it might also be informative and evocative. Of the three, the one that is dominant in a given speech is known as the **general purpose** of that speech. Once you identify your general purpose, you are ready to begin the next step of developing your presentation by focusing on your audience.

Understanding Your Audience   Because the speaking event is a transactional process between you and your audience, it is important to learn as much as possible about your audience as you develop your speech. In public speaking this is called **audience analysis**. Understanding and relating to your audience are crucial aspects of public speaking because, regardless of purpose or goals, the success of your presentation depends on its appropriateness for your audience.

Audience analysis involves learning as much as you can in response to the following four questions.

1. What does the audience already know about your topic? What do they want to know?

special-occasion speeches
Evocative speeches intended to entertain, inspire, celebrate, commemorate, or build community.

general purpose
Whichever of three goals—to inform, persuade, or entertain—dominates a speech.

audience analysis
The process of determining what an audience already knows or wants to know about a topic, who they are, what they know or need to know about the speaker, and what their expectations might be for the presentation.

2. What do your listeners know about you? What do they need to know about you?

3. What expectations do your listeners have for the presentation?

4. Who are your audience members in terms of identity characteristics such as age, gender, race and ethnicity, education, socioeconomic status, and group membership? These characteristics are known as audience demographics, and the process of investigating them is known as **demographic analysis**.

▲ Audiences can be complex groups of people who may share some interests but differ on others. Demographic information can be helpful, but avoid playing into stereotypes.

Although it may seem difficult to obtain answers to these questions, it is easy to see that if your audience consists of people you have already met—such as fellow students in your class—you may already be able to provide many answers. You can also ask them about various aspects of these audience analysis questions, either in informal conversations or by developing an audience analysis questionnaire. If you are speaking to an unfamiliar group of listeners and do not have an opportunity to meet them before the speech, ask the person who invited you to speak. Like most facets of public speaking, audience analysis is a rich topic in itself, but we hope these essentials will enable you to approach the task effectively.

demographic analysis
The portion of an audience analysis that considers the ages, races, sexes, sexual orientations, religions, and social classes of the audience.

Selecting Your Topic   Selecting a topic can be the most interesting and the most difficult part of any speech presentation. Assuming that the topic is not already determined for you, here are some guidelines to help you choose:

- Consider the communication event. What are the expectations for your presentation? What types of topics would be appropriate to speak about?

- Consider your interests. Take a personal inventory. What are some unusual experiences you've had? What subjects do you know a lot about? What topics do you feel strongly about? What would you like to learn more about?

- Consider your relationship to the communication event. Why are you being asked to speak? Do you have a special relationship to someone—for example, the bride at a wedding or the deceased at a funeral? If so, you may have special insight into topics the audience would consider appropriate and effective. Have you been chosen because you are an expert in a particular area? If so, the audience will expect you to demonstrate that expertise and to answer questions effectively.

Critical Thinking Prompt
If you had to give a speech today to the graduating class of the high school you attended, what topics might you consider for your speech?

We'll return to the development of speech topics when we guide you through the important process of narrowing a broad topic to an appropriately focused one.

Identifying a Specific Purpose   Once you know the general purpose of your speech and have selected your speech topic, you can begin focusing on the specific purpose of your speech. As discussed previously, your general purpose may be to inform, persuade, or evoke a certain feeling from your audience. Your **specific purpose** focuses on what you would like to inform or persuade your audience about, or what type of feelings you want to evoke. Identifying your specific purpose helps you focus your topic and establish your organizational structure.

specific purpose
What a speaker wants to inform or persuade an audience about, or the type of feelings the speaker wants to evoke.

COMMUNICATION IN SOCIETY
Communication Event Checklist

What other details might you need to know for a particular speaking event?

_____ 1. When will you speak (date and time), and how long is your speech supposed to last?

_____ 2. Where will you speak (address, directions), and what will the size and physical layout of the room be?

_____ 3. What is the general purpose of your speech? The specific purpose?

_____ 4. What do you know about your audience?

_____ 5. Have you arranged for any computer or audiovisual equipment you will need?

_____ 6. Do you have the name and phone number of a person in charge whom you can contact in case a question or emergency arises?

The specific purpose of your speech should be a "nutshell" summary of what you want your audience to take away. Here are some examples of specific purposes for informative, persuasive, and evocative speeches.

- My specific purpose is to inform my audience about the cost of private preschools in our local area.

- My specific purpose is to inform my audience about the history of immigration at Ellis Island.

- My specific purpose is to persuade my audience that our public school system should raise taxes to institute a universal preschool program.

- My specific purpose is to persuade my audience to donate money to the Ellis Island Museum.

- My specific purpose is to evoke a humorous mood regarding parents' anxiety over their children's performance in preschool interviews.

- My specific purpose is to evoke nostalgia with the story of my great-grandfather's immigration experience at Ellis Island.

Once you have a specific purpose, you need to research your topic, gather evidence for your claims, and organize your speech. We will turn to those steps next. But first, to make sure you've obtained all the preliminary "nuts and bolts" information you need to prepare your speech, refer to _Communication in Society: Communication Event Checklist._

Researching and Organizing Your Presentation

Once you have laid the foundation for developing your speech, you are ready to craft your thesis statement, locate supporting materials, and decide how to organize your message.

thesis statement
A statement of the topic of a speech and the speaker's position on it.

Crafting Your Thesis Statement   By rephrasing your specific purpose as a **thesis statement**, you create a statement of your topic and your position on it. The thesis statement is important because it is the foundation on which you construct your presentation. For example, if your specific purpose is to argue that voting should be mandatory, you might articulate your thesis statement this way: "Voting should be mandatory in the United States." This is an effective thesis statement because it clearly sets out the proposition to be considered. Each of the main points you want to convey should clearly connect to and develop your thesis statement.

supporting materials
Information that supports the speaker's ideas.

Finding Supporting Materials   Some topics require extensive research, particularly those on which you are not an expert. However, all speech preparations should include some research to find **supporting materials** that support your ideas.

Supporting materials are available from at least three sources: electronic, print, and personal. You can start with the electronic card catalog in your library, accessing databases and online journals. You will also want to search the Internet, which is increasingly an excellent and acceptable source for research, even scholarly studies. One caution about Internet sources, however: You must evaluate them carefully, as you should any source. Referring to credible sources is especially important for informative and persuasive speeches.

Print sources include books, magazines, and newspapers. Again, evaluate the source. Newspapers such as *The Wall Street Journal* or the *Washington Post* are considered highly reliable on certain topics. Note that some print materials (e.g., *The New American, The Nation, Ms. Magazine*) have a specific point of view. You may use such sources to support your point, but you should acknowledge their viewpoint or bias in your speech. You can find magazines that address every topic imaginable—from general news (e.g., *Newsweek*) to specific hobbies (e.g., *Model Railroader, Scrapbooking, Sky and Telescope*). Use Internet databases such as EBSCO or NexisLexis® to help you locate print magazine articles that address your speech topic. In addition to newspapers and magazines, there are encyclopedias and other reference works (e.g., *Statistical Abstract of the United States, People's Almanac, Guinness Book of World Records*) that offer a wealth of information on a variety of topics.

A final source of supporting materials can be personal interviews. You might want to interview people who can give you facts, opinions, and background information on your topic. In addition, you can use interviews to find leads to other sources, including the faculty at your college or university. Most professors have a wealth of information in several areas of expertise and enjoy sharing that information, including where you might do further research. Before any interview, be sure to prepare well. Know what kind of information you're looking for, contact potential interviewees in advance to make appointments, and be able to explain why you chose them (this shows you've done some homework).

As you identify and use any of these kinds of sources, take careful notes because you may need to refer to them. Moreover, some instructors require that references be submitted with a speaking outline. We'll discuss different types of outlines when we discuss organizing speeches.

Once you have a collection of relevant sources, what kinds of material do you look for within them? Statistics, examples, and personal narratives can all be useful in bolstering your points. Visual aids also provide effective support, especially when a topic is complex. Let's look at the uses for each of these types of support materials.

Statistics Statistics can highlight the size of a problem and help the audience understand a contrast or comparison. However, they can be overwhelming or confusing if they are too complex for the audience to follow. If you are dealing with large numbers, it is often best to round them off. For example, according to the Australian Bureau of Statistics (2020), the population of Australia is estimated to be 25,705,216 as of September 25, 2020. Your audience is more likely to remember the population if you round it off and say that there are almost 26 million people in Australia.

When citing statistics, however, be careful about attributing meaning to them because the reasons for statistical differences are not always apparent or reported with the statistical data. For example, the Pew Research Center came out with a study that showed that about 23 percent of Hispanics have heard of the term *Latinx* but only 3 percent use it (Noe-Bustamante et al., 2020). This bilingual study focused on U.S. Hispanics and showed that younger people were more familiar with the term than older people. Women were more likely to use the term *Latinx* than men. Although this is interesting information that may be useful in a speech about changing identity labels, it is important to be aware that the Pew survey did not attribute any causes to these differences. We don't know why the survey respondents answered as they did, so you would not want to mislead your audience by adding attributions of your own unless you clearly state that such attributions are your own opinion.

Examples   A second type of supporting material, examples, can also add power to a presentation. A speaker might give a brief example to illustrate a point in passing or use a more extended example, woven throughout a speech. Examples provide a concrete and realistic way of thinking about a topic and clarifying it. If you were to speak about nonfiction television programming, for example, your audience may better understand your point if you name specific programs, such as *60 Minutes, Nova,* or *Monday Night Football.* Without these examples, some audience members might think you are referring to reality television programs, such as *Survivor, Amazing Race,* and *Big Brother.*

Personal Narratives   A third kind of support for your presentation—personal narratives and testimony of others—can give your speech a human touch. For example, if you are speaking about non-English languages in the United States and you describe your own family's struggle to retain its non-English language, your story adds emotional texture to the issue. See *It Happened to Me: Lisa* to read how a personal narrative can influence your audience.

It Happened to Me
Lisa

We once had a speaker in class who told us about her family's struggle with diabetes. I had never really thought about diabetes before, and the statistics about diabetes didn't impact me as much as her story. I didn't know that some diabetics had to have their feet amputated, but now that I know, I am much more sensitive to the struggles of diabetics.

Visual Aids   As a student in elementary school, you may have used visual aids in show-and-tell speeches. In these speeches, the visual aid—perhaps a favorite toy, gift, or souvenir—was at the center. As part of your college coursework, your instructors may also require that you use visual aids in speeches. Even if you are not required to do so, you should consider whether visual aids would enhance the clarity of your presentation or make it more memorable or more interesting. **Visual aids** are any audiovisual materials that help you reach your speech goals. Some of the most common kinds are video or audio clips, photographs and drawings, charts and graphs, and PowerPoint slides.

visual aids
Audiovisual materials that help a speaker reach intended speech goals.

Always select and incorporate visual aids carefully, remembering that their purpose is to augment and enhance your presentation, not to detract from your presentation. They are also not a substitute for content, as Edward Tufte instructs in *Alternative View: PowerPoint Is Evil: Power Corrupts. PowerPoint Corrupts Absolutely.*

To determine whether a visual aid is going to augment or detract, ask yourself why you are using it and how it will support your speech goals. Here are some tips for handling visual aids effectively:

1. Prepare visual aids in advance.
2. Make sure your visual aids are easy for all audience members to see.
3. Make sure the equipment you need will be available when you speak.
4. Make sure your speech can stand on its own in case of a technology failure.

In using a visual aid during your speech, follow these three steps: (a) introduce the visual aid to your audience members by explaining what they will see, (b) point to the parts of the visual

▼ Visual aids can be helpful in explaining ideas and instructions. In this photo, students receive hands-on training in CPR.

ALTERNATIVE VIEW

PowerPoint Is Evil: Power Corrupts. PowerPoint Corrupts Absolutely

Have you ever sat through a horrible PowerPoint presentation? PowerPoint is a tool that can be very helpful and effective in presentations, but—like any tool—it can be used in ways that are counterproductive. Bad PowerPoint presentations can turn audiences away from the presentation and sometimes turn against the presenter. We've all been subjected to bad PowerPoint presentations, but you can avoid making one by following some important tips.

1. Do not put your text on the slides and then read to the audience. Audiences can often read faster than you can read aloud and you risk losing the audience. They may read the slides and then, while you continue reading to them, they may check their smartphones, send text messages, daydream and so on.
2. Think about the number of slides that you use. While it is often easy to include a lot of slides, audiences can get overwhelmed by a large number of slides. Keep the focus of the presentation on your content.
3. Be careful not to overload your audience with too much information. Much of the information in a presentation does not need to be reflected on PowerPoint slides.

4. Don't forget the affective or emotional aspects of your presentation, especially if your goal is to persuade as in a sales talk. Emotions can be powerful motivators and PowerPoint slides may draw away from those emotional appeals.
5. Consider what the strengths of PowerPoint are and how you can best use this tool. For example, a PowerPoint slide can show an image that would be much more difficult to explain verbally. Images can also help audiences spark emotional responses of childhood, family, home and more which you can then use to draw your audience toward the direction that you wish to take them.

Overall, remember that PowerPoint is a tool to help you with your presentation. It should not overwhelm or distract the audience away from your talk. Keep your talk at the center of the presentation and use the PowerPoint to assist you in the goals of the presentation. PowerPoint should never be a substitution for your presentation. An audience should never feel that they would have been better off if you had just printed out your PowerPoint slides and distributed them.

SOURCE: Tufte, E. (2003, September). PowerPoint is evil. *Wired Magazine*, 118–119. Reprinted by permission from Edward R. Tufte, *The Cognitive Style of PowerPoint*. Graphics Press.

---

aid that you want them to focus on, and (c) reaffirm the major point of the visual aid, thus pointing audience members to the conclusion you want them to draw.

Organizing Your Message   Once you have gathered enough information and evidence to build your speech, you need to organize the presentation in a clear manner. Organizing an effective presentation means choosing and following a pattern that is compatible with your topic and that will make sense to your audience. It also involves creating an outline that can serve as the framework for your material. To anchor your organizational structure, you will develop an introduction, a conclusion, and transitions.

Organizational Patterns   In most cases, a speech should be organized around three to five main points. If you have fewer than three points, you may not yet have sufficiently thought about or researched your topic. Once you have identified your main points, divide them into subpoints. These subpoints should all clearly relate to their corresponding main points. Once you have all your main points and subpoints, you need to consider how to arrange them. Speakers generally follow one of five organizational patterns: chronological, spatial, topical, problem–solution, or cause–effect.

A **chronological pattern** follows a timeline; for example, a speech on the life of a famous person lends itself well to a chronological outline.

chronological pattern
An organization that follows a timeline.

Here is an example of a chronological pattern:

Topic: Life of Susan B. Anthony

    I. Her birth and formative years (1820–1840)

    II. Her fight to end slavery (1840–1860)

    III. Her fight for women's rights (1860–her death in 1906)

spatial pattern
An organization that arranges points by location and can be used to describe something small.

A **spatial pattern** arranges points by location and can be used to describe something small (for example, parts of a flower—moving from the edge to its center) or something large (for example, the immigration center buildings at Ellis Island—moving along a central hallway).

Here is an example of a spatial pattern:

Topic: A Tour of Ellis Island

    I. The Baggage Room

    II. The Registry Room

    III. The Hearing Room

    IV. The Bunk Room

topical pattern

An organization that has no innate organization except that imposed by the speaker.

A **topical pattern** of organization, the most common, is used when your main points have no innate pattern except the one you impose on them. This situation requires more thinking because the points have no predetermined relationship, and you will need to find the scheme that is most logical and will work best for your audience.

Here is an example of a topical pattern:

Topic: MERS (Middle Eastern Respiratory Syndrome)

    I. What is MERS?

    II. Who is most at risk?

    III. How can you prevent MERS?

problem–solution pattern

An organization in which the speaker describes various aspects of a problem and then proposes solutions.

In the **problem–solution pattern**, you describe various aspects of a problem and then propose solutions; it is frequently used in persuasive speeches.

Here is an example of a problem–solution pattern:

Topic: Childhood Obesity

    I. Problem: Increasing obesity rates in U.S. children

    II. Solution: Eat healthier foods and drink water

    III. Solution: Increase amount of exercise, sports activities, and general physical activity

cause–effect pattern

An organization used to create understanding and agreement, and sometimes to argue for a specific action.

A final approach to organization, the **cause–effect pattern**, is often used to create understanding and agreement or to argue for a specific action in light of the cause that is associated with a given result.

Here is an example of a cause–effect pattern:

Topic: Climate Change

    I. Causes

        Subpoints: energy consumption, overpopulation, increasing consumption

    II. Effects

        Subpoints: extreme weather events, rising sea levels, melting ice caps

    III. How to slow climate change

Outlining Your Speech   Once you have selected your pattern, you will have a good idea of the order in which you want to present your points. Thus, you are ready to create your outline. You are probably already familiar with how to outline. In the past, you may have used outlining chiefly to organize your written compositions. However, outlining also is useful in organizing a public-speaking presentation. An outline should be considered a working document, so you shouldn't hesitate to change it again and again. The idea is to create a sound organizational structure and a road map from which you can best build your presentation.

Introduction, Body, and Conclusion   After you have developed your outline, arranging your points and subpoints according to the pattern you have chosen, you will need to develop this skeleton into a full-bodied presentation. In doing so, you will pay special attention to your introduction and conclusion. Audiences usually remember much more about these opening and closing elements than they do about the body of the speech.

From your **introduction**, audience members gain a first impression of your speech's content and of you as the speaker, so both the content and presentation of the introduction are important. You'll want to start with a bang, not a whimper. To do this, your introduction should: (1) gain audience attention, (2) focus their attention on your topic by relating it to them, (3) give them an overview of your organizational pattern, and (4) help them understand your thesis.

You can gain audience attention with a snappy quotation, a startling fact, a personal example, or a shocking statistic connected to your speech topic.

Once you have gotten the audience's attention, you need to focus it on your specific topic. Your next task is to present your thesis statement so the audience understands the point of the speech. In the final part of your introduction, you would preview the overall organization of the presentation.

Moving on to the body of your speech, you will want to insert transitions to help your audience understand your organization as you progress from main point to main point, and from subpoint to subpoint. These transitions, called **signposts**, tell the audience where you are in the overall organization, thus making it easier for them to follow along and stay oriented. Common signposts include phrases such as "my second point is" or "a second stage of the" or "in addition." These devices are not merely mechanical. You can use them in an artful way to help your words and ideas flow together gracefully.

The transition into your conclusion needs to be marked by a major signpost so that the audience knows you are preparing to end your speech. The **conclusion** should accomplish several goals. First, it should review the three to five main points in the body of your presentation. Second, if you are giving a persuasive speech, during the conclusion, you will challenge the audience to act. Actions may include finding out more about the topic or becoming more involved in the issue—for example, by registering to vote, donating blood, or signing a petition. As you formulate this challenge, or call the audience to action, consider how you want your presentation to impact their lives. Do you want them to vote a particular way? Change their eating habits? Use sunscreen? Finally, the conclusion should leave the audience with a positive view of you and your topic.

Whatever closing technique you choose, remember that public speaking is an art that requires artistic judgment. There is no one right or wrong way to do it, only more effective and less effective ones. See Figure 12.1 for an outline of the basic speech structure that has just been described.

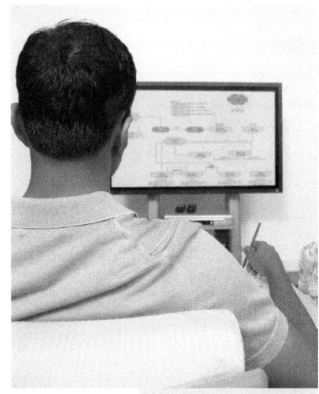

▲ Outlining your speech is a very important part of the public-speaking process. Your outline will form the basis of your speaking notes.

introduction

Opening material of a speech from which the audience members gain a first impression of the speech's content and of the speaker.

signposts

Transitions in a speech that help an audience understand the speaker's organization, making it easier for them to follow.

conclusion

Closing material of a speech where the speaker reviews the main points, may challenge the audience to act, and leaves the audience with a positive view of speaker and topic.

Figure 12.1 Basic Speech Structure

I. Introduction
  A. Attention-getting step
  B. Connection to audience
  C. Thesis statement
  D. Preview of main points
  E. Transition to first point
II. First Main Point
  A. Signpost your first point.
  B. Make your point (include supporting material).
  C. Transition to your next point.
	III. Second Main Point
	  A. Signpost your second point.
	  B. Make your point (include supporting material).
	  C. Transition to your next point.
	IV. Third Main Point
	  A. Signpost your third point.
	  B. Make your point (include supporting material).
	  C. Transition to conclusion.
	V. Conclusion
	  A. Review main points.
	  B. Connect back to audience.
	  C. Create a memorable conclusion.

Rehearsing and Delivering Your Speech

After you have developed, researched, and organized your materials, you are ready to consider the presentation of your speech. Many people think of public speaking as being all about delivery, but delivery is, as we hope you have seen, only one aspect of the entire process. In the context of public speaking, **delivery** refers to the presentation of the speech you have researched, organized, outlined, and practiced. Delivery *is* important, of course, because it is what is most immediate to the audience. In this section, we focus on three important aspects of delivery: being aware of time, developing a speaking persona, and finally, putting your speech into action.

delivery
The presentation of a speech before an audience.

Being Aware of the Time   In the United States, we often think about time as absolute, a phenomenon that can be broken down into clearly measurable units: seconds, minutes, and hours. Yet communication scholars have repeatedly shown that notions of time are relative. Many public speakers experience this relative nature of time, feeling like they have been speaking for a long time, whereas their audience may feel that they have heard only a short speech, or vice versa.

Knowing for how long to speak is an important aspect of the art of public speaking. The length of any speech should be guided by audience expectations in a particular context as well as by the content of your message. In some instances, the guidelines are rather loose, such as speeches at weddings and retirements. In other cases, the time limits are strict, and you may be cut off before you finish. For example, a citizen advocating a position in city council meetings often faces strict time limits. In classroom speech situations, you are often told how long to speak, and your audience will expect you to stay within those limits.

If your speech is significantly longer than expected, your audience may become restless, impatient, or even hostile. On the other hand, if your speech is significantly shorter than the time expected, your audience may leave feeling disappointed or short-changed because they may have made a significant effort to attend your presentation. If your speech is part of a larger program, the planners will be depending on you to fill a particular time slot.

One way to make sure you comply is to time yourself when you practice. Doing this will ensure that you know how long your speech runs and whether you need to adjust it. If you have prepared, practiced, and timed your speech, you should have no problem meeting your time requirement.

Projecting a Persona   Developing a persona, or the image a speaker conveys, is one of the most artistic aspects of public speaking. If you have seen Ellen DeGeneres on her talk show, you know that she projects a down-to-earth, almost naïve persona. She dresses casually and jokes with her audience. Her nonverbal communication is informal and relaxed. She makes direct eye contact with her audience and the television camera; she sometimes slouches in the chair and even does a little dance at the beginning of every show. These elements together contribute to her public persona.

As you create your public persona, consider a few factors that shape it. First, the speed at which you speak will shape your persona and how people perceive you. There is no one ideal speaking rate; it should vary to fit your message. For example, speaking slowly and deliberately can be effective if you want to highlight the gravity of a situation. At other times, you may wish to speak more quickly, particularly for a light, humorous presentation. You may also vary your speed as you move from point to point, slowing down, perhaps, to emphasize one item in particular.

Eye contact is another important element of creating your persona. Making **eye contact** is one of the most direct ways to show your engagement with your audience, and it can lend credibility to your presentation. If you watch *Law & Order: SVU* on television, you may have noticed that the lawyers make direct eye contact with the jury in their closing remarks. Gestures and movement also contribute to one's persona.

eye contact
Looking directly into the eyes of another.

One of the best ways to ensure that your gestures and movement are smooth and natural-looking is to practice them along with your speech.

Finally, although you may think that your delivery begins when you stand up to speak, you begin to present your persona well before that. In some cases, for example, speakers are part of a panel, seated at a table in front of the audience, or a single speaker is introduced by someone else. In both cases, the speakers are constructing their personas while they wait to speak. Fidgeting, rolling the eyes, yawning, chewing gum, being late, and displaying other unflattering nonverbal behaviors will detract from the persona you want to project. Assume that you are "on stage" from the moment you walk into the room until the moment you leave.

Rehearsing Your Speech   One of the best ways to become an effective public speaker is to practice. However, going over the points silently in your head does not count as practice. Practice means giving your speech out loud, standing up and speaking as if you were in front of an audience. In fact, it is ideal to practice in front of an audience—ask one or two of your friends to watch, listen, and give you feedback. To see yourself as others will see you, it is helpful to practice in front of a mirror or to record yourself with audio or video equipment. Do this as many times as necessary to ensure that you are familiar with your speech and feel comfortable delivering it.

Rehearsing will enable you to identify and avoid any distracting nervous mannerisms you may have, and to improve your signposting, your speaking rate, and your eye contact. In other words, you can work on projecting the type of public persona you desire. Each time you practice your speech, you can focus on a different aspect—one time on your gestures, one time on clear enunciation, and so on—until you feel comfortable with the persona and style you have developed. See *It Happened to Me: Tamara* to learn how one speaker approaches practice.

It Happened to Me
Tamara

I have had to deliver several speeches this year, and I discovered that I like to practice the beginning of my speech a little bit more than the middle or end. Why? I've learned that if I do well at the beginning, after a few minutes, I feel confident, I get into the rhythm, and I even relax a bit.

Although you may practice your speech many times, your goal is not to memorize it. A memorized speech often sounds like a recording rather than a real human being. In addition, if you work strictly from memory and you stumble over a word or phrase, you may lose your place and find it difficult to recover. Instead, during practice, focus on a delivery that is enthusiastic, vibrant, and engaging. Each time you practice, you will come out with different phrasing, different wording, and different movements. When the time comes to give your speech "for real," yet another version may appear, but this time, it will likely be a version that you are comfortable presenting.

Speech Delivery and Overcoming Anxiety   When the day comes for you to give your speech, be sure to arrive early enough to check out the room and any audiovisual or computer equipment you have arranged for. Have alternative plans in mind in case anything goes wrong with your equipment.

It's likely that you will be nervous, but if you have prepared well, you will be able to speak confidently despite any apprehension you may feel. In fact, seasoned performers depend on nerves for an extra boost of energy when they are in front of an audience. Remember that your listeners want you to do well. Focus on the faces in the audience who look friendly and who may be smiling or nodding in agreement. The peak anxiety time for most speakers is the first moment of confronting the audience (Behnke & Sawyer, 1999, 2004). Receiving positive reinforcement early on is an excellent way to get over this initial anxiety. Before you know it, your speech will be over and you'll be beaming as the audience applauds.

▲ With practice, you can develop a delivery style that is enthusiastic, vibrant, and engaging.

If you are troubled by performance anxiety, you may want to try using relaxation techniques just before speaking. Although the fear may be in your head, it manifests itself in physiological changes in your body: Your muscles tense, your breathing becomes shallow, and adrenaline pumps through your system (Behnke & Sawyer, 2004). Effective relaxation techniques for such situations include taking several deep, even breaths; yawning once or twice to relax your throat; smiling, shaking hands and talking with attendees; taking sips of water (avoid caffeine); and looking at your notes. Visit the Great Speaking Center's "Stage Fright Strategies" at http://www.antion.com/articles/stagefright.htm for many more suggestions. Although you may feel nervous, your inner anxiety is not often easy for your audience members to see. Do not assume they see how nervous you feel, and it's best not to mention it. Project confidence, and you will feel more confident as you speak.

Finally, the strategy most public speaking instructors and students use to overcome anxiety is to take the opportunity to give lots of speeches (Levasseur et al., 2004). Public speaking becomes easier and easier with each speech. As one seasoned speaker said, "Learning to become a confident speaker is like learning to swim. You can watch people swim, read about it, listen to people talk about it, but if you don't get into the water, you'll never learn" (Sanow, 2005). Take opportunities to hone your public-speaking skills. Volunteer to give speeches or become a member of Toastmasters International or a local group of public speakers.

The public speaking process involves a lot of preparation and practice. We hope that these guidelines will help you become a more effective rhetor.

Journal Prompt 12.6: Purposes for Public Speaking
Identify three general purposes in public speaking. How is the general purpose different from the specific purpose? Provide some examples.

SUMMARY

12.1 Describe some of the key issues in rhetorical communication.

- Rhetoric is important in our society for at least three reasons: it is vital to the functioning of a democracy; it plays an important role in finding justice; and it helps us understand our world.

12.2 Identify cultural and social influences on the development of rhetoric.

- Rhetoric is tied intimately to the social, cultural, and historical environment in which it functions.
- It has been defined differently in different societies, cultures, and historical eras.

12.3 Identify and define the three artistic proofs of ethos, pathos, and logos.

- Characteristics of rhetors play an important role in effective public communication.
- These include use of ethos, pathos, and logos; position in society; and relationship to the audience.
- Organizations, institutions, and corporations can also be rhetors. Rhetoric gives meaning and shape to public thinking about major events, and it can serve vital democratic functions. Rhetoric also can bring about justice and provide momentum for major social changes.

12.4 Explain four functions of rhetoric: reaffirming cultural values, increasing democratic participation, securing justice, and promoting social change.

- Rhetoric allows us to reaffirm our cultural values through the celebration or denunciation of events around us.
- Rhetoric serves to increase democratic participation through advocating for and against changes in laws and policies as well as politicians.
- Securing justice is another function of rhetoric, such as through courtroom arguments for or against finding parties guilty and the appropriate punishments for the guilty.
- Rhetoric also promotes social change through advocating change through social movements, such as Black Lives Matter.

12.5 Understand the ethical issues facing rhetors and audience members.

- To be an ethical receiver of rhetoric, one should be willing to: listen with an open mind, speak out when one disagrees, and change one's mind based on persuasive evidence.

12.6 Identify the basic steps in preparing a speech.

- One can become a more effective rhetor by practicing the art of public speaking.
- Effective rhetors understand the communication event, have focused their topics and purpose with the audience in mind, have researched and organized their speeches, and have practiced their delivery to be aware of the time, project a persona, and overcome anxiety.

KEY TERMS

rhetoric p. 313
rhetorical critic p. 316
sophists p. 317
orator p. 318
rhetor p. 319
artistic proofs p. 320
ethos p. 320
persona p. 321
pathos p. 321
logos p. 321
social position p. 322
rhetorical audience p. 323

rhetorical event p. 324
epideictic rhetoric p. 324
deliberative rhetoric p. 325
public sphere p. 325
forensic rhetoric p. 325
social movement p. 327
special-occasion speeches p. 330
general purpose p. 330
audience analysis p. 330
demographic analysis p. 331
specific purpose p. 331
thesis statement p. 332

supporting materials p. 332
visual aids p. 334
chronological pattern p. 335
spatial pattern p. 335
topical pattern p. 336
problem–solution pattern p. 336
cause–effect pattern p. 336
introduction p. 337
signposts p. 337
conclusion p. 337
delivery p. 338
eye contact p. 338

APPLY WHAT YOU KNOW

1. **Create a List of Ten Speakers You Have Heard**
   This list might include politicians such as Donald Trump, Nancy Pelosi, Rand Paul, or Barack Obama; entertainers such as Margaret Cho, Jon Stewart, or Oprah Winfrey; and so on. Put these speakers in order of most to least effective and powerful, and be clear about your reasons for ranking them in this way. Then without revealing your order, exchange lists with a classmate. Rank each other's speakers and see how your rankings compare. If they differ, discuss your reasons. Think about the criteria that you are using.

2. **Research the Characteristics of a Particular Kind of Speech**
   Ask your family and friends what they might expect from a speaker who is giving a eulogy, a graduation speech, or a retirement speech. How long would they expect the presentation to be? What level of formality do they expect? Do the people you ask differ in their opinions? What did you learn from this exercise? Compile your findings in a presentation to your class, following the steps outlined in this chapter.

3. **Watch a Video of Someone You Consider to Be a Good Speaker**
   Possibilities include Martin Luther King Jr., Malcolm X, John F. Kennedy, Ronald Reagan, Barack Obama, or Pete Buttigieg. Analyze the speech, the style, and the delivery. How do your favorite speakers organize their speeches? Do they project a particular persona or use a particular style? Take notes as you watch them and compile your notes into a report that identifies some public-speaking skills that you would like to incorporate.

4. **Research Some Ways That Public Speaking Functions in Other Cultures**
   How might culture influence how we speak in public?

Mass Media and Communication

 LEARNING OBJECTIVES

> *"The economics of media production shapes mass communication and gives it a unique and powerful role in our society."*

When Peacock, an over-the-top (OTT) television service, was launched in 2020, Charee decided to sign up and watch some shows on this platform. Peacock is owned by NBC Universal and offers many of the NBC shows that she can find on her local NBC channel. Charee decided to join to gain access to the original content that is available on Peacock, including Brave New World, but also international programming such as Noughts & Crosses from the BBC, Five Bedrooms from Australia, and Departure from Canada. Charee needs to watch these television programs from her computer rather than her television, as she earlier decided to "cut the cord," or cancel her cable TV subscription. She still watches television programming and films, but over the Internet through Hulu, Netflix, and more.

Charee's experience points to the rapidly changing concept of mass media. These television programs and films are still very important to her, and streaming services give her the freedom to watch the programs that she wants when she wants. When you think about this behavior on the individual level, you probably view it as a matter of choice or taste. When communication scholars analyze television viewing on the social level, however, they examine the influence media have on individuals and how media messages exert influence. In 2010, *Law & Order: SVU* ran an episode that highlighted the backlog of untested rape kit samples (Rubin, 2010). Rape kits store the evidence collected after a reported rape to help convict suspected rapists. Actress Mariska Hargitay, who plays a detective on that show, testified before a House committee about this issue (Dwyer & Jones, 2010). Although her television character is fictional, Hargitay uses her image to be an advocate. In 2013, she received a star on the Hollywood Walk of Fame, and Dick Wolf, creator of *Law & Order: SVU*, noted that she "has a role and an influence beyond her on-screen TV persona" (Scott, 2013). She has gone on to found the Joyful Heart Foundation to help "survivors of sexual assault, domestic violence and child abuse" (Scott, 2013). Television programs, like other types of mass media from radio to film, can influence people's lives in important ways.

In this chapter, we first look at the importance of media in everyday life. We then briefly examine the major forms of mass media. Next, we investigate how individuals use media and the influence that media messages have on individuals. Then we consider media usage within the context of the societal framework and explore the influence media have on society overall. Finally, we discuss media activism as a means for individuals to express media ethics, and we introduce guidelines for becoming more effective consumers of media. Although the Internet is also a type of media, we address that topic in Chapter 14, where we will focus on the role of interactive mediated communication.

The Importance of Mass Media

13.1 Identify the issues facing mass media.

Media hold an important place in our society. As an indication of their importance to you, consider these questions. If you met someone who did not watch television shows, see or rent movies, or listen to the radio, would you be surprised? What if the same person had never heard of Lady Gaga, Stephen Colbert, Oprah Winfrey, LeBron James, or J. Lo? Would knowing this change your interaction with that person? What topics could you and couldn't you discuss? If you concluded that many topics would be off-limits, you can see that media messages serve important social functions. For example, they help people bond with others who like or dislike the same shows, movies, advertisements, singers, or actors. Media messages and images also help shape how people view the world and what they understand—and perhaps misunderstand—about events around the globe. Because people are so deeply immersed in this media environment, however, they rarely think about their participation in it. Nevertheless, it is indeed an interaction because individuals participate in the communication process by selecting certain programs and agreeing or disagreeing with what they hear or see.

Why are media studies important? To begin with, U.S. Americans watch an enormous amount of television, although the exact number of hours is difficult to pin down. In 2016, Nielsen reported that U.S. adults spent a little over 32 hours per week watching television, followed by over 15 hours per week on their smartphones. When combining television, radio, PCs, TV-connected devices (e.g., DVDs, game consoles), tablets, and smartphones, adults spend about 74.5 hours per week using these various media (Nielsen, 2017b).

People turn to communication media for both information and entertainment. For example, most U.S. Americans turned to television to learn the results of the 2016 presidential elections. Eighty-four percent turned to television, while 48 percent used online platforms and a smaller number, 21 percent, turned to social media, such as Facebook and Twitter. The numbers add up to more than 100 percent because many people used more than one media. Thirty-seven percent used both television and the Internet to learn about the election results (Anderson, 2016). Although more people are turning to the Internet, it is important to recognize that television remains the primary information source. Of course, not all people turn to television. People at work may not have access to television but can check frequently for news on the Internet while working at their computers. People traveling by car rely on radio for their information.

▼ Smart TVs increase the choices for viewers. Are they making television even more important in our lives?

Media scholars today recognize that they work during an era of rapid media change and development. For example, communication scholars Jennings Bryant and Dorina Miron (2004) identified six kinds of changes that are currently affecting and being affected by mass communication:

1. new form, content, and substance in mass communication;
2. new kinds of interactive media, such as the Internet;
3. new media ownership patterns in a global economy;
4. new viewing patterns and habits of audiences;
5. new patterns in family life; and
6. new patterns of interactive media use by youth.

Because of the rapid pace of these changes, measuring and studying their influence can be a challenge.

We live in an age when media consumers have more options than ever. In the United States, the average household in 2019 fell to 179.5 channels, which continues a trend of decreasing channels (Barr, 2019). Despite having so many channels, the average U.S. household only watched 12.7 channels (Mandese, 2020). So more choices do not necessarily mean that consumers are becoming more fragmented in their viewing.

Nielsen also recognizes that we are becoming increasingly diverse demographically as well as in the ways we are consuming media. According to another Nielsen report, "Changes in the population are creating a younger, more diverse, more tech-savvy consumer base. But connecting with them has become more complicated due to an exploding number of viewing options" (Nielsen, 2014, May 12). The rise of the Internet and the many choices that we now have led some to discuss the "end" of mass media, with some going so far as to claim, "The mass-media era now looks like a relatively brief and anomalous period that is coming to an end" ("Coming full circle," 2011). Some claim that the economic model for mass media is no longer viable and that spells the end of mass media (Greenslade, 2016), but others do not agree.

In contrast, others are seeing the Internet as another way for consumers to continue to consume even more television programming in many more places at many more times than ever before. As the Internet incorporates television programming, Shira Ovide, a *New York Times* technology writer, notes: "As home entertainment is being dragged into the digital world, I'm struck by how many holdovers have stuck around" (2020). She notes that much programming remains locked into 30- and 60-minute episodes, and she asks, "Sure, the internet changed everything. But also, has it?" and ultimately concludes that "the new watching 'TV' still feels a lot like watching TV" (Ovide, 2020). Services like Hulu and Amazon Prime are becoming popular as ways that more people can watch television programming. The Internet is an important way that traditional broadcasting corporations are reaching wider audiences. Instead of killing the traditional broadcasting corporations, the Internet is seen by some as an increasingly important medium for traditional broadcasters to reach more audiences.

We see this influence, for example, when we look at Netflix, which many people view as a provider of movies. While it is widely known that "Netflix is secretive about viewing figures," it is estimated that they spent an estimated $13 billion on original content in 2018. Yet, "80% of Netflix streams are for licensed content that first aired elsewhere, with 42% of viewers never viewing original content" (Iqbal, 2020). Although some of this television programming is created by Netflix (e.g., *The Baby-sitters Club, Feel Good, Girl/Haji*), these shows are all destined for a mass audience who can watch them whenever they wish, wherever they wish. Netflix is also internationalizing U.S. television offerings by adding TV "series from Argentina, Britain, Canada, Japan, Mexico, South Korea, Spain and Turkey to its American offerings" (Hale, 2017).

The coming years will reveal what happens to mass media. Will audiences become further fragmented as more choices become available across a range of platforms? Or will media consumption be driven by popularity among audiences so that television programming continues to draw mass audiences—although not all people are watching at the same time or on the same screens? Or will different media take different paths with the Internet?

Although it is difficult to measure the precise power of media messages, these messages surround and influence people every day. The importance of media in our everyday lives and in our society has been rapidly increasing. The rise of the Internet, cell phones, and other "new media" has led to a distinction being made between "mass media" and "new media." In this chapter, we will focus on mass media, and in Chapter 14, we explore interactive media. To help you to understand the term *mass media*, we discuss this topic next.

Journal Prompt 13.1: Mass Media and Change
What are six kinds of changes currently affecting or being affected by mass media?

What Are Mass Media?

13.2 Identify the main forms of mass media.

Mediated communication refers to communication that is transmitted through a channel, such as television, film, radio, and print. We often refer to these channels of communication more simply as *media*.

The word **media** is the plural form of *medium*. Television is one communication medium; others include film, radio, magazines, advertisements, and newspapers. When you pick up the telephone to speak to someone, you are using yet another communication medium. When you write a letter, your communication is mediated by the form of letter writing. Even the voice and the body can be considered media of communication.

media
The plural form of *medium*; a channel of communication.

For all the complexity and variety of media studies, its focus typically falls on **mass media**, or mediated communication intended for a large audience. Mass-mediated messages are usually produced and distributed by large organizations or industries in the business of mass communication. Mass media businesses are also known as **culture industries** because they produce television shows, made-for-television movies, video games, and other cultural products as an industry. The creation of these cultural products is not driven by individual artists, but by large groups of workers in for-profit (and some nonprofit) organizations.

mass media
Mediated communication intended for large audiences.

culture industries
Large organizations in the business of mass communication that produce, distribute, or show various media texts (cultural products) as an industry.

The study of media is often a moving target because changes in media continually occur. Part of understanding the influence of media on our everyday lives entails understanding the changes that have occurred and what media were available in other time periods. Historically, communication has been framed by the media available during a given time. Let's now look at some of these industries and the media texts they produce.

One of the first media addressing a large public was newspapers. During the nineteenth century, many newspapers grew in distribution and readership as the cost of mass printing declined. As expansion westward continued in the United States, the newspaper played a critical role in community building. Newspapers flourished during this period in staggering numbers. For example, "Before the end of 1867, at least four newspapers had been published in Cheyenne, a town that still had a population well under 800, in the Wyoming Territory" (Boorstin, 1965, p. 131). These numbers are all the more impressive in view of today's decline in newspaper readership. As you can see, different eras embraced different communication media.

Today, when most people think of newspapers, they first think of large-circulation papers in large metropolitan areas, such as *The New York Times, Washington Post,* and *Los Angeles Times.* They might also think about smaller, local papers, including the *Corvallis Gazette-Times,* the *Nome Nugget,* and the *Knoxville News Sentinel.* Because large-circulation newspapers serve different needs from local papers, many readers subscribe to both. Other newspapers target specific demographic groups, such as immigrant communities, ethnic and racial communities, LGBTQIA+ communities, or retirees. Some are bilingual. Others are referred to as the "alternative" press. These alternative-press newspapers attempt to present perspectives and voices that may not be heard in the mainstream press. Examples of alternative papers include the *Seattle Stranger*, the *San Francisco Bay Guardian*, and New York City's *Village Voice*.

Another development that followed the lowered cost of mass printing was the development of the magazine. Magazines are produced weekly, monthly, bimonthly, or quarterly. Some, such as *Time, Harper's, Reader's Digest*, and *Smithsonian*, target broad, general audiences. Other magazines focus on more limited audiences—*Ebony, Latina, Men's Health*, and *Woman's World*, for example—and still others on specific topics, as shown by the titles *Bon Appetit, Hot Rod*, and *Rhode Island Monthly*. Like newspapers, magazines offer important forums for political discussions, but they also address distinct interests, such as crafts, hobbies, or travel. Like newspapers, magazines have generally seen declining revenue in their print formats and have been moving increasingly to online digital formats. However, the Pew Research Center reports that "2013 and early 2014 brought a level of energy to the news industry not seen for a long time. Even as challenges of the past several years continue and new ones emerge, the activities this year have created a new sense of optimism—or perhaps hope—for the future of American journalism" (Mitchell, 2014). Newspapers and magazines are adjusting to the new digital world and feeling more optimistic about their future as new revenues are coming in to digital news platforms. Investors sense that digital formats will bring a positive return on their investments. Even after President Trump tweeted that *The New York Times* was "fake news" and its subscribers "dwindling," the newspaper reported that it added 276,000 digital and 25,000 print subscribers in the fourth quarter of 2016 (Pallotta, 2017). Since then, digital revenues have been increasing. One example is *The Guardian:* "Today, 55 percent of *Guardian* revenue comes from digital sources, a real feat of transition," while *The New York Times* is expected to get over 50 percent of

▼ Some magazines offer important forums for political discussions. Others address distinct interests, such as sports, travel, beauty, and fashion.

its revenue from digital sources in 2020 (Benton, 2019). As magazines and newspapers move online, their digital presence will become increasingly important for readers as well as revenue streams.

Popular books are another medium addressed to a large audience. Sometimes called **mass-market paperbacks**, these books include romance novels, self-help books, and comic books as well as other genres that are produced in large numbers and distributed widely. **E-books** (electronic books) constitute another type of mass media. E-books are books read on a computer screen or e-readers (such as Amazon's Kindle) instead of a printed page. Sales of e-books have taken off, with 69 million sold in 2010 to over 335 million sold in 2019 (Watson, 2020). Although e-reader devices are becoming increasingly user-friendly, many readers still say they prefer the printed page.

Motion pictures, first shown commercially in the 1890s, flourished throughout the twentieth century. Although today people can make movies relatively cheaply with digital video, high-quality productions that draw large audiences cost millions of dollars to produce, distribute, and advertise. Therefore, movie studios with adequate resources dominate the motion picture industry. Although some documentary movies do become popular, such as *Tiger King, I Am Not Your Negro,* and *On the Record*, most best-selling movies are purely entertainment-oriented, such as *Little Women, Deadpool, Parasite,* and *Ad Astra*. Typically, large-budget films receive the widest distribution and the most publicity, but small-budget films can also reach audiences and sometimes offer alternative views of important social issues.

Like movies, radio technology emerged in the late nineteenth century. At first, it had important applications at sea, but in the 1920s stations sprang up all over the United States. As journalism professor Jane Chapman notes, "Radio's take-off was swift, and public enthusiasm for it peaked during the 'golden age' of the 1930s and 1940s" (2005, p. 147). Radio programming included not only news and commentary but also quiz shows, dramas, and situation comedies. With the rise of television, the Internet, and other competing media, radio broadcasting has become much more specialized, with radio stations serving specific audiences by broadcasting classical music, jazz, country music, news, sports, or other focused content. Audiences for these specialized programs are often targeted based on identities, such as age, socioeconomic class, race and ethnicity, or language. Today, radio is also broadcast over the Internet, via satellite, and through podcasts. And although commercial enterprises dominate radio in the United States, nonprofit radio, such as National Public Radio and Pacifica, also exists.

Popular music, another form of mass media, existed long before radio, and people listened to it live in public and private venues and, later, on gramophones and record players. Popular music now also plays on television and via other communication media, such as CDs, DVDs, and MP3 players. Streaming music services are increasingly how many people listen to music, as traditional music sales have declined. There are many streaming platforms for listening to music, with Spotify and Apple Music among the most popular. People choose how to stream music based on their own situations. If you have high-quality audio equipment, you may want to listen to music over Tidal rather than Pandora. Those people who like to listen to classical music might choose Idagio, but "Idagio doesn't have music that falls outside the realm of classical music, so you're out of luck if you like a little Springsteen with your Stravinsky" (Germain, 2020). The market for streaming music is growing as Amazon, SiriusXM, YouTube, and others are competing for this market. In spite of the pandemic, streaming music revenues are expected to continue to grow past $1 billion in the United States alone (Stassen, 2020).

Television is among the most familiar forms of communication media. Early in its development, in the mid-twentieth century, networks such as ABC, CBS, and NBC dominated because they were the only providers of content. The rise of cable television, with its multiple specialized channels, has taken significant market share away from the networks, yet they remain important and continue to draw large audiences. Since its inception, cable television has expanded to include pay channels such as HBO,

mass-market paperbacks
Popular books addressed to a large audience and widely distributed.

e-books
Electronic books read on a computer screen instead of a printed page.

Critical Thinking Prompt
Should consumer-created media such as blogs, Twitter, and video sites like YouTube and Vimeo be considered mass media? Why or why not? In what ways are their functions similar to, or different from, those of mass media created by larger organizations?

Showtime, and Cinemax. In addition, satellite television is challenging cable television. Because television programming is expensive, the medium is dominated by commercial enterprises; however, the United States also has nonprofit television stations, many of which belong to the Public Broadcasting network or to the satellite network Deep Dish TV. In addition, cable TV stations are required to provide public, educational, and government-access channels.

With the developments of mass media online, many people have decided to cancel their cable subscriptions and opt for online viewing instead. At the beginning of the chapter, we saw that Charee "cut cable." The trend is very clear: "The number of pay-TV households peaked in 2010 at 105 million; now it's down to approximately 82.9 million. And a study last year by eMarketer forecast that number to dip to 72.7 million by 2023" (Schneider & Aurthur, 2020). Yet, as we saw earlier, the new streaming TV is very similar to the older forms of TV.

All told, these many forms of mass media saturate our world and penetrate deeply into our individual consciousness, yet we still have some choices regarding which messages to accept. Let's see how this works.

The Individual and Mass Media

13.3 Describe various models of media.

Media scholars are interested in the impact media messages have on individuals, but they are also interested in how individuals decide which media messages to consume or avoid. Marketers and media producers especially want to know how they might predict and characterize individuals' choices so that they can more effectively influence consumer choice. In this section, we'll explore both aspects of individual media consumption—how media messages influence us and how we become **active agents**, or active seekers, of various media messages and resisters of others. With the term *active agent*, we stress that even though people inhabit a densely media-rich environment, they need not be passively bombarded by media messages.

How Media Messages Affect the Individual

One approach to studying the influence of media messages relies on the linear model. Recall that in Chapter 1 we described how early models conceived of communication as a linear process involving the transfer of information without feedback from one person to another. Similarly, when it comes to media, there is a traditional linear model that portrays communication as a process that occurs in a linear fashion—for example, on a path from the television to the viewer (see Figure 13.1). In this traditional approach, scholars focus on the sender, the medium, the audience, and the effect of the message. This model views media communication as a process that moves from one source to many receivers. Although researchers who use this approach recognize that people are not passive viewers or consumers of media messages, they are interested only in measuring the influence of media messages on the individual, not vice versa.

By understanding the effects of media messages, communication scholars in the linear tradition hope to assist public policy debates about media regulation. For example, their research findings might be used in debates about the effects on viewers of violence

Journal Prompt 13.2: Common Mass Media
What are some of the most common forms of mass media?

active agents
Seekers of various media messages and resisters of others.

Figure 13.1 The Linear Model

The linear model emphasizes the effect of media messages on the individual. Communication in this model is largely (although not entirely) one way.

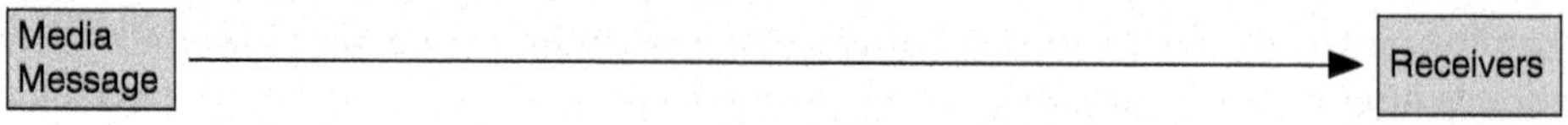

| Media Message | ⟶ | Receivers |

or sexuality in the media. So, on a societal level, research based on the linear model often influences public policy decision making. On an individual level, this kind of research may help you select the types of television shows you watch or the movies you allow your children to see.

As an analytic tool, the linear model of media analysis has its limits. For example, critics argue that its simplicity cannot account for the multiple ways people respond to media messages (Sproule, 1989). Viewers are neither merely passive receivers of messages, these critics say, nor do the viewers necessarily believe or imitate everything they watch or read. Those who watched *Modern Family*, for example, did not necessarily model their family behaviors on the show's characters. Nor did everyone who watched the trial of Casey Anthony, accused of murdering her daughter Caylee, agree with the jury's verdict (Hightower & Sedensky, 2011).

On the other hand, the linear model does highlight the power and influence of media messages. Some people did try to imitate the antics of Johnny Knoxville on the MTV television show *Jackass*, resulting in serious injuries despite televised warnings against trying to imitate the stunts. And in a classic example, a mass panic was set off when thousands of listeners to Orson Welles's 1938 Halloween radio broadcast, *War of the Worlds*, believed that Martians were landing in New Jersey.

Scholars who study media influence work in an area called **mass media effects**. The study of mass media effects has undergone significant changes over the years, as researchers have disagreed about how much effect a particular media message has on people's everyday lives (McQuail, 1987). In the 1930s, Paul Lazarsfeld and his colleagues studied radio's effect on listeners and, in particular, its effect on voting behavior. This study, titled *The People's Choice* (Lazarsfeld et al., 1948), argued that media had limited effects because they found that radio tended to reinforce preexisting beliefs rather than shape new ones.

mass media effects
The influence that media have on people's everyday lives.

Today, the focus on effects remains important in media research. For example, contemporary researchers have examined media images of beautiful bodies and how those images influence people's perceptions of their own bodies and their resultant behavior in response to those images, including dieting, working out, taking diet pills, and undergoing cosmetic surgery. Author and comedian Lindy West writes about the very negative effects on women of popular media images of the "perfect body", which she says, of course, doesn't exist. In their study on media effects and Black Lives Matter, Danielle Kilgo and Rachel Mourão (2019) found that viewing conservative media outlets tended to increase negative views of the movement's goals while viewing mainstream and more liberal media outlets did not result in more positive views of the movement's goals.

Another area of inquiry among media effects scholars involves media images of violence. In their study of media usage among middle-school children in 10 regions in the United States, Michael Slater and his colleagues (2003) found that aggressive young people seek out violent media and that exposure to media violence can predict aggression. Thus, they see media violence and aggression as mutually reinforcing and call their model a *downward spiral model* to describe the powerful, negative influence the interaction has on youth. Those youth who are prone to violent behaviors seek out violent media that reinforce more violent behavior. More recently, Bushman and Gibson (2011) have also found that aggression continues long after engaging with violent video games.

Promoting health through media messages is another significant area of inquiry among scholars seeking to understand media effects. In one study on antidrug advertisements for adolescents, Hunyi Cho and Franklin J. Boster (2008) compared antidrug messages framed around the costs of using drugs (loss) versus the benefits of avoiding them (gain). The study found that framing loss rather than gain was more effective among adolescents who had friends who used drugs. There was no difference among adolescents whose friends did not use drugs. To engage the most effective communication messages to promote public health, media effects scholars are also trying to better understand how media messages can be more effective.

How Individuals Choose Media Messages

Advertisers, political campaign strategists, and communication scholars all want to understand which groups of people consume which media texts. They want to know who watches *Grey's Anatomy*, who reads *The New York Times*, and who reads *People* magazine. As you might guess, this type of information enables advertisers to target their messages more accurately toward certain consumers. It also enables campaign strategists to focus their message to attract more votes. But why would media scholars be interested in this information?

Media scholars need this information so that they can correctly target their research. For example, if scholars want to study the effect of a particular **media text**—for example, a television show, advertisement, or movie—they need to know which audience group to study. If they want to know how people interpret a particular media text, they need to know the audience of that text. Or if scholars want to know about the economic influence of particular media texts, they need to know which audience groups advertisers target with these messages.

As an individual, you are constantly faced with media choices, and your choices have increased considerably in the past decade as a result of the increased predominance of online news and blogging as well as instant downloads of movies and TV episodes. Researchers are interested in not only *what* we choose but *how* we choose. See how one of our students considers this in *It Happened to Me: Andrew*.

Although Andrew doesn't mention it explicitly, both what people choose and how they choose are related to their identities. And, as we noted in Chapter 2, identities are not fixed; they are dynamic across time and situations. With them, media choices change as well. For example, as a child, Andrew may have been a fan of Saturday morning cartoons or *Sesame Street*, but as an adult, perhaps he prefers *Monday Night Football* or HBO's *Lovecraft Country*. Andrew's age and the ages of his friends likely influence the television shows and movies he selects. But age is only one aspect of identity and perhaps one of the simplest factors that influence media choices. Other aspects, such as regional identity, might also have an effect, but they are more difficult to correlate with media tastes.

media text
A television show, advertisement, movie, or other media event that a media scholar isolates for study.

> ## It Happened to Me
> ### Andrew
>
> I enjoy watching a lot of different types of movies. I like historical pieces, such as *1917*, a historical film about World War I, and *Little Women*, which is set in the nineteenth century. But sometimes I follow the filmmaker. I enjoyed watching *Get Out*, a film by Jordan Peele, so when his next film came out, *Us*, I knew that I wanted to see it, too. Sometimes I also look at the ratings on *Rotten Tomatoes* or other websites, and I saw that *Knives Out* was well received, so I was interested in that movie, too.

selective exposure
The idea that people seek media messages or interpret media texts in ways that confirm their beliefs and, conversely, resist or avoid messages that challenge their beliefs.

Selective Exposure **Selective exposure** theories help us understand how identity plays a role in media tastes and preferences. These theories are based on the idea that people seek media messages and interpret media texts in ways that confirm their beliefs—and, conversely, that they resist or avoid messages that challenge their beliefs. Depending on their personal and political beliefs, some people enjoyed watching the inauguration of President Trump. Others chose not to watch the inauguration. (See *Communication in Society: Watching or Not Watching* 12 Years a Slave.)

One television show that was studied heavily in terms of selective exposure is *The Cosby Show*, a prime-time situation comedy that ran from 1984 to 1992. According to selective exposure theory, if someone believes racism no longer exists, then they are likely to interpret media messages as confirming or reinforcing this perception. In a classic study of *The Cosby Show*, Sut Jhally and Justin Lewis (1992) set up focus groups. Twenty-six of these focus groups were composed of White viewers of the show, and 23 were composed of African American viewers. In analyzing the White

COMMUNICATION IN SOCIETY
Watching or Not Watching *12 Years a Slave*

12 Years a Slave is a 2013 movie that is based on the slave narrative of a free man, Solomon Northrup, who was sold into slavery in the 1840s. It won a number of awards, including three Oscars (Academy Awards), notably Best Picture. Given the widespread attention that this film received, what were the most important reasons that you decided to watch or not to watch it? What might be reasons that influenced others' decisions to watch or not watch this film? Do you think that racial identities may have influenced some people's decisions? Let's take a look at some of the discussions about watching or not watching this film.

Despite the critical acclaim that the film received, its box office receipts did not match those of other films, such as *Captain Phillips*, *Gravity*, and *Frozen*. A film critic for the *Los Angeles Times* explains why this film may not have drawn the audiences that other films did: "The racial legacy we struggle with today lives inside '12 Years a Slave.' Slavery on our soil is painful to remember, painful to admit, difficult to discuss, almost unbearable to watch—and that is why so many choose not to. It will take more than an Oscar win on Sunday to change that" (Sharkey, 2014).

The racial history that envelopes all of us led one woman to struggle with whom to go to see the movie: "I'm not a racist. But I do have a race problem. I finally owned up to it as I was anticipating seeing *12 Years a Slave*. In the weeks leading up to its opening in my state of North Carolina, I tried to think of whom among my friends I could see this film with. I have a number of racially and ethnically diverse friends and acquaintances who would love to see it, and yet, I knew I could only

see this movie alone or with another dark-skinned person" (Okoro, 2013). In the end, she went to see the movie alone because she didn't want to have to engage in explaining or discussing anything in the film.

One of the controversies that arose in relation to the Academy Awards is that some of the voting members did not watch the film. One of these voting members admitted that the film was too difficult to watch. There are many painful scenes in this film, and many people chose not to subject themselves to the violent and disturbing scenes in the film. Some people felt that they already knew about the ugly history of slavery in the United States and did not need to subject themselves to the film. Everyone is an active consumer of mass media, and some people are willing to watch films that others are not willing to watch.

As you can see, there are many complex reasons why people decided to watch or not watch this film. As you think about media consumption, it is important to remember that we are active agents who are consciously making decisions about what or what not to watch, and with whom to watch it.

SOURCES: Feinberg, S. (2014, March 2). Brutally honest Oscar voter ballot no. 7. *The Hollywood Reporter.* http://www.hollywoodreporter.com/race/brutally-honest-oscar-voter-ballot-684839

Okoro, E. (2013, November 27). Why I wouldn't see *12 Years a Slave* with a white person. *The Atlantic.* http://www.theatlantic.com/entertainment/archive/2013/11/why-i-wouldnt-see-em-12-years-a-slave-em-with-a-white-person/281883/

Sharkey, B. (2014, February 27). Oscars 2014: For many, "12 Years a Slave" is too hard to watch. *Los Angeles Times.* http://articles.latimes.com/2014/feb/27/entertainment/la-et-mn-12-years-a-slave-notebook-20140227/2

focus group responses, Jhally and Lewis found that Whites were more likely to think that *The Cosby Show* proved African Americans can succeed; therefore, they said, African Americans who did not succeed were to blame for their own failure. In other words, as the White focus groups saw it, personal failings, rather than discrimination or racism, were what blocked success. In contrast, African American respondents saw *The Cosby Show* as a "cultural breakthrough" in terms of positive portrayals of African American culture (p. 121). Thus, they expressed far more concern about the pervasive negative images of African Americans in media and the influences of those images on viewers. As you can see, although both racial groups were watching the same television show, their interpretations were different.

The *Cosby* study was a very influential study, but selective exposure has continued to explore other aspects of media usage. For example, in their study on young women and the sexualized images of women in music videos, Karsay and Matthes (2020) found that "the use of sexually objectifying music videos may result in a spiraling effect" (p. 444) in which young women who watched music videos with highly sexualized images turn to other media content with highly sexualized images. These young women "tended to describe themselves with more body-related statements" than young women who were not exposed to highly sexualized music videos.

Selective exposure theories point to the ways that both groups interpret the show to confirm their own beliefs and views. Those who subscribe to selective exposure theory argue that people rarely inhabit a media environment that challenges their social identities, including their religious and political beliefs, notions about gender, or ideas about race. Not all scholars subscribe to this theory, however: see *Alternative View: Hostile Media Effect*.

Another line of media research, called **uses and gratifications** studies, explores how people use media messages and what types of gratifications they find in some media texts rather than others. Working within this approach, researchers might want to know why viewers watch *The Bachelor* instead of *Dancing with the Stars*, *Chicago PD* instead of *Chicago Med*, or *48 Hours* instead of *60 Minutes*. For example, a researcher might want to know why some people enjoyed watching *Saturday Night Live* during the Donald Trump presidency versus other presidential periods. What parts of the show satisfy particular needs or wants? What is satisfying about the portrayals of President Trump, Vice President Pence, and other administration officials? Denis McQuail and his colleagues (1972) suggested four general uses and gratifications that audiences have for media texts:

- information
- personal identity
- integration and social interaction
- entertainment

The first motivation, information seeking, is straightforward: audiences want to learn from some media presentations, as in the case of a news event. The second

ALTERNATIVE VIEW
Hostile Media Effect

In what ways do you selectively expose yourself to media messages? Do you generally listen to the same news commentators rather than seeking alternative voices? Do you watch the same shows your friends watch, or do you look for something different?

Selective exposure theories tell us that people tend to consume media that reinforce or support their own views. Yet, some media researchers counter this idea. Why? Researchers have found that people on both sides of an issue can be exposed to the same media coverage, and when asked what they thought of the coverage, both groups say that it was biased against their views. If both sides find the same coverage biased, it may undermine the idea that people only seek messages that confirm their views. Thus, the researchers concluded that although bias in media news stories surely does occur, another kind of bias rests with the viewer—a phenomenon called the "hostile media effect" because it reflects a general hostility toward media.

In their study, Albert C. Gunther and Kathleen Schmitt (2004) used the controversy over genetically modified foods to understand the hostile media effect. In part, their study found that regardless of respondents' position on genetically modified foods, they viewed news media stories as biased against them. However, when respondents saw the same information in a student essay format, the hostility tended to be absent or at least minimal. The researchers conclude, then, that the hostile media effect is created by the

perception that a media message has the potential to influence large numbers of people for or against a particular viewpoint.

In a more recent study that takes into account social media, Brian Weeks and his colleagues (2019) looked at the social media postings of the 2016 presidential candidates. They found that the social media presence increased emotional feelings—positive and negative—for the candidates. In an increasingly mistrustful environment, many people may turn to the candidates' social media for information, which may fuel further distrust of the media and the hostile media effect.

If the selective exposure theory is correct and people tend to select media messages that support their own views, then why would they interpret these messages to be biased against them? What role does social media play in interpreting media messages? There is no easy answer, but perhaps questions of bias and media selection need to be thought about in more complicated ways. When charges of bias arise against a media source, how often do we consider that the bias may be our own?

SOURCES: Gunther, A. C., & Schmitt, K. (2004). Mapping boundaries of the hostile media effect. *Journal of Communication, 54*, 55–70.

Weeks, B. E., Kim, D. H., Hahn, L. B., Diehl, T. H., & Kwok, N. (2019). Hostile media perceptions in the age of social media: Following politicians, emotions, and perceptions of media bias. *Journal of Broadcasting and Electronic Media, 63*(3), 374–392.

motivation, personal identity, refers to the idea that viewers may use media messages to affirm some aspect of their personal identity—for example, as mothers, consumers, or political conservatives. The third motivation, integration and social interaction, underscores the role that media can play in helping people connect with others, as they do when discussing sports or the events on a soap opera. Finally, the entertainment motivation refers to the use of media for pleasure, or the desire simply to be entertained. Of course, these motivations can overlap, so that we can watch a program for information while at the same time using it as a topic for conversation with others, which would fit within McQuail's third motivation.

According to selective exposure theories, people seek out media that confirm what they already believe. What political views might be different among viewers of different channels?

Cultural Values in Media Consumption

Understanding why some groups choose one program over another highlights the cultural values at work in the consumption of media. In his study of television preferences among Israeli adults, Jonathan Cohen (2002) examined viewing habits and choice. He found that factors influencing media selection included loyalty to particular channels, preferences for certain types of shows, and even the language of the programs, because programming in Israel is available in Hebrew, English, and other languages. His conclusion was that "[m]ost Israeli viewers seem to prefer native programming, whether due to language problems or to cultural resonance" (p. 218). Cohen suggests that Israeli audiences use television not only for entertainment but also to affirm their Israeli identities and as a context for social interaction with other Israelis.

Determining why people seek specific media texts and not other texts is important from an economic perspective. After all, a media corporation does not want to spend a lot of money on a television show or magazine if it is going to fail. However, it is notoriously difficult to predict which media texts will become popular and which will not. *This Is Us*, for example, was described as "the more surprising show that looks as if it's going to be a hit" (Yahr, 2016). Despite major investments in market research, there is no completely foolproof way to predict audience response.

Of course, the inability to accurately predict audience response does not mean that media producers have no information on trends. In certain eras, viewers are more interested in Westerns or police dramas, reality shows, or evening soap operas than they are during other periods. Today, reality shows are quite popular. Furthermore, advertisers know that some groups prefer to consume certain kinds of media. For example, the advertising that appears during televised football games or *Dancing with the Stars* reveals what advertisers have learned about those audiences through careful market research and analysis.

How Individuals Resist Media Messages

Although media messages bombard people every day, individuals do not necessarily, or even easily, accept all that they receive. In addition, people actively resist certain media texts. For example, some people sought out and watched the *Harry Potter* films, *A Beautiful Day in the Neighborhood, Moonlight,* and *Knives Out.* Others actively avoided them. Why? We resist media texts every day for many reasons, including something as hard to quantify as individual taste and something as personal as what we see as negative portrayals of our political, moral, or religious views; our interests, age, or level of education; or our gender, sexuality, and racial and ethnic identities. Other far less political reasons can create consumer resistance as well, as our student reveals in *It Happened to Me: Alyssa*.

It Happened to Me
Alyssa

When *Antebellum* was made available very quickly online due to the COVID-19 pandemic, I was curious about watching it. I like Janelle Monáe, but as an African American, I was also worried about watching more "slavery porn" in which African Americans are brutalized by cruel Whites. I really didn't enjoy *12 Years a Slave* for that reason. I want to read more reviews and hear from my friends before I decide if I am going to watch it.

Resisting media messages entails much more than simply whether we go to a particular movie or watch a particular video. It is also about how we resist the power of media to shape our identities. For example, in one study, Meenakshi Gigi Durham (2004) interviewed South Asian immigrant teenage girls living in the United States. She explored the question of how these girls dealt with traditional Indian notions of female gender expectations in the context of available media. She found that the only mainstream U.S. show they liked to watch was *Friends*, which they found to be funny, and that they disliked *Dawson's Creek*, which they thought was unrealistic. In general, they distanced themselves from mainstream U.S. media. In contrast, they consumed large amounts of media (films, popular music) from India, which they rented from Indian grocery stores and restaurants, borrowed from others, and watched or downloaded from the Internet. They particularly identified with the narratives in *Mississippi Masala, Bend It Like Beckham*, and *American Desi*, which are three Indian films with narratives involving "taboo relationships between Indian girls and men of different racial/cultural backgrounds" (p. 154). Durham concludes that these adolescent girls use media to create new identities and that these identities do not conform to stereotypes of either Asian Indian women or U.S. American women.

In another example, it has been reported that former President Obama refuses to watch any of the videos showing U.S. Americans being beheaded that are posted by the Islamic State of Iraq and Syria (ISIS). His decision not to watch these videos is explained by his desire to avoid playing into the propaganda of ISIS ("Has Obama seen," 2014). Given his social and political position as president of the United States at that time, his avoidance and resistance to this type of media are very public and have important implications for how we interpret and deal with these media messages. All of us must make decisions about media consumption and resistance that are based on our many identities.

As you have seen through our discussion, communication researchers are interested in all aspects of the relationship between individuals and the media messages that surround them. First, they wonder what effect media messages have on individuals; and second, they explore how individuals choose, resist, and interpret these messages. Research has revealed that the answers to both questions involve complex processes related to individual identity, individual needs, and individual taste. Audiences respond to and interpret texts based on both their individual and social identities, and therefore, different social groups can consume the same text while being affected by it differently and interpreting it differently. However, all individual responses and choices occur in a larger social context. Thus, to provide a more complete picture, we now shift our attention to the role of media at the societal level.

Journal Prompt 13.3: Selecting Mass Media
What strategies do media consumers use to select and reject media texts? Why might audiences prefer to watch media texts that affirm the values and beliefs they already hold?

The Individual, Mass Media, and Society

13.4   Understand five issues in media studies: social identities, understanding the world, media events, media violence, and media economics.

Why do media play such an important role in society? One reason is that they often serve as the voice of the community. In this way, media offer people a means of thinking about themselves, their places in the world, and the societal forces around them. As individuals, we can only choose from among the media choices available. Societal forces, including the government, economics, media organizations, and advertisers, largely determine which media options are available. In the following section, we'll look at three important roles that media play in society: confirming social identities, helping people understand the world, and helping individuals understand important public events. And finally, because no discussion of media and society would be complete without a discussion of media violence and media economics, we will conclude with these topics.

▲ Content analysis can provide data on factors such as media representation of various groups, media violence, and the kinds of topics covered and the way in which they are covered in the media.

Confirming Social Identities

As we've noted, media representations influence our understanding of social identities, such as gender or age identity, as well as the identities of others. This is one of the functions of media usage we examined as we discussed uses and gratifications. For example, images we see on television and in films, magazines, and newspapers shape our sense of what it is to be a man or woman. These views generally create or enforce a hierarchy of identities, often portraying men as more powerful than women. Audiences can be critical of negative messages about various identities, and after a controversy arose over the possible use of a racist term on the 2020 *Big Brother All-Stars* show, CBS issued a statement: "Hate speech will not be tolerated, and those who violate the policy will be removed from the Big Brother house" (qtd. in Nolan, 2020). This policy was welcomed by some who noted that the show "has hosted an incredible amount of hate speech, including overtly racist language and racial slurs, uttered by everyone from winners to players no one remembers" (Denhart, 2020). The 2020 season also came under criticism for some contestants mocking Ian Terry, another contestant, who has autism. Since no one was removed for those comments, it creates a hierarchy in which racism is not tolerated but making fun of a disability is tolerated.

One approach to understanding how and what media communicate about various social identities is content analysis. **Content analysis** focuses on some specific aspect of a text's content. Bernard Berelson (1952/1971), a behavioral scientist, explains that content analysis took off during the late 1930s, with the work of Harold Laswell and his colleagues (see Chapter 1), who were concerned with "propaganda and public opinion and the emergence of radio as a great mass medium of communication."

How does content analysis work? To begin, a researcher might want to know how many non-White characters appear on the television show *NCIS: Los Angeles*, a show set in a city where Whites are a minority population. The researcher would thus watch a number of episodes, count the number of non-White characters, note the kinds of roles they play and which characters are central, and finally, draw conclusions based on these data. Actress Geena Davis became quite concerned about the imbalance between males and females in media representations. In two large studies on television programs and films, males outnumbered females by 70 percent to 30 percent (Belkin, 2010). To try to understand these content differences and their impact on children, she founded the Geena Davis Institute on Gender and Media (https://seejane.org).

content analysis
Approach to understanding media that focuses on a specific aspect of the content of a text or group of texts.

Further, researcher Caroline Aoyagi (2004) conducted a content analysis of TV shows set in the state of Hawaii and concluded the following:

> No one can blame the big television networks for their love affair with the beautiful islands of Hawaii, but as several new shows are set to launch or are already on air, the lack of Asian Pacific Americans in the shows' casts have many wondering: what Hawaii is this?
>
> In a state where Asian Pacific Islander Americans [APIA] make up more than 80 percent of the population and whites are considered the minority, a look at the new line-up of shows for FOX, the WB network, and NBC show no APIA lead actors and only one or two APIAs in supporting roles. (p. 1)

A content analysis of television shows, thus, can provide data on racial representation in media. Content analysis also can reveal the kinds of topics that arise most often, the way episodes and conflicts are resolved most frequently, the number and types of conflicts that occur, and many other issues. In their analysis of the news media coverage of the U.S.–Mexico border, Jill Fleuriet and Mari Castellano focused on articles from 2015 to 2017 in major U.S. news media. They looked at the ways the metaphor of the border shifted under President Donald Trump and how the metaphor gained particular meanings. To create the image of the border as "unmanageable, corrupt, and dangerous" (p. 891) has implications beyond the media coverage. In part, they point to the August 2019 mass shooting in El Paso, Texas, of Latina/os by a white supremacist using "the same language as President Trump when referring to Mexican immigrants" (p. 891). Their study, however, is not a media effects study; instead, they look at the discursive climate created by President Trump. They conclude that "the question of who gets to define the border is more important now than ever" (p. 892).

Content analysis by itself does not reveal why viewers choose to watch particular television shows or consume other kinds of media messages. Collecting demographic information about an audience's racial, ethnic, or age composition may give some insight as to which groups are drawn to what kind of content, but, again, this is not the primary purpose of content analysis. For example, in Fleuriet and Castellano's study, they did not try to explain why many U.S. Americans were drawn to these descriptions of the U.S.–Mexico border or why the news media report these kinds of news. What their study does show is that the border, as a metaphor, is given problematic meanings that have consequences.

Some studies use a more detailed analysis of media messages than content analysis does, and this approach can help us better understand which social identities are being confirmed and elevated. Such studies, which rely on textual analysis, typically focus on fewer media texts than content analyses do. Researchers who conduct textual analyses of media messages take an approach similar to literary critics when they explore meanings in a literary work. However, in textual analysis, any kind of media image can be considered a text. For example, in her study of the news coverage of Freaknik, a spring break event that used to draw African American college students to Atlanta, Marian Meyers (2004) looked closely at the news reports of sexual violence against African American women perpetrated by African American men. "In essence," she wrote, "the news criminalized Black men primarily with respect to property damage while decriminalizing them concerning their abuse of women. The safety of Black women appears of less consequence than that of property" (p. 113). Thus, these news reports confirmed an identity of Black men as criminals while undermining the identity of Black women as crime victims.

In her study of masculinity, Helene Shugart (2008) focused on the media construction of the "metrosexual" in the context of commercialism. Metrosexuals are men who are meticulous about their appearance—not only their physiques, but also their clothing, hair styles, and so forth. In her textual analysis of the metrosexual, Shugart found that metrosexuality "bore all the hallmarks of a fad or a trend" (p. 295), but metrosexuality also "served a vital and strategic rhetoric function as part of a much larger and ongoing cultural discourse about masculinity(ies)" (p. 295). Because commercialism has threatened traditional masculinity by insisting on enhancing masculinity through the purchase of various products, metrosexuality helped to reconcile the contradiction between the commercial masculinity and a more traditional or normative masculinity.

Thus, what people see, hear, and read in the media can confirm identities, but so can their media choices. Although our social identities are not absolute predictors of media choices,

▲ Images of male beauty are socially constructed.

trends do emerge if we look at the correlations between media consumption and various social identities. Nielsen Media Research has studied the most popular television shows among all U.S. Americans and among African Americans as a subgroup, revealing that their choices are similar in some respects and different in others and, thus, that racial identities do somewhat correlate with media consumption.

In addition, people often choose media images that not only confirm their identities but also help them deal with the various issues involved in any identity. For example, some African American women are drawn to the ABC shows *How to Get Away with Murder* and *Scandal*, which feature strong women characters—one working as a law professor and attorney and the other as a media consultant—who work in male-dominated environments. These characters help women envision how they can operate successfully in White, masculine environments and retain their gender and racial identities.

How does media coverage favor some identities over others? The amount of coverage, as revealed by content analysis, is sometimes the controlling factor. For example, in their study of the Salt Lake City Olympics in 2002, Billings and Eastman (2003) found that NBC devoted more time to reporting on male athletes and White athletes than on other groups. The potential effect of this imbalance is that the identities of particular viewers are reinforced, while the identities of other viewers are undermined.

As you learned in Chapter 2, social identities help shape individuals' outlook on the world; at the same time, individuals interpret media texts from their identity positions. Media critics have been instrumental in bringing to the public's attention these issues of identity confirmation and media bias in portraying identities. As a result, many with identities that media portray less positively have come to recognize their exclusion. The effect can be anger or disengagement when few, if any, images exist of one's own social group acting in positive ways.

Understanding the World

Media play a key role in helping people understand the world. Most people will never travel to Russia, North Korea, Iraq, Kenya, Indonesia, Syria, or Brazil, but they can learn something about these places through media. They may see these distant regions on the Travel Channel or in *National Geographic* magazine, or they may see news about them on CNN, MSNBC, Fox News, or other news channels.

However, the texts that media organizations produce can distort the images of far-away places as well as enhance them, especially if viewers have never been to the parts of the world represented. In her study of AP wire photographs of Afghan women—both during and after the Taliban regime—Shahira Fahmy (2004) found that "1 percent of [published] AP photographs portrayed women revealing their face and hair." Thus, even after the fall of the Taliban, Afghan women are depicted wearing their burqas—despite the fact that many photos exist that portray "images of Afghan women removing their burqas as a sign of liberation" (p. 110). In this study, Fahmy brings to light the discrepancy between the pool of available AP photographs and the ones selected for publication in the United States, noting that the ones that editors select shape and sometimes distort our impressions of the subject.

As another example of the media's power to shape knowledge and understanding, prior to the current Syrian Civil War, there had been little U.S. news coverage of Syria. Many U.S. Americans did not know the difference between Aleppo and Raqqa and the involvement of Al Qaeda, ISIS, and the government of Bashir al-Assad. When President Trump decided to withdraw troops from Northern Syria in 2019, many U.S. Americans may not have known the impact that would have on the Kurds or that the Kurds were U.S. allies. In contrast, media provide U.S. audiences with extensive detail on the British royal family and the departure of Harry and Meghan as well as international celebrities, such as Shakira and Ed Sheeran. As you can see, by choosing what to cover and how extensively, media shape audience understanding of what is and isn't important in the world.

In his 1974 work *Frame Analysis*, Erving Goffman argued that we have "two broad classes of primary frameworks: natural and social" (p. 22). We view the world through these frames, and this concept has been extended to understanding media frames through which we interpret and understand events. **Frame analysis** in mass media studies focuses on the power media frames have to shape how we understand various events and, ultimately, the world.

In her study of feminicides in Ciudad Juárez, Mexico, a city across the border from El Paso, Texas, Michelle Holling (2019) looked at 14 years of U.S. print media coverage of the murders of women and girls. She found three dominant frames: (1) "city of two faces," (2) "victims, bodies, and murdered women," and (3) "grieving mothers." She concludes that these frames "engender discursive violence, the effacement or masking of other forms of violence" (p. 264). Readers are led to view Ciudad Juárez as dangerous without any contextualizing of "the cultural, economic, political and social shifts that occurred in Juárez" (p. 265).

In a recent study out of Nigeria, Jude Ogbodo and colleagues (2020) studied media coverage of the COVID-19 crisis from December 2019 to April 2020 in media reports from North America, Europe, Asia, and Africa. They found that the significant media frames were economic consequences, human interest, conflict, morality/religion, attribution of responsibility, politicization, ethnicization, and fear/scaremongering. They concluded that these themes were common across media coverage, but the focus on breaking news tended to increase, rather than decrease, fear.

This approach to studying media is closely tied to content analysis as well as agenda-setting research, which we will look at next.

Agenda-Setting Capacity

This power of media coverage to influence individuals' view of the world is referred to as its **agenda-setting capacity**. Thus, in agenda-setting research, scholars focus on audience perceptions of reality and attempt to discover how or whether media coverage correlates with these audience perceptions. For example, Lowry and colleagues (2003) studied correlations between crime rates, news coverage on crime, and public attitudes about crime from 1978 to 1998. Existing data indicated that in March 1992, only 5 percent

frame analysis
Studies on the constructions of media frames that shape how we interpret and understand various events.

agenda-setting capacity
The power of media coverage to influence individuals' view of which topics are more salient than others.

of the public thought that crime was the most important problem. By August 1994, however, 52 percent felt that way. What accounted for this jump? By correlating the amount of television news coverage with the crime rates, the researchers found that the amount of news coverage was far more influential than actual crime rates in this change in public perception. By focusing so much attention on crime reporting, the theory goes, media set the public agenda for what was important. Agenda-setting studies often look at long time periods, as the crime-coverage study did, to correlate media coverage to changes in audience perceptions.

▲ Cultivation theory has been used to emphasize the role of news coverage of crime in the perceptions of crime rates.

In another study using an agenda-setting perspective, Jochen Peter (2003) focused on the issue of 14 European nations and their integration into the European Union (EU). Here, however, he did not find a simple correlation between more news coverage of EU integration and public attitudes about the importance of this issue. Instead he found that when political elites agreed about integration, public involvement or interest in the issue declined. Coverage of disagreement among political elites over EU integration did correlate, though, with increased public involvement in the issue. Thus, controversy and the degree of exposure does play a role in setting the public's agenda.

Cultivation Theory   Media messages also play a critical role in acculturating individuals. **Cultivation theory** proposes that long-term immersion in a media environment leads to "cultivation," or enculturation, into shared beliefs about the world. Unlike other approaches that focus on specific media messages, television programs, movies, or other kinds of text, "Cultivation analysis is concerned with the more general and pervasive consequences of cumulative exposure to cultural media" (Morgan & Signorielli, 1990, p. 16). Initiated by George Gerbner (2002) and his colleagues, cultivation analysis seeks to uncover how television, in particular, influences those who are heavy viewers. Those who watch television news, the theory goes, will share certain beliefs or distortions about the world. Moreover, this theory argues that media coverage shapes attitudes about one's own society and the issues it faces. For example, although crime rates have gone down overall in recent years, many U.S. Americans feel more insecure than ever. In their study on fear of crime, Daniel Romer and colleagues (2003) surveyed 2,300 Philadelphia residents. Within that population group, they found a relationship between the widespread belief that crime is a significant problem and the amount of local television news coverage of crimes. The point of the study is that Philadelphia media coverage cultivates attitudes and beliefs that shape everyday life in the city, with a key element of daily life being an exaggerated fear of crime. The studies on Philadelphia are well known today in relation to cultivation theory. Research using cultivation theory continues by exploring gender and finding that "the overall relationship between television exposure and self-protective behavior does not differ between genders" (Custers et al., 2017), as well as studies on television news coverage of public health issues and how it cultivates community values, beliefs, and norms (Gollust et al., 2019).

cultivation theory
The idea that long-term immersion in a media environment leads to "cultivation," or enculturation, into shared beliefs about the world.

In another cultivation study, Jeff Niederdeppe and his colleagues (2010) studied the ways that local television news covers cancer prevention because the "sheer volume of news coverage about cancer causes and prevention has led to broad speculation about its role in promoting fatalistic beliefs" (p. 231). Niederdeppe and colleagues developed three hypotheses comparing local television news coverage with local newspaper coverage of various cancer issues, and their fourth hypothesis focused on the relationship between local TV news viewing and fatalistic beliefs about cancer prevention. They found that there is "a tendency for local TV news to focus on aspects of cancer that are likely to cultivate the beliefs that everything causes cancer or that there are too many recommendations about cancer prevention" (p. 246). It creates the fatalistic sense that nothing can be done to avoid cancer. In both these studies, then, immersion in the television environment shaped, or cultivated, a particular view of the world.

Media Hegemony   A different way of explaining how media influence how we understand the world is through **hegemony**. Hegemony refers to the process by which people consent to particular understandings as reflected in media representations. For instance, we come to understand what "mother" means through often idealized images of mothers on television programs, films, and other media. Although there are no laws that regulate what a "mother" must do, we consent to these images of motherhood and we expect mothers to engage in certain behaviors, such as throwing birthday parties for their children. In contrast, our hegemonic understanding of "fathers" does not include that kind of activity. Fathers can, of course, throw birthday parties for their children, but it is not part of the hegemonic construction of fatherhood.

Masculinity, as represented in media content, has been a rich site for investigating how hegemony functions. For example, in his work on hegemony, communication scholar Nick Trujillo (1991) studied the media representations of Nolan Ryan, a baseball pitcher, to show how masculinity is constructed. He found five features of how Ryan was portrayed: (1) male athletic power, (2) ideal image of the capitalist worker, (3) family patriarch, (4) White rural cowboy, and (5) symbol of male (hetero)sexuality. Trujillo asks that we consider the negative consequences of this construction of masculinity. In his study of male action heroes in films such as *The Fast and the Furious, The Expendables,* and various *James Bond* films, Kelvin Ke (2020) looked at how the aging heroes develop different attributes as they age. This changing notion of the aging hero is seen as positive, as he gains wisdom and maturity. His analysis focuses on aging as a process that can be positive rather than negative. Hegemony is a process by which we all participate in the social construction of ourselves and others. If we violate these hegemonic notions, we risk alienation. This approach to the study of media content helps us better understand the contours and limits of how we might present ourselves and interpret others because hegemony outlines what is acceptable, normal, or even ideal.

Interpreting Media Events

The term **media event** applies to those occasions or catastrophes that interrupt regular programming. Like rhetorical events, which we discussed in the previous chapter, media events create vast numbers of media messages. Examples include the funeral of John F. Kennedy, the Olympics, Princess Diana's funeral, or the attacks of September 11, 2001. Media scholars are interested in the coverage of such events because such coverage can shape viewers' understanding of what has occurred and create powerful responses. For example, Daniel Dayan and Elihu Katz (1992) found that media events bring society closer together. As a new form of "high holidays of mass communication" (p. 1), these events both reinforce and celebrate national identity.

Some media events are staged by public relations officers to garner media attention on a particular issue. When the president of the United States calls a press conference, for example, he is creating a media event. Then, of course, the representatives of

hegemony
The process by which we consent to social constructions, rather than having them imposed on us.

media event
Occasions or catastrophes that interrupt regular programming.

various news media are present to report what he says. In these cases, the president and his public relations staff carefully control many aspects of the conference—where it will be staged, what kinds of issues will be raised, who will be present, what video images will be shown, and so on. Other politicians, movie stars, and lawyers in high-profile cases also commonly create media events to bring attention to themselves or their causes.

Not everyone, however, can attract this kind of media attention. People seeking media attention who lack notoriety or celebrity must use other measures. For example, during the World Trade Organization meetings in Seattle in 1999, protestors used the Internet and alternative newspapers to plan a large march in downtown Seattle. The violence that erupted between police and some protesters drew considerable media attention and was broadcast widely (DeLuca & Peeples, 2002). More recently, when President Donald Trump signed a travel ban on people from some Middle East countries, protests took place at airports around the United States which drew media attention. Following the inauguration of President Trump, the Women's March took place in January 2017 and a number of other protests followed. These public protests drew crowds that made them media events.

Not all media events are staged. In 2019, a former student at Marjory Stoneman Douglas High School in Parkland, Florida, opened fire and killed 17 people and injured 17 others (Laughland et al., 2018). This mass shooting became a media event with the ensuing discussions about guns in U.S. society. In a speech titled "We Call B.S.," Emma González, a student at the school, coined the term *Parkland kid*. In his analysis of this media event, Justin Eckstein (2020) analyzed how González worked to shift our understanding of this event by focusing on generational differences and experiences with guns. Eckstein notes that "the kid is no longer a passive object, but an active stakeholder in gun policy" (p. 171) and the "Parkland kid" has now entered into many other discussions on guns.

Media events are filled with messages that shape one's view of the world and invite one to view the world in a particular way. The funerals of Yasser Arafat and Ronald Reagan, the inaugurations of Barack Obama and Donald Trump, and many other media events are worthy of examination for the underlying assumptions and meanings they communicate beyond reporting the facts. For example, in addition to explaining what occurred, such events can stimulate nationalistic feelings, celebrate a nation's history or values, or reinforce specific political beliefs and positions. Another example of a powerful media event was the 2010 earthquake in Haiti and the 2011 earthquake and tsunami in Japan. Media played a key role in bringing attention to these human tragedies, which in turn prompted huge numbers of people to make donations to relief organizations.

Monitoring Media Violence

Representations of violent acts in media are common and are an increasingly important area of research, as well as a concern among parents and other groups. As you might surmise, our society is ambivalent about **media violence**, as indicated by the range of responses to it. On the one hand, a large number of people must be entertained by it, or why would there be so many violent books, movies, and video games? On the other, media producers and editors make intentional decisions to keep certain violent images out of the public view (beheadings, coffins, bodies). In addition, we are inventing tools such as parental control devices for television to protect certain members of society from witnessing violence. These conflicting trends reveal tensions between the principles of censorship, freedom of the press, and protection of children.

Although no clear-cut definition of violence exists, most people generally consider shootings, stabbings, and other kinds of killings and attempted killings to be violent. Slapping, hitting, and fighting of all types also constitute violence. Most of the concern

media violence
Representations of violent acts in media.

about media violence focuses on its impact on children. The American Academy of Pediatrics, for example, is particularly concerned about the influence of media violence on children under eight years of age; they have concluded that media violence has the following effects on children:

- increased aggressiveness and antisocial behavior,
- increased fear of becoming victims,
- less sensitivity to violence and to victims of violence, and
- increased appetite for more violence in entertainment and in real life.

These concerns are not new. People, especially parents, began to worry about media violence in television almost as soon as broadcasting began in 1946. Also, as we noted previously, numerous studies have shown that "media violence contributes to a more violent society" (Anderson & Bushman, 2002, p. 2377). Research has also demonstrated that although cartoons are far more violent than prime-time television, an intervention by parents and adults can influence how children respond to those violent images. For example, in her study of five- to seven- and 10- to 12-year-old children, Amy Nathanson (2004) found that when parents and other adults simply discussed the production techniques of a program, this either had no effect on children or it increased the influence of the violent images. In contrast, when parents underscored the fictional nature of a program's characters, the children were better able to deal with the violence and were less afraid.

In response to concerns about children and television content, in 1998 the Federal Communications Commission (2003) mandated that half of all new televisions 13 inches or larger manufactured after July 1, 1999, and *all* sets 13 inches or larger manufactured after January 1, 2000, must have a **V-chip** installed. A V-chip identifies program ratings by content and can block programming that is designated by the owner, typically the parent(s). For example, a parent who does not want a child to watch programs with TV-14 ratings can block such programs from being shown. Similar systems have been developed to block access to certain kinds of websites on the Internet and other media.

Of course, not all violent images presented in media are fictional. Television news journalists must decide what is and is not too horrifying to broadcast. Internet broadcasts of hostages in Iraq being beheaded in 2014–2015 were not shown on U.S. network television. Images of people leaping to their deaths from the World Trade Center towers on September 11, 2001, also were considered too troubling to broadcast.

The Federal Communications Commission has oversight of the appropriateness of television programming, but it focuses more on the major network channels than on cable channels. Moreover, the commission can fine broadcasters for presenting inappropriate materials, but these fines are typically for indecency rather than violence. Sometimes broadcasters warn audiences that an upcoming image may not be suitable for all audiences—one approach to dealing with extremely violent

V-chip
Device that identifies television program ratings by content and can block programming designated by the owner.

▼ Parents play an important role in their children's media viewing as well as the way in which their children interpret the programs they watch.

images. For example, some television newscasters provided such warnings before showing the numerous bodies of victims of the 2004 Indian Ocean tsunami. Some offer similar warnings before showing fatal shootings, or material that some parents may not want their children to see. Cable broadcasts, particularly pay-per-view, have more leeway in their programming because the assumption is that viewers have actively sought out and paid for a particular type of programming.

Analyzing Media Economics

Mass communication today is dominated by the large corporations that produce and distribute media messages. Thus, the economics of media production shapes mass communication and gives it a unique and powerful role in our society. No individual can easily compete with a multinational corporation in producing and distributing media messages. Therefore, these huge media corporations determine which messages are available, and this ownership can have consequences for society in important ways. The Walt Disney Company, one of the world's largest media conglomerates, owns several television networks as well as TV and movie production and distribution companies; these, together with its publishing and merchandising divisions and Disney character licensing, give the company enormous influence on the messages that fill the media environment. One example is what happened to the Fantastic Four (see *Alternative View: The Fantastic Four and the Disney/Fox Merger*).

In the area of media studies concerned with economic issues, scholars focus on **political economy**, or the ways in which media institutions produce texts in a capitalist system and the legal and regulatory frameworks that shape their options for doing so. Political economists also examine how these media products are marketed

Critical Thinking Prompt
How well does the V-chip serve its intended purpose? What measures do you think society should take to limit children's exposure to inappropriate media content?

political economy
The ways in which media institutions produce texts in a capitalist system and the legal and regulatory frameworks that shape their options for doing so.

ALTERNATIVE VIEW

The Fantastic Four and the Disney/Fox Merger

How much should we pay attention to media ownership? What impact does ownership have on the media products that we consume? In a recent study, Robert Brookey and Nan Zhang (2021) looked at the ways that fan culture and corporate ownership worked in the production of the Fantastic Four products. Initially launched as comic book characters, the Fantastic Four quickly gained a fan base. The film rights to these characters were eventually obtained by Constantin Films, a German company. They "partnered with 20th Century Fox to produce the big-budget *Fantastic Four* release in 2005 and the *Fantastic Four: Rise of the Silver Surfer* in 2007" (p. 156).

While both of these films had significant budgets of $100 million and $130 million, the box office returns were "moderately successful" (p. 156). Fox decided to create and sell video games of the Fantastic Four. Given the mediocre revenues, "Fox passed on the option for a third film in the franchise. Fox decided to reboot the franchise with the 2015 release, a film that was [. . .] savaged by the critics" (p. 156). The revenues for this film were only about $167 million worldwide.

Despite a strong fanbase, the Fantastic Four franchise has not fared well under the ownership of Constantin Films and 20th Century Fox. In comparison to the Avengers, Spiderman, and Black Panther—Marvel creations—the Fantastic Four has not achieved the same success. When Disney bought out significant portions of Fox in 2018, the Fantastic Four was only one part of a much larger deal. Now, Disney has international distribution rights, which significantly impacts the value of Constantin's film production rights. Interestingly, in 2018, Marvel comics relaunched the Fantastic Four comics.

What's important to understand from Brookey and Zhang's study is that we need to pay attention to both media industries and the legal and economic interests at stake as well as the audiences and fans of particular media products. The Fantastic Four has a long-standing fan base, but those fans may not be enough for more products. Brookey and Zhang note, however, that the Fantastic Four cartoons from the early 1990s are now available on Disney+, which may foreshadow a return of the Fantastic Four in the future.

SOURCE: Brookey, R. A., & Zhang, N. (2021). The not-so *Fantastic Four* franchise: A critical history of the comic, the films, and the Disney/Fox merger. In A. Rauscher, D., Stein, & J.-N. Thon (Eds.), *Comics and video games: From hybrid medialities to transmedia expansions* (pp. 149–163). Routledge.

to understand what they reveal about our society. This approach is an extension of the work of Karl Marx, the influential nineteenth-century socialist thinker, and it emphasizes the economics of media rather than its messages or audiences, although all those components are interrelated. An example of this theory's application can be seen in one researcher's analysis of the decision by ABC to cease broadcasting the Miss America pageant. After all, the researcher noted, "a little more than a decade ago [this pageant] had copped about 27 million viewers; last month it drew a record-low 9.8 million" (de Moraes, 2004). With a small viewing audience, the demand for and price of advertising during the pageant also dropped. Thus, the theory goes, economic factors largely determine what media content people are exposed to.

Previously in this chapter, we introduced the term *culture industries* to refer to organizations that produce, distribute, or show various media texts. In the United States, these culture industries most often are media corporations or media industries that operate for profit. In some other countries, however, culture industries are more like U.S. public television—meaning that they are nonprofit media organizations—and this economic structure affects content and programming. Consider for a moment how a nonprofit media organization might develop programming as compared with a for-profit organization. What factors might guide their decision making? PBS, for example, needs to please the public and the government, both of which fund it. President Trump proposed ending all federal funding for public broadcasting, which is not the first time such a proposal has been made (Stelter, 2017). In contrast, for-profit networks need to please shareholders and advertisers by drawing large audiences.

Although television networks have historically been identified with specific nations—for example, CBC with Canada and BBC with Britain—globalization has recently sparked and sustained transnational television networks. Many media corporations with significant financial backing are moving in this direction. Though initial attempts at transnational broadcasting in the early 1980s to mid-1990s faced many difficulties and most did not survive (Chalaby, 2003), today, transnational television networks are growing, and some of these include U.S.-based networks such as CNN International and MTV. Some are European-based, such as BBC World, Deutsche Welle, Euronews, France24, and Skynews. And in Asia, NHK World-Japan serves a similar function. More studies need to be done to determine how this global flow of information and entertainment may be influencing societies.

In China, another kind of change has been occurring in the mass media system, related in part to globalization. As the Chinese economy has moved toward a capitalist or free-enterprise model, the state-owned mass media system has experienced changes, including the "rise of semi-independent newspapers and broadcasting stations, the proliferation of private Internet content providers and unlicensed cable networks, and increasing cross-investment by the media into other commercial enterprises, including joint ventures with international media giants" (Akhavan-Majid, 2004, p. 553). In her study of these new Chinese media, Akhavan-Majid argues that "non-state actors (e.g., citizens, journalists, entrepreneurs)" (2004, p. 554) have used loopholes in official Chinese policies to creatively open new media opportunities. As you can see, changes in political and economic structures can be intimately intertwined with changes in mass media.

Political economists also analyze the mergers and acquisitions that occur in the media industry as a way of understanding changes in programming. For example, when NBC acquired the Bravo channel (2001), it added performing arts and art films to its roster, as well as some riskier programs, including *Boy Meets Boy* (2003), *Queer Eye for the Straight Guy* (2003–2007), and *Girl* (2008). In a news release related to this sale, Bob Wright, vice chairman of General Electric and chairman and CEO of NBC, noted that "Bravo, with its desirable demographic, is a perfect strategic addition to our portfolio, providing a particularly good fit with NBC's network and cable viewers"

(Cablevision, 2000). In analyzing these developments, a political economist might focus on the economic reasons behind this acquisition and the potential future revenues to be generated by appealing to this desirable demographic group ("desirable" typically refers to an audience with the size and demographic profile to bring in high advertising revenues). As Bravo continues to search for desirable audiences, the network has moved to new television programming, including *Top Chef, Below Deck,* the *Million Dollar Listing* franchise, and *The Real Housewives* franchise.

Another desirable demographic is Millennials. As the largest generational group, Millennials are expected to become an important market for advertisers. In order to capture this market, it's important to understand what they are watching as well as how they are watching media texts. In 2017, Nielsen released a report, "Millennials on Millennials," that looked at their media consumption. Traditional TV viewing still dominates the media consumption of Millennials, but less than older generations. Millennials have migrated to other screens—for example, tablets, smartphones, and other digital streaming devices—to watch various media. They also tend to multitask while watching programs, change the channel less often, and remember fewer of the advertisements. These viewing habits are important for advertisers to understand as they try to make money selling to this generation.

Of course, political economists cannot predict the kinds of media texts that will emerge from any specific merger. They know that television stations seek viewers who are more affluent so they can attract more advertisers, but political economists do not know (nor does anyone) what kinds of shows will attract affluent viewers. Although television production companies try to create—and television networks try to buy—television programs that will draw large audiences, they do not always succeed. Political economists cannot and do not predict such successes, either. Instead, they focus on the ways that corporate media influence the information we get, the consequences of capitalist media corporations on society, and the demands that this political and economic structure places on journalists, broadcasters, and other media workers.

In the context of the 2003 Federal Communications Commission's decision to relax restrictions on ownership of media, understanding and unraveling the complex relationships among media economics, media ownership, and media content can be crucial. For example, because news is sold for profit, the profit motive shapes what readers consider "news." This commercial pressure influences the work of journalists as well as the way media organizations are run. One leading scholar in this area, Robert McChesney (1998), raised this alarm more than two decades ago:

> The American media system is spinning out of control in a hyper-commercialized frenzy. Fewer than 10 transnational media conglomerates dominate much of our media; fewer than two dozen account for the overwhelming majority of our newspapers, magazines, films, television, radio, and books. With every aspect of our media culture now fair game for commercial exploitation, we can look forward to the full-scale commercialization of sports, arts, and education, the disappearance of notions of public service from public discourse, and the degeneration of journalism, political coverage, and children's programming under commercial pressure. (p. 4)

By focusing on the political and economic structures in which media industries operate, political economists offer a unique perspective on the influence of media in our lives. Their analysis of areas that many people ignore reveals the potential consequences of the business of media on all of us.

Societal issues very much influence individuals' interactions with media. Moreover, both personal and social identities are important to one's interactions with media and how one interprets media violence. Given the profits to be made, media economics ensures that media violence will remain pervasive as long as people continue to purchase products with violent content.

**Journal Prompt 13.4:
Mass Media Issues**
What are five issues in the study of mass media and how do each of these relate to the individual and to society at large?

Ethics and Mass Media

13.5   Identify five ethical issues with mass media.

media activism
The practice of organizing to communicate displeasure with certain media images and messages as well as to force change in future media texts.

Because media messages are so powerful, they can generate powerful responses. One potential response is **media activism**, or the practice of organizing to communicate displeasure with certain media images and messages as well as to advocate for change in future media texts. The issues that media activists address are important because they highlight many significant ethical questions surrounding mediated communication. Media activism, of course, is not limited to the United States. Media activist groups have mobilized around the world to express ethical concerns about media coverage on a range of issues.

Voicing ethical concerns through media activism is not a recent phenomenon. People have been concerned about media content and images for centuries. The notions of freedom of speech and freedom of the press articulated in the U.S. Constitution reflect one response to media control. In the early twentieth century, as silent movies became popular entertainment, concerns about their racy content and the transition to talking movies led to calls for government regulation of media. In an attempt to avoid government regulation, Hollywood established the Hays Office to create its own system of regulation. The **Hays Code**, which was published in 1930, established strict rules for media content with the goal of wholesome entertainment. Some of the Hays regulations still apply today, such as the ban on exposing children's sex organs. Other regulations, however, have become outdated, such as the ban against portraying sexual relationships between interracial couples or using vulgar expressions or profanity, which the code specified as including the words "God, Lord, Jesus, Christ (unless used reverently); cripes; fairy (in a vulgar sense)."

Hays Code
Self-imposed rules for Hollywood media content instituted in 1930 with the goal of creating "wholesome entertainment."

The Hays code came about because of media activism in the 1920s, and it continued to set industry standards until the late 1960s, when the Motion Picture Association of America (**MPAA**) devised its rating codes. The MPAA represents the six major Hollywood studios. These codes have changed slightly since then, but most people are familiar with the G, PG, PG-13, R, and NC-17 ratings.

MPAA
Motion Picture Association of America is a film sector industry representing the six major Hollywood studios.

Today, media activism has concentrated largely on the ethics of five areas: children's programming, representations of cultural groups, bias in news reporting, alternative programming, and the use of media as an activist strategy. Let's look at each of these in turn.

The first area of ethical focus of media activism is the concern over the impact of media images on children. Complaints about content in television shows and its influence on children led to the creation of the **TV Parental Guidelines** (TV Parental Guidelines Monitoring Board, n.d.), which are a self-regulating system of the television industry. These guidelines rate programs in terms of appropriateness for particular age groups. You have probably noticed the rating codes in the upper-left corner of the television screen. (An explanation of the ratings is available at http://www.tvguidelines.org/ratings.htm.) This kind of rating system is voluntary, so unless an adult activates the V-chip or an adult is present to change the channel or turn off the television, the rating system may not work as it was intended.

TV Parental Guidelines
A self-regulating system of the television industry that rates programs in terms of appropriateness for particular age groups.

The second ethical focus of media activists has been distortions perpetrated or reinforced by media. The concern here is that such portrayals create stereotypes and misunderstandings. Minority groups, in particular, have had such concerns, as we can see in the number of media activist groups focused on media representations of racial and sexual minorities. On record with *Newsweek*, Martin Reynolds of the Maynard Institute for Journalism Education, a nonprofit that promotes diversity in the newsroom, has asserted, "The black press and the ethnic press as a whole have consistently maintained far more credibility in their communities than their mainstream counterparts" (Celis, 2017). Yet that is not to say that minority groups have the same alternative viewpoints about mainstream news.

Media activism has recently taken on more meaning since the "fake news" phenomenon which has been causing confusion among Americans (Barthel et al., 2016). Media activism has traditionally been understood as alternative outlets using media to spark and sustain social movements. But in a world where journalists are no longer the exclusive "gatekeepers" of information, mainstream media channels are increasingly seeing themselves as activists. Media activism, then, now refers to media owners repurposing what it means to disseminate news to the public (Ward, 2015). In fact, some media insiders increasingly see themselves as activists against privately disseminated fake news.

These activists argue that when people have limited contact with minority groups,

▲ The GLAAD Media Awards is an annual event that honors responsible and accurate media images of lesbians, gays, transgendered individuals, and bisexuals. *Pose* won the "Outstanding Drama Series" award in 2020.

they are likely to gain false impressions from media misrepresentations. In turn, these distorted images may lead to hate crimes or discriminatory government policies, such as racial profiling. Media activist groups that monitor media producers and challenge them to create responsible and accurate images include Media Action Network for Asian Americans (MANAA) and Gay and Lesbian Alliance Against Defamation (GLAAD) as well as organizations that have broader goals but that include a media activist focus, such as the National Organization for Women (NOW) and the League of United Latin American Citizens (LULAC).

A third category of activist groups has focused on structural issues in media industries and the consequences for how news content is constructed and broadcast to consumers. Within a profit-making environment, does making money influence what stories are covered, and how they are covered for wealthier consumers? For example, organizations such as Fairness and Accuracy in Reporting (FAIR), the Annenberg Public Policy Center's factcheck.org, the Arthur W. Page Center for Integrity in Public Communication, and the National Public Radio program *On the Media* are some of the organizations that focus on the news media and their accuracy and fairness in reporting various issues and the inclusion of diverse viewpoints.

The fourth ethical focus of media activists has been to find and provide media texts that offer alternatives to mainstream sources. Many newspapers, radio programs, and Internet sites are available for those who want alternatives to mainstream news media coverage so that they can hear a diversity of voices and opinions. Previously, we discussed the alternative press, but there is also alternative radio programming, such as the Progressive Radio Network, and other alternative media outlets, such as Amy Goodman and Juan Gonzalez's daily television program *Democracy Now!* Other alternative views are expressed as humor in print, online in *The Onion*, and on television on *The Daily Show* and *Last Week Tonight with John Oliver*. Alternative media outlets are not the same as fake news, in that they do not present false facts but focus more on alternative interpretations of facts and report news that is not covered in mainstream media outlets.

Finally, some activists use media to communicate specific ethical concerns and messages to a wide audience. Thus, despite the fact that they lack the backing of huge media conglomerates, activists have used media to educate or influence audiences regarding cruelty to animals; the situations in Palestine, Guantánamo, and Afghanistan; violence against women; anti-Semitism; genocide; racism; and more. To get their messages out, these groups set up websites and webcasts, solicit funds to run advertisements on television or in mainstream newspapers or magazines, and sometimes organize demonstrations at strategic times and places.

As new media outlets develop (for example via the Internet, cable TV, and satellite radio) and the world continues to confront new challenges, new ethical issues and new ways of communicating will continue to emerge. We cannot forecast the future, but we do know that the ongoing process of change in the media environment shows no signs of abating. Media activists will continue to try to shape the media messages we receive, while at the same time, media producers will continue to try to sell what people are interested in purchasing. And so, bombarded as you are by media and the messages of a range of media activists, how can you become a responsible media consumer? Let's explore this topic next.

Journal Prompt 13.5: Mass Media Ethics
What are the five ethical focuses in mass media?

Becoming a More Effective Media Consumer

13.6 Describe three ways to be a more effective consumer of media messages.

As a potential consumer of practically nonstop messages coming from radio, television, newspapers, magazines, advertisements, movies, and so on, you need strategies for dealing with this complex media environment. The solution cannot be boiled down to a set of simple guidelines, of course, but here are some ideas to consider when interacting with media. To become more effective in your media consumption, be an active agent in your media choices, be mindful of the media choices you make, and speak out if you find media content offensive.

Be an Active Agent

How can you become an active consumer of media? First, don't just watch or read whatever is available. Make deliberate choices about media you expose yourself to so that you can better control the effect that media messages have on you. As you become more selective, you express a set of media-related values, which in turn indicates to media providers what type of media programming they should be providing.

As an active agent, then, seek out those media that meet your needs and avoid or resist others. To be a truly active agent, however, you have to think about the basis for your media choices. Are you avoiding some media messages simply because they challenge your beliefs? If so, this probably is not the best way to navigate through the media environment. Sometimes, you can benefit from being open-minded about the views and perspectives of others.

Broaden Your Media Horizons

People often live within the confines of a particular media environment and, like a fish in water, can't see the limits. With the vast possibilities now available via the Internet, in libraries, and through other media outlets, you have access to practically the whole world. Even if your only language is English, you have many media options available to you.

As you work to broaden your horizons, obtain a range of views on world events. Try to understand why other people view the world the way they do, no matter how different their views are from your own. Try to understand the rising anti-Americanism coming from around the world. You may disagree with what you hear, or even find it offensive, but by seeing the complexity of issues involved you can gain a better understanding of the world we live in.

Overall, being a responsible and effective consumer of media is not easy. It certainly extends far beyond lounging around watching whatever is on television. Becoming an active partner in this complex communication process is a challenge, one we hope you will take up.

Critical Thinking Prompt
How can media consumers find a range of media outlets from which to get news and information? How would you define an adequate and well-balanced "diet" of media consumption?

Talk Back

You can benefit from talking back or challenging the messages you receive via news commentators, politicians, reporters, or even characters in television programs. In other words, if you hear something you disagree with or that sounds wrong, point this out, even if only to yourself. For example, suppose you hear a reporter covering a natural disaster refer to "innocent victims." What, you might ask yourself, is a "guilty victim" in the context of an earthquake, or in any context for that matter? Noticing and questioning these kinds of empty phrases makes you a more active consumer of media. As you watch or listen, you might also consider why one news story is given more time than another one, or why a particular story is reported at all, and what that prioritizing and selection communicates about what is and isn't valued.

Talking back also includes being attentive to the ethical implications of media to which you are exposed, particularly if it promotes some social identities at the expense of others. More specifically, be aware of the ways that, for example, women and racial minorities, sexual minorities, and religious minorities are portrayed and what influences these images may have on the groups depicted. If you watch movies that mock particular cultural or religious groups, that denigrate women, or that misrepresent the experiences of certain individuals, consider the implications. You not only ratify this depiction by your attendance, but you also encourage the production of more of this type of media with your dollars.

▲ As an active media consumer, you can talk back to your television as well as discuss media messages with family and friends.

Talking back, however, can involve much more than talking to the images that come to you in media or making choices about which images to support or resist. If you find something particularly objectionable, you can contact the television station, magazine, or newspaper that has offended you. For example, if you believe that specific programs manipulate or attempt to unfairly influence children, use the "contact us" information on the station's website to let the producers of those programs, and the companies that advertise in that medium, know exactly how you feel. Or you can complain to the Federal Communications Commission, the federal agency that regulates radio, television, wire, cable, and satellite. On the other hand, if you believe specific media have a positive influence and should be more widely produced or distributed, let advertisers and media companies know that as well. Certainly, praising a job well done is as important a form of talking back as raising objections.

In general, few consumers are sufficiently deliberate about the media messages they select. But because media messages have such a powerful impact on consumers, and because you can have some influence on the availability of specific types of media, you benefit society when you become an active and critical media consumer.

Journal Prompt 13.6: Mass Media Activism
How do media activists respond to media messages they find objectionable? What are some concerns that contemporary media activists have raised?

SUMMARY

13.1 Identify the issues facing mass media.

- Media influence how we see ourselves and the world around us.
- *Mediated communication* are mediated, or transmitted, through a channel, such as television, film, radio, or print.
- Mass media communication refers to communication that is directed at a mass audience.
- Individuals choose what types of media texts to watch, read, listen to, purchase, or avoid.

13.2 Identify the main forms of mass media.

- The main forms of mass media are: newspapers, magazines, mass market paperbacks and e-books, motion pictures or movies, radio, popular music, and television.

13.3 Describe various models of media.

- The linear model focuses on media effects.
- Selective exposure theory emphasizes how people choose media that confirm their views and avoid media that challenge those beliefs.
- Uses and gratifications studies focus on how people use media to satisfy their need for information, personal identity, social interaction, and entertainment.
- People also resist media, as they are active agents.

13.4 Understand five issues in media studies: social identities, understanding the world, media events, media violence, and media economics.

- Media confirm our social identities, help us understand the world, help us understand important media

events, and shape the images of real and imagined violence.
- Media are influenced by and function within a capitalist economic system.

13.5 Identify five ethical issues with mass media.

- Media activism is one way that people express their ethical views and respond to objectionable media messages and powerful media corporations.
- Media activists are concerned about children's programming.
- Media activism is also focused on how cultural groups are represented or stereotyped.
- Media activism is also concerned about news reporting and fake news.
- Media activism can also produce alternative programming.

13.6 Describe three ways to be a more effective consumer of media messages.

- Be an active agent and aware of your own media consumption habits.
- Broaden your media horizons and be active in making your choices.
- Talk back when media content is offensive or problematic.

KEY TERMS

media p. 347
mass media p. 347
culture industries p. 347
mass-market paperbacks p. 349
e-books p. 349
active agents p. 350
mass media effects p. 351
media text p. 352

selective exposure p. 352
uses and gratifications p. 354
content analysis p. 357
frame analysis p. 360
agenda-setting capacity p. 360
cultivation theory p. 361
hegemony p. 362
media event p. 362

media violence p. 363
V-chip p. 364
political economy p. 365
media activism p. 368
Hays Code p. 368
MPAA p. 368
TV Parental Guidelines p. 368

APPLY WHAT YOU KNOW

1. **Media Texts**
   Research a popular media text—for example, a magazine, television show, or newspaper—that targets an identity group different from your own. What elements differ from a text targeted at one of your identity groups?

2. **Media Events**
   Select and study a media event such as the Super Bowl, Miss America Pageant, or a famous murder trial, and identify the rituals that surround this event. How does the media event affirm U.S. cultural values?

3. **Media Activism**
   Select a media activist group to study. Go to their webpage and identify their concerns about media. What strategies do they use to promote their messages? Who is their audience? How do they plan to change media in the ways that concern them?

Communicating through Social and Other Interactive Media

CHAPTER

14

 LEARNING OBJECTIVES

> *"Experts predict the Internet will become 'like electricity'—less visible, yet more deeply embedded in people's lives for good and ill."*
>
> — Janna Anderson and Lee Rainie, "Digital Life in 2025," *Pew Research Center*, 2014

At the end of the day, Charee sits down on the couch facing her bookshelf and realizes this is the first time all day she has not been utilizing media. First thing this morning, she scrolled through Twitter for the latest news and then TikTok to see what was new with her friends. She then attended two classes on Zoom with a group project meeting after that on Google Hangouts. As the group leader, she was tasked with emailing the professor for clarification about the assignment. She had a Teams virtual meeting with two coworkers (wishing she could meet with them in person) and then headed to the gym for a quick workout. On her way there, she started listening to the "How to Do Everything" podcast, which she has been following for a few weeks because of its helpful tips for adulting, but was interrupted with an urgent message from her mother asking her to please make dinner as she had a work emergency. After gym she checked out her favorite recipe blogger and ordered the groceries needed through her phone app to be delivered. After following the YouTube "How To" video for dinner, she checked in with her grandma on FaceTime, once her grandmother's nurse got her iPad working.

Now Charee's thinking about her constant connectivity and all the different choices she has with the various communication technologies and wonders how long the "remote" and "online" life will last. She's worried about her grades this semester because sometimes she has a hard time concentrating online. She isn't convinced that remote learning is for her. She wants to participate in class discussions, but she is worried about keeping her camera turned on because she lives at home; she's worried about her little sister interrupting her or having her parents in the background. They always want to check in and see what she is learning in class, but she's embarrassed about having her parents be seen on camera. She also misses the social connection of going to class and the physical aspects of seeing friends there.

Charee's communication choices illustrate a number of issues we will address in this chapter. For example, given the many choices we have to connect with people every day, how do we decide which is the most appropriate? Can there be too much connectivity and online interaction? How do people use technology to communicate in different contexts and with different people? How has the pervasiveness of technology impacted the way we communicate with others? And how does the constant "connectivity" to others affect our identities and our interpersonal relationships?

In the previous chapter, we focused on mass media. The focus of mass media is one-way mediated communication produced by large industries intended for a large audience, such as television, radio, and films. In this chapter, we focus on **interactive media**, or mediated communication, which relies on technologies such as the Internet and mobile phones and other devices. First, we describe how interactive media play an important role in our lives and define what we mean by interactive media. As you'll see, social media is the largest group of interactive media—which is why it is included in the title of this chapter. Then we examine individuals' use of interactive media, including identity issues and impacts on personal and work relationships. We then shift the focus to societal forces—examining how gender, race/ethnicity, and socioeconomic class impact interactive media use and who does (and does not) have access to these and other communication technologies. Finally, we discuss ethical issues related to interactive media use and conclude with suggestions for improving your own skills in using communication technologies.

interactive media
A collection of mediated communication technologies that are digital and converging and tend to be mobile.

The Importance of Interactive and Social Media

14.1 Identify three reasons for learning about interactive media.

Interactive media are a constant reality in our lives and affect our daily activities in multiple ways. This pervasiveness provides the first and primary reason for learning more about this topic. A second reason is that understanding interactive media and having good media skills provide opportunities for self-expression and can help you be more successful personally. And a third reason is that understanding and using social media effectively in your professional life can help ensure career success.

First, we say that interactive media are pervasive because most of us interact with these communication technologies almost constantly and increasingly access them on mobile devices (Auxier et al., 2019). Recently, people have to rely on interactive media more than ever; because of remote work/learning/health environments, there has been a shift in thinking of interactive media as entertainment for pleasure to thinking of it as something we need in our daily lives for school and professional purposes (Vogels et al., 2020). You probably know that social media use has grown dramatically over your lifetime. In 2005, just 5 percent of U.S. Americans used social media, compared to today when 75 percent of all adults and almost 90 percent of young people (ages 18–29) use social media. Although communication technologies are a huge boon for many people around the globe, they present challenges to communication researchers (and textbook authors) in trying to understand and study the implications of these interactive media in our daily lives. Communication technologies come and go at a rapid rate. By the time researchers design a study, the particular technology may have lost prominence, and the study results can then seem irrelevant. In addition, it's difficult to predict which technologies will be important in the future or how we will use current ones differently.

That said, we have to start somewhere to describe the role of interactive media in our everyday lives, and most experts agree that we currently use communication technologies primarily for (1) connecting with others in various ways, through social networks, media sharing, social blogging, and discussion/community blogging and (2) consuming content (verbal and visual). These interactive media offer many ways to stay connected and, as Charee discovered, present many communication choices. Our friends can know immediately what movies we're streaming and what brand of sunscreen we've purchased as well as the restaurant where we're eating. Digital apps help us connect with new friends who share our interests (e.g., Meetup, Meet My Dog, Nextdoor) and potential sexual or romantic partners (e.g., Grindr, Tinder, Scruff, Bumble, OkCupid). Perhaps more importantly, social media can provide a quick way to notify friends and loved ones that we're safe during natural or human caused disasters (e.g., Facebook's Safety Check).

Of course, different social media platforms have different audiences that require different approaches. What you post on LinkedIn, for example, differs from what you post on Instagram or TikTok. We are constantly making choices about which information we want to share with which friends/acquaintances/colleagues and in which medium. Throughout this chapter, we will examine how this pervasive connectivity can affect our communication choices as well as our sense of identity, personal privacy, and romantic, work, and acquaintance relationships.

Connecting with others can provide opportunities for civic engagement and activism. Interacting on social media (e.g., Twitter) offers opportunities for closer access to political leaders and celebrities. Some journalists say this direct access has upset the traditional role of journalists. But social media also presents opportunities for civic engagement and political activism. For example, one analysis found that the #MeToo hashtag had been used more than 19 million times on Twitter from October 15, 2017 (when actress Alyssa Milano tweeted, urging victims of sexual harassment to reply "me too"), through September 30, 2018 (Auxier et al., 2019). And the #BlackLivesMatter campaign started with one tweet after the murder of Trayvon Martin and Michael Brown in 2012, gathered momentum over the years, and led to the 2020 massive protests after the killing of George Floyd.

Activism that takes less effort, or "slacktivism," involves supporting a cause merely by connecting with others on social media (e.g., by changing a profile image, retweeting an opinion, or using a trending hashtag). It turns out that "slacktivism" or "clicktivism" (a less negative term) is actually more effective than we might assume. By spreading little-known ideas and publicizing non-mainstream notions, these actions collectively can provide momentum to fledgling social and political movements (Fisher, 2020). Even seemingly insignificant daily social media activities can provide social solidarity and be a gateway to political participation (Stewart & Schultze, 2019; Yamamoto et al., 2019).

In addition to organizing and promoting social causes, interactive media have been used successfully to raise money through **crowdfunding** to support individuals, charities, or start-up companies. People can contribute to crowdfunding requests with no expectation of repayment, or companies can offer shares of the business to contributors. Kickstarter, the most popular crowdfunding site, has raised over $5 billion with more than 182,000 projects funded since its inception in 2009. Indiegogo and Causes are popular for nonprofit fundraising, and GoFundMe is used to raise money for personal causes (soliciting money, for example, for healthcare costs or travel). Kiva enables people from developing countries who cannot afford bank loans to crowdfund temporary loans (Nguyen, 2020).

crowdfunding
The process of raising money online— often many small amounts from a large number of people.

Another important interactive media activity is searching for information/consuming content (visual and verbal). Some activities may be less interactive (e.g., reading news reports; getting directions; reading reviews of restaurants, movies, or home repair professionals; obtaining stock quotes or weather reports; watching funny cat videos), but others are quite interactive, like commenting on political/news/opinion blogs, posting your own opinions and reviews, or sharing a funny TikTok video to a friend along with your comments (see *Communication in Society: The Role of Social Media in a National Health Crisis*).

Searching for information presents a choice: When do you do a Google search, post a question on Quora (crowdsourcing), or ask friends on Instagram? One group of researchers found that people carefully choose their platform based on the nature of their question and the audience they're interested in. People used Facebook to ask questions when they wanted opinions from their friends, were seeking very specific information, or were asking friends to supplement information from a search engine. They tended to use Twitter when they needed a broader audience or were seeking information they thought inappropriate (too sensitive or too controversial) for other social media friends. They used search engines when they didn't think their Facebook friends would have the answer or the topic was too sensitive for social media (Oeldorf-Hirsch et al., 2014). How do you choose?

Closely related to crowdfunding, discussed earlier, is **crowdsourcing.** While crowdfunding seeks to obtain money, crowdsourcing is a way of getting information or opinions from a large group of people through interactive media. Originally, crowdsourcing was used like a Google search for general information; it is now increasingly monetized, used by businesses or marketing firms to solicit new business or raise capital. Individuals who respond to the crowdsourcing questions may be paid employees or freelancers hired to promote organizations/businesses, often by including links (to those businesses/organizations) in their answers.

crowdsourcing
The practice of engaging a "crowd" or group online for a common goal—often for information or problem solving.

A second reason for learning more about interactive media is that developing good digital skills can help in your personal life, for example, by helping overcome the challenges of problematic interactive media use (Busch & McCarthy, 2020; Tanega & Downs, 2020). As we'll discuss in more detail later in the chapter, knowing how to use social media effectively can lead to better self-esteem (Firth et al., 2019), better mental health,

COMMUNICATION IN SOCIETY

The Role of Social Media in a National Health Crisis

In a national health crisis, some people panic, and some remain calm. Why is there this variation, and what types of official messages are most effective in helping citizens deal with such a crisis? Can you relate this information to national health issues today?

Communication scholars Glowacki and Taylor (2020) investigated this topic by examining 400 social media responses (Facebook posts and Tweets) to three different media sources during the three-month crisis when the deadly Ebola virus entered the United States in 2014. The three sources represented a range of political/cultural positions: (1) the Centers for Disease Control and Prevention (CDC), viewed as a scientific and relatively neutral source; (2) the White House (WH), with a progressive Democratic President Obama; and (3) Alex Jones's show *Infowars*, a politically far-right, self-proclaimed conspiracy theorist known for stoking fear and concern from followers.

As expected, the messages from the CDC were focused on explanations of the virus and the health situation, the WH's messages on calming fears. However, these attempts at informing and calming citizens were often met with social media responses of criticism, distrust, and scepticism (e.g., the CDC was incompetent, hadn't provided best practices for handling the virus, and so on).

Not surprisingly, messages on *Infowars'* Facebook page stoked fear and anxiety. For example, some messages accused the U.S. government of "draconian powers" and detaining Americans. Other messages accused the CDC of a "hidden" past, saying that the CDC knew Ebola had mutated into an airborne virus much earlier in 1989. Not surprisingly, social media responses to these messages centered on distrust of the government rather than concerns over Ebola (e.g., accusing the government of intentionally bringing Ebola into the United States and withholding treatment).

The CDC continued to send out facts and advice about the virus, quickly countering *Infowars'* false information; responses of accusations and blame slowly turned to scepticism and frustration, and finally the tide seemed to turn and responses to the CDC messages were more thankful and even asking for guidance. Responses to *Infowars'* fearmongering messages became sceptical, with some labeling the messages as "scare tactics."

Glowacki and Taylor draw several conclusions: (1) When faced with a potential health crisis, citizens respond to fear with "hyperbolic" (exaggerated) rhetoric: scepticism and blame, apprehension, and/or an unwillingness to comply with the prescribed guidelines. (2) This hyperbolic rhetoric seems to feed off of established patterns but "has a shelf life, lacks the endurance to withstand prolonged discussion." Suggestions for health officials: Monitor social media posts to get a sense of what the public perceives as concerning. Use specific rather than vague language when communicating about health recommendations and practices. The CDC's vague language at the beginning of the crisis seemed to lead to panic, mistrust, and scepticism.

SOURCE: Glowacki, E. M., & Taylor, M. A. (2020). Health hyperbolism: A study in health crisis rhetoric. *Qualitative Health Research, 30*(12), 1953–1964.

and emotional well-being (Faelens et al., 2021). Understanding the challenges of virtual relationships (romantic and friendships) can lead to safer interpersonal relationships and higher relational satisfaction (Verduyn et al., 2021).

Finally, you may not choose a career in social media (e.g., social influencer, digital marketer), but knowing how to use social media effectively to find and secure a job or using social media and other communication technologies in your chosen career will enhance your chances of professional success. For example, recent research shows a strong relationship between professional success and active use of social media such as LinkedIn. It appears that users of these platforms report more timely access to resources and referrals to career opportunities than nonusers do. (LinkedIn explicitly promises to connect its members with professionals from all over the world.) These professional informational benefits are positively related to career satisfaction, which is also linked to overall life satisfaction (Utz & Breuer, 2019).

Understanding the role that interactive media can play in employer–employee relationships and understanding organizational rules and practices involving interactive media, including surveillance, privacy concerns, and "netiquette," will serve you well. You have probably read news reports about employees who lost their jobs or were penalized as a result of not understanding the informal or formal rules about media behavior in the workplace (Doyle, 2020). Perhaps you wonder when employers can (and cannot) terminate employees for social media practices. We will discuss this question later in the chapter as well as various challenges and guidelines for effective interactive media use in work contexts (Miller, 2018).

Many experts worry about our overreliance on interactive media for information and identify three issues:

1. **Challenges in evaluating the information we access.** According to recent reports by the Pew Research Center, 93 percent of all Americans get some news online and most young Americans get their news primarily from social media (Stocking, 2019). Research confirms that those who get their news from social media are less aware of current events and also more likely to hear fringe or conspiracy theories and unproven

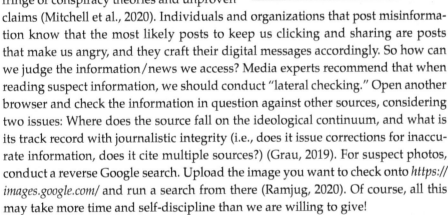

▲ Interactive media are a constant reality in our lives and affect our daily activities in multiple ways.

claims (Mitchell et al., 2020). Individuals and organizations that post misinformation know that the most likely posts to keep us clicking and sharing are posts that make us angry, and they craft their digital messages accordingly. So how can we judge the information/news we access? Media experts recommend that when reading suspect information, we should conduct "lateral checking." Open another browser and check the information in question against other sources, considering two issues: Where does the source fall on the ideological continuum, and what is its track record with journalistic integrity (i.e., does it issue corrections for inaccurate information, does it cite multiple sources?) (Grau, 2019). For suspect photos, conduct a reverse Google search. Upload the image you want to check onto *https:// images.google.com/* and run a search from there (Ramjug, 2020). Of course, all this may take more time and self-discipline than we are willing to give!

2. **Reduction in memory, attention/focus, or critical thinking skills.** We don't need to remember anything, we're never lost, or we don't need to take risks or figure things out because there's an app for everything. Apparently, having information available at our fingertips online and via smartphones makes us think we know more than we do. Studies show that these illusions of self-knowledge are evident when individuals are unable to remember information that they had previously searched for and say they know. Other research indicates that relying on digital searching may impede cognitive memory processes and that constant "media multitasking"—engaging with the limitless stream of different forms of digital media through hyperlinks, notifications, and prompts—make us less able to focus attention on other cognitive tasks. This seems to be especially detrimental in young children. However, some recent research is more hopeful, suggesting that relying on the Internet for memory storage may actually "free up" other cognitive resources, allowing us to use our newly available storage for more ambitious tasks.

3. **"Echo chamber syndrome."** As with mass media selective exposure discussed in Chapter 13, we (and social media platform administrators) often tailor the material we access on interactive media to conform to our particular tastes and opinions, cutting ourselves off from a range of views and opinions (Smith, 2018). As we discussed in Chapter 7, some communication scholars say that the echo chamber is a bit overstated, that if one only consumes news from social media, one is likely to encounter those with similar ideas, but in a complex, multimedia environment—which is the way people live now because of the Internet—you instead find people consuming a lot of different media.

Journal Prompt 14.1: Professional Communication Skills
What are three reasons to learn more about interactive media?

What Are Interactive Media?

14.2 Define *interactive media*.

We define *interactive media* as a collection of mediated communication technologies that are digital and converging and tend to be mobile, all accessed on a variety of devices, from desktop and laptop computers, smartphones, tablets, and other mobile devices. Let's unpack this definition a little further and distinguish interactive media from mass media—the topic covered in Chapter 13. In contrast to in-person communication, both mass media and interactive media are mediated forms of communication, meaning that the messages are carried through an *intervening* system of **digital** electronic storage before being transmitted between two or more people.

In contrast to mass media, in which messages are generally one-to-many, interactive media messages converge, meaning that they can be sent one to one, one to many, or many to many. Also in contrast to mass media, they are interactive, meaning that communication goes both ways and permits individuals to connect and interact with others. So what are examples of interactive media? There are many, but the easiest description is: Interactive media include social media, online games [e.g., **massively multiplayer role-playing online games (MMORPGs)**], messaging apps, remote learning platforms, virtual reality, and email.

Social media is "a group of Internet-based, web applications that allow the creation and exchange of user-generated content" (Kaplan & Haenlein, 2010, p. 61). For our purposes, social media include social networking sites (SNS), like Facebook, Twitter, and LinkedIn; media sharing networks, like Instagram, Pinterest, and YouTube; social blogging networks, like Tumblr; discussions, like Reddit and Quora; and review networks, like Yelp and TripAdvisor. These categories are not set in stone. Twitter, for example, is an SNS but is also categorized as a microblog. Snapchat is a messaging app but functions like a social media platform. Remember, in addition to social media, interactive media also include mobile messaging and email.

One of the characteristics of interactive media is new versions are always emerging. It is a dynamic form of communication, and increasingly mobile. Distinctions between mass and interactive media are becoming more and more blurred. For example, some mass media forms like television reality shows viewed on mobile devices incorporate audience reaction and participation. And some media, like podcasts, may not allow interaction, functioning in a way that is similar to traditional mass media. For the purposes of this chapter, we focus on the *interactive* elements of media, where the "real give and take of social life" in cyberspace occurs (Walther & Parks, 2002, p. 3).

How do this mobility and this constant connection with others and information sources through interactive media affect our communication choices and uses? Before addressing this question, we need to understand how various communication technologies differ from each other and from in-person communication—the topic we turn to next.

How Does Interactive Media Use Affect Our Communication Choices?

14.3 Describe the dimensions of interactive media and how these dimensions help us understand and choose among various media.

Because interactive media are rapidly changing forms of communication, it is difficult to arrive at definitive conclusions about their exact role in everyday life. Researching these forms of communication can be like trying to hit a moving target. Still, with a basic

---

digital
Information that is transmitted in a numerical format based on only two values (0 and 1).

massively multiplayer role-playing online games (MMORPGs)
Text-based "virtual reality" games in which participants interact with enrichments, objects, and other participants.

social media
Group of Internet-based applications that allow the creation and exchange of user-generated content.

Journal Prompt 14.2: Defining Interactive Media
What is the definition of interactive media?

understanding of what interactive media are and some of the ways they can differ, we can get some sense of their increasingly important role.

To begin, let's consider Charee's constant connectivity and her reaction to the various interactive media. Why do online classes and remote work frustrate her to some degree? Why is she happy to consult her cooking video and order her groceries online? Like Charee, perhaps you find yourself happy to engage with certain interactive media and not others. Or perhaps you have had an issue to discuss with a friend or acquaintance and were unsure what the most effective mode of communication would be. If so, you had good reason to feel unsure. Interactive media differ in important ways, and these differences can affect your response, the outcome of your interaction, and even your sense of well-being and happiness. One way to understand these reactions and choices is to examine the characteristics of various media and how they vary along two dimensions.

Media Characteristics

There are two characteristics that can differentiate various interactive media. First, some forms of communication technologies lack the capability to carry nonverbal cues. As we discussed in Chapter 5, nonverbal cues play an important role in understanding the totality of a person's message. When we speak in person to someone, we see the other person's gestures, facial expressions, and attire, we hear their sighs, accent, or dialect; these are just a few of the many cues we use to fully understand what a person means. Some interactive media, however—like mobile messages and tweets—eliminate those cues that help us to determine what is being communicated.

Second, some interactive media are asynchronous in nature, which means a delay may occur between the time the message is sent and when it is responded to. Other interactive media, like videoconferencing, are synchronous and afford immediate feedback. It seems that people increasingly prefer asynchronous messages in some interpersonal contexts, and phone calls are sometimes considered intrusive. Experts suggest that this is because we can be reached anywhere, at possibly a very inconvenient time (having a romantic dinner, in the middle of class, at a dentist appointment). One way to draw some boundaries around our "constant connectivity" is to schedule a voice or video call through an asynchronous mobile message (Paul, 2015).

Three theories can help us understand the range and impact of these characteristics in various interactive media: media richness theory, media synchronicity theory, and uses and gratification. **Media richness theory** describes the potential information-carrying capacity of a communication medium (Daft & Lengel, 1984, 1986; Ishii et al., 2019). According to this theory, in-person communication is the richest medium for communicating because you can see facial expressions and body gestures as well as hear the tone, speed, and quality of a person's voice. All these factors relay a tremendous amount of information and allow for **social presence**, the feelings of psychological closeness or immediacy that people experience when they interact with each other (Short et al., 1976). This richness and social presence allow you to interpret and respond to messages more accurately. You not only hear the words or the content of the message, but you also receive the relational messages that are being sent nonverbally and that reveal how that person feels about you. If the other person is smiling, leaning toward you, and maintaining eye contact, you probably infer that the person is happy or glad to talk with you. If the person is scowling and avoiding eye contact, you might infer that they are angry or unhappy with you. Some experts think we need to return to the richer communication of in-person conversation (see *Alternative View: Reclaiming Conversation*).

media richness theory
Theory that describes the potential information-carrying capacity of a communication medium.

social presence
Degree of psychological closeness or immediacy engendered by various media.

ALTERNATIVE VIEW
Reclaiming Conversation

Do you think that pervasive connectivity makes us less connected to other people and less competent at conversation? Why or why not?

Sherry Turkle, a pioneer in studying communication technologies and digital life, challenges us to reexamine our assumptions about technology being the answer to relational intimacy. She thinks that although we are constantly communicating with each other—*tethered* to our technology—we sometimes choose technologies that merely substitute for human intimacy and, ultimately, technology is taking us "places we don't want to go." In an early TED (Technology Entertainment Design) talk, Turkle describes the creation of furry stuffed animal–like social robots designed to comfort lonely older people. Dr. Turkle thinks this is proof that we're abdicating our human responsibility and what makes us human: the ability to connect with and care for others in intimate ways. We substitute technology for intimacy.

In her book based on extensive interviews with individuals in homes, schools, and workplaces, Turkle argues that we are constantly coming to a better understanding of where our technology can and cannot take us and that now is the time to reclaim conversation. According to Turkle, in our technological universe, we have sacrificed conversation for mere connection.

She describes a typical dinner table scene where parents occasionally look up from their phones to answer children's questions or social outings with our friends where we have become skillful at talking with each other in between text messages and emails. At work, "we retreat to our screens although it is conversation at the water cooler that increases not only productivity but commitment to work."

She suggests that we stop running from conversation and strive to reestablish intimate and authentic connections with others. She advises that the place to begin is with some "necessary conversations of solitude and self-reflection" to help us stop relying on others to give us a sense of who we are and then to reclaim the joys and benefits of in-person conversations, such as empathy, friendship, love, and even increased professional productivity and commitment. She extols the virtues of in-person conversations as timeless and says that "our most basic technology, talk, responds to our modern challenges. We have everything we need to start, we have each other."

SOURCES: Turkle, S. (2015). *Reclaiming conversation: The power of talk in a digital age.* Penguin Books.

Turkle, S. (2012, February). *TED talk: Connected, but alone?* http://www.ted .com/talks/sherry_turkle_alone_together#t-755215.

▼ Some experts think that pervasive digital connectivity actually makes us less connected to other people and less competent at conversation.

According to media richness theory, some types of mediated communication (videoconferencing, Zoom, Skype) do allow for a certain amount of richness and social presence. However, as we pointed out in Chapter 6, when we communicate via these interactive media, we are not receiving *all* the information we can acquire when we talk in person. Although we do catch some nonverbal cues, we rarely see all of the person and have to rely solely on facial cues. Thus, we rarely see the other in motion, missing immediate context cues, such as body posture or gestures. A voice phone call is a less rich medium, revealing some paralinguistic cues (for example, tone of voice) but no facial expression, eye gaze, or gestures.

The least-rich media that is also low in social presence (according to media richness theory) are text-based messages—email, messaging, and tweets. But nonverbal cues aren't completely absent here, either. Some relational/nonverbal information *can* be communicated in these text-based media; messages can be made "richer" by emoji, bitmoji, Facebook's recently added "care" button, gifs, altering the font color, using particular punctuation, or emphasizing or repeating certain words (Moffitt et al., 2020).

Media synchronicity theory (MST) extends media richness theory, adding context and feedback to the understanding of media choice. That is, MST says it is not just the degree of richness that determines the choice of a particular medium but whether the context calls for immediate feedback—for synchronous or asynchronous communication (Dennis & Valacich, 1999). In-person communication and media, like the telephone/FaceTime and Zoom, are **synchronous**; that is, messages are sent and received at the same time, and feedback is immediate. However, interactive media like blogs, Facebook, or Instagram posts are **asynchronous**; that is, messages may be read by the receiver at a later, more convenient time with no immediate feedback. The distinction between synchronous and asynchronous messages can be blurred. Mobile messaging may be synchronous or not, depending on how quickly the other person acknowledges or responds to the message. In some instances, one can choose to make a media interaction asynchronous (e.g., sending phone calls directly to voicemail, saving Snapchats).

Researchers using MST theory point out that context is very important in media choice. Some contexts may call for immediate feedback, and synchronous communication would be the best choice. In other contexts, delayed feedback may be more effective. For example, highly emotional messages may be more effective in asynchronous media, giving the receiver time to reflect and construct a response. Online class discussion on race relations seems to be more productive on discussion boards than on Zoom. The same seems to be true for virtual group work (Robert et al., 2018). In discussion boards, shy participants can't see the nonverbal responses of others and thus may be encouraged to participate more often. Also, asynchronous messages often work better for non-native speakers as they have time to craft their message, perhaps consulting a dictionary or rechecking their grammar and spelling.

A final theory that helps us understand interactive media use is **uses and gratifications**, which was introduced in Chapter 13 and helps explain why people select certain types of media over others. The underlying assumption is that individuals choose media that meet their goals; individuals are aware of their needs, and media allows for those needs to be fulfilled. For example, uses and gratifications has been used to explain why some fans engage with eSports over traditional sports. Watching eSports on a laptop is more interactive and engaging than watching traditional sports on TV, and having a second screen or device for viewing eSports on social media enhances the experience (Brown et al., 2018). Also, the uses and gratifications framework is used to explain how families use different types of social media in maintaining long-distance relationships. One study showed that chat/messaging tools were helpful for resolving conflict and that video calls were better at creating "ambient co-presence" (social presence) since they were able to go about daily activities while having other family members in the virtual background. In addition, Facebook and Instagram allowed for distant family members to interact with posts asynchronously when immediate feedback wasn't necessary (Abel et al., 2020).

These frameworks/theories can be useful in at least three ways: First, they show the tremendous number and variation of communication opportunities we have in our everyday lives. Second, they can help us understand our own responses and reactions to various interactive media, why we prefer some and not others, or why we prefer some in certain contexts and not others. Third, they can be used to help us think through and guide our communication choices—in terms of how to present ourselves to others and how much social presence or media richness we desire in particular contexts. Individuals make many different choices every day. Consider Charee's reaction and choices in the opening vignette. In talking with her grandmother she chose FaceTime, knowing that social presence/media richness was necessary for that interaction. By contrast, when contacting her professor she assumed that social presence and synchronicity were not

media synchronicity theory (MST)
The ability of media to support synchronicity, a shared pattern of coordinated behavior among individuals.

synchronous
Communication in which messages are sent and received at the same time.

asynchronous
Communication in which messages are sent and received at different times.

uses and gratifications
The idea that people use media messages and find various types of gratifications in some media texts rather than in others.

Critical Thinking Prompt
Think of a recent conflict you had and describe how it might have been different if the communication media had been different. How might the conflict have been handled on Zoom? In person? Via mobile messaging?

---

required, so emailing would be a fine choice. A person may choose to switch media in the same conversation, depending on the topic. Our student Rosemary started getting into an argument with a friend on Instagram and then switched to private messaging to continue the discussion. Sometimes the authors of this textbook will start a discussion via text message and then switch to phone or Zoom to be more efficient when immediate feedback is needed.

In addition to considering the content and context of a particular message, it is also helpful to consider carefully the other communicator. For example, how do you interpret a lean, asynchronous message (e.g., direct message) that isn't responded to? Or a cryptic message from a friend after you send a message that you're feeling bad and you assume she knows you want some in-person time? How do you communicate to a romantic partner that you don't want to be in the relationship anymore? Or that you don't want so much "together time"? Perhaps the tried-and-true rhetorical guideline of "know your audience" is useful here. For example, Youngju knows that one of her friends is always on Instagram and that it's the best way to contact her and she'll respond quickly there; another friend is a single mom, is rarely on Instagram or TikTok, but responds quickly to text messages. Youngju has another friend who just doesn't respond very quickly to any messages. It can be several days before she responds to one of Youngju's messages. Knowing her audience helps her make decisions about interpreting and sending interactive media messages.

Another complicating issue of some interactive media is that your communication can potentially be seen and received by many different audiences. With in-person encounters, you know to whom you are addressing your message. When Charee is talking to her mother or grandmother in person or on FaceTime, she tailors her messages specifically to them (and may use different communication styles and word choices than she would use with her close friends). However, when she posts on Instagram or TikTok or sends a tweet or a snap, these messages can potentially be seen by many (even the snaps and chats), and she can't easily adapt her message to all these potential audiences. Scholar danah boyd (2014) describes this phenomenon as "**collapsing contexts**"—meaning we don't always know exactly to whom we are speaking (what the communication context is) when we send a message on social media, and this leads to another characteristic of social media—"**spreadability**," which is the ease with which content can be spread. That is, our messages can be reposted, shared, retweeted, and quickly seen by hundreds of people, complicating our communication choices even more! Some people create different social media accounts, one with their real name that is more public and professional and another with a name that only close friends can see, or use multiple social media platforms for various "imagined audiences." Our communication choices today are clearly challenging. We'll discuss further the topic of these communication choices in the next section on identity.

Although experts mostly agree on these characteristics of various media, they do not always agree on the specific impacts these characteristics have on our communication choices and relationships. Some experts point to the positive and some point to the negative aspects. Some experts suggest that the digital future is only bright—bringing more connectivity, maximizing human potential, more civic engagement, democracy, and equality. Others point to the downside, and researchers even identify two types of digital stressors encountered by young people: (1) common forms of relational hostility online (e.g., mean personal attacks, public shaming and humiliation, impersonating someone else in order to harass them), which we will discuss in the following sections and (2) stressful challenges in forming and maintaining intimacy (feeling smothered, pressure to provide access to accounts or nude photos, and breaking and entering into digital accounts and devices) (Weinstein & Selman, 2016).

However, seeing interactive media and technology in general as all good or all evil for human interaction is too simplistic. What is clear is that they play an important role in our lives and that people use multiple media in addition to in-person interactions to

collapsing contexts
In social media, not knowing exactly who is reading one's posts.

spreadability
The ease with which content can be spread on social media.

fit their social needs and lifestyles. It seems more useful to view these media through a dialectical lens. As we described in Chapters 8 (Communication across Cultures) and 9 (Communicating in Close Relationships), a dialectical perspective emphasizes simultaneous contradictory truths, recognizing that things may be "both/and"—both good and bad, strong and weak—and that we each have to navigate this media landscape, making the best choices we can. This complexity of choice should not be a surprise, considering the pace of technology development and how much we still must learn about interactive media capacities. With these thoughts in mind, let's look at a related topic—how personal identity is performed and managed in interactive media use.

Journal Prompt 14.3:
Interactive Communication
What are key differences among various interactive media and in-person communication? What is the dialectical perspective on the benefits and challenges of interactive media?

Interactive Media and the Individual

14.4 Describe issues that can arise in identity and relationship development when using interactive media.

Clearly, interactive media use presents us with a range of choices, and those choices can have a powerful impact on communication between individuals in terms of identity, and in turn, personal relationships. Let's examine the way this works.

Managing Identity

The range of communication choices in interactive media has profound implications for how we manage our identity online. Social media provides many opportunities to be seen and admired and to self-disclose. At the same time, some media (Twitter, Internet forums) allow us to control the amount of information we disclose about ourselves. All these options provide a fluidity to our identities that we don't have with in-person communication. As we noted in Chapter 2, one's identity or self-concept is developed and expressed through communication with others. How do you present yourself and manage impressions that others have of you on various interactive media sites, given the characteristics and range of possibilities discussed in the previous section?

Self-Presentation Online   In using interactive media, you often make decisions about what kind of information to reveal about yourself. There seem to be three (overlapping) types of information that can be disclosed:

1. Standard information (for example, name, gender, profile picture);
2. Sensitive personal information—details that could be used to locate/identify or to threaten or harm (for example, email address, birthday, birth year, employer, job position, profile picture, photo albums);
3. Potentially stigmatizing information—information that could result in stigmatization within society (for example, religious views, political views, birth year, sexual orientation, photos).

Some important questions in deciding how much and what type of information to disclose: Who are your intended/"imagined" audiences? Which interactive media do you use as a professional platform, almost like a résumé, where potential employers can read about (or view) your academic achievements and work experiences? Which media do you use as a place to hang out with good friends and discuss the latest partying activities? Is there overlap in the information you provide in various media?

For young people working out issues around their sexual identity or sexual practices, participation in interactive media can be tricky. On the one hand, it can provide communities of support where they can develop identities consistent with their desires. For example, Jen, a 21-year-old Midwest transgender woman with a disapproving parent, appreciated the hundreds of transgender-themed websites, blogs, and TikTok videos where she could follow other transgender individuals talking about their transitions and their daily lives. She created an Instagram page with her evolving female identity and found spaces to vent and relax that were safer than the places she went in public with her support group, where people would gawk and make hateful comments (Cavalcante, 2016). On the other hand, for LGBTQIA+ individuals, interactive media, especially given collapsing contexts, exposes them to potential discrimination or reactions from people they may not want to see certain aspects of their identity development (Dhoest & Szulc, 2016).

Perhaps one of the biggest challenges in how to present yourself and manage your online identity is that you don't know exactly who might be listening or reading. It's easier on some social media than others. Relatively speaking, your Instagram and Snapchat audiences are more known to you than your TikTok audience, so you're probably more careful about your self-disclosure and self-presentation there than other media.

Sometimes young people have their intended self-presentation sabotaged by others—when friends tag them in photos or post photos of them engaging in activities they'd rather not have others see. Or they have been embarrassed (often intentionally) by their parents—who post inappropriate photos and/or comments (Hindman, 2016). Another consequential audience is the **lurkers**, people who see and read social media material posted on SNSs but don't comment. Most lurkers are harmless, but underage users should remember that accepting "followers" they don't know could result in their photos and videos ending up on pedophile websites.

lurkers
People who read, observe, but do not actively participate in online communities/sites.

Some decisions about what to reveal on social media may be related to a person's age; some research shows that older people tend to disclose more information than some younger people. Some say members of the Millennial generation seem less inclined to make their lives an open book, are more selective in what they post, and opt for less public sharing. Oversharing can also have negative professional impacts; as we noted in Chapter 1, potential employers and college admissions officers can access your (and your friends') profile information, and many employers and admission committees admit to dismissing a candidate from consideration because of what they found on social networking sites (e.g., profanity, illegal/questionable behavior).

How do you make decisions about what to disclose? In addition to considering your "imagined audience," you might think about the impact of the information of others. Disclosing information on social media is also related to other factors. For example, perhaps not surprisingly, people with low self-esteem, who are lonely or stressed, who feel they need to connect constantly with others, or who lack the ability to identify their audience tend to reveal more information about themselves (Lusinski, 2020; Zhang & Fu, 2020). These factors do not necessarily pertain to professional social media influencers, whose livelihood involves sharing huge amounts of personal information.

There is some suggestion that currently people are oversharing less and are perhaps more cautious about having a permanent record of everything they've shared. According to some social media experts, while the impulse to share may not have gone away, people are now more aware of its consequence, and social media companies provide features that allow more intimate sharing, like Instagram's "Close Friends" feature, which allows users to choose who gets to view their content; Apple's "shared album" feature, which allows users to post photos privately; or "finsta," a separate, fake Instagram account that is entirely private (Meyerson, 2020).

Critical Thinking Prompt
How many personal details do you think people should disclose on social media pages? Is there any information that you think should be routinely disclosed? Never disclosed? How much do you disclose? Why?

Anonymity and Psuedoanonymity When you communicate via some interactive media, others may not know your age, gender, race, nationality, or many of the other cues that affect perceptions of individuals. However, it seems that there is increasingly less opportunity for anonymity online as more and more of our lives and information about our "real" selves is posted, persistent, and available for searching. The old adage of "There are no erasers on the Internet" is still very true. Getting rid of information once it's out on the Internet can be difficult, if not impossible. The degree to which people should be able to remain anonymous online has been vigorously debated. When Facebook instituted a "real name policy" in 2014, saying that real names allow people to better connect to their offline friends, there was vigorous opposition from various groups including the ACLU of California, Human Rights Watch, and others. For example, drag queens, locked out of their Facebook accounts for using "fake" names, protested that forcing them and other "gender nonnormative people" to use their legal names was discriminatory. Likewise, victims of abuse, stalking, or bullying use aliases to hide from perpetrators (MacAulay & Moldes, 2016). In response, Facebook relaxed its policy in 2015 (Holpuch, 2015).

There are at least three issues in the complex relationship between anonymity and identity in online communication. The first has to do with the informative aspect of the identity. On the one hand, knowing something about the person sending information gives a context for judging their messages. If you know, for example, that the person answering your medical question online is a doctor, that person seems more credible than a person who does not have a medical degree. On the other hand, because information on age, gender, and race can form the basis for stereotyping and prejudice, some anonymity presents the possibility of interactions somewhat free of prejudice.

A second issue regarding anonymity is its capacity to liberate speech. For example, without knowing who has issued a statement, the legal restrictions on speech are difficult to enforce. So, if someone is misrepresenting oneself online and makes racist or libelous statements, it is almost impossible to implement legal sanctions. On the other hand, anonymity can give people courage to express unpopular opinions or question conventional wisdom, which they might be afraid to do in offline interactions (e.g., 4Chan) (van der Nagel & Frith, 2015). Some young people find anonymity gives a sense of freedom that they don't have on social media where parents or other authority figures are always watching, or even on sites or online games where they construct a pseudo identity.

The third and final issue related to anonymity is that in some ways, the freedom that people feel as a result of their anonymity may lead them to be less responsible communicators. Several of these irresponsible behaviors (there are many more) are discussed in the following paragraphs: trolling, phishing, cyberbullying, doxing, canceling and deceptive messages.

Trolling　Anonymity can lead to irresponsible and destructive online behavior, like **trolling** (Navarro-Carillo et al., 2021). Recent examples include how male online players denigrate, harass, and drive off female would-be gamers and how anti-Chinese racism is expressed in hostile in-game interactions and in YouTube rants (Cisneros & Nakayama, 2015; Nakayama, 2017).

trolling
Posting Internet messages meant to intentionally anger or frustrate in order to provoke reactions from others.

Phishing　The practice of trying fraudulently to get consumer banking/credit card or other personal information, such as usernames, passwords, and Social Security numbers, known as **phishing**, is another problem for interactive media users. This leads to a good reason to be careful about how much personal information to disclose on social media; spammers have used freely accessible profile data from SNSs to craft phishing schemes that appear to originate from a friend on the network. Targets are much more likely to give away information to this "friend" than to a perceived "stranger." Phishing messages can also lead to ransomware attacks in which hackers deny access to computer systems or sensitive data until ransom is paid, via prepaid cash service, money transfers, or gift cards.

phishing
The practice of trying fraudulently to get consumer banking and credit card information.

Cyberbullying　Another form of bad behavior online is **cyberbullying**, introduced in Chapter 11 and defined as "repetitive and aggressive behavior transmitted through mediated channels aimed at directing malice toward a victim with a to-harm goal" (Palomares & Wingate, 2020). Cyberbullying differs from traditional bullying partly because it can be anonymous, it can occur anywhere (through voice, text, picture, or video messages on cell phones and through social networking sites, blogs, and so on), and an infinite number of viewers can observe or participate. Research shows that cyberbullying can have many negative consequences for victims, ranging from psychological problems such as depression, anxiety, and low self-esteem to disastrous consequences, including victims committing suicide. Some experts report that approximately 25 percent of minors are victims of cyberbullying and about 15 percent

cyberbullying
The deliberate and repeated misuse of communication technology by an individual or group to threaten or harm others.

admit that they cyberbullied others, leading many schools to implement cyberbullying prevention programs. Communities are also beginning to seriously enforce anti-cyberbullying laws (Ferman, 2014; Patchin, 2014). LGBTQIA+ students are often the targets of bullies, and some experts suggest that bullying is not always just aggressive behavior but often reflects the socially accepted norm of marginalizing those outside the norm. They propose rethinking intervention programs to include challenges to the culturally accepted and perpetuated inequities regarding gender, racial, ethnic, and sexual identities (Payne & Smith, 2013).

doxing

Searching for and publishing the personal information of a private individual.

Doxing, a heightened form of cyberbully, is the practice of searching for and publishing the personal information of a private individual. Doxxers use these attacks to threaten or intimidate their targets. For example, Kyle Quinn, a biomedical engineer at the University of Arkansas, was identified by overzealous civil rights activists as taking part in a neo-Nazi rally. These activists doxed him (made public his home address and phone number). However, it was simply a case of mistaken identity—he only resembled one of the neo-Nazi marchers. "Once doxxers got involved, his life, that of his family, friends, and colleagues became hell" (Cooper, 2020).

canceling

Withdrawing support, often for public figures and companies, after they have done or said something considered objectionable or offensive.

Canceling "Canceling" is another hostile behavior on interactive media and is usually a reaction to things said or done—by a well-known person or organization/company. It begins when someone (sometimes activists) describe the "bad" behavior and suddenly everyone goes after the person or organization by posting nasty, hateful messages on its social media page. Sometimes there's a boycott, depending on the target. For example, author J. K. Rowling got "canceled" for a tweet that was seen as transphobic (Camero, 2020). But it is more commonly used now to shun anyone and anything that does or represents something offensive to particular people, cultures, or ideologies.

Deception The final form of bad online behavior related to anonymity is deception. If you have represented yourself as something you are not on a social media profile, you are not alone. Many people say they put false information on their social networking sites and they give many reasons for doing so. In some cases, it's a strategy for projecting a more positive image (e.g., lying about one's salary, weight, achievements), or for some, it's about achieving privacy because they become more and more aware of the consequences of having their posted information taken out of context. Fabricating data on these sites may protect from unwanted advances from strangers, but for young people, it can also fake out their parents (boyd, 2014) or be a strategy for finding out what "friends" think of them by starting an online conversation about oneself using a false identity.

However, some children lie about their age to create social media accounts and engage in other risky online behaviors, leaving them open to fraud and predators (Notten & Nikken, 2016), although some experts think the media focus on online risks to children is misplaced. They say that children and teens who engage in risky behavior online are often struggling offline (with unsafe home environments, addicted parents, etc.) and that in fact technology can often help keep children safe (boyd, 2014).

▲ Players of MMORPGs invent new identities by creating avatars.

Beyond anonymity is the phenomenon of **pseudoanonymity**, or projecting a "false" identity. For example, people can invent identities through acceptable means in online discussion sites (e.g., Reddit) where users create a screen name that follows them across the site or on virtual worlds where they create **avatars**. These sites afford people the opportunity to construct alternate identities, different from those in their offline world of school and work. There are rarely negative consequences because this "deception" is expected.

To summarize, interactive media technologies afford many possibilities for performing and managing identities, but these possibilities should be balanced with consideration of safety and ethical concerns as well as impression management concerns. Let's now turn our attention to how relationships develop and are maintained through interactive media.

Relationship Development

You probably have a few relationships that exist only online, such as with acquaintances you met in an online course or on social media, although it appears most people's relationships now exist both in person and virtually. Let's consider the impact of interactive media on three types of relationships: friendships, romantic relationships, and relationships in the workplace.

Friendships   Although online and offline relationships have much in common, interactive media can affect our relational development in at least a couple significant ways. First, you can encounter many more people online than you ever would in person, so online relationships may offer many more potential partners than offline life.

Second, through interactive media, relational interaction overcomes limits of time and space. If you have to relocate to a faraway place, the relationship may not be affected. You do not have to (ever) be in close proximity to these people and you do not (ever) have to exchange messages at the same time, and you can stay in close contact almost 24/7. What are the implications of these characteristics for these relationships?

There has been much debate about whether social media have overall positive or negative effects on relationships. A summary of recent research suggests that social media have a range of positive psychological outcomes, providing greater feelings of belonging and keeping up with friends and providing shy individuals with a sense of social support (Faelens et al., 2021; Zhu & Stephens, 2019). In fact, recent findings confirmed the similarity between online and offline social relationships. Research examining friendship connections (posting patterns and exchanges within Twitter, Facebook, and even online gaming platforms) indicates a similar average number of friendships online and in person and also that social connections formed in the online world are processed socio-psychologically in similar ways to those of the offline world. It appears then that, with all the pervasiveness of virtual interaction, "the basic operations of human social networks appear to remain relatively unchanged" (Firth et al., 2019, p. 125). In addition, other evidence suggests that social media use (e.g., comparing heavy and light smartphone users' offline interactions/relationships) does *not* replace or reduce intimacy of offline relationships (Verduyn et al., 2021).

However, there are two cautionary notes. First, there is the negative impact of the common tendency to make upward social comparisons in both online and in-person encounters. That is, there is a tendency to compare ourselves unfavorably with those who are "better" than we are—those perceived as having more resources, being better looking, leading more exciting lives, or being better parents. There is more opportunity to make these negative comparisons with friends or acquaintances on interactive media, and they can produce "unrealistic expectations of oneself—leading to poor body image and negative self-concept" and depression, particularly for younger people and young girls (Firth et al., 2019, p. 125).

A second downside is the potential for **problematic social media use (PSMU)**—a strong dependency on social media and, in extreme cases, excessive use, with symptoms similar to chemical and other behavioral addictions. It seems that PSMU is more often

pseudoanonymity
Projecting a false identity.

avatars
Digital alter egos or versions of oneself, used in MMORPGs.

problematic social media use (PSMU)
A strong, sometimes excessive, dependency on social media.

found in younger women, those who tend to be introverted or very lonely, and those who have low self-control (Busch & McCarthy, 2020; Kircaburun et al., 2020). In fact, some experts estimate that a substantial number of young people are at risk for PSMU and emphasize that social media companies invest heavily in behavioral engineering strategies "designed solely to maximize user time on their platforms, and perhaps even entice users to become addicted" (Tanega & Downs, 2020, p. 159).

It should be clear by now that we cannot assume that interactive media have all positive (or negative) effects on communication or relationships. Continuing our dialectical view, let's examine how interactive media can *both* weaken *and* strengthen relationships. For example, too much videoconferencing or interacting only virtually seems likely to weaken personal relationships, a result of having extended encounters that lack information richness, social presence, and synchronicity. The notion of friendship includes shared experiences, feelings, and activities. So, when you receive terrific news that you want to share with your best friend, telling them through a delayed message (if your friend does not immediately respond to your message) or not being able to hug your friend or see her jump for joy does not have the same impact that an in-person conversation would.

Interactive media can cause some relationships to become more fragile, as some people drop out because they find the pressures of social media "performance" too stressful (agonizing over how to present themselves, which photos to post, whether their photos and music picks are "cool" enough, getting depressed by constant upward comparisons, and so on). Or sometimes discussions become too politically contentious, damaging personal relationships. As one Facebook user posted after the 2016 presidential election: "The election was the last straw for me. In the days after, all I saw was hate. From both sides. . . . I decided that day to get rid of my original Facebook and create my 'new' Facebook . . . full of running, bikes, breweries, cat videos, satire, art, music, hiking, food, and good people. . . . (Selyukh, 2016). Given these pressures of social media engagement, some users find it useful to take a break from time to time, recently including some celebrities. Gwyneth Paltrow's Goop outlines how to do a "digital detox" (Meyerson, 2020).

Asynchronous mediated messages can also have positive effects, even possibly strengthening relationships. They can give people time to formulate a message, which can be helpful for shy people and others (e.g., non-native speakers). In fact, in one study, young people explained that although there were often misunderstandings, they sometimes preferred mobile messaging over other forms of communication partly because it gave them more time to reflect, process received messages, and think about how they were going to respond (Coyne et al., 2011). Now that we've discussed some aspects of the role of interactive media in friendships, let's examine the influence of interactive media in romantic relationships.

Romantic Relationships   A benefit of online romance is the same as for other virtual relationships—you can encounter many more people online than you ever would in person, so online connections may offer many more potential romantic partners than offline life. Another benefit is the ease of finding similar others and of achieving intimate exchanges, as there is already information known about the other (physical characteristics, hobbies, political and religious attitudes, etc.) prior to meeting. Online dating apps serve an important function during the pandemic, as many in-person encounters are restricted. (See *It Happened to Me: Jacqueline*). Dating experts advise that developing romantic relationships remotely or with social distancing may require special considerations.

It Happened to Me
Jacqueline

My friends recently convinced me to join Bumble because I've been single for a while and I've been getting tired of Tinder since it's used primarily for hookups. I've been talking with a match on Bumble for a few days and recently started following him on Instagram because he is also into food and trying new recipes like I am, so I like seeing his posts. We have been exchanging messages for a while now and seem to have a good connection, but I'm not sure how to take it to the next level and meet in person. I wish it were easier to meet people out in the world because all of the back-and-forth messaging gets to be exhausting!

(See *Did You Know?: Online Dating in a Pandemic*.)

According to one survey, about 30 percent of U.S. American adults have used a dating site or app, and these sites/apps are especially popular among lesbian, gay, and bisexual (LGB) individuals, who are twice as likely to use apps than heterosexual individuals (Anderson, 2020b). Many online dating apps feature a scientific approach, which often includes compatibility and personality testing and seems to cover all ages and income levels (e.g., Match, OkCupid, eHarmony, Coffee Meets Bagel, and Bumble). Some focus more on hookups than dating per se (e.g., Tinder) or specialize in niche marketing focusing on religion (Jewish, Catholic, Christian), race/ethnicity (interracial, Black, Latino), or age (OurTime for singles older than 50). Others use matching activities, such as music (Tastebuds) or social gaming (Tagged), or physical location (Tinder, Happn).

▲ During the pandemic, Zoom socializing became more common.

Some dating apps present challenges for lesbian, bisexual, trans, and gender-fluid women, who want to communicate their preferences for partners but may not want to share these preferences with all social media audiences. For example, some lesbian, bisexual, trans, and gender-fluid women are hesitant to use Tinder because Tinder is owned by Facebook, and so these women are required to register for Tinder through Facebook. Facebook also owns other social media platforms (e.g., Instagram and Spotify), which means that these women's information posted on Tinder (and thus Facebook) is potentially accessible to audiences beyond Tinder. In one study, lesbian, bisexual, trans, and gender-fluid women were interviewed and reported to researchers that Tinder's connection to other social media (e.g., Instagram and Spotify) makes it difficult for them to use Tinder in certain ways. For example,

DID YOU KNOW?
Online Dating in a Pandemic

Online dating sites/apps serve an important function during the pandemic, as many in-person encounters are restricted. Dating experts provide the following advice for those considering (or involved in) online dating now:

- Be more selective; the stakes may be higher, as health risks may be involved at some point, so don't waste time on those you know are not potential partners. In some ways the pandemic and social distancing may be beneficial in forcing you to focus on what you really want in a partner.
- Invest in enough remote meetings prior to in-person meetings. Remote conversations can be informative—without the distractions of a bar/restaurant setting.
- Ask key questions early (don't wait until you have already invested too much effort before asking important questions)

and don't be afraid to ask about priorities in life, relationships, career, and so on, as well as dating and sexual history.
- When setting up an in-person meeting, agree on health precautions for meeting (facial coverings or not? social distancing? virus/testing history?).
- As in any initial in-person romantic encounter, consider personal safety; meet in a public place and tell a friend where you'll be meeting.

SOURCE: Lee, B. Y. (2020, August 23). 12 pandemic dating tips, how to do romance with the Covid-19 Coronavirus. *forbes.com*. https://www.forbes.com/sites/brucelee/2020/08/23/12-pandemic-dating-tips-how-to-do-romance-with-the-covid-19-coronavirus/#2f961f342b37

in order to protect their privacy, they may prefer to use to use a fake identity on Tinder, which creates problems with their true identity on Facebook. According to these women, the potential wider accessibility to their personal details has resulted in frequent (unwanted) encounters with cisgender-presenting men, predatory accounts, couples, and heterosexual women. The researchers conclude that there is an enduring need for LGBTQIA+-specific digital dating spaces (Ferris & Duguay, 2020).

General challenges when searching for romance online include deception and potential harassment. Online daters report that they usually assume some deception and learn to "correct" for it: "One woman mentioned that if a profile said a man was 5'11" she would assume he was probably 5'9"; a man said that if a woman said she was 'average' body type, he would assume she was slightly heavy" (Heino et al., 2010). More serious deception is the practice of **catfishing** (introduced in Chapter 2)—creating an intentionally deceptive social media profile, sometimes even including fake photos, bios, friends, and so on, often with the goal of making a romantic connection (D'Costa, 2014). More sinister are criminal motives; people have been swindled out of money by someone posing as a potential suitor and then asking for money after gaining the trust and interest of a dating partner. Dating sites or apps can also be a place for harassment and problematic behavior, especially for young women. More than 50 percent of women using these sites report being sent unwanted sexually explicit messages or images (Anderson et al., 2020b). There have also been accusations that these sites reflect and sometimes encourage racism by including filters that allow users to categorically reject potential partners from specific ethnic (or racial or gender) groups and profiles that state "no Asians" or "I'm not attracted Asians" (Stokel-Walker, 2019). Dating apps like Grindr, Tinder, and Bumble are grappling with how to reduce racism and some have considered removing the ethnicity filters.

In spite of the challenges, online romance is common, and many close, lasting relationships are initiated online. Many of the same things that make offline romantic relationships work, discussed in Chapter 9, are important in online relationships, like intimacy, trust, and communication satisfaction. In fact, it appears that interactive media and constant connectivity *can* strengthen romantic relationships. Although not replacing in-person expressions of affection, a quick mobile message to say "I luv u" or a phone call while doing routine errands enables couples to continue expressing affection throughout the day; couples in long-distance relationships or during temporary separations can stay in touch with FaceTime, Zoom, or other videoconferencing tools.

However, there are also downsides to the constant connectivity of new media in maintaining romantic relationships. Experts have found that using some social media is associated with increased jealousy in romantic relationships and relational dissatisfaction. For example, one young woman describes how her boyfriend reads all her messages when she's not looking. Similarly, the connectedness of mobile messaging can be seen as stifling or even as harassing if one partner insists on constant communication: "So my boyfriend is constantly txting me every minute of everyday . . . he's becoming really clingy with it. what should i do???" (Weinstein & Selman, 2016). And some individuals (more than 40 percent of respondents in one study!) complain that their partners are too distracted by cell phones. Others argue about the amount of time their partners spend on particular online activities (Lenhart & Duggan, 2014).

Terminating romantic relationships, given all the communication choices, can be particularly challenging, and many young people admit to breaking up with someone over text message or being dumped with a text message (Howard & Steber, 2020). Breaking up can produce anxiety, and one can never totally anticipate how the other person will react, so it may be understandable why someone would choose to avoid all the drama and just send a message. Some social media experts suggest that this avoidance is not surprising because pervasive connectivity can make us less connected to other people and less capable of in-person conversation (see *Alternative View: Reclaiming Conversation*).

After a breakup, it's much more difficult to digitally disconnect from a former partner. This is probably why around 2014, clauses called "social media clauses" began appearing

catfishing
Creating an intentionally deceptive social media profile.

in prenuptial agreements, protecting exes from potentially embarrassing aftermaths with belated releases of demeaning photographic or textual data (Rothenburg, 2014).

Work Relationships   Most workers report that communication technologies have improved their ability to do their job, share ideas with coworkers, and work in a flexible way. For example, one software company has seventeen employees at three locations: Phoenix, Arizona; Cape Cod, Massachusetts; and Philadelphia, Pennsylvania. All their documents are in cloud storage; they communicate regularly using Teams software. They have monthly videoconference meetings and meet in person from time to time. These interactive technologies mean that none of the employees had to relocate when they were hired, and through media technologies, they stay connected and productive. Although interactive technologies generally have positive effects on work relationships, some concerns exist. As we discussed in Chapter 11, many workers think that these technologies result in longer hours and increased stress levels—depending, in part, on employees' perception of the utility of "digital work interruptions" (Morris, 2017). The impact of technology on work varies, however, depending on the type of relationship— whether it is a superior–subordinate relationship or a peer relationship.

Superior–Subordinate Communication   Given the striking increase in remote working and virtual communication in most work situations, it is interesting that some employees, especially Gen Zers, generally want to have more in-person communication with their supervisors (and other workers) (Schawbel, 2017). In one study, employees described in-person communication as being higher quality than virtual communication (except in some specific situations where asynchronous messaging was better suited), and the frequency of in-person interaction with superiors was strongly connected with employee job satisfaction (Braun et al., 2019).

At least three areas of concern center on interactive media in the workplace: status and boundary issues, surveillance issues, and confidentiality issues. A major impact of online communication in the workplace is its status-leveling effect. Currently, anyone can have instant digital access to superiors, and this status leveling can raise boundary issues: How much digital interaction is appropriate between boss and employees? Should you ask to friend your boss on Facebook? Should a supervisor request to friend a subordinate? Every CEO or colleague will have an opinion about this. Some CEOs like to connect with employees and colleagues on social media, as a way to build relationships outside the office, but most experts say don't. As one CEO explained, "it's not a good idea because it can blur work-personal relationships in unproductive ways. For example, personal information about employees or tagged photos can be posted by others without employees' knowledge or consent. There is just too little control over one's image on social media. So, I instruct our management team to refrain from accepting or submitting friend requests from those employees that they supervise."

Communication technologies also give superiors a way of checking up on subordinates. Technological surveillance occurs in many ways in the workplace. In fact, some "monitoring" happens prior to being hired. According to one report, more than 70 percent of employers reported that they use social networking sites to research job candidates before hiring them; nearly half (48 percent) check up on current employees on social media (Hayes, 2018). However, they must be careful about accessing certain information (e.g., any legally protected characteristics including age, disability, pregnancy, race, religion, and so on that would not otherwise be apparent in an in-person interview) as an applicant could claim that a decision not to hire was based on that characteristic (Choi, 2014).

Employee surveillance is increasingly common and sophisticated, especially in larger companies. Some employers monitor communications; employers can see photos, text messages, or emails sent by employees on company computers and phones and also monitor their social media use. In the United States, employers have the legal right to not disclose what they are tracking. "Companies are increasingly sifting through texts, Slack chats and, in some cases, recorded and transcribed phone calls on mobile devices" (Krouse, 2019). Technologies such as GPS and employee badges with radio frequency identification (RFID) tags also provide employee monitoring. These tracking systems can record, display, and archive the exact location of any employee—both inside and outside the office—at any time. These monitoring policies are somewhat controversial. Some say that keeping an eye on employees (including employees' social media use) helps companies protect themselves, as disgruntled employees can easily go on social media and criticize customers or harass subordinates, damaging a company's reputation. The data can also be used productively to measure employee productivity, management efficacy, and employee work–life balance.

Others say no, that monitoring is too often a fishing expedition that wastes important time and resources (i.e., employees, especially Millennials, are experts at controlling and manipulating their online presence) and should only be done when there is a solid reason to suspect employee wrongdoing (Kumar, 2015). Human resources experts advise that employees can be fired in some instances for their social media posts—for example, if actions violate stated company policy, divulge confidential information, or give information that proves the employee has lied to the organization. The best advice: Be aware of your company's policy and be careful not to violate it (Doyle, 2020).

Another issue concerns decisions about what should be handled in person or virtually. Just as in romantic relationships, bad news (termination, negative job performance reviews) should probably be communicated in person or, if that is impossible, in as rich a medium as possible (e.g., video).

Peer Communication   Although interactive media may make the communication between workers more efficient and effective, access to certain kinds of information often decreases when one relies only on online communication. For example, as discussed in Chapters 10 and 11, in-person work contexts provide more informal opportunities to observe colleagues in the next office, in halls, or in kitchen conversations, whereas communicating only online provides less information about colleagues, which can increase uncertainty as well as the potential for disagreements and misunderstanding, as one of our students describes in *It Happened to Me: Mei-Lin*. As we discussed in Chapter 10, to minimize these misunderstandings and build trust among personnel, some employers try to arrange periodic in-person meetings or even promote social networking communication among coworkers.

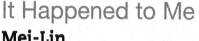

It Happened to Me
Mei-Lin

I sent an urgent Slack message to a colleague requesting information for a report I was writing. He didn't respond, and I became very irritated at his lack of response. A few days later, I found out that his child had been in a serious accident and that he had missed work for several days. If we had been located in the same office, I would have known immediately what was wrong, would have responded more appropriately to his absence, and could have gotten the information I needed in some other way.

Journal Prompt 14.4: Anonymity Concerns
What are three identity concerns that result from the anonymity afforded by some new media forms? How do these concerns relate to staying safe when using social media?

To summarize, interactive media provides opportunities and challenges for relationship development and maintenance, and each type of relationship, whether a friendship, a romance, or a work relationship, has unique challenges. When we expand the frame of reference beyond individuals, as we do in the next section, we encounter a new set of new media-related issues and challenges—those posed by societal forces.

The Individual, Interactive Media, and Society

14.5   Understand the role of power and privilege in interactive media use.

All media activities—whether for fun, socializing, or information seeking—are enacted by humans within a social context and the larger society. These activities both reflect and influence larger societal norms. For example, some of the same social hierarchies that exist in the larger society also exist in the realm of interactive media. When we sort people out by various identities (for example, gender, ethnicity, or race), we find differences not only in how many of them use communication technologies, but also in how they are perceived to use these media. In this section, we'll first look at how various identities influence technology use and then examine some of the inequalities in communication technologies use.

Gender, Age, Ethnicity, and Technology Use

Does technology use vary with gender, along traditional gender roles—with men being more action oriented and females more interpersonally oriented? The answer, it turns out, is somewhat. Males are more likely than females to play online games and to play a larger variety of games, although female players are increasing in numbers (Lopez-Fernando et al., 2019). Hacking also seems to be a predominantly male activity (Holt et al., 2019). Not surprisingly, more men than women tend to major in and pursue careers in computer science or other technology-related fields (Vitores & Gil-Juárez, 2016).

Women tend to access more social networking sites in general, and this is particularly true of Pinterest (Perrin & Anderson, 2020). Nevertheless, some of the conventional stereotypes about gender are unfounded. For example, some evidence shows males and females having equal levels of computer skills (Gebhardt et al., 2019), and it seems that both genders are equally likely to shop online and take online courses. Taken together, then, this evidence suggests that the use of communication technologies only partially reflects and reinforces gender roles and stereotypes.

It should be noted, however, that while gender inequality in uses has lessened, societal norms about what is acceptable or unacceptable online behavior vary greatly, especially when it comes to sexting and related activities. Focus group studies show that young men's sharing digital photos of their own nudity, their bodily functions or even sharing female friends' nude photos without permission are often viewed as funny, daring, even part of male bonding, and with little negative consequence. In contrast, young women engaging in the same behaviors are labeled "attention sluts" or whores and are socially shamed and humiliated (Salter, 2016).

How do other identities—such as age—interact with interactive media use? As one might expect, young people are still more comfortable with new technologies than older folks, and they tend to use communication technologies in more and different ways (Perrin & Anderson, 2019). The younger you are, the more likely you are to use a variety of social media (Snapchat, Instagram, TikTok) and messaging apps (WhatsApp) than are older people (Perrin & Anderson, 2020). However, the stereotype of older people avoiding technology is somewhat inaccurate, as the number of older people (age 50 and older) who use social media and smartphones has increased significantly in the last few years (Vogels, 2019).

Social media use also varies somewhat with race. It turns out that the Black American presence on Twitter is significant and is often focused on political activism,

▼ The number of older people who visit SNSs has increased significantly in the past few years.

feeding a loop of online and offline actions and demonstrations. For example, #Black-LivesMatter mentioned earlier in the chapter and also #OscarsSoWhite in 2015, protesting the complete lack of any person of color in four major acting categories, led to national visibility and eventually some actors boycotting the Oscar event (Anderson et al., 2020a; Wortham, 2016). Some experts suggest that Twitter is particularly conducive to the strong participative oral traditions within many Black communities—the "call and response" between minister and congregation or the "playin' the dozens," which are playful back-and-forth insults (Florini, 2014).

Concerning race and gender in online gaming—the gaming population is more diverse now because smartphones and tablets make gaming more accessible and the population of gamers worldwide includes female gamers, people of different racial and cultural backgrounds, and gamers of varying ages (Yanev, 2020). Stereotypes of ethnic, racial, and gender groups still persist; studies show that characters in video games are overwhelmingly White and male. Outside of sports video games, only a few Black characters exist, and they are mostly portrayed as sidekicks, athletes, rappers, and gangsters. Latinos and Native Americans are extremely underrepresented as video game characters, probably because game developers are overwhelmingly White and they draw from their own experiences (Peckham, 2020). Female characters are more likely to be represented by partially nude avatars of an unrealistic body type (Zarrilla, 2010).

As you can see, people use social media in different ways and not everyone is equally represented in the communication technology revolution, nor does everyone have equal access to digital life and cyberspace, which is perhaps the most important way that societal forces affect interactive media use.

Power, Access, and Digital Inequalities

It would be a mistake to think that the United States is the most technologically advanced country. For example, South Koreans did their banking by mobile phone years ago and have more mobile phones per capita than in almost any other country. Also years ago, in Singapore and other Asian cities, restaurant goers ordered their food from a tableside computer tablet menu, and tourists were provided smartphones during their stay for easy access to the Internet and for texting (prior to easy international phone calling on cell phones) (Woodhouse, 2015). On the highways in the Gauteng urban region in South Africa, overhead electronic camera tracking (e-tolling) monitors individual motorists (through e-tags on license plates) and eliminates tollbooths and related traffic slowdowns. However, in many other countries, only a tiny fraction of the population has access to computers and the Internet, and there are also many Americans who do not have access to the Internet.

digital divide
Inequity of access between the technology "haves" and "have nots."

The inequality of access between the technology "haves" and the "have nots"—once referred to as the **digital divide**—is probably more accurately viewed now as a continuum of digital inequalities rather than a divide (Wei, 2012). These inequalities exist within the United States and also on a global scale. For example, in Africa, Internet connectivity is about 40 percent, compared with about 70 percent in Latin and South America, 80 percent in East Asia, and 90 percent in Europe, Australia/New Zealand, and North America (InternetWorldStats.com, 2020). Many developing countries lack landline services, but their mobile phone usage is growing exponentially; it's estimated that 90 percent of the world's population now owns a cell phone, and many have mobile connectivity to the Internet (Silver, 2019).

The issues of who does and does not have access to digital technologies and whose culture dominates it are relevant in our current global economy. Why? Some activists and policymakers hope that new communication technologies and economic globalization (increased mobility of goods, services, labor, and capital) can lead to a more democratic and equitable world. And some evidence supports this hope. For example, outsourcing American jobs to overseas locations has provided income opportunities for many in English-speaking countries such as India. And despite some governments' attempts to limit their citizens' access to new media, the Internet provides information, world news, and possibilities for interpersonal communication that were not available previously.

Why do differences in digital access and use matter? In a global information society, information is an important commodity that everyone needs to function. In addition, to function effectively in society, people need **cultural capital** (Bourdieu, 1986), or certain bodies of cultural knowledge and cultural competencies. Those with the most power in a society decide what constitutes cultural capital, and it is passed down from parents to children, just as economic capital is.

▲ Cultural capital includes the knowledge enabling people to make use of interactive media.

cultural capital
Cultural knowledge and cultural competencies that people need to function effectively in society.

technocapital
Access to technological skills and resources.

In the United States and much of the world, cultural capital includes the ability to use communication technologies in appropriate ways, and digital exclusion is one of the most damaging forms of exclusion in our increasingly digitized world, especially critical during the pandemic, when most Americans find digital connections essential (Vogels, 2020a; Vogels et al., 2020).

What hinders people from acquiring **technocapital**, that is, access to technological skills and resources? Without these skills and knowledge, one can feel disconnected from the center of society. For example, a researcher told of a man who had little experience with computers. When the man went for a haircut, he was told to check in online, either with his phone or on the computer at the counter. He was too embarrassed to admit not knowing how to do this, so he left the shop without getting a haircut. Why is this man on the far side of the digital inequalities continuum? What factors keep him, and others, from having digital technocapital?

Who Has Access to Interactive Media?   Inequalities in digital access and usage are decreasing in some ways. For example, gender differences in digital access—once a feature underlying the digital divide in the United States—have all but disappeared, and cell phone ownership is almost universal. Racial and ethnic disparities are also shrinking for some media use, especially the more recent technologies. However, some experts say that disparities based on race, income, education, rural/urban address, and physical ability persist. Let's look more closely at what they mean by this statement.

Although all smartphone users can access the Internet by phone, Blacks and Latinos are more likely than Whites to rely *only* on mobile phones because they are less likely to have access to a computer or broadband Internet at home, therefore being "smartphone dependent." The same is true for less educated and lower-income and disabled Americans in all ethnic and racial groups—people who make less than $30,000 and people with less than a high school education (Anderson, 2019). What are the implications? It is difficult or impossible to accomplish some important activities easily with a smartphone, such as updating a résumé and conducting a job search online. In addition, they are more likely than other users to run up against data-cap limits and more frequently have to cancel or suspend service due to financial constraints. Thus, these ethnic/racial and socioeconomic groups are at a disadvantage, which illustrates the new configuration of digital inequalities; it has to do with how one *uses* interactive media. Communication scholar Lu Wei suggests that to understand digital inequalities, we should measure the number of online activities one engages in (**multimodality**), not just whether one has access to the Internet or a particular media device (like a smartphone). That is, the more digital activities one pursues (e.g., check email, log on to Instagram, write on Twitter, share a video on TikTok, post a picture on Tumblr, move money from one account to another on a banking site, and update and post a résumé on LinkedIn), the more digitally empowered one is (Gui & Büchi, 2019).

multimodality
The range or breadth of Internet activities.

▲ Gender, race, ethnicity, and age influence technology use to varying degrees.

Reducing Digital Inequalities   To understand how to reduce these digital inequalities we need to better understand why some people lack technocapital. One important aspect is limited access to the Internet, available to some only through smartphones. Approximately 10 percent of Americans have no access to the Internet today, and some experts say that the number is vastly underestimated (Sonnemaker, 2020; "Who's not online," 2020). According to Kathryn deWit of the Pew Charitable Trusts, the vast majority are in rural areas, but others affected are in cities and suburbs all throughout the country and are more likely to be older (65 and older), have no high school degree, and have an annual income of less than $30,000 (Anderson & Kumar, 2019).

But the inequalities extend beyond Internet access, and one way to view them is by describing the many ways that the COVID-19 pandemic highlighted and exacerbated the serious digital inequalities in the United States, which some termed the "COVID-igital Divide" (Levander & Decherney, 2020). Pre-pandemic, two groups with the least digital access were the poor and minority communities. During the pandemic, college-educated, middle-class individuals were most likely to work remotely (teachers, lawyers, therapists, physicians). The working poor and many minorities could not because their jobs were either eliminated or deemed "essential," demanding in-person contact (also making them more vulnerable to disease) (Kochhar & Passel, 2020). The K–12 children of these individuals, pre-pandemic, were already behind in many educational metrics due to the inequality of education in the United States. They had less access to digital hardware/software and Internet connections at home. According to a 2020 survey, many poor and minority parents reported worries about how their children would be

▲ Many parents and children were challenged when education shifted to online learning.

able to complete their homework when education shifted to online learning because they lacked access to computers at home, would have to use public Wi-Fi to finish their schoolwork, or would have to do their schoolwork on a cell phone. In addition, parents were often unable to be at home and supervise the children's learning (Vogels, 2020b). College-age students faced similar problems when courses were shifted online. "This combination of negative forces puts economically disadvantaged students and students of color at greater risk of not being able to attend college . . . due to illness and personal finances" (Levander & Decherney, 2020). These examples show how acquiring technocapital is not a given for many individuals, and the impact of this lack on the young can limit their future educational and professional achievements.

How to eliminate these inequalities? Having access to the Internet and making computers, mobile devices, and applications available are important first steps but not enough. Experts suggest that to survive and thrive in the digitized world, people must acquire four levels of access to technocapital (Carlson & Isaacs, 2018):

1. **Awareness.** Perhaps the most important level of technocapital and easiest to overcome, awareness relates to the extent to which an individual is conscious of a particular technology and its potential utility.

2. **Material access to digital hardware.** Most public policy currently focuses on material access to digital hardware and is defined as the extent to which a particular technology is available to an individual. Many U.S. states are trying to address the digital inequities highlighted by the pandemic. For example, in some places, buses equipped with Wi-Fi park in school and library parking lots where area residents can drive up and get online. Some libraries lend hotspots, and some schools are lending or giving laptops to their students ("Who's not online," 2020). On a more global scale, computer hardware and software developers have developed inexpensive sturdy laptops and tablets for developing countries' markets (Maity & Ramesh, 2020).

3. **Knowledge.** Knowledge means knowing how to use a variety of computer applications. Many nonusers view a lack of digital readiness as a barrier, and frustration levels can be significant. **Digital readiness** involves confidence in using computers, facility with getting new technology to work, use of digital tools for learning, and ability to determine the trustworthiness of online information. Older, poorer, and less-educated people use the Internet for limited basic applications. For example, learning to build a website, navigate social media, or conduct online banking takes more know-how than using the computer to play games or send email. One barrier here is lack of user-friendly technology, and in order to facilitate knowledge, hardware and software developers must better understand the minds of users, taking into consideration their diverse cultural communication norms and practices (Horrigan, 2016). An example of one such project is led by communication scholar Uttaran Dutta, who has collaborated with indigenous community members in rural India. Together, they co-developed a computer application to help those who were illiterate access useful information regarding local weather, employment, education and health care. The information

digital readiness
People's preparedness and comfort in using digital tools.

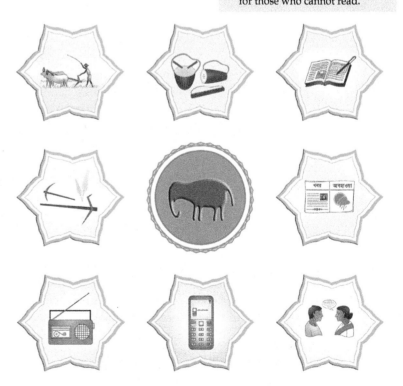

▼ Communication scholar Uttaran Dutta, along with indigenous community members in India, developed this computer application with signs and symbols for those who cannot read.

is conveyed through sounds, pictures, symbols, and signs they can understand (Dutta, 2021).

4. **Technological capacity of the individual's social collective.** This access refers to the extent to which other members of an individual's network see the importance of and use the particular information technologies. A related theory, the **diffusion of innovations**, explains how ideas (innovations) spread over time through groups of people and explains why some people accept new technologies and others don't. Developed by communication scholar Everett Rogers (2003), the theory suggests that for people to accept a new technology such as a computer or a smartphone, they have to see it as useful and compatible with their values and lifestyle. Moreover, if people important to the individual (e.g., an adolescent's peers) adopt the innovation first, then the individual is more likely to adopt it. Furthermore, once a certain number of individuals have adopted a new technology and there is a "critical mass," others in their networks will shortly follow suit. The theory has been used recently to explain how older and younger journalists accept and use social media differently (Wu, 2019) and how and why the Uber mobile app is adopted/accepted by some individuals, showing that an important factor in adopting the technology was if they saw their friends/family using the app (Min et al., 2019).

diffusion of innovations theory
Theory that explains how, over time, an idea or product diffuses (or spreads) through (a) specific population(s).

Journal Prompt 14.5: Digital Inequalities
What is digital inequality? What are the most important factors that determine digital inequalities?

Ethics and Interactive Media

14.6 Identify four ethical challenges involving interactive media use.

One message we hope you take from this chapter is that interactive media are not good or bad in themselves, nor better or worse than offline communication. They are simply different. However, these differences can allow for irresponsible, thoughtless, or even unethical communication. How can you become an ethical user of social media?

There are at least four areas of ethical consideration: (1) presentation of identity online, (2) privacy issues, (3) posting ethical messages, and (4) building online relationships.

Ethics and Online Identity

As we discussed previously, the issue of identity and ethics online is complex, and one can take various positions on the issue. An extreme position would be that one should never misrepresent oneself. By contrast, some interactive media (e.g., MMOR-PGs) clearly offer legitimate opportunities to take on a new identity or pseudo-identity, and in some cases, social media users have good reasons to mask their true identity (for example, victims of cyberbullying, domestic abuse, or online harassment). It's fairly common to assume a pseudonym/handle on Tumblr or Twitter, that reflects your interests, or because your preferred nickname may be already taken. Perhaps a more challenging issue is deciding when to set up a second social media page with a pseudo-identity because you don't want all your posts to be seen by all your potential audiences, or you want to post opinions that may be unaccepted by some of your friends/acquaintances. One general principle might be "Do no harm" and do not engage in behavior that is deceitful.

Communication, of course, is interactive and reciprocal; it takes two people to engage in any interaction, and both have responsibility. Among the receiver's responsibilities is the duty to harbor a certain amount of skepticism for messages that may be questionable. In the case of interactive media, skepticism should focus on how people present their identity—particularly in certain contexts (e.g., on social media, online forums, or other interactive media sites).

Privacy Issues

A second ethical issue concerns online privacy, and the general guideline of doing no harm can also apply here. Specifically, ethical interactive media use includes respecting others' privacy and not snooping around social media or digital messages that are not intended for you. There is increasing opportunity for privacy violation as we own more mobile devices (tablet, phones, and so on).

Finally, if you accidentally access private information, you should consider carefully the consequences of sharing this information with others—would the owner of the information want this information to be shared? Will others be harmed by sharing the information? Of course, the harm could be mild (sharing news about a friend that they would not want shared) to much more drastic consequences (sharing personal identity information that could result in cyberbullying or identity theft).

Respecting others' privacy extends to making others' private lives public by sharing information about them without their knowledge and/or permission. This includes posting a photo or video you took with other people in it, forwarding information from others, posting a link to someone's video or even "liking" a post, and tagging photos or posts with a person's name. All these actions make it easier for others to access this information. Photos that can seem harmless to the person posting about her bachelorette party may be incriminating for others. For example, a picture of a teacher consuming alcohol could have negative repercussions on their credibility. Even without explicit tags, facial recognition systems can also be at play.

Posting Ethical Messages

A third ethical issue is the incivility of messages posted on SNSs, blogs, and especially Twitter. When bloggers disclose their feelings and opinions, they become vulnerable to personal attacks via comments left by readers. One writer described the prevalence of the "very bad, hateful, awful things" one encounters in these comments (Lange, 2018). Women or LGBTQIA+ individuals seem to be frequent targets of vulgar or insulting comments—from death threats to manipulated photos (Humphreys & Vered, 2014). It can be tempting to retweet or repost a link that will give you lots of likes or retweets. With the prevalence of media in our lives today, the news that we post has the potential to impact hundreds or thousands of strangers, depending on our networks. This gives us a responsibility to double-check the authenticity of a news story so that we don't contribute to the spreading of nonsense or fake news. In a deeper sense, it is also worth taking a moment to think about the impact we will have on people's days with the content that we share. It doesn't take more than a moment to ask yourself, "Am I spreading mostly negative stories, or a balance of critical, thought-provoking, and uplifting stories?" If you retweet an opinion piece that claims that students don't need to attend classes in university like they did in high school, what are you hoping to accomplish by spreading this, besides gathering likes?

Some website and software developers have suggested that a set of guidelines for conduct be created and implemented to "bring civility to the web" (Bryson, 2013). Some progress is being made as bloggers control if and when they will allow anonymous comments by strangers, and they often make explicit which behaviors they will (and will not) tolerate. However, an ethical stance is a balanced one. Some bloggers become so obsessed with policing comments that their blogs cease to become anything but an echo chamber because any dissenting comment is labeled as a violation of the rules of the blog. Discussion needs to be civil, but when disagreement of any kind is labeled as offensive trolling, then discussion becomes impossible.

Another ethical issue unfamiliar to many social media users concerns copyright violation. If you share another's work on a personal website, not a business site that makes any money from that image, consider that someone somewhere created it and owns it. For example, Instagram accounts that share posts made by other people may be sharing copyrighted material. Think before you just grab a screen capture and then repost it without any kind of credit or link back. As media experts explain, there are specific, legal rules to follow when sharing others' work (Jatania, 2019).

Building Ethical Mediated Relationships

The first step in building ethical relationships is to remember the characteristics of interactive media—the variations in media richness, social presence, feedback, opportunities for anonymity, deception, and so on. First, present yourself as honestly and truthfully as you can and behave as you would in real life. How you act online may be the most direct way that people—including potential employers as well as love interests— will perceive you. You also need to give recipients of your message enough information to discern the "tone" of your message. For example, you may have to explain in words (or emoji) the humorous tone that in person you would communicate with facial expressions or gestures.

It Happened to Me
Cruzita

My boss writes novels, so I picked up her most recent mystery book and read it over the weekend. One of the characters—Amy—goes missing and is never found. On Monday morning, I emailed her in all capital letters, "WHAT HAPPENED TO AMY?," thinking she would immediately get the reference and have a good laugh. Unfortunately, I forgot that we work with an Amy. My boss called Amy to find out what was wrong only to learn Amy was totally fine. She then called me, and I had to backtrack and explain the whole situation. It was very embarrassing.

A second step is to consider which form of communication is appropriate for your message. Here, relevant factors are your relationship with the receiver and the purpose of the message. For example, in a work context, a lean email message can convey essential information. However, personal messages may be better delivered in person, especially if miscommunication is likely and you need immediate feedback to make sure you are understood. (See *It Happened to Me: Cruzita*.)

A final thought about ethical digital behavior. Based on extensive interviews with young people, media scholar Carrie James (2016) identifies three ways to approach online privacy, property, and participation: *self-focused thinking*, concerned mostly about consequences for herself; *moral thinking*, concerned about the consequences for people one knows; or *ethical thinking*, concerned about unknown individuals and larger communities. James offers a vision of *conscientious connectivity*, which involves ethical thinking skills but, perhaps more important, is marked by sensitivity to the dilemmas posed by online life, a motivation to wrestle with them, and a sense of moral agency that supports socially positive online actions.

Journal Prompt 14.6: Ethical Self-Presentation
Which of these ethical guidelines do you think is most important in presenting *your* identity online?

Improving Your Mediated Communication Skills

14.7 Discuss ways to improve your own mediated communication skills.

What should you take from this chapter that can help you be a better communicator? First, you can strive to communicate more effectively in educational, personal, and professional contexts. Just as we have norms of courtesy for traditional, in-person communication, we also have etiquette for virtual communication.

Educational Contexts

Consider these guidelines for effective virtual communication in classroom contexts and with instructors:

* Follow guidelines for technology use (turning video on/off, muting oneself, using the raise hand feature).

- Be prepared for some awkwardness and be adaptable. It may take a little time to feel comfortable (knowing exactly when to unmute, trying not to interrupt, etc.).
- Wait a bit longer before speaking to avoid interruptions (due to digital delays).
- Consider what you say during a live class session since lectures are often recorded.
- Don't record your instructor/other students without their permission (e.g., don't record a Zoom class session with your phone).
- Consider with some care what you put in the chat box since all conversations (even ones that you think are private) go to the host.

Because email is still prevalent in school contexts (for example, contacting professors), it is worth considering how to increase its effectiveness. Remember that what you put in writing can never be unwritten and that others besides the intended recipient may see it. The most effective email messages to your instructor most likely:

- Contain a specific subject line and not "FYI" or "Hi." Consider adding your course number/title.
- Address the recipient appropriately, probably with your instructor's title (unless you are securely on a first-name basis) and not with "Hey!," "Hi there," or "I need to talk with you about my grade."
- Use correct grammar and accurate spelling.

Interpersonal Contexts

The overarching principle for communicating interpersonally using interactive media is to be considerate of others' time and convenience. Put yourself in the place of the person receiving your message and ask yourself, "Would I appreciate the way this message has been worded and transmitted?" If the answer is yes, you are probably doing all right. Consider these specific suggestions:

- Focus on self-care when you're using so much screen time; make sure you are taking breaks from screen time, engaging with people, and putting your phone down for a while.
- Take a break from social media for a few days.
- Consider how upward social comparisons might affect you when reading social media posts, tweets, and messages.
- Be thoughtful about whom you follow.
- Think about your privacy settings. Remember that anyone, from your future employer to your communication professor, can see your posts. If your account isn't private, tweet like your grandmother is reading.
- Don't overuse hashtags, type in all capital letters, or post the same thing on every social media platform.
- Consider the guidelines for ethical messages—sharing, privacy, and civility.
- Consider your audience. Does a certain person usually reply to emails within the same day or within several days? What is your relationship to that person?

Professional Contexts

Social media are playing an increasingly important role in job searches for both employers and job applicants. How can you use mediated messages effectively in searching for employment?

- First, network. Get the word out that you're looking (but, of course, be discreet if you don't want your current employer to know). Use as many media platforms as possible—Facebook, Twitter, LinkedIn. Create relevant profiles for yourself that include your job history. In general, the more visible you are, the more likely you are to make the contacts that will lead to a job while meeting a lot of professionals

▲ Consider how your mediated messages can have an impact on your job search. Research shows that your coworkers are more likely to discover information on social media that lowers their opinion of you than improves it.

who share your same career aspirations. New and old friends are likely to yield information about openings before they are posted, and people you know might be able to fast-track you to the interview. And you never know where *the* contact might happen.

- Look at organizations' social media to get a feel for their cultures and their positions. Following companies and engaging in their social media are ways to show support and build relationships. This could also be a way to interact and network with their social media employees.

- Conduct an extensive virtual search to find job postings (e.g., Indeed, LinkedIn, Glassdoor, CareerBuilder). But don't rely only on job sites. Experts say that companies are much more likely to hire applicants from internal sources, such as referrals, recruiter outreach, and internal job boards.

- Be thoughtful and considerate in contacting and following up with potential employers. After a meeting or interview, follow up with a short thank-you email. Similarly, be sure to thank anyone who helps you by giving you leads or recommendations.

- Practice interviews by videoing yourself answering questions.

- Be aware of how you are portrayed online (set a Google alert for your name so you will be notified when you appear in searches).

- Remember to help others. Be known as a resource. In your job search, you may come across information or contacts that may not be relevant to your search but might be helpful to a friend, colleague, or online acquaintance. What goes around comes around—the person you help today may be in a position to do you a favor next week or next year.

- Consider the guidelines for ethical (civil, respectful) messages. While you are certainly entitled to your opinions, think before you respond to an email or post a comment on another's post in an inflammatory way. Research shows that your coworkers are more likely to discover information on social media that lowers their opinion of you than improves it. Remember that no argument is ever won on social media.

As one CEO put it, "for me, it boils down to showing respect: respecting each other's privacy, respecting the company that employs you and respecting one another's viewpoints, even if you don't agree. Basically, treat people online the way you would treat them in person" (Krouse, 2019). Interactive media are deeply embedded in the ways we do business and in the ways we socialize and connect with others. Clearly, we have much to think about as we use these tools in every context to communicate responsibly, ethically, equitably, and with social awareness.

Journal Prompt 14.7: Interactive Media Etiquette
What are some guidelines for improving your interactive media etiquette?

SUMMARY

14.1 Identify three reasons for learning about interactive media.

- Interactive media is pervasive and constant in our daily lives.
- Understanding and having good media skills will help you be more successful personally and professionally.

14.2 Define *interactive media*.

- Interactive media are defined as a collection of mediated communication technologies that are digital and converging and tend to be interactive.
- Interactive media include social media, online games, messaging platforms, and virtual reality and present us with many communication choices in our everyday lives.
- These media are neither good nor bad, but better viewed through a dialectical lens—as having potentially both beneficial and harmful impacts.

14.3 Describe the dimensions of interactive media and how these dimensions help us understand and choose among various media.

- Interactive media can vary in two media characteristics (media richness and syncronicity/asychronicity).
- Three theories—media richness theory, media synchronicity, and uses and gratifications—help us understand and can guide our interactive media choices.

14.4 Describe issues that can arise in identity and relationship development when using interactive media.

- Interactive media choices have implications for how we present ourselves online (self-presentation, anonymity, and pseudoanonymity).

- Interactive media afford access to many more potential relationships, and these relationships are not bound by time or space. Interactive media impact friendships, as well as romantic and work relationships.
- Using a dialectical lens, interactive media can strengthen and weaken interpersonal relationships as they are both durable and fragile.

14.5 Understand the role of power and privilege in interactive media use.

- Digital inequalities—differential access and knowledge about interactive media—often vary along income, geographical address (rural/urban), educational, ethnic/racial, and national lines.
- Power also comes into play in digital inequalities, as it does in other parts of society because the most powerful are the ones who develop and define computer literacy and expertise—sometimes excluding those from less powerful groups.
- Two theories are proposed to help us understand and reduce these inequalities: technocapital and diffusion of innovation.

14.6 Identify four ethical challenges involving interactive media use.

- The four challenges include ethics and online identity, ethics and privacy issues, posting ethical messages, and building ethical online relationships.

14.7 Discuss ways to improve your own mediated communication skills.

- Be thoughtful and consider guidelines when using interactive media in educational, interpersonal, and professional contexts.

KEY TERMS

interactive media p. 375
crowdfunding p. 377
crowdsourcing p. 377
digital p. 380
massively multiplayer role-playing
   online games (MMORPGs) p. 380
social media p. 380
media richness theory p. 381
social presence p. 381
media synchronicity theory (MST)
   p. 383

synchronous p. 383
asynchronous p. 383
uses and gratifications p. 383
collapsing contexts p. 384
spreadability p. 384
lurkers p. 386
trolling p. 387
phishing p. 387
cyberbullying p. 387
doxing p. 388
canceling p. 388

pseudoanonymity p. 389
avatars p. 389
problematic social media use
   (PSMU) p. 389
catfishing p. 392
digital divide p. 396
cultural capital p. 397
technocapital p. 397
multimodality p. 398
digital readiness p. 399
diffusion of innovations theory p. 400

APPLY WHAT YOU KNOW

1. **Take a Digital Break**
    Don't use any interactive media for 24 hours and then
    answer the following questions. To what extent did
    you miss these forms of communication? What did you
    miss most and least? What might you conclude about
    the role interactive media play in *your* everyday life and
    relationships? How do you view those who have lim-
    ited access to new communication technologies?

2. **Analyze a Digital Identity**
    Select any personal page from any individual blog
    and describe the identity you think the person is try-
    ing to project. Describe the elements that contribute
    to this identity. What kind of information is pre-
    sented? What information is missing?

Glossary

absolutism   The belief that there is a single correct moral standard that holds for everyone, everywhere, every time.

active agents   Seekers of various media messages and resisters of others.

active-empathic listening (AEL)   Listening skills that involve active engagement with the speaker and putting themselves emotionally in the speaker's shoes, not only on understanding information but also "listening" to others' feelings.

adaptors   Gestures used to manage emotions.

affiliative conversationalists   Style of conversation that focuses on the other person, encourages others to participate in the conversation, and attempts to elicit ideas and involvement from the speaker's partners.

African American English (AAE)   American English dialect used primarily by African American conversationalists.

African American Vernacular English   A version of English that has its roots in West African, Caribbean, and U.S. slave languages.

age identity   A combination of self-perception of age along with what others understand that age to mean.

agenda-setting capacity   The power of media coverage to influence individuals' view of which topics are more salient than others.

analysis paralysis   Potential pitfall in small group interaction; occurs when excessive analysis prevents a group from moving toward a solution.

analytical listening style   Listening style that systematically focuses on the facts and the logical consistency of a speaker's message and withholds judgment until all information is presented.

androcentrism   The use of male experience as normative for humanity and female experience as emphasizing gender difference.

appropriateness   Following the rules, norms and expectations for specific situations or relationships.

argot   A type of jargon used by marginalized or stigmatized communities.

artifacts   Physical objects including cars, clothing, and other material items.

artistic proofs   Artistic skills of a rhetor that influence effectiveness.

assertive conversationalists   Style of conversation that directs attention to themselves, seeks to control the conversation, and attempts to influence the speaking partner's ideas or actions.

assertiveness   Expressing one's opinions forcefully without offending or challenging others.

assimilation   The communicative, behavioral, and cognitive processes that influence individuals to join, identify with, become integrated into, and (occasionally) exit an organization.

asynchronous   The ability of media to support synchronicity, a shared pattern of coordinated behavior among individuals.

attraction theory   Theory that explains the primary forces that draw people together.

attractiveness   The appeal one person has for another based on physical appearance, personality, or behavior.

attribution theory   Explanation of the processes we use to judge our own and others' behavior.

attributional bias   A cognitive bias that refers to the systematic errors made when people evaluate or try to find reasons for their own and others' behaviors.

audience analysis   The process of determining what an audience already knows or wants to know about a topic, who they are, what they know or need to know about the speaker, and what their expectations might be for the presentation.

authoritarian leader   Leader who takes charge, makes all the decisions, and dictates strategies and work tasks.

avatars   Digital alter egos or versions of oneself, used in MMORPGs.

avoiding   Stage of romantic relational dissolution in which couples try not to interact with each other.

bandwagon effect   Arguing that many or even most people have done what the manipulator wants you to do.

behavioral de-escalation   Avoiding the partner.

BIPOC   Acronym for Black, Indigenous, People of Color.

bonding   Stage of romantic relational development characterized by public commitment.

border dwellers   People who live between cultures and often experience contradictory cultural patterns.

brainstorm   To generate as many ideas as possible without critiquing them.

bullying   Repeated hostile behaviors that are or are perceived to be intended to harm parties who are unable to defend themselves.

burnout   A chronic condition that results from the accumulation of daily stress, which manifests itself in a specific set of characteristics, including exhaustion, cynicism, and ineffectiveness.

canceling   Withdrawing support, often for public figures and companies, after they have done or said something considered objectionable or offensive.

categorization   A cognitive process used to organize information by placing it into larger groupings of information.

catfishing   Creating an intentionally deceptive social media profile.

cause–effect pattern   An organization used to create understanding and agreement, and sometimes to argue for a specific action.

channel   The means through which a message is transmitted.

charismatic leadership   A leadership style in which extremely self-confident leaders inspire unusual dedication to themselves by relying on their strong personalities and charm.

Chicano English (ChE)   American English dialect spoken predominantly by Mexican American conversationalists.

chronemics   The study of the way people use time as a message.

chronological pattern   An organization that follows a timeline.

circumscribing   Stage of romantic relational dissolution in which couples discuss safe topics.

cisgender   Someone whose gender identity matches their biological sex.

cocultural group   A significant minority group within a dominant majority that does not share dominant group values or communication patterns.

cocultural theory   Explores the role of power in daily interactions.

code switching The practice of changing language or dialect to accommodate to the communication situation.

cognitive complexity The degree to which a person's constructs are detailed, involved, or numerous.

cognitive representation The ability to form mental models of the world.

cohort effect The influence of shared characteristics of a group that was born and reared in the same general period.

collapsing contexts In social media, not knowing exactly who is reading one's posts.

collectivistic orientation A value orientation that stresses the needs of the group.

communicating information Using nonverbal behaviors to help clarify verbal messages and reveal attitudes and motivation.

communication competence The ability to adapt one's communication to achieve one's goals.

communication ethics The standards of right and wrong that one applies to messages that are sent and received.

conclusion Closing material of a speech where the speaker reviews the main points, may challenge the audience to act, and leaves the audience with a positive view of speaker and topic.

confirming communication Comments that validate positive self-images of others.

congruent Verbal and nonverbal messages that express the same meaning.

connotative meaning The affective or interpretive meanings attached to a word.

constructive marginal people People who thrive in a border-dweller life, while recognizing its tremendous challenges.

constructs Categories people develop to help them organize information.

content analysis Approach to understanding media that focuses on a specific aspect of the content of a text or group of texts.

content meaning The concrete meaning of the message and the meanings suggested by or associated with the message, as well as the emotions triggered by it.

contextual awareness Sensitivity to the circumstances in which a conversation occurs, including participant variables, the social situation, and social norms.

contradicting Verbal and nonverbal messages that send conflicting messages.

conversation Informal, in-person, spoken interaction in which participants exchange ideas, information, and feelings through talking with one another.

conversational awareness Familiarity with the conversational rules a culture has as well as how to adhere them.

conversational manipulation Persuasion attempts that intend to fool, control, or convince a person into doing, believing, or buying something that provides no benefit.

critical listening style Listening style that focuses on the accuracy of the content and reflects a preference for error-free and well-organized speaking.

crowdfunding The process of raising money online—often many small amounts from a large number of people.

crowdsourcing The practice of engaging a "crowd" or group online for a common goal—often for information or problem solving.

cultivation theory The idea that long-term immersion in a media environment leads to "cultivation," or enculturation, into shared beliefs about the world.

cultural capital Cultural knowledge and cultural competencies that people need to function effectively in society.

cultural values Beliefs that are so central to a cultural group that they are never questioned.

culture Learned patterns of perceptions, values, and behaviors shared by a group of people.

culture industries Large organizations in the business of mass communication that produce, distribute, or show various media texts (cultural products) as an industry.

culture shock A feeling of disorientation and discomfort as a result of the lack of familiar environmental cues.

cyberbullying Repetitive and aggressive behavior transmitted through mediated channels and intended to harm a victim.

de-escalation strategies A broad category that includes promising some continued closeness and suggesting that the couple might reconcile in the future.

decoding Receiving a message and interpreting its meaning.

deep acting When employees work to actually *feel* the emotion required.

deliberative rhetoric The type of rhetoric used to argue what courses of action a society should take in the future.

delivery The presentation of a speech before an audience.

demand touching A type of touch used to establish dominance and power.

democratic leader Leader whose style is characterized by considerable input from group members.

demographic analysis The portion of an audience analysis that considers the ages, races, sexes, sexual orientations, religions, and social classes of the audience.

denotative meaning The dictionary, or literal, meaning of a word.

dialect A variation of a language distinguished by its vocabulary, grammar, and pronunciation.

dialectical approach Recognizes that things need not be perceived as "either/or" but may be seen as "both/and."

diaspora The movement, migration, or scattering of a people away from an established or ancestral homeland.

dichotomous thinking Thinking in which things are perceived as "either/or"—for example, "good or bad," "big or small," "right or wrong."

differentiating Stage of romantic relational dissolution in which couples increase their interpersonal distance.

diffusion of innovations theory Theory that explains how, over time, an idea or product diffuses (or spreads) through (a) specific population(s).

digital Information that is transmitted in a numerical format based on only two values (0 and 1).

digital divide Inequity of access between the technology "haves" and "have nots."

digital readiness People's preparedness and comfort in using digital tools.

disability identity Identification with physical or mental impairment that substantially impact everyday life.

disconfirming communication Comments that reject or invalidate a positive or negative self-image of our conversational partners.

disruptive or individual-oriented roles Roles that focus more on individuals' own interests and needs than on those of the group.

downward communication In a traditional conduit model of communication, communication with subordinates.

doxing Searching for and publishing the personal information of a private individual.

e-books Electronic books read on a computer screen instead of a printed page.

effectiveness Achieving one's goals successfully.

ego-defensive function The role prejudice plays in protecting individuals' sense of self-worth.

emblems Gestures that stand for a specific verbal meaning.

emergence phase The third phase of the decision-making process; occurs when group members express a cooperative attitude.

employee dissent When an employee perceives an inconsistency in what was promised by the organization and subsequently objects to, questions, or disagrees with circumstances.

empowerment Feeling capable of performing a job and having the authority to decide how to perform it well.

enacting identities Performing scripts deemed proper for particular identities.

enby Someone who does not identify as either male or female, or non-binary (NB).

encapsulated marginal people People who feel disintegrated by having to shift cultures.

encoding Converting ideas into messages.

epideictic rhetoric The type of rhetoric that reaffirms cultural values through praising and blaming.

equity Perception that one's costs (or inputs) are balanced by one's rewards (or outputs).

equity theory Theory that argues that people are more satisfied in relationships they perceive as fair, that is, where their costs are balanced by their rewards.

establishing social control Using nonverbal communication to exercise influence over other people.

ethnic identity Identification with a particular group with which one shares some or all of these characteristics: national or tribal affiliation, religious beliefs, language, and/or cultural and traditional origins and background.

ethnocentrism The tendency to view one's own group as the standard against which all other groups are judged.

ethos The rhetorical construction of character.

evaluating Assessing your reaction to a message.

evasion Giving irrelevant, rambling, or vague responses.

experimenting Stage of romantic relational development in which both people seek to learn about each other.

expressing and managing intimacy Using nonverbal behaviors to help convey attraction and closeness.

eye contact Looking directly into the eyes of another.

feedback The response to a message.

field of experience The education and experiences that a communicator possesses.

forensic rhetoric Rhetoric that addresses events that happened in the past with the goal of setting things right after an injustice has occurred.

formal communication channels Officially designated channels of communication, reflecting explicit or desired patterns of interaction.

frame Assumptions and attitudes that we use to filter perceptions to create meaning.

frame analysis Studies on the constructions of media frames that shape how we interpret and understand various events.

friendship touch Touch that is more intimate than social-polite touch and usually conveys warmth, closeness, and caring.

function The goals and effects of communication.

functional (situational) theory A theory that assumes that leadership behaviors can be learned.

functional touch The least intimate type of touch; used by certain workers, such as dentists, hairstylists, and hospice workers, as part of their livelihood; also known as *professional touch*.

fundamental attribution error The tendency to attribute others' negative behavior to internal causes and their positive behaviors to external causes.

gaslighting A tactic used to exert power or control over another person by encouraging them to question their reality.

gatekeeping The practice of admitting some people but not others to a societal group.

gender fluid Someone whose gender identity is not fixed but is dynamic and changes in different contexts at different times.

gender identity How and to what extent one identifies with the social construction of masculinity and femininity.

general purpose Whichever of three goals—to inform, persuade, or entertain—dominates a speech.

general systems theory Theory that organizations are a system composed of many subsystems and embedded in larger systems, and that organizations should develop communication strategies that serve both.

generalized other The collection of roles, rules, norms, beliefs, and attitudes endorsed by the community in which a person lives.

gestures Nonverbal communication made with part of the body, including actions such as pointing, waving, or holding up a hand to direct people's attention.

ghosting Having someone you view as a friend or have been dating suddenly cease communicating with you without warning.

globalization The increasing connectedness of the world in economic, political, and cultural realm.

grammar The structural rules that govern the generation of meaning in a language.

group processes The methods, including communication, by which a group accomplishes a task.

group roles The shared expectations group members have regarding each individual's communication behavior in the group.

grouphate The distaste and aversion that people feel toward working in groups.

groupthink A negative, and potentially disastrous, group process characterized by "excessive concurrence thinking."

haptics The study of the communicative function of touch.

hate speech Use of verbal communication to attack others based upon some social category.

Hays Code Self-imposed rules for Hollywood media content instituted in 1930 with the goal of creating "wholesome entertainment."

hearing The stage when listeners pick up the sound waves directed toward them.

hegemony The process by which we consent to social constructions, rather than having them imposed on us.

heterogeneous Diverse.

heuristic Use of language to acquire knowledge and understanding.

hierarchy A power structure in which some members exercise authority over others.

homogeneity High degree of similarity.

horizontal communication In a traditional conduit model of communication, communication with peers.

hostile work environment   An intimidating, hostile, or offensive workplace atmosphere created by unwelcome and inappropriate sexually based behavior.

human communication   A transactional process in which people generate meaning through the exchange of verbal and nonverbal messages in specific contexts, influenced by individual and social forces, and embedded in culture.

human–nature value orientation   The perceived relationship between humans and nature.

hurtful messages   Conversations in which one criticizes, teases, rejects, or otherwise causes an emotional injury to another person.

identity   Who a person is; composed of individual and social categories a person identifies with as well as the categories that others identify with that person.

illustrators   Signals that accompany speech to clarify or emphasize the verbal message.

imaginative   Use of language to express oneself artistically or creatively.

immediacy   How close or involved people appear to be with each other.

individualistic orientation   A value orientation that respects the autonomy and independence of individuals.

indulgence versus restraint   A value orientation that reflects a subjective feeling of happiness. The indulgence orientation emphasizes relatively free gratification of basic and natural human drives related to enjoying life and having fun. Restraint emphasizes suppressing gratification of needs and regulates it by means of strict social norms.

informal communication channels   Patterns of interaction that develop spontaneously based on personal relationships and contacts.

informational listening   Listening skills that are useful in situations requiring attention, in general, to content.

informative   Use of language to communicate information or report facts.

ingratiation   Behavior and communication designed to increase liking.

initiating   Stage of romantic relational development in which both people behave so as to appear pleasant and likeable.

innovation   A function of organizational communication by means of which systems are changed.

instrumental   Use of language to obtain what you need or desire.

integrating   Stage of romantic relational development in which both people portray themselves as a couple.

intensifying   Stage of romantic relational development in which both people seek to increase intimacy and connectedness.

intensity   Degree of emphasis with which a speaker makes their claim.

intentional messages   Messages that are perceived as purposely causing harm to the recipient.

interactional   Use of language to establish and define social relationships.

interactive media   A collection of mediated communication technologies that are digital and converging and tend to be mobile.

intercultural communication   Communication that occurs in interactions between people who are culturally different.

interpersonal aggression   Behaviors that attempt to inflict physical and psychological/social harm on family, friends, romantic partners and acquaintances.

interpretation   The act of assigning meaning to sensory information.

intersectionality   How different identities combine to shape our communication experiences.

intimate distance   (zero to eighteen inches) The space used when interacting with those with whom one is very close.

intimate partner violence   Physical violence against one's romantic partner.

introduction   Opening material of a speech from which the audience members gain a first impression of the speech's content and of the speaker.

jargon   The specialized terms that develop in many professions.

justification strategies   Providing a reason or excuse for ending the relationship.

kinesics   Nonverbal communication sent by the body, including gestures, posture, movement, facial expressions, and eye behavior.

Knapp's stage model   Model of romantic relationship development that views relationships as occurring in "stages" and that focuses on how people communicate as relationships develop and decline.

label   A name assigned to a category based on one's perception of the category.

laissez-faire   A leadership style characterized by complete freedom for the group in making decisions.

lexical choice   Vocabulary.

linguistic profiling   The act of using conversational style to attribute specific characteristic to a particular group.

listening   The process of receiving, constructing meaning from, and responding to spoken and/or nonverbal messages.

listening style   A set of attitudes, beliefs, and predispositions about the how, where, when, who, and what of the information receiving and encoding process.

logos   Rational appeals; the use of rhetoric to help the audience see the rationale for a particular conclusion.

long-term orientation   A value orientation in which people stress the importance of virtue.

long-term versus short-term orientation   The dimension of a society's value orientation that reflects its attitude toward virtue or truth.

looking-glass self   The idea that self-image results from the images others reflect back to an individual.

love-intimate touch   The touch most often used with one's romantic partners and family.

lurkers   People who read, observe, but do not actively participate in online communities/sites.

lying   Concealment, distortion, or dishonesty in communication.

Machiavellian tactics   Having a third party convey one's unhappiness about a relationship.

maintenance   A function of organizational communication in which the stability of existing systems is preserved.

mass media   Mediated communication intended for large audiences.

mass media effects   The influence that media have on people's everyday lives.

mass-market paperbacks   Popular books addressed to a large audience and widely distributed.

Massively Multiplayer Role-Playing Online Games (MMORPGs)   Text-based "virtual reality" games in which participants interact with enrichments, objects, and other participants.

matching hypothesis   The tendency to develop relationships with people who are approximately as attractive as we are.

media   The plural form of *medium*; a channel of communication.

media activism The practice of organizing to communicate displeasure with certain media images and messages as well as to force change in future media texts.

media event Occasions or catastrophes that interrupt regular programming.

media richness theory Theory that describes the potential information-carrying capacity of a communication medium.

media synchronicity theory (MST) The ability of media to support synchronicity, a shared pattern of coordinated behavior among individuals.

media text A television show, advertisement, movie, or other media event that a media scholar isolates for study.

media violence Representations of violent acts in media.

messages A transactional process in which people generate meaning through the exchange of verbal and nonverbal messages in specific contexts, influenced by individual and social forces, and embedded in culture.

micro expressions Unconscious and fleeting facial expressions that convey suppressed emotions and feelings.

microaggressions Brief and commonplace daily verbal, behavioral, and environmental indignities, whether intention or unintentional that communicate hostile, derogatory, or negative prejudicial slights and insults toward any group, particularly marginalized groups.

minimization Denying one's behavior or intent and trying to rationalize it.

monochronically Engaging in one task or behavior at a time.

monotheistic Belief in one god.

motivation Feeling personally invested in accomplishing a specific activity or goal.

MPAA Motion Picture Association of America is a film sector industry representing the six major Hollywood studios.

multimodality The range or breadth of Internet activities.

multiracial identity One who self-identifies as having more than one racial identity.

mutable Subject to change.

naïve realism The human tendency to believe that we see the world objectively and that those who disagree are uninformed, irrational, or biased.

national identity A person's citizenship.

negative identity management Communicating in ways that arouse negative emotions to make the other person upset enough to agree to break off the relationship.

new social contract Assumes that loyalty is not expected by workers or organizations and that job security is unlikely.

noise Any stimulus that can interfere with or degrade the quality of a message.

nominalists Those who argue that any idea can be expressed in any language and that the structure and vocabulary of the language do not influence the speaker's perception of the world.

nonverbal behavior All the nonverbal actions people perform.

nonverbal codes Distinct, organized means of expression that consists of symbols and rules for their use.

nonverbal communication The sending and receiving of information through appearance, objects, the environment, and behavior.

olfactics The communicative functions associated with the sense of smell.

openness Sharing ideas as well as listening to others in a way that avoids conveying negative or disconfirming feedback.

openness Straightforwardly explaining why the relationship is ending.

orator A public speaker.

organization The procedure by which one recognizes what sensory input represents.

organizational climate How organizational members feel about, or experience, the organization's culture.

organizational culture A pattern of shared beliefs, values, and behaviors.

organizational identification The stage of assimilation that occurs when an employee's values overlap with the organization's values.

organizations The set of interactions that members of purposeful groups use to accomplish their individual and common goals.

overattribution Selecting an individual's most obvious characteristic and using it to explain almost anything that person does.

overbenefitted Overbenefitted people perceive that their rewards exceed their costs.

paralinguistics All aspects of spoken language except for the words themselves; includes rate, volume, pitch, and stress.

participants The people interacting during communication.

particular others The important people in an individual's life whose opinions and behavior influence the various aspects of identity.

passing away Process by which relationships decline over time.

passive-aggressive communication Indirectly communicating negative feelings and reactions instead of openly talking about them.

pathos The rhetorical use of emotions to affect audience decision making.

peacebuilding Working toward stability in a region to prevent conflicts from escalating into war.

perception A sense-making process in which we attempt to understand our environment so we can respond to it appropriately.

performance of identity The process or means by which we show the world who we think we are.

persona The identity one creates through one's public communication efforts.

personal distance (eighteen inches to four feet) The space used when interacting with friends and acquaintances.

personal language Use of language to express individuality and personality.

perspective taking Understanding the world from another's point of view.

persuasion Exerting effort to cause another person to do or believe something through reasoning or argument.

phishing The practice of trying fraudulently to get consumer banking and credit card information.

phonology The study of the sounds that compose individual languages and how those sounds communicate meaning.

political economy The ways in which media institutions produce texts in a capitalist system and the legal and regulatory frameworks that shape their options for doing so.

polychronically Engaging in multiple activities simultaneously.

polytheistic Belief in more than one god.

positive tone strategies Communicating concern for the rejected partner and trying to make the person feel better.

posture and movement Kinesics behaviors that communicate messages by how immediate or relaxed they are.

power distance A value orientation that refers to the extent to which less powerful members of institutions and organizations within a culture expect and accept an unequal distribution of power.

pragmatics   Field of study that emphasizes how language is used in specific situations to accomplish goals.

predicted outcome theory   Theory that attempts to explain how reducing uncertainty can lead to attraction or repulsion.

preferred personality   A value orientation that expresses whether it is more important for a person to "do" or to "be."

prejudice   Experiencing aversive or negative feelings toward a group as a whole or toward an individual because she or he belongs to a particular group.

primacy effect   The tendency to form a judgment or opinion based on the first information received.

primary tension   The uncertainty commonly felt in the beginning phase of decision making.

problem–solution pattern   An organization in which the speaker describes various aspects of a problem and then proposes solutions.

problematic social media use (PSMU)   A strong, sometimes excessive, dependency on social media.

production   A function of organizational communication in which activity is coordinated toward accomplishing tasks.

professional touch   The least intimate type of touch; used by certain workers, such as dentists, hairstylists, and hospice workers, as part of their livelihood; also known as *functional touch*.

prototype   A representative or idealized version of a concept.

proxemics   The study of how people use spatial cues, including interpersonal distance, territoriality, and other space relationships, to communicate.

proximity   How physically close one is to others.

pseudoanonymity   Projecting a false identity.

psychological/social aggression   Behavior designed to cause harm to another by attacking their psychological and/or social well-being.

public distance   (twelve to twenty-five feet) The distance used for public ceremonies such as lectures and performances.

public sphere   The arena in which deliberative decision making occurs through the exchange of ideas and arguments.

quid pro quo   Requests for sexual favors as a condition of getting or keeping a job or benefit.

racial identity   Identification with a particular racial group.

rationality   The ability to communicate through reasoning, bargaining, coalition building, and assertiveness.

recency effect   The tendency to form a judgment or opinion on the most recent information received.

reference group   Others to whom we compare ourselves to make judgments about our identities.

reflected appraisals   The idea that people's self-images arise primarily from the ways that others view them and from the many messages they have received from others about who they are.

regulating interaction   Using nonverbal behaviors to help manage conversational interaction.

regulators   Gestures used to control conversations.

regulatory   Use of language to control or regulate the behaviors of others.

reinforcement phase   The final phase of the decision-making process when group members reach consensus and members feel a sense of accomplishment.

relational listening style   Listening style that is associated with friendly, open communication and an interest in establishing ties with others.

relational maintenance   Behaviors couples perform that help maintain their relationships.

relational roles   Roles that help establish a group's social atmosphere.

relational trajectory models   Relationship development models that view the development process as more variable than do stage models.

relationship meaning   What a message conveys about the relationship between the parties.

relativism   The belief that moral behavior varies among individuals, groups, and cultures and across situations.

relativists   Those who argue that language not only serves as a way for us to voice our ideas but "is itself the shaper of ideas, the guide for the individual's mental activity."

relaxation   The degree of tension displayed by the body.

religious identity   Aspect of identity defined by one's spiritual beliefs.

responding   Showing others how you regard their message.

reverse culture shock/re-entry shock   Culture shock experienced by travelers on returning to their home country.

rhetor   A person or institution that addresses a large audience; the originator of a communication message but not necessarily the one delivering it.

rhetoric   Communication that is used to influence the attitudes or behaviors of others; the art of persuasion.

rhetorical audience   Those people who can take the appropriate action in response to a message.

rhetorical critic   An informed consumer of rhetorical discourse who is prepared to analyze rhetorical texts.

rhetorical event   Any event that generates a significant amount of public discourse.

role expectations   The expectation that one will perform in a particular way because of the social role occupied.

Sapir-Whorf hypothesis   Idea that the language people speak determines the way they see the world (a relativist perspective).

schemas   Cognitive maps that help us organize information.

script   A relatively fixed sequence of events that functions as a guide or template for communication or behavior.

secondary (recurring) tension   Conflict or tension found in the second or conflict phase of the decision-making process.

selection   The procedure of choosing which sensory information to focus on.

selective attention   Consciously or unconsciously attending to just a narrow range of the full array of sensory information available.

selective exposure   The idea that people seek media messages or interpret media texts in ways that confirm their beliefs and, conversely, resist or avoid messages that challenge their beliefs.

self-concept   The understanding of one's unique characteristics as well as the similarities to and differences from others.

self-esteem   Part of one's self-concept; arises out of how one perceives and interprets reflected appraisals and social comparisons.

self-fulfilling prophecy   When an individual expects something to occur, the expectation increases the likelihood that it will, as the expectation influences behavior.

self-presentation   Influencing others' impressions by creating an image that is consistent with one's personal identity.

self-respect   Treating others and expecting to be treated with respect and dignity.

self-serving bias   The tendency to give one's self more credit than is due when good things happen and to accept too little responsibility for those things that go wrong.

semantics   The study of meaning.

servant leadership A leadership style that seeks to ensure that other people's highest-priority needs are being served to increase teamwork and personal involvement.

service-task functions Using nonverbal behavior to signal close involvement between people in impersonal relationships and contexts.

setting The physical surroundings of a communication event.

sexual coercion Unwanted sexual activity that occurs when one is pressured, tricked, manipulated, threatened, or forced in a non-physical way.

sexual consent An agreement between participants to engage in sexual activity.

sexual identity Which of the various categories of sexuality one identifies with.

shared (collaborative or distributed) leadership A type of leadership style in which functional leadership is extended to an organizational level; all members are equal partners and share responsibility for the work of the group.

short-term orientation A value orientation that stresses the importance of possessing one fundamental truth.

signposts Transitions in a speech that help an audience understand the speaker's organization, making it easier for them to follow.

similarity Degree to which people share the same values, interests, and background.

small group communication Communication among a small number of people who share a common purpose or goal, who feel connected to each other, and who coordinate their behavior.

social class identity An informal ranking of people in a culture based on their income, occupation, education, dwelling, child-rearing habits, and other factors.

social distance (four to twelve feet) The distance most U.S. Americans use when they interact with unfamiliar others.

social exchange theory Theory that explains the development and longevity of relationships as a result of individuals' ability to maximize the rewards and minimize the costs of their relationships.

social media Group of Internet-based applications that allow the creation and exchange of user-generated content.

social movement A large, organized body of people who are attempting to create social change.

social norms The informal rules or expectations that govern behavior in groups.

social penetration theory Theory that proposes that relationships develop through increases in self-disclosure.

social position Place in the social hierarchy, which comes from the way society is structured.

social presence Degree of psychological closeness or immediacy engendered by various media.

social role The specific position or positions one holds in a society.

social-polite touch Touch that is part of daily interaction in the United States; it is more intimate than professional touch but is still impersonal.

socioeconomic status One's position in the economic hierarchy of society based on a combination of annual income, educational attainment, and occupational prestige.

sophists The first group to teach persuasive speaking skills in the Greek city-states.

soundscape The everyday sounds in our environments.

spatial pattern An organization that arranges points by location and can be used to describe something small.

special-occasion speeches Evocative speeches intended to entertain, inspire, celebrate, commemorate, or build community.

specific purpose What a speaker wants to inform or persuade an audience about, or the type of feelings the speaker wants to evoke.

speech act theory Branch of pragmatics that suggests that when people communicate, they do not just say things, they also *do* things with their words.

spreadability The ease with which content can be spread on social media.

stagnating Stage of romantic relational dissolution in which couples try to prevent change.

standard American English (SAE) American English dialect spoken by most White conversationalists.

stereotype threat Process in which reminding individuals of stereotypical expectations regarding important identities can impact their performance.

stereotyping Creating schemas that overgeneralize attributes of a specific group.

strategy control Assessing the available information and options to increase one's understanding of the conflict and the other party.

structure Recurring patterns of interaction among organizational members.

style theory Theory that asserts that a leader's manner or style determines their success.

sudden death Process by which relationships end without prior warning for at least one participant or due to a betrayal.

supporting materials Information that supports the speaker's ideas.

supportiveness Providing subordinates with access to information and resources.

surface acting When employees express the required emotion without the accompanying feeling.

symbol Something that represents something else and conveys meaning.

symbolic interactionism A theory that describes how we develop meaning and identities through our communication with others.

synchronous Communication in which messages are sent and received at the same time.

Synergetic Model A transactional model that emphasizes how individual and societal forces, contexts, and culture interact to affect the communication process.

syntax The rules that govern word order.

task roles Roles that are directly related to the accomplishment of group goals.

task-oriented listening style Listening style that reflects an interest in listening as simply a transaction, focused on the substance, the point of the message.

technocapital Access to technological skills and resources.

terminating Stage of romantic relational dissolution in which couples end the relationship.

thesis statement A statement of the topic of a speech and the speaker's position on it.

topical pattern An organization that has no innate organization except that imposed by the speaker.

trait theory A theory that assumes leaders are born, not made.

transformational leadership A leadership style that empowers group members to work independently from the leader by encouraging group cohesion.

transgender Someone whose gender identity does not match their biological sex.

trolling   Posting Internet messages meant to intentionally anger or frustrate in order to provoke reactions from others.

turning point model for romantic couples   Model of relationship development in which couples move both toward and away from commitment over the course of their relationship.

turning point model of friendship   Model of relationship development where friends move toward or away from closeness over the course of their relationship.

TV Parental Guidelines   A self-regulating system of the television industry that rates programs in terms of appropriateness for particular age groups.

uncertainty reduction theory   Theory that argues relationship development is facilitated or derailed by participants' efforts to reduce their uncertainty about each other.

underbenefitted   Underbenefitted people perceive that their costs exceed their rewards.

understanding   Interpreting the messages associated with sounds or what the sounds mean.

unintentional messages   Messages that are not intended to hurt the recipient.

upward communication   In a traditional conduit model of communication, communication with superiors.

urgent organizations   Companies that try to shorten the time it takes to develop new products and respond to customer demands.

uses and gratifications   The idea that people use media messages and find various types of gratifications in some media texts rather than in others.

V-chip   Device that identifies television program ratings by content and can block programming designated by the owner.

value-expressive function   The role played by prejudice in allowing people to view their own values, norms, and cultural practices as appropriate and correct.

view of human nature   A value orientation that expresses whether humans are fundamentally good, evil, or a mixture.

virtual small group   A small group whose members interact through electronic communication media.

virtuality   The degree to which groups work through electronic communication media.

visual aids   Audiovisual materials that help a speaker reach intended speech goals.

vocalizations   Uttered sounds that do not have the structure of language.

voice qualities   Qualities such as pitch, rhythm, vocal range, and articulation that make up the "music" of the human voice.

withdrawal/avoidance   Friendship termination strategy in which friends spend less time together, don't return phone calls, and avoid places where they are likely to see each other.

work–life conflict   Difficulty balancing job and home responsibilities.

World English   English in its many forms internationally.

References

Chapter 1

Alberts, J. K., Yoshimura, C. G., Rabby, M. K., & Loschiavo, R. (2005). Mapping the topography of couples' daily interaction. *Journal of Social and Personal Relationships, 22,* 299–323.

Andersen, P. A., Lustig, M. W., & Andersen, J. F. (1990). Changes in latitude, changes in attitude: The relationship between climate and interpersonal communication predispositions. *Communication Quarterly, 38,* 291–311.

Anderson, K. E., & Tompkins, P. S. (2015). *Practicing communication ethics: Development, discernment, and decision-making* (pp. 127–152). Routledge.

Buck, R., & VanLear, C. A. (2002). Verbal and nonverbal communication: Distinguishing symbolic, spontaneous and pseudo-spontaneous nonverbal behavior. *Journal of Communication, 52,* 522–541.

Burgoon, J. K., Buller, D. B., & Woodall, W. G. (1996). *Nonverbal communication: The unspoken dialogue.* Harper & Row.

Cupach, W., Canary, D., & Spitzberg, B. (2009). *Competence in interpersonal conflict.* Waveland Press.

Danilyuk, J. (2019, September 25). Academic cheating statistics say there's lots of work to do. *unicheck.com.* https://unicheck.com/blog/academic-cheating-statistics

DePaulo, B. (2011, September 6). Who lies? Frequent liars. What kinds of people lie most often? *Psychology Today.* http://www.psychologytoday.com/blog/living-single/201109/who-lies

Dickens, T. E. (2003). General symbol machines: The first stage in the evolution of symbolic communication. *Evolutionary Psychology, 1,* 192–209.

Diener, M. (2002, January). Fair enough: To be a better negotiator, learn to tell the difference between a lie and a *lie. Entrepreneur Magazine.* http://www.Entrepreneurmagazine.com/article/47442

Dixon, M., & Duck, S. W. (1993). Understanding relationship processes: Uncovering the human search for meaning. In S. W. Duck (Ed.), *Understanding relationship processes, Vol. 1: Individuals in relationships* (pp. 175–206). Sage.

Duck, S. (1994). *Meaningful relationships: Talking, sense and relating.* Sage.

Eisenberg, E. M., Goodall, H. L., Jr., & Trethewey, A. (2010). *Organizational communication: Balancing creativity and constraints.* St. Martin's.

Emanuel, R. (2007). Humanities: Communication's core discipline. *American Communication Journal, 9*(2). http://www.acjournal.org/holdings/vol9/summer/articles/discipline.html

Friedrich, G. W. (1994). Essentials of speech communication. *SCA Rationale Kit: Information supporting the speech communication discipline and its programs* (pp. 9–12). Speech Communication Association.

Fritz, J. M. H. (2020). Honesty as ethical communicative practice: A framework for analysis. In C. B. Miller & R. West (Eds.), *Integrity, honesty, and truth-seeking.* Oxford University Press.

Gergen, K. J. (1982). *Toward transformation in social knowledge.* Springer.

Hendrickson, M. (2020, June 12). Judge says new charges against Jussie Smollett not double jeopardy. *Chicago Sun-Times.* https://chicago.suntimes.com/crime/2020/6/12/21289507/jussie-smollett-empire-actor-charges-hate-crime-lying-police

Jussie Smollett: Timeline of the actor's alleged attack and arrest (2020, February 12). *BBC News.* https://www.bbc.com/news/newsbeat-47317701

Kant, I. (1949). *Fundamental principles of the metaphysic of morals.* (T. K. Abbott, Trans.). Bobbs-Merrill. (Original work published 1785)

Laswell, H. D. (1948). The structure and function of communication in society. In L. Bryson (Ed.), *The Communication of Ideas.* Harper.

Lipari, L. (2009). Ethics theories. In S. W. Littlejohn & K. A. Foss (Eds.), *Encyclopedia of communication theory* (pp. 352–355). Sage Publications.

Martin, J. N. & Nakayama, T. K. (2018). *Intercultural communication in contexts* (7th ed). McGraw-Hill.

McCornack, S. A., & Parks, M. R. (1986). Deception detection and relationship development: The other side of trust. In M. L. McLaughlin (Ed.), *Communication yearbook 9* (pp. 377–389). Sage. http://www.natcom.org/policies/External/EthicalComm

Mead, G. H. (1934). *Mind, self, and society.* University of Chicago Press.

National Endowment for Financial Education® (NEFE®) (2018, February 14). Celebrate relationships, but beware of financial infidelity *.nefe.org.* Retrieved October 22, 2020 from https://www.nefe.org/news/polls/2018/celebrate-relationships-but-beware-of-financial-infideltiy.aspx

National Communication Association. (2003). What is communication? *Pathways.* http://www.natcom.org/nca/Template2.asp?bid=339

Nolen-Hoeksema, S., Wisco, B., & Lyubomirsky, S. (2008). Rethinking rumination. *Perspectives on Psychological Science, 3,* 400–424.

Passer, M. W., & Smith, R. E. (2004). *Psychology: The science of mind and behavior* (2nd ed.). McGraw-Hill.

Paul, R., & Elder, L. (2008). *The miniature guide to critical thinking concepts and tools.* Foundation for Critical Thinking Press.

Reilly, K. (2020, March 12). A year after the college admissions scandal, here's what has (and has not) changed. *Time.* https://time.com/5801167/college-admissions-scandal-changes/

Robinson-Smith, G. (2004). Verbal indicators of depression in conversations with stroke survivors. *Perspectives in Psychiatric Care, 40,* 61–69.

Rogers, E. M., & Chafee, S. H. (1983). Communication as an academic discipline: A dialogue. *Journal of Communication, 3,* 18–30.

Schwartz-Mette, R. A., & Smith, R. L. (2018). When does co-rumination facilitate depression contagion in adolescent friendships? Investigating intrapersonal and interpersonal factors. *Journal of Clinical Child & Adolescent Psychology, 47*(6), 912–924.

Sartre, J. P. (1973). *Existentialism and humanism* (P. Mairet, Trans.) Methuen Ltd. (Original work published 1946)

Shannon, C. E., & Weaver, W. (1949). *A mathematical model of communication.* University of Illinois Press.

Warren, S. F., & Yoder, P. J. (1998). Facilitating the transition to intentional communication. In A. Wetherby, S. Warren, & J. Reichle (Eds.), *Transitions in prelinguistic communication* (pp. 39–58). Brookes Publishing.

Watzlawick, P., Beavin, J., & Jackson, D. D. (1967). *Pragmatics of human communication.* W. W. Norton.

Wokutch, R. E., & Carson, T. L. (1981). The ethics and profitability of bluffing in business. In Lewickis, Saunders, & Minton (Eds.), *Negotiation: Readings, exercises, and cases* (pp. 341–353). Irwin/McGraw-Hill.

Chapter 2

A quick guide for non-binary dating. (2020, July 9). *OkCupid.* https://help.okcupid.com/article/207-a-quick-guide-for-non-binary-dating

Abrams, J., O'Connor, J., & Giles, H. (2002). Identity and intergroup communication. In W. B. Gudykunst & B. Mody (Eds.), *Handbook of international and intercultural communication* (2nd ed., pp. 225–240). Thousand Oaks, CA: Sage.

Adams, T. E., & Berry, K. (2013). Size matters: Performing (il)logical male bodies on FatClub.com. *Text and Performance Quarterly, 33*(4), 308–325.

Allen, B. (2004). *Difference matters: Communicating social identity.* Waveland.

Americans with Disabilities Act of 1990, as amended with Amendments of 2008. http://www.ada.gov/pubs/adastatute08.htm

Arana, M. (2008, November 30). He's not black. *Washington Post.* http://www.washingtonpost.com/wp-dyn/content/article/2008/11/28/AR2008112802219.html

Baker, C. (2003, November 30). What is middle class? *The Washington Times.* http://www.washtimes.com/specialreport/2003112910585 57412r.htm

Bennett-Haigney, B. (1995, August). Faulkner makes history at the Citadel. *NOW Newsletter.* http://www.now.org/nnt/08-95/citadel.html

Blake, J. (2020, August 2). How 'good White people' derail racial progress. *CNN.* https://www.cnn.com/2020/08/01/us/white-liberals-hypocrisy-race-blake/index.html?utm_source=pocket-newtab

Blumer, H. (1969). *Symbolic interactionism: Perspective and method.* Prentice Hall.

Bock, G. (1989). Women's history and gender history: Aspects of an international debate. *Gender & History, 1*(1), 7–30.

Bourdieu, P. (1984). *Distinction: A social critique of the judgment of taste.* (R. Nice, Trans.). Routledge & Kegan Paul.

Butler, J. (1990). *Gender trouble: Feminism and the subversion of identity.* Routledge.

Butler, J. (1993). *Bodies that matter: On the discursive limits of "sex."* Routledge.

Campbell, H. A. (Ed.). (2013). *Digital religion: Understanding religious practice in new media worlds.* Routledge.

Capatides, C. (2020, July 8). Why saying "all lives matter" communicates to Black people that their lives don't. *CBS News.* https://www.cbsnews.com/news/all-lives-matter-black-lives-matter/

Carbaugh, D. (2007). Commentary: Six basic principles in the communication of social identities: The special case of discourses and illness. *Communication & Medicine, 4*(1), 111–115.

Carbaugh, D. (2007). Cultural discourse analysis: Communication practices and intercultural encounters. *Journal of Intercultural Communication Research, 36*(3), 167–182.

Cardillo, L. W. (2010). Empowering narratives: Making sense of the experience of growing up with chronic illness or disability. *Western Journal of Communication, 74*(5), 525–546.

Coaston, J. (2019, May 28). The intersectionality wars. *Vox.* https://www.vox.com/the-highlight/2019/5/20/18542843/intersectionality-conservatism-law-race-gender-discrimination

Cooley, C. H. (1902). *Human nature and the social order.* Scribner's.

Corey, F. C. (2004). A letter to Paul. *Text and Performance Quarterly, 24,* 185–190.

Corey, F. C., & Nakayama, T. K. (2004). Introduction: Religion and Performance. [Special issue]. *Text and Performance Quarterly, 24,* 209–211.

Cornell University. (2004). Fear factor: 44 percent of Americans queried in Cornell national poll favor curtailing some liberties for Muslim Americans. *Cornell News.* http://www.news.cornell.edu/releases/Dec04/Muslim.Poll.bpf.html

Crenshaw, K. (1989). Demarginalizing the intersection of race and sex: A Black feminist critique of antidiscrimination doctrine, feminist theory and antiracist politics. *University of Chicago Legal Forum, 1989*(1), Article 8. http://chicagounbound.uchicago.edu/uclf/vol1989/iss1/8

Croizet, J., & Claire, T. (1998). Extending the concept of stereotype threat to social class: The intellectual underperformance of students from low socioeconomic backgrounds. *Personality and Social Psychology, 24*(5), 588–594.

Davies, R., & Ikeno, O. (Eds.). (2002). *The Japanese mind: Understanding contemporary culture.* Tuttleman.

Edwards, R. (1990). Sensitivity to feedback and the development of the self. *Communication Quarterly, 38,* 101–111.

Eguchi, S., & Washington, M. (2016). Race-ing queerness: Normative intimacies in LOGO's *DTLA. Journal of Communication Inquiry, 40*(4), 408–423.

Fassett, D. L., & Morella, D. L. (2008). Remaking (the) discipline: Marking the performative accomplishment of (dis)ability. *Text and Performance Quarterly, 28*(1–2), 139–156.

Foucault, M. (1988). *History of sexuality* (R. Hurley, Trans.). Vintage Books.

Fussell, P. (1992). *Class: A guide through the American status system.* Touchstone.

Garcia, S. E. (2020, June 17). Where did BIPOC come from? *The New York Times.* https://www.nytimes.com/article/what-is-bipoc.html

Gecewicz, C. (2020, April 30). Few Americans say their house of worship is open, but a quarter say their faith has grown amid pandemic. *Pew Research Center.* https://www.pewresearch.org/fact-tank/2020/04/30/few-americans-say-their-house-of-worship-is-open-but-a-quarter-say-their-religious-faith-has-grown-amid-pandemic/

Guzmán, I. M., & Valdivia, A. N. (2004). Brain, brow, and booty: Latina iconicity in U.S. popular culture. *Communication Review, 7,* 205–221.

Hacker, A. (2003). *Two nations: Black and white, separate, hostile, unequal.* Scribner.

Harwood, J. (2006). Communication as social identity. In G. J. Shepherd, J. St. John, & T. Striphas (Eds.), *Communication as . . . : Perspectives on theory* (pp. 84–90). Sage.

Hecht, M. L., Jackson R. L., III, & Ribeau, S. A. (2003). *African American communication: Exploring identity and culture.* (2nd ed.). Lawrence Erlbaum Associates.

Henderson, B., & Ostrander, R. N. (2008). Introduction to special issue on disability studies/performance studies. *Text and Performance Quarterly, 28*(1–2), 1–5.

Hirschman, C. (2003, May). *The rise and fall of the concept of race.* Paper presented at the annual meeting of the Population Association of America, Minneapolis, MN.

Hobeika, M. O. N., & Nakayama, T. K. (2020). Check-mate: The MENA/Arab double-bind. In H. Bhabra, F. Z. C. Alaoui, S. Abdi, & B. M. Calafell (Eds.), *Negotiating identity & transnationalism: Middle Eastern and North African Communication and Critical Cultural Studies* (pp. 17–30). Peter Lang.

Horn, D. (2013, April 14). Middle class a matter of income, attitude. *USA Today.* http://www.usatoday.com/story/money/business/2013/04/14/middle-class-hard-define/2080565/

Horowitz, J. M., Igielnik, R. & Kochhar, R. (2020, January 9). Trends in income and wealth inequality. *Pew Research Center.* https://www.pewsocialtrends.org/2020/01/09/trends-in-income-and-wealth-inequality/

In U.S., decline of Christianity continues at a rapid pace. (2019, October 17). *Pew Research Center.* https://www.pewforum.org/2019/10/17/in-u-s-decline-of-christianity-continues-at-rapid-pace/

Jackson, D. (2019, April 3). Ariana Grande responds to bisexual rumors sparked by new song "Monopoly." *Newsweek.* https://www.newsweek.com/ariana-grande-bisexual-rumors-monopoly-1385531

Johnson, A. G. (2001). *Privilege, power and difference.* McGraw-Hill.

Jones, N. A., & Smith, A. S. (2001). The two or more races population. *Census 2000 Brief (U.S. Census Bureau Publication No. C2KBR/01-6).* U.S. Government Printing Office.

Kimmel, M. S. (2005). *The history of men: Essays in the history of American and British masculinities.* State University of New York Press.

Koshy, S. (2004). *Sexual naturalization: Asian Americans and miscegenation.* Stanford University Press.

Kraybill, D. B. (1989). *The riddle of Amish culture.* Johns Hopkins University Press.

Lagarde, D. (2005, September 22–28). Afghanistan: La loi des tribus. *L'Express International,* 30–37.

Lang, C. (2020, July 6). How the "Karen Meme" confronts the violent history of white womanhood. *Time.* https://time.com/5857023/karen-meme-history-meaning/

Lindemann, K. (2008). "I can't be standing up out there": Communicative performances of (dis)ability in wheelchair rugby. *Text and Performance Quarterly, 28*(1–2), 98–115.

Loden, M., & Rosener, J. B. (1991). *Workforce America: Managing workforce diversity as a vital resource.* Business One Irwin.

Lucas, K. (2011). Socializing messages in blue-collar families: Communication pathways to social mobility and reproduction. *Western Journal of Communication, 75*(1), 95–121.

Lum, Z.-A. (2017, February 2). Joël Lightbound urges no more silence over Islamophobia after Quebec City mosque attack. *Huffington Post Canada.* http://www.huffingtonpost.

ca/2017/02/02/joel-lightbound-quebec-shooting_n_14575968.html

Mack, A. N., & McCann, B. J. (2019). Recalling Persky: White rage and intimate publicity after Brock Turner. *Journal of Communication Inquiry, 43*(4), 372–393.

Macur, J. (2020, June 10). Former athletes file sex abuse lawsuits against U.S.A. Swimming. *The New York Times*. https://www.nytimes.com/2020/06/10/sports/olympics/swimming-abuse-coaches-lawsuit.html

Manczak, D. W. (1999, July 1). Raising your child's self-esteem. *Clinical Reference Systems, 1242.*

Marshall, G. A. (1993). Racial classification: Popular and Scientific. In S. G. Harding (Ed.), *The "racial" economy of science: Toward a democratic future* (pp. 116–127). Indiana University Press.

Martin, J. N., & Harrell, T. (1996). Reentry training for intercultural sojourners. In D. Landis & R. S. Bhagat (Eds.), *Handbook of intercultural training* (2nd ed., pp. 307–326). Sage.

McGlone, M. S., & Aronson, J. (2006). Stereotype threat, identity salience, and spatial reasoning. *Journal of Applied Development Psychology, 27*(5), 486–493.

McHugh, M. (2013, August 23). It's catfishing season! How to tell lovers from liars online, and more. *Digital Trends*. http://www.digitaltrends.com/web/its-catfishing-season-how-to-tell-lovers-from-liars-online-and-more/#ixzz2uvnrrkOx

Mead, G. H. (1934). *Mind, self, and society*. University of Chicago Press.

Meatto, K. (2019, May 2). Still separate, still unequal: Teaching about school segregation and educational inequality. *The New York Times*. https://www.nytimes.com/2019/05/02/learning/lesson-plans/still-separate-still-unequal-teaching-about-school-segregation-and-educational-inequality.html

Mikkelsen, E. G., & Einarsen, S. (2001). Bullying in Danish work-life: Prevalence and health correlates. *European Journal of Work and Organizational Psychology, 10*, 393–413.

Next UK census may ask about sexuality and gender identity. (2016, May 23). *The Guardian*. https://www.theguardian.com/uk-news/2016/may/23/next-uk-census-may-ask-about-sexuality-and-gender-identity

Nittle, N. K. (2019, April 30). 5 ways to make your racially segregated church more diverse. *ThoughtCo*. https://www.thoughtco.com/diversify-your-racially-segregated-church-2834542

Office for National Statistics. (2012, December 11). *Ethnicity and national identity in England and Wales*. http://www.ons.gov.uk/ons/dcp171776_290558.pdf

Online Glossary. (2005, January). Prentice Hall. www.prenhall.com/rm_student/html/glossary/a_gloss.html

Palladino, G. (1996). *Teenagers: An American history*. Basic Books.

Papalia, D. E., Olds, S. W., & Feldman, R. D. (2002). *A child's world: Infancy through adolescence*. McGraw-Hill.

Philipsen, G. (1992). *Speaking culturally: Explorations in social communication*. State University of New York Press.

Rawls, J. (1995). Self-respect, excellence, and shame. In R. S. Dillon (Ed.), *Dignity, character, and self-respect* (pp. 125–131). Routledge.

Roland, C. E., & Foxx, R. M. (2003). Self-respect: A neglected concept. *Philosophical Psychology, 16*(2), 247–288.

Rosenblith, J. F. (1992). *In the beginning: Development from conception to age two*. Sage.

Sanders, W. B. (1994). *Gangbangs and drive-bys: Grounded culture and juvenile gang violence*. Aldine de Gruyter.

Seippul, Ø. (2017). Sports and nationalism in a globalized world. *International Journal of Sociology, 47*(1), 43–61.

Shih, M., Pittinsky, T. L., & Ambady, N. (1999). Stereotype susceptibility: Identity salience and shifts in quantitative performance. *Psychological Science. 10*(1), 80–83.

Sloop, J. M. (2004). *Disciplining gender: Rhetoric of sex identity in contemporary U.S. culture*. University of Massachusetts Press.

Smith, J. L., & White, P. H. (2002). An examination of implicitly activated, explicitly activated, and nullified stereotypes on mathematical performance: It's not just a women's issue. *Sex Roles, 47*(3–4), 179–191.

Smith, T. L. (2020, June 29). Saying 'All Lives Matter' doesn't make you racist, just extremely ignorant. *Cleveland.com*. https://www.cleveland.com/entertainment/2020/06/saying-all-lives-matter-doesnt-make-you-racist-just-extremely-ignorant.html

Steele, C. M., & Aronson, J. (1995). Stereotype threat and intellectual test performance of African Americans. *Journal of Personality and Social Psychology, 69*(5), 797–811.

Stokes, B. (2017, February 1). What it takes to truly be "one of us." *Pew Research Center*. https://www.pewresearch.org/global/2017/02/01/what-it-takes-to-truly-be-one-of-us/

Sullivan, H. S. (1953). *The interpersonal theory of psychology*. Norton.

Sullivan, T. A., Warren, E., & Westbrook, J. (2001). *The fragile middle class: Americans in debt*. Yale University Press.

Taylor, J. (2005, June 6). Between two worlds: How many Americans really attend church each week? [Blog post]. http://theologica.blogspot.com/2005/06/how-many-americans-really-attend.html

Teeman, T. (2018, November 9). Michael C. Hall on his "fluid" sexuality, "Dexter," death, and David Bowie. *The Daily Beast*. https://www.thedailybeast.com/michael-c-hall-sexuality-dexter-death-bowie-and-me

Ting-Toomey, S. (1999). *Communicating across cultures*. Guilford.

Trammell, K. (2019, September 4). Lil Nas X tried to explain why he came out as gay. Then Kevin Hart interrupted him. *CNN*. https://www.cnn.com/2019/09/04/entertainment/lil-nas-x-kevin-hart-homosexuality-trnd/index.html

Trethewey, A. (2001). Reproducing and resisting the master narrative of decline: Midlife professional women's experiences of aging. *Management Communication Quarterly, 15*, 183–226.

Vevea, N. (2008). *Body art: Performing identity through tattoos and piercing*. Paper presented at the annual meeting of the NCA 94th Annual Convention, TBA, San Diego, CA Online. http://www.allacademic.com/meta/p258244_index.html

Waring, O. (2018, March 18). What is catfishing and how can you spot it? *Metro* (UK). https://metro.co.uk/2018/03/18/catfishing-can-spot-7396549/

Waters, M. C. (1990). *Ethnic options: Choosing identities in America*. University of California Press.

Wax, E. (2005, September 26–October 2). Beyond the pull of the tribe: In Kenya, some teens find unity in contemporary culture. *Washington Post*, National Weekly Edition, 22(49), 8.

Weber, P. (2014, February 21). Confused by all the new Facebook genders? Here's what they mean. *Slate*. http://www.slate.com/blogs/lexicon_valley/2014/02/21/gender_facebook_now_has_56_categories_to_choose_from_including_cisgender.html

Chapter 3

Abramov, I., Gordon, J., Feldman, O., & Chavarga, A. (2012a). Sex and vision I: Spatio-temporal resolution. *Biology of Sex Differences, 3*(21). https://bsd.biomedcentral.com/articles/10.1186/2042-6410-3-20

Abramov, I., Gordon, J., Feldman, O. & Chavarga, A. (2012b). Sex and vision II: Color appearance of monochromatic lights. *Biology of Sex Differences, 3*(21). https://link.springer.com/article/10.1186/2042-6410-3-21

Applegate, J. (1982). The impact of construct system development on communication and impression formation in persuasive contexts. *Communication Monographs, 49*, 277–289.

Bradbury, T. N., & Fincham, F. D. (1988). Individual difference variables in close relationships: A contextual model of marriage as an integrative framework. *Journal of Personality and Social Psychology, 54*, 713–721.

Braithwaite, C. (1990). Communicative silence: A cross-cultural study of Basso's hypothesis. In D. Carbaugh (Ed.), *Cultural communication and intercultural contact* (pp. 321–327). Lawrence Erlbaum Associates.

Branson-Potts, H., Chabria, A., Campa, A. J., & Vega, P. (2020, May 8). At protests, mostly white crowds show how pandemic has widened racial and political divides. *LA Times*. https://www.latimes.com/california/story/2020-05-08/california-coronavirus-protests-race

Brislin, R. (2000). *Understanding culture's influence on behavior* (2nd ed.). Wadsworth.

Burgoon, J. K., Berger, C. R., & Waldron, V. R. (2000). Mindfulness and interpersonal communication. *Journal of Social Issues, 56*, 105–127.

Burleson, B. R., & Caplan, S. E. (1998). Cognitive complexity. In J. C. McCroskey, J. Daly, & M. M. Martin (Eds.), *Communication and personality: Trait perspectives.* Hampton.

CDC. (2020, June 25). COVID-19 in racial and ethnic minority groups. *Coronavirus disease 2019 (COVID-19).* https://www.cdc.gov/coronavirus/2019-ncov/need-extra-precautions/racial-ethnic-minorities.html

Chapin, J. (2001). It won't happen to me: The role of optimistic bias in African American teens' risky sexual practices. *Howard Journal of Communication, 12,* 49–59.

Classen, C. (1990). Sweet colors, fragrant songs: Sensory models of the Andes and the Amazon. *American Ethnologist, 14,* 722–735.

Columbia Journalism Review. (2019, Summer). *The reach of #MeToo.* https://www.cjr.org/special_report/reach-of-metoo.php

Cox, W. T. L., Abramson, L. Y., Devine, P. G., & Hollon, S. D. (2012). Stereotypes, prejudice, and depression: The integrated perspective. *Perspectives on Psychological Science 7*(5), 427–449. https://doi.org/10.1177/1745691612455204

Deutsch, F. M., Sullivan, L., Sage, C., & Basile, N. (1991). The relations among talking, liking, and similarity between friends. *Personality and Social Psychology Bulletin, 17,* 406–411.

Dijk, T. A., van. (1977). *Text and context: Explorations in the semantics and pragmatics of discourse.* Longman.

Dillard, J. P., Solomon, D. H., & Samp, J. A. (1996). Framing social reality: The relevance of relational judgments. *Communication Research, 23,* 703–723.

Durfeel, J. (2006). "Social change" and "status quo" framing effects on risk perception: An exploratory experiment. *Science Communication 27*(4), 459–495. https://doi.org/10.1177/1075547005285334

Ehrenreich, B. (2001). *Nickel and dimed: On (not) getting by in America.* Metropolitan Books.

Fehr, B., Baldwin, M., Collins, L., Patterson, S., & Benditt, R. (1999). Anger in close relationships: An interpersonal script analysis. *Personality and Social Psychology, 25*(3), 299–312. https://doi.org/10.1177/0146167299025003003

Goldstein, E. B. (2010a). *Encyclopedia of perception* (8th ed.). Sage Publications.

Goldstein, E. B. (2010b). *Sensation and perception* (9th ed.). Wadsworth.

Granello, D. H. (2010). Cognitive complexity among practicing counselors: How thinking changes with experience. *Journal of Counseling and Development, 88*(1), 92–100. https://doi.org/10.1002/j.1556-6678.2010.tb00155

Greenough, W. T., Black, J. E., & Wallace, C. S. (1987). Experience and brain development. *Child Development, 58,* 539–559.

Griffin, E. (1994). *A first look at communication theory.* McGraw-Hill.

The Guardian. (September 25, 2014). Ohio Walmart video reveals moments before officer killed John Crawford. https://www.theguardian.com/world/2014/sep/24/surveillance-video-walmart-shooting-john-crawford-police

Gueguen, N., & De Gail, M. (2003). The effect of smiling on helping behavior: Smiling and good Samaritan behavior. *Communication Reports, 16*(2), 133–140.

Harvey, P., & Martinko, M. J. (2010). Attribution theory and motivation. In N. Borkowski (Ed.), *Organizational behavior in health care* (2nd ed., pp. 147–164). Jones and Bartlett.

Hehman, E., Carpinella, C. M., Johnson, K. L., Leitner, J. B., & Freeman, J. B. (2014). Early processing of gendered facial cues predicts the electoral success of female politicians. *Social Psychology and Personality Science, 5*(7), 815–824.

Heider, F. (1958/2013). *The psychology of interpersonal relations.* Wiley.

Heine, S. J., & Lehman, D. R. (2004). Move the body, change the self: Acculturative effects on self-concept. In A. Schaller & C. Crandall (Eds.), *The psychological foundations of culture* (pp. 305–331). Erlbaum.

Holmstrom, A. J., & Burleson, B. R. (2010). An initial test of a cognitive-emotional theory of esteem support messages. *Journal of Counseling and Development, 88*(1), 92–100.

Hurley, R. W., & Adams, M. C. B. (2008). Sex, gender and pain: An overview of a complex field. *Anesthesia and Analgesia, 107,* 309–317.

Kanizsa, G. (1979). *Organization in vision.* Praeger.

Kellerman, K. (2004). A goal-direct approach to compliance-gaining: Relating differences among goals to differences in behavior. *Communication Research, 31,* 345–347.

Kelley, H. H. (1973). The processes of causal attribution. *American Psychologist, 28,* 107–128.

Kim, M. S. (2002). *Non-Western perspectives on human communication.* Sage.

Kirouac, G., & Hess, U. (1999). Group membership and the decoding of nonverbal behavior. In R. S. Feldman & P. Philippot (Eds.), *The social context of nonverbal behavior* (pp. 182–210). Cambridge University Press.

Krivonos, P. D., & Knapp, M. L. (1975). Initiating communication: What do you say when you say hello? *Central States Speech Journal, 26,* 115–125.

Lakoff, G. (1987). *Women, fire, and dangerous things: What categories reveal about the mind.* University of Chicago Press.

Langer, E. J. (1978). Rethinking the role of thought in social interaction. In J. H. Harvey, W. Ickes, & R. F. Kidd (Eds.), *New directions in attribution research* (Vol. 2, pp. 3–58). Wiley.

Levinthal, D., & Gavetti, G. (2000, March). Looking forward and looking backward: Cognition and experiential search. *Administrative Science Quarterly,* 1–9.

Link, B. G., & Phelan, J. C. (2001, August). Conceptualizing stigma. *Annual Review of Sociology, 27,* 363–385.

Lupfer, M. B., Weeks, M., & Dupuis, S. (2000). How pervasive is the negativity bias in judgments based on character appraisal? *Personality and Social Psychology Bulletin, 26,* 1353–1366.

Manusov, V., & Spitzberg, B. (2008). Attributes of attribution theory: Finding good cause in the search for a theory. In D. O. Braithwaite & L. A. Baxter (Eds.), *Engaging theories in interpersonal* (pp. 37–49). Sage.

Markus, H. R., Mullally, P. R., & Kitayama, S. (1997). Selfways: Diversity in modes of cultural participation. In U. Neisser & D. A. Jopling (Eds.), *The conceptual self in context* (pp. 13–59). Cambridge University Press.

Middle of the class. (July 14, 2005). [Special report: America]. *Economist.* http://www.economist.com/displayStory.cfm?Story_id=4148885

Morgan, M. J. (1977). *Molyneux's question: Vision, touch and the philosophy of perception.* Cambridge University Press.

Morton-Cooper, A. (2004). *Health care and the autism spectrum: A guide for health professionals, parents and careers.* Jessica Kingsley.

NBC News. (July 7, 2020). White woman who called police on black bird watcher in Central Park faces false report charge. https://www.nbcnews.com/news/nbcblk/white-woman-who-called-police-black-bird-watcher-central-park-n1233006

Neale, M. A., & Bazerman, M. H. (1991). *Cognition and rationality in negotiation.* Free Press.

Olivier, C., Leyens, J.-P., Yzerbyt, V. Y., & Walther, E. (1999). Judgeability concerns: The interplay of information, applicability, and accountability in the over-attribution bias. *Journal of Personality and Social Psychology, 76*(3), 377–387. https://doi.org/10.1037/0022-3514.76.3.377

Operario, D., & Fiske, S. T. (2003). Stereotypes: Content, structures, processes, and contexts. In R. Brown & S. L. Gaertner (Eds.) *Blackwell handbook of social psychology: Intergroup processes* (pp. 22–44). Blackwell.

Owen, J. (2012). Men and women really do see things differently. *National Geographic.* https://www.nationalgeographic.com/news/2012/9/120907-men-women-see-differently-science-health-vision-sex/Pearce, W. B. (1994). *Interpersonal communication: Making social worlds.* HarperCollins.

Planalp, S. (1993). Communication, cognition, and emotion. *Communication Monographs, 60,* 3–9.

Putnam, L. L., & Holmer, M. (1992). Framing, reframing and issue development. In L. L. Putnam & M. E. Roloff (Eds.), *Communication and negotiation* (pp. 128–155). Sage.

Rothenberg, P. S. (1992). *Race, class, and gender in the United States.* St. Martin's Press.

Samter, W., & Burleson, B. R. (1984). Cognitive and motivational influences on spontaneous comforting behavior. *Human Communication Research, 11,* 231–260.

Schwarz, N. (2006). Attitude research: Between Ockham's razor and the fundamental attribution error. *Journal of Consumer Research, 33,* 19–21.

SciTechDaily. (2012). *Biology News*. Females distinguish colors better while men excel at tracking fast moving objects. https://scitechdaily.com/females-distinguish-colors-better-while-men-excel-at-tracking-fast-moving-objects/

Scollon, R., & Wong-Scollon, S. (1990). Athabaskan-English interethnic communication. In D. Carbaugh (Ed.), *Cultural communication and intercultural contact* (pp. 259–287). Erlbaum.

Seligman, M. (1998). *Learned optimism*. Simon & Schuster.

Sherwood, B. (2009). *The survivor's club*. Grand Central Publishing.

Shore, B. (1996). *Culture in mind: Cognition, culture and the problem of meaning*. Oxford University Press.

Sillars, A. L., Roberts, L. J., Leonard, K. E., & Dun, T. (2000). Cognition during marital conflict: The relationship of thought and talk. *Journal of Social and Personal Relationships, 17*, 479–502.

Sillars, A. L., Roberts, L. J., Leonard, K. E., & Dun, T. (2002). Cognition and communication during marital conflicts: How alcohol affects subjective coding of interaction in aggressive and nonaggressive couples. In P. Noller & J. A. Feeney (Eds.), *Understanding marriage: Developments in the study of couples' interaction* (pp. 85–112). Cambridge University Press.

Siu, W. L. W., & Finnegan, J. R. (2004, May). *An exploratory study of the interaction of affect and cognition in message evaluation*. Paper presented at the International Communication Association Convention, San Francisco, CA.

Smith, S. W., Kopfman, J. E., Lindsey, L., Massi, Y. J., & Morrison, K. (2004). Encouraging family discussion on the decision to donate organs: The role of the willingness to communicate scale. *Health Communication, 16*, 333–346.

Snyder, M. (1998). Self-fulfilling stereotypes. In P. S. Rothenberg (Ed.), *Race, class and gender in the U.S.: An integrated study* (pp. 452–457). St. Martin's Press.

Solender, A. (April 30, 2020). Armed protesters storm Michigan state house over COVID-19 lockdown. *Forbes Magazine*. https://www.forbes.com/sites/andrewsolender/2020/04/30/armed-protesters-storm-michigan-state-house-over-covid-19-lockdown/#3f9a146369b5

Starkey, J. C., Koerber, A., Sternadori, M., & Pitchford, B. (August 13, 2019). #MeToo goes global: Media framing of silence breakers in four national settings. *Journal of Communication Inquiry, 43*(4), 437–461. https://doi-org.ezproxy1.lib.asu.edu/10.1177/0196859919865254

Stephan, C., & Stephan, W. (1992). Reducing intercultural anxiety through intercultural contact. *International Journal of Intercultural Relations, 16*, 89–106.

Than, K. (2005). Rare but real: People who feel, taste and hear color. *LiveScience*. Retrieved December 15, 2014, from http://www.livescience.com/169-rare-real-people-feel-taste-hear-color.html

Ting-Toomey, S. (1999). *Communicating across cultures*. New York: Guilford.

U.S. National Research Council. (1989). *Improving risk communication*. Committee on risk perception and communication. National Academy Press.

Weick, K. (1995). *Sensemaking in organizations*. Sage.

Chapter 4

Abbott, E. (2020, January 9). Why learning another language can change your life. *The Hill*. https://thehill.com/changing-america/enrichment/education/477414-why-learning-another-language-can-change-your-life

Académie Française. (2017, February 2). *Self-service*. http://www.academie-francaise.fr/self-service

American Civil Liberties Union. (1994). *Free speech: Hate speech on campus*. http://www.aclu.org/free-speech/hate-speech-campus

Anderson, J. F., Beard, F. K., & Walther, J. B. (2010). Turn-taking and the local management of conversation in a highly simultaneous computer-mediated communication system. *Language@Internet*. http://www.languageatinternet.org/articles/2010/2804

Arana, G. (2013, January 10). Creaky voice: Yet another example of young women's linguistic ingenuity. *Atlantic.com*. http://www.theatlantic.com/sexes/archive/2013/01/creaky-voice-yet-another-example-of-young-womens-linguistic-ingenuity/267046/

Asmelash, L. (2020, May 16). Arbiters of the French language say "Covid" is feminine. *CNN*. https://www.cnn.com/2020/05/16/world/academie-franciase-covid-feminine-trnd/index.html

Austrian woman convicted under law that makes Holocaust denial illegal. *Jewish Telegraphic Agency*. http://www.jta.org/2017/02/19/news-opinion/world/austrian-woman-convicted-under-law-that-makes-holocaust-denial-illegal

Aylor, B., & Dainton, M. (2004). Biological sex and psychological gender as predictors of routine and strategic relational maintenance. *Sex Roles: A Journal of Research, 50*, 689–697.

Bippus, A. M., & Young, S. L. (2005). Owning your emotions: Reactions to expressions of self versus other-attributed positive and negative emotions. *Journal of Applied Communication Research, 33*, 26–45.

Bond, S. (2020, July 1). Over 400 advertisers hit pause on Facebook, threatening $70 billion juggernaut. *National Public Radio*. https://www.npr.org/2020/07/01/885853634/big-brands-abandon-facebook-threatening-to-derail-a-70b-advertising-juggernaut

Bowen, S. P. (2012). Jewish and/or woman: Identity and communicative styles. In A. González, M. Houston, & V. Chen. (Eds.), (5th ed., pp. 47–52). Oxford University Press.

Boxer, D. (2002). Nagging: The familial conflict arena. *Journal of Pragmatics, 34*, 49–61.

Burrell, N. A., Donohue, W. A., & Allen, M. (1988). Gender-based perceptual biases in mediation. *Communication Research, 15*, 447–469.

Caughlin, J. P. (2002). The demand/withdraw pattern of communication as a predictor of marital satisfaction over time: Unresolved issues and future directions. *Human Communication Research, 28*, 49–85.

Chomsky, N. (1957). *Syntactic structures*. Mouton.

Cohen, R. (2014, March 12). In defense of *I can't even*. *Slate.com*. http://www.slate.com/blogs/lexicon_valley/2014/03/12/language_i_can_t_even_is_just_the_newest_example_of_an_old_greek_rhetorical.html

"Covid-19" bald im Duden? (2020, May 9). *Taggeschau.de*. https://www.tagesschau.de/inland/corona-duden-101.html#:~:text=Social%20Distancing%2C%20Corona%2DParty%20oder,einigen%20Wochen%20noch%20unbekannt%20waren.&text=%22Hei%C3%9Fer%20Kandidat%20f%C3%BCr%20die%20Aufnahme,Redaktion%2C%20Kathrin%20Kunkel%2DRazum

Crystal, D. (2003). *The Cambridge encyclopedia of the English language*. Cambridge University Press.

Dance, F. E. X., & Larson, C. E. (1976). *The functions of human communication*. Holt, Rinehart, & Winston.

Deutscher, G. (2010). *Through the language glass: Why the world looks different in other languages*. Metropolitan Books.

Duke, M. P., Fivush, R., Lazarus, A., & Bohanek, J. (2003). *Of ketchup and kin: Dinnertime conversations as a major source of family knowledge, family adjustment, and family resilience* [Working Paper #26]. http://www.marial.emory.edu/research/

Edwards, J. V. (2004). Foundations of bilingualism. In T. K. Bhatia & W. C. Ritchie (Eds.), *The handbook of bilingualism* (pp. 7–31). Blackwell.

Ellis, A., & Beattie, G. (1986). Variations within a language. *The psychology of language and communication*. (pp. 109–114). Psychology Press.

Fromkin, V., & Rodman, R. (1983). *An introduction to language*. Holt, Rinehart, and Winston.

Gamp, O. (2017, February 12). Online giant Amazon facing pressure over Holocaust denial books. *International Business Times*. http://www.ibtimes.co.uk/online-giant-amazon-facing-pressure-over-holocaust-denial-books-1606130

Gong, G. (2012). When Mississippi Chinese talk. In A. González, M. Houston, & V. Chen (Eds.), *Our voices: Essays in culture, ethnicity, and communication* (5th ed., pp. 104–111). Oxford University Press.

Gray, J. (2012). *Men are from Mars, women are from Venus* (20th anniversary ed.). HarperCollins.

Hannah, A., & Murachver, T. (2007). Gender preferential responses to speech. *Journal of Language and Social Psychology, 26*(3), 274–290.

Hecht, M. L., Jackson, R. L., II, & Ribeau, S. A. (2003). *African American communication*. Lawrence Erlbaum Associates.

Hegarty, P., & Buechel, C. (2006). Androcentric reporting of gender differences in APA journals: 1965–2004. *Review of General Psychology*, *10*(4), 377–389.

Heilman, M. E. (2001). Description and prescription: How gender stereotypes prevent women's ascent up the organizational ladder. In "Gender, hierarchy and leadership," Ed. L. Carli & A. Eagly. *Journal of Social Issues*, *57*(4), 657–674.

Heilman, M. E., Caleo, S., & Halim, M. L. (2010). Just the thought of it! Effects of anticipating computer-mediated communication on gender stereotyping. *Journal of Experimental Social Psychology*, *46*(4), 672–675.

Hern, A. (2020, June 29). How hate speech campaigners found Facebook's weak spot. *The Guardian*. https://www.theguardian.com/technology/2020/jun/29/how-hate-speech-campaigners-found-facebooks-weak-spot

Hess, A. (2016, March 29). Who's 'they'? *New York Times*. https://www.nytimes.com/2016/04/03/magazine/whos-they.html

Hoijer, H. (1994). The Sapir-Whorf hypothesis. In L. Samovar & R. E. Porter (Eds.), *Intercultural communication: A reader* (pp. 194–200). Wadsworth.

Holmes, S. (2017, February 12). Dozens of books claiming the Holocaust was a HOAX are available on Amazon for as little as 99 p. *Daily Mail*. http://www.dailymail.co.uk/news/article-4216568/Dozens-books-claiming-Holocaust-hoax-Amazon-buy.html

Hsu, T., & Lutz, E. (2020, August 1). More than 1,000 companies boycotted Facebook. Did it work? *New York Times*. https://www.nytimes.com/2020/08/01/business/media/facebook-boycott.html

Hudson, R. A. (1983*). Sociolinguistics*. Cambridge University Press.

Hyde, J. S. (2006). Gender similarities still rule. *American Psychologist*, *61*(6), 641–642.

Kikoski, J. F., & Kikoski, C. K. (1999). *Reflexive communication in the culturally diverse workplace*. Praeger.

Kim, M. S. (2002). *Non-Western perspectives on human communication*. Sage.

Kohonen, S. (2004). Turn-taking in conversation: Overlaps and interruptions in intercultural talk. *Cahiers*, *10*(1), 15–32.

Kubany, E. S., Bauer, G. B., Muraoka, M., Richard, D. C., & Read, P. (1995). Impact of labeled anger and blame in intimate relationships. *Journal of Social and Clinical Psychology*, *14*, 53–60.

Labov, W. (1980). The social origins of sound change. In W. Labov (Ed.), *Locating language in time and space* (pp. 251–265). Academic Press.

Labov, W. (Ed.). (2005). *Atlas of North American English*. Walter De Gruyter.

Leaper, C., & Ayres, M. M. (2007). A meta-analytic review of gender variation in adults' language use: Talkativeness, affiliative speech, and assertive speech. *Personality and Social Psychology Review*, *11*(4), 328–363.

Levenson, M. (2020, February 29). Mother and daughter attacked for speaking Spanish, prosecutor says. *New York Times*. https://www.nytimes.com/2020/02/29/us/east-boston-hate-crime-attack.html

Liptak, A. (2008). Hate speech or free speech? What much of West bans is protected in U.S. *New York Times*. http://www.nytimes.com/2008/06/11/world/americas/11iht-hate.4.13645369.html

Martin, J. N., Krizek, R. L., Nakayama, T. K., & Bradford, L. (1999). What do white people want to be called? A study of self-labels for white Americans. In T. K. Nakayama & J. N. Martin (Eds.), *Whiteness: The communication of social identity* (pp. 27–50). Sage.

Media Awareness Network. (n.d.). Online hate and free speech. http://mediasmarts.ca/online-hate/online-hate-and-free-speech

Mehl, M. R., & Pennebaker, J. W. (2003). The sounds of social life: A psychometric analysis of students' daily social environments and natural conversations. *Journal of Personality and Social Psychology*, *84*, 857–870.

Mey, J. L. (2001). *Pragmatics: An introduction* (2nd ed.). Blackwell Publishing.

Mulac, A., Bradac, J. J., & Gibbons, P. (2001). Empirical support for the gender-as-culture hypothesis: An intercultural analysis of male/female language differences. *Human Communication Research*, *27*, 121–152.

Nofsinger, R. (1999). *Everyday conversation*. Waveland.

Orbe, M. P. (1998). *Constructing co-cultural theory: An explication of culture, power, and communication*. Sage.

Panko, B. (2016, December 2). Does the linguistic theory at the center of the film 'Arrival' have any merit? *Smithsonian Magazine*. https://www.smithsonianmag.com/science-nature/does-century-old-linguistic-hypothesis-center-film-arrival-have-any-merit-180961284

Paramasivam, S. (2007). Managing disagreement while managing not to disagree: Polite disagreement in negotiation discourse. *Journal of Intercultural Communication Research*, *36*(2), 91–116.

Park, J. E. (2016). Turn-taking in Korean conversation. *Journal of Pragmatics*, *99*, 62–77.

Pennebaker, J. W., & Stone, L. D. (2003). Words of wisdom: Language use across the life span. *Journal of Personality and Social Psychology*, *82*, 291–301.

Philips, S. U. (1990). Some sources of cultural variability in the regulation of talk. In D. Carbaugh (Ed.), *Cultural communication and intercultural contact* (pp. 329–344). Erlbaum.

Piaget, J. (1952). *The origins of intelligence in children*. International Universities Press.

Pinker, S. (2007). *The stuff of thought: Language as a window into human nature*. Viking.

Pinto, D., & Raschio, R. (2007). A comparative study of requests in heritage speaker Spanish, L1 Spanish, and L1 English. *International Journal of Bilingualism*, *11*(2), 135–155.

Polari: The secret language gay men used to survive. (2018, February 12). *BBC News*. https://www.bbc.com/culture/article/20180212-polari-the-code-language-gay-men-used-to-survive

Preston, D. R. (2003). Where are the dialects of American English at anyhow? *American Speech*, *78*, 235–254.

Ramírez-Esparza, N., Gosling, S. D., Benet-Martínez, V., Potter, J. D., & Pennebaker, J. W. (2006). Do bilinguals have two personalities? A special case of cultural frame switching. *Journal of Research in Personality*, *40*, 99–120.

Reid, S. A., Keerie, N., & Palomares, N. A. (2003). Language, gender salience, and social influence. *Journal of Language and Social Psychology*, *22*, 210–233.

Ruben, D. L. (2003). Help! My professor (or doctor or boss) doesn't talk English! In J. N. Martin, T. K. Nakayama, & L. A. Flores (Eds.). *Readings in intercultural communication* (2nd ed., pp. 127–138). McGraw-Hill.

Sacks, H., Schegloff, E., & Jefferson, G. (1978). A simplest systematics for the organization of turn-taking for conversation. In J. Schenkein (Ed.), *Studies in the organization of conversational interaction* (pp. 7–55). Academic Press.

Sagrestano, L. M., Heavey, C. L., & Christensen, A. (1998). Theoretical approaches to understanding sex differences and similarities in conflict behavior. In D. J. Canary & K. Dindia (Eds.), *Sex differences and similarities in communication: Critical essays and empirical investigations on sex and gender in interaction* (pp. 287–302). Erlbaum.

Sauerbrey, A. (2013, September 25). How do you say "blog" in German? *New York Times*. http://www.nytimes.com/2013/09/26/opinion/how-do-you-say-blog-in-german.html?_r=0

Sbisa, M. (2002). Speech act in context. *Language & Communication*, *22*, 421–436.

Schegloff, E. A. (2000). Overlapping talk and the organization of turn-taking for conversation. *Language in Society*, *29*, 1–63.

Scheibel, D. (1995). Making waves with Burke: Surf Nazi culture and the rhetoric of localism. *Western Journal of Communication*, *59* (4), 253–269.

Sedivy, J. (2012, March 28). Votes and vowels: A changing accent shows how language parallels politics. *Discover*. http://blogs.discovermagazine.com/crux/2012/03/28/votes-and-vowels-a-changing-accent-shows-how-language-parallels-politics/#.UxoiICifNiF

Sellers, J. G., Woolsey, M. D., & Swann, J. B. (2007). Is silence more golden for women than men? Observers derogate effusive women and their quiet partners. *Sex Roles*, *57*(7–8), 477–482.

Sharma, D. (2019, November 25). British people still think some accents are smarter than others—what that means in the workplace. *The Conversation*. https://theconversation.com/british-people-still-think-some-accents-are-smarter-than-others-what-that-means-in-the-workplace-126964

Sharon, J. (2019, February 13). "Landmark decision" in UK upholds conviction for Holocaust denial. *The Jerusalem Post*. https://www

.jpost.com/diaspora/landmark-decision-in-uk-upholds-conviction-for-holocaust-denial-580589

Shutiva, C. (2012). Native American culture and communication through humor. In A. González, M. Houston, & V. Chen (Eds.), *Our voices: Essays in culture, ethnicity, and communication* (5th ed., pp. 134–138). Oxford University Press.

Social Mobility Commission. (2017, January 26). New research uncovers "class pay gap" in Britain's professions. https://www.gov.uk/government/news/new-research-uncovers-class-pay-gap-in-britains-professions

U.S. Department of Health and Human Services. (n.d.). *What is cyberbullying?* http://www.stopbullying.gov/cyberbullying/what-is-it/

Walker, J. L. (2010). *You are an African American, so why are you talking like a white person?* P.T.C.E, Inc.

Weger, H., Jr. (2005). Disconfirming communication and self-verification in marriage: Associations among the demand/withdraw interaction pattern, feeling understood, and marital satisfaction. *Journal of Social and Personal Relationships, 22,* 19–31.

Where are the world's best English-speakers? (2019, December 4). *The Economist.* https://www.economist.com/graphic-detail/2019/12/04/where-are-the-worlds-best-english-speakers

White, D. (2020, January 14). Woman attacks nail salon worker with knife for not speaking English, Oklahoma cops say. *The Kansas City Star.* https://www.kansascity.com/news/nation-world/national/article239277303.html

Why the family meal is important. (2020). *Stanford Children's Health.* https://www.stanfordchildrens.org/en/topic/default?id=why-the-family-meal-is-important-1-701

Willsher, K. (2016, February 5). Not the oignon: Fury as France changes 2,000 spellings and drops some accents. *The Guardian.* https://www.theguardian.com/world/2016/feb/05/not-the-oignon-fury-france-changes-2000-spellings-ditches-circumflex

Wissing, R. (2020, Summer). The secret language used by LGBTQ people in Turkey. *Attitude.* https://attitude.co.uk/article/the-secret-language-used-by-lgbtq-people-in-turkey-1/23524/?s=09

Wood, J. T. (2002). *Gendered lives: Communication, gender and cultures.* Wadsworth.

Chapter 5

Abu-Ghazzeh, T. M. (2000). Environmental messages in multiple family housing: Territory and personalization. *Landscape Research, 25,* 97–114.

Als, H. (1977). The newborn communicates. *Journal of Communication, 2,* 66–73.

Axtell, R. (1993). *Do's and taboos around the world.* Wiley.

Becker, F. D. (1973). Study of special markers. *Journal of Personality and Social Psychology, 26,* 429–445.

Birdwhistell, R. L. (1985). *Kinesics and context: Essays in body motion communication.* University of Philadelphia Press.

Boone, R. T., & Cunningham, J. G. (1998). Children's decoding of emotion in expressive body movement: The development of cue attunement. *Developmental Psychology, 34,* 1007–1016.

Briton, N. J., & Hall, J. A. (1995). Beliefs about female and male nonverbal communication. *Sex Roles, 32,* 79–90.

Burgoon, J. K., & Guerrero, L. K. (1994). Nonverbal communication. In M. Burgoon, F. G. Hunsaker, & E. J. Dawson (Eds.), *Human communication* (pp. 122–171). Sage.

Burgoon, J. K., & Hale, J. L. (1988). Nonverbal expectancy violations: Model elaboration and application to immediacy behaviors. *Communication Monographs, 55,* 58–79.

Burgoon, J. K., & Le Poire, B. A. (1993). Effects of communication expectancies, actual communication, and expectancy disconfirmation on evaluations of communicators and their communication behavior. *Human Communication Research, 20*(1), 67–96.

Burgoon, J. K., Buller, D. B., & Woodall, W. G. (1996). *Nonverbal communication: The unspoken dialogue.* Harper & Row.

Business Wire. (2020, March 20). *Global cosmetic skin care market 2020–2024: Evolving opportunities.* http://businesswire.com/news/home/20200302005469/en/Global-Cosmetic-Skin-Care-Market-2020-2024-Evolving

Capella, J. (1985). The management of conversations. In M. L. Knapp & G. R. Miller (Eds.), *Handbook of interpersonal communication* (pp. 393–435). Sage.

Centers for Disease Control and Prevention. (2020, July 5). Social distancing. *Coronavirus disease 2019 (COVID-19).* https://www.cdc.gov/coronavirus/2019-ncov/prevent-getting-sick/social-distancing.html

Chartrand, T. L., & Bargh, J. A. (1999). The chameleon effect: The perception-behavior link and social interaction. *Journal of Personality and Social Psychology, 76,* 893–910.

Chemaly, S. (2018). *Rage becomes her: The power of women's anger).* Atria Books.

Chiang, L. H. (1993, October). *Beyond the language: Native Americans' nonverbal communication.* Paper presented at the annual meeting of the Midwest Association of Teachers of Educational Psychology, Anderson, IN: October 1–2.

Cicca, A. H., Step, M., & Turkstra, L. (2003, December 16). Show me what you mean: Nonverbal communication theory and application. *ASHA Leader, 34,* 4–5.

Dié, L. (2008, November 9). Obama: Speech patterns analyzed. *News Flavor: U. S. Politics.* http://newsflavor.com/category/politics/us-politics/

Dijksterhuis, A., & Smith, P. K. (2005). What do we do unconsciously? And how? *Journal of Consumer Psychology 15*(3), 225–229.

Duke, L. (2002). Get real! Cultural relevance and resistance to the mediated feminine ideal. *Psychology and Marketing, 19,* 211–234.

Eibl-Eibesfeld, I. (1972). Similarities and differences between cultures in expressive movement. In R. A. Hinde (Ed.), *Nonverbal communication* (pp. 297–314). Cambridge University Press.

Ekman, P. (2003). *Emotions revealed: Recognizing faces and feelings to improve communication and emotional life.* Times Books.

Ekman, P., & Friesen, W. V. (1969). The repertoire of nonverbal behavior: Categories, origins, usage and coding. *Semiotica, 1,* 49–98.

Ekman, P., & Friesen, W. V. (1986). A new pan-cultural expression of emotion. *Motivation and Emotion, 10*(2), 159–168.

Elfenbein, H. A. (2006). Learning in emotion judgments: Teaching and the cross-cultural understanding of facial expressions. *Journal of Nonverbal Communication, 30,* 21–36.

Elfenbein, H. A., Maw, D. F., White, J., Tan, H. H., & Aik, V. C. (2007). Reading your counterpart: The benefit of emotion recognition accuracy for effectiveness in negotiation. *Journal of Nonverbal Behavior, 31,* 205–223.

Eskritt, M., & Lee, K. (2003) Do actions speak louder than words? Preschool children's use of the verbal-nonverbal consistency principle during inconsistent communication. *Journal of Nonverbal Behavior, 27,* 25–41.

Field, T. (2002). Infants' need for touch. *Human Development, 45,* 100–104.

Fussell, P. (1992). *Class: A guide through the American status system.* Touchstone Books.

Givens, D. B. (2005). *The nonverbal dictionary of gestures, signs, and body language cues.* Center for Nonverbal Studies Press.

Grammer, K., Fink, B., Joller, A., & Thornhill, R. (2003). Darwinian aesthetics: Sexual selection and the biology of beauty. *Biological Reviews, 78,* 385–408.

Guerrero, L. K., & Andersen, P. A. (1991). The waxing and waning of relational intimacy: Touch as a function of relational stage, gender, and touch avoidance. *Journal of Social and Personal Relationships, 8,* 147–165.

Guerrero, L. K., & Andersen, P. A. (1994). Patterns of matching and initiation: Touch behavior and touch avoidance across romantic relationship stages. *Journal of Nonverbal Behavior, 18,* 137–153.

Guerrero, L. K., & Ebesu, A. S. (1993, May). While at play: An observational analysis of children's touch during interpersonal interaction. Paper presented at the annual conference of the International Communication Association, Washington, DC.

Gundersen, D. F. (1990). Uniforms: Conspicuous invisibility. In J. A. Devito & M. L. Hecht (Eds.), *The nonverbal communication reader* (pp. 172–178). Waveland.

Hall, E. T. (1966). *The hidden dimension.* Doubleday.

Hall, E. T. (1983). *The dance of life.* Doubleday.

Hall, E. T., & Hall, M. R. (1987). *Hidden differences: Doing business with the Japanese.* Anchor.

Hall, E. T., & Hall, M. R. (1990). *Understanding cultural differences: Germans, French and Americans.* Intercultural Press.

Hanzal, A., Segrin, C., & Dorros, S. M. (2008). The role of marital status and age on men's and women's reactions to touch from a relational partner. *Journal of Nonverbal Behavior, 32,* 21–35.

Harrison, S. (2014, May 21). The most charisma-free actors. *TV Guide.* https://www.tvguide.com/galleries/charisma-free-actors-1081847/3/

Isaacson, L. A. (1998). Student dress codes. *ERIC Digest, 117.* http://eric.uoregon.edu/publications/digests/digest117.html

Johnson, A. G. (2001). *Privilege, power, and difference.* McGraw-Hill.

Jones, S. E., & LeBaron, C. D. (2002). Research on the relationship between verbal and nonverbal communication: Emerging integration. *Journal of Communication, 52,* 499–521.

Kemmer, S. (1992). Are we losing our touch? *Total Health, 14,* 46–49.

Knapp, M. L., & Hall, J. A. (1992). *Nonverbal communication in human interaction* (3rd ed.). Holt, Rinehart and Winston.

Knapp, M. L., & Hall, J. A. (2001). *Nonverbal communication in human interaction.* Wadsworth.

Koerner, A., & Fitzpatrick, M.A. (2002). Nonverbal communication and marital adjustment and satisfaction: The role of decoding relationship relevant and relationship irrelevant affect. *Communication Monographs, 68*(1), 33–51.

Kraus, M., & Keltner, D. (2009). Signs of socio-economic status: A thin-slicing approach. *Psychological Science, 20,* 99–106.

Lord, T. L. (2009). *The relationship of gender-based public harassment to body image, self-esteem, and avoidance behavior.* (Unpublished dissertation). Indiana University of Pennsylvania.

Manusov, V. (1995). Reacting to changes in nonverbal behaviors: Relational satisfaction and adaptation patterns in romantic dyads. *Human Communication Research, 21,* 456–477.

Manusov, V., & Patterson, M. (2006). *Handbook of nonverbal communication.* Sage.

Marketdata LLC. (2019). The U.S. weight loss & diet control market. *Research and Markets.* Research and Markets.

Mast, M. S., & Hall, J. A. (2004). Who is the boss and who is not? Accuracy of judging status. *Journal of Nonverbal Behavior, 28,* 145–165.

Matsumoto, D. (2006). Culture and nonverbal behavior. In V. Manusov & M. Patters (Eds.), *Handbook of nonverbal communication* (pp. 219–235). Sage.

McLaughlin, C., Olson, R., & White, M. (2008). Environmental issues in patient care management: Proxemics, personal space, and territoriality. *Rehabilitation Nursing, 33*(4), 143–147.

Mehrabian, A. (1971). *Nonverbal communication.* Aldine-Atherton.

Mehrabian, A. (2007). *Nonverbal communication.* Aldine de Gruyter.

Mehrabian, A., & Weiner, M. (1967). Decoding of inconsistent communication. *Journal of Personality and Social Psychology, 6,* 109–114.

Meltzoff, A. N., & Prinz, W. (2002). *The imitative mind: Development, evolution, and brain bases.* Cambridge University Press.

Montepare, J. M., Goldstein, S. B., & Clausen, A. (1987). The identification of emotions from gait information. *Ethology and Sociobiology, 6,* 237–247.

Müller, C., Cienki, A., Fricke, E., Ladewig, S., McNeill, D., & Tessendorf, S. (2014). Ring-gestures across cultures and times: Dimensions in variation. In C. Müller, A. Cienki, E. Fricke, S. Ladewig, D. McNeill, & J. Bressem (Eds.), *Body–Language–Communication* (pp. 1511–1522). De Gruyter Mouton.

Newport, F. (1999). Americans agree that being attractive is a plus in American society. *Gallup Poll Monthly, 408,* 45–49.

Ohl, A. (2012). *Personal space and friendship in Asperger and neurotypical adolescents.* Doctoral dissertation, Proquest LLC, New York.

Parasuram, T. V. (2003, October 23). Sikh shot and injured in Arizona hate crime. *Sikh Times.* http://www.sikhtimes.com/news_052103a.html

Patterson, M. L. (1982). A sequential functional model of nonverbal exchange. *Psychological Bulletin, 89,* 231–249.

Patterson, M. L. (1983). *Nonverbal behavior.* Springer.

Patterson, M. L. (2003). Commentary. Evolution and nonverbal behavior: Functions and mediating processes. *Journal of Nonverbal Behavior, 27,* 201–207.

Phillips, J. (1998). Personal space in a virtual community. In C. M. Carat & A. Lund (Eds.), *Summary of the conference in human factors in computing systems* (pp. 347–348). ACM.

Richards, V., Rollerson, B., & Phillips, J. (1991). Perceptions of submissiveness: Implications for victimization. *Journal of Psychology, 125*(4), 407–411.

Richeson, J. A., & Shelton, J. N. (2005). Brief report: Thin slices of racial bias. *Journal of Nonverbal Behavior, 29,* 75–86.

Rutstein, A. (2019, March). On a woman being told to smile. *Women in Higher Education, 28*(3), 6.

Samovar, L., & Porter, R. (2004). *Communication between cultures.* Thomson, Wadsworth.

Schwartz, L. M., Foa, U. G., & Foa, E. B. (1983) Multichannel nonverbal communication: Evidence for combinatory rules. *Journal of Personality and Social Psychology, 45,* 274–281.

Segerstrale, U., & Molnár, P. (Eds.). (1997). *Nonverbal communication: Where nature meets culture* (pp. 27–46). Erlbaum.

Shelp, S. (2002). Gaydar: Visual detection of sexual orientation among gay and straight men. *Journal of Homosexuality, 44,* 1–14.

Swales, V. (2019, December, 15). When the o.k. sign is no longer ok. *New York Times.* https://www.nytimes.com/2019/12/15/us/ok-sign-white-power.html

Tiedens, L., & Fragale, A. (2003). Power moves: Complementarity in dominant and submissive nonverbal behavior. *Journal of Personality and Social Psychology, 84,* 558–568.

Trost, M. R., & Alberts, J. K. (2006). How men and women communicate attraction: An evolutionary view. In D. Canary & K. Dindia (Eds.), *Sex, gender and communication: Similarities and differences* (2nd ed., pp. 317–336). Lawrence Erlbaum.

Tuleja, T. (2012). In the wink of an eye: Gestures and posture. *Curious customs.* Stonesong Press.

Watson, O., & Graves, T. (1966). Quantitative research in proxemic behavior. *American Anthropologist, 68,* 971–985.

Wing Sue, D. (2010). *Microaggressions in everyday life: Race, gender, and sexual orientation.* Wiley.

Wise, T. (2005, October 23). Opinions on NBA dress code are far from uniform. *Washington Post,* p. A01. http://www.washingtonpost.com/wp-dyn/content/article/2005/10/22/AR2005102201386.html

Wolburg, J. M. (2001). Preserving the moment, commodifying time, and improving upon the past: Insights into the depiction of time in American advertising. *Journal of Communication, 51,* 696–720.

Wolf, C. (2020, June 29). The NBA's new relaxed dress code kisses the suit goodbye. *GQ.* https://www.gq.com/story/nba-dress-code-orlando-bubble

Young, R. L. (1999). *Understanding misunderstandings.* University of Texas Press.

Chapter 6

American Debate League. (n.d.). What is debate? https://www.americandebateleague.org/what-is-debate.html#/

Azvier, H., Trope, Y., & Todorov, A. (2012). Body cues, not facial expressions, discriminate between intense positive and negative emotions. *Science, 338*(6111), 1225–1229.

Bates, T. (2016, January 17). Sexual coercion of men often unreported, misunderstood. *Rome Sentinel.* https://romesentinel.com/stories/sexual-coercion-of-men-often-unreported-misunderstood,37366

Baugh, J. (2003). Linguistic profiling. In A. Ball, S. Makoni, G. Smitherman, & A. K. Spears (Eds.), *Black linguistics: Language, society, and politics in Africa and the America* (pp. 155–168). Routledge.

Beres, M. A. (2014). Rethinking the concept of consent for anti-sexual violence activism and education. *Feminism & Psychology, 24*(3), 373–389.

Blatt, B., LeLacheur, S. F., Galinsky, A., Simmens, S. J. & Greenberg, L. (2010). Does perspective taking increase patient satisfaction in medical encounters? *Academic Medicine, 85*(9), 1445–1452.

Bowles, H. R., & Babcock, L. (2007). Social incentives for divergences in the propensity to initiate negotiations: Sometimes it does hurt to ask. *Organizational Behavior and Human Decision Processes, 103,* 84–103.

Consent conversations. (n.d.). Sexual Assault Centre of Edmonton. https://www.sace.ca/learn/consent-conversations/

Cote, S., Kraus, M., Piff, P. K., Beerman, U., Keltner, D. (2014). Social class clash: A dyadic model of social affiliation in cross-class and same-class interactions. *Rotman School of Management Working Paper No. 2503031,* 1–69.

Croy, I., Buschhüter, D., Seo, H. S., Negoias, S., & Hummel, T. (2010). Individual significance of olfaction: Development of a questionnaire. *European Archives of Oto-Rhino-Laryngology, 267*(1), 67–71. https://doi.org/10.1007/s00405-009-1054-0

de Groot, J. S. B., Simen, G. R., & Smeets, M. A. M. (2014). I can see, hear and smell your fear: Comparing olfactory and audiovisual media in fear communication. *Journal of Experimental Psychology, 143*(2), 825–834.

Dragojevic, M., Giles, H., Beck, C., & Tatum, N. T. (2017). The fluency principle: Why foreign accent strength negatively biases language attitudes. *Communication Monographs, 84*(3), 385–405.

Duffy, J. (2019). The power of perspective taking. *Psychology Today.* https://www.psychologytoday.com/nz/blog/the-power-personal-narrative/201906/the-power-perspective-taking

Dunleavy, K. N., Goodboy, A., Booth-Butterfield, M., Sidelinger, R. J., & Banfield, S. (2009). Repairing hurtful messages in marital relationships. *Communication Quarterly, 57*(1), 67–84.

Ekman, P. (2004). *Emotions revealed: Recognizing faces and feelings to improve communication and emotional life.* Holt McDougal.

Fields, J. (n.d.) The line between persuasion and manipulation. https://www.jonathanfields.com/the-line-between-persuasion-and-manipulation/

Folkes, V. F. (1982). Communicating the reasons for social rejection. *Journal of Experimental Social Psychology, 18*(3), 235–252.

Franzoi, S. L., Davis, M. H., & Young, R. D. (1985). The effects of private self-consciousness and perspective taking on satisfaction in close relationships. *Journal of Personality and Social Psychology, 48*(6), 1584–1594. https://doi.org/10.1037/0022-3514.48.6.1584

French, B. H., Tilghman, J. D., & Malebranche, D. A. (2015). Sexual coercion context and psychosocial correlates among diverse males. *Psychology of Men & Masculinity, 16*(1), 42–53. https://doi.org/10.1037/a0035915

Galinsky, A. D., Ku, G., & Wang, C. S. (2005). Perspective-taking and self-other overlap: Fostering social bonds and facilitating social coordination. *Group Processes and Intergroup Relations, 8*(2), 109–124.

Galinsky, A. D., & Moskowitz, G. B. (2000). Perspective-taking: Decreasing stereotype expression, stereotype accessibility, and ingroup favoritism. *Journal of Personality and Social Psychology, 78*(4), 708–724. https://doi.org/10.1037/0022-3514.78.4.708

Gehlbach, H., Young, L. V., & Roan, L. K. (2012) Teaching social perspective taking: How educators might learn from the Army. *Educational Psychology, 32*(3), 295–309. https://doi.org/10.1080/01443410.2011.652807

Goldfarb, Z. A. (2014). *Economic policy.* https://www.washingtonpost.com/news/wonk/wp/2014/03/05/these-four-charts-show-how-the-sat-favors-the-rich-educated-families/?arc404=true

Goldschmidt, O. T., & Weller, L. (2011). "Talking emotions": Gender differences in a variety of conversational contexts. https://onlinelibrary.wiley.com/doi/abs/10.1525/si.2000.23.2.117

Grant, A. M. & Berry, J. W. The necessity of others is the mother of invention: Intrinsic and prosocial motivations, perspective taking, and creativity. *Academy of Management, 54*(1), 73–96.

Grogger, J. (2019). Speech and wages. *Journal of Human Resources, 54*(4), 926–952.

Guadagno, R. B., & Cialdini, R. E. (2007). Gender differences in impression management in organizations: A qualitative review. *Sex Roles 56,*483–494. https://doi.org/10.1007/s11199-007-9187-3Heilmen, M. E., Wallen, A. S., Fuchs, D., & Tamkins, M. M. (2004). Penalties for success: Reactions to women who succeed at male gender-typed tasks. *Journal of Applied Psychology, 89*(3), 416–427. https://doi.org/10.1037/0021-9010.89.3.416

Herz, R. S., & Inzlicht, M. (2002). Sex differences in response to physical and social factors involved in human mate selection: The importance of smell for women. *Evolution and Human Behavior, 23*(5), 359–364. https://doi.org/10.1016/S1090-5138(02)00095-8

Hoever, I. J., van Knippenberg, D., van Ginkel, W. P., & Barkema, H. G. (2012). Fostering team creativity: Perspective taking as key to unlocking diversity's potential. *Journal of Applied Psychology, 97*(5), 982–996. https://doi.org/10.1037/a0029159

Holmes, J., & Stubbe, M. (1997). Good listeners: Gender differences in New Zealand conversation. *Women and Language, 20*(2), 7–14.

Hummel, T., Kobal, G., Gudziol, H., & Mackay-Sim, A. (2007). Normative data for the "Sniffin' Sticks" including tests of odor identification, odor discrimination, and olfactory thresholds: An upgrade

based on a group of more than 3,000 subjects. *European Archives of Oto-Rhino-Laryngology, 264*(3), 237–243.

Hyde, J. & Grieve, R. (2018). The dark side of emotion at work: Manipulation in everyday and work place contexts. *Personality and Differences, 129,* 108–113.

Jin, B. (2013). Hurtful texting in friendships: Satisfaction buffers the distancing effects of intention, *Communication Research Reports, 30*(2), 148–156.

Johnson, F. L., & Aries, E. J. (2012). Conversational patterns among same-sex pairs of late-adolescent close friends. *Journal of Genetic Psychology, 142,* 225–238.

Korneliussen, I. (2012). Women smell better than men. *Science Nordic.* http://sciencenordic.com/women-smell-better-men

Kraus, M. W., Torrez, B., Park, J. W., & Ghayebi, F. (2019). Evidence for the reproduction of social class in brief speech. *Proceedings of the National Academy of Sciences of the United States of America, 116*(46), 22998–23003.

Krauss, R. M., & Fussell, S. R. (1991). Perspective-taking in communication: Representations of others' knowledge in reference. *Social Cognition, 9*(1), 2–24. https://doi.org/10.1521/soco.1991.9.1.2

Leaper, C., & Ayres, M. M. (2007). A meta-analytic review of gender variations in adults' language use: Talkativeness, affiliative speech, and assertive speech. *Personality and Social Psychology, 11*(4), 328–363.

Lord, C. G., Lepper, M. R., & Preston, E. (1984). Considering the opposite: A corrective strategy for social judgment. *Journal of Personality and Social Psychology, 47*(6), 1231–1243. https://doi.org/10.1037/0022-3514.47.6.1231

Maccaby, E. E., & Jacklin, C. N. (1978). *The psychology of sex differences.* Stanford University Press.

Martini, T. S., Grusec, J. E., & Bernardini, S. C. (2001). Effects of interpersonal control, perspective taking, and attributions on older mothers' and adult daughters' satisfaction with their helping relationships. *Journal of Family Psychology, 15,* 688–705.

McCoy, N. & Pitino, L. (2002). Pheromonal influences on sociosexual behavior in young women. *Physiology and Behavior, 75*(3), 367–375.

McEwen, W. J., & Greenberg, B. S. (1970). The effects of message intensity on receiver evaluations of source, message, and topic. *Journal of Communication, 20,* 340–350.

McLeod, L. (2015). Towards a culture of consent: Sexual consent styles and contemporary social interventions. (Unpublished thesis). James Cook University, Cairns, Australia.

McNeal, A., Fiallo, K., Jones, A., Jones, S., Laureano, S., Monjarrez, M. & Xu, Y. (2019). "Sounding Black": The legal implications of linguistic profiling. *Northeastern University Working Papers in Linguistics, 4.* https://cos.northeastern.edu/wp-content/uploads/2016/07/MacNeal-et-al-2019.pdf#_ga=2.51975273.1139904720.1604948485-2036969815.1604948485

Merrill, N., Gallo, E., & Fivush, R. (2015). Gender differences in family dinnertime conversations. *Discourse Processes, 52*(7), 533–588.

Mills, R. S. L., Nazar, J., & Farrell, H. M. (2002). Child and parent perceptions of hurtful messages. *Journal of Social and Personal Relationships, 19*(6), 731–754.

Muehlenhard, C. L., Humphreys, T. P., Jozkowski, K. N., & Peterson, Z. D. (2016). The complexities of sexual consent among college students: A conceptual and empirical review. *Journal of Sex Research, 54*(4–5), 457–487.

Myers, S. A., & Bryant, L. (2008). Adult siblings' use of verbally aggressive messages as hurtful messages. *Communication Quarterly, 56*(3), 268–283.

Myers, S. A., Schrodt, P., & Rittenour, C. E. (2006). The impact of parents' use of hurtful messages on adult children's self-esteem and educational motivation. In L. H. Turner & R. West (Eds.), *The family communication sourcebook* (p. 425–445). Sage Publications, Inc. https://doi.org/10.4135/9781452233024.n23

Nofsinger, R. E. (1991). *Everyday conversation.* Sage Publications, Inc.

Nour, L. (2019, January 31). Understanding linguistic discrimination: Consequences and policy responses. *Policy Perspectives.* https://policy-perspectives.org/2019/01/31/understanding-linguistic-discrimination-consequences-and-policy-responses

Oakley, J. G. (2000). Gender-based barriers to senior management positions: Understanding the scarcity of female CEOs. *Journal of Business Ethics, 27,* 321–334.

Park, H. S., & Raile, A. N. (2010). Perspective taking and communication satisfaction in coworker dyads. *Journal of Business and Psychology, 25*(4), 569–581.

Perrachione, T. K., Chiao, J. Y., & Wong, P. C. M. (2010). Asymmetric cultural effects on perceptual expertise underlie an own-race bias for voices. *Cognition, 114*(1), 42–55.

Popp, D., Donovan, R. A., Crawford, M., Marsh, K., & Peele, M. (2003). Gender, race, and speech style stereotypes. *Sex Roles, 48*, 317–325.

Purkiss, S. L. S., Perrewe, P. L., Gillespie, T. L., Mayes, B. T., & Ferris, G. R. (2003). Implicit sources of bias in employment interview judgments and decisions. *Organizational Behavior and Human Decision Processes, 101*(2), 152–167.

Purnell, T., Idsardi, W., & Baugh, J. (1999). Perceptual and phonetic experiments on American English dialect identification. *Journal of Language and Social Psychology, 18*, 10–30.

Ridgeway, C. L. (2014). Why status matters for inequality. *American Sociological Review, 79*(1), 1–16.

Schawbel, D. (2017). 10 workplace trends you'll see in 2018. *Forbes.* https://www.forbes.com/sites/danschawbel/2017/11/01/10-workplace-trends-youll-see-in-2018/?sh=eeb9dca4bf22

Schlamp, S., Gerpott, F. H., & Voelpel, S. C. (2020). Same talk, different reaction? Communication, emergent leadership and gender. *Journal of Managerial Psychology.* https://www.emerald.com/insight/content/doi/10.1108/JMP-01-2019-0062/full/html

Schneider, E. W. (2000). From region to class to identity: "Show me how you speak, and I'll tell you who you are." *American Speech, 7*(4), 359–361.

Schroder-Abe, M. & Schutz, A. (2011). Walking in each other's shoes: Perspective taking mediates effects of emotional intelligence on relationship quality. *European Journal of Personality.* https://onlinelibrary.wiley.com/doi/abs/10.1002/per.818

Shinn, L. K., & O'Brien, M. (2008). Parent–child conversational styles in middle childhood: Gender and social class differences. *Sex Roles, 59*, 61–67.

Singh, D. & Bronstad, M. (2001). Female body odor is a potential cue to ovulation. *Proceedings of the Royal Society B: Biological Sciences, 268*, 797–801.

Smith-Lovin, L., & Robinson, D. T. (1992). Gender and conversational dynamics. In C. L. Ridgeway (Ed.), *Gender, interaction and equality* (pp.122-156). Springer.

Street, R. L. (1992). Communicative styles and adaptations in physician-parent consultations. *Social Science and Medicine, 34*, 1155–1163. https://doi.org/10.1016/0277-9536(92)90289-3

Struckman-Johnson C., & Struckman-Johnson, D. (1994). Men pressured and forced into sexual experience. *Archives of Sex Behavior, 23*, 93–114. https://doi.org/10.1007/BF01541620

Subtirelu, N. (2014). *Shibboleths of social class: On the obscurity of SAT vocabulary.* https://linguisticpulse.com/2014/04/18/shibboleths-of-social-class-on-the-obscurity-of-sat-vocabulary/

Thornhill, R., & Gangestad, S. W. (1999). The scent of symmetry: A human sex pheromone that signals fitness? *Evolution and Human Behavior, 20*, 175–201.

Todd, A. R., Bodenhausen, G. V., Richeson, J. A., & Galinsky, A. D. (2011). Perspective taking combats automatic expressions of racial bias. *Journal of Personality and Social Psychology, 100*(6), 1027–1042.

Tracy, K., Van Dusen, D., & Robinson, S. (1987). "Good" and "bad" criticism: A descriptive analysis. *Journal of Communication, 37*(2), 46–59.

Turkle, S. (2015). *Reclaiming conversation: The power of talk in a digital age.* Penguin.

U.S. Department of Health and Human Services. (n.d.). *Sexual coercion. Office of women's health.* https://www.womenshealth.gov/relationships-and-safety/other-types/sexual-coercion

Van Edwards, V. (2014, September 22). 57 killer conversation starters so you can start a conversation with anyone, anytime. *Science of People.* https://www.scienceofpeople.com/conversation-starters-topics/

Vangelisti, A. L. (1994). Messages that hurt. In W. R. Cupach, & B. H. Spitzberg (Eds.), *The dark side of interpersonal communication* (pp. 53–82). Erlbaum.

Vangelisti, A. L. (2007). Communicating hurt. In B. Spitzberg & W. Cupach (Eds.), *The dark side of close relationships* (pp. 121–142). Erlbaum.

Vangelisti, A. L., & Young, S. L. (2000). When words hurt: The effects of perceived intentionality on interpersonal relationships. *Journal of Social and Personal Relationships, 17*, 393–424.

Vangelisti, A. L., Young, S. L, Carpenter, K. E., & Alexander, A. L. (2005). Why does it hurt? The perceived causes of hurt feeling. *Communication Research, 32*(4), 443–477.

Wade, L. (2012). The correlation between income and SAT scores. *The Society Pages.* https://www.washingtonpost.com/news/wonk/wp/2014/03/05/these-four-charts-show-how-the-sat-favors-the-rich-educated-families/?arc404=true

Willems, S., De Maesschalck, S., Deveugele, M., Derese, A., & De Maeseneer, J. (2005). Socio-economic status of the patient and doctor–patient communication: Does it make a difference? *Patient Education and Counseling, 56*(2), 139–146.

Wilson, M. (2020, May 26). 20 facts about the class of 2020 that will blow your mind. *Insider.* https://www.insider.com/facts-about-the-graduating-class-of-2020

Young, S. L., & Bippus, A. M. (2001). Does it make a difference if they hurt you in a funny way? Humorously and non-humorously phrased hurtful messages in personal relationships. *Communication Quarterly, 49*(1), 35–52.

Young, Y. K., & Sax, L. J. (2009). Student–faculty interaction in research universities: Differences by student gender, race, social class, and first-generation status. *Research in Higher Education, 50*, 437–459.

Zhang, S. (2009). Sender–recipient perspectives of honest but hurtful evaluative messages in romantic relationships. *Communication Reports, 22*(2), 89–101.

Chapter 7

Ahern, K., & Mehlenbacher, A. (2019). Response: Listening to new voices: Silence, repair, hybridity. *International Journal of Listening (Special Issue): Listening in Unusual Ways in Unusual Spaces: Ethics, Listening and Place), 33*(3), 168–172.

Alda, A. (2017). *If I understood you, would I have this look on my face?* Random House.

Barker, L., & Watson, K. (2000). *Listen up: How to improve relationships, reduce stress, and be more productive by using the power of listening.* St. Martin's Press.

Battell, C. (2006). *Effective listening.* ASTD Press.

Beall, M. L. (2010). Perspectives on intercultural listening. In A. D. Wolvin (Ed.), *Listening and human communication in the 21st century* (pp. 232–238). Wiley-Blackwell.

Beard, D. (2009). A broader understanding of the ethics of listening: Philosophy, cultural studies, media studies and the ethical listening subject. *The International Journal of Listening, 23*(1), 7–20.

Bodie, G. D. (2010). Treating listening ethically. *International Journal of Listening, 24*(3), 185–188.

Bodie, G. D., & Fitch-Hauser, M. (2010). Quantitative research in listening: Explication and overview. In A. D. Wolvin (Ed.), *Listening and human communication in the 21st century* (pp. 46–93). Wiley-Blackwell.

Bodie, G. D., Worthington, D. L., & Gearhart, C. C. (2013a). The listening styles profile-revised (LSP-R): A scale revision and evidence for validity. *Communication Quarterly, 61*, 72–90.

Bodie, G. D., Vickery, A. J., & Gearhart, C. C. (2013b). The nature of supportive listening, I: Exploring a relation between supportive listeners and supportive people. *The International Journal of Listening, 27*(1), 39–49.

Bodie, G. D., Worthington, D., Imhof, M., & Cooper, L. (2008). What would a unified field of listening look like? A proposal linking past perspectives and future endeavors. *The International Journal of Listening, 22*, 103–122.

Brownell, J. (2015). *Listening: Attitudes, principles, and skills* (6th ed.). Pearson.

Carnevale, A. P. (2013). *21st century competencies for college and career readiness.* NCDA Career Developments. https://repository.library.georgetown.edu/bitstream/handle/10822/559289/CD_21stCenturyCompetencies.pdf?sequence=1

Cheong, P. H., Shuter, R., & Suwinyattichaiporn, T. (2016). Managing student digital distractions and hyperconnectivity: Communication strategies and challenges for professorial authority. *Communication Education, 65*(3), 272–289.

Clark, A. (2005). Listening to and involving young children: A review of research and practice. *Early Child Development and Care, 175*(6), 489–505.

Cooper, L. O., & Buchanan, T. (2010). Listening competency on campus: A psychometric analysis of student listening. *International Journal of Listening, 24*(3), 141–163.

Diamond, L. E. (2007). *Rule #1: Stop talking! A guide to listening.* Listeners Press.

Dubois, E., & Blank, G. (2018). The echo chamber is overstated: The moderating effect of political interest and diverse media. *Communication & Society, 70,* 1–12.

Emanuel, R., Adams, J., Baker, K., Daufin, E. K., Ellington, C., Fitts, E., . . . & Okeowo, D. (2008). How college students spend their time communicating. *The International Journal of Listening, 22*(1), 13–28.

Ferrari-Bridgers, F., Stroumbakis K., Drini, M., Lynch, B., & Vogel, R. (2017a). Assessing critical-analytical listening skills in math and engineering students: An exploratory inquiry of how analytical listening skills can positively impact learning. *International Journal of Listening, 31,* 121–141.

Ferrari-Bridgers, F., Vogel, R., & Lynch, B. (2017b). Fostering and assessing critical listening skills in the speech course. *International Journal of Listening, 31*(1), 19–32.

Floyd, J. (2010). Provocation: Dialogic listening as reachable goal. *International Journal of Listening, 24*(3), 170–173.

Floyd, K. (2014). Empathic listening as an expression of interpersonal affection. *International Journal of Listening, 28,* 1–14.

Froemming, K. J., & Penington, B. A. (2011). Emotional triggers: Listening barriers to effective interactions in senior populations. *The International Journal of Listening, 25,* 113–131.

Fujii, Y. (2008). You must have a wealth of stories: Cross-linguistic differences between addressee support behaviour in Australian and Japanese. *Multilingua, 27*(4), 325–370.

Gearhart, C. C., Denham, J. P., & Bodie, G. D. (2014). Listening as a goal-directed activity. *Western Journal of Communication, 78*(5), 668–684.

Genette, J., Olson, C. D., & Linde, J. (2017). *Hot topics, cool heads: A handbook on Civil Dialogue®.* Kendall Hunt.

Gilmore, J. (2019). Design for everyone: Apple AirPods and the mediation of accessibility. *Critical Studies in Media Communication, 36*(5), 482–494.

Gottfried, J., & Shearer, E. (2016). News use across social media platforms 2016. *Pew Research Center Report.* http://www.journalism.org/2016/05/26/news-use-across-social-media-platforms-2016/

Hanson, K. (2019). Beauty "therapy": The emotional labor of commercialized listening in the salon industry. *International Journal of Listening, 33*(3), 148–153.

Hearing Loss Association of America. (2016, December 15). *Quick statistics.* https://www.hearingloss.org/hearing-help/hearing-loss-basics/

Holba, A. M. (2019). Listening in leisure: Enacting chora to cultivate understanding. *International Journal of Listening, 33*(3), 173–180.

Imhof, M. (2001). How to listen more efficiently: Self-monitoring strategies in listening. *The International Journal of Listening, 5,* 2–19.

Imhof, M. (2004). Who are we as we listen? Individual listening profiles in varying contexts. *The International Journal of Listening, 18,* 39–44.

Imhof, M. (2010). Listening to voices and judging people. *International Journal of Listening, 24*(1), 19–33.

Imhof, M., & Janusik, L. A. (2006). Development and validation of the Imhof-Janusik listening concepts inventory to measure listening conceptualization differences between cultures. *Journal of Intercultural Communication Research, 35,* 79–98.

International Listening Association. (1995, April). An ILA definition of listening. *ILA Listening Post, 53,* 1–4.

Itzchakov, G., Kluger, A. N., Emanuel-Tor, M., & Gizbar, H. K. (2014). How do you like me to listen to you? *International Journal of Listening, 28*(3), 177–185.

Janusik, L., & Imhof, M. (2017). Intercultural listening: Measuring listening concepts with the LCI-R. *International Journal of Listening, 31*(2), 80–97.

Janusik, L. A., & Wolvin, A. D. (2009). 24 hours in a day: A listening update to the time studies. *International Journal of Listening, 23*(2), 104–120.

Klein, L. (2020). The value of listening during the pandemic. *Mercurynews.com.* https://www.mercurynews.com/2020/07/03/opinion-listening-during-the-covid-19-pandemic/

Kluger, A. N., & Zaidel, K. (2013). Are listeners perceived as leaders? *International Journal of Listening, 27*(2), 73–84.

Lacey, K. (2013). *Listening publics: The politics and experience of listening in the media age.* Polity.

Lange, J. (2018). Let us lurk. *theweek.com.* https://theweek.com/articles/804466/let-lurk

Linde, J. Genette, J., & Olson, C. D. (2014). *Civil Dialogue: Producing civility through the process of dialogue.* https://www.civil-dialogue.org/publications.html

Lipetz, L., Kluger, A., & Bodie, G. (2020). Listening is listening is listening: Employees' perception of listening as a holistic phenomenon. *International Journal of Listening, 34*(2), 71–96.

Lloyd, K. J., Boer, D., Kluger, A. N., & Voelpel, S. C. (2015). Building trust and feeling well: Examining intraindividual and interpersonal outcomes and underlying mechanisms of listening. *International Journal of Listening, 29*(1), 12–29.

Manusov, V., Stofleth, D., Harvey, J. A., & Crowley, J. P. (2020). Conditions and consequences of listening well for interpersonal relationships: Modeling active-empathic listening, social-emotional skills, trait mindfulness, and relational quality. *International Journal of Listening, 34*(2), 110–126.

McNeil, J. (2020). *Lurking: How a person became a user.* MCD.

Nichols, M. P. (2009). *The lost art of listening* (2nd ed.). The Guilford Press.

Olson, C. D., Genette, J., & Linde, J. (n.d.). *Civility in urban spaces: The use of Civil Dialogue® in urban controversies.* http://www.civil-dialogue.com/civil-dialogue-in-urban-controversies.html

Pasupathi, M., & Billitteri, J. (2015). Being and becoming through being heard: Listener effects on stories and selves. *International Journal of Listening, 29*(2), 67–84.

Pearce, C. G., Johnson, I. W., & Barker, R. T. (2003). Assessment of the Listening Styles Inventory: Progress in establishing reliability and validity. *Journal of Business and Technical Communication, 17*(1), 84–113.

Pence, M. E., & James, T. A. (2015). The role of sex differences in the examination of personality and active-empathic listening: An initial exploration. *International Journal of Listening, 29,* 85–94.

Perrin, A., & Anderson, M. (2019, April 10). Share of U.S. adults using social media, is mostly unchanged since 2018. *Pew Research Center FactTank.* https://www.pewresearch.org/fact-tank/2019/04/10/share-of-u-s-adults-using-social-media-including-facebook-is-mostly-unchanged-since-2018/

Ramos Salazar, L. R. (2017). The influence of business students' listening style on their compassion and self-compassion. *Business and Professional Communication Quarterly, 80*(4), 426–442.

Robertson, K. (2005). Active listening: More than just paying attention. *Australian Family Physician, 34*(12), 1053–1055.

Roebuck, D., Bell, R., Raina, R., & Lee, C. (2016). Comparing perceived listening behavior differences between managers and nonmanagers living in the United States, India, and Malaysia. *International Journal of Business Communication, 53*(4), 485–518.

Rosenfeld, L. B., & Berko, R. (1990). *Communicating with competency.* Scott, Foresman/Little.

Sagon, C. (2017, September 8). Hearing loss hits a younger generation. *chicagotribune.com.* https://www.chicagotribune.com/lifestyles/health/sc-hlth-young-hearing-loss-0913-story.html

Shafir, R. Z. (2003). *The Zen of listening* (2nd ed.). Quest Books.

Shafran-Tikva, S., & Kluger, A. N. (2018). Physician's listening and adherence to medical recommendations among persons with diabetes. *International Journal of Listening, 32*(3), 140–149.

Shotter, J. (2009). Listening in a way that recognizes/realizes the world of "the other." *The International Journal of Listening, 23*(1), 21–43.

Sims, C. M. (2017). Do the Big-Five personality traits predict empathic listening and assertive communication? *International Journal of Listening, 31*(3), 163–188.

Smiles, D. (2019). Listening to Native Radio. *International Journal of Listening, 33*(3), 142–147.

Tannen, D. (1994). *Talking from 9 to 5.* William Morrow.

Underwood, M. K., & Ehrenreich, S. E. (2017). The power and the pain of adolescents' digital communication: Cyber victimization and the perils of lurking. *The American Psychologist, 72*(2), 144–158.

Wang, I. C., Ahn, J. N., Kim, H. J., & Lin-Siegler, X. (2017). Why do international students avoid communicating with Americans? *Journal of International Students, 7*(3), 555–582.

Watson, K. W., Barker, L. L., & Weaver, J. B. (1995). The Listening Styles Profile (LSP-16): Development and validation of an instrument to assess four listening styles. *Journal of the International Listening Association, 9*, 1–13.

Welch, S. A., & Mickelson, W. T. (2013). A listening competence comparison of working professionals. *International Journal of Listening, 27*(2), 85–99.

Welch, S. A., & Mickelson, W. (2020). Listening across the life span: A listening environment comparison. *International Journal of Listening, 34*(2), 97–109.

Wilson, B. L. (2020, June 8). I'm your black friend, but I won't educate you about racism. That's on you. *washingtonpost.com.* https://www.washingtonpost.com/outlook/2020/06/08/black-friends-educate-racism/

Wolvin, A. (2013). Understanding the listening process: Rethinking the "one size fits all" model. *International Journal of Listening, 27*(2), 104–106.

Wolvin, A. D. (2017, July). Listenability: A missing link in the basic communication course. *Listening Education*, 13–21.

Chapter 8

Allen, B. (2011). *Difference matters: Communicating social identity* (2nd ed). Waveland Press.

Allison Nafziger Travel Blog. Reprinted by permission of Allison Nafziger.

America's reckoning on racism spreads beyond policing. (2020, June 10). *nytimes.com.* https://www.nytimes.com/2020/06/10/us/protests-black-lives-matter-george-floyd.html

Balachandran, M. (2016, January 15). *weforum.org.* Which country has the largest diaspora? https://www.weforum.org/agenda/2016/01/which-country-has-the-largest-diaspora/

Barboza, T. (2013, May 7). Water war between Klamath River farmers: Tribes poised to erupt. *LA Times.* http://articles.latimes.com/2013/may/07/local/la-me-klamath-20130507

Bellah, R. N., Madsen, R., Sullivan, W. M., Swidler, A., & Tipton, S. M. (2007). *Habits of the heart: Individualism and commitment in American life, with a new preface.* University of California Press.

Bennett, J. M. (1998). Transition shock: Putting culture shock in perspective. In M. J. Bennett (Ed.), *Basic concepts in intercultural communication: Selected readings* (pp. 215–224). Intercultural Press. First published in 1977 in N. C. Jain (Ed.), *International and Intercultural Communication Annual, 4,* 45–52.

Bond, M. (1991). *Beyond the Chinese face.* Oxford University Press.

Bond, M. (Ed.). (2010). *The Oxford handbook of Chinese psychology.* Oxford University Press.

Braskamp, L. A., Braskamp, D. C., & Merrill, K. C. (2009). Assessing progress in global learning and development of students with education abroad experiences. *Frontiers: The Interdisciplinary Journal of Study Abroad, 13,* 101–118.

Broome, B. J. (2004). Building a shared future across the divide: Identity and conflict in Cyprus. In M. Fong and R. Chuang (Eds.), *Communicating ethnic and cultural identity* (pp. 275–294). Rowman and Littlefield, Publishers.

Broome, B. J. (2013). Building cultures of peace: The role of intergroup dialogue. In J. G. Oetzel & S. Ting-Toomey (Eds.), *Sage handbook of conflict communication: Integrating theory, research, and practice* (2nd ed., pp. 737–762). Sage.

Broome, B. J. (2014). Dialogue across the divide: Bridging the separation in Cyprus. In N. Haydari & P. Holmes (Eds.), *Case studies in intercultural dialogue* (pp. 39–54). Kendall Hunt Publishers.

Broome, B. J. (2015). Empathy. In J. M. Bennett (Ed.), *The SAGE Encyclopedia of Intercultural Competence* (pp. 287–291). SAGE Publications, Inc.

Broome, B. J., & Collier, M. J. (2012). Culture, communication, and peacebuilding: A reflexive multi-dimensional contextual framework. *Journal of International and Intercultural Communication, 5*(4), 245–269.

Broome, B. J., & Hatay, J. (2010). Building peace in divided societies: The role of intergroup dialogue. In J. Oetzel & S. Ting-Toomey (eds.), *Handbook of conflict communication* (pp. 627–662). Sage Publications.

Brzozowski, A. (2019, November 20). Far right terrorism has more than tripled over last four years, report warns. *euractiv.com.* https://www.euractiv.com/section/justice-home-affairs/news/far-right-terrorism-has-more-than-tripled-over-last-four-years-report-warns/

Buchanan, L., Bui, Q., & Patel, J. K. (2020, July 3). Black Lives Matter may be the largest movement in U.S. history. *nytimes.com.* https://www.nytimes.com/interactive/2020/07/03/us/george-floyd-protests-crowd-size.html

Carlson, B. (2013). Why big American businesses fail in China. *nbcnews.com.* https://www.nbcnews.com/news/china/why-big-american-businesses-fail-china-flna4B11231213

Cheung, H., Feng, Z. & Deng, B. (2020, May 27). Coronavirus: What attacks on Asians reveal about American identity. *bbc.com.* https://www.bbc.com/news/world-us-canada-52714804

Chinese Culture Connection. (1987). Chinese values and the search for culture-free dimensions of culture. *Journal of Cross-Cultural Psychology, 18,* 143–164.

Colby, S. L., & Ortman, J. M. (2015). *Projections of the size and composition of the U.S. population: 2014-2060.* U.S. Census Bureau. https://www.census.gov/content/dam/Census/library/publications/2015/demo/p25-1143.pdf

Collman, A. (2018, November 15). Michelle Obama tells her side of the story about the time she broke royal protocol and touched Queen Elizabeth. *businessinsider.com.* Retrieved November 4, 2020 from www.businessinsider.com/michelle-obama-touched-queen-elizabeth-her-story-2018-11

Cowan, G. (2005). Interracial interactions of racially diverse university campuses. *Journal of Social Psychology, 14,* 49–63.

Custer, C. (2015, May 20). The 3 biggest reasons foreign companies fail in China. *Techinasia.com.* https://www.techinasia.com/3-biggest-reasons-foreign-companies-fail-china

De La Garza, A. T., & Ono, K. (2015). Retheorizing adaptation: Differential adaptation and critical intercultural communication. *Journal of International & Intercultural Communication, 8*(4), 269–289.

DeTurk, S. (2001). Intercultural empathy: Myth, competency, or possibility for alliance building? *Communication Education, 50*(4), 374–384.

DiAngelo, R. (2018). *White fragility: Why it's so hard for white people to talk about racism.* Beacon Press.

Eagle aviary allows American Indians to continue heritage. (2005, March 3). *Newswise.com.* http://www.newswise.com/articles/eagle-aviary-allows-american-indians-to-continue-heritage

Engen, D. (2012). Invisible identities: Notes on class and race. In A. González, M. Houston, & V. Chen (Eds.), *Our voices: Essays in culture, ethnicity and communication* (5th ed., pp. 223–239). Oxford University Press.

Flores, L. A. (1996). Creating discursive space through a rhetoric of difference: Chicana feminists craft a homeland. *Quarterly Journal of Speech, 82,* 142–156.

Gareis, E., (2012). Intercultural friendship: Effects of home and host region. *Journal of International & Intercultural Communication, 5*(4), 309–329.

Geeraert, N., Demoulin, S., & Demes, K. A. (2014). Choose your (international) contact wisely: A multilevel analysis on the impact of intergroup contact while abroad. *International Journal of Intercultural Relations, 38*(2014), 86–96.

Geiger, A. W. & Livingston, G. (2019, February 13). 8 facts about love and marriage in America. *pewresearch.org.* https://www.pewresearch.org/fact-tank/2019/02/13/8-facts-about-love-and-marriage/

Guéguen, N., Lourel, M., Charron, C., Fischer-Lokou, J., & Lamy, L. (2009). A web replication of Snyder, Decker, and Bersheid's (1977) experiment on the self-fulfilling nature of social stereotypes. *Journal of Social Psychology, 149*(5), 600–602.

Hall, B. J. (1997). Culture, ethics and communication. In F. L. Casmir (Ed.), *Ethics in intercultural and international communication* (pp. 11–41). Erlbaum.

Hanasono, L. K., Chen, L., & Wilson, S. R. (2014). Identifying communities in need: Examining the impact of acculturation on perceived discrimination, social support, and coping amongst racial minority members in the United States. *Journal of International and Intercultural Communication 7*(3), 216–237.

Hartig, H. (2018, May 24). Republicans turn more negative toward refugees as number admitted to U.S. plummets. *pewresearch.org*. https://www.pewresearch.org/fact-tank/2018/05/24/republicans-turn-more-negative-toward-refugees-as-number-admitted-to-u-s-plummets/

Hecht, M., Sedano, M., & Ribeau, S. (1993). Understanding culture, communication, and research: Application to Chicanos and Mexican Americans. *International Journal of Intercultural Relations, 17*, 157–165.

Hecht, M. L., Jackson, R. L., II, & Ribeau, S. (2002). *African American communication: Exploring identity and culture* (2nd ed.). Erlbaum.

Hegde, R. S. (1998). Swinging the trapeze: The negotiation of identity among Asian Indian immigrant women in the United States. In D. V. Tanno & A. González (Eds.), *Communication of identity across cultures* (pp. 34–55). Sage.

Hegde, R. S. (2012). Hybrid revivals: Ethnicity and South Asian celebration. In A. González, M. Houston, & V. Chen (Eds.), *Our voices: Essays in culture, ethnicity and communication* (5th ed., pp. 158–163). Oxford University Press.

Ho, M. K., Rasheed, J. M., & Rasheed, M. N. (2004). *Family therapy with ethnic minorities* (2nd ed). Sage.

Hofstede, G., Hofstede, G. J., & Minkov, M. (2010). *Cultures and organizations: Software of the mind* (3rd ed.). McGraw-Hill.

Holloway, K. (2015, April 14). Black people are not here to teach you: What so many white Americans just can't grasp. *salon.com*. https://www.salon.com/2015/04/14/black_people_are_not_here_to_teach_you_what_so_many_white_americans_just_cant_grasp_partner/

Holmes, P., & O'Neill, G. (2012). Developing and evaluating intercultural competence: Ethnographies of intercultural encounters. *International Journal of Intercultural Relations, 36*, 707–718.

Hudson, T. (2018). Random roommates: Supporting our students in developing friendships across difference. *About Campus: Enriching the Student Learning Experience, 23*(3), 13–22.

Hulse, E. (1996). Example of the English Puritans. *Reformation Today, 153*. http://www.puritansermons.com/banner/hulse1.htm

Infoplease Staff. (2020, October 7). *Native Americans by the numbers*. https://www.infoplease.com/history/native-american-heritage/native-americans-by-the-numbers

Institute of International Education. (2020). *Open doors 2019: International education*. http://www.iie.org/Research-and-Publications/Open-Doors/Data/US-Study-Abroad/Infographic

Jaret, C. (1999). Troubled by newcomers: Anti-immigrant attitudes and action during two eras of mass immigration to the United States. *Journal of American Ethnic History, 18*(3), 9–40.

Johnson, A. J. (2017). Privilege, power and difference (2nd ed.). Sage.

Johnson, B. R., & Jacobson, C. K. (2005). Context in contact: An examination of social settings on whites' attitudes toward interracial marriage. *Journal of Social Psychology, 68*, 387–399.

Kahna, S., Alessib, E., Woolnera, L., Kima, H., & Olivieric, C. (2017). Promoting the wellbeing of lesbian, gay, bisexual and transgender forced migrants in Canada: Providers' perspectives. *Culture, Health & Sexuality, 19*(10), 1165–1179.

Kim, Y. Y. (2005). Adapting to a new culture: An integrative communication theory. In W. B. Gudykunst (Ed.), *Theorizing about intercultural communication* (pp. 375–400). Sage.

Kim, Y. Y., & McKay-Semmler, K. (2013). Social engagement and cross-cultural adaptation: An examination of direct and mediated interpersonal communication activities of educated non-natives in the United States. *International Journal of Intercultural Relations, 37*, 99–112.

Kluckhohn, F., & Strodtbeck, F. (1961). *Variations in value orientations*. Row, Peterson & Co.

Landgrave, L. (2019, September 17). Immigrants learn English. *cato.org*. https://www.cato.org/publications/immigration-research-policy-brief/immigrants-learn-english-immigrants-language

Lee, B. Y. (2020, May 26). Over 1700 reports of coronavirus-related discrimination against Asian Americans since March 19. *forbes.com*. https://www.forbes.com/sites/brucelee/2020/05/26/covid-19-coronavirus-continues-to-expose-anti-asian-bigotry-how-to-stop-it/#6334fcc4148a

Linker, L. (2020, May 6). American individualism is a suicide pact. *theweek.com*. https://theweek.com/articles/912853/american-individualism-suicide-pact

Loewen, J. W. (2010). *Teaching what really happened*. Teachers College, Columbia University.

Lu, J., Hafenbrack, A., Eastwick, P., Wang, D., Maddux, W., & Galinsky, A. (2017). "Going out" of the box: Close intercultural friendships and romantic relationships spark creativity, workplace innovation, and entrepreneurship. *Journal of Applied Psychology, 102*(7), 1091–1108.

Martin, J. N., & Nakayama, T. K. (2018). *Experiencing intercultural communication: An introduction* (7th ed.). McGraw-Hill.

Massey, D. S. (2016). Residential segregation is the linchpin of racial stratification. *City & Community, 15*(1), 3–7.

Mather, M., & Lee, A. (2020, February 10). Children are at the forefront of U. S. racial and ethnic change. *prb.org*. https://www.prb.org/children-are-at-the-forefront-of-u-s-racial-and-ethnic-change/

McGrath, A. R., Tsunokai, G. T., Schultz, M., Kavanagh, J., & Tarrence, J. A. (2016). Differing shades of colour: Online dating preferences of biracial individuals. *Ethnic & Racial Studies, 39*(11), 1920–1942.

Moon, D. G. (2016). "Be/coming" white and the myth of white ignorance: Identity projects in white communities. *Western Journal Of Communication, 80*(3), 282–303.

Orbe, M. P. (1998). *Constructing co-cultural theory: An explication of culture, power, and communication*. Sage.

Orbe, M., & Roberts, T. L. (2012). Co-cultural theorizing: Foundations, applications, and extensions. *Howard Journal of Communications, 23*(4), 293–311.

Orta, D., Murguia, E., & Cruz, C. (2019). From struggle to success via Latina sororities: Culture shock, marginalization, embracing ethnicity, and educational persistence through academic capital. *Journal of Hispanic Higher Education, 18*(1), 41–58.

Park, J. (2015). Signs of social change on the bodies of youth: Tattoos in Korea. *Visual Communication, 15*(1), 71–92.

Parker, J., Morin, R., Horowitz, J. M., Lopez, M. H., & Rohal, M. (2015). *Multiracial in America: Proud, diverse and growing in numbers*. http://www.pewsocialtrends.org/files/2015/06/2015-06-11_multiracial-in-america_final-updated.pdf

Pendery, D. (2008). Identity development and cultural production in the Chinese diaspora to the United States, 1850–2004: New perspectives. *Asian Ethnicity, 9*(3), 201–218.

Phillips, K. W. (2014, October 1). How diversity makes us smarter. *Scientificamerican.com*. http://www.scientificamerican.com/article/how-diversity-makes-us-smarter/

Piff, P. K., Kraus, M. W., Côté, S., Cheng, B. H., & Keltner, D. (2010). Having less, giving more: The influence of social class on prosocial behavior. *Journal of Personality and Social Psychology, 99*(5), 771–784.

Pitts, M. J. (2016). Sojourner reentry: A grounded elaboration of the integrative theory of communication and cross-cultural adaptation. *Communication Monographs, 83*(4), 419–445.

Porter, T. (2002). The words that come before all else. *Native Americas, 19*, 7–10.

Reiter, M. J., & Gee, C. B. (2009). Open communication and partner support in intercultural and interfaith romantic relationship: A relational maintenance approach. *Journal of Social and Personal Relationships, 25*(4), 539–599.

Robertson, C. (2019, April 25). Crime is down, yet U.S. incarceration rates are still among the highest in the world. *nytimes.com*. https://www.nytimes.com/2019/04/25/us/us-mass-incarceration-rate.html

Rosenstone, R. A. (2005). My wife, the Muslim. *Antioch Review, 63*, 234–246.

Rothman, L. (2012, July 8). Essence Fest 2012: Is reality TV still not diverse enough? *Time.com*. http://entertainment.time.com/2012/07/08/essence-reality-tv-family-panel/

Sahagun, L. (2014, February 24). Northern spotted owls are being ousted by barred owl invaders. *LA Times*. http://www.latimes.com/science/sciencenow/la-sci-sn-barred-owl-invasion-20140224,0,4292055.story

Sanchez-Burks, J., Lee, F., Choi, I., Nisbett, R., Zhao, S., & Koo, J. (2003). Conversing across cultures: East-West communication styles in work and nonwork contexts. *Journal of Personality and Social Psychology: Personality Processes and Individual Differences, 85*(2), 363–372.

Schaeffer, K. (2019, November 20). In a rising number of U.S. counties, Hispanic and black Americans are the majority. *pewresearch.org.* https://www.pewresearch.org/fact-tank/2019/11/20/in-a-rising-number-of-u-s-counties-hispanic-and-black-americans-are-the-majority/

Schaeffer, K. (2020, March 4). Far more Americans see "very strong" partisan conflicts now than in the last two presidential election years. *pewresearch.org.* https://www.pewresearch.org/fact-tank/2020/03/04/far-more-americans-see-very-strong-partisan-conflicts-now-than-in-the-last-two-presidential-election-years/

Scott, K. D. (2013). Communication strategies across cultural borders: Dispelling stereotypes, performing competence, and redefining black womanhood. *Women's Studies in Communication, 36,* 312–329.

Scott, B. (2016, May 19). America's schools are still segregated by race and class. That has to end. *The Guardian.* https://www.theguardian.com/commentisfree/2016/may/19/america-schools-segregation-race-class-education-policy-bobby-scott

Shear, M. D., & Kanno-Youngs, Z. (2019, September 26). Trump slashes refugee cap to 18,000, curtailing U.S. role as haven. *nytimes.com.* https://www.nytimes.com/2019/09/26/us/politics/trump-refugees.html

Shenhav, S., Campos, B., & Goldberg, W. A. (2017). Dating out is intercultural: Experience and perceived parent disapproval by ethnicity and immigrant generation. *Journal of Social and Personal Relationships, 34*(3), 397–422.

Sobré-Denton, M. (2011). The emergence of cosmopolitan group cultures and its implications for cultural transition: A case study of an international student support group. *International Journal of Intercultural Relations, 35,* 79–91.

Telford, T. (2019, September 26). Income inequality is the highest it's been since the Census Bureau started tracking it, data shows. *washingtonpost.com.* https://www.washingtonpost.com/business/2019/09/26/income-inequality-america-highest-its-been-since-census-started-tracking-it-data-show/

Ting-Toomey, S. (1999). *Communicating across cultures.* Guilford.

Ting-Toomey, S. (2010). Applying dimensional values in understanding intercultural communication. *Communication Monographs, 77*(2), 169–180.

Triandis, H. C. (1995). *Individualism & collectivism.* Westview Press.

Trompenaars, F., & Hampden-Turner, C. (2012). *Riding the waves of culture: Understanding diversity in global business* (3rd ed.). McGraw-Hill.

United Nations High Commissioner for Refugees. (2020). *Refugee statistics.* https://www.unhcr.org/refugee-statistics/

UNTWO. (2020, January 19). World Tourism Barometer #18, January 2020. *untwo.org.* https://www.unwto.org/world-tourism-barometer-n18-january-2020

USA Study Abroad. (2020). United States Department of State. https://studyabroad.state.gov/value-study-abroad/study-abroad-data

U.S. Census Bureau. (2019). Population estimates. *Quick facts.* https://www.census.gov/quickfacts/fact/table/US/PST045219

Ward, C. (2008). Thinking outside the Berry boxes: New perspectives on identity, acculturation and intercultural relations. *International Journal of Intercultural Relations, 32,* 105–114.

Waterston, A. (2005). Bringing the past into the present: Family narratives of holocaust, exile, and diaspora: The story of my story: An anthropology of violence, dispossession, and diaspora. *Anthropological Quarterly, 78,* 43–61.

Wilson, B. L. (2020, June 8). I'm your black friend, but I won't educate you about racism. That's on you. *washingtonpost.com.* https://www.washingtonpost.com/outlook/2020/06/08/black-friends-educate-racism/

Woodard, C. (2012). *American nations: A history of the eleven rival regional cultures of North America.* Penguin Books.

Yako, R. M., & Biswas, B. (2014). "We came to this country for the future of our children. We have no future": Acculturative stress among Iraqi refugees in the United States. *International Journal of Intercultural Relations, 38,* 133–141.

Yamato, G. (2001). Something about the subject makes it hard to name. In M. L. Andersen & P. H. Collins (Eds.), *Race, class, and gender: An anthology* (4th ed., pp. 90–94). Wadsworth.

Zoppo, A., Santos, A. P., & Hudgins, J. (2017, February 14). *nbcnews.com.* Here's the full list of Donald Trump's executive orders. https://www.nbcnews.com/politics/white-house/here-s-full-list-donald-trump-s-executive-orders-n720796

Chapter 9

Aboud, F. E., & Mendelson, M. J. (1996). Determinants of friendship selection and quality: Developmental perspectives. In W. M. Bukowski, A. F. Newcomb, & W. W. Hartup (Eds.), *The company they keep: Friendship in childhood and adolescence* (pp. 87–112). Cambridge University Press.

Alberts, J., Yoshimura, C., Rabby, M., & Loschiavo, R. (2005). Mapping the topography of couples' everyday interaction. *Journal of Social and Personal Relationships, 22,* 299–322.

Allan, G. (1977). Class variation in friendship patterns. *British Journal of Sociology, 28,* 389–393.

Altman, I., & Taylor, D. (1987). Communication in interpersonal relationships: Social penetration theory. In M. E. Roloff & G. R. Miller (Eds.), *Interpersonal processes: New directions in communication research* (pp. 257–277). Sage.

Altman, I., & Taylor, D. A. (1973). *Social penetration: The development of interpersonal relationships.* Holt, Rinehart, & Winston.

American Civil Liberties Union. (2015, October). *Highlights: Responses from the field.* https://www.aclu.org/report/highlights-responses-field

Anglin, K., & Holtzworth-Munroe, A. (1997). Comparing the responses of maritally violent and nonviolent spouses to problematic marital and nonmarital situations: Are the skills deficits of physically aggressive husbands and wives global? *Journal of Family Psychology, 11,* 301–313.

Argyle, M., & Henderson, M. (1984). The rules of friendship. *Journal of Social and Personal Relationships, 1,* 211–237.

Balsam, K., Beauchaine, T., & Rothblum, E. (2005). Victimization over the lifespan: Comparison of lesbian, gay, bisexual and heterosexual siblings. *Journal of Consulting and Clinical Psychology, 73,* 477–487.

Baxter, L. A. (1982). Strategies for ending relationships: Two studies. *Western Journal of Speech Communication, 46,* 233–242.

Baxter, L. A. (1988). A dialectical perspective on communication strategies in relationship development. In S. W. Duck, D. F. Hay, S. E. Hobfoll, W. Ickes, & B. Montgomery (Eds.), *Handbook of personal relationships* (pp. 257–273). Wiley.

Baxter, L. A. (1991). Gender differences in the heterosexual relationship rules embedded in break-up accounts. *Journal of Social and Personal Relationships, 3,* 289–306.

Baxter, L. A., & Bullis, C. (1986). Turning points in developing romantic relationships. *Human Communication Research, 12,* 469–493.

Becker, J. A. H., Johnson, A. J., Craig, E. A., Gilchrist, E., Haigh, M. M., & Lane, L. L. (2009). Friendships are flexible not fragile: Turning points in geographically-close and long-distance friendships. *Journal of Social and Personal Relationships, 26*(4), 347–369.

Bennet, D. C., Guran, E. L., Ramos, M. C., & Margolin, G. (2011). College students' electronic victimization in friendship and dating relationships: Anticipated distress and associations with risky behavior. *Violence and Victims, 26*(4), 409–430.

Bennhold, K. (2012, June 12). Equality and the end of marrying up. *New York Times.* http://www.nytimes.com/2012/06/13/world/europe/13ihtletter13.html?pagewanted=all&_r=0

Berg, J. H., & Piner, K. E. (1990). Social relationships and the lack of social relationships. In S. Duck & R. C. Silver (Eds.), *Personal relationships and social support* (pp. 140–158). Sage Publications.

Berger, C. R., & Calabrese, R. J. (1975). Some explorations in initial interaction and beyond: Toward a developmental theory of interpersonal communication. *Human Communication Theory, 1,* 99–112.

Berger, C. R., & Kellerman, N. (1994). Acquiring social information. In J. Daly & J. Wiemann (Eds.), *Strategic interpersonal communication* (pp. 1–31). Lawrence Erlbaum.

Berscheid, E., & Reis, H. T. (1998). Attraction and close relationships. In D. Gilbert, S. Fiske, & G. Lindzey (Eds.), *Handbook of social psychology* (Vol. 2, 4th ed., pp. 193–281). McGraw-Hill.

Bleske-Rechek, A., & Lighthall, M. (2010). Attractiveness and rivalry in women's friendships with women. *Human Nature, 21*(1), 82–97.

Blieszner, R., & Adams, R. G. (1992). *Adult friendship.* Sage.

Bogle, K. (2008). *Hooking up: Sex, dating and relationships on campus.* New York University Press.

Bowker, A. (2004). Predicting friendship stability during early adolescence. *Journal of Early Adolescence, 24,* 85–112.

Bureau of Labor Statistics, (2013). Marriage and divorce: Patterns by gender, race and educational attainment. https://www.bls.gov/opub/mlr/2013/article/marriage-and-divorce-patterns-by-gender-race-and-educational-attainment.htm

Burgoon, J. K., & Bacue, A. E. (2003). Nonverbal communication skills. In J. O. Greene & B. R. Burleson (Eds.), *Handbook of communication and social interaction skills* (pp. 179–188). Lawrence Erlbaum.

Burgoon, J. K., Buller, D. B., Ebesu, A., & Rockwell, P. (1994). Interpersonal deception: V. Accuracy in deception detection. *Communication Monographs, 61*(4), 303–325.

Burleson, B. R., & Samter, W. (1996). Similarity in the communication skills of young adults: Foundations of attraction, friendship, and relationship satisfaction. *Communication Reports, 9,* 127–137.

Buss, D. M. (1985). Human mate selection. *American Scientist, 73,* 47–51.

Buss, D. M., Shackelford, T. K., Kirkpatrick, L. A., & Larsen, R. J. (2001). A half century of mate preferences: The cultural evolution of values. *Journal of Marriage and the Family, 63,* 491–503.

Byrne, D. (1997). An overview (and underview) of research and theory within the attraction paradigm. *Journal of Social and Personal Relationships, 14,* 417–431.

Canary, D. J., & Spitzberg, B. H. (1985). Loneliness and relationally competent communication. *Journal of Social and Personal Relationships, 2,* 387–402.

Canary, D. J., & Stafford, L. (1992). Relational maintenance strategies and equity in marriage. *Communication Monographs, 51*(3), 342–267.

Center for American Progress. (2011). *Domestic violence in the LGBT community: A fact sheet.* http://www.americanprogress.org/issues/lgbt/news/2011/06/14/9850/domestic-violence-in-the-lgbt-community/

Centers for Disease Control and Prevention. (2019, February 26). *Preventing intimate partner violence.* https://www.cdc.gov/violenceprevention/intimatepartnerviolence/fastfact.html

Centers for Disease Control and Prevention. (2020, January 17). *Preventing sexual violence.* https://www.cdc.gov/violenceprevention/sexualviolence/fastfact.html

Chung, C. (2016, July 21). Why Chinese parents don't say I love you. *The Sydney Morning Herald.* http://www.smh.com.au/lifestyle/life-and-relationships/real-life/why-chinese-parents-dont-say-i-love-you-20140304-341ws.html

Cody, M. J. (1982). A typology of disengagement strategies and an examination of the role intimacy, reactions to inequity and relational problems play in strategy selection. *Communication Monographs, 49,* 148–170.

Cordova, J. V., Jacobsen, N. S., Gottman, J. M., Rushe, R., & Cox, G. (1993). Negative reciprocity and communication in couples with a violent husband. *Journal of Abnormal Psychology, 102,* 559–564.

Dainton, M. A., Zelley, E., & Langan, E. (2003). Maintaining friendships throughout the lifespan. In D. J. Canary & M. Dainton (Eds.), *Maintaining relationships through communication* (pp. 79–102). Erlbaum.

Donaghue, N., & Fallon, B. J. (2003) Gender-role self-stereotyping and the relationship between equity and satisfaction in close relationships. *Sex Roles, 48,* 217–230.

Duck, S. (1991). *Understanding relationships.* Guilford Press.

Duck, S. W. (1982). Social and cognitive features of the dissolution of commitment to relationships. In S. W. Duck (Ed.), *Personal relationships 4: Dissolving personal relationships* (pp. 51–73). Academic Press.

Duck, S. W. (1988). *Relating to others.* Dorsey Press.

Dwyer, L. (2015, September 9). The surprising reality of hook-up culture on campus. *Teen Vogue.* http://www.teenvogue.com/story/hookup-culture-myth-dating-college

Emmers-Sommers, T. M. (2004). The effect of communication quality and quantity indicators on intimacy and relational satisfaction. *Journal of Social and Personal Relationships, 21*(4), 399–411.

Essau, C. A., Conradt, J., & Petermann, F. (1999). Frequency and comorbidity of social phobia and fears in adolescents. *Behavior Research and Therapy, 37,* 831–843.

Felmlee, D. H. (1995). Fatal attractions: Affections and disaffections in intimate relationships. *Journal of Social and Personal Relationships, 12,* 295–311.

Ferraro, K. (1996). The dance of dependency: A genealogy of domestic violence discourse. *Hypatia, 11,* 72–91.

Fingerhut, A. W. & Peplau, L. A. (2013). Same-sex romantic relationships. In C. J. Patterson & A. R. D'Augelli (Eds.), *Handbook of psychology and sexual orientation* (pp. 165-178). Oxford University Press.

Gierveld, J., & Tilburg, T. (1995). Social relationships, integration and loneliness. In C. P. M. Knipscheer, J. Gierveld, T. Tilburg, & P. A. Dykstra (Eds.), *Living arrangements and social networks among older adults* (pp. 95–113). VU University Press.

Goodwin, R., & Tang, D. (1991). Preferences for friends and close relationships partners: A cross-cultural comparison. *Journal of Social Psychology, 131,* 579–581.

Haas, S. M., & Stafford, L. (1998). An initial examination of relationship maintenance behaviors in gay and lesbian relationships. *Journal of Social and Personal Relationships, 15,* 846–855.

Hall, J. (2018). How many hours does it take to make a friend? *Journal of Social and Personal Relationships, 36*(4), 1278-1296.

Hays, R. B. (1988). Friendship. In S. W. Duck (Eds.), *Handbook of personal relationships* (pp. 391–408). Wiley.

Henningsen, D. D. (2004). Flirting with meaning: An examination of miscommunication in flirting interactions. *Sex Roles, 50,* 481-489.

Hinsz, V. B. (1989). Facial resemblance in engaged and married couples. *Journal of Social and Personal Relationships, 6,* 223–229.

Holt-Lunstad, J., Birmingham, W., & Jones, B. Q. (2008). Is there something unique about marriage? The relative impact of marital status, relationship quality, and network support on ambulatory blood pressure and mental health. *Annals of Behavioral Medicine, 35,* 239–244.

Holt-Lunstad, J., Smith, T. B., & Layton, J. B. (2010). Social relationships and mortality risk: A meta-analytic review. http://www.plosmedicine.org/article/info%3Adoi%2F10.1371%2Fjournal.pmed.1000316

Janz, T. A. (2000). The evolution and diversity of relationships in Canadian families. *Canadian Journal of Higher Education.* http://www.lcc.gc.ca/research_project/00_diversity_1-en.asp

Johnson, A. J., Haigh, M. M., Becker, J. A. H., Craig, E. A., & Wigley, S. (2008). College students' use of relational management strategies in email in long-distance and geographically close relationships. *Journal of Computer-Mediated Communication, 13*(2008), 381–404.

Johnson, A. J., Wittenberg, E., Haigh, M., & Wigley, S. (2004). The process of relationship development and deterioration: Turning points in friendships that have terminated. *Communication Quarterly, 52,* 54–68.

Kalmijn, M. (1994). Assortative mating by cultural and economic occupational status. *American Journal of Sociology, 100*(2), 422–452.

Kelley, H. H., Berscheid, E., Christensen, A., Harvey, J., Huston, T., Levinger, G., . . . & Peterson, D. (1983). *Close relationships.* Freeman.

Kimmel, M. S. (2002). Male victims of domestic violence: A substantive and methodological research review. *Violence Against Women, 8*(11), 1332–1363.

Knapp, M. L. (1978). *Social intercourse: From greeting to goodbye.* Allyn & Bacon.

Knapp, M. L., & Vangelisti, A. (1997*). Interpersonal communication and relationships* (2nd ed.). Allyn & Bacon.

Knight, K. (September, 2014). Communicating dilemmas in adults' friends with benefits relationships: Challenges to relational talk. *Emerging Adulthood.* http://eax.sagepub.com/content/early/2014/09/19/2167696814549598

Kurdek, L. A. (1991). The dissolution of gay and lesbian couples. *Journal of Social and Personal Relationships, 8,* 265–278.

Kurt, J. E., & Sherker, J. L. (2003). Relationship quality, trait similarity, and self-other agreement on personality ratings in college roommates. *Journal of Personality, 71*, 21–40.

LaFollette, H. (1996). *Personal relationships: Love, identity, and morality.* Blackwell Publishers.

Lever, J., Groy, C., Royce, T., & Gillespie, J. (2008). Searching for love in all the "write" places: Exploring internet personals use by sexual orientation, gender, and age. *International Journal of Sexual Health, 20*(4), 233–246.

Little, A. C., Burt, D. M., & Perret, D. I. (2006). Assortive mating for perceived facial personality traits. *Personality and Individual differences, 40*, 973–984.

Lloyd, S. A. (1990). Conflict types and strategies in violent marriages. *Journal of Family Violence, 5*, 269–284.

Lloyd, S. A., & Emery, B. C. (2000). The context and dynamics of intimate aggression against women. *Journal of Social and Personal Relationships, 17*(4–5), 503–521.

Long, J., Long, N., &, Whitson, S. (2016). *The angry smile: Effective strategies to manage passive-aggressive behaviors at home, at school, in marriages and close relationships, the workplace and online.* The LSCI Institute.

Lutgen-Sandvik, P., Tracey, S. J., & Alberts, J. K. (2007). Burned by bullying in the American workplace: Prevalence, perception, degree and impact. *Journal of Management Studies.* https://onlinelibrary.wiley.com/doi/abs/10.1111/j.1467-6486.2007.00715.x

McCormick, N. B., & Jones, J. J. (1989). Gender differences in nonverbal flirtation. *Journal of Sex Education and Therapy, 15*, 271–282.

McCoy, K., & Oelschlager, J. (n.d.) Sexual coercion awareness and prevention. *Florida Institute of Technology.* http://www.fit.edu/caps/documents/SexualCoercion_000.pdf

McCroskey, L. L., McCroskey, J. C., & Richmond, V. P. (2006). Analysis and improvement of the measurement of interpersonal attraction and homophily. *Communication Quarterly, 54*(1), 1–31.

Menning, C., & Holtzman, M. (2014). Process and patterns in gay, lesbian and bisexual assault: A multmethodological assessment. *Journal of Interpersonal Violence, 29*(6), 1071–1093.

Miller, R. S. (2002). Suicidal and death ideation in older primary care patients with depression, anxiety, and at-risk. *American Journal of Geriatric Psychiatry, 10*, 417–427.

Starmer-Smith, C. (2004, March 13). Indonesia to ban kissing in public. *The Telegraph.* https://www.telegraph.co.uk/travel/729911/Indonesia-to-ban-kissing-in-public.html#:~:text=Travellers%20caught%20kissing%20in%20public,face%20five%20years%20in%20jail.&text=The%20suggested%20jail%20terms%20for,rupiah%20(%C2%A316%2C000)%20fine

Muehlenhard, C. L., & Hollabough, L. C. (1988). Do women sometimes say no when they mean yes? The prevalence and correlates of women's token resistance to sex. *Journal of Personality and Social Psychology, 54*, 872–879.

Nardi, P. M. (1992). That's what friends are for: Friends as family in the gay and lesbian community. In K. Plummer (Ed.), *Modern homosexualities: Fragments of lesbian and gay experience* (pp. 108–120). Routledge.

Nardi, P. M. (2007). Friendship, sex, and masculinity. In M. Kimmel (Ed.), *The sexual self* (pp. 49–60). Vanderbilt University Press.

National Coalition Against Domestic Violence. (2015). *National statistics domestic violence fact sheet.* www.ncadv.org/learn-more/statistics

Noller, P., & Fitzpatrick, M. A. (1990). Marital communication in the eighties. *Journal of Marriage and the Family, 52*, 832–843.

O'Brien, E., & Foley, L. (1999). The dating game: An exercise illustrating the concepts of homogamy, heterogamy, hyperogamy, and hypogamy. *Teaching Sociology, 27*(2), 145–149.

Payne, E., & Smith, M. (2013). LGBTQ kids, school safety and missing the big picture: How the dominant bullying discourse prevents school professionals from thinking about systemic marginalization or . . . why we need to rethink LGBTQ bullying. *QED: A Journal in GLBTQ Worldmaking, Inaugural issue*, 1–36.

Peplau, A. (2009). Gay, lesbian, and bisexual relationships. In the *Encyclopedia of Human Relationships.* http://www.sage-reference.com/humanrelationships/Article_n238.html

Pew Research Center. (2015, September). U.S. Catholics open to non-traditional families. *Religion and Public Life.* https://www.pewforum.org/2015/09/02/u-s-catholics-open-to-non-traditional-families/

Pogrebin, L. C. (1992). The same and different: Crossing boundaries of color, culture, sexual preference, disability, and age. In W. B. Gudykunst & Y. Y. Kim (Eds.), *Readings on communicating with strangers* (pp. 318–336). McGraw-Hill.

Pugachevsky, J., & Andrews, T. (2020, May 27). 11 apps that will help you make friends because, help, it's hard. https://www.cosmopolitan.com/sex-love/a24799641/best-friendship-app

Rawlins, W. K. (1992). *Friendship matters.* Aldine de Gruyter.

Rawlins, W. R., & Holl, M. (1987). Communicative achievement of friendship during adolescence: Predicaments of trust and violation. *Western Journal of Communication, 51*(4), 345–363.

Reeder, H. (1996). *What Harry and Sally didn't tell you.* (Unpublished Doctoral dissertation). Arizona State University, Tempe, AZ.

Rohrbaugh, J. R. (2006). Domestic violence in same-gendered relationships. *Family Court Review, 44*, 287–299.

Root, M. P. (2001). *Love's revolution: Interracial marriage.* Temple University Press.

Sabourin, T. C. (1996). The role of communication in verbal abuse between spouses. In D. D. Cahn & S. A. Lloyd (Eds.), *Family violence from a communication perspective* (pp. 199–217). Sage.

Sailer, S. (2003). Race and marriage. *Financial Review.* https://www.afr.com/politics/race-and-marriage-19971010-k7pr8

Sarkis, S. A. (2017, January 22). 11 warning signs of gaslighting. *Psychology Today.* https://www.psychologytoday.com/us/blog/here-there-and-everywhere/201701/11-warning-signs-gaslighting

Schafer, R. B., & Keith, P. M. (1990). Matching by weight in married couples: A life cycle perspective. *Journal of Social Psychology, 130*(5), 657–664.

Sias, P. M., & Cahill, D. J. (1998). From coworkers to friends: The development of peer friendships in the workplace. *Western Journal of Communication, 62*, 273–299.

Sollors, W. (Ed.). (2000). *Interracialism: Black and white intermarriage in American history, literature and law.* Oxford University Press.

Spitzberg, B. (1998). Sexual coercion in courtship relationships. In B. Spitzberg & W. Cupach (Eds.), *The dark side of close relationships.* Erlbaum.

Sprecher, S. (1998). Insiders' perspectives on reasons for attraction to a close other. *Social Psychology Quarterly, 61*, 287–300.

Sprecher, S. & Hatfield, E. (2009). Matching hypothesis. In H. Reis & S. Sprecher (Eds.) *Encyclopedia of human relationships.* Sage.

Sprecher, S., & Regan, P. (2002). Liking some things (in some people) more than others: Partner preferences in romantic relationships and friendships. *Journal of Social and Personal Relationships, 19*, 463–481.

Stafford, L. (2010). Geographic distance and communication during courtship. *Communication Research, 37*(2), 275–297.

Struckman-Johnson, C. J., Struckman-Johnson, B. L., & Anderson, B. (2003). Tactics of sexual coercion: When men and women won't take no for an answer. *Journal of Sex Research, 40*(1), 76–86.

Sunnafrank, M. (1986). Predicted outcome value in initial conversations. *Communication Research Reports, 5*(2), 169–172.

Surra, C. (1987). Reasons for changes in commitment: Variations by courtship type. *Journal of Social and Personal Relationships, 4*, 17–33.

Thibault, J. W., & Kelley, H. H. (1959). *The Social Psychology of Groups.* John Wiley & Sons.

Vilhauer, J. (2015, November 27). Why ghosting hurts so much. *Psychology Today.* https://www.psychologytoday.com/us/blog/living-forward/201511/why-ghosting-hurts-so-much

Vorauer, J., & Ratner, R. (1996). Who's going to make the first move? *Journal of Social and Personal Relationships, 13*, 483–506.

Walster, E., Berscheid, E., & William. G. (1973). New directions in equity research. *Journal of Personality and Social Psychology, 25*(2), 151–176.

Walzer, S. (1996). *Thinking about the baby: Gender and transitions into parenthood (women in the political economy)* (pp. 1–209). Temple University Press.

Watson, D., Klohnen, E., Casillas, A., Simms, E., Haig, J., & Berry, D. (2004). Assortative mating in married couples. *Journal of Personality, 72*(5), 1029–1068.

Weber, A. L. (1998). Losing, leaving and letting go: Coping with nonmarital breakups. In B. H. Spitzberg & W. R. Cupach (Eds.), *The dark side of close relationships* (pp. 267–306). Erlbaum.

Willan, V. J., & Pollard, P. (2003). Likelihood of acquaintance rape as a function of males' sexual expectations, disappointment, and adherence to rape-conducive attitudes. *Journal of Social and Personal Relationships, 20,* 637–661.

Wright, D. E. (1999). *Personal relationships: An interdisciplinary approach.* MountMayfield Publishing.

Young, J. E. (1981). Cognitive therapy and loneliness. In G. Emery, S. D. Hollon, & R. C. Bedrosian (Eds.), *New directions in cognitive therapy: A casebook* (pp. 139–159). Guilford Press.

Zarefsky, M. (2020, August 18). Why anxiety, depression are prevalent during COVID -19. *American Medical Association.* https://www.ama-assn.org/delivering-care/public-health/why-depression-anxiety-are-prevalent-during-covid-19

Chapter 10

Bakken, R. (2018, August 23). Challenges to managing virtual teams and how to overcome them. *blog.dce.harvard.edu.* https://blog.dce.harvard.edu/professional-development/challenges-managing-virtual-teams-and-how-overcome-them

Abrams, K. M., Wang, Z., Song, Y. J., & Galindo-Gonzalez, S. (2015). Data richness trade-offs between face-to-face, online audiovisual, and online text-only focus groups. *Social Science Computer Review, 33*(1), 80–96.

Adams, S. (2014, November 12). The 10 skills employers most want in 2015 graduates. *Forbes.* https://www.forbes.com/sites/susan-adams/2014/11/12/the-10-skills-employers-most-want-in-2015-graduates/?sh=6e0c36af2511

Allen, T. H., & Plax, T. G. (2002). Exploring consequences of group communication in the classroom. In L. R. Frey (Ed.), *New directions in group communication* (pp. 219–234). Sage.

Arrow, H., McGrath, J. E., & Berdahl, J. L. (2000). *Small groups as complex systems.* Sage.

Barge, J. K. (1989). Leadership as medium: A leaderless group discussion model. *Communication Quarterly, 37,* 237–247.

Benne, K. D., & Sheats, P. (1948). Functional roles of group members. *Journal of Social Issues, 4,* 41–49.

Bernier, A., & Stenstrom, C. (2016). Moving from chance and "chemistry" to skills: Improving online student learning outcomes in small group collaboration. *Education for Information, 32*(1), 55–69.

Blum, S. (2020, April 22). Why we're exhausted by Zoom. *insiderhighed.com.* https://www.insidehighered.com/advice/2020/04/22/professor-explores-why-zoom-classes-deplete-her-energy-opinion

Bono, J. E., & Judge, T. A. (2004). Personality and transformational and transactional leadership: A meta-analysis. *Journal of Applied Psychology, 89*(5), 901–910.

Braun, M. T., Kozlowski, S. W. J., Brown, T. A. (Rench), & DeShon, R. P. (2020). Exploring the dynamic team cohesion–performance and coordination–performance relationships of newly formed teams. *Small Group Research, 51*(5), 551–580.

Cain, S. (2013). *Quiet: The power of introverts in a world that can't stop talking.* Broadway Books.

Cater III, J. J., & Young, M. (2020). An examination of the leadership roles of senior generation women in family firms: How does servant leadership apply? *Journal of Leadership, Accountability and Ethics, 17*(2), 25–52.

Caya, O., Mortensen, M., & Pinsonneault, A. (2013). Virtual teams demystified: An integrative framework for understanding virtual teams. *International Journal of e-collaboration, 9*(2), 1–33.

Chahine, S., Cristancho, S., Padgett, J., & Lingard, L. (2017). How do small groups make decisions?: A theoretical framework to inform the implementation and study of clinical competency committees. *Perspectives on Medical Education, 6*(3), 192–198.

Choi, H.-S., Seo, J.-G., Hyun, J., & Bechtoldt, M. (2019). Collectivistic independence promotes group creativity by reducing idea fixation. *Small Group Research, 50*(3), 381–407.

Covey, S. R. (1989). *The seven habits of highly effective people: Restoring the character ethic.* Simon and Schuster.

Cragan, J. F., & Wright, D. W. (1999). *Communication in small groups: Theory, process, skills* (5th ed.). Wadsworth.

Crown, D. F. (2007). The use of group and groupcentric individual goals for culturally heterogeneous and homogeneous task groups: An assessment of European work teams. *Small Group Research, 38*(4), 489–508.

Daft, R. L. (2015). *The leadership experience* (6th ed.). Cengage Higher Education.

Denhardt, R. B., & Denhardt, J. V. (2004). *The dance of leadership.* M. E. Sharpe.

de Wit, F. R. C., Greer, L. L., & Jehn, K. A. (2012). The paradox of intragroup conflict: A meta-analysis. *Journal of Applied Psychology, 97*(2), 360–390.

Eisenberg, J., Post, C., & DiTomaso, N. (2019). Virtual team dispersion and performance: The role of team communication and transformational leadership. *Small Group Research, 50*(3), 348–380.

Five ways to effectively handle conflict in a virtual team. (2020). *thevirtualhub.com.* https://www.thevirtualhub.com/blog/5-ways-to-effectively-handle-conflict-in-virtual-teams/

Ferrazzi, K. (2012, November 19). How to manage conflict in virtual teams. HBR Blog Network. http://blogs.hbr.org/2012/11/how-to-manage-conflict-in-virt/

Fiedler, F. E. (1981). *Leader Attitudes and Group Effectiveness.* Greenwood Publishing Group.

Fiedler, F. E., & Garcia, J. E. (1987). *New approaches to leadership, cognitive resources and organizational performance.* John Wiley and Sons.

Five tips for running inclusive virtual meetings. *globesmart.com.* https://www.toolbox.com/hr/mobile-workforce/guest-article/inclusive-virtual-meetings/

Foels, R., Driskell, J. E., Mullen, B., & Salas, E. (2000). The effects of democratic leadership on group member satisfaction: An integration. *Small Group Research, 31,* 676–701.

French, J. R., Jr., & Raven, B. H. (1959). The bases of social power. In D. Cartwright (Ed.), *Studies in social power* (pp. 150–167). Institute for Social Research.

Frey, L. R. (1994). The call of the field: Studying communication in natural groups. In L. R. Frey (Ed.), *Group communication in context: Studies of natural groups* (pp. ix–xiv). Erlbaum.

Garcia, C., & Badia, A. (2017). Information problem-solving skills in small virtual groups and learning outcomes. *Journal of Computer Assisted Learning, 33*(4), 382–392.

Gladwell, M. (2008). *Outliers.* Little, Brown and Company.

Gloor, P. A. (2006). *Swarm creativity: Competitive advantage through collaborative innovative networks.* Oxford University Press.

Gloor, P. A., & Colladon, A. F. (2020). Heart beats brain: Measuring moral beliefs through e-mail analysis. In A. Przegalinska, F. Grippa, & P. A. Gloor (Eds.), *Digital transformation of collaboration* (pp. 85–99). Springer.

Gollent, M. (2007, June 6). Why are leadership skills important—for everyone? http://ezinearticles.com/?why-are-leadership-skills-important—for-everyone?&id=591333

Greenleaf, R. (1970/1991). *The servant as leader* (pp. 1–37). The Robert K. Greenleaf Center.

Greenleaf, R. K. (2016). *Center for servant leadership.* https://www.greenleaf.org/what-is-servant-leadership/

Handke, L., Klonek, F. E., Parker, S. K., & Kauffeld, S. (2020). Interactive effects of team virtuality and work design on team functioning. *Small Group Research, 51*(1), 3–47.

Handke, L., Schulte, E.-M., Schneider, K., & Kauffeld, S. (2019). Teams, time, and technology: variations of media use over project phases. *Small Group Research, 50*(2), 266–305.

Hansen, R. S. (2011, September 12). 15 quick tips for excelling at work. *Quintzine.com, 12*(9). http://www.quintcareers.com/15_excelling_work_tips.html

Hargrove, R. (1998). *Mastering the art of creative collaboration.* Business-Week Books.

Henningsen, D. D., & Henningsen, M. L. M. (2006). Examining the symptoms of groupthink and retrospective sensemaking. *Small Group Research, 37*(1), 36–64.

Hirokawa, R. Y., & Salazar, A. J. (1999). Task-group communication and decision-making performance. In L. R. Frey, D. S. Gouran, & M. S. Poole (Eds.), The *handbook of group communication theory and research* (pp. 167–191). Sage.

Jaeger, E. L. (2020). Not the desired outcome: Groupthink undermines the work of a literacy council. *Small Group Research, 51*(4), 517–541.

Jobidon, M.-E., Turcotte, I., Aubé, C., Labrecque, A., Kelsey, S., & Tremblay, S. (2016). Role variability in self-organizing teams working in crisis management. *Small Group Research, 48*(1), 62–92.

Johnson, B. R., & D'Lauro, C. J. (2018). After brainstorming, groups select an early generated idea as their best idea. *Small Group Research, 49*(2), 177–194.

Judge, T. A., & Cable, D. M. (2004). The effect of physical height on workplace success and income: Preliminary test of a theoretical model. *Journal of Applied Psychology, 89*, 428–441.

Judge, T. A., Bono, J. E., Ilies, R., & Gerhardt, M. W. (2002). Personality and leadership: A qualitative and quantitative review. *Journal of Applied Psychology, 87*, 765–780.

Judge, T. A., Colbert, A. E., & Ilies, R. (2004). Intelligence and leadership: A quantitative review and test of theoretical propositions. *Journal of Applied Psychology, 89*, 542–552.

Jung, D. I., & Sosik, J. J. (2002). Transformational leadership in work groups: The role of empowerment, cohesiveness, and collective-efficacy on perceived group performance. *Small Group Research, 33*, 313–336.

Keyton, J. (1999). Relational communication in groups. In L. R. Frey, D. S. Gouran, & M. S. Poole (Eds.), *Handbook of group communication theory and research* (pp. 199–222). Sage.

Keyton, J. (2000). Introduction: The relational side of groups. *Small Group Research, 34*, 387–396.

Keyton, J., Harmon, N., & Frey, L. R. (1996, November). *Grouphate: Implications for teaching group communication.* Paper presented at the Annual Meeting of the National Communication Association, San Diego, CA.

Klocke, U. (2007). How to improve decision making in small groups: Effects of dissent and training interventions. *Small Group Research, 38*(3), 437–468.

Koeslag-Kreunen, M., Van den Bossche, P., Hoven, M., Van der Klink, M., & Gijselaers, W. (2018). When leadership powers team learning: A meta-analysis. *Small Group Research, 49*(4), 475–513.

Kramer, M. W. (2006). Shared leadership in a community theater group: Filling the leadership role. *Journal of Applied Communication Research, 34*(2), 141–162.

Lambertz-Berndt, M., & Blight, M. (2016). You don't have to like me, but you have to respect me: The impacts of assertiveness, cooperativeness, and group satisfaction in collaborative assignments. *Business and Professional Communication Quarterly, 79*(2), 180–199.

Levine, K. J., Muenchen, R. A., & Brooks, A. M. (2010). Measuring transformational and charismatic leadership: Why isn't charisma measured? *Communication Monographs, 77*(4), 576–591.

Lewis, L. K., Isbell, M. G., & Koschmann, M. A. (2010). Collaborative tensions: Practitioners' experiences of interorganizational relationships. *Communication Monographs, 77*(4), 462–481.

Lowry, P. B., Roberts, T. L., Romano, N. C., Cheney, P. D., & Hightower, R. T. (2006). The impact of group size and social presence on small-group communication: Does computer-mediated communication make a difference? *Small Group Research, 37*(6), 631–661.

MacNeil, A., & McClanahan, A. (2005). *Shared leadership, The Connexions Project.* http://cnx.org/content/m12923/latest/

Matha, B., & Boehm, M. (2008). *Beyond the babble: Leadership communication that drives results.* Jossey-Bass.

Martinic, A., Fertalj, K., & Kalpic, D. (2012). Methodological framework for virtual team project management. *International Journal of Innovation, Management and Technology, 3*(6), 702–707.

Mitchell, T. D., Hu, J., & Johnson, L. (2019). Diminishing returns of leadership behaviors on leadership emergence. *Small Group Research, 50*(6), 759–773.

Moore, K. (2012). Introverts no longer the quiet followers of extroverts. *Forbes.* http://www.forbes.com/sites/karlmoore/2012/08/22/introverts-no-longer-the-quiet-followers-of-extroverts/

Myers, S. A., & Goodboy, A. K. (2005). A study of grouphate in a course on small group communication. *Psychological Reports, 97*(2), 381–386.

Nishimura, K. (2020, June 11). Investing in diversity can deliver bottom-line benefits, experts say *sourcingjournal.com.* https://sourcingjournal.com/topics/retail/psfk-diversity-inclusion-retail-black-consumers-melissa-gonzalez-lionesque-215323/

Northouse, P. G. (2012). *Leadership: Theory and practice* (6th ed.). Sage.

Oetzel, J. G. (1998). Explaining individual communication processes in homogeneous and heterogeneous group through individual-collectivism and self-construal. *Human Communication Research, 25*, 202–224.

Oetzel, J. G. (2001). Self-construals, communication processes, and group outcomes in homogeneous and heterogeneous groups. *Small Group Research, 32*, 19–54.

Oetzel, J. G. (2005). Effective intercultural workgroup communication theory. In W. B. Gudykunst (Ed.), *Theorizing about intercultural communication* (pp. 351–371). Sage.

Ostergaard, C., Timmermans, B., & Kristinsson, K. (2011). Does a different view create something new? The effect of employee diversity on innovation. *Research Policy, 40*(3), 500–509.

Paletz, S. B. F., Peng, K., Erez, M., & Maslach, C. (2004). Ethnic composition and its differential impact on group processes in diverse teams. *Small Group Research, 35*, 128–158.

Park, H. S., & Shin, S.-Y. (2015). The role of the star player in a cohesive group. *Small Group Research, 46*(4), 415–430.

Pavitt, C. (1999). Theorizing about the group communication-leadership relationship. In L. R. Frey, D. S. Gouran, & M. S. Poole (Eds.), *Handbook of group communication theory and research* (pp. 313–334). Sage.

Peterson, R. S., & Behfar, K. J. (2003). The dynamic relationship between performance feedback, trust, and conflict in groups: A longitudinal study. *Organizational Behavior and Human Decision Processes, 92*, 102–112.

Phadnis, S., & Caplice, C. (2013). Global virtual teams: How are they performing? *Supply Chain Management Review, 17*(4), 8–9.

Phillips, K. W. (2014, October 1). How diversity makes us smarter. *Scientific American.* http://www.scientificamerican.com/article/how-diversity-makes-us-smarter/

Posner, C. (2018, February 6). BlackRock advocates that at least two women be on each company board. *cooleypubco.com.* https://cooleypubco.com/2018/02/06/blackrock-advocates-that-at-least-two-women-be-on-each-company-board/

Poole, M. S. (1983). Decision development in small groups: A study of multiple sequences in decision-making. *Communication Monographs, 50*, 206–232.

Poole, M. S., & Garner, J. T. (2006). Workgroup conflict and communication. In J. G. Oetzel & S. Ting-Toomey (Eds.), *The Sage handbook of conflict communication* (pp. 267–292). Sage.

Rothwell, J. D. (2019). *In mixed company: Communicating in small groups and teams.* Oxford University Press.

Rowold, J., & Heinitz, K. (2007). Transformational and charismatic leadership: Assessing the convergent, divergent and criterion validity of the MLQ and the CKS. *The Leadership Quarterly, 18*, 121–133.

Schultz, B. G. (1999). Improving group communication performance. In L. R. Frey, D. S. Gouran, & M. S. Poole (Eds.), *Handbook of group communication theory and research* (pp. 371–394). Sage.

Sell, J., Lovaglia, M. J., Mannix, E. A., Samuelson, C. D., & Wilson, R. K. (2004). Investigating conflict, power, and status within and among groups. *Small Group Research, 35*, 44–72.

Sengupta, S. (2020, January 21). Greta Thunberg's message at Davos Forum: "Our house is still on fire." *nytimes.com.* https://www.nytimes.com/2020/01/21/climate/greta-thunberg-davos.html

Shepard, J. (2009). *The meaning of Matthew: My son's murder in Laramie and a world transformed.* Penguin Group.

Sharma, M., Bhatia, G., & Scarr, S. (2019, December 18). Dangerous heights. *graphics.reuters.com.* http://graphics.reuters.com/NEPAL-EVEREST/0100B4S22JR/index.html

Sims, C. M., & Morris, L. R. (2018). Are women business owners authentic servant leaders? *Gender in Management: An International Journal, 33*(5), 40–45.

Sleesman, D. J., Hollenbeck, J. R., Spitzmuller, M., & Schouten, M. E. (2018). Initial expectations of team performance: specious speculation or framing the future? *Small Group Research, 49*(5), 600–635.

Stauffer, D. C., & Maxwell, D. L. (2020). Transforming servant Leadership, organizational culture, change, sustainability, and courageous leadership. *Journal of Leadership, Accountability & Ethics, 17*(1), 105–116.

Stogdill, R. M. (1974). *Handbook of leadership: A survey of theory and research.* Free Press.

Van der Haar, S., Koeslag-Kreunen, M., Euwe, E., & Segers, M. (2017). Team leader structuring for team effectiveness and team learning in command-and-control teams. *Small Group Research, 48*, 215–248.

Van Swol, L. M. (2009). Discussion and perception of information in groups and judge-advisor systems. *Communication Monographs, 76*(1), 99–120.

Virtual work trends for 2020. (2020, June 2). *flashhub.io.* https://www.flashhub.io/virtual-work-trends-for-2020-you-need-to-know/

Talke, K., Salomo, S., & Rose, K. (2010). How top management team diversity affects innovativeness and performance via the strategic choice to focus on innovation fields. *Research Policy, 39*(7), 907–918.

Walker, R., Cardon, P., & Aritz, J. (2018). Enhancing global virtual small group communication skills. *Journal of Intercultural Communication Research: Bringing International Perspectives to the Communication Curriculum in the Age of Globalization, 47*(5), 421–433.

Wang, S., Homan, A. C., & Jehn, K. (2020). Individual task conflict asymmetry and peer ratings of member effectiveness. *Small Group Research, 51*(3), 402–426.

Westover, J. H. (2020, April 20). Creating a workplace culture of belonging, diversity and inclusivity. *Forbes.* https://www.forbes.com/sites/forbescoachescouncil/2020/04/20/creating-a-workplace-culture-of-belonging-diversity-and-inclusivity/#15d77200276e

Wheelan, S. A., Davidson, B., & Tilin, F. (2003). Group development across time: Reality or illusion? *Small Group Research, 34*, 223–245.

Chapter 11

Aeberhard-Hodges, J. (1996). Sexual harassment in employment: Recent judicial and arbitral trends. *International Labor Review, 135*(5), 499–533.

Alberts, J. K., Lutgen-Sandvik, P., & Tracy, S. J. (2005, May). *Bullying in the workplace: A case of escalated incivility. Organizational Communication Division.* The International Communication Association Convention, New York, NY.

Alberts, J. K., Tracy, S., & Trethewey, A. (2011). An integrative theory of the division of domestic labor: Threshold level, social organizing, and sensemaking. *Journal of Family Communication, 11*, 271–238.

Altman, S. A. (2020, May 20). Will Covid-19 have a lasting impact on globalization? *Harvard Business Review.* https://hbr.org/2020/05/will-covid-19-have-a-lasting-impact-on-globalization

Baker, M. (2020, June 8). 9 Future of work trends post-COVID 19. *Gartner.com.* https://www.gartner.com/smarterwithgartner/9-future-of-work-trends-post-covid-19/

Baker, M. & Fink, S. (2020, March 31). At the top of the Covid-19 curve, how do hospitals decide who gets treatment? *The New York Times.* https://www.nytimes.com/2020/03/31/us/coronavirus-covid-triage-rationing-ventilators.html

Barley, S. R., & Kunda, G. (1992). Design and devotion: Surges of rational and normative ideologies of control in managerial discourse. *Administrative Science Quarterly, 37*, 363–399.

Berger, C. (1979). Beyond initial interaction. In H. Giles & R. St. Clair (Eds.), *Language and psychology* (pp. 122–144). Basil Blackwell.

Bisel, R. (2010). A communicative ontology of organization? A description, history, and critique of CCO theories for organization science. *Management Communication Quarterly, 24*(1), 124–131.

Bisel, R., & Adame, E. (2018). Encouraging upward ethical dissent in organizations: The role of reference to embodied expertise. *Management Communication Quarterly, 33*(2), 139–159.

Brown, M. (1989, Winter). Ethics in organizations. *Issues in Ethics, 2*(1). http://www.scu.edu/ethics/publications/iie/v2n1/homepage.html

Brummans, B. H. J. M., Cooren, F., Robichaud, D., & Taylor, J. R. (2014). Approaches to the communicative constitution of organizations. In L. L. Putnam & D. K. Mumby (Eds.), *The SAGE handbook of organizational communication: Advances in theory, research, and methods* (pp. 173–194). Sage.

Canary, D., & Lakey, S. L. (2012). *Strategic conflict.* Routledge.

Casey, M. K. (1998). *Communication, stress and burnout: Use of resource replacement strategies in response to conditional demands in community-based organizations.* (Doctoral dissertation). Michigan State University, East Lansing, MI.

Chambers, B., Moore, A. B., & Bachtel, D. (1998). Role conflict, role ambiguity and job satisfaction of county extension agents in the Georgia Cooperative Extension Service. *AERC Proceedings.* http://www.edst.educ.ubc.ca/aercd1998/98chambers.htm

Cheney, G. (1995). Democracy in the workplace: Theory and practice from the perspective of communication. *Journal of Applied Communication Research, 23*, 167–200.

Cheney, G., Christensen, L. T., Zorn, T. E., Jr., & Ganesh, S. (2004). *Organizational communication in an age of globalizations: Issues, reflections, practices.* Waveland.

Cheung, H. K., Goldberg, C. B., King, E. B., & Magley, V. J. (2018). Are they true to the cause? Beliefs about organizational and unit commitment to sexual harassment awareness training. *Group and Organizational Management, 43*(4), 531–560.

Chilton, K., & Weidenbaum, M. (1994, November). *A new social contract for the American workplace: From paternalism to partnering.* Center for the Study of American Business.

Clair, R. (1996). The political nature of a colloquialism, "a real job": Implications for organizational assimilation. *Communication Monographs, 63*, 249–267.

Clarke, H. M. (2020). Organizational failure to ethically manage sexual harassment: Limits to #metoo. *Business Ethics: A European Review, 29*, 544–556.

Conrad, C., & Witte, K. (1994). Is emotional expression repression oppression? *Communication Yearbook, 17*, 417–428.

Cowan, R. L., & Horan, S. M. (2014). Why are you dating him? Contemporary motives for workplace romances. *Qualitative Research Reports in Communication, 15*(1), 9–16.

Coy, P., Conlin, M., & Herbst, M. (2010, January 7). The disposable worker. *Bloomberg Business Week.* http://www.businessweek.com/magazine/content/10_03/b4163032935448.htm

Daniels, T. D., Spiker, B. K., & Papa, M. J. (1996). *Perspectives on organizational communication* (4th ed.). Brown & Benchmark.

Derks, J., Bakker, A. B., & Gorgievski, M. (2021). Private smartphone use during worktime: A diary study on the unexplored costs of integrating the work and family domains. *Computers in Human Behavior, 114.*

De Ruiter, M., Blomme, R., & Schalk, R. (2016). Manager responses to employee dissent about psychological contract breach: A dyadic process approach. *Management Communication Quarterly, 30*(2), 188–217.

Dockery, T. M., & Steiner, D. D. (1990). The role of the initial interaction in leader-member exchange. *Group and Organization Studies, 15*, 395–413.

Eisenberg, E., Goodall, H. L., & Trethewey, A. (2010). *Organizational communication: Balance, creativity and constraint.* Bedford/St. Martin's.

Eisenberg, J., Post, C., & DiTomaso, N. (2019). Virtual team dispersion and performance: The role of team communication and transformational leadership. *Small Group Research, 50*(3), 348–380.

Equal Employment Opportunity Commission. (1980). Guidelines on discrimination because of sex (Sect. 1604.11). *Federal Register, 45,* 74676–74677.

Everbach, T. (2007). The culture of a women-led newspaper: An ethnographic study of the *Sarasota Herald-Tribune. Journalism and Mass Communication Quarterly, 83*, 477–493.

Faiola, A. (2020, June 26). The virus that shut down the world. *The Washington Post.* https://www.washingtonpost.com/graphics/2020/world/coronavirus-pandemic-globalization/

Fay, M., & Kline, S. (2011). Coworker relationships and informal communication in high-intensity telecommuting. *Journal of Applied Communication Research, 39*(2), 144–163.

Fetherston, M. (2017). Information seeking and organizational socialization: A review and opportunities for anticipatory socialization research. *Annals of the International Communication Association, 41*(3–4), 258–277.

Fishman, C. (2006). *The Wal-Mart effect.* Penguin Press.

Follett, M. P. (1942). *Dynamic administration.* Harper & Row.

Gailliard, B., Myers, K., & Seibold, D. (2010). Organizational assimilation: A multidimensional reconceptualization and measure. *Management Communication Quarterly, 24*(4), 552–578.

Ganesh, S., Zoller, H., & Cheney, G. (2005). Transforming resistance, broadening our boundaries: Critical organization meets globalization from below. *Communication Monographs, 72*(2), 169–191.

Gelfand, M., Gordon, S., Li, C., Choi, V., & Prokopowicz, P. (2018, October 2). One reason mergers fail: The two cultures aren't compatible. *hbr.org*. https://hbr.org/2018/10/one-reason-mergers-fail-the-two-cultures-arent-compatible

Gioia, D. A., & Patvardhan, S. (2012). Identity as process and flow. In M. Schultz, S. Maguire, A. Langley, & H. Tsoukas (Eds.), *Constructing identity in and around organizations* (pp. 50–62). New York, NY: Oxford University.

Golembiewski, R. T., Boudreau, R. A., Sun, B. C., & Luo, H. (1998). Estimates of burnout in public agencies: Worldwide how many employees have which degrees of burnout, and with what consequences? *Public Administration Review, 58,* 59–65.

Graen, G., & Graen, J. (2006). *Sharing network leadership.* Information Age Publishing.

Hochschild, A. (1983). *The managed heart.* University of California Press.

Holt, J. (2020, February 3). How Boeing lost its way. *Forbes.* https://www.forbes.com/sites/josephholt/2020/02/03/how-boeing-lost-its-way/#3c2499c3f14d

Igbaria, M., & Guimaraes, T. (1993). Antecedents and consequences of job satisfaction among information center employees. *Journal of Management Information Systems, 9*(4), 145–155.

Jablin, F. M. (1979). Superior–subordinate communication: The state of the art. *Psychological Bulletin, 86,* 1201–1222.

Jablin, F. M. (2001). Organizational entry, assimilation, and exit. In F. M. Jablin & L. L. Putnam (Eds.), *The new handbook of organizational communication: Advances in theory, research, and methods* (pp. 732–828). Sage.

Jablin, F. M., & Sias, P. M. (2001). Communication competence. In F. M. Jablin & L. Putnam (Eds.), *The new handbook of organizational communication* (pp. 819–864). Sage.

Jacobson, R. K., & Eaton, A. A. (2018). How organizational policies influence bystander likelihood of reporting moderate and severe sexual harassment at work. *Employee Responsibilities and Rights Journal, 30,* 37–62.

Jenner, L. (1994). Work-family programs: Looking beyond written programs. *HR Focus, 71,* 19–20.

Jia, M., Cheng, J., & Hale, C. (2017). Workplace emotion and communication: Supervisor nonverbal immediacy, employees' emotion experience, and their communication motives. *Management Communication Quarterly, 31*(1), 69–87.

Kenny, C. (2018, October 18). LGBTQ youth share their stories, offer advice to adults to end bullying. *glaad.org.* https://www.glaad.org/amp/lgbtq-youth-share-stories-offer-advice-adults-to-end-bullying

Khanna, P. & Francis, D. (2016). Rise of the Titans. *Foreign Policy, 217,* 50–55.

Kirby, E. L., & Krone, K. J. (2002). "The policy exists but you can't really use it": Communication and the structuration of work-family polices. *Journal of Applied Communication Research, 30,* 50–77.

Knight, R. (2018, January 29). How to ask for a promotion. *hbr.org.* https://hbr.org/2018/01/how-to-ask-for-a-promotion

Koniarek, J., & Dudek, B. (1996). Social support as a barrier in the stress–burnout relationship. *International Journal of Stress Management, 3,* 99–106.

Kram, K. E., & Isabella, L. A. (1985). Mentoring alternatives: The role of peer relationships in career development. *Academy of Management Journal, 28,* 110–132.

Kreps, G. (1991). *Organizational communication: Theory and practice* (2nd ed.). Longman.

Krugman, P. (2002). *The great unraveling: Losing our way in the new century.* W. W. Norton.

Larson, J., Jr. (1989). The dynamic interplay between employees: Feedback-seeking strategies and supervisors' delivery of performance feedback. *Academy of Management Review, 14,* 408–422.

Larson, G., & Pearson, A. (2012). Placing identity: Place as a discursive resource for occupational identity work among high-tech entrepreneurs. *Management Communication Quarterly, 26*(2), 241–266.

Lutgen-Sandvik, P., Tracy, S., & Alberts, J. (2005, February). *Burned by bullying in the American workplaces: A first time study of U.S. prevalence and delineation of bullying "degree."* Paper presented at the Western States Communication Convention, San Francisco, CA.

Madan, A. O. (2014). Cyber aggression, cyber bullying and the dark triad: Effect on workplace behavior and performance. *International*

Journal of Social, Management, Economics and Business Engineering, 8(6), 1682–1687.

Martin, J. (2002). *Organizational culture: Mapping the terrain.* Sage.

Martin, J. (2012). That's how we do things around here: Organizational culture (and change) in libraries. http://www.inthelibrarywiththeleadpipe.org/2012/thats-how-we-do-things-around-here/

Maslach, C. (2003). Job burnout: New directions in research and intervention. *Current Directions in Psychological Science, 12*(5), 189–192.

Maslach, C., & Leiter, M. (1997). *The truth about burnout: How organizations cause personal stress and what to do about it.* Jossey-Bass.

Matthews, C., & Gandel, S. (2015, December 27). The 5 biggest corporate scandals of 2015. *Fortune.* http://fortune.com/2015/12/27/biggest-corporate-scandals-2015/

McGrath, J. E. (1976). Stress and behavior in organizations. In M. D. Dunnette (Ed.), *Handbook of industrial and organizational psychology.* Consulting Psychologists Press.

McNamara, C. (2008). *Field guide to leadership and supervision.* Authenticity Publishing.

Miller, V. D., & Jablin, F. (1991). Information seeking during organizational entry: Influence, tactics and a model of the process. *Academy of Management Review, 16,* 522–541.

McPhee, R. D., & Zaug, P. (2009). The communicative constitution of organization: A framework for explanation. In L. L. Putnam & A. M. Nicotera (Eds.), *Building theories of organization: The constitutive role of communication* (pp. 21–48). Routledge.

Men, L. R., & Jiang, H. (2016). Cultivating quality employee-organization relationships: The interplay among organizational leadership, culture, and communication. *International Journal of Strategic Communication, 10*(5), 462–479.

Miller, K. (2015). *Organizational communication: Approaches and processes* (7th ed). Cengage Learning.

Monge, P. R., & Contractor, N. S. (2001). Emergence of communication networks. In F. M. Jablin & L. L. Putnam (Eds.), *The new handbook of organizational communication* (pp. 440–502). Sage.

Morgan, H., & Milliken, F. J. (1992). Keys to action: Understanding differences in organizations' responsiveness to work-and-family issues. *Human Resource Management, 31,* 227–248.

Namie, G. (2017). *The 2017 WBI U.S. workplace bullying survey.* https://workplacebullying.org/research-wbi/

Onibada, A. (2020, June 2). TikTok tells Black creators: "We know we have work to do to regain and repair that trust." *buzzfeed.com.* https://www.buzzfeednews.com/article/adeonibada/tiktok-apology-black-creators-racism-blm-george-floyd

Pacanowsky, M. L., & Trujillo, N. (1983). Organizational communication as organization performance. *Communication Monographs, 50,* 126–147.

Palomares, N. W. & Wingate, N. V. (2020). Victims' goal understanding, uncertainty reduction, and perceptions in cyberbullying: Theoretical evidence from three experiments. *Journal of Computer-Mediated Communication, 5*(4), 253–273.

Pappas, V. & Chikumbu, K. (2020, June 24). Progress report: How we're supporting Black communities and promoting diversity and inclusion. https://newsroom.tiktok.com/en-us/progress-report-how-were-supporting-black-communities-and-promoting-diversity-and-inclusion

Paul, G. D., & Putnam, L. L. (2017). Moral foundations of forgiving in the workplace. *Western Journal of Communication, 81*(1), 43–63.

Powers, S. R. & Myers, K. K. (2020). Work-related emotional communication model of burnout: An analysis of emotions for hire. *Management Communication Quarterly, 34*(2) 155–187.

Privitera, C., & Campbell, M. A. (2009). Cyberbullying: The new face of workplace bullying. *Cyber Psychology & Behavior, 12*(4), 395–400.

Rapoport, R., & Bailyn, L. (1996). *Relinking life and work.* Ford Foundation.

Rawlins, W. K. (1994). Being there and growing apart: Sustaining friendships during adulthood. In D. Canary & L. Stafford, *Communication and relational maintenance* (pp. 275–294). Academic.

Richardsen, A. M., & Martinussen, M. (2004). The Maslach burnout inventory: Factorial validity and consistency across occupational groups in Norway. *Journal of Occupational and Organizational Psychology, 77,* 1–20.

Rizzo, J. R., House, R. J., & Lirtzman, S. L. (1970). Role conflict and ambiguity in complex organizations. *Administrative Science Quarterly, 15,* 150–163.

Roberts, B. S., & Mann, R. A. (2000, December 5). Sexual harassment in the workplace: A primer. *Akron Law Review*. http://www3.uakron.edu/lawrev/robert1.html

Roose, K. (2014, April 24). The sharing economy isn't about trust, it's about desperation. *New York Magazine*. http://nymag.com/daily/intelligencer/2014/04/sharing-economy-is-about-desperation.html

Schneider, B., Ehrhart, K. H., & Ehrhart, M. G. (2005). Organizational climate. In C. L. Cooper (Ed.), *The Blackwell Encyclopedia of Management*, XI, 270–272. http://www.blackwellreference.com/public/tocnode?id=g9780631233176_chunk_g978063123536119_ss2-8#citation

Scott, C., & Myers, K. (2005). The emotion of socialization and assimilation: Learning emotion management at the firehouse. *Journal of Applied Communication Research, 33*(1), 67–92.

Shuler, S., & Sypher, B. D. (2000). Seeking emotion labor: When managing the heart enhances the work experience. *Management Communication Quarterly, 14*, 50–89.

Sias, P. M. (2005). Workplace relationship quality and employee information experiences. *Communication Studies, 56*(4), 375–395.

Sias, P. M., & Cahill, D. J. (1998). From coworkers to friends: The development of peer friendships in the workplace. *Western Journal of Communication, 62*, 273–279.

Sias, P., & Duncan, K. (2019). "I know it's not your job but . . . ": Extra-role tasks, communication, and leader-member exchange relationships. *Communication Quarterly, 67*(4), 355–382.

Sias, P. M., & Jablin, F. M. (1995). Differential superior–subordinate relations: Perceptions of fairness, and coworker communication. *Human Communication Research, 22*, 5–38.

Sias, P. M., Smith, G., & Avdeyeva, T. (2003). Sex and sex-composition differences and similarities in peer workplace friendship development. *Communication Studies, 54*, 322–340.

Sigal, J., Braden-Maguire, J., Patt, I., Goodrich, C., & Perrino, C. S. (2003). Effect of coping response, setting, and social context on reactions to sexual harassment. *Sex Roles, 48*(3–4), 157–166.

Solomon, C. (1994). Work/family's failing grade: Why today's initiatives aren't enough. *Personnel Journal, 73*(5), 72–87.

Steele, G. A., & Plenty, D. (2015). Supervisor–subordinate communication competence and job and communication satisfaction. *International Journal of Business Communication, 52*(3), 294–318.

Stephens, K., Jahn, J., Fox, S., Charoensap-Kelly, P., Mitra, R., Sutton, J., Waters, E., Xie, B., & Meisenbach, R. (2020). Collective sensemaking around COVID-19: Experiences, concerns, and agendas for our rapidly changing organizational lives. *Management Communication Quarterly, 34*(3), 426–457.

Teresi, M., Pietroni, D. D., Barattucci, M., Gianella, V. A., & Pagliaro, S. (2019). Ethical climate(s), organizational identification, and employees' behavior. *Frontiers in Psychology, 10.* http://10.3389/fpsyg.2019.01356

Thomas, P., Chaney, S., & Cutter, C. (2020, Aug 28). New Covid-19 layoffs make job reductions permanent. *wsj.com*. https://www.wsj.com/articles/new-covid-19-layoffs-make-job-reductions-permanent-11598654257

Thomson, K. (2020). Slow motion revolution or assimilation? Theorizing "entryism" in destabilizing regimes of inequality. *Current Sociology, 68*(4), 499–519.

Thurnell, R., & Parker, A. (2008). Men, masculinities and firefighting: Occupational identity, shop-floor culture and organisational change. *Emotion, Space and Society, 1*(2), 127–134.

Tracy, S. J. (2000). Becoming a character for commerce: Emotion labor, self-subordination and discursive construction of identity in a total institution. *Management Communication Quarterly, 14*, 90–128.

Tracy, S. J. (2005). Locking up emotion: Moving beyond dissonance for understanding emotion labor discomfort. *Communication Monographs, 72*, 261–238.

Tracy, S. J., Franks, T. M., Brooks, M. M., & Hoffman, T. K. (2015). An OPPT-in approach to relational and emotional organizational communication pedagogy. *Management Communication Quarterly, 29*(2), 322–328.

Trethewey, A., & Corman, S. (2001). Anticipating k-commerce: E-Commerce, knowledge management, and organizational communication. *Management Communication Quarterly, 14*, 619–628.

Van Gilder, B. J. (2019). Femininity as perceived threat to military effectiveness: How military service members reinforce hegemonic masculinity in talk. *Western Journal of Communication, 83*(2), 151–171.

Vault. (2003). *Vault office romance survey.* http://www.vault.com/nr/newsmain.jsp>nr_page=3dch_id=420d.article_id=16513021

von Bertalanffy, L. (1968). *General systems theory.* Braziller.

Waldron, V. R. (1994). Once more, with feeling: Reconsidering the role of emotion in work. In S. Deetz (Ed.), *Communication yearbook, 17,* 388–416. Sage.

Wayne, S. G., & Ferris, G. R. (1990). Influence tactics, affect and exchange quality in supervisor-subordinate interactions: A laboratory experiment and field study. *Journal of Applied Psychology, 75,* 487–499.

Wen, J., Huang, S., & Hou, P. (2019). Emotional intelligence, emotional labor, perceived organizational support, and job satisfaction: A moderated mediation model. *International Journal of Hospitality Management, 81,* 120–130.

Westman, M., & Etzion, D. (2005). The crossover of work-family conflict from one spouse to the other. *Journal of Applied Social Psychology, 35*(9), 1936–1957.

Whetton, D. A., & Cameron, K. S. (2002). *Developing managerial skills* (6th ed.). Prentice Hall.

Wright, K., Abendschein, B., Wombacher, K., O'Connor, M., Hoffman, M., Dempsey, M., Krull, C., Dewes, A., & Shelton, A. (2014). Work-related communication technology use outside of regular work hours and work life conflict: The influence of communication technologies on perceived work life conflict, burnout, job satisfaction, and turnover intentions. *Management Communication Quarterly, 28*(4), 507–530.

Yin, P., Ou, C. X. J., Davison, R. M., & Wu, J. (2018). Coping with mobile technology overload in the workplace. *Internet Research, 28*(5), 1189–1212.

Zillman, C. (2017, October). A new poll on sexual harassment suggests why "Me Too" went so insanely viral. *fortune.com*. https://fortune.com/2017/10/17/me-too-hashtag-sexual-harassment-at-work-stats/

Zuckerman, M. B. (2011, June 20). Why the job situation is worse than it looks. *U.S. News and World Report*. http://www.usnews.com/opinion/mzuckerman/articles/2011/06/20/why-the-jobs-situation-is-worse-than-it-looks

Chapter 12

Aguilera, J. (2020, June 9). Confederate statues are being removed amid protests over George Floyd's death. Here's what to know. *Time*. https://time.com/5849184/confederate-statues-removed/

Aristotle. (1991). *On rhetoric: A theory of civic discourse* (G. A. Kennedy, Trans.). Oxford University Press.

Arrigo, A. F. (2018, December 24). What Aristotle can teach us about Trump's persuasive rhetoric. *Newsweek*. https://www.newsweek.com/donald-trump-aristotle-donald-trump-rhetoric-us-president-barack-obama-1270496

Australian Bureau of Statistics. (2020). Population clock. https://www.abs.gov.au/ausstats/abs%40.nsf/94713ad445ff1425ca25682000192af2/1647509ef7e25faaca2568a900154b63?OpenDocument

Behnke, R., & Sawyer, C. (1999). Milestones of anticipatory public speaking anxiety. *Communication Education, 48*, 165–173.

Behnke, R., & Sawyer, C. (2004). Public speaking anxiety as a function of sensitization and habituation processes. *Communication Education, 53*, 164–173.

Bitzer, L. (1968). The rhetorical situation. *Philosophy and Rhetoric, 1*, 1–14.

Blake, A. (2020, September 1). Trump's illuminating defense of Kyle Rittenhouse. *The Washington Post*. https://www.washingtonpost.com/politics/2020/08/31/trumps-illuminating-defense-kyle-rittenhouse/

Change.org (2019). *Impact report 2019.* https://static.change.org/brand-pages/impact/reports/2020/2020_Impact+Report_Change_EN_final.pdf

Conger, K. (2020, July 21). Twitter takedown targets QAnon accounts. *The New York Times*. https://www.nytimes.com/2020/07/21/technology/twitter-bans-qanon-accounts.html

Conley, T. (1994). *Rhetoric in the European tradition.* University of Chicago Press.

Darsey, J. (1991). From "gay is good" to the scourge of AIDS: The evolution of gay liberation rhetoric, 1977–1990. *Communication Studies, 42*, 43–66.

Darsey, J. (1994). Must we all be rhetorical theorists? An anti-democratic inquiry. *Western Journal of Communication, 58,* 164–181.

Dehghan, S. K. (2011, July 31). Iranian woman blinded by acid attack pardons assailant as he faces same fate. *Guardian.* http://www.guardian.co.uk/world/2011/jul/31/iran-acid-woman-pardons-attacker

Delgado, F. (1995). Chicano movement rhetoric: An ideographic interpretation. *Communication Quarterly, 43,* 446–455.

DeLuca, K. M. (1999). *Image politics: The new rhetoric of environmental activism.* Guilford.

Douglass, F. (1852, July 5). *The meaning of July Fourth for the Negro.* http://www.pbs.org/wgbh/aia/part4/4h2927t.html

Effron, O. (2020, July 31). David Duke has been banned from Twitter. *CNN Business.* https://www.cnn.com/2020/07/31/tech/david-duke-twitter-ban/index.html

Ehninger, D. (1967). On rhetoric and rhetorics. *Western Speech, 31,* 242–249.

Erdbrink, T. (2008, December 14). Woman blinded by spurned man invokes Islamic retribution. *Washington Post,* p. A1.

Gayle, B. M. (2004). Transformations in a civil discourse public speaking class: Speakers' and listeners' attitude change. *Communication Education, 53,* 174–185.

Haskins, E. (2006). Choosing between Isocrates and Aristotle: Disciplinary assumptions and pedagogical implications. *Rhetoric Society Quarterly, 36*(2), 191–201. http://www.jstor.org/stable/3886176

Haskins, E. (2013). On the term "Dunamis" in Aristotle's definition of rhetoric. *Philosophy & Rhetoric, 46*(2), 234–240. http://www.jstor.org/stable/10.5325/philrhet.46.2.0234

Infante, D. A., Rancer, A. S., & Womack, D. F. (1990). *Building communication theory.* Waveland.

Jackson, S. J., Bailey, M., & Welles, B. F. (2020). *#HashtagActivism: Networks of race and gender justice.* MIT Press.

Johannesen, R. L. (1997). Diversity, freedom, and responsibility in tension. In J. M. Makau & R. C. Arnett (Eds.), *Communication ethics in an age of diversity* (pp. 157–186). University of Illinois Press.

Kennedy, G. A. (1998). *Comparative rhetoric: An historical and cross-cultural introduction.* Oxford University Press.

King, J. L. (2002). Cultural differences in the perceptions of sports mascots: A rhetorical study of Tim Giago's newspaper columns. In J. N. Martin, T. K. Nakayama, & L. A. Flores (Eds.), *Readings in intercultural communication: Experiences and contexts* (pp. 205–212). McGraw-Hill.

Levasseur, D. G., Dean, K. W., & Pfaff, J. (2004). Speech pedagogy beyond the basics: A study of instructional methods in the advanced public speaking course. *Communication Education, 53,* 234–252.

Lucaites, J. L., Condit, C. M., & Caudill, S. (1999). *Contemporary rhetorical theory: A reader.* Guilford.

Maffesoli, M. (1996). *The time of the tribes: The decline of individualism in mass society.* Sage.

Makau, J. M. (1997). Embracing diversity in the classroom. In J. M. Makau & R. C. Arnett (Eds.), *Communication ethics in an age of diversity* (pp. 48–67). University of Illinois Press.

McKerrow, R. E., Gronbeck, B. E., Ehninger, D., & Monroe, A. H. (2003). *Principles of public speaking* (15th ed.). Allyn & Bacon.

Nakamura, L., & Chow-White, P. A. (Eds.). (2012). *Race after the internet.* Routledge.

Noe-Bustamante, L., Mora, L., & Lopez, M. H. (2020, August 11). About one-in-four U.S. Hispanics have heard of Latinx, but just 3% use it. *Pew Research Center.* https://www.pewresearch.org/hispanic/2020/08/11/about-one-in-four-u-s-hispanics-have-heard-of-latinx-but-just-3-use-it/

O'Hair, D., Stewart, R., & Rubenstein, H. (2004). *A speaker's guidebook* (2nd ed.). Bedford/St. Martin's.

Osterman, R. (2005, May 23). "Soft skills" top list of what area employers desire. *Sacramento Bee,* p. D1.

Ray, R. (2020, June 19). What does "defund the police" mean and does it have merit? *Brookings.* https://www.brookings.edu/blog/fixgov/2020/06/19/what-does-defund-the-police-mean-and-does-it-have-merit/

Sanow, A. (2005, March 3). *How I overcame the fear of public speaking.* http://www.expertclick.com/NewsReleaseWire/default.cfm?Action=ReleaseDetail&ID=8372&NRWid=1698

Sprague, J., & Stuart, D. (2005). *The speaker's handbook.* Wadsworth/Thomson.

Tavernise, S., & Oppel, R. A., Jr. (2020, March 23). Spit on, yelled at, attacked: Chinese-Americans fear for their safety. *The Washington Post.* https://www.nytimes.com/2020/03/23/us/chinese-coronavirus-racist-attacks.html

Thomas, D., & Horowitz, J. M. (2020, September 16). Support for Black Lives Matter has decreased since June but remains strong among Black Americans. *Pew Research Center.* https://www.pewresearch.org/fact-tank/2020/09/16/support-for-black-lives-matter-has-decreased-since-june-but-remains-strong-among-black-americans/

Thomas, S. (n.d.). *From slave to abolitionist/editor.* http://www.history.rochester.edu/class/douglass/part2.html

Tostevin, R. (2014, March 14). Online activism: It's easy to click, but just as easy to disengage. *The Guardian.* http://www.theguardian.com/media-network/media-network-blog/2014/mar/14/online-activism-social-media-engage

Tufte, E. (2003, September). PowerPoint is evil. *Wired Magazine,* 118–119. Reprinted by permission from Edward R. Tufte, *The Cognitive Style of PowerPoint.* Graphics Press.

VanHoose, B. (2020, August 13). Va. mayor apologizes for calling Kamala Harris racist nickname: "Wrong, offensive & unbecoming." *People.* https://people.com/politics/virginia-mayor-apologizes-after-calling-kamala-harris-aunt-jemima/

Wallace, G. (2016, November 30). Voter turnout at 20-year low in 2016. *CNN.* http://edition.cnn.com/2016/11/11/politics/popular-vote-turnout-2016/

Weaver, R. (1985). *The ethics of rhetoric.* Routledge.

Westring, L. (2019, February 18). Comment: How pathos helps leaders like Trump reign supreme. *The Scotsman.* https://www.scotsman.com/news/opinion/columnists/comment-how-pathos-helps-leaders-trump-reign-supreme-113461

Chapter 13

Akhavan-Majid, R. (2004). Mass media reform in China: Toward a new analytical perspective. *Gazette: The International Journal for Communication Studies, 66,* 553–565.

Anderson, C. A., & Bushman, B. J. (2002, March 29). The effects of media violence on society. *Science, 295,* 2377–2378. http://www.psychology.iastate.edu/faculty/caa/abstracts/2000-2004/02AB2.pdf

Anderson, M. (2016, November 21). TV still the top source for election results, but digital platforms rise. *Pew Research Center.* http://www.pewresearch.org/fact-tank/2016/11/21/tv-still-the-top-source-for-election-results-but-digital-platforms-rise/

Aoyagi, C. (2004, July 2–15). TV networks' current fascination with Hawaii often doesn't translate into more roles for APAs. *Pacific Citizen, 139,* 1.

Barr, J. (2019, July 31). Why Americans are watching fewer TV channels. *Forbes.* https://www.forbes.com/sites/jonathanberr/2019/07/31/why-americans-are-watching-fewer-tv-channels/#1b087e771330

Barthel, M., Mitchell, A., & Holcomb, J. (2016, December 15). *Many Americans believe fake news is sowing confusion.* http://www.journalism.org/2016/12/15/many-americans-believe-fake-news-is-sowing-confusion/

Belkin, L. (2010, December 14). Wanted: More girls on screen. *New York Times.* http://parenting.blogs.nytimes.com/2010/12/14/wanted-more-girls-on-screen/

Benton, J. (2019, May 1). Want to see what one digital future for newspapers looks like? Look at The Guardian, which isn't losing money anymore. *Nieman Lab.* https://www.niemanlab.org/2019/05/want-to-see-what-one-digital-future-for-newspapers-looks-like-look-at-the-guardian-which-isnt-losing-money-anymore

Berelson, B. (1952/1971). *Content analysis in communication research.* Hafner Publishing Co.

Billings, A. C., & Eastman, S. T. (2003). Framing identities: Gender, ethnic, and national parity in network announcing of the 2002 Olympics. *Journal of Communication, 53,* 569–586.

Boorstin, D. J. (1965). *The Americans: The national experience.* Random House.

Brookey, R. A., & Zhang, N. (2021). The not-so *Fantastic Four* franchise: A critical history of the comic, the films, and the Disney/

Fox merger. In A. Rauscher, D. Stein, & J. N. Thon (Eds.), *Comics and video games: From hybrid medialities to transmedia expansions* (pp. 149–163). Routledge.

Bryant, J., & Miron, D. (2004). Theory and research in mass communication. *Journal of Communication, 54*, 662–704.

Bushman, B. J., & Gibson, B. (2011). Violent video games cause an increase in aggression long after the game has been turned off. *Social Psychological and Personality Science, 2*, 29–32.

Cablevision. (2002, November 4). *NBC to acquire Bravo from Cablevision Systems Corporation.* http://www.cablevision.com/index.jhtml?id=2002_11_04

Celis, B. (2017, March 12). The time's right for a new wave of Black media activism. *Newsweek.* http://www.newsweek.com/time-right-new-wave-black-media-activism-565377

Chalaby, J. K. (2003). Television for a new global order: Transnational television networks and the formation of global systems. *Gazette: The International Journal for Communication Studies, 65*, 457–472.

Chapman, J. (2005). *Comparative media history.* Polity Press.

Cho, H., & Boster, F. J. (2008). Effect of gain versus loss frame antidrug ads on adolescents. *Journal of Communication, 58*, 428–446.

Cohen, J. (2002). Television viewing preferences: Programs, schedules, and the structure of viewing choices made by Israeli adults. *Journal of Broadcasting & Electronic Media, 46*, 204–221.

Coming full circle: The end of mass media. (2011, July 7). *The Economist.* http://www.economist.com/node/18904158

Custers, K., Hall, E. D., Bushnell Smith, S., et al. (2017). The indirect association between television exposure and self-protective behavior as a result of worry about crime: The moderating role of gender. *Mass Communication and Society, 20*(5), 637–662.

Dayan, D., & Katz, E. (1992). *Media events: The live broadcasting of history.* Harvard University Press.

DeLuca, K. M., & Peeples, J. (2002). From public sphere to public screen: Democracy, activism, and the "violence" of Seattle. *Critical Studies in Media Communication, 19*, 125–151.

de Moraes, L. (2004, October 21). No more Miss America pageantry for ABC. *Washington Post,* p. C7. http://www.washingtonpost.com/wp-dyn/articles/A50114-2004Oct20.html

Denhart, A. (2020, September 18). Big Brother now bans racial slurs. But what about BB22's implicit racism or autism-mocking? *Reality Blurred.* https://www.realityblurred.com/realitytv/2020/09/big-brother-cbs-racial-slur-ban-bb22-racism-autism-mocking

Durham, M. G. (2004). Constructing the "new ethnicities": Media, sexuality, and diaspora identity in the lives of South Asian immigrant girls. *Critical Studies in Media Communication, 21*, 140–161.

Dwyer, D., & Jones, L. (2010, May 20). Rape kit testing backlog thwarts justice for victims. *ABC News.* http://abcnews.go.com/Politics/sexual-assault-victims-congress-solve-rape-kit-backlog/story?id=10701295

Eckstein, J. (2020) Sensing school shootings. *Critical Studies in Media Communication 37*(2), 161–173.

Fahmy, S. (2004). Picturing Afghan women: A content analysis of AP wire photographs during the Taliban regime and after the fall of the Taliban regime. *Gazette: The International Journal for Communication Studies, 66*, 91–112.

Federal Communications Commission. (2003, July 8). *V-chip: Viewing television responsibly.* http://www.fcc.gov/vchip/

Feinberg, S. (2014, March 2). Brutally honest Oscar voter ballot no. 7. *The Hollywood Reporter.* http://www.hollywoodreporter.com/race/brutally-honest-oscar-voter-ballot-684839

Fleuriet, K. J., & Castellano, M. (2020). Media, place-making, and concept-metaphors: The U.S.-Mexico border during the rise of Donald Trump. *Media, Culture & Society, 42*(6), 880–897.

Gerbner, G. (2002). *Against the mainstream: The selected works of George Gerbner.* M. Morgan (Ed.). Peter Lang.

Germain, T. (2020, August 24). Best music streaming services. *Consumer Reports.* https://www.consumerreports.org/streaming-music-services/best-music-streaming-service-for-you

Goffman, E. (1986). *Frame analysis: An essay on the organization of experience.* Northeastern University Press. Originally printed 1974.

Gollust, S. E., Fowler, E. F., & Niederdeppe, J. (2019). Television news coverage of public health issues and implications for public health policy and practice. *Annual Review of Public Health, 40*, 167–185.

Greenslade, R. (2016, May 31). Mass media is over, but where does journalism go from here? *The Guardian.* https://www.theguardian.com/media/greenslade/2016/may/31/mass-media-is-over-but-where-does-journalism-go-from-here

Gunther, A. C., & Schmitt, K. (2004). Mapping boundaries of the hostile media effect. *Journal of Communication, 54*, 55–70.

Hale, M. (2017, March 13). On Netflix, the borders remain open. *New York Times.* https://www.nytimes.com/2017/03/13/arts/television/netflix-fauda-nobel-review.html?_r=0

Has Obama seen ISIS execution videos? (2014, September 5). http://abcnews.go.com/Politics/video/obama-isis-execution-videos-25258267?utm_source=twitterfeed&utm_medium=twitter

Hightower, K., & Sedensky, M. (2011, July 10). Anger over Casey Anthony verdict pours out online. *USA Today.* http://www.usatoday.com/news/topstories/2011-07-09-2575323558_x.htm

Holling, M. A. (2019). Rhetorical contours of violent frames and the production of discursive violence. *Critical Studies in Media Communication, 36*(3), 249–271.

Iqbal, M. (2020, June 23). Netflix revenue and usage statistics (2020). *Business of Apps.* https://www.businessofapps.com/data/netflix-statistics/#:~:text=Average%20daily%20time%20spent%20with%20Netflix%20in%20US&text=Nielson%20audience%20stats%20published%20in,6%25%20of%20total%20television%20time

Jhally, S., & Lewis, J. (1992). *Enlightened racism: The Cosby show, audiences, and the myth of the American dream.* Westview Press.

Karsay, K., & Matthes, J. (2020). Sexually objectifying pop music videos, young women's self-objectification, and selective exposure: A moderated mediation model. *Communication Research, 47*(3), 428–450.

Ke, K. (2020). Rehabilitating hegemonic masculinity with the bodies of aging action heroes. In G. Sar, (Ed.), *Gender and diversity representation in mass media* (pp. 178–196). IGI Global.

Kilgo, D., & Mourão, R. R. (2019). Media effects and marginalized ideas: Relationships among media consumption and support for Black Lives Matter. *International Journal of Communication, 13*, 4287–4305.

Laughland, O., Luscombe, R., & Yubas, A. (2018, February 15). Florida school shooting: At least 17 people dead on "horrific, horrific day." *The Guardian.* https://www.theguardian.com/us-news/2018/feb/14/florida-shooting-school-latest-news-stoneman-douglas

Lazarsfeld, P. F., Berelson, B., & Gaudet, H. (1948). *The people's choice: How the voter makes up his mind in a presidential campaign.* Columbia University Press.

Lowry, D. T., Nio, T. C. J., & Leitner, D. W. (2003). Setting the public fear agenda: A longitudinal analysis of network TV crime reporting, public perceptions of crime and FBI crime statistics. *Journal of Communication, 53*, 61–73.

Mandese, J. (2020, February 13). Number of TV channels received by U.S. households falls dramatically. *Mediapost.* https://www.mediapost.com/publications/article/347034/number-of-tv-channels-received-by-us-households.html

McChesney, R. (1998). Making media democratic. *Boston Review, 23*, 4–10, 20. http://www.bostonreview.net/BR23.3/mcchesney.html

McQuail, D., Blumler, J. G., & Brown, J. R. (1972). The television audience: a revised perspective. In McQuail, D. (ed.), *Sociology of Mass Communication* (pp. 135–165). Penguin.

McQuail, D. (1987). *Mass communication theory: An introduction* (2nd ed.). Sage Publications.

Meyers, M. (2004). African American women and violence: Gender, race, and class in the news. *Critical Studies in Media Communication, 21*, 95–118.

Mitchell, A. (2014, March 26). State of the news media 2014. *Pew Research Journalism Project.* http://www.journalism.org/2014/03/26/state-of-the-news-media-2014-overview/

Morgan, M., & Signorielli, N. (1990). Cultivation analysis: Conceptualization and methodology. In N. Signorielli & M. Morgan (Eds.), *Cultivation analysis: New directions in media effects research* (pp. 13–34). Sage Publications.

Nathanson, A. (2004). Factual and evaluative approaches to modifying children's responses to violent television. *Journal of Communication, 54*, 321–336.

Niederdeppe, J., Fowler, E. F., Goldstein, K., & Pribble, J. (2010). Does local television news coverage cultivate fatalistic beliefs about cancer prevention? *Journal of Communication, 60*, 230–253.

Nielsen. (2014, May 12). *Advertising and audiences: State of the media.* http://www.nielsen.com/us/en/reports/2014/advertising-and-audiences-state-of-the-media.html

Nielsen. (2017a, March 2). *Millennials on millennials: A look at viewing behavior, distraction and social media stars.* http://www.nielsen.com/us/en/insights/news/2017/millennials-on-millennials-a-look-at-viewing-behavior-distraction-social-media-stars.html

Nielsen. (2017b). *The Nielsen comparable metrics report, Q3 2016.* http://www.nielsen.com/content/dam/corporate/us/en/reports-downloads/2017-reports/q3-2016-comparable-metrics-report.pdf

Nolan, E. (2020, September 18). "Big Brother's" Memphis Garrett cleared of using racial slur, many fans unconvinced. *Newsweek.* https://www.newsweek.com/big-brother-memphis-garrett-cleared-racial-slur-david-alexander-cbs-1532820

Ogbodo, J. N., Onwe, E. C., Chukwu, J., Nwasum, C. J., Nwakpu, E. S., Nwankwo, S. U., Nwamini, S., Elem, S., & Ogbaeja, N. I. (2020). Communicating health crisis: A content analysis of global media framing of COVID-19. *Health Promotion Perspectives, 10*(3), 257–269.

Okoro, E. (2013, November 27). Why I wouldn't see *12 Years a Slave* with a white person. *The Atlantic.* http://www.theatlantic.com/entertainment/archive/2013/11/why-i-wouldnt-see-em-12-years-a-slave-emwith-a-white-person/281883/

Ovide, S. (2020, July 2). New "TV" is a lot like TV. *New York Times.* https://www.nytimes.com/2020/07/02/technology/internet-tv.html

Pallotta, F. (2017, February 2). New York Times touts subscriber growth with a jab at Trump. *CNN Money.* http://money.cnn.com/2017/02/02/media/new-york-times-subscribers-trump/

Peter, J. (2003). Country characteristics as contingent conditions of agenda setting: The moderating influence of polarized elite opinion. *Communication Research, 30,* 683–712.

Romer, D., Jamieson, K. H., & Aday, S. (2003). Television news and the cultivation of fear of crime. *Journal of Communication, 53,* 88–104.

Rubin, S. (2010, October 6). Rape kit backlog hits primetime on "SVU." *Ms. Magazine.* http://msmagazine.com/blog/blog/2010/10/06/rape-kit-backlog-hits-primetime-on-svu/

Schneider, M., & Aurthur, K. (2020, July 21). R.I.P. cable TV: Why Hollywood is slowly killing its biggest moneymaker. *Variety.* https://variety.com/2020/tv/news/cable-tv-decline-streaming-cord-cutting-1234710007

Scott, D. C. (2013, November 9). Mariska Hargitay: A Hollywood star for an actress—and activist. *The Christian Science Monitor.* http://www.csmonitor.com/The-Culture/2013/1109/Mariska-Hargitay-A-Hollywood-star-for-an-actress-and-activist-video

Sharkey, B. (2014, February 27). Oscars 2014: For many, "12 Years a Slave" is too hard to watch. *Los Angeles Times.* http://articles.latimes.com/2014/feb/27/entertainment/la-et-mn-12-years-a-slave-notebook-20140227/2

Shugart, H. (2008). Managing masculinities: The metrosexual moment. *Communication and Critical/Cultural Studies, 5,* 280–300.

Slater, M. D., Henry, K. L., Swaim, R. C., & Anderson, L. L. (2003). Violent media content and aggressiveness in adolescents: A downward spiral model. *Communication Research, 30,* 713–736.

Sproule, J. M. (1989). Progressive propaganda critics and the magic bullet myth. *Critical Studies in Mass Communication, 6,* 225–246.

Stassen, M. (2020, September 10). Music streaming revenues on course to grow by over $1bn in the U.S. in 2020, despite everything. *Music Business Worldwide.* https://www.musicbusinessworldwide.com/music-streaming-revenues-in-the-us-are-on-course-to-grow-by-over-a-billion-dollars-in-2020

Stelter, B. (2017, March 16). PBS and NPR are ready to fight budget cuts—again. *CNN Money.* http://money.cnn.com/2017/03/16/media/public-media-pbs-npr-budget-cuts/

Trujillo, N. (1991). Hegemonic masculinity on the mound: Media representations of Nolan Ryan and American sports culture. *Critical Studies in Mass Communication, 8,* 290–308.

TV Parental Guidelines Monitoring Board. (n.d.). *Understanding the TV ratings.* http://www.tvguidelines.org/ratings.htm

Ward, B. (2015, September 25). "I can't ever unsee that": Which unforgettable moments should a journalist choose to cover? *Poynter.* https://www.poynter.org/2015/i-cant-ever-unsee-that-which-unforgettable-moments-should-a-journalist-choose-to-cover/374171/

Watson, A. (2020 August 27). Estimated number of e-books sold in the United States from 2010 to 2019. *Statista.* https://www.statista.com/statistics/426799/e-book-unit-sales-usa

Weeks, B. E., Kim, D. H., Hahn, L. B., Diehl, T. H., & Kwok, N. (2019). Hostile media perceptions in the age of social media: Following politicians, emotions, and perceptions of media bias. *Journal of Broadcasting and Electronic Media, 63*(3), 374–392.

Yahr, E. (2016, October 19). NBC's 'This Is Us' is officially the surprise breakout hit of the fall TV season. *Washington Post.* https://www.washingtonpost.com/news/arts-and-entertainment/wp/2016/10/19/nbcs-this-is-us-is-officially-the-surprise-breakout-hit-of-the-fall-tv-season/?utm_term=.f7a8f9d09aa0

Chapter 14

Abel, S., Machin, T., & Brownlow, C. (2020). Social media, rituals, and long-distance family relationship maintenance: A mixed-methods systematic review. *New Media & Society.* Advance online publication.

Anderson, J. & Rainie, L.(2014, March 11) Digital divide in 2025. *pewresearch.org.* https://www.pewresearch.org/internet/2014/03/11/digital-life-in-2025/

Anderson, M. (2019, June 20). Mobile technology and home broadband 2019. *pewresearch.org.* https://www.pewresearch.org/internet/2019/06/13/mobile-technology-and-home-broadband-2019

Anderson, M., & Kumar, M. (2019, June 5). Digital divide persists even as lower-income Americans make gains in tech adoption. *pewresearch.org.* https://www.pewresearch.org/fact-tank/2019/05/07/digital-divide-persists-even-as-lower-income-americans-make-gains-in-tech-adoption

Anderson, M., Barthel, M., Perrin, A., & Vogels, E. A. (2020a, June 10). #BlackLivesMatter surges on Twitter after George Floyds death. *pewresearch.org.* https://www.pewresearch.org/fact-tank/2020/06/10/blacklivesmatter-surges-on-twitter-after-george-floyds-death/

Anderson, M., Vogels, E. A., & Turner, E. (2020b, February 6). The virtues and downsides of online dating. *pewresearch.org.* https://www.pewresearch.org/internet/2020/02/06/the-virtues-and-downsides-of-online-dating

Auxier, B., Anderson, M., & Kumar, M. (2019, December 20). 10 tech related trends that shaped the decade. *pewresearch.org.* https://www.pewresearch.org/fact-tank/2019/12/20/10-tech-related-trends-that-shaped-the-decade

Bourdieu, P. (1986). The forms of capital. In J. G. Richardson (Ed.), *Handbook of theory and research for the sociology of education* (pp. 241–258). Greenwood.

boyd, d. (2014). *It's complicated: The social lives of networked teens.* Yale University Press.

Braun, S., Bark, A. H., Kirchner, A., Stegmann, S., & van Dick, R. (2019). Emails from the boss—curse or blessing? Relations between communication channels, leader evaluation, and employees' attitudes. *International Journal of Business Communication, 56*(1), 50–81.

Brown, K. A., Billings, A. C., Murphy, B., & Puesan, L. (2018). Intersections of fandom in the age of interactive media: eSports fandom as a predictor of traditional sport fandom. *Communication & Sport, 6*(4), 418–435.

Bryson, D. (2013, July 23). What is web civility. *Endurance International Group.* http://enduranceinternational.com/our-mission/web-civility/what-is-web-civility

Busch, P. A., & McCarthy, S. (2020). Antecedents and consequences of problematic smartphone use: A systematic literature review of an emerging research area. *Computers in Human Behavior* (Journal Pre-Proof). doi: https://doi.org/10.1016/j.chb.2020.106414

Camero, K. (2020, July 8). What is "cancel culture"? J.K. Rowling controversy leaves writers, scholars debating. *miamiherald.com.* https://www.miamiherald.com/news/nation-world/national/article244082037.html

Carlson, A., & Isaacs, A. M. (2018). Technological capital: An alternative to the digital divide. *Journal of Applied Communication Research, 46*(2), 243–265.

Cavalcante, A. (2016). "I did it all online": Transgender identity and the management of everyday life. *Critical Studies in Media Communication, 33*(1), 109–122.

Choi, C. (2014). 5 Best practices for lawfully monitoring your employees' social media activities. *Philadelphia Business Journal*. http://www.bizjournals.com/philadelphia/blog/guest-comment/2014/10/5-best-practices-for-lawfully-monitoring-your.html

Cisneros, J. D., & Nakayama, T. K. (2015). New media, old racisms: Twitter, Miss America, and cultural logics of race. *Journal of International & Intercultural Communication, 8*(2), 108–127.

Cooper, S. (2020, July 30). What is doxing? *comparitech.com*. https://www.comparitech.com/blog/vpn-privacy/what-is-doxxing-how-to-avoid/#:~:text=A%20number%20of%20celebrities%20have,to%20SWATTING%20and%20flawed%20doxxing

Coyne, S. M., Stockdale, L., Busby, D., Iverson, B., & Grant, D. M. (2011). "I luv u :)!": A descriptive study of the media use of individuals in romantic relationships. *Family Relations, 60*, 150–162.

Daft, R. L., & Lengel, R. H. (1984). Information richness: A new approach to managerial behavior and organization design. *Research in Organizational Behavior, 6*, 191–233.

Daft, R. L., & Lengel, R. H. (1986). A proposed integration among organizational information requirements, media richness, and structural design. *Management Science, 32*(5), 544–571.

D'Costa, K. (2014, April 25). Catfishing: The truth about deception online. *Scientific American*. http://blogs.scientificamerican.com/anthropology-in-practice/2014/04/25/catfishing-the-truth-about-deception

Dennis, A. R., & Valacich, J. S. (1999, January). Rethinking media richness: Towards a theory of media synchronicity. *Proceedings of the 32nd Annual Hawaii International Conference on Systems Sciences. 1999. HICSS-32. Abstracts and CD-ROM of Full Papers* (pp. 1-10). IEEE.

Dhoest, A., & Szulc, L. (2016, October–November). Navigating online selves: Social, cultural and material contexts of social media use by diasporic gay men. *Social Media + Society*, 1–10.

Doyle, A. (2020, July 21), You can get fired for what you post online. *thebalancecareers.com*. https://www.thebalancecareers.com/posting-information-online-can-get-you-fired-2062154

Dutta, U. (2021). Communication design for social change: Co-creating information solutions in indigenous Global South. In S. Melkote & A. Singhal (Eds.), *Handbook of communication and development*. Elgar Original Reference.

Faelens, L., Hoorelbeke, K., Soenens, B., Van Gaeveren, K., De Marez, L., De Raedt, R., & Koster, E. H. W. (2021). Social media use and well-being: A prospective experience-sampling study. *Computers in Human Behavior, 14*, 1–10.

Ferman, R. (2014, April 1). Cyber-bullying: Taking on the tormentors. *The Huffington Post*. http://www.huffingtonpost.com/risa-ferman/cyberbullying-taking-on-t_b_5064537.html

Ferris, L., & Duguay, S. (2020). Tinder's lesbian digital imaginary: Investigating (im)permeable boundaries of sexual identity on a popular dating app. *New Media & Society, 22*(3), 489–506.

Firth, J., Torous, J., Stubbs, B., Firth, J. A., Steiner, G. Z., Smith, L., Alvarez-Jimenez, M., Gleeson, J., Vancampfort, D., Armitage, C. J., & Sarris, J. (2019). The "online brain": How the Internet may be changing our cognition. *World Psychiatry, 18*(2), 119–129.

Fisher, R. (2020). The subtle ways that clicktivism shapes the world. *bbc.com*. https://www.bbc.com/future/article/20200915-the-subtle-ways-that-clicktivism-shapes-the-world

Florini, S. (2014). Tweets, tweeps, and signifyin': Communication and cultural performance on "Black Twitter." *Television & New Media, 15*(3), 223–237.

Glowacki, E. M., & Taylor, M. A. (2020). Health hyperbolism: A study in health crisis rhetoric. *Qualitative Health Research, 30*(12), 1953–1964.

Grau, M. (2019, June 13). Prominent journalists and social media influencers join Poynter-led digital media project, MediaWise. *poynter.org*. https://www.poynter.org/news-release/2019/prominent-journalists-and-social-media-influencers-join-poynter-led-digital-literacy-project-mediawise

Gui, M., & Büchi, M. (2019). From use to overuse: Digital inequality in the age of communication abundance. *Social Science Computer Review*, 1–10.

Hayes, L. N. (2018, August 9). More than half employers have found content on social media . . . . *careerbuilder.com*. http://press.careerbuilder.com/2018-08-09-More-Than-Half-of-Employers-Have-Found-Content-on-Social-Media-That-Caused-Them-NOT-to-Hire-a-Candidate-According-to-Recent-CareerBuilder-Survey

Heino, R. D., Ellison, N. B., & Gibbs, J. L. (2010). Relationshopping: Investigating the market metaphor in online dating. *Journal of Social and Personal Relationships, 27*, 427–447.

Hindman, K. L. (2016, May). 15 parents who embarrassed their kids on social media. http://www.thethings.com/15-parents-who-embarrassed-their-kids-on-social-media/

Holpuch, A. (2015, December 15). Facebook adjusts controversial "real name" policy in wake of criticism. *The Guardian*. https://www.theguardian.com/us-news/2015/dec/15/facebook-change-controversial-real-name-policy

Holt, T. J., Navarro, J. N., & Clevenger, S. (2019). Exploring the moderating role of gender in juvenile hacking behaviors, *Crime & Delinquency, 66*(11), 1533–1555.

Horrigan, J. B. (2016, September 20). *Digital readiness gaps*. http://www.pewinternet.org/2016/09/20/digital-readiness-gaps/

Howard, L., & Steber, C. (2020, July 16). Experts explain why breaking up over text is so common. *bustle.com*. https://www.bustle.com/life/is-it-ok-to-break-up-with-someone-over-text-why-its-so-common-according-to-relationship-experts-7823100

Humphreys, S., & Vered, K. O. (2014). Reflecting on gender and digital networked media. *Television & New Media, 15*(1), 3–13.

Ishii, K., Lyons, M. M., & Carr, S. A. (2019). Revisiting media richness theory for today and future. *Human Behavior and Emerging Technologies, 1*(2), 124–131.

InternetWorldStats.com. (2020, March 31). *Internet world stats: Usage and population statistics*. http://internetworldstats.com

James, C. (2016). *Disconnected: Youth, new media and the ethics gap*. MIT Press.

Jatania, L. (2019, September 3). What do you mean its not legal? *mediasmarts.ca*. https://mediasmarts.ca/blog/what-do-you-meme-it%E2%80%99s-not-legal

Kaplan, A. M., & Haenlein, M. (2010). Users of the world, unite! The challenges and opportunities of social media. *Business Horizons, 53*, 59–68.

Kircaburun, K., Alhabash, S., Tosuntaş, Ş. B., & Griffiths, M. D. (2020). Uses and gratifications of problematic social media use among university students: A simultaneous examination of the Big Five of personality traits, social media platforms, and social media use motives. *International Journal of Mental Health and Addiction, 18*(3), 525–547.

Kochhar, R., & Passel, J. S. (2020, May 6). Telework may save U.S. jobs in COVID-19 downturn especially among college graduates. *pewresearch.org*. https://www.pewresearch.org/fact-tank/2020/05/06/telework-may-save-u-s-jobs-in-covid-19-downturn-especially-among-college-graduates

Krouse, S. (2019, July 19). The new ways your boss is spying on you. *wsj. com*. https://www.wsj.com/articles/the-new-ways-your-boss-is-spying-on-you-11563528604

Kumar, S. (2015, May 22). Why monitoring employees' social media is a bad idea. *time.com*. https://time.com/3894276/social-media-monitoring-work/

Lange, J. (2018). Let us lurk. *theweek.com*. https://theweek.com/articles/804466/let-lurk

Lee, B. Y. (2020, August 23). 12 pandemic dating tips, how to do romance with the Covid-19 Coronavirus. *forbes.com*. https://www.forbes.com/sites/brucelee/2020/08/23/12-pandemic-dating-tipshow-to-do-romance-with-the-covid-19-coronavirus/#2f961f342b37

Lenhart, A., & Duggan, M. (2014, February 11). *Couples, the Internet and social media*. http://pewinternet.org/Reports/2014/Couples-and-the-internet.aspx

Levander, C., & Decherney, P. (2020, June 10). The COVID-igital divide. insidehighered.com. https://www.insidehighered.com/digital-learning/blogs/learning-time-corona/covid-igital-divide

Lopez-Fernando, O., Williams, A. J., & Kuss, D. (2019). Measuring female gaming: Gamer profile, predictors, prevalence, and characteristics. *Frontiers in Psychology, 10*, Article 898. https://www.frontiersin.org/articles/10.3389/fpsyg.2019.00898/full

Lusinski, N. (2020, July 30). Why do people overshare? *mic.com*. http://mic.com/p/why-do-people-overshare-the-psychology-behind-revealing-personal-details-17909502

MacAuley, M., & Moldes, M. D. (2016). Queen don't compute: Reading and casting shade on Facebook's real names policy. *Critical Studies in Media Communication, 33*(1), 6–22.

Maity, S. Q. A., & Ramesh, S. (2020, July 02). Best laptops under rs30000 in India. *Techradar.com*. https://www.techradar.com/news/best-laptops-under-rs-30000-in-india

Meyerson, C. (2020, March 3). Is this the end of oversharing? *wired.com*. https://www.wired.com/story/is-this-the-end-of-oversharing

Miller, B. (2018). Can you fire an employee over social media posts? *hrdailyadvisor.blr.com*. hrdailyadvisor.blr.com/2018/09/12/can-you-fire-an-employee-over-social-media-posts

Min, S., So, K. K. F., & Jeong, M. (2019). Consumer adoption of the Uber mobile application: Insights from diffusion of innovation theory and technology acceptance model. *Journal of Travel & Tourism Marketing, 36*(7), 770–783.

Mitchell, A., Jurkowitz, M., Oliphant, J. B., & Shearer, E. (2020, July 30). *pewresearch.org*. http://journalism.org/2020/07/30/in-addition-to-lower-awareness-of-current-events-social-media-news-users-hear-more-about-some-unproven-claims

Moffitt, R. L., Padgett, C., & Grieve, R. (2020). Accessibility and emotionality of online assessment feedback: Using emoticons to enhance student perceptions of marker competence and warmth. *Computers & Education, 143*, N.PAG. https://doi-org.ezproxy1.lib.asu.edu/10.1016/j.compedu.2019.103654

Morris, D. Z. (2017). New French law bars work email after hours. *Fortune*. http://fortune.com/2017/01/01/french-right-to-disconnect-law/

Nakayama, T. K. (2017). What's next for whiteness and the Internet. *Critical Studies in Media Communication, 34*(1), 68–72.

Navarro-Carrillo, G. Torres Marin, J., Carretero-Dios, H. (2021). Do trolls just want to have fun? Assessing the role of humor-related traits in online trolling behaviour. *Computers in Human Behavior, 114*.

Nguyen, S. (2020, September 15). The best crowdfunding sites of 2020. *thebalancesmb.com*. https://www.thebalancesmb.com/best-crowdfunding-sites-4580494

Notten, N., & Nikken, P. (2016). Boys and girls taking risks online: A gendered perspective on social context and adolescents' risky online behavior. *New Media & Society, 18*(6), 966–988.

Oeldorf-Hirsch, A., Hecht, B., & Morris, M. R. (2014). *To search or to ask: The routing of information needs between traditional search engines and social networks*. Proceedings of the CSCW 2014, Baltimore, MD.

Palomares, N. W., & Wingate, N. V. (2020). Victims' goal understanding, uncertainty reduction, and perceptions in cyberbullying: Theoretical evidence from three experiments. *Journal of Computer-Mediated Communication, 5*(4), 253–273.

Patchin, J. W. (2014, April 9). *Summary of our research (2004–2014)*. http://cyberbullying.us/summary-of-our-research/

Paul, F. (2015, September 1). The real reason everyone hates making phone calls today. *networkworld.com*. https://www.networkworld.com/article/2978859/the-real-reason-everyone-hates-making-phone-calls-today.html

Payne, E., & Smith, M. (2013). LGBTQ kids, school safety and missing the big picture: How the dominant bullying discourse prevents school professionals from thinking about systemic marginalization or . . . why we need to rethink LGBTQ bullying. *QED: A Journal in GLBTQ Worldmaking, Inaugural issue*, 1–36.

Peckham, E. (2020, June 21). Confronting racial bias in video games. *techcrunch.com*. https://techcrunch.com/2020/06/21/confronting-racial-bias-in-video-games

Perrin, A., & Anderson, M. (2020, April 10). Share of U.S. adults using social media including Facebook is mostly unchanged since 2018. *pewresearch.org*. https://www.pewresearch.org/fact-tank/2019/04/10/share-of-u-s-adults-using-social-media-including-facebook-is-mostly-unchanged-since-2018

Ramjug, P. (2020, September 30). Fake news vs factual news: Think twice about what's in your feed. *news.northeastern.edu*. https://news.northeastern.edu/2020/09/25/fake-news-vs-factual-news-think-twice-about-whats-in-your-feed

Robert, L. P., Dennis, A. R., & Ahuja, M. (2018). Differences are different: Examining the effects of communication media on the impacts of racial and gender diversity in decision-making teams, *Information Systems Research, 29*(3), 525–545.

Rogers, E. M. (2003). *Diffusion of innovations* (5th ed.). The Free Press.

Rothenberg, K. (2014). Prenups evolving to include new "social media clause." Fox News. http://www.foxnews.com/us/2014/06/22/prenups-evolving-to-include-new-social-media-clause.html

Salter, M. (2016). Privates in the online public: Sex(ting) and reputation on social media. *New Media & Society, 18*(11), 2723–2739.

Selyukh, A. (2016, November 20). Postelection, overwhelmed Facebook users unfriend, cut back. *NPR*. http://www.npr.org/sections/alltechconsidered/2016/11/20/502567858/post-election-overwhelmed-facebook-users-unfriend-cut-back

Schawbel, D. (2017, November 1). 10 Workplace trends you'll see in 2018. *forbes.com*. https://www.forbes.com/sites/danschawbel/2017/11/01/10-workplace-trends-youll-see-in-2018/#3f92f0de4bf2

Short, J., Williams, E., & Christie, B. (1976). *The social psychology of telecommunications*. Wiley.

Silver, L. (2019, February 5). Smartphone ownership is growing rapidly around the world, but not always equally. *pewresearch.org*. https://www.pewresearch.org/global/2019/02/05/smartphone-ownership-is-growing-rapidly-around-the-world-but-not-always-equally

Smith, A. (2018, June 8). Public attitudes toward media companies. *pewresearch.org*. https://www.pewresearch.org/internet/2018/06/28/public-attitudes-toward-technology-companies

Sonnemaker, T. (2020, March 12). The number of Americans without reliable internet access may be way higher than the government's estimate—and that could cause major problems in 2020. *businessinsider.com*. https://www.businessinsider.com/americans-lack-of-internet-access-likely-underestimated-by-government-2020-3

Stewart, M., & Schultze, U. (2019). Producing solidarity in social media activism: The case of my stealthy freedom. *Information and Organization, 29*(3), 100251–100275.

Stocking, G. (2019, November). Digital fact sheet. *pewresearch.org*. https://www.journalism.org/fact-sheet/digital-news/

Stokel-Walker, C. (2018, Sept 29). Why is it OK for online daters to block whole ethnic groups? *theguardian.com*. https://www.theguardian.com/technology/2018/sep/29/wltm-colour-blind-dating-app-racial-discrimination-grindr-tinder-algorithm-racism

Tanega, C., & Downs, A. (2020). Addictive technology: Prevalence and potential implications of problematic social media use. *Psi Chi Journal of Psychological Research, 25*(2), 151–161.

Turkle, S. (2012, February). *TED talk: Connected, but alone?* http://www.ted.com/talks/sherry_turkle_alone_together#t-755215

Turkle, S. (2015). *Reclaiming conversation: The power of talk in a digital age*. Penguin Books.

Utz, S., & Breuer, J. (2019). The relationship between networking, LinkedIn use, and retrieving informational benefits. *Cyberpsychology, Behavior and Social Networking, 22*(3), 180–185.

van der Nagel, E., & Frith, J. (2015). Anonymity, pseudonymity, and the agency of online identity. *FirstMonday, 20*(3). http://firstmonday.org/article/view/5615/4346

Vitores, A., & Gil-Juárez, A. (2016). The trouble with "women in computing": A critical examination of the deployment of research on the gender gap in computer science, *Journal of Gender Studies, 25*(6), 666–680.

Verduyn, P., Schulte-Strathaus, J., Kross, E., & Hülsheger U. (2021). When do smartphones displace face-to-face interactions and what to do about it? *Computers in Human Behavior, 114*. https://www.sciencedirect.com/science/article/pii/S0747563220303009

Vogels, E. A. (2019, September 9). Millennials stand out for their technology use, but older generations also embrace digital life. *pewresearch.org*. https://www.pewresearch.org/fact-tank/2019/09/09/us-generations-technology-use

Vogels, E. A. (2020a, April 30). From virtual parties to ordering food, how Americans are using the internet during COVID-19. *pewresearch.org*. https://www.pewresearch.org/fact-tank/2020/04/30/from-virtual-parties-to-ordering-food-how-americans-are-using-the-internet-during-covid-19

Vogels, E. A. (2020b, September 10). 59% of U.S. parents with low incomes say their child may face digital obstacles in schoolwork. *pewresearch.org*. https://www.pewresearch.org/fact-tank/2020/09/10/59-of-u-s-parents-with-lower-incomes-say-their-child-may-face-digital-obstacles-in-schoolwork/

Vogels, E. A., Perrin, A. Wallenstein, A., Rainie, L., & Anderson, M. (2020, April 30). 53% of Americans say the internet has been essential during the COVID 19 outbreak. *pewresearch.org*. https://www.pewresearch.org/internet/2020/04/30/53-of-americans-say-the-internet-has-been-essential-during-the-covid-19-outbreak

Walther, J. B., & Parks, M. R. (2002). Cues filtered out, cues filtered in: Computer-mediated communication and relationships. In M. L. Knapp & J. A. Daly (Eds.), *Handbook of interpersonal communication* (pp. 529–563). Sage.

Wei, L. (2012). Number matters: The multimodality of Internet use as an indicator of the digital inequalities. *Journal of Computer-Mediated Communication, 17*, 303–318.

Weinstein, E. C., & Selman, R. L. (2016). Digital stress: Adolescents' personal accounts. *New Media & Society, 18*(3), 391–409.

Who's not online today. (2020, May 19). *Interview with Kathryn deWit, manager, Broadband Research Initiative*. https://www.pewtrusts.org/en/research-and-analysis/articles/2020/05/29/whos-not-online-in-america-today

Woodhouse, A. (2015, December 8). Tink labs wants to bring its Handy smartphones to hotel rooms in Europe. *South China Morning Post*. https://www.scmp.com/tech/start-ups/article/1886783/tink-labs-wants-bring-its-handy-smartphones-hotel-rooms-europe

Wortham, J. (2016, September). Black tweets matter. *Smithsonian, 47*(5), 1–4.

Wu, Y. (2019). How age affects journalists' adoption of social media as an innovation: A multi-group SEM analysis. *Journalism Practice, 13*(5), 537–557.

Yamamoto, M., Nah, S., & Bae, S. Y. (2019). Social media prosumption and online political participation: An examination of online communication processes. *New Media & Society, 22*(10), 1885–1902.

Yanev, V. (2020, July 25). Who plays video games in 2020? *techjury.net*. https://techjury.net/blog/video-game-demographics/#gref

Zarrilla, M. (2020). Video games and gender. *Radford.edu*. https://www.radford.edu/~mzorrilla2/thesis/gamerepresentation.html

Zhang, R., & Fu, J. S. (2020). Privacy management and self-disclosure on social network sites: The moderating effects of stress and gender. *Journal of Computer-Mediated Communication, 25*(3), 236–251.

Zhu, Y., & Stephens, K. K. (2019). Online support group participation and social support: Incorporating identification and interpersonal bonds. *Small Group Research, 50*(5), 593–622.

Credits

Photo Credits

p. 337: IS184/Image Source/Alamy Stock Photo; **p. 339:** OLJ Studio/Shutterstock; **p. 340:** Al Goldis/AP Images.

Chapter 13 Page 343: Patti McConville/Alamy Stock Photo; **p. 345:** JHPhoto/Alamy Stock Photo; **p. 348:** Megapress/ Alamy Stock Photo; **p. 352:** Shao-Chun Wang/123RF Ltd; **p. 355:** Paul Bradbury/OJO Images Ltd/Alamy Stock Photo; **p. 356:** Samuel Borges Photography/Shutterstock; **p. 357:** Shutterstock; **p. 359:** Stacy Walsh Rosenstock/Alamy Stock Photo; **p. 361:** Digital Vision/Getty Images; **p. 364:** Eric Audras/ONOKY – Photononstop/Alamy Stock Photo; **p. 369:** Stewart Cook/FX/ Picturegroup/Shutterstock; **p. 371:** Darren Baker/Shutterstock.

Chapter 14 Page 374: Eric Audras/ONOKY – Photononstop/ Alamy Stock Photo; **p. 379:** ESB Professional/Shutterstock; **p. 382:** Dean Drobot/123RF; **p. 388:** Cathy Yeulet/123RF GB Ltd; **p. 390:** Kent Weakley/Shutterstock; **p. 391:** Vadym Pastukh/ Shutterstock; **p. 395:** stylephotographs/123RF GB Ltd; **p. 397:** Prasit Rodphan/Shutterstock; **p. 398(top):** Rawpixel.com/ Shutterstock; **p. 398(bottom):** BaanTaksinStudio/Shutterstock; **p. 402:** ESB Basic/Shutterstock; **p. 404:** Cathy Yeulet/123RF.

Text Credits

Chapter 1 Page 3: Nolen-Hoeksema S., Wisco B., & Lyubomirsky S. Rethinking rumination. (2008). Perspectives on Psychological Science, 3, 400–424.; Schwartz-Mette, R. A., & Smith, R. L. (2018). When does co-rumination facilitate depression contagion in adoles-cent friendships? Investigating intrapersonal and interpersonal factors. Journal of Clinical Child & Adolescent Psychology, 47(6), 912–924.; **p. 4:** Passer, M. W., & Smith, R. E. (2004). Psychology: The science of mind and behavior (2nd ed.). New York: McGraw-Hill.; **p. 12:** Warren, S. F., & Yoder, P. J. (1998). Facilitating the transition to intentional communication. In A. Wetherby, S. Warren, & J. Reichle (Eds.), Transitions in Prelinguistic Communication, (pp. 39–58). Baltimore: Brookes Publishing.; Watzlawick, P., Beavin, J., & Jackson, D. D. (1967). Pragmatics of human communication. New York: W. W. Norton.

Chapter 2 Page 26: Harwood, J. (2006). Communication as social identity. In G. J. Shepherd, J. St. John, & T. Striphas (Eds.), Communication as . . . : Perspectives on theory (pp. 84–90). Thousand Oaks, CA: Sage.; **p. 28:** Abrams, J., O'Connor, J., & Giles, H. (2002). Identity and intergroup communication. In W. B. Gudykunst & B. Mody (Eds.), Handbook of international and intercultural communication (2nd ed., pp. 225–240). Thousand Oaks, CA: Sage.; **p. 34:** Smith, T. L. (2020, June 29). Saying 'all lives matter' doesn't make you racist, just extremely ignorant. Cleve-land.com Retrieved July 13, 2020 from https:// www.cleveland.com/entertainment/2020/06/saying-all-lives-matter-doesnt-make-you-racist-just-extremely-ignorant.html.; Adams, T. E., & Berry, K. (2013). Size matters: Performing (il) logical male bodies on FatClub.com. Text and Performance Quarterly, 33 (4): 308–325.; **p. 35:** Macur, J. (2020, June 10). Former athletes file sex abuse lawsuits against U.S.A. Swimming. The New York Times. Retrieved July 13, 2020 from https://www .nytimes.com/2020/06/10/sports/olympics/swimming-abuse-coaches-lawsuit.html.; **p. 37:** Office for National Statistics. (2012, December 11). Ethnicity and national identity in England and Wales. Retrieved March 2, 2014, from http://www.ons.gov.uk/ ons/dcp171776_290558.pdf.; Hobeika, M. O. N. & Nakayama, T. K. (2020). Check-mate: The MENA/Arab double-bind. In H. Bhabra, F. Z. C. Alaoui, S. Abdi & B.M. Calafell (Eds.), Negotiating identity & transnationalism: Middle Eastern and North African communication and critical cultural studies (pp. 17–30). New York: Peter Lang.; Marshall, G. A. (1993). Racial classification: Popular and Scientific. In S. G. Harding (Ed.), The "racial" economy of science: Toward a democratic future (pp. 116–127). Bloomington: Indiana University Press.; **p. 38:** Arana, M. (2008, November 30). He's not black. Washington Post, p. B1. Retrieved December 31, 2008, from: www .washingtonpost.com/wp-dyn/content/article/2008/11/28/ AR2008112802219.html.; Arana, M. (2008, November 30). He's not black. Washington Post, p. B1. Retrieved December 31, 2008, from: www.washingtonpost.com/wp-dyn/content/ article/2008/11/28/AR2008112802219.html.; Seippul, Ø. (2017). Sports and nationalism in a globalized world. International Journal of Sociology, 47(1), 43-61.; Stokes, B. (2017, February 1). What it takes to truly be "one of us." Pew Research Center. Retrieved July 14, 2020 from https://www.pewresearch.org/ global/2017/02/01/what-it-takes-to-truly-be-one-of-us/.; **p. 39:** Wax, E. (2005, September 26–October 2). Beyond the pull of the tribe: In Kenya, some teens find unity in contemporary culture. Washington Post, National Weekly Edition, 22(49), 8.; **p. 40:** Garcia, S. E. (2020, June 17). Where did BIPOC come from? The New York Times. Retrieved July 14, 2020 from https://www .nytimes.com/article/what-is-bipoc.html.; A quick guide for non-binary dating. (2020, July 9). OkCupid. Retrieved July 14, 2020 from https://help.okcupid.com/article/207-a-quick-guide-for-non-binary-dating.; **p. 41:** Weber, P. (2014, February 21). Confused by all the new Facebook genders? Here's what they mean. Slate. Retrieved March 2, 2014, from http://www.slate.com/blogs/ lexicon_valley/2014/02/21/gender_facebook_now_has_56_ categories_to_choose_from_including_cisgender.html.; Jackson, D. (2019, April 3). Ariana Grande responds to bisexual rumors sparked by new song 'Monopoly'. Newsweek. Retrieved July 14, 2020 from https://www.newsweek.com/ariana-grande-bisexual-rumors-monopoly-1385531.; **p. 44:** Lucas, K. (2011). Socializing messages in blue-collar families: Communication pathways to social mobility and reproduction. Western Journal of Communication, 75(1), 95-121. p. 95.; Americans with Disabilities Act of 1990, as amended with Amendments of 2008. Retrieved May 13, 2011, from http://www.ada.gov/pubs/adastatute08 .htm.; Fassett, D. L., & Morella, D. L. (2008). Remarking (the) discipline: Marking the performative accomplishment of (dis) ability. Text and Performance Quarterly, 28(1-2), 139-156. p. 144.; **p. 45:** Henderson, B., & Ostrander, R. N. (2008). Introduction to special issue on disability studies/performance studies. Text and Performance Quarterly, 28(1–2), 1–5.; Lindemann, K. (2008). "I can't be standing up out there": Communicative performances of (dis)ability in wheelchair rugby. Text and Performance Quarterly, 28(1-2), 98-115.; Cardillo, L. W. (2010). Empowering narratives: Making sense of the experience of growing up with chronic illness or disability. Western Journal of Communication, 74(5), 525-546. p. 539.; Gecewicz, C. (2020, April 30). Few Americans say their house of worship is open, but a quarter say their faith has grown amid pandemic. Pew Research Center. Retrieved July 14, 2020 from https://www.pewresearch.org/fact-tank/2020/04/30/ few-americans-say-their-house-of-worship-is-open-but-a-quarter-say-their-religious-faith-has-grown-amid-pandemic/.; Corey, F. C. (2004). A letter to Paul. Text and Performance Quarterly, 24, 185–190.; **p. 46:** Corey, F. C., & Nakayama, T. K. (2004). Introduction. Special issue "Religion and Performance." Text and Performance Quarterly, 24, 209–211.; Campbell, H. A., ed. (2013). Digital religion: Understanding religious practice in new media worlds. New York: Routledge.; Coaston, J. (2019, May 28). The intersectionality wars. Vox. Retrieved July 14, 2020 from https://www.vox.com/the-highlight/2019/5/20/18542843/ intersectionality-conservatism-law-race-gender-discrimination.; **p. 47:** Lang, C. (2020, July 6). How the 'Karen Meme' confronts the violent history of white womanhood. Time. Retrieved July 14, 2020 from https://time.com/5857023/karen-meme-history-meaning/.; Lum, Z. A. (2017, February 2). Joël Lightbound urges no more silence over Islamophobia after Quebec City mosque attack.

Huffington Post Canada. Retrieved February 10, 2017 from http://www.huffingtonpost.ca/2017/02/02/joel-lightbound-quebec-shooting_n_14575968.html.; **p. 49:** Waring, O. (2018, March 18). What is catfishing and how can you spot it? Metro (UK). Retrieved July 14, 2020 from https://metro.co.uk/2018/03/18/catfishing-can-spot-7396549/.; McHugh, M. (2013, August 23) It's catfishing season! How to tell lovers from liars online, and more. Digital Trends. Retrieved March 3, 2014, from http://www.digitaltrends.com/web/its-catfishing-season-how-to-tell-lovers-from-liars-online-and-more/#ixzz2uvnrrkOx.

Chapter 3 Page 54: SciTechDaily. (2012). Biology News. Females distinguish colors better while men excel at tracking fast moving. objects. Retrieved July, 12, 2020, from https://scitechdaily.com/females-distinguish-colors-better-while-men-excel-at-tracking-fast-moving-objects/.; Abramov, I., Gordon, J., Feldman, O.,& Chavarga, A. (2012) Sex and vision I: Spatio-temporal resolution. Biology of SexDifferences, 3 (21). Retrieved July 12, 2020 from https://bsd.biomedcentral.com/articles/10.1186/2042-6410-3-20.; Abramov, I., Gordon, J., Feldman, O. ,& Chavarga, A. (2012). Sex and vision II: Color appearance of monochro-matic lights. Biology of Sex Differences, 3 (21). Retrieved July 12, 2020from https://link.springer.com/article/10.1186/2042-6410-3-21.; SciTechDaily. (2012).Females distinguish colors better while men excel at tracking fast moving. objects. Biology News.Retrieved July, 12, 2020 fromhttps://scitechdaily.com/females-distinguish-colors-better-while-men-excel-at-tracking-fast-moving-objects/.; Owen, J. (2012). Men and women really do see things differently. National Geographic. Retrieved July 11, 2020 fromhttps://www.nationalgeographic.com/news/2012/9/120907-men-women-see-differently-science-health-vision-sex/.; **p. 70:** Ting-Toomey, S. (1999). Communicating across cultures. New York: Guilford. p. 149.

Chapter 4 Page 80: Académie française. (2017, February 2). Self-service. Retrieved February 20, 2017, from: http://www.academie-francaise.fr/dire-ne-pas-dire.; Asmelash, L. (2020, May 16). Arbiters of the French language say "Covid" is feminine. CNN.Retrieved July 24, 2020, from https://www.cnn.com/2020/05/16/world/academie-franciase-covid-feminine-trnd/index.html.; Covid-19" bald im Duden? (2020, May 9). Taggeschau.de. Retrieved August 9, 2020, from https://www.tagesschau.de/inland/corona-duden-101.html#:~:text=Social%20Distancing%2C%20Corona%2DParty%20oder,einigen%20Wochen%20noch%20unbekannt%20waren.&text=%22Hei%C3%9Fer%20Kandidat%20f%C3%BCr%20die%20Aufnahme,Redaktion%2C%20Kathrin%20Kunkel%2DRazum.; Sauerbrey A. (2013, September 25). How do you say "blog" in German? New York Times. Retrieved March 6, 2014, from http://www.nytimes.com/2013/09/26/opinion/how-do-you-say-blog-in-german.html?_r=0.; Willsher, K. (2016, February 5). Not the oignon: Fury as France changes 2,000 spellings and drops some accents. The Guardian. Retrieved May 28, 2017, from https://www.theguardian.com/world/2016/feb/05/not-the-oignon-fury-france-changes-2000-spellings-ditches-circumflex.; **p. 86:** Heilman, M. E. (2001). Description and prescription: How gender stereotypes prevent women's ascent up the organizational ladder. In "Gender, hierarchy and leadership," Ed. L. Carli & A. Eagly. Journal of Social Issues, 57(4), 657–674.; **p. 88:** Sedivy, J. (2012, March 28). Votes and vowels: A changing accent show how language parallels politics. Discover. Retrieved March 7, 2014, from http://blogs.discovermagazine.com/crux/2012/03/28/votes-and-vowels-a-changing-accent-shows-how-language-parallels-politics/#.UxoiICifNiF.; **p. 89:** Survey Data Courtesy of ALan McConchie Visit WWW.pepvsoda.com to participate.; **p. 90:** Hecht, M. L., Jackson, R. L., II, & Ribeau, S. A. (2003). African American communication. Mahwah, NJ: Lawrence Erlbaum Associates.; **p. 91:** Wissing, R. (2020, Summer). The secret

language used by LGBTQ people in Turkey. Attitude. Retrieved July 27, 2020, from https://attitude.co.uk/article/the-secret-language-used-by-lgbtq-people-in-turkey-1/23524/?s=09.; Polari: The secret language gay men used to survive. (2018, February 12). BBC News. Retrieved July 27, 2020 from https://www.bbc.com/culture/article/20180212-polari-the-code-language-gay-men-used-to-survive.; Wissing, R. (2020, Summer). The secret language used by LGBTQ people in Turkey. Attitude. Retrieved July 27, 2020 from https://attitude.co.uk/article/the-secret-language-used-by-lgbtq-people-in-turkey-1/23524/?s=09.; **p. 92:** Hoijer, H. (1994). The Sapir-Whorf hypothesis. In L. Samovar & R. E. Porter (Eds.), Intercultural communication: A reader (pp. 194–200). Belmont, CA: Wadsworth.; Panko, B. (2016, December 2). Does the linguistic theory at the center of the film 'Arrival' have any merit? Smithsonian Magazine. Retrieved August 8, 2020, from https://www.smithsonianmag.com/science-nature/does-century-old-linguistic-hypothesis-center-film-arrival-have-any-merit-18096.; **p. 95:** Social Mobility Commission. (2017, January 26). New research uncovers "class pay gap" in Britain's professions. Retrieved February 20, 2017, from https://www.gov.uk/government/news/new-research-uncovers-class-pay-gap-in-britains-professions.; Sharma, D. (2019, November 25). British people still think some accents are smarter than others--what that means in the workplace. The Conversation. Retrieved August 9, 2020, from https://theconversation.com/british-people-still-think-some-accents-are-smarter-than-others-what-that-means-in-the-workplace-126964.; **p. 96:** Abbott, E. (2020, January 9). Why learning another language can change your life. The Hill. Retrieved August 9, 2020, from https://thehill.com/changing-america/enrichment/education/477414-why-learning-another-language-can-change-your-life.; Where are the world's best English-speakers? (2019, December 4). The Economist. Retrieved August 9, 2020, from https://www.economist.com/graphic-detail/2019/12/04/where-are-the-worlds-best-english-speakers.; **p. 98:** Levenson, 2020. Mother and Daughter Attacked for Speaking Spanish, Prosecutor Says.; Hern, A. (2020, June 29). How hate speech campaigners found Facebook's weak spot. The Guardian. Retrieved August 10, 2020 from https://www.theguardian.com/technology/2020/jun/29/how-hate-speech-campaigners-found-facebooks-weak-spot.; Bond, S. (2020, July 1). Over 400 advertisers hit pause on Facebook, threatening $70 billion juggernaut. National Public Radio. Retrieved August 10, 2020, from https://www.npr.org/2020/07/01/885853634/big-brands-abandon-facebook-threatening-to-derail-a-70b-advertising-juggernaut.; Hsu, T. and Lutz, E. (2020, August 1). More than 1,000 companies boycotted Facebook. Did it work? The New York Times. Retrieved August 10, 2020 from https://www.nytimes.com/2020/08/01/business/media/facebook-boycott.html.

Chapter 5 Page 107: Müller, C., Cienki, A., Fricke, E., Ladewig, S., McNeill, D., and Tessendorf, S. (2014). Ring-gestures across cultures and times: Dimensions in variation. In Body – Language – Communication. In Müller, C. Cienki, A., Fricke, E., Ladewig, S., McNeill, D., and Bressem, J., Eds. Berlin: De Gruyter Mouton, 1511–1522.; Swales, V. (December, 15, 2019). When the o.k. sign is no longer ok. New York Times. Retrieved August 16, 2020, from https://www.nytimes.com/2019/12/15/us/ok-sign-white-power.html.; Tuleja, T. (2012). Tuleja, Tad (2012).In the wink of an eye: Gestures and posture. Curious Customs. NY, NY: Stonesong Press.; **p. 108:** Manusov, V., & Patterson, M. (2006). Handbook of nonverbal communication. Thousand Oaks, CA: Sage.; **p. 109:** Birdwhistell, R. L. (1985). Kinesics and context: Essays in body motion communication. Philadelphia: University of Philadelphia Press.; Mehrabian, A. (1971). Nonverbal communication. Chicago, IL: Aldine-Atherton.; Mehrabian, A. (2007). Nonverbal communication. Chicago, IL: Aldine de Gruyter.; **p. 114:** Trost, M. R., & Alberts, J. K. (2006). How men and women communicate attraction: An evolutionary view. In D. Canary & K. Dindia (Eds.), Sex, gender and communication: Similarities and differences (2nd ed.; pp. 317–336). Mahwah, NJ: Lawrence Erlbaum.; **p. 116:** Burgoon, J. K., & Hale, J. L. (1988). Nonverbal expectancy violations: Model elaboration and application to immediacy behaviors. Communication Monographs, 55, 58–79.; Burgoon, J. K., & Le Poire, B. A. (1993). Effects of Communication expectancies, actual communication, and expectancy disconfirmation on evaluations of communicators and their communication behavior. Human Communication Research, 20(1), 67–96.; **p. 118:** Lord, T. L. (2009). The relationship of gender-based public harassment to body image, self-esteem, and avoidance behavior. Unpublished dissertation. Ann Arbor, MI: ProQuest.; **p. 125:** Wolf, C. (June 29, 2020). The NBA's new relaxed dress code kisses the suit goodbye. GQ. Retrieved on August 7, 2020, at https://www.gq.com/story/nba-dress-code-orlando-bubble.; **p. 126:** Wing Sue, D. (2010). Microaggressions in everyday life: Race, gender, and sexual orientation (p. xvi). Hoboken, NJ: Wiley.

Chapter 6 Page 132: Turkle, S. (2015). Reclaiming conversation: The power of talk in a digital age. London, UK: Penguin.; **p. 156:** Zachary A. Goldfarb (2014) These four charts show how the SAT favors rich, educated families, Washington Post March 5, 2014 Retrieved from https://www.washingtonpost.com/news/wonk/wp/2014/03/05/these-four-charts-show-how-the-sat-favors-the-rich-educated-families/?arc404=true.;

Chapter 7 Page 167: Carnevale, A. P. (2013). 21st century competencies for college and career readiness. San Francisco, CA: NCDA Career Developments. Available at https://repository.library.georgetown.edu/bitstream/handle/10822/559289/CD_21stCenturyCompetencies.pdf?sequence=1.; **p. 168:** International Listening Association. (1995, April). An ILA Definition of Listening. ILA Listening Post, 53, 1–4.; p. 169: Quote by Alan Alda.; McNeil, J. (2020). Lurking: How a Person Became a User. NYC: MCD.; Lange, J. (2018). Let us lurk. theweek.com. Retrieved July 25, 2020, from https://theweek.com/articles/804466/let-lurk.; **p. 170:** Cooper, L. O., & Buchanan, T. (2010). Listening competency on campus: A psychometric analysis of student listening. International Journal of Listening, 24(3), 141–163.; Watson, K. W., Barker, L. L., & Weaver, J. B. (1995). The Listening Styles Profile (LSP-16): Development and validation of an instrument to assess four listening styles. Journal of the International Listening Association, 9, 1–13.; Watson, K. W., Barker, L. L., & Weaver, J. B. (1995). The Listening Styles Profile (LSP-16): Development and validation of an instrument to assess four listening styles. Journal of the International Listening Association, 9, 1–13.; **p. 173:** Klein, L. (2020). The value of listening during the pandemic. Mercurynews.com. Retrieved August 9, 2020, from https://www.mercurynews.com/2020/07/03/opinion-listening-during-the-covid-19-pandemic/.; **p. 174:** Janusik, L., & Imhof, M. (2017). Intercultural listening: Measuring listening concepts with the LCI-R. International Journal of Listening, 31(2), 80–97.; **p. 176:** (2016, December 15). Hearing Loss Association of America. Quick Statistics. Retrieved August 5, 2020, from https://www.hearingloss.org/hearing-help/hearing-loss-basics/.; **p. 177:** Shafir, R. Z. (2003). The Zen of listening (2nd ed). Wheaton, IL: Quest Books.; Genette, J., Olson, C. D., & Linde, J. (2017). Hot topics, cool heads: A handbook on Civil Dialogue®. Dubuque, IA: Kendall Hunt.; Linde, J. Genette, J., & Olson, C. D. (2014). Civil dialogue: Producing civility through the process of dialogue. Retrieved August 31, 2020, from at https://www.civil-dialogue.org/publications.html.; **p. 179:** Algeria K. Wilson. July 8, 2020, We don't need white saviors." A Black social worker calls her white colleagues to action.Michigan Radio.; **p. 181:** Weblink for Smithsonian Institution.; **p. 184:** Alda, A. (2017). If I understood you, would I have this look on my face? New York, NY: Random House.; Nichols, M. P. (2009). The lost art of listening (2nd ed.). New York: The Guilford Press.

Chapter 8 Page 188: Allison Nafziger Travel Blog. Reprinted by permission of Allison Nafziger.; **p. 189:** U.S. Census Bureau projections.; **p. 191:** Broome, B. J., & Collier, M. J. (2012). Culture, communication, and peacebuilding: A reflexive multi-dimensional contextual framework. Journal of International and Intercultural Communication, 5(4), 245–269.; **p. 193:** Kim, Y. Y. (2005). Adapting to a new culture: An integrative communication theory. In W. B. Gudykunst (Ed.), Theorizing about intercultural communication (pp. 375–400). Thousand Oaks, CA: Sage.; Yako, R. M., & Biswas, B. (2014). "We came to this country for the future of our children. We have no future": Acculturative stress among Iraqi refugees in the United States. International Journal of Intercultural Relations, 38, 133–141.; **p. 194:** De La Garza, A. T., & Ono, K. (2015). Retheorizing adaptation: Differential adaptation and critical intercultural communication. Journal of International & Intercultural Communication, 8(4), 269–289.; Hartig, H. (2018, May 24). Republicans turn more negative toward refugees as number admitted to U.S. plummets. pewresearch.org. Retrieved August 20, 2020, from https://www.pewresearch.org/fact-tank/2018/05/24/republicans-turn-more-negative-toward-refugees-as-number-admitted-to-u-s-plummets/.; Landgrave, L. (2019, September 17). Immigrants learn English. cato.org. Retrieved August 20, 2020, from https://www.cato.org/publications/immigration-research-policy-brief/immigrants-learn-english-immigrants-language.; **p. 196:** Rosenstone, R. A. (2005). My wife, the Muslim. Antioch Review, 63, 234–246.; **p. 197:** Linker, L. (2020, May 6). American individualism is a suicide pact. theweek.com. Retrieved June 22, 2020, from https://theweek.com/articles/912853/american-individualism-suicide-pact.; **p. 202:** Cheung, H., Feng, Z. & Deng, B. (2020, May 27). Coronavirus: What attacks on Asians reveal about American identity. bbc.com. Retrieved August 17, 2020, from https://www.bbc.com/news/world-us-canada-52714804.; Cheung, H., Feng, Z. & Deng, B. (2020, May 27). Coronavirus: What attacks on Asians reveal about American identity. bbc.com. Retrieved August 17, 2020, from https://www.bbc.com/news/world-us-canada-52714804.; **p. 204:** Rothman, L. (2012, July 8). Essence Fest 2012: Is reality TV still not diverse enough? Time.com. Retrieved March 22, 2014, from http://entertainment.time.com/2012/07/08/essence-reality-tv-family-panel/.; **p. 206:** Wilson, B. L. (2020, June 8). I'm your black friend, but I won't educate you about racism. That's on you. washingtonpost.com. Retrieved August 18, 2020, from https://www.washingtonpost.com/outlook/2020/06/08/black-friends-educate-racism/.; **p. 209:** Scott, K. D. (2013). Communication strategies across cultural borders: Dispelling stereotypes, performing competence, and redefining black womanhood. Women's Studies in Communication, 36, 312–329.

Chapter 9 Page 218: Knight, K. (September, 2014). Communicating dilemmas in adults' friends with benefits relationships: Challenges to relational talk. Emerging Adulthood. Retrieved November 25, 2014, from http://eax.sagepub.com/content/early/2014/09/19/2167696814549598.; **p. 220:** Knapp, M. L., & Vangelisti, A. (1997). Interpersonal communication and relationships (2nd ed.). Boston: Allyn & Bacon.; **p. 221:** Rawlins, W. R. & Holl, M. (1987). Communicative achievement of friendship during adolescence: Predicaments of trust and violation. Western Journal of Communication, 51(4), 345-363.; **p. 222:** Baxter, L. A., & Bullis, C. (1986). Turning points in developing romantic relationships. Human Communication Research, 12, 469–493.; Johnson, A. J., Wittenberg, E., Haigh, M., & Wigley, S. (2004). The process of relationship development and deterioration: Turning points in friendships that have terminated. Communication Quarterly, 52, 54–68.; **p. 223:** Reeder, H. (1996). What Harry and Sally didn't tell you. (Unpublished Doctoral dissertation). Arizona State University, Tempe, AZ.; **p. 225:** Adapted from Dwyer, L. (September 9, 2015). The surprising reality of hook-up culture on campus. Teen Vogue.

Retrieved March 22, 2017, from http://www.teenvogue.com/story/hookup-culture-myth-dating-college.; **p. 229:** Canary, D., Stafford, L., Hause, K., & Wallace, L. (1993). An inductive analysis of relational maintenance strategies: Comparisons among lovers, relatives, friends, and others. Communication Research Reports, 10, 5–14.; Johnson, A.J., Haigh, M. M., Becker, J.A.H., Craig, E. A., & Wigley, S.(20080. College students' use of relational management strategies in email in long-distance and geographically close relationships. Journal of Computer-Mediated Communication, 13 (2008) 381-404.; **p. 232:** Cody, M. J. (1982). A typology of disengagement strategies and an examination of the role intimacy, reactions to inequity and relational problems play in strategy selection. Communication Monographs, 49, 148–170.; **p. 235:** Struckman-Johnson, C. J., Struckman-Johnson, B. L., & Anderson, B. (2003). Tactics of sexual coercion: When men and women won't take no for an answer. Journal of Sex Research, 40(1), 76–86.; CDC. (2020, January 17). Preventing sexual violence. In Centers for Disease Control and Prevention. Retrieved August 17, 2020, from https://www.cdc.gov/violenceprevention/sexualviolence/fastfact.html.; McCoy, K., & Oelschlager, J. (n.d.) Sexual coercion awareness and prevention. Florida Institute of Technology. Retrieved May 17, 2011, from http://www.fit.edu/caps/documents/SexualCoercion_000.pdf.

Chapter 10 Page 247: Arrow, H., McGrath, J. E., & Berdahl, J. L. (2000). Small groups as complex systems. Thousand Oaks, CA: Sage.; **p. 251:** Thecouchmanager.com. (September, 2020). Retrieved September 16, 2020, and adapted from https://www.thecouchmanager.com/the-ultimate-list-of-virtual-team-technology-tools/.; **p. 252:** Lawrence Frey (1994).; **p. 253:** Benne, K. D., & Sheats, P. (1948). Functional roles of group members. Journal of Social Issues, 4, 41–49.; Benne, K. D., & Sheats, P. (1948). Functional roles of group members. Journal of Social Issues, 4, 41–49.; Benne, K. D., & Sheats, P. (1948). Functional roles of group members. Journal of Social Issues, 4, 41–49.; **p. 256:** Gollent, M. (2007, June 6). Why are leadership skills important—for everyone? Retrieved March 30, 2011, from http://ezinearticles.com/?why-are-leadership-skills-important—for-everyone?&id=591333.; Daft, R. L. (2010). The Leardership experience (5th Ed). Mason, OH: Thomson Higher Education. p. 5.; **p. 258:** Cain, S. (2013). Quiet: The power of introverts in a world that can't stop talking. New York: Broadway Books.; Moore, K. (2012). Introverts no longer the quiet followers of extroverts. Forbes.com. Retrieved February 22, 2017, from http://www.forbes.com/sites/karlmoore/2012/08/22/introverts-no-longer-the-quiet-followers-of-extroverts/.; **p. 259:** Foels, R., Driskell, J. E., Mullen, B., & Salas, E. (2000). The effects of democratic leadership on group member satisfaction: An integration. Small Group Research, 31, 676–701.; **p. 260:** Eisenberg, J., Post, C., & DiTomaso, N. (2019). Virtual team dispersion and performance: The role of team communication and transformational leadership. Small Group Research, 50(3), 348–380.; **p. 266:** Ferrazzi, K. (2012, November 19). How to Manage Conflict in Virtual Teams. HBR Blog Network. Retrieved March 1, 2017, from http://blogs.hbr.org/2012/11/how-to-manage-conflict-in-virt/.; Five ways to effectively handle conflict in a virtual team. (2020). thevirtualhub.com. Retrieved September 16, 2020, from https://www.thevirtualhub.com/blog/5-ways-to-effectively-handle-conflict-in-virtual-teams/.; **p. 267:** Wang, S., Homan, A. C., & Jehn, K. (2020). Individual task conflict asymmetry and peer ratings of member effectiveness. Small Group Research, 51(3), 402–426.; **p. 270:** Five Tips for Running Inclusive Virtual Meetings. globesmart.com. Retrieved July 15, 2020, from https://www.globesmart.com/wp-content/uploads/2020/04/QG-Running-Inclusive-Virtual-Meetings.pdf.; Phillips, K. W. (2014, October 1). How diversity makes us smarter. Scientific American. Retrieved February 6, 2017, from http://www.scientificamerican.com/article/how-diversity-makes-us-smarter/.; **p. 271:** Gloor, P. A. (2006). Swarm creativity: Competitive advantage through collaborative innovative networks. Oxford: Oxford University Press.; **p. 273:** Oetzel, J. G. (2005). Effective intercultural workgroup communication theory. In W. B. Gudykunst (Ed.), Theorizing about intercultural communication (pp. 351–371). Thousand Oaks, CA: Sage.

Chapter 11 Page 282: Kramer & Bisel, 2017. Organizational Communication A Lifespan Approach. p. 133.; **p. 286:** Gelfand, M., Gordon, S., Li, C., Choi, V. & Prokopowicz, P. (2018, October 02). One reason mergers fail: The two cultures aren't compatible. hbr.org. Retrieved September 7, 2020, from https://hbr.org/2018/10/one-reason-mergers-fail-the-two-cultures-arent-compatible.; **p. 289:** Clair, R. (1996). The political nature of a colloquialism, "A real job": Implications for organizational assimilation. Communication Monographs, 63, 249–267.; **p. 298:** Stephens, K., Jahn, J., Fox, S., Charoensap-Kelly, P., Mitra, R., Sutton, J., Waters, E., Xie, B., & Meisenbach, R. (2020). Collective sensemaking Around COVID-19: Experiences, concerns, and agendas for our rapidly changing organizational lives. Management Communication Quarterly, 34(3), 426–457.; **p. 302:** Eisenberg, E., Goodall, H. L., & Trethewey, A. (2010). Organizational communication: Balance, creativity and constraint. Boston, MA: Bedford/St. Martin's.; **p. 303:** Namie, G. (2017). The 2017 WBI U. S. workplace bullying survey. Retrieved October 7, 2020 from https://workplacebullying.org/research-wbi/.; Palomares, N. W. & Wingate, N. V. (2020). Victims' goal understanding, uncertainty reduction, and perceptions in cyberbullying: Theoretical evidence from three experiments, Journal of Computer-Mediated Communication, 5(4), 253–273.

Chapter 12 Page 313: Tavernise, S. & Oppel, R. A., Jr. (2020, March 23). Spit on, yelled at, attacked: Chinese-Americans fear for their safety. The Washington Post. Retrieved on September 23, 2020, from https://www.nytimes.com/2020/03/23/us/chinese-coronavirus-racist-attacks.html.; **p. 314:** Tostevin, R. (2014, March 14). Online activism: It's easy to click, but just as easy to disengage. The Guardian. Retrieved May 18, 2014 from: http://www.theguardian.com/media-network/media-network-blog/2014/mar/14/online-activism-social-media-engage.; **p. 315:** Blake, A. (2020, September 1). Trump's illuminating defense of Kyle Rittenhouse. The Washington Post. Retrieved September 22, 2020, from https://www.washingtonpost.com/politics/2020/08/31/trumps-illuminating-defense-kyle-rittenhouse/.; **p. 317:** Thomas, S. (n.d.). From slave to abolitionist/editor. Retrieved June 26, 2006, from http://www.history.rochester.edu/class/douglass/part2.html.; Douglass, F. (1852, July 5). The meaning of July Fourth for the Negro. Retrieved June 26, 2006, from www.pbs.org/wgbh/aia/part4/4h2927t.html.; **p. 318:** Aristotle. (1991). On rhetoric: A theory of civic discourse (G. A. Kennedy, trans.) New York: Oxford University Press, (p. 42)(Original work written about 350 B.C.E).; **p. 319:** George Kennedy, (1998). Comparitive rhetoric: An historical and cross cultural introduction. New York: Oxford University Press (p. 215).; **p. 321:** Westring, L. (2019, February 18). Comment: How pathos helps leaders like Trump reign supreme. The Scotsman. Retrieved September 22, 2020, from https://www.scotsman.com/news/opinion/columnists/comment-how-pathos-helps-leaders-trump-reign-supreme-113461.; Arrigo, A. F. (2018, December 24). What Aristotle can teach us about Trump's persuasive rhetoric. Newsweek. Retrieved September 22, 2020, from https://www.newsweek.com/donald-trump-aristotle-donald-trump-rhetoric-us-president-barack-obama-1270496.; **p. 322:** Janis King (2002) Cultural differences in the perceptions of sports mascots: A rhetoric study og Tim Giago's newspaper columns. In J. N. Martin, T. K. Nakayama, L . A. Flores (Eds), Reading in intercultural communication : Experiences and context (pp. 205–212) New York: McGraw-Hill(p. 211).; **p. 323:** Thomas &

Horowitz, 2020. Support for Black Lives Matter has decreased since June but remains strong among Black Americans. © Pew Research Centre.; **p. 326:** Aguilera, J. (2020, June 9). Confederate statues are being removed amid protests over George Floyd's death. Here's what to know. Time. Retrieved September 24, 2020, from https://time.com/5849184/confederate-statues-removed/.; Thomas Erdbrink (2008) Iranian Woman Blinded by Spurned Suitor Persuades Court to Punish Him Similarly. Washington Post.; **p. 327:** Jackson, S. J., Bailey, M. & Welles, B. F. (2020). #HashtagActivism: Networks of race and gender justice. Cambridge, MA: MIT Press.; **p. 328:** VanHoose, B. (2020, August 13). Va. mayor apologizes for calling Kamala Harris racist nickname: 'Wrong, offensive & unbecoming'. People. Retrieved September 24, 2020, from https://people.com/politics/virginia-mayor-apologizes-after-calling-kamala-harris-aunt-jemima/.; **p. 335:** Tufte, E. (2003, September). PowerPoint is evil. Wired Magazine, (pp. 118–119). Reprinted by permission from Edward R. Tufte, The Cognitive Style of PowerPoint. Cheshire, CT: Graphics Press.; **p. 340:** Sanow, A. (2005, March 3). How I overcame the fear of public speaking. Retrieved June 26, 2006, from http://www.expertclick.com/NewsreleaseWire/default.cfm?Action=ReleaseDetail&ID-8372&NRWid=1698.

Chapter 13 Page 344: Scott, D. C. (2013, November 9). Mariska Hargitay: A Hollywood star for an actress—and activist (+video). The Christian Science Monitor. Retrieved June 6, 2014, from: http://www.csmonitor.com/The-Culture/2013/1109/Mariska-Hargitay-A-Hollywood-star-for-an-actress-and-activist-video.; **p. 346:** Ovide, S. (2020, July 2). New 'TV' is a lot like TV. The New York Times. Retrieved October 15, 2020, from https://www.nytimes.com/2020/07/02/technology/internet-tv.html.; Iqbal, M. (2020, June 23). Netflix revenue and usage statistics (2020). Business of Apps. Retrieved October 15, 2020, from https://www.businessofapps.com/data/netflix-statistics/#:~:text=Average%20daily%20time%20spent%20with%20Netflix%20in%20US&text=Nielson%20audience%20stats%20published%20in,6%25%20of%20total%20television%20time.; Hale, M. (2017, March 13). On Netflix, the borders remain open. New York Times. Retrieved from: https://www.nytimes.com/2017/03/13/arts/television/netflix-fauda-nobel-review.html?_r=0.; Nielsen. (2014, May 12). Advertising and audiences: State of the media. Retrieved June 6, 2014, from: http://www.nielsen.com/us/en/reports/2014/advertising-and-audiences-state-of-the-media.html.; Coming full circle: The end of mass media. (2011, July 7). The Economist. Retrieved June 6, 2014, from: http://www.economist.com/node/18904158.; **p. 347:** Boorstin, D. J. (1965). The Americans: The national experience. New York: Random House.; **p. 348:** Mitchell, A. (2014, March 26). State of the news media 2014. Pew Research Journalism Project. Retrieved June 11, 2014, from: http://www.journalism.org/2014/03/26/state-of-the-news-media-2014-overview/.; **p. 349:** Chapman, J. (2005). Comparative media history. Malden, MA: Polity Press.; Germain, T. (2020, August 24). Best music streaming services. Consumer Reports. Retrieved October 5, 2020, from https://www.consumerreports.org/streaming-music-services/best-music-streaming-service-for-you.; **p. 350:** Schneider, M. & Aurthur, K. (2020, July 21). R.I.P. Cable TV: Why Hollywood is slowly killing its biggest moneymaker. Variety. Retrieved October 15, 2020, from https://variety.com/2020/tv/news/cable-tv-decline-streaming-cord-cutting-1234710007.; **p. 353:** Sharkey, B. (2014, February 27). Oscars 2014: For many, "12 Years a Slave" is too hard to watch. Los Angeles Times. Retrieved June 9, 2014, from http://articles.latimes.com/2014/feb/27/entertainment/la-et-mn-12-years-a-slave-notebook-20140227/2.; Okoro, E. (2013, November 27). Why I wouldn't see 12 Years a Slave with a white person. The Atlantic. Retrieved June 9, 2014, from http://www.theatlantic.com/entertainment/archive/2013/11/why-i-wouldnt-see-em-12-years-a-slave-em-

with-a-white-person/281883/.; Feinberg, S. (2014, March 2). Brutally honest Oscar voter ballot no. 7. The Hollywood Reporter. Retrieved June 9, 2014, from: http://www.hollywoodreporter.com/race/brutally-honest-oscar-voter-ballot-684839.; **p. 354:** Gunther, A. C., & Schmitt, K. (2004). Mapping boundaries of the hostile media effect. Journal of Communication, 54, 55–70.; Weeks, B. E., Kim, D. H., Hahn, L. B., Diehl, T. H., & Kwok, N. (2019). Hostile media perceptions in the age of social media: Following politicians, emotions, and perceptions of media bias. Journal of Broadcasting and Electronic Media, 63(3): 374–392.; Yahr, E. (2016, October 19). NBC's 'This Is Us' is officially the surprise breakout hit of the fall TV season. The Washington Post. Retrieved from: https://www.washingtonpost.com/news/arts-and-entertainment/wp/2016/10/19/nbcs-this-is-us-is-officially-the-surprise-breakout-hit-of-the-fall-tv-season/?utm_term=.f7a8f9d09aa0.; **p. 355:** Cohen, J. (2002). Television viewing preferences: Programs, schedules, and the structure of viewing choices made by Israeli adults. Journal of Broadcasting & Electronic Media, 46, 204–221.; **p. 356:** Durham, M. G. (2004). Constructing the "new ethnicities": Media, sexuality, and diaspora identity in the lives of South Asian immigrant girls. Critical Studies in Media Communication, 21, 140–161.; **p. 357:** Nolan, E. (2020, September 18). 'Big Brother's' Memphis Garrett cleared of using racial slur, many fans unconvinced. Newsweek. Retrieved October 3, 2020, from https://www.newsweek.com/big-brother-memphis-garrett-cleared-racial-slur-david-alexander-cbs-1532820.; Denhart, A. (2020, September 18). Big Brother now bans racial slurs. But what about BB22's implicit racism or autism-mocking? Reality Blurred. Retrieved October 3, 2020, from https://www.realityblurred.com/realitytv/2020/09/big-brother-cbs-racial-slur-ban-bb22-racism-autism-mocking.; **p. 358:** Aoyagi, C. (2004, July 2–15). TV networks' current fascination with Hawaii often doesn't translate into more roles for APAs. Pacific Citizen, 139, 1.; Meyers, M. (2004). African American women and violence: Gender, race, and class in the news. Critical Studies in Media Communication, 21, 95–118.; **p. 359:** Shugart, H. (2008). Managing masculinities: The metrosexual moment. Communication and Critical/Cultural Studies, 5, 280–300.; **p. 360:** Fahmy, S. (2004). Picturing Afghan women: A content analysis of AP wire photographs during the Taliban regime and after the fall of the Taliban regime. Gazette: The International Journal for Communication Studies, 66, 91–112.; Fahmy, S. (2004). Picturing Afghan women: A content analysis of AP wire photographs during the Taliban regime and after the fall of the Taliban regime. Gazette: The International Journal for Communication Studies, 66, 91–112.; Holling, M. A. (2019) Rhetorical contours of violent frames and the production of discursive violence. Critical Studies in Media Communication, 36(3): 249-271.; **p. 361:** Morgan, M., & Signorielli, N. (1990). Cultivation analysis: Conceptualization and methodology. In N. Signorielli & M. Morgan (Eds.), Cultivation analysis: New directions in media effects research (pp. 13–34). Newbury Park, CA: Sage Publications.; Custers, K, Hall, ED, Bushnell Smith, S, et al. (2017) The indirect association between television exposure and self-protective behavior as a result of worry about crime: The moderating role of gender. Mass Communication and Society 20(5): 637–662.; **p. 362:** Niederdeppe, J., Fowler, E. F., Goldstein, K., & Pribble, J. (2010). Does local television news coverage cultivate fatalistic beliefs about cancer prevention? Journal of Communication, 60, 230–253.; **p. 363:** Eckstein, J. (2020) Sensing school shootings. Critical Studies in Media Communication 37:2, 161-173.; **p. 364:** Anderson, C. A., & Bushman, B. J. (2002, March 29). The effects of media violence on society. Science, 295, 2377–2378. Retrieved May 1, 2006, from: http://www.psychology.iastate.edu/faculty/caa/abstracts/2000-2004/02AB2.pdf.; **p. 365:** Brookey, R. A. & Zhang, N. (2021). The not-so Fantastic Four franchise: A critical history of the comic, the films, and the Disney/Fox merger. In Rauscher, A., Stein, D. & Thon, J.-N., eds. Comics and video games: From hybrid medialities to transmedia expansions (pp. 149–163). New York: Routledge.; **p. 366:** de Moraes, L. (2004, October 21). No more Miss America pageantry for ABC. Washington Post, p. C7. Retrieved June 24, 2006, from: http://www.washingtonpost.com/wp-dyn/articles/A50114-2004Oct20.html.; Akhavan-Majid, R. (2004). Mass media reform in China: Toward a new analytical perspective. Gazette: The International Journal for Communication Studies, 66, 553–565.; Cablevision. (2000, November 4). NBC to acquire Bravo from Cablevision Systems Corporation. Retrieved June 24, 2006, from:http://www.cablevision.com/index.jhtml?id=2002_11_04.; **p. 367:** McChesney, R. (1998). Making media democratic. Boston Review, 23, 4–10, 20. Retrieved June 24, 2006, from: http://www.bostonreview.net/BR23.3/mcchesney.html.; **p. 368:** Celis, B. (2017, March 12). The time's right for a new wave of Black media activism. Newsweek. Retrieved from: http://www.newsweek.com/time-right-new-wave-black-media-activism-565377.

Chapter 14 Page 375: Digital Life in 2025, Pew Report, 2014 —J. G. Ballard.; **p. 378:** Glowacki, E. M., & Taylor, M. A. (2020). Health hyperbolism: A study in health crisis rhetoric. Qualitative Health Research, 30(12), 1953-1964.; **p. 380:** Kaplan, A. M., & Haenlein, M. (2010). Users of the world, unite! The challenges and opportunities of social media. Business Horizons, 53, 59–68.; **p. 382:** Turkle, S. (2015). Reclaiming conversation: The power of talk in a digital age. New York: Penguin Books.; Turkle, S. (2012, February). TED talk: Connected, but alone? Retrieved September 29, 2020 from http://www.ted.com/talks/sherry_turkle_alone_together#t-755215.;

p. 388: Cooper, S. (2020, July 30). What is doxing? comparitech.com. Retrieved September 26, 2020, from https://www.comparitech.com/blog/vpn-privacy/what-is-doxxing-how-to-avoid/#:~:text=A%20number%20of%20celebrities%20have,to%20SWATTING%20and%20flawed%20doxxing.; **p. 389:** Firth, J., Torous, J., Stubbs, B., Firth, J. A., Steiner, G. Z., Smith, L., Alvarez-Jimenez, M., Gleeson, J., Vancampfort, D., Armitage, C. J., & Sarris, J. (2019). The "online brain": How the Internet may be changing our cognition. World Psychiatry, 18(2), 119–129.; **p. 390:** Tanega, C., & Downs, A. (2020). Addictive technology: Prevalence and potential implications of problematic social media use. Psi Chi Journal of Psychological Research, 25(2), 151–161.; Selyukh, 2016. Postelection, Overwhelmed Facebook Users Unfriend, Cut Back. NPR.; **p. 391:** Yee, B. Y. (2020, August 23). 12 pandemic dating tips, how to do romance with the Covid-19 Coronavirus. forbes.com. Retrieved September 27, 2020, from https://www.forbes.com/sites/brucelee/2020/08/23/12-pandemic-dating-tips-how-to-do-romance-with-the-covid-19-coronavirus/#.; **p. 392:** Heino, R. D., Ellison, N. B., & Gibbs, J. L. (2010). Relationshopping: Investigating the market metaphor in online dating. Journal od Social and Personal Relationships, 27, 427-447.; Weinstein, E. C. & Selman, R. L. (2016). Digital Stress: Adolescents' personal accounts. New Media & Society, 18(3), 391–409.; **p. 393:** Krouse, S. (2019, July 19). The new ways your boss is spying on you. wsj. com. Retrieved September 25, 2020, from https://www.wsj.com/articles/the-new-ways-your-boss-is-spying-on-you-11563528604.; **p. 399:** Levander, C., & Decherney, P. (2020, June 10). The COVID-igital divide. insidehighered.com. Retrieved September 17, 2020, from https://www.insidehighered.com/digital-learning/blogs/education-time-corona/covid-igital-divide.

Index